Ties that Bind

Cornell University

Trần Ngọc Angie

Ties that Bind
Cultural Identity, Class, and Law in Vietnam's Labor Resistance

SOUTHEAST ASIA PROGRAM PUBLICATIONS
Southeast Asia Program
Cornell University
Ithaca, New York
2013

Cornell Southeast Asia Program Publications
640 Stewart Avenue, Ithaca, NY 14850-3857

Studies on Southeast Asia No. 62

Printed in the United States of America

ISBN: hc 978-0-87727-792-7
ISBN: pb 978-0-87727-762-0

Cover: designed by Kat Dalton

DEDICATION

Thương Kính Tặng Ba Mẹ và Ông Bà

TABLE OF CONTENTS

Acknowledgments   ix

Map of Ho Chi Minh City and Surrounding Districts   xiii

Map of Viet Nam   xiv

Introduction: Issues for Labor Organizing and Protests   1

Chapter 1
  Peasant and Migrant Workers under French Colonial Rule (1880–1954)   15

Chapter 2
  Labor Protests in the Republic of Vietnam (1954–75)   63

Chapter 3
  State Institutions and the Legal Framework: Their Influence on   111
  Labor–Management Relations since *Đổi Mới* (1986 to Present)

Chapter 4
  State Worker Agency in State-Owned and Equitized Enterprises   153

Chapter 5
  Labor Organizing and Protests in Foreign–Direct Investment Factories   181

Chapter 6
  Workers' Activism in Vietnamese Private and Underground   225
  Foreign-Investment Factories

Chapter 7
  Internal State Contradictions, Workers, and the Rule of Law   261

Chapter 8
  Conclusion   291

Appendices   303
  Appendix A, Glossary of Terms and Acronyms   303
  Appendix B, Thirty-three Cases Classified by Protest Type   304
  Appendix C, Huê Phong Factory (1992–2008): A Representative Sample   307
    of Protests and Intervention by the Media and State Agencies
  Appendix D, Danh Sách Công Ty Nợ Bảo Hiểm Xã Hội   311

Selected Bibliography   313

Index   331

ACKNOWLEDGMENTS

This book is truly a labor of love: a ten-year effort to bring together research materials that I obtained from numerous fieldwork trips to Vietnam with money cobbled from a variety of sources. I am deeply grateful to many people without whom this book might not have seen the light of day. First are the workers in Vietnam who trusted me and poured their hearts out to me so I would have firsthand understanding of their plight. It is to the heroic efforts of workers, of over a hundred years of labor movements, that I dedicate this book. Second are the many journalists in Vietnam who over the years explained to me the realities on the ground and shared with me important, and at times confidential, materials. For that reason, I have kept their identities anonymous to preserve their well-being. (Those journalists who gave me some of the photos that appear in this book did, of course, give me permission to publish their names).

My deep appreciation also goes to many wonderful colleagues—Nguyễn-võ Thu Hương, Vân Nguyễn-Marshall, Huỳnh thị Ngọc Tuyết, Bùi Đức Hải, Donald K. Emmerson, and Benedict J. Tria Kerkvliet—who read my manuscript, gave excellent feedback, shared resources and archival materials (including rare materials from the Republic of Vietnam), and connected me to some important people-in-the-know to interview in Vietnam. I also took to heart the constructive critiques of three anonymous manuscript reviewers whose guidance was invaluable in pushing me to sharpen my arguments and in bringing this book to fruition.

I was deeply saddened by the sudden death of Melanie Beresford in February 2013, whose encouragement, guidance, and collaboration over the twenty-five years of knowing her is acknowledged in this book. Her death is such a tremendous loss, not only to her colleagues, students, and the people of Southeast Asia, but also to me: first, as a mentor, then as a colleague, then as a very dear friend and a spiritual sister.

My transnational extended family provides me with constant support (despite the continuous, concerned questions like: "when will your book *ever* come out?"). My cousins from the north of Vietnam (Chị Đoàn Thị Như Mai, Anh Phạm Anh Tuấn, Chị Vũ Thị Phương Sao) obtained and took photos of some important historical and archival materials, and connected me to some elderly cadres (all were in their late eighties) who had participated directly in labor organizing and strikes in Nam Định, or had witnessed historic labor-related events. I seized the opportunities and interviewed Bác Nguyễn Tiến Cảnh, a Nam Định resident and an anti-French revolutionary who knew labor issues there intimately, and was happy to share his wisdom and knowledge with me for hours in person and by phone before, sadly, he passed away in November 2012. I also interviewed Bác Trần Thị Kim Đường and Bác Phạm Khánh Hội, who worked in Nam Định textile combine during the colonial French era, and generously shared their knowledge about Nam Định workers then. My cousins from the south of Vietnam were always eager to help with a smile: Chị Doãn Thị Cẩm Liên connected me with some interview sources in the south; Chị Doãn Thị Kim Khánh painstakingly pored over the 300-page manuscript to proofread and check the Vietnamese diacritics, and Anh Doãn Quốc Vinh made substantive artistic suggestions to SEAP on the cover design.

Ultimately, my parents (Ông Trần Quang Phong, Bà Doãn Thị Quý) are the ones who gave me daily spiritual support through the ebbs and flows of this long process. Not only did they cheer me on during every step of the way, read through my manuscript, and help with translations of some of the materials (especially my mother, with the poetry), but they also checked the final galleys for any mistakes with the Vietnamese diacritical marks. They are the best parents any scholar could dream to have!

I'm grateful for the many sources of institutional and financial support that allowed me to do fieldwork in Vietnam and to get access to Southeast Asia archival centers (especially the Cornell University Echols Collection, the Hoover Institution Archives, the Australian National University Library, and the National University of Singapore Library), and those that gave me the best gift—time—to analyze my materials and write. They include: the Lee Kong Chian National University of Singapore–Stanford University Distinguished Fellow on Southeast Asia, the Henry Luce Post-Doc Fellowship at the Research School of Pacific and Asian Studies–Australian National University, Senior Visiting Fellowship at the Centre for Asia Pacific Social Transformation Studies (CAPSTRANS) at the University of Wollongong NSW as part of the Australian Research Council Grant, and several CSU Research, Scholarship, and Creative Activity Awards. Other travel grants and affiliations enabled me to participate in global conferences to exchange ideas with other colleagues, such as the Center for Asian and Pacific Studies and College of Law, University of Iowa (to present at the Fourth Symposium on Contemporary Vietnam: Symposium on Labor, Enterprises, Entrepreneurs and the State in Vietnam, Paris), the Southeast Asia Program at Cornell University (to present at the Global Companies–Global Unions–Global Research–Global Campaigns Conference), and the Center for Southeast Asia Studies at the University of California–Berkeley. As an isolated Vietnam/Southeast Asia scholar at a primarily teaching institution, I deeply appreciate these invaluable opportunities to interchange with the best minds on labor-management-state relations issues in Southeast Asia.

I could not have completed this book without the loving support of my wonderful colleagues in the Social Behavioral and Global Studies Division at California State University, Monterey Bay (CSUMB). Gerald Shenk has been consistently supportive from the get-go and also helped with the proofreading; Kathryn Poethig has always been interested in my work and asked excellent questions; Yong Lao helped me make beautiful maps of Vietnam and the south where most strikes took place; Lilly Martinez and Heather Wilde are always cheerful and helpful with all administrative tasks that facilitated both my teaching and writing. Other CSUMB colleagues—Marsha Moroh and Ken Wanderman, Renee Curry, Diana Garcia, Rebecca Bergeon, and the Inter-Library Loan staff, and the Navarro family—provided faithful support, cheered me on, and were very patient with my preoccupation with this book project. The friendly staff members at CSUMB Otter Aquatic Center were always so nice to me and often allowed me to swim some extra laps at the end of a long working day! A lot of new insights came to me while I was in the water, walking along the trail, or riding my bike around the beautiful Monterey peninsula.

I'm very thankful to freelance editor Paula Douglas, who did a great job of making this bilingual manuscript read smoothly and with eloquent prose. I'm also grateful to Cornell SEAP Publications editors Deborah Homsher and Fred Conner who offered superb copyediting: their good, critical questions encouraged me to be even more concise and analytical at the end of each chapter. They have been very respectful of the Vietnamese language and attentive to accurate diacritics in the book and on the book cover. I am especially grateful to Fred for working patiently and closely with me to the very end of this editing process and for accommodating my requests on visuals and photos that I have accumulated over a long period of time. Of course, responsibility for any and all unintentional mistakes and oversights remains with me. I also wish to thank Fran Benson of the ILR imprint of Cornell University Press, who encouraged me and guided me to this successful relationship with SEAP.

Last but not least, my loving partner, Joseph Lubow, has supported me during every step of this long process. We discussed and dissected all aspects of my book at any time of day or night; his critical and insightful questions required me to strengthen and clarify my arguments for the general public. As hard a labor as this has been throughout this long journey, we always remembered to have fun along the way with our dear friends and families, and to sustain ourselves with our shared passion for great conversation, nature, music, museums, films, and the arts.

Ho Chi Minh City and Surrounding Districts

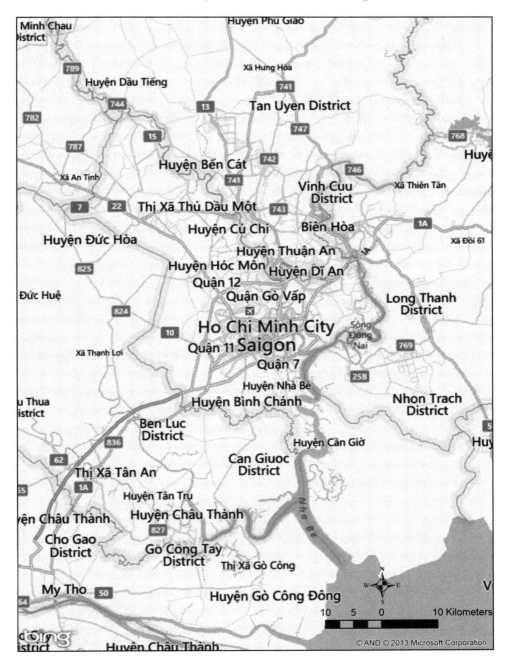

Map of Viet Nam

INTRODUCTION:
ISSUES FOR
LABOR ORGANIZING AND PROTESTS

Labor activism has been a hallmark of modern Vietnamese history, dating from French colonial rule to the modern-day one-party socialist state system. This in-depth study focuses on the rise of labor activism and the necessary conditions for its success. It shows the political and economic significance of wage workers, especially domestic migrant workers—the majority of the Vietnamese manufacturing workforce—who produce for the twenty-first-century global supply chain. This analysis of labor in Vietnam, covering more than one hundred years, examines the role of cultural identity in the labor process and, through migrant workers' own voices and real-life experiences, their power to improve their working and living conditions by finding effective ways to protest.

Two November 2010 newspaper articles from *Người Lao Động* (Laborer) revealed the complexities of labor-management-state relations in socialist Vietnam. The first article was about an increase in the minimum wage, a topic that continues to attract people's attention and directly affects millions of people in Vietnam. Thanks to the worker-led minimum-wage strikes in 2006, the government mandated annual, inflation-adjusted nationwide increases in the minimum wage. A new minimum wage was announced each November and took effect in January of the following year. But the paper reported that the most significant change in this round of state response to worker-led strikes was an additional increase in the minimum wage in the four districts near Ho Chi Minh City (HCMC), including the two hot spots for strikes: Hóc Môn and Củ Chi districts, places well known for their past revolutionary activities.[1]

The second article was about workers' direct action, especially about initiating strikes in the Hóc Môn and Củ Chi districts. The article served to raise awareness of so-called "cicada factories"[2] that came about when foreign factory owners declared bankruptcy, abruptly closed the factory, attempted to remove all the machinery and anything of value, and left behind an empty shell—the factory buildings. When this happened, the workers were stranded without being paid for their work, and no employers' contributions were sent to the state funds for workers' social security, health, and unemployment benefits. Taking direct action, more than one hundred

---

[1] Hoàng Hà, "Đồng loạt điều chỉnh lương tối thiểu từ ngày 1-1-2011," [Uniformly Adjusting the Minimum Wage from January 1, 2011], *Người Lao Động*, November 9, 2010, http://nld.com.vn/20101109015453591P0C1010/dong-loat-dieu-chinh-luong-toi-thieu-tu-ngay-112011.htm, accessed November 10, 2010.

[2] "Kim tuyền thoßát xác" (shedding of the golden cicada skin) is terminology popular within Vietnamese pro-labor circles. This imagery refers to an escapee who used a shell to fool predators and escape danger. But the modern cicada is a predator itself, equivalent to the "footloose" strategy of capital.

workers in a Taiwanese-owned factory stood guard around the factory to ensure that the fleeing owner did not remove the machinery and equipment from the building. These workers knew very well that such property—the only tangible things left in most of these cases—could be sold to compensate for the back pay and benefits owed to the workers.[3]

With attention to such top-down and bottom-up initiatives, this book examines the conditions that foment protests in Vietnam, putting workers' perspectives and their actions at the center of the analysis. Starting with the period of French colonial rule and ending with the *Đổi Mới* period (after 1986 to the present), this study uses the historical record, interviews (recent and some from long ago), and letters written by workers. I show how workers see themselves as independent thinkers who have relied on and continue to rely on elements of their cultural identity (native place, gender, ethnicity, and religion) and other factors (historical legacy, knowledge, and skills) to enable collective action in moments of crisis or desperation.

My overarching argument is that workers utilize the nexus of elements of their cultural identity to connect with each other in both productive relations inside and social relations outside the factory. In moments of crisis, this nexus enables labor mobilization and makes possible workers' awareness of belonging to the working class and of their shared interests. In other words, certain forms of cultural bonding among workers come first; then, in times of desperation or crisis, relying on the comfort and security derived from their cultural networks, workers may come to recognize a form of collective consciousness, including class consciousness. They engage in diverse types of resistance, including Marxist, Polanyian, and the use of law.

However, not all elements of cultural identity are central in all protests. While bonding based on native place is central for migrant workers who work far away from home, this type of bonding was not characteristic of local workers who commuted each day to work. Similarly, ethnicity and religion played a role in some historical protests, but not in all. Thus, workers bond with each other based on some cultural commonalities and some form of collective consciousness at particular historical moments. When the crisis is resolved, workers return to their daily lives in a comfort zone based on shared aspects of their cultural identity.

As socialist Vietnam has increased its participation in the free-market system, it has gradually relinquished many social contracts, benefits, and the job security it had established for its workers. Thus, finding answers to these three broad questions is relevant to understanding the contemporary labor scene in Vietnam:

1. What is the significance of cultural identity factors with respect to Vietnamese workers, and how did these factors coalesce to foster the development of social ties in different historical contexts (during the French colonial rule, in the Republic and the Democratic Republic of Vietnam, and in the Socialist Republic of Vietnam)?
2. To what extent did the workers' nexus of cultural identity and social ties enable labor mobilization and make possible "moments of class consciousness" in times of crisis and desperation?

---

[3] Vĩnh Tùng, "Lương thấp, tranh chấp tăng" [Low Wages, Rising Conflicts], *Người Lao Động*, November 11, 2010, http://nld.com.vn/2010111010141698P0C1010/luong-thap-tranh-chap-tang.htm, accessed August 6, 2012.

3. What are the *types of protest* that workers used to demand their rights, entitlements, and human dignity at particular historical moments?

In this book, I examine the meaning of class and the issues of consciousness that come into play during times of protest as well as the meaning and impact of the rule of law as it applies to three economic sectors (state, foreign direct investment, and domestic private).

STATE CONTRADICTIONS AND THE RULE OF LAW

Attention to the rule of law beginning with *Đổi Mới* in 1986 (the onset of economic renovation in Vietnam) is important in gaining an understanding of contemporary labor-capital-state relations. The socialist state uses the law to sustain its legitimacy and to govern labor and capital; the workers appeal to the law to justify their grievances and to advance their protests aimed at improving working conditions; the unions and the media cite the law to demand worker rights and entitlements, as well as to protect themselves from state censorship and capital retaliation.

Since *Đổi Mới* and, more prominently, since Vietnam's acceptance into the World Trade Organization (WTO) in 2006, the state has been legislating laws and issuing decrees, decisions, and directives to sustain "a market economy with a socialist orientation." In other words, the state, using the legal structure/framework, is attempting to maintain its socialist legitimacy while engaging in the capitalist mode of production.

Vietnam's joining the WTO in January 2007 firmly integrated the nation into the global market system, which has forced the Communist party that runs the state to face many internal contradictions. The state's claim that Vietnam has "a market economy with a socialist orientation" brings forth memories of internal battles that have shaken the country's very foundation—a Marxist-Leninist ideology. With the surge of capital entering Vietnam by way of foreign direct investment (FDI), which has more than doubled since 2006, and the privatization of state-owned enterprises, which began in 2000, the state is becoming less and less of a (self-proclaimed) government acting on behalf of the people; at times, some state organs/institutions are in alliance with the capitalists.

Many scholars agree that the state's use of the law as an instrument of governance and a source of legitimacy intensified in the global neoliberal era. Jean and John Comaroff argued that the language of the law affords a neutral medium through which different people (defined by their cultures, social endowments, material circumstances, and personal identities) can make claims on each other and the polity. The law allows the state to represent itself as the custodian of civility and social harmony against disorder.[4] Aihwa Ong explained how governments make exceptions to their usual governing practices to compete in the neoliberal global economy.[5] The state has the power and flexibility to grant privileges and protections

---

[4] Jean Comaroff and John L. Comaroff, "Millennial Capitalism: First Thoughts on a Second Coming," *Public Culture* 12,2 (2000): 328–29, http://publicculture.dukejournals.org/content/12/2/291.full.pdf+html, accessed August 6, 2012.

[5] Aihwa Ong, *Neoliberalism as Exception: Mutations in Citizenship and Sovereignty* (Durham, NC, and London: Duke University Press, 2006).

to certain groups of citizens (as determined by laws regarding zones of development such as special economic zones, export processing zones, and urban development zones) in order to engage with global capitalists and attract their investment.[6] In the case of Vietnam, the government selected the low-skilled segments of the population and advertised "compliant and low-cost labor"—primarily for working on assembly lines—in order to attract foreign investment in manufacturing. Ching Kwan Lee also discussed how the Chinese state has used the law to create and sustain its legalistic legitimacy. She distinguished between the "regime's project of 'rule by law' rather than a 'rule of law' system," and asserted that the Chinese state refuses "to subject itself to the constraints of the law."[7]

Scholars have noted that the Vietnamese state's need to establish a legal system dated back to the late 1980s, during their quest to integrate into the global capitalist market system. They also pointed out the gap between the "rule *by* law" and the "rule *of* law," which explains the challenges of implementing the rule *of* law.

Melanie Beresford argued that the state used the law to control the population, yet was not willing to subject itself to the law. Rule *by* law refers to the state's intention to create a legal framework to engage with the neoliberal market economy, that is, to rule by law rather than by decree. Overall, the practice of rule by law is preferable to rule by decree (by the Politburo, leaders of the Vietnamese Communist Party [VCP]); since joining the global market system, the Vietnamese National Assembly has ratified many laws, especially regarding labor-capital relations, commerce, and foreign investment. On the other hand, rule *of* law implies a separation of powers between government and judiciary, making the state subject to the law, which is not the intention of the Vietnamese state.[8]

More than a decade later, Nguyễn Quốc Việt elaborated on that contradiction in Vietnam's legal system: the difference between rule *of* law (the intent) and rule *by* law (how the state bends its own rules). He chronicled how the socialist rule of law was adopted with the establishment of the 1992 Constitution. In particular, Article 12 articulates and mandates governance by means of law (*quản lý bằng pháp luật*), emphasizing that "all State organs … and all citizens must seriously abide by the Constitution and the law. … All infringements of State interests, of the rights and legitimate interests of collectives and individual citizens, shall be dealt with in accordance with the law."[9] The Eighth Party Congress strengthened this rule of law in 1996, and the Ninth Party Congress accepted the term "socialist state governed by the rule of law" in the legal system in 2001.[10] John Gillespie made a similar argument and called the post-1992 Vietnam the "law-based state" (*Nhà nước pháp quyền*).[11]

---

[6] Ibid, pp. 7, 78–79.

[7] Ching Kwan Lee, *Against the Law: Labor Protests in China's Rustbelt and Sunbelt* (Berkeley, CA: University of California Press, 2007), pp. 117, 202.

[8] Melanie Beresford, review of Carlyle A. Thayer and David G. Marr, *Vietnam and the Rule of Law*, in *The Journal of Asian Studies* 54,3 (August 1995): 910–12.

[9] Nguyễn Quốc Việt, "Explaining the Transition to the Rule of Law in Vietnam: The Role of Informal Institutions and the Delegation of Powers to Independent Courts" (PhD dissertation in Law and Economics, Kassel University, Germany, 2006), pp. 50–51, http://kobra.bibliothek.uni-kassel.de/bitstream/urn:nbn:de:hebis:34-2006070313842/1/VietDiss-final.pdf, accessed August 6, 2012.

[10] Ibid.

[11] John Gillespie, "Understanding Legality in Vietnam," in *Vietnam's New Order: International Perspectives on the State and Reform in Vietnam*, ed. Stéphanie Balme and Mark Sidel (New York,

Now we examine how the state is not subject to its own mandates. Nguyễn explained about the main obstacle to the rule of law: arbitrary discretion of the state. Arbitrary discretion means that the communist state, especially the Politburo executive branch, exploits its power, thereby weakening the power of the other two branches of government. Consequently, Nguyễn argued, the legal system is inconsistent, and no effective mechanism exists to enforce the laws and to protect people's rights.[12] He argued that "widespread arbitrary discretion of government impedes the rule of law reform, infringes individual rights, and therefore hinders the transformation to a market economy in Vietnam." He pointed out that most of the laws in Vietnam are drafted by various ministries, not by the National Assembly members (who represent broader interests); consequently, these laws tend to reflect state interests rather than those of the masses.[13] Moreover, to implement a law, the state must provide under-law guidelines—instructions on how to implement a particular law properly—however, often such guidelines are not available until several years after the law is enacted. The legal hierarchical structure of seven levels of legal paperwork is cumbersome and does not facilitate the rule of law.[14] However, Nguyễn's examples focus primarily on how the use of state power infringes on the rights of business and capital;[15] he did not discuss how state arbitrariness impacts workers.

Focusing on economic relations, Adam Fforde and Stefan de Vylder explained how the socialist state needed to develop a legal system to control these economic relations but faced challenges in doing so. The authors recognized that the transitional period in the 1980s—from a system of central state planning and control to more of a market-based system—was chaotic, with the breakdown of the Soviet economy in 1989 affecting the Vietnamese decision to abolish central planning.[16] Focusing on that early period (even before Vietnam joined the WTO), Fforde and de Vylder cited other Vietnamese legal studies in the 1980s that pointed out the challenges posed by the "non-implementability" of the law in a "formally unreformed central-planning model with extensive bottom-up decentralization." They pointed out that studies by some influential Vietnamese scholars in the late 1980s indicated the need for economic contract law with "a system of business courts that could be more independent of local political interests." They also analyzed the situation from the state perspective and found that the shift to such a legal infrastructure—or a rule of law—would have curtailed state executive (ministerial) control over the powerful state economic sector, including major import-export bank holdings and construction projects (including new hotels) in the late 1980s.[17]

Mark Sidel acknowledged the gap between textual intent and implementation of the laws on labor and industrial relations in a globalized market system. He argued that in Vietnam, this gap creates contradictory effects stemming from the

---

NY: Palgrave Macmillan, 2006), pp. 143, 148, 150. Gillespie brought attention to the influence of the 1960s Soviet doctrine on the Vietnamese state that the state is the source of the law.

[12] Nguyễn Quốc Việt, "Explaining the Transition to the Rule of Law in Vietnam," pp. 16–17.

[13] Ibid., pp. 71–72.

[14] Ibid., p. 73. Note: in recent years the state has provided legal guidelines more promptly.

[15] Ibid., pp. 74, 77.

[16] Adam Fforde and Stefan De Vylder, *From Plan to Market: The Economic Transition in Vietnam* (Boulder CO: Westview Press, 1996), p. 148.

[17] Ibid., pp. 153, 166.

introduction of economic and labor laws, which, on the one hand, strengthen Vietnam's integration into the global economy, yet, on the other hand, restrict rights and opportunities for the working poor in Vietnam. He found that while the intent of Vietnam's legal reforms genuinely supported both duties and rights, their implementation often enforced duties while leaving rights unprotected.[18]

In summary, these scholarly works consistently identify the existence of a gap between policy and implementation and the different implications of rule *of* law and rule *by* law. Even with the "rule by law" practice, the one-party government has acted arbitrarily by enforcing some laws and not others. The government has not respected the supposed separation of powers (separating the Politburo, the National Assembly, and the judiciary), a characteristic of the rule *of* law.

I analyze this gap and consequences of state arbitrariness throughout this book. In particular, I explain how workers appeal to the rule of law in good faith, and how the state's arbitrary enforcement (rule by law) creates the gap between the legal intention and the real implementation of laws. Moreover, I show how this discrepancy has effectively circumscribed workers' resistance, as well as the efforts of labor journalists and labor unions to assist workers in achieving their rights, which concern wages, work hours, overtime hours, and compensation, as well as benefits such as social, health, and unemployment insurances, and allowances.[19]

CLASS AND THE CULTURAL–IDENTITY APPROACH TO LABOR RESISTANCE

Another issue that is central to the book is the notion that class and cultural identity can have a profound influence on labor resistance. When collective action is undertaken by a multitude of workers, the question of class and class consciousness becomes inevitably significant. To what extent is class consciousness a condition at the beginning of a collective action or an outcome that tends to arise from the process? A review of Marxist arguments with regard to labor processes and protests shows a complex picture: Trần Văn Giàu stresses the leadership role of the Marxist-Leninist worker party and labor union without recognizing the role of cultural identities in the formation of class consciousness.[20] E. P. Thompson recognizes the role of cultural factors in labor organizing and in fomenting class consciousness, and he suggests that class consciousness will be achieved at the end of the process, not at the beginning.[21]

---

[18] Mark Sidel, *Law and Society in Vietnam: The Transition from Socialism in Comparative Perspective* (Cambridge: Cambridge University Press, 2008), pp. 92, 116, 118.

[19] These allowances date back to the socialist era and are very important to workers. They include the common practice of paying workers a thirteenth-month salary (or year-end bonus). Also, laid-off state workers were supposed to receive severance packages from the government when government officials privatized state-owned enterprises (more in Chapter 3).

[20] Trần Văn Giàu. *Giai Cấp Công Nhân Việt Nam: Sự Hình Thành và Sự Phát Triển của Nó từ Giai Cấp 'Tự Mình' đến Giai Cấp 'Cho Mình,'* [The Vietnamese Workers' Class: Its Formation and Development from 'Class-In-Itself' to 'Class-For-Itself'] (Hanoi: Sự Thật Publisher, 1961), pp. 69, 84–85.

[21] Edward Palmer Thompson, "The Making of Class," in *Class*, ed. Patrick Joyce (Oxford and New York, NY: Oxford University Press, 1995), p. 131. Edward Palmer Thompson, "Class and Class Struggle," in *Class*, ed. Patrick Joyce, p. 136.

At the same time, we must consider the concept of "false consciousness," defined as forms of consent and capitulation among workers to the dominant ideology, hegemonic order, and/or state policies that reproduce their subordination in capitalist production relations.[22] In particular, James C. Scott analyzes two forms of false consciousness: the thick form, which claims consent; and the thin form, which settles for resignation. He defines the thick version of false consciousness by saying that "a dominant ideology works its magic by persuading subordinate groups to believe actively in the values that explain and justify their own subordination" and that "ideological state apparatuses," such as schools, church, media, and institutions of parliamentary democracy, secure active consent of subordinate groups "to the social arrangements that reproduce their subordination."[23] He describes the thin version of false consciousness as a kind of surrender: "The dominant ideology achieves compliance by convincing subordinate groups that the social order in which they live is natural and inevitable." Scott argues that the ruling elites define for subordinate groups what is realistic and produce consent *without* changing people's values: They persuade the underclass that their positions, life chances, and tribulations are inevitable and unchangeable.[24]

Focusing on the manufacturing/factory setting, Michael Burawoy argues that worker consent is voluntary. He discusses the "games" that workers play with management with respect to organizing and enforcing the rules regarding minimum wages and acceptable profit margins. In that context, workers engage in such "games" by coming to work and abiding by these rules once at work. He argues that the production process defines the rules of the game, and such game-playing can generate consent to the social relationships between labor and management within that production process. Relative satisfaction that workers derive from such subordination would be considered "voluntary servitude," or consent.[25] In each chapter, I discuss the relevance of these different meanings of "false consciousness" with regard to labor-management-state relations in Vietnam.

In examining the factors that enable labor mobilization and collective action, I find that the identity-based approach provides a broad framework that incorporates not only class but also cultural-identity factors—gender, native place, ethnicity, religion, and skills—which are keys to explaining the labor process and protests.[26] This broad-based framework provides a structure for describing and interpreting

---

[22] James C. Scott, *Domination and the Arts of Resistance: Hidden Transcripts* (New Haven, CT, and London: Yale University Press, 1990).

[23] Ibid., pp. 72–74.

[24] Ibid.

[25] Michael Burawoy, *Manufacturing Consent: Changes in the Labor Process under Monopoly Capitalism* (Chicago, IL, and London: The University of Chicago Press, 1979), pp. 80–82.

[26] For more discussion on this approach, see Comaroff and Comaroff, "Millennial Capitalism"; Thompson, "The Making of Class" and "Class and Class Struggle"; Aihwa Ong, *Spirits of Resistance and Capitalist Discipline: Factory Women in Malaysia* (Albany, NY: State University of New York Press, 1987); Aihwa Ong, "The Gender and Labor Politics of Postmodernity," in *The Politics Of Culture in the Shadow of Capital*, ed. Lisa Lowe and David Lloyd (Durham, NC, and London: Duke University Press, 1997); Elizabeth J. Perry, *Shanghai on Strike: The Politics of Chinese Labor* (Palo Alto, CA: Stanford University Press, 1997); Edward Palmer Thompson, "Time, Work-Discipline, and Industrial Capitalism," *Past and Present Society* 38 (December 1967): 56–97; Edward Palmer Thompson, "Eighteenth Century English Society: Class Struggle without Class?" *Social History* 3 (1978): 133–65.

Vietnamese labor organizing and protests that span more than one hundred years (from the 1880s to the present), an analysis that will unfold in the remaining chapters of this book.

However, not all cultural-identity factors are central to labor organizing, since workers rely on relevant cultural resources available to them in particular historical conditions and use them to overcome challenges. For local workers, native-place identification is not explicit in their rhetoric, whereas native-place identification is significant for migrant workers, who live and work far away from home (chapters 1, 5, 6). Overall, gender identification is important for both local and migrant workers.

A particular historical condition in the tumultuous US–Vietnam war era (1954–1975) gave workers a relevant cultural resource: religious consciousness that transcended class and ethnicity. Progressive Catholic priests and lay people in the South of Vietnam spearheaded a broad-based, social-justice platform that lent workers' protests two broad objectives: promoting democracy and people's welfare.

Why do workers protest in Vietnam? I find that, together, Karl Polanyi's and Marx's works explain the objectives of resistance, and hence, the motivation to protest. A Polanyi-type struggle is not based on class interests, but rather on the need to protect social substances imperiled by the "self-regulating" market.[27] In Vietnam, it means fighting against labor commodification for human dignity, justice, and self-preservation. A Marx-type struggle is based on class, and on the fight against capitalist exploitation for better wages and other labor rights. In the context of socialist Vietnam, labor resistance also reminds the state to fulfill its socialist contract. Overall, underlying all types of protest, workers use the law to protect themselves and their rights.

Reviewing Lee, I analyze how the state uses the legal system to legitimize the regime and how workers use the law to protect their rights and benefits.[28] But different from Lee's study, this book brings out the flexible nature of protests in Vietnam—the intermingling of both Marxist- and Polanyi-type protests carried out by workers in all types of factories: state-owned, domestic–private, foreign, and joint-venture factories. The chapters trace various ways in which workers have appealed to and used the rule of law, from citing violations of the laws in public-court settings to sending collective protest letters and petitions to newspapers, to informing the state apparatuses (state offices, labor unions, newspapers) about their plight, to filing lawsuits in the labor courts. I provide evidence from the French colonial time (Chapter 1), from the time of the regime of the US-supported government of the Republic of Vietnam, south of the seventeenth parallel (Chapter 2), and from practices of the Socialist Republic of Vietnam.

Again, critical analysis of the gap between legal intention and implementation is important for understanding the Vietnam case. Throughout the book, I assess how the arbitrary discretion of the state (rule *by* law) has effectively constrained workers'

---

[27] Karl Polanyi, *The Great Transformation: The Political and Economic Origins of Our Time* (Boston, MA: Beacon Press, 1944), p. 162. Unlike Marx, Polanyi argues that class interests offer only a limited explanation of long-run movements in society: "… the chances of classes in a struggle will depend upon their ability to win support from outside their own membership, which again will depend upon their fulfillment of tasks set by interests wider than their own. Thus, neither the birth nor the death of classes, neither their aims nor the degree to which they attain them; neither their co-operations nor their antagonisms can be understood apart from the situation of society as a whole" (p. 152).

[28] Lee, *Against the Law.*

resistance (appealing to rule *of* law). Moreover, the state has curtailed the efforts of some state apparatuses, such as the media and the labor unions, in assisting workers' struggles. While Chapter 3 presents the formation of the legal framework with a focus on laws regarding labor-capital relations in the *Đổi Mới* period, chapters 4, 5, and 6 examine historical incidents and consequences of arbitrary state discretion that affected labor-capital-state relations in the three economic sectors (state, foreign, and domestic private), respectively. Chapter 7 concludes with an analysis of internal state conflicts and their social consequences: how workers use the laws to fight for their rights and how labor journalists rely on the laws to protect themselves in championing workers' rights.

Different combinations of cultural-identity factors in specific historical conditions gave rise to different forms of protest that demonstrate flexible worker responses to specific conditions, during moments of class consciousness, against the capitalists and, at times, the state. The varied nature of these protests in Vietnam is reflected by a wide range of methods of protest. Throughout the book, I demonstrate both overt and covert forms of resistance to show their scope, range, and nuances in factories controlled by various types of owners. Showing a wide spectrum of protest methods, I present both public and "hidden" messages[29] communicated in a range of actions, including through strikes, slow-downs, factory toilet-stall graffiti with strike messages, letters of complaint to the state media and other state agencies, boycotts of contaminated factory meals, singing to disrupt lunch and nap hours, squatting in front of the factory gate, committing sabotage, and using poetry and collective language in their protest letters and petitions.

METHODOLOGY AND DATA SOURCES

Workers' voices constitute the key source of information that offers likely answers to the questions posed at the beginning of this introduction. Narratives of workers are loud and clear throughout the book: they come to us from interviews, archival materials, newspaper articles, and workers' poetry. The narratives are accompanied by photos of protest messages and collective actions.

In the analysis of workers' utterances (in their letters, petitions, complaints, and interviews with me), for Marx-type protests, I include workers' use of collective, class language—such as "we, us, sisters, brothers, workers, collective," and words that evoke their expectation of the fulfillment of the "socialist contract" in a worker state. For Polanyi-type protests, I focus on words or concepts that uphold the preservation of labor, life, and human decency and dignity. Moreover, I look for expressions that communicate the workers' love and care for the well-being of their fellow workers and demand for proper compensation when they are hurt or killed on the job or in protests.

Between 1998 and 2012, I amassed both quantitative and qualitative information that shed light on all forms of protests, especially protests in the state sector that were not reported by the media and the conditions that made the workers organize. However, without consistently available representative data, I cannot make generalizations based on my findings. I do intend to show the scope, range, and nuances of the labor protests in state and non-state factories. When permitted by representative data, I will show some patterns of protests throughout Vietnam.

---

[29] James C. Scott, *Weapons of the Weak* (New Haven, CT: Yale University Press, 1990).

I use a combination of qualitative—ethnography with in-depth interviews, participant observation, and factory visits—and quantitative methods (basic descriptive statistics) to illustrate labor practices, labor-management relations, and labor protests throughout Vietnam. During more than a decade of fieldwork, I interviewed hundreds of stakeholders in Vietnam, but in this book I feature forty-one interviewees and correspondents: fifteen workers (including strike participants, labor organizers, and leaders in textile, garment, and shoe factories, where most of the protests occurred); six state and union officials; four managers and owners (one foreign and three domestic entrepreneurs); and two international labor officials. Additionally, I present rare interviews with eight activists and cadres who witnessed and experienced labor organizing and protests that took place during eras ranging from the French colonial period to the socialist period following the introduction of *Đổi Mới*: two *Hoa* labor and communist activists who were embedded in factories in the South before 1975; two progressive Catholics (a former priest and a labor organizer) who promoted social justice in light of liberation theology during the US–Vietnam war; and four communist cadres (three are in their eighties; one, in his late fifties). Moreover, I corresponded with six journalists who provided invaluable insights and understanding regarding the role of the state media in state-labor-capital relations.

Throughout the chapters, except for state officials and other respondents who preferred that their real names be used, I strictly use pseudonyms to protect the interviewees' safety and well-being. I also present and analyze thirty-three protest case studies. Appendix B summarizes the role of cultural identity, class, and types of protest for each of these cases.

To supplement these empirical data, I analyzed fifteen years of strike data (1995–2010), compiled by the Vietnamese General Confederation of Labor and the General Statistics Office of Vietnam. These show patterns of strikes by ownership type, origins of capital, and geographical location throughout the country. Focusing on the South, where most protests have erupted, I used the compilation of sixteen years of labor protests in HCMC (1995–2011; provided by the HCMC Labor Federation) to illustrate different forms of dissent in the state sector (which encompasses workplaces ranging from 100 percent state-owned enterprises to factories that have been privatized), and the private sector (including domestic-private, FDI, and joint-ventures).

I use many original works of Vietnamese scholarship from sources including archival materials from the Nam Định Textile Museum and various government agencies/offices of the Republic of Vietnam, as well as contemporary studies by Vietnamese scholars. I also examine some valuable, internally circulated contemporary reports at the district- and city-government levels to offer insights into internal dynamics and contradictions among state agencies in the Socialist Republic of Vietnam. Additionally, I found two sources of *samizdat*[30] in the South (under the RVN government) that shed light on labor organizing and protests from progressive Catholic perspectives between 1954 and 1975: the ĐD journal and the *Bản Tin Lao Động* newsletter.

---

[30] In terminology borrowed from the former Soviet Union, *samizdat* means banned or underground literature. In one of these two sources, the publisher changed the title often to avoid government persecution, but his publication always carried a code—the same abbreviation for the title—to identify itself to supporters.

I performed in-depth content analyses of original petitions, complaints, and letters, including a sample of thirty-nine worker complaint letters and petitions submitted to newspapers in the South in 2005 and 2006, and workers' petitions in the North in 1998 and 1999. These years have no special significance; they were the times when I was able to meet and talk with workers and respondents who had given me these valuable resources. I do not include the identities of these sources, but use pseudonyms for interviewees (with the exception of some officials who asked to be identified) as a matter of ethical imperative, for the protection of their anonymity and safety.

Both workers and journalists supplied writings that documented these protest letters, some of which were published in newspapers. For these, I will mention the senders and the recipients when possible (in many cases senders did not write down their names). If the complaints were not published officially, I do not mention names to protect all involved. In all cases, I provide as much context and the general identities of the senders and recipients as I have available, without violating human-subject protection protocols.

ORGANIZATION OF THIS BOOK

The organization of this book reflects one important aspect of the labor-capital dynamics: All foreign capital is not the same; it has different *identities*. Foreign investment in different types of factories demonstrates different characteristics, beyond the oft-cited culturally distinct characteristics and management styles. These different capital identities are based on relevant historical legacies (such as the return of Taiwanese and Korean capitalists to Vietnam in the late 1980s), the ethnicity of the enterprise's capital owner, the role and location of the enterprise in the global supply chain (as multinationals, or suppliers, or subcontractors), as well as the method of investment (formal, underground, or via a third country). To aid in understanding the impact of these diverse investors, I have organized the chapters of this book to show capital variability based on time and the aforementioned factors, spanning from the French colonial and American imperialist periods to the present global market system.

This book is divided into three parts. Part I focuses on Voices of History and Forms of Consciousness, that is, how history illuminates the role of cultural identities in the process of arriving at some forms of consciousness from the era of French colonial rule to the reunification of Vietnam in 1975. Chapter 1 focuses on peasant and migrant workers under French colonial rule (1880s–1954). Chapter 2 examines labor movements and protests in the Republic of Vietnam (1954–1975).

The topic of Part II is State Policies, State Capital, and Worker Response since *Đổi Mới*, that is, how the socialist state has used the rule of law to manage labor-capital relations since opening up to the global capitalist market in 1986 and how state workers have responded to different forms of state capital—from 100 percent state-owned to joint-ventures to privatized state factories. Chapter 3 focuses on the rule of law with regard to policies in Socialist Vietnam since *Đổi Mới* (1986–present). Chapter 4 explains the transformation of state-owned enterprises into private, joint-stock companies and various forms of labor protest in both state-owned and privatized state enterprises.

Part III analyzes Mobilized Labor and Morphing Private Capital since *Đổi Mới*, that is, in the neoliberal context, examining how workers respond to various forms of *private* capital—from foreign-direct investment to domestic private, including underground investment. Chapter 5 examines labor organizing and protests in foreign-direct-investment factories. Chapter 6 focuses on workers' activism in domestic-private and underground foreign-investment factories. Finally, synthesizing previous chapters, Chapter 7 analyzes the internal state conflicts and their social consequences, workers' use of laws to fight for their rights, and labor journalists' and labor unions' use of laws to champion workers' rights and to protect themselves.

The Conclusion summarizes responses to those three broad questions on cultural identity and class, flexible resistance, and the rule of law, and discusses implications for future research. Finally, it suggests the theoretical implications and a critique of the approach and conclusions of some scholars with respect to the labor process and the false consciousness concept.

SUMMARY OF THE FINDINGS

From abundant evidence of more than one hundred years of labor movements, I found support for the identity-based approach to labor resistance. To understand what enables development of a class consciousness, we need to analyze the totality of migrant workers' experiences in the whole labor process, not only in the workplace and at the point of production, but also in their living spaces where the nexus of cultural-identity factors—native place, gender, ethnicity, and religion— plays an important role. Workers find support among persons of their own gender. Also, in both good times and times of struggle, migrant workers bond with fellow workers who have the same birthplace (native-place bonding). It is unclear, however, whether native-place bonding occurs among local, commuter-workers, who did not explicitly remark about native place in our interviews. But evidence from both quantitative and qualitative data mentioned above shows that they do rely on other cultural-identity factors, depending on particular historical conditions.

My interviews and secondary sources also evince that class consciousness did develop during what I call "class moments." During these times of struggle, workers brought together by cultural bonds became aware of belonging to the working class and of their shared interests. The "we workers" language was prevalent in both state and private factories throughout the hundred-year period addressed by this analysis, notably, among such groups as the brown-shirted peasant workers, the torn-shirt group, and the collective of male and female fiber technicians/workers, as well as the contract workers, weaving workers, industrial workers, and the "sister" and "brother" workers.

Evidence confirms the diverse nature of protests in Vietnam—the combination of both Marxist- and Polanyi-type protests by workers in all types of factories: state-owned, domestic-private, and foreign-owned as well as joint-ventures. While state workers used more Marx-type rhetoric and actions than Polanyi-type, private workers—the growing sector of the labor force—utilized Marx-type and Polanyi-type rhetoric and actions about equally (Appendix B).

Workers always have appealed to the rule of law to fight for their rights and human dignity, even under French colonial rule (appealing, for example, to the contract law and the labor code as early as 1929, to the free trade union system and the right to strike in the RVN from 1954 to 1975, and to minimum wage laws in socialist Vietnam). In the twenty-first century, workers in all sectors have used legalistic language, in addition to class-based language, and appealed to legal remedies as their first line of offense and defense.

Evidence from my sources also shows that the state maintains the privilege to act arbitrarily, using the law to govern labor-capital relations in the neoliberal era but still not respecting the "socialist state governed by the rule of law" endorsed by the Ninth Party Congress since 2001.[31] This has greatly circumscribed workers' gains—whether big or small—and limited the effectiveness of workers' allies (the labor newspapers and local unions) when they tried to crack open more space for workers' voices in their struggles for their rights and interests.

Last but not least, I am grateful to the many workers who trusted me, invited me into their homes, and shared their heartfelt trials, tribulations, and triumphs. While this book is dedicated to the workers, I am always conscious of the unintended power disparities between myself and them. I never can resolve such power differences, but my sincere goal is to bring their voices out in the open while doing my utmost not to jeopardize them in any way. I can only hope that this book will shed light on their courageous struggles and help bring them justice.

---

[31] Nguyễn Quốc Việt, "Explaining the Transition to the Rule of Law in Vietnam," pp. 50–51.

CHAPTER 1

PEASANT AND MIGRANT WORKERS UNDER FRENCH COLONIAL RULE (1880–1954)

French Indochina, which included Vietnam, was established in the 1880s and lasted until 1954, except for a short period of Japanese control during World War II. Foreign investment in rubber, fiber, textile, and other village-based industries began in the early years of French colonization, but Vietnam remained primarily agricultural throughout this era. While modern-day Vietnam has changed dramatically since those years, the roots of Vietnam's labor unrest, which began in the factories and fields of colonial times, play an important role in feeding the spirit of today's workers, who call upon that heritage of resistance and solidarity to stand up to factory owners throughout the nation.

I have paid particular attention to the port town of Nam Định in northeast Vietnam—known as the birthplace of the labor movement in the North. By relying on interviews and archival materials, I have attempted to capture some historical perspectives in the words of those who lived during the years when labor practices and the labor movement were taking shape. Included here are interviews with surviving communist cadres who organized in Nam Định, as well as with some elderly Vietnamese with knowledge of the Nam Định Textile Combine.[1] I walked through the streets of Nam Định, following the path of those rural migrant workers a century earlier, to imagine their arduous, daily, six- to twelve-mile (roundtrip) walk between home and factory. I visited the Nam Định Museum to gain access to workers' own words—via archival materials, such as petition letters, transcriptions of oral poems, memoirs, and leaflets—and accounts from scholars and historians.

Without the opportunity to talk to those workers directly, I had to interpret the events and intentions based on existing evidence, while weighing all available alternative perspectives. I was allowed access to the Nam Định archives for a very limited time. I was permitted, however, to take photos of all the documents that were available to me there, including pamphlets, poetry, newspaper articles, photos, and other texts. Examining those photos at length afterward, I was able to garner a wealth of information that is not readily available to researchers.[2]

---

[1] The French used Vietnamese labor to build this integrative compound, which included both fiber and weaving plants to process raw fiber to finished fabrics.

[2] When I returned there in 2009 and tried to visit the Nam Định Textile Combine Museum again, I was told that it was closed to the public due to a planned relocation of the factory to outside of Nam Định city. As of 2013, however, I learned that the museum was still at the same location, although its public access is very limited.

As background to understanding Vietnam's labor history, I first present the broad political-economic context of French colonial rule in Vietnam and its key policies affecting labor and capital.

FRENCH POLICIES AND THE RISE OF CONTRACT WORKERS (1880–1954)

French colonial rule in Indochina from 1880 to 1954 encompassed the three geographic sections of Vietnam: Tonkin, An Nam, and Cochin China (northern, central, and southern Vietnam, respectively).[3] The colonies were rich in valuable natural resources, and the French government and capitalists exploited colonial workers to extract those raw materials. Moreover, the colonizers invested money in factories and production enterprises over which the Europeans wielded total control. These were common practices of colonial governments and capitalists. Fiber and textile production was a key manufacturing sector. By 1900, French capitalists already had invested in the profitable fiber and textile industries in Nam Định, in collaboration with Hoa[4] merchants who had established their handicraft in small-scale fiber factories in the late-nineteenth century.[5]

In the period leading up to World War I, the French government and French capitalists (finance corporations) invested idle francs in wartime industries and commerce, such as coal, rubber, mining, and transportation throughout Indochina and in parts of Africa.[6] The devalued franc was tied to Indochinese piasters (which were backed by silver). The French invested their devalued currency in labor-intensive industries, such as textile and garment. They exploited the labor of women and children, as demonstrated by the case of Nam Định textile factory, described below. After World War I, with heavy debts to the United States, the French had to make a transition from a wartime to a peacetime economy. The worldwide boom in demand for rubber rescued them: the French met this increased world demand by establishing about a dozen rubber plantations in the South of Vietnam and extracting raw rubber from these plantations using "contract workers."[7] Saigon, then, became a

---

[3] During the French colonial administration, Vietnam was divided into three geographically arbitrary territories: Tonkin protectorate (in the north), An Nam protectorate (in the central region), and the colony of Cochinchina (in the south). The two protectorate territories had a dual system of French and (nominal) Vietnamese administration.

[4] Hoa are ethnic Chinese Vietnamese born and raised in Vietnam.

[5] Nam Định Textile Combine Party Executive Committee, *Lịch Sử Đảng Bộ Công Ty Dệt Nam Định 1930–1975* (The History of the Party at Nam Dinh Textile Combine 1930–1975) (Nam Định: Nam Định Publisher, 2000), pp. 10–11.

[6] Before World War II, 78 percent of total private investment in Indochina came from France. See Bửu Hoàn, "A Study of the Consequences of the Geneva Peace for the Vietnamese Economy," *Far Eastern Economic Review* XXV,24 (December 11, 1958): 753–57; XXV,25 (December 18, 1958): 789–98; and XXV,26 (December 25, 1958): 839–42. This private investment from France was for French interests, not for its colonies. Flooding its colonial markets with French final products while exploiting the colonies' raw materials and labor created economic dependency on France in those colonies. Trần Văn Giàu, *Giai Cấp Công Nhân Việt Nam: Sự Hình Thành và Sự Phát Triển của Nó từ Giai Cấp 'Tự Mình' đến Giai Cấp 'Cho Mình'* (The Vietnamese Workers' Class: Its Formation and Development from 'Class-In-Itself' to 'Class-For-Itself') (Hanoi: Su That Publisher, 1961), pp. 129–35.

[7] Nguyễn Thị Mộng Tuyền, "Phong Trào Đấu Tranh Của Công Nhân Cao Su Thủ Dầu Một Trong 30 Năm Chiến Tranh Giải Phóng (1945-1975)" [The Struggle Movement of the Thủ Dầu Một Rubber Plantation Workers in 30-Year Liberation War (1945–1975)] (PhD dissertation, Vietnam Academy for Social Sciences/Southern Institute of Sustainable Development, 2010),

global center of commercial rubber production.[8] The raw product was shipped to France for refinement and the manufacturing of rubber products.

To meet an increased demand for labor, both before and after the war, the French used a worker contract system to supply labor in Vietnam's mines, plantations, and factories. Since these industries were located in rural areas, a recruitment system was developed to import laborers from other parts of the colony. In many instances, recruiters were sent to find and bring workers to the jobs.

Most contract workers (*công nhân công tra*) were originally peasants who migrated to work far away from their home villages, especially those from poor provinces in the northern and central regions.[9] Unable to find work locally, these workers went to where the jobs were, often hundreds of miles away. They looked for work in far-flung industrial towns, such as Hanoi, Nam Định, Hải Phòng, and Saigon-Chợ Lớn, and where rubber was plentiful, such as Phước Long.[10]

The labor contract system facilitated this labor migration nationwide, which resulted in the development of the peasant-turned-worker, or *công nhân áo nâu* (brown-shirted workers) as they were called in factories, mines, and plantations. These early migrant workers were the most vulnerable workers: the contract offer came without any labor-union rights (the case studies below demonstrate some of the shady practices used to fool workers into signing these long-term contracts). This practice continued during the Great Depression and throughout the 1930s, when wages fell even further.[11]

Peasants coming from the same villages often worked together in the same factories or were forced to stay in the same makeshift living quarters. Such ways of working and living contributed to workers' spontaneous collective action. In the 1920s, at least 600,000 peasants lost their land and, thus, went looking for work in mines, plantations, factories, and government public works projects.[12]

Peasant workers—most of whom were illiterate—were tricked into signing three-year contracts to work in the South. Many ruthless Vietnamese or French Vietnamese recruiters assisted these efforts. The contracts required three-year commitments to slave-like working conditions for extremely low wages, leaving the trapped workers with no hope of earning or saving enough to pay off even small debts (for food and housing, for example). Moreover, the French capitalists often paid workers late, thus plunging them even deeper into a vicious cycle of indebtedness, poverty, and misery.

The French used a combination of daily pay and piece-rate remuneration in early 1900s factory work. Workers got paid by the day, based on a minimum number (target) of finished products that they had to produce. After the target was achieved,

---

pp. 231–32, www.sugia.vn/index.php?mod=news&cpid=12&nid=669&view=detail, accessed October 2, 2010.

[8] Mark Cleary, "Land Codes and the State in French Cochinchina c. 1900–1940," *Journal of Historical Geography* 29 (July 2003): 356–75.

[9] Jean Chesneaux, "Stages in the Development of the Vietnam National Movement 1862–1940," *Past and Present* 7 (April 1955): 71.

[10] Hồ Sơn Đài, "Introduction," in *Lịch Sử Phong Trào Công Nhân Cao Su Dầu Tiếng* [History of the Labor Movement in Dầu Tiếng Rubber Plantation], ed. Lê Văn Khoa (Ho Chi Minh City: Nhà Xuất Bản Lao Động, 2000), pp. 14–17; Trần Văn Giàu, *Giai Cấp Công Nhân Việt Nam*, pp. 473–74.

[11] Chesneaux, "Stages in the Development," p. 72.

[12] David Marr, *Vietnamese Tradition on Trial: 1920–1945* (Berkeley, CA: University of California Press, 1981), pp. 30, 318.

workers could produce additional products and earn more money at the piece rate, but the rate was set very low. This system effectively controlled workers in two ways. First, there was real fear of displacement: a reserve of peasant workers waited outside the factory gate and could be drawn on to replace less-productive workers or protesters at any time. This put tremendous pressure on workers inside the factory, and some worked until they collapsed for fear of losing their jobs. Second, with low piece rates, workers worked themselves to exhaustion under minimal supervision.[13] This was not "voluntary servitude," and workers did not consent to the unfair remuneration structure:[14] workers participated simply in order to survive.

Migrant workers, their families, and their friends concentrated in factories, mines, or plantations, and lived in nearby makeshift housing.[15] By the end of 1929, an estimated 220,000 workers were marginally employed throughout Vietnam: 39 percent worked in industrial and commercial enterprises; 37 percent on rubber plantations; and 24 percent in coal mines.[16] An unintended consequence of worker concentration in "industrial towns," which had flagship factories, was that these factories became a type of incubator conducive to promulgating strikes nationwide. For example, more than four thousand workers were at Nam Định Textile Combine; three thousand workers at Hải Phòng cement factory; one thousand railroad workers in Vinh, and one thousand workers at Ba Son Shipyard.[17]

Since there were no labor unions or collective-bargaining negotiations to resolve labor-management conflicts, the French colonial government was able to suppress workers as soon as strikes and protests erupted.[18] Worse yet, the global economic crisis between 1929 and 1933 led to falling wages and increasing costs of living (because the colonial piaster was tied to the franc). This inflation hurt the local poor and peasants while benefiting the French. The reason was that French capitalists had already been investing their devalued/idle franc in textile and garment factories, mining, and rubber plantations in Vietnam since World War I, so they continued to benefit from these investments while the workers suffered from the inflation and falling wages.[19]

The three case studies that follow—Nam Định Textile Combine and the Dầu Tiếng and Phú Riềng rubber plantations—demonstrate how workers' cultural identities regarding native place, gender, and ethnicity created a foundation for their networking and labor activism; the stories are told in the workers' own voices using interviews I conducted with the individuals, as well as archival materials. I selected the Nam Định Textile Combine (in the North) because it was the largest combine in

---

[13] Nam Định Textile Combine Party Executive Committee, *Công Ty Dệt Nam Định*, pp. 20, 28, 30.

[14] Michael Burawoy, *Manufacturing Consent: Changes in the Labor Process under Monopoly Capitalism* (Chicago, IL, and London: The University of Chicago Press, 1979), pp. 80–81.

[15] Trần Văn Giàu, *Giai Cấp Công Nhân Việt Nam*, p. 502.

[16] Hoàng Quốc Việt, *The Trade Union Movement in Vietnam* (Hanoi: Foreign Languages Publishing House/Vietnam Federation of Trade Unions, 1988), p. 14.

[17] Trịnh Chi, *Questions and Answers about the History of Vietnamese Communist Party* (Hanoi: Thanh Niên Publisher, 1978), p. 14; Trần Văn Giàu, *Giai Cấp Công Nhân Việt Nam*, p. 135.

[18] Trịnh Quang Quỹ, *Phong Trào Lao Động Việt Nam* [The Labor Movement in Vietnam] (Saigon: np, 1970), p. 25; Nam Định Textile Combine, *Lịch Sử Đảng Bộ*, p. 20.

[19] Chesneaux, "Stages in the Development," pp. 71–72; Trần Văn Giàu, *Giai Cấp Công Nhân Việt Nam*, pp. 112–26, 236-60.

Indochina and employed peasants who walked to the factory from their nearby villages; I chose the two rubber plantations (in the South) because they exemplify the working and living conditions of local peasant workers and migrant contract workers from the North and the Central.

ROLE OF ETHNICITY: THE FRENCH, THE KINH, AND THE HOA

To understand the roles of the key players in colonial Vietnam's labor history, I start with ethnicity—a factor of cultural identity—and analyze how it intersects with other cultural factors in influencing labor organizing and protests.[20]

For this analysis, out of fifty-four distinct ethnic groups recognized by the Vietnamese state, I focus on the two relevant ethnic groups: the Kinh (commonly called Người Việt in Vietnam), which accounts for more than 86 percent of the Vietnamese population, and the Hoa (ethnic Chinese who were born and raised in Vietnam), which accounts for only 1.1 percent of the population. However, the economic power and global networking of the Hoa date back as far as one thousand years, through the period of Chinese domination of Vietnam, and the Hoa continue to have influence in present-day Vietnam.

Based on common usage in Vietnam, I will refer to Kinh and Hoa to denote these two ethnic groups when the discussion centers on ethnicity. For other topics, I use Việt or Vietnamese to refer collectively to the whole population. In all cases, I use "ethnic Chinese" to refer to Chinese investors coming from East and Southeast Asia, especially Taiwan and Hong Kong.

Focusing on the relations between the Kinh and the Hoa across classes, I examine the history of the Hoa in Vietnam, the alliance between the French and the Hoa merchant class, and labor organizing efforts of both the Kinh and Hoa working class. Scholars have found two different alliances: between the French and the Hoa capitalist class, and between the Kinh and the Hoa working class.[21]

From the mid-eighteenth century to the mid-nineteenth century, many Chinese nationals migrated to Vietnam, primarily congregating in the area of Saigon surrounding Chợ Lớn (meaning large market), the key hub of the Hoa community in the city. Their network and bonding were based on native place and kinship (đồng hương, đồng tộc), as well as skills in trade and commerce.[22] These Chinese immigrants

---

[20] I am conscious that ethnicity is different from race and that racial/ethnic divisions can hinder labor organizing. In the US context, David Roediger's classic work focuses on whiteness and the identities of white workers as the center of his analysis, and their relationships with workers of different races, such as Whites and Blacks (a distinction that was significant in the St. Louis general strike in 1877, for example), and Whites and Asians (the distinction most significant in a movement initiated in San Francisco for the eight-hour working day and the spread of railroads throughout the nation in the late 1870s). David Roediger, *The Wages of Whiteness: Race and the Making of the American Working Class* (London and New York, NY: Verso, 1991).

[21] Nghị Đoàn, "Đồng Bào Hoa tại Thành Phố Hồ Chí Minh Dưới Sự Lãnh Đạo của Đảng Cộng Sản Việt Nam" [The Hoa in Hồ Chí Minh City under the Leadership of the Vietnamese Communist Party], in *Người Hoa Tại Thành Phố Hồ Chí Minh* (Hồ Chí Minh City: Nhà Xuất Bản Sở Văn Hoá Thông Tin, 2007), pp. 30–31; and Huỳnh Ngọc Trảng, "Người Hoa ở Thành Phố Hồ Chí Minh," in ibid., p. 78.

[22] Trần Khánh, "Tìm hiểu các tổ chức xã hội và nghiệp đoàn truyền thống của người Hoa ở Việt Nam trong lịch sử" [Understanding Traditional Social Associations and Trade Unions of the Hoa in Vietnam in Historical Perspective], *Tạp Chí Dân Tộc Học* [Ethnology Journal] 116 (February 2002): 5.

controlled fruit orchards, handicrafts, and, most importantly, the river transportation necessary for rice, various fruits, and most food distribution throughout the Mekong River delta region.[23] These immigrants established their commercial trading networks in the mid-nineteenth century by buying small-scale Vietnamese artisanal products and, in turn, selling industrial and raw materials along land and sea routes.[24]

These Hoa sustained their stronghold in the local economy, especially in the South, and were tolerated by the French.[25] Relying on trust (*chữ tín*) in credit and lending has served them well over time.[26] They invested in rice production, a strategically vital crop and the top agricultural export of Indochina and, subsequently, of the Republic of Vietnam (1954–1975). The Hoa in Chợ Lớn effectively had a vertical monopoly of the rice trade: from milling, wharf labor, and land and river transport to making and fixing jute rice containers. The Hoa owned large steam-engine-powered–rice-milling factories and processing plants for preparing rice for export.[27]

The Hoa formed trade associations (*hội nghề nghiệp*), worker unions (*nghiệp đoàn công nhân*), and some underground associations (such as Thiên Địa Hội; these associations, in general, were partly anti-French, partly pro-ethnic Chinese merchant/capitalist) while under French rule, which developed further under the Republic of Vietnam rule between 1954 and 1975.[28] Trade associations developed around such industries as garment, barber/hair cutting, weaving, Chinese medicine, finance and banking, and commercial transportation. The chamber of commerce of the Hoa was recognized by the French in 1903 and developed into the sophisticated and multifunctional Chợ Lớn Chamber of Commerce in 1924 (which operated until 1975). The development of the chamber of commerce created by the Hoa in the early twentieth century laid the groundwork for the solid commercial and economic foundation that would support the return of ethnic-Chinese capital investment in Vietnam's Đổi Mới era of the late twentieth and twenty-first centuries (Chapters 5 and 6).

From the very beginning of French colonial rule, the French tried to divide and conquer the Kinh and the Hoa, using both class and ethnic divisions. First, the French formed a capitalist alliance at the transnational level. The French signed several key

[23] Nguyễn Tuấn Triết and Trịnh Thị Kiều Oanh, "Truyền Thống Đấu Tranh Cách Mạng và Thành Tựu Xây Dựng Chủ Nghĩa Xã Hội của Đồng Bào Hoa ở Quận 6 Thành Phố Hồ Chí Minh" [Revolutionary Tradition and Achievement in Building Socialism of the Hoa in District 6 in Hồ Chí Minh City], in *Người Hoa ở Quận 6—Thành Phố Hồ Chí Minh,* ed. Phan An (Hồ Chí Minh City, Vietnam: Mặt Trận Tổ Quốc Việt Nam Quận 6, 1990), pp. 39–40.

[24] Trần Văn Giàu, *Giai Cấp Công Nhân Việt Nam,* pp. 26–27; Phan An and Phan Xuân Biên, "Người Hoa trong hoạt động kinh tê của Miên Nam Việt Nam Trước Năm 1975" [The Hoa in the South of Vietnam's Economic Activities before 1975], *Phát Triển Kinh Tế* [Economic Development Journal] 12 (October 1991), pp. 21–22.

[25] Trần Khánh, *The Ethnic Chinese and Economic Development in Vietnam* (Singapore: Institute of Southeast Asian Studies, 1993), p. 106.

[26] Clifton Barton, "Trust and Credit: Some Observations Regarding Business Strategies of Overseas Chinese Traders in South Vietnam," in *The Chinese in Southeast Asia, Volume 1: Ethnicity and Economic Activity,* ed. Linda Y. C. Lim and Peter Gosling (Singapore: Maruzen Asia, 1983 , pp. 46–64.

[27] Trần Văn Giàu, *Giai Cấp Công Nhân Việt Nam,* p. 53.

[28] Trần Khánh, "Tìm hiểu các tổ chức xã hội và nghiệp đoàn truyền thống," pp. 9–10, 13.

agreements with the Chinese government, which granted Chinese investors privileges to invest in and monopolize some vital industries (such as banking, hotels, restaurants, small retail stores, and rice production) at the expense of local Vietnamese.[29] In 1885, the French and the Chinese governments signed the Treaty of Peace, Friendship, and Commerce between France and China, in which the emperor of China recognized French colonial rule in Vietnam.[30] For its part, France recognized the rights of Chinese citizens in Vietnam: "Chinese, settlers, or soldiers, who live peaceably in An Nam, engaging in agriculture, industry, or commerce ... shall enjoy, both in their persons and property, the same security as French dependents."[31] This treaty recognized the common interests of the emperor of China and the French Republic, which completely governed commerce and trade, including the export and import of opium, between China and French-controlled regions (Tonkin, An Nam). Nowhere did the treaty mention the interests and the rights of the Vietnamese in these French-controlled regions.

Then, the Tianjin Commercial Convention—signed in 1886, between the French and the emperor of China—gave the Chinese citizens freedom to do business in Vietnam and extended the same rights to the French in China. Article IV states:

> Chinese shall have the right to possess land, construct buildings, open business establishments, and have stores throughout An Nam. For their persons, their families, and their property, protection and security equal to that of subjects of the most favored European nation will prevail and, as with these latter, they shall not be the object of any ill-treatment ... Frenchmen shall receive the same treatment from China.[32]

This convention, in particular, opened the floodgates to Chinese investment in Vietnam when the °French needed to use Chinese compradors (middlemen) to transform Indochina into a huge market for consumer goods and cheap labor as well as a center for rice export, mostly controlled by Chinese investors.[33] Articles XI and XV clearly show how this convention promoted the export of food—rice and grains in particular—from Vietnam to China, benefiting Chinese businessmen exporting food from Vietnam and importing it in China. Moreover, the convention also helped the French government's tax revenue by allowing the imposition of an import duty on Chinese products exported to Vietnam.[34] Finally, two separate articles of the

---

[29] Huỳnh, "Người Hoa ở Thành Phố Hồ Chí Minh," p. 78; Trần Khánh, *The Ethnic Chinese and Economic Development in Vietnam*, pp. 46–47.

[30] "China's External Relations—A History," http://www.chinaforeignrelations.net/taxonomy/term/4, accessed April 2012.

[31] "Treaty of Peace, Friendship, and Commerce between France and China [1885]," http://www.chinaforeignrelations.net/node/164, accessed April 2012.

[32] Convention of Tientsin [Tianjin], 1886 (Ratified by France by the Law of 30 November 1888), http://www.chinaforeignrelations.net/node/165, accessed April 2012.

[33] Huỳnh argued further that this treaty legitimized the Chinese government's intervention in Vietnam in order to protect their Chinese citizens. Huỳnh, "Người Hoa ở Thành Phố Hồ Chí Minh," pp. 77–78.

[34] ARTICLE XI: "Products of Chinese origin brought into Tonkin via the land frontier shall pay the import duty of the Franco-Annamese Tariff. They need pay no export duty upon leaving Tonkin." ARTICLE XV: "The export of rice and grains will be banned in China. The importation of these items will be free of duty ..."

convention (articles IV and XVI) stress the protection of Chinese citizens as the "subjects of the most favored European nation."[35] On the other hand, out of nineteen articles of the convention, the interests of Vietnamese (or Annamites) are mentioned only once in one article.[36]

The Nanjing Agreement, signed in 1930, between the French and the Chinese Nationalist Kuomintang (KMT) government, extended the scope of the foreign trade and industrial activities of the Chinese citizens in Vietnam.[37] In 1946, the signing of the Chongqing Treaty granted Chinese citizens further privileges and the same status as that of the French, with exemptions, such as from military service.[38] Moreover, the Chongqing Treaty cemented commercial rights already established in the 1886 Tianjin Commercial Convention that gave the Chinese the right to engage in mining, to buy and develop land, and to put up buildings. With this transnational commercial alliance in place, the French focused on class and ethnic divisions to foment resentment between the Kinh and the Hoa (by 1946, many Chinese citizens had been in Vietnam for more than sixty years, since 1885), as is discussed in depth, later.

The French shared some common economic interests with the Hoa capitalists, so both benefited by allying with the other.[39] The French needed local compradors to deal with local Vietnamese, and the Hoa fulfilled that need in several key industries—fiber/textile, rice, river transport, and, especially, banking. The French and the Hoa capitalists dominated the banking system in Indochina. In 1875, the French founded the Indochina Bank, which totally controlled banking for the benefit of French, Hoa, and Kinh businessmen and merchants.[40] By 1922, the Hoa and French capitalists had joined forces to form the Franco-Chinese bank; then, the Hoa formed six Chinese commercial banks and insurance companies in the South before 1955.[41] In an agriculturally based economy, these financial institutions essentially controlled credit extended to rice merchants and Vietnamese farmers from the period of colonial French rule to the fall of the Republic of Vietnam. As of 1906, French and Chinese capital monopolized all three economic sectors: 70 percent of capital in the agricultural and industrial sectors was French; 62 percent of capital in the domestic-trade sector was Hoa.[42] The French granted the Hoa monopoly power in some key

---

[35] ARTICLE XVI: "Chinese residents in An Nam shall, in matters of criminal jurisdiction, fiscal or otherwise, [hold] the same status as subjects of the most favored nation."

[36] ARTICLE III: "It is agreed, on both sides, that in the localities to which the Consuls are sent, the respective authorities will exert themselves to facilitate the establishment of these agents in honorable housing. Frenchmen may settle in the localities open to commerce on the Chinese frontier under the conditions anticipated by Articles 7, 10, 11, 12, and others of the Treaty of 27 June 1858. Annamites will also enjoy the same privileged treatment in these localities."

[37] Trần Khánh, *The Ethnic Chinese and Economic Development in Vietnam*, p. 41; Peter Zarrow, "The Nanjing Decade, 1928–1937: The Guomindang Era," in *China in War and Revolution, 1895-1949*, ed. Peter Zarrow (London: Routledge, 2005), pp. 248–70.

[38] Trần Khánh, *The Ethnic Chinese and Economic Development in Vietnam*, p. 46; Stein Tønnesson, *Vietnam 1946: How the War Began* (Berkeley, CA: University of California Press, 2010).

[39] Trần Văn Giàu, *Giai Cấp Công Nhân Việt Nam*, pp. 39, 48, 53–54.

[40] While the complete takeover of the whole country was accomplished in 1883, the French had already established factories in the South, since the 1860s. Trần Văn Giàu, *Giai Cấp Công Nhân Việt Nam*, pp. 44–45.

[41] Trần Khánh, *The Ethnic Chinese and Economic Development in Vietnam*, pp. 59-60.

[42] Ibid., pp. 44, 46.

industries: shopping centers, wine/alcohol/opium production and distribution, rice processing, and heavy and light factories, such as textile and garment, dyeing, fiber, and battery manufacturing.[43]

Relations between the Kinh and Hoa were complicated. From the start of their rule, the French used the divide-and-conquer strategy by promoting the unity of the Hoa living in Vietnam—in terms of their ethnicity—and reinforcing the differences and the division between the Hoa and the Kinh.[44] The French employed Hoa merchants as middlemen to deal with local Kinh in key economic and social functions: taxation, migration, and household registration, as well as the critical credit and banking services, supplied by the Franco-Chinese bank and the six Chinese commercial banks mentioned earlier.[45] In manufacturing, the French located a major naval base for the Indochina region in Hải Phòng province. Thus, Hải Phòng became a bustling commercial port city with a shipbuilding industry as well as light industries, such as textile, cement, glass, and porcelain.[46] Moreover, the French allowed the Hoa investors to play a major role in exploring mines in the North, but took over those enterprises when they made profits. The French also allowed the Hoa to monopolize the making and selling of alcohol. In these cases as well, the French capitalists took over when the business venture made profits.[47]

In the early 1920s, the French tried to provoke a sense of nationalism, which pitted the Kinh against the Hoa. This effort did have some effects, especially among students and small shop owners who engaged in various boycotting activities, such as "the boycott campaign against the Hoa merchants; An Nam people traded with other An Nam folks" (*Phong trào tẩy chay các chú, người An Nam mua bán với người An Nam*).[48] But Trần Văn Giàu—a historian and high-ranking Vietnamese Communist Party member—was quick to dismiss the Kinh actions as stemming from bourgeois sentimentality and argued that Hoa workers fought alongside Kinh workers in moments of need.[49]

To be sure, class division existed within the Hoa community in the development of the market system both during and after the French era.[50] Evidence can be found in their trade and commerce associations. The leaders of these associations were rich,

---

[43] Nguyễn Tuấn Triết and Trịnh Thị Kiều Oanh, "Truyền Thống Đấu Tranh Cách Mạng," pp. 41–42.

[44] Nghị Đoàn, *Người Hoa ở Việt Nam—Thành Phố Hồ Chí Minh* [The Hoa in Vietnam—Ho Chi Minh City] (Ho Chi Minh City: Thanh Pho Ho Chi Minh Publisher, 1999), p. 24; Nghị Đoàn, "Đồng Bào Hoa tại Thành Phố Hồ Chí Minh Dưới Sự Lãnh Đạo của Đảng Cộng Sản Việt Nam" [The Hoa in Ho Chi Minh City under the Leadership of the Vietnamese Communist Party], in *Người Hoa Tại Thành Phố Hồ Chí Minh* (Ho Chi Minh City: Sở Văn Hoá Thông Tin Publisher, 2007), pp. 30–31.

[45] Trần Khánh, "Tìm hiểu các tổ chức xã hội và nghiệp đoàn truyền thống," p. 4; Trần Văn Giàu, *Giai Cấp Công Nhân Việt Nam*, p. 54.

[46] Trần Văn Giàu, *Giai Cấp Công Nhân Việt Nam*, p. 35. About Hải Phòng province, see *The Columbia Encyclopedia, Sixth Edition* (New York, NY: Columbia University Press, 2004), as quoted on Questia.com, http://www.questiaschool.com/library/encyclopedia/haiphong.jsp?l=H&p=1, accessed June 8, 2009.

[47] Trần Văn Giàu, *Giai Cấp Công Nhân Việt Nam*, p. 54.

[48] Ibid., p. 270.

[49] Ibid., p. 269.

[50] Nghị Đoàn, ""Đồng Bào Hoa tại Thành Phố Hồ Chí Minh"; Nguyễn Tuấn Triết and Trịnh Thị Kiều Oanh, "Truyền Thống Đấu Tranh Cách Mạng."

powerful, and influential Hoa merchants who were also the heads of their kinship/native-place *bang* (organization). These leaders strategically integrated both economic functions (finance and banking) and vital social functions (financing schools and hospitals, and establishing various types of social insurance for Hoa rights), thus enhancing their power and influence both within and beyond their communities before 1975.[51]

Even with class and ethnic divisions intensified by French strategies, however, historical evidence shows that some level of solidarity existed between Kinh and Hoa workers as far back as the late nineteenth century. In April 1861, Hoa cooks joined Kinh cooks in trying to poison French soldiers in Saigon. In the latter part of the 1800s, Hoa welders (*thợ rèn*) fought side-by-side with the Kinh welders against the French when they took over Biên Hòa in the south.[52] Since 1920, some districts, such as districts 5, 6, 8, and 11, were populated by the Hoa. For instance, over half of the workforce in District 6 in the south comprised Hoa workers, who led many collective actions against the local owners and the French. In 1920, hundreds of Hoa together with more than forty thousand Kinh workers in District 6 went on strike to demand decent working and living conditions and disciplinary actions against exploitative foremen in factories. In 1922, the work stoppage by more than six hundred dyers (*thợ nhuộm*)—both Kinh and Hoa—in dozens of handicraft and small Chợ Lớn dyeing units showed cooperation across ethnic lines, as well as effective labor-organizing efforts to bring them together.[53]

In sum, according to available evidence, there was some level of solidarity across ethnicities of the same class: Kinh and Hoa workers fought together against management (both Hoa and Kinh members of the merchant class), even when the French attempted to divide them. But there were conflicts *across* classes: members of the Hoa merchant class opposed Hoa workers who aligned with Kinh co-workers.

Then, in the late 1920s, the Vietnamese Communist Party (VCP) began to play an increasingly influential role in labor organizing. In 1927, Red Trade Union members operated underground in a Bình Tây alcohol distillery and other factories.[54] By then, one started to see the emergence of a key strike agenda of Kinh and Hoa protestors: demanding democracy (as a political system opposed to an authoritarian state) and ensuring livelihoods (watching out for workers' welfare, or people's welfare broadly defined) (*dân chủ, dân sinh*). Trade associations—in public and semi-public arenas— were formed among workers in key industries and businesses controlled by the Hoa merchants. Those key industries and businesses included producing small types of machinery, weaving, glassmaking, and printing; restaurants and coffee shops; and making rubber, cigarettes, and silver items (especially jewelry). Through these associations, the VCP organized strikes and work stoppages in the Saigon and Chợ Lớn areas[55]: at the Bình Tây alcohol distillery in 1931; in twelve factories in Chợ Lớn in 1932, involving more than five hundred weavers; and in twelve rice-husking (*xay*

---

[51] Trần Khánh, "Tìm hiểu các tổ chức xã hội và nghiệp đoàn truyền thống," pp. 11–12.

[52] Trần Văn Giàu, *Giai Cấp Công Nhân Việt Nam*, p. 49.

[53] Ibid., p. 348; Nguyễn Tuấn Triết and Trịnh Thị Kiều Oanh, "Truyền Thống Đấu Tranh Cách Mạng," p. 42.

[54] Nguyễn Tuấn Triết and Trịnh Thị Kiều Oanh, "Truyền Thống Đấu Tranh Cách Mạng," p. 43.

[55] Phan An, *Người Hoa ở Nam Bộ* [The Hoa in the South of Vietnam] (Hồ Chí Minh City: Nhà Xuất Bản Khoa Học Xã Hội—Viện Khoa Học Xã Hội Vùng Nam Bộ, 2005), p. 102; Nghị Đoàn, *Người Hoa Tại Thành Phố Hồ Chí Minh*, p. 36.

lúa) factories in Chợ Lớn in 1934, involving hundreds of workers. The scale of the strikes increased in 1938: about 2,500 workers participated in strikes in thirty-five rice-husking factories in Chợ Lớn. Strikers demanded improvements to their working conditions and an eight-hour workday, and the activism spread to other workers in Saigon and Chợ Lớn.

A political and economic connection between Taiwan and the Hoa in Vietnam existed then (and still exists today), which is a useful point of reference with which to compare later periods. Starting in 1927, the Nationalist Party government of China, led by Chiang Kai-shek (who would take the government to Taiwan twenty years later), gave support to the Association of the Hoa in Vietnam (Hội Hoa Kiều Việt Nam). This umbrella organization brought together many trade associations and kinship *bang* of the Hoa in southern Vietnam.[56] From 1956 to the fall of the Republic of Vietnam in 1975, the Nationalist Party government in Taiwan used the *bang* to spread their political agenda to the Hoa in Vietnam in exchange for the Taiwanese government's formal protection of and assistance to the Hoa capitalists in finance, technology, education, health, and commerce.[57] This arrangement accelerated the Hoa investment in strategic industries—rice milling, weaving and making garments, food processing, and chemical-product manufacturing—and supported the Hoa's trading activities, which proved useful when they chose to return to Vietnam after their expulsion decades later.[58]

SPONTANEOUS PROTESTS, 1900 TO MID-1920S

Spontaneous protests erupted between 1885 and 1891 and sporadically until the early 1920s, before the formation of the Red Trade Union in the latter part of that decade. Based on available data and interviews with an elder cadre,[59] these protests were sparked by the need to preserve labor in terms of protecting the well-being and dignity of workers in general, and, especially, of women workers.

Karl Polanyi stressed the need to preserve labor, which is not a commodity for sale, but life itself. He then warns about the deleterious effects of an unchecked market:

> To allow the market mechanism to be sole director of the fate of human beings and their natural environment, indeed, even of the amount and use of purchasing power, would result in the demolition of society.[60]

According to Polanyi, active participation in a sustained social process is important in effecting changes and protecting people from the negative effects of the "self-

[56] Trần Khánh, "Tìm hiểu các tổ chức xã hội và nghiệp đoàn truyền thống," p. 5.

[57] Ibid., p. 6.

[58] Ngô Quang Định, "Về Thế Mạnh Kinh Tế Của Người Hoa ở Quận 5 và Khu Vực Chợ Lớn Trước Năm 1975" [About the Economic Strength of Ethnic Chinese in District 5 and Cholon Area before 1975], *University of Social Science and Humanities* 22,15 (n.d.); Trần Khánh, "Tìm hiểu các tổ chức xã hội và nghiệp đoàn truyền thống."

[59] "Cadre" is the word that often describes an active member of a revolutionary party, or the Vietnamese Communist Party in this case.

[60] Karl Polanyi, *The Great Transformation: the Political and Economic Origins of Our Time* (Boston, MA: Beacon Press, 1944), pp. 72–73.

regulating market system." In particular, Polanyi discusses the double movement as being supported by two organizing principles in society. The first of these principles is *economic liberalism*, which advocates a self-regulating market—maintained with support from the trading classes—that relies on laissez-faire and free trade as its methods. The second is *social protection,* the countermovement to check the action of the market with respect to the factors of production: labor and land. The countermovement aims at the conservation of man and nature and of productive organization, relying on the support of the working and landed classes (the two classes most affected by the deleterious action of the market) and using protective legislation, restrictive associations, and other instruments of intervention as its methods.[61]

To be sure, colonial French rule was much worse than a self-regulating market of the sort Polanyi criticizes. Workers started with individual protests; then they fought collectively. They engaged in individual walk-outs, collective work stoppages, slowdowns, sabotage, and shouting matches with bosses when being insulted and beaten. Rank-and-file workers in the north spontaneously organized the first waves of strikes in the early 1900s. The first strike took place in May 1909, at L'Union Commerciale Indochinoise (L'UCI) in Hanoi, the seat of power of the biggest French commercial corporation. When L'UCI management found that twenty kilograms of lead had disappeared, they immediately assumed that the Vietnamese workers had stolen it, so they disciplined all two hundred workers by charging each a fine of five days' wages. This triggered collective action by the workers—a spontaneous strike against this injustice.[62] The L'Annam-Tonkin newspaper reported this strike on May 18, 1909, portending a lot more to come:

> Hundreds of L'UCI workers had stopped work and acted as one. With this proud and spontaneous action, they had declared their independence right to the colonialists ... This work-stoppage went beyond the limit of a mundane/common event ... It is a variation of a dangerous psychology which was reflected violently in a food-poisoning case in Hanoi ...[63]

Between 1900 and 1918, strikes broke out in heavy industries in the north: in the mining, railroad, construction, and armament industries;[64] strikes then spread to other industries throughout the country. Between 1909 and 1926, strikes broke out in the light manufacturing industries as well: at least eight protests erupted spontaneously in various factories. In the factories of the Nam Định Textile Combine, even before the VCP wielded influence, a party source admitted that skilled workers—blue-shirted workers (*công nhân áo xanh*)—who worked in technical and

---

[61] Ibid., pp. 131–33.

[62] Đỗ Quang Hưng, *Công Hội Đỏ Việt Nam* [The Vietnamese Red Trade Union] (Hanoi: Labor Publisher, 2004), p. 100.

[63] Ngô Văn Hòa and Dương Kinh Quốc, *Giai Cấp Công Nhân Việt Nam Những Năm Trước Khi Thành Lập Đảng* [The Working Class before the Establishment of the Vietnamese Communist Party] (Hanoi: Khoa Hoc Xa Hoi Publisher and Uy Ban Khoa Hoc Xa Hoi Vietnam, 1978), pp. 161–62. The food poisoning targeted the French in June 1908 and was planned and carried out by an alliance of workers, soldiers, and Đề Thám nationalist revolutionaries. See Đỗ Quang Hưng, *Công Hội Đỏ Việt Nam*, p. 100.

[64] Trần Văn Giàu, *Giai Cấp Công Nhân Việt Nam*, pp. 103–9; Patrice Morlat, *La repression coloniale au Vietnam (1908–1940)* (Paris: L'Harmattan, 1990).

electrical departments had led the brown-shirted workers of the fiber and weaving assembly lines out on strike.[65] Then strikes spread beyond the textile factory to other factories that produced necessities, such as bottles, woven mats, and lamps, and to the electricity and water providers.[66]

Respect for women workers' dignity and workers' well-being had been the causes that rallied both male and female workers against French managers. In 1903, women workers in Cửa Ông factory (which manufactured winnowing machinery, *máy sàng*) turned off their machines and engaged in a work stoppage to demand that management send their fellow woman worker, who had miscarried while at work, to the hospital.[67] On May 1, 1909 (May Day), women workers in the bottle factory protested against body searches at the gate, which they considered a violation of their dignity. To understand this protest, I interviewed Nguyễn Tiến Cảnh, who was eighty years old at the time of the interview and who had been a high-ranking cadre of the people's committee[68] of Nam Định province (he served as a judge of Nam Định province). He said, "Workers were very upset and protested against these violations toward women [*phản đối hành vi xâm phạm phụ nữ*]." On January 2, 1922, workers at the silk factory protested against a foreman's brutality against workers. On February 27, 1924, more than one hundred silk factory employees stopped work. Then, on September 14, 1924, when a French foreman, named Mandolet, single-handedly eliminated the night meal (bread) for weaving workers and drastically reduced their subcontracting rates, 250 peasant workers in Nam Định Textile Combine shut down their machines in protest.[69] These worker-led strikes culminated in a general strike on April 30, 1925, with 2,500 workers in the textile/fiber factory protesting against the lay-offs of three hundred workers who had participated in earlier strikes.[70] The strikes at the textile/fiber factory spread to Hải Phòng cement factories and to Quảng Ninh mines.

Apparently, workers' class interest or consciousness was not a condition at the beginning of their protests necessary to the processes that fomented change. Identification with other members of one's class may arise as an outcome of these processes. Polanyi argues, "The process in question may decide about the existence of the class itself."[71] This is consistent with Thompson's argument that workers don't commence their struggle with a class consciousness, but they may arrive at class consciousness—as an outcome—at the end of a historical, social process such as a struggle. Thompson uses the terms "class" and "class-consciousness" interchangeably and defines class not as a group of people, but as a historical phenomenon that happens in human relationships, among real people in real experiences. Through their common experiences, people come to articulate the

---

[65] Nam Định Textile Combine Party Executive Committee, *Công Ty Dệt Nam Định*, p. 49.

[66] Phone Interview with Nguyễn Tiến Cảnh, June 2010, Nam Định.

[67] Ngô Văn Hoà and Dương Kinh Quốc, *Công Nhân Việt Nam Trước Khi Thành Lập Đảng*, p. 160.

[68] People's committees are the executive arms of administrative units of all levels of government in Vietnam (such as ward/district, city/province), responsible for implementing policy in those units.

[69] Nam Định Textile Combine Party Executive Committee, *Công Ty Dệt Nam Định*, p. 29.

[70] Ibid., p. 30.

[71] Polanyi, *The Great Transformation*, p. 153.

identity of their interests and that of opposing interests.[72] When they experience exploitation and struggle to protect their interests, they discover class-consciousness as an outcome of this whole experience. So, class-consciousness is triggered and sustained not only by workers' ability to identify their interests (class identity) *and* opposing ones, but also by their active participation in the struggle (with some implied organization) to fight for those interests.[73]

In the Vietnam case, Trần Văn Giàu—a historian and high-ranking Vietnamese Communist Party member who wrote about labor movements in Vietnam—linked the class issue to open class struggle. In particular; his analysis did not take cultural factors into consideration. He defined two aspects of class—"class-in-itself" and "class-for-itself"—and applied them to labor organizing and protests in Vietnam.[74] During this period, before the communist party began to influence workers, Trần Văn Giàu recognized and attributed a sense of class in these collective actions as activities of a "class-in-itself" (*giai cấp tự mình*); workers entered into social relations and protests when they realized they were being abused. Giàu did not trust that workers would bring about changes to capitalist exploitation by themselves. For the working poor to become "class-for-itself" (*giai cấp cho mình*), Giàu argued that they must first recognize that they were different from other classes because they had different rights and potentials (*triển vọng*) to play a specific role in history.[75] He argued that the worker party and Marxism-Leninism helped workers to achieve such class consciousness.[76] (I analyze this claim in the Red Trade Union section later in this chapter.)

Giàu commented that "the level of workers' unity [*tính chất đoàn kết*] was strong" and provided abundant evidence on diverse forms of protests—strikes, work stoppages, slow downs, sabotage, and insubordination demonstrated by yelling— spawned by worker abuse.[77] These spontaneous worker protests, he argued, have characteristics of "class-in-itself": Workers protested when they realized that they

---

[72] E. P. Thompson, "The Making of Class," in *Class*, ed. Patrick Joyce (Oxford and New York, NY: Oxford University Press, 1995), p. 131.

[73] "To put it bluntly: classes do not exist as separate entities, look around, find an enemy class, and then start to struggle. On the contrary, people find themselves in a society structure in determined ways (crucially, but not exclusively, in productive relations), they experience exploitation (or the need to maintain power over those whom they exploit), they identify points of antagonistic interest, they commence to struggle around these issues, and in the process of struggling they discover themselves as classes, they come to know this discovery as class-consciousness. Class and class-consciousness are always the last, not the first, stage in the real historical process." E. P. Thompson, "Eighteenth Century English Society: Class Struggle without Class?," *Social History* 3 (1978), pp. 147, 149–50.

[74] In class analysis, "class-in-itself" has to do with class formation/structure: workers would enter into social relations and protests when they realized they were abused; whereas "class-for-itself" has to do with consciousness, organization, and class action: workers become conscious of their own class and other classes in politics and struggle. Patrick Joyce, "Introduction," in *Class*, p. 11.

[75] This definition is consistent with Braverman's definition of the consciousness of the working class. He says: "class consciousness is that state of social cohesion reflected in the understanding and activities of a class or a portion of a class," and "it is only through consciousness that a class becomes an actor on the historic stage." See Harry Braverman, *Labor and Monopoly Capital: The Degradation of Work in the Twentieth Century* (New York, NY: Monthly Review Press, 1974), p. 29.

[76] Trần Văn Giàu, *Giai Cấp Công Nhân Việt Nam*, pp. 69, 84–85.

[77] Ibid., p. 339.

were being exploited, but they had not yet identified the interests of the opposing class nor did they have the organization for collective action. Through these acts of resistance, they did win some concessions. In 1925, the workday was reduced from fifteen hours (prevalent from 1900 to 1924) to twelve hours, but still workers had no meal break. Then, a decree issued on October 25, 1927, stipulated the ten-hour workday for contracted workers with one day off per week (or two days off every other week). Moreover, for plantation workers, the new ten-hour workday included travel time to and from work, a clear victory for them. However, non-contract workers were not at all protected by this decree.[78] Overall, workers won some limited, small-scale, short-term, and regional victories, such as wage increases, abolition of wage deductions as a penalty, and days off.

During this period of spontaneous protests, workers demonstrated that they could organize protests by themselves effectively. Labor representatives, who were themselves workers (but not yet VCP members), identified the strike agenda; some participated in fund-raising activities and then allocated the funds to various tasks; and some stopped the strikebreakers when workers were on strike.[79] So, strikes spread and expanded in scope, beyond the initial sparks in textile factories. Over 2,700 individual protests of all forms were reported between 1919 and 1923.[80] These included strikes, slow-downs, collective resolutions delivered to bosses, verbal disturbances (yelling), and physical brawling against French managers and Vietnamese foremen.

One interesting characteristic of these worker-led strikes and work stoppages is that those who were committed to the labor movement and respected by their fellow workers operated openly to mobilize the masses.[81] This stands in contrast to the actions of labor organizers involved in modern-day protests in Vietnam, as those leaders tend to work underground, concealing their identities from the state and corporate managers (although they are known to the workers) to avoid arrest and further suppression.

Many of these protests in the 1920s involved migrant workers who were fooled into signing long-term contracts to work on often remote southern rubber plantations far from their hometowns in the north and central regions; many ended their contracts early and physically tackled their abusive foremen. There were twenty-five worker-led stoppages between 1920 and 1925 in some key rubber plantations in the south.[82] Trần Văn Giàu did not analyze the important role of cultural-identity factors with respect to these migrant workers who were able to foment protests in the south. I fill in that gap by analyzing migrant workers in the Dầu Tiếng and Phú Riềng rubber plantation case studies in the next section.

Some evidence suggests that these class-in-itself, worker-led collective actions prompted the formation of a communist party in Vietnam. Nguyễn Tiến Cảnh argued that it was the participation of many factories in the April 30, 1925, general strike that surprised the French middle class and expedited the establishment of a communist party in Vietnam.[83] Cảnh cited the example of Nguyễn An—a Vietnamese

---

[78] Ibid., pp. 208-9, 247.

[79] Ibid., p. 360.

[80] Ibid., pp. 65, 69.

[81] Ibid., pp. 84–85, 102–10.

[82] Ibid., p. 339.

[83] Phone Interview with Nguyễn Tiến Cảnh, Nam Định, June 2010.

revolutionary representative at the Sixth Congress of the Communist International in August 1928—who showcased this general strike as evidence of the maturity of the working class in Vietnam, and its readiness for a revolution. Nguyễn An used that general strike to advocate for the formation of the Indochina Communist Party and the Red Trade Union in Vietnam.[84]

NAM ĐỊNH PEASANT WORKERS: *CÔNG NHÂN ÁO NÂU*

Who were the peasant workers under French colonial rule? What were their working and living conditions? How did their cultural identities—native place, gender, religion—bring them together, at work and outside of work? How did they organize? What made possible their resistance? Before exploring these questions, I present a history of a significant place, Nam Định.

History of Nam Định Textile Combine

To be in workers' "sandals" a century after the fact, during my fieldwork in 2004, I walked through many Nam Định streets, passing by the compound that included the fiber plants (*nhà máy sợi*) and the weaving plants (*nhà máy dệt*). I was able to live in the space and time of those "brown-shirted" peasant workers, the *công nhân áo nâu*. A factory bell still punctuated the passage of time throughout the day and controlled workers' lives, as a similar bell did in America for the "Lowell mill girls" in Massachusetts in the 1830s and 1840s.[85] But in 2004, the bell rang more often: the shuttles were bringing workers for three shifts per day to produce for the global supply chain.[86]

In the late nineteenth century, Nam Định profited from its silk artisanal production and trade, but it did not really have a well-known weaving tradition compared to that of Hải Phòng. What it had was a large pool of potential workers—the poor peasants who had lost their land and needed to work. The French intended to monopolize fabric production while recruiting those desperate local peasants. First, in 1900, French capitalists took over a small fiber factory with about one hundred workers, owned by a Hoa merchant. Next, the French made use of Nam Định's most important asset: "abundant local peasants in nearby villages who were useful for French investors."[87] Then, after successfully putting small Nam Định weavers and Hải Phòng textile factory workers out of business, between 1900 and

---

[84] Nam Định Textile Combine Party Executive Committee, *Công Ty Dệt Nam Định*, pp. 30–31. However, when I checked the Communist International website, I cannot find his name or his presentation (www.marxists.org/history/international/comintern/index.htm, checked on August 10, 2010).

[85] They were the female operatives who worked in the cotton mills of Lowell, Massachusetts, in the 1840s. These young women came from the surrounding farms and villages of New England, but they became dissatisfied by the mid-1840s after experiencing the long work hours and poor working conditions in the mills, and the strict regulations of the boarding houses. Joanne Weisman Deitch, *The Lowell Mill Girls: Life in the Factory—Perspectives on History Series* (Lowell, MA: Discovery Enterprises Ltd., 1991).

[86] While the global supply chain system encompasses both textile and garment production, running the machines twenty-four hours per day for seven days is more a feature of textile production—not garment production. (I was told that this continuous textile operation increases productivity.)

[87] Phone Interview with Nguyễn Tiến Cảnh, Nam Định, June 2010.

1931, the French hired the landless peasants to build the largest textile complex in Indochina: the Nam Định Textile Combine. This integrative system consisted of eight factories that connected all stages of textile production: spinning, weaving, dyeing, and finishing.[88] By 1930, this combine had not only woven fabrics using its own raw cotton fiber, but also manufactured simple finished products, such as blankets and cotton balls to serve wartime needs in other French colonies. By 1940, this combine employed the largest number of workers in Indochina, 14,400, more than 70 percent of whom were women and children.[89] These poor peasants came from Nam Định's outlying villages and local areas. The majority of them (more than 10,500) walked to work everyday. Once settled in the combine, workers formed one of the earliest communist cells.[90]

Gender, Place, and Historical Motivation

Giàu's historical analysis does not examine the role of cultural identities in labor organizing and protests before and after the communist party began to gain real influence in Vietnam. But including an identity-based approach incorporates cultural factors that help to explain what makes labor organizing possible in the first place.

Thompson argues that "class consciousness is the way in which experiences (inherited or shared experiences, maybe exploitation of capital, in which they can articulate that their interests are different from those of capital) are *handled in cultural terms*: embodied in traditions, value-systems, ideas, and institutional forms" (my emphasis).[91] For migrant workers in Vietnam who live and work far away from home, their shared experiences are those that stem not only from the work they do together (productive relations), but also from their living arrangements (social relations), where cultural factors play important roles. By envisioning both social and work relations in open labor struggles, Thompson's argument connects with the identity-based approach to labor resistance to explain the totality of migrant workers' experiences in Vietnam.

Aihwa Ong, one of the practitioners of the identity-based approach, stressed that workers' struggles and resistance are more often linked to kinship and gender than to class.[92] Her focus is on cultural identifiers—such as kinship, gender, and ethnicity—and the covert, not class, struggle of Malaysian female factory workers against Japanese factory owners in rural Malaysia. While I agree with Ong about the significance of cultural identifiers in facilitating workers' activism, I argue that cultural identifiers can also become a basis for "class moments" in open protests in Vietnam, with clear economic and social agendas.

---

[88] There were two fiber plants, three weaving plants, one cotton processing factory, one washing/dyeing factory, and one blanket factory. Moreover, the factory complex included auxiliary support systems for production, including one electricity-generating power plant and one machine shop, as well as its own transportation network. Ibid., pp. 12–13, 17.

[89] Phone interview with Cảnh, June 2010; Nam Định, pp. 23, 41.

[90] Nam Định Textile Combine Party Executive Committee, *Công Ty Dệt Nam Định*, pp. 16, 18.

[91] Thompson, "The Making of Class," p. 131.

[92] Aihwa Ong, *Spirits of Resistance and Capitalist Discipline: Factory Women in Malaysia* (Albany, NY: State University of New York Press, 1987); Aihwa Ong, "The Gender and Labor Politics of Postmodernity," in *The Politics of Culture in the Shadow of Capital*, ed. Lisa Lowe and David Lloyd (Durham, NC, and London: Duke University Press, 1997).

In the case of Vietnam, native place and gender are strong identity markers among migrant workers. Workers see themselves as natives from the same towns/villages (*đồng hương*), working far away from their home base. As sisters (*chị, em*) and brothers (*anh, em*), they help each other out during good and bad times, providing advice and sharing experiences with younger workers involved in negotiating with the bosses, and finding appropriate ways to address their immediate concerns and improve their conditions through protest.[93]

In the colonial French era, most workers in the Nam Định Textile Combine were peasants originating from three villages near downtown Nam Định—Mỹ Lộc, Nam Trực, and Trực Ninh—who walked to work and back home each day. Only a few were residents of Nam Định city.[94]

I talked with Trần Thị Kim Đường, a cadre who worked closely with the textile workers, about the identities of those peasant workers. She was one of the first cadres from the liberated zone who returned in 1955 to take inventory of and control (*kiểm kê*) the property of the Nam Định Textile Combine. She said:

> Some lived in downtown; most were from the outlying villages. They walked to work and walked home after their shift, from five to ten kilometers [about 3.1 to 6.2 miles]. They had to take care of their own housing since there was no collective dormitory [*khu tập thể*] back then. If they worked the afternoon shift, they left home in the morning, walked to work, and then walked back home at around 10 pm. A smaller percentage (30 percent) [her own estimate] of workers lived in the city. Only the peasants who lost their land (or never had any) had to work in the factories. On the other hand, city folks preferred to engage in commerce and retail shops rather than working in the factories. These peasant workers had a very rough life: there was no cafeteria in the factory, so they had to bring packed rice [*cơm nắm*] for their meals and worked continuously during their shift (there was no break).[95]

Until 1926, the French management of the textile combine built some makeshift, thatched-roof living quarters near the factory for some of these peasant workers. But this was not an act of kindness: they also created a network of informers to monitor worker activities day and night and to create fear among workers in order to suppress any potential protests.[96]

The evidence in the narratives of those local peasant workers (most were from Nam Định, either in the city or nearby villages) does not specifically mention the role of native place. But the long-lasting effect of historical legacy and power of tradition

---

[93] Bùi Thị Thanh Hà, *Industrial Workers in Joint-Ventures in Vietnam in the Renovation Era* [Công nhân công nghiệp trong các doanh nghiệp liên doanh ở nước ta thời kỳ đổi mới] (Hanoi: Social Science Publishing House, 2003); Huỳnh Thị Ngọc Tuyết, "Báo Cáo Kết Quả Cuộc Khảo Sát Về 'Phòng Chống Mua Bán Phụ Nữ—Trẻ Em' và 'Tăng Cường Trách Nhiệm Xã Hội'" [Findings of the Survey on the Trafficking of Women and Children and Strengthening Social Responsiblity] (Ho Chi Minh City: Go Vap District People's Committee, ActionAid Vietnam [Southern Office], and Development Assistance Project, 2005); Nghiêm Liên Hương, "Work Culture, Gender, and Class In Vietnam: Ethnographies of Three Garment Workshops in Hanoi" (PhD Dissertation, University of Amsterdam, 2006).

[94] Correspondence with Nguyễn Tiến Cảnh, Nam Định, July 2010.

[95] Phone Interview with Trần Thị Kim Đường, Vũng Tàu, July 2010.

[96] Nam Định Textile Combine Party Executive Committee, *Công Ty Dệt Nam Định*, p. 25.

play an important role. David Harvey talks about "motivational power of tradition" as a force generated by the workers' attachment to a place well-known for its revolutionary tradition, but he worries that this place-bound identity is difficult to maintain "in the face of all the flux and ephemerality of flexible accumulation."[97] Similarly, Jean Comaroff and John Comaroff were concerned that the changing relationship of labor to capital and the global dispersal of manufacturing would erode the conditions that give rise to class opposition, and fragment class consciousness and class alliance.[98] However, I found that the "motivational power of tradition" has been alive and well among thousands of Nam Định migrant workers who moved to the South in the twentieth and twenty-first centuries to work in the factories there and carried with them this historical legacy and influence; many had mobilized other workers to fight for their rights (see chapters five and six).

Archival materials demonstrate consistent efforts to preserve workers' dignity, and suggest that gender bonding was strong. Local workers networked based on gender—both in terms of women workers helping each other and all workers (men and women alike) rushing to the aid of women workers under duress—to protest unambiguously against the inhumane working conditions and the disrespectful treatment toward women workers. Workers' expressions of activism were numerous in their poetry, leaflets, and petitions. In particular, I showcase some popular poems expressing workers' sentiment and determination to protect their fellow women workers who were beaten by the bosses.

Industrial Discipline, Women, and Child Labor

The French institutionalized the factory system using the time bell in all Nam Định factories in 1900. For whom did the bell toll? It called those brown-shirted peasant workers and thrust them into industrial life. This form of factory control managed workers' lives before and during work shifts: one long alarm marked an hour before each shift to "call" these peasant workers, since most lived in nearby villages; one short alarm indicated the end of the shift.[99]

Peasants workers had to deal with a difficult transition from the rhythm of village life to the rhythm of industrial life centered on the factory's shifts as defined by the bells. For many workers who lived in nearby villages and did not own any clocks, getting to work on time was a challenge. Many left their villages when it was still dark, for fear that they would be late for work. They walked to the factory, and, if they were early, many caught up on their sleep in the bushes near the factory until awakened an hour before their shift began by the factory bells' long alarms.[100]

The French manipulated time on the factory floor to make their employees work a longer and faster day. Some French line-leaders literally sped up the assembly line at the beginning of the work shift and slowed it down when workers were about to finish their workday. The effect was to force workers to work faster when they were

---

[97] David Harvey, *The Condition of Postmodernity: An Enquiry into the Origins of Cultural Change* (Cambridge, MA, and Oxford: Blackwell, 1990), pp. 302–3.

[98] Jean Comaroff and John L. Comaroff, "Millennial Capitalism: First Thoughts on a Second Coming," *Public Culture* 12,2 (2000): 302.

[99] Phone Interview with Nguyễn Tiến Cảnh, Nam Định, July and August 2004.

[100] Nam Định Textile Combine Party Executive Committee, *Công Ty Dệt Nam Định*, pp. 21–23; phone interview with Trần Thị Kim Đường, Vũng Tàu, June 2010.

still alert, and only relent when workers were exhausted at the end of the day. The managers also adjusted the clock accordingly: fast at the beginning of the shift and slow at the end.[101] So the Marxist concept of labor exploitation, or surplus value extraction (products/services from workers), can be applied here, given the lengthening of the workday (for the capitalists to obtain absolute surplus value) and acceleration of the assembly line in a normal workday (for the capitalists to obtain relative surplus value) in the classic factory setting. Speeding up work resulted in many otherwise avoidable tragic accidents on the factory floor, because management did not put in place safety measures so as to profit from increased labor productivity while keeping operating costs low. For instance, when textile workers designed bamboo-woven shields to protect their eyes and faces from flying shuttles in the weaving process, management removed them, arguing that they slowed down the work process. As a result of workplace hazards, in the years 1926–30 there were 417 work accidents that left eight workers dead, and others maimed and seriously injured for the rest of their lives.[102]

The French were keen on hiring women workers, on the basis that they were "hardworking, perseverant, and [had] nimble fingers." The French also hired children as young as twelve years old.[103] Photos of child workers in the factory registry clearly indicate that the children were *coulines*, a French word for hard-labor workers.[104] Women and child workers often bore the brunt of exploitative work conditions, and they joined forces in protests.

Child workers were known to foment strikes themselves, without the Vietnamese Communist Party leadership. For example, two young workers, fifteen and sixteen years old, initiated and inspired a work stoppage in two Nam Định fiber plants that lasted more than a week, between March 20 and March 29, 1929. They protested against French management for laying off half of the workforce (twenty-four out of forty-eight), while demanding that the same amount of work be performed at the same pay. After witnessing his older friend being hit savagely by the French manager in his office, the fifteen-year-old called for a work stoppage, starting in Fiber Factory A, where workers joined in solidarity and convinced all other workers in Fiber Factory B to stop working. The French then posted on the factory floor two messages representing their two-pronged coping strategy: on the one hand, threatening to fire striking workers and, on the other hand, trying to corrupt them by offering some bonuses. In response, workers posted their own resolution alongside the French announcements so that other workers could compare them, and this sustained the strike. Finally, the French gave in and provided a small wage increase for workers in both fiber factories. There were no details about the fate of the sixteen-year-old boy who was beaten.[105] Clearly, these protests showed no workers' consent to the "rule of the game" imposed by the French management, and labor resistance became more sophisticated over time, with open economic and political agenda items and expanding scope and tactics.

---

[101] Nam Định Textile Combine Party Executive Committee, *Công Ty Dệt Nam Định,* p. 21.

[102] Ibid., p. 22. These are French statistics, numbers which may be underestimated.

[103] Ibid., pp. 23, 82.

[104] Nam Định Archives—photo of Nguyễn Văn Ty with number 612 and "coulines" stated as his occupation.

[105] Nam Định Textile Combine Party Executive Committee, *Công Ty Dệt Nam Định*, pp. 40–41.

Skills, Experiences, Gender

Elizabeth Perry's insightful study on the politics of production and open labor resistance in Shanghai argues that native place of origin, gender, skills, and social networks (such as artisan guilds, mutual aid societies, sisterhoods, brotherhoods, and gangs) of workers bound these Chinese laborers together in open protests against management years before the arrival of Chinese Marxist organizers. She identified different organizations, protest patterns, and demands of skilled craftsmen versus unskilled laborers.[106]

In the context of analyzing labor organizing, I define the concept of "aristocracy of labor" broadly as a division between skilled, highly paid workers—who are organized in the formal sector—and low-skilled workers—who are in the informal sector or in agriculture and are not organized.[107] I find little evidence that this distinction was sharply drawn in Vietnam. The blurred line separating peasants from industrial workers—the brown-shirted peasant workers who came to labor in the factories—mediated such division. Also, it should be noted that skilled electricians, mechanics, and drivers went around the Nam Định Textile Combine and other factories to organize workers of all skill levels, another piece of evidence that "labor aristocrats" were not separated from their fellow workers in Vietnam. This egalitarianism distinguishes Vietnamese workers of the 1920s from Shanghai silk weavers in the 1920s and 1930s.[108]

In Vietnam, the skill factor works differently than it did in Perry's Shanghai study: it enables labor organizing regardless of skill levels. Trần Văn Giàu argued that the participation of professional (skilled) workers (*công nhân chuyên nghiệp*) at the beginning of each new act of resistance brought more success to labor protests, although once the protests were underway, the "brown-shirted workers" (*thợ áo nâu*) participated more strongly.[109] Most labor organizers and strike leaders, from the colonial French era to the US-Vietnam war period, were skilled workers. As electricians, machinists, and truck drivers employed by the factories, they had more flexibility to roam around the factories and spread the word to organize low-skilled workers for collective action. The low-skilled Vietnamese weavers demanded a wage increase from four sous per day to six sous per day, unlike the low-skilled Chinese workers, who protested against wage cuts instead of demanding a wage increase (a common demand of skilled Chinese artisans).[110] Also, in controlling some critical

---

[106] Elizabeth Perry, *Shanghai on Strike: the Politics of Chinese Labor* (Palo Alto, CA: Stanford University Press, 1993), pp. 46–47, 61, 215.

[107] Bellin also argues that, in the context of labor surplus and mass poverty, a minority of the organized workers in the formal sector are likely to be more privileged—compared to the unorganized poor—and their unions' interests are different from those of the poor. Eva R. Bellin, "Contingent Democrats: Industrialists, Labor, and Democratization in Late-Developing Countries," *World Politics* 52,2 (January 2000), pp. 183–84.

[108] Elizabeth Perry, *Challenging the Mandate of Heaven: Social Protest and State Power in China* (London: M. E. Sharpe, 2002), pp. 135, 161.

[109] Trần Văn Giàu, *Giai Cấp Công Nhân Việt Nam*, p. 352. Also, according to documents from the Nam Định Archives, the list of seven cadres in Nam Định Textile Combine—who joined the Revolutionary Youth League in June 1927—were all skilled (men) workers: one electrician, three mechanics, one truck/car driver, one postal worker, and one employee at the Indochina Bank.

[110] Perry, *Shanghai on Strike*, pp. 61, 261, 263.

steps of shoe and apparel production, skilled workers could stall the whole assembly line in modern-day Vietnam. However, I'm conscious of the brevity of the data I have and the need for a larger and more representative sample for comparative purposes.

Socially constructed gender roles existed, which led to skills differentiation between male and female workers. Women workers were often channeled to low-skilled tasks. When I asked about gender division of labor, Trần Thị Kim Đường said:

> There were more women workers in the weaving section than men. On the other hand, men operated machinery such as *máy hồ* [fabric coating machine], *máy lờ* [spinning machine], transport, fixing machinery, big machines. Over two-thirds of women workers specialized in the weaving machine, *máy suốt* [spindle machine], *máy ống* [another type of spindle machine], sewing machine, and cleaning the facility including the toilet. Men workers were assigned to maintaining machinery and equipment.[111]

This account is consistent with both written and archival materials that I obtained.[112] Skills differentiation between male and female workers (often based on socially constructed gender roles in a patriarchal society) did not hinder labor organizing in the textile/garment factories in this period. Male workers—often channeled to high-skill positions such as electrician, machine operator, and driver—earned more and, as mentioned above, could use their ability to move about the factories to mobilize lower- or semi-skilled workers, both males and females. Under such conditions, this "skill" factor benefited both male and female workers.

There was no evidence that wage differentials between skilled and low-skilled workers divided them. To start with, wage differentials were small between Vietnamese skilled and unskilled workers. On the basis of twenty-six workdays per month, weavers (assumed to be semi-skilled) earned thirty-four sous per day (or 9.8 piasters per month with twenty-six workdays); mechanics (assumed to be skilled) earned seventy sous per day (or 18.2 piasters per month).[113] However, these wage differences did not hinder labor organizing and protests, as shown in these spontaneous collective actions.

For instance, a French foreman (signed "Et-sam") confirmed this solidarity across skill level. In a letter to his boss, Marchand, on April 1, 1929, he reported what he found in the factory under his watch: "Attached to this letter are some leaflets found on the night of January 31 in the weaving plant. An unknown worker had concealed these leaflets inside the weaving machines. The suspect may be an electrician working his night shift. Signed Et-Sam."[114] Thus, it is not surprising that the first group of strike leaders in 1927 consisted of all-male party cadres who were

---

[111] Phone Interview with Trần Thị Kim Đường, Vũng Tàu, June 2010.

[112] Nam Định Textile Combine Party Executive Committee, *Công Ty Dệt Nam Định*, p. 82.

[113] There were 100 sous per one piaster. *So Sánh Đồng Lương Giữa Người Thợ Việt Nam Với Đốc Công Người Pháp* [Comparison between the Wages of Vietnamese Workers and those of French Foremen], Nam Định Archives. A much larger wage gap is evident when the low wages paid to skilled and unskilled workers are compared to what a French foreman earned, that is, from 200 to 450 piasters per month.

[114] *Report on April 1, 1929, to Marchand about the Leaflets Found in the Factory*, Nam Định Archives (translated into English from Vietnamese by the author).

embedded as skilled workers in the Nam Định combine. The top leader was an electrician of the whole combine; three cadre members were machinists in the fiber plant; one was the factory truck driver; and the other two leaders were employed at a post office and a bank.[115]

Most female workers were assigned to low-skill tasks, which constrained their freedom of movement. Yet, even with such lack of mobility, the bonding among female workers as "sisters" was still strong and based on their knowledge and experiences. Most weavers were women, who had to stay next to their machines all the time. However, experienced female leaders, who tended critical textile machinery, used their knowledge about the whole production cycle, especially the strategic stage, to organize workers. As soon as strikes erupted, rank-and-file female and child workers rose to the occasion and were proactive in seizing opportunities to help.[116]

The experienced (often older) workers knew how to hurt French management the most: by stalling the production flow at a critical step. The oldest female worker in that combine explained to younger female workers, as among sisters, about the important first step of weaving: spooling, or the preparation of the textile fiber by transferring it from smaller to larger spools before weaving. Without large spools of fiber, the weaving process would stall:

> Operating *máy lờ* [a type of spinning machine that draws and combines textile fiber onto larger spools] is an important first step of the production line; if this step is stalled, then other steps such as hồ [a form of coating the fiber] and weaving cannot continue. Moreover, since very few people know how to operate this type of machine, if we were to stop work, the bosses [could not] hire workers from outside to replace us.[117]

The women's skills in operating certain machines gave them power, since it was difficult to find other employees capable of replacing them. So these strikers were not too concerned that strikebreakers would come in to claim their jobs.

Ethnicity

Few materials can be found on the role of ethnicity in labor organizing in Vietnam during this period. Most textile workers who worked in Nam Định back then had passed away by the time I conducted my fieldwork. Therefore, in dealing with this issue, I rely on interviews with two older cadres who gained some knowledge through their discussions with Hoa and Kinh workers, as well as on secondary sources.

On the factory floor in Nam Định Textile Combine, the French created a division of labor to divide and conquer workers by assigning the French to management (*quản đốc*), Kinh to foremen positions (*cai*), and some Hoa to engineering, technical, and clerical positions (e.g., inventory clerk, *thủ kho*). While a source claimed that the French assigned Hoa to mid-level leadership positions—as foremen, for example—to

---

[115] Nam Định Textile Combine Party Executive Committee, *Công Ty Dệt Nam Định*, p. 35.

[116] Interview with Lan, August 2004; Nam Định Textile Combine Party Executive Committee, *Công Ty Dệt Nam Định*, pp. 19, 24–25, 35.

[117] Ibid., p. 40.

monitor Kinh workers on the assembly lines,[118] interviews with Nguyễn Tiến Cảnh and Trần Thị Kim Đường revealed otherwise. They said such monitoring jobs were the function of Kinh foremen and French managers, rather than Hoa, whose population in the factory was small. Most Hoa workers were assigned to technical positions—such as technician, inventory clerk, or head of a technical field in production (*trưởng ngành*)—not to supervising workers or monitoring the production line.

Based on interviews with Cảnh, there was no division between the Hoa and the Kinh workers in the Textile Combine at this time. An eighty-two-year-old of Hoa ethnicity in Nam Định confirmed this point in her brief conversation with Cảnh in June 2010. She said that there were only about two hundred to three hundred Hoa in Nam Định Textile Combine during the 1920s, and they participated in strikes when the majority of workers went on strike. Back then, most of them stayed in Phố Hoa Kiều (Chinatown, near the main market in downtown Nam Định).[119]

When asked about the relations between Kinh and Hoa workers in protests in Nam Định Textile Combine, Cảnh said: "From my viewpoint, if you were workers during that time, you were exploited, all the same. So, most workers cooperated with each other [*hòa hợp với nhau*]. If there was any division, that was with the Hoa leaders [in technical positions], not with the Hoa workers."[120]

THE RED TRADE UNION

Trần Văn Giàu stressed the leadership role of the VCP and the Red Trade Union in fomenting class consciousness and developing the labor movement during and after French colonial rule. Giàu used a Leninist justification when arguing in support of control by the "vanguard" and the party, and said that the VCP knew better than the Vietnamese workers themselves about their interests and consciousness in applying "Marxist-Leninist" ideology to Vietnam.[121]

In the 1920s, the Indochina Communist Party (ICP), later renamed the Vietnamese Communist Party, focused on the twin goals of instigating class struggle and achieving political/national liberation in their appeals to the masses.[122] They implemented these by clandestinely embedding key youth cadres in small units called cells (*chi bộ ghép*) in factories, plantations, and mines; these cadres fomented

[118] Ibid., pp. 25–26.

[119] Then, beginning with the Hoa exodus in 1978, many returned to China. Tom Lam, "The Exodus of Hoa Refugees from Vietnam and their Settlement in Guangxi: China's Refugee Settlement Strategies," *Journal of Refugee Studies* 13,4 (2000): 374–90.

[120] Phone Interview with Nguyễn Tiến Cảnh, Nam Định, June 2010.

[121] I agree with Thompson's general critique of the Leninist justification for "the politics of substitution" in that the "vanguard" and the party know better than the class itself what their true interests are and what consciousness ought to be. E. P. Thompson, "Class and Class Struggle," in *Class*, p. 134.

[122] This is based on official Vietnamese Communist Party political writing. At that time, members of Thanh Niên Cách Mạng Đồng Chí Hội (Revolutionary Youth League of Vietnam) were still in the process of forming the Indochina Communist Party, the predecessor of the Vietnamese Communist Party. Đinh Lực, *Lịch Sử Đảng Cộng Sản Việt Nam, Tập 1* [History of the Vietnamese Communist Party, Volume 1] (Hanoi: Nhà Xuất Bản Chính Trị Quốc Gia, 1993), pp. 36–39, 82.

strikes with better organization and longer-term victories than had been possible for workers who organized themselves.[123]

The work stoppage of 2,500 workers in April 1925, in the Nam Định fiber plant, demanded an increase in their daily wage from four sous to six sous, a moratorium on beating workers, and an end to layoffs of striking workers. The employees won their demands; word of victories in this strike spread and inspired other protests nationwide.[124] After 1925, workers' protests, petitions, and leaflets demonstrated higher levels of organization and concrete public agendas were being used in the pursuit of their rights and interests.

Between 1925 and 1927, most party and union leaders (over two hundred cadres of middle-class background) were sent to China to learn Marxism-Leninism and revolutionary strategies and tactics. Returning to Vietnam in the late 1920s, they engaged in the "proletarianization" process of "eating and living together" with the peasant workers in order to instill in them the Marxist-Leninist ideas and to facilitate class consciousness. They also planted members in industrial associations (*công hội*) and, subsequently, in July 1929, formed the Red Trade Union as a public organization to mobilize workers.[125]

Many original leaders of the VCP came from Nam Định, trained in China, and returned to organize and lead the labor unions on the factory floor. For example, Nguyễn Đức Cảnh, a Nam Định student, studied Marxist-Leninist theories and strategies in China in 1926.[126] Together with other students and intellectuals, he joined the Revolutionary Youth League of Vietnam (formed in 1928); he then became the first leader of the Red Trade Union, and a member of the Central Committee.[127] His work, along with the work of the embedded VCP cells in the Nam Định plants, was to organize and foment workers' strikes and demonstrations, which culminated in victory during the August 1945 Revolution.

The Red Trade Union Federation (RTUF) went public in 1929 after waves of factory and mining workers' strikes in factories in Saigon, Hải Phòng, Hanoi, and Nam Định that dated back to the early 1900s. The RTUF established their branches in all three regions of Vietnam (Tonkin, An Nam, and Cochin China) and in different economic sectors and industries: shipyards (Ba Son in Saigon), railroads (Tràng Thi, Vinh in the north), cement factories (Hải Phòng in the north), a textile/garment combine (Nam Định in the north), and rubber plantations (Dầu Tiếng and Phú Riềng

[123] The key members of the Revolutionary Youth League of Vietnam were planted in venues that had big strikes. They were, for example, Ngô Gia Tự, who worked as a wharf worker/porter in Saigon; Nguyễn Văn Cừ, who worked in Mao Khe mine; Hoàng Quốc Việt, who worked for Nhà Bè Oil (and who was president of the General Confederation of Labor from 1950–61); Hoàng thị Ái, who worked in a Đà Nẵng factory; Nguyễn Đức Cảnh (the first president of the Red Trade Union Federation), who worked in the Hải Phòng cement factory; Khuất Duy Tiến and Mai Thị Vũ Trang, who worked at the Nam Định spinning mill; and Vũ Thị Mai and Lê Thanh Nghị, who worked at Hòn Gai factories. See: Trịnh Chi, *Questions and Answers about the History of Vietnamese Communist Party* (Hanoi: Thanh Niên Publisher, 1978), pp. 24–25; and Đinh Lực, *Lịch Sử Đảng*, p. 91.

[124] Nam Định Textile Combine Party Executive Committee, *Công Ty Dệt Nam Định*, p. 30.

[125] Trịnh Chi, *Questions and Answers,* pp. 16, 24–25; Hoàng Quốc Việt, pp. 8–9, 47–48; Đinh Lực, *Lịch Sử Đảng*, pp. 76, 82–83; and Nam Định Textile Combine Party Executive Committee, *Công Ty Dệt Nam Định*, p. 34.

[126] Vũ Ngọc Lý, *The Ancient Capital* (Nam Định: Sở Văn Hóa Thông Tin, 1997), pp. 301–4.

[127] Đinh Lực, *Lịch Sử Đảng*, p. 89.

in the south). Organized with more sophisticated strategies and tactics, strikes spread throughout Vietnam in different industries. From the late 1920s to 1939, embedded VCP cadres instigated strikes by organizing huge meetings, rallies, and marches, and by expanding strike agendas, which included political goals as well as economic demands, such as "democracy and people's welfare; freedom to form labor unions; increased wages; and elimination of all forms of physical discipline."[128]

Since the mid 1920s, the party cadres and labor organizers were behind many types of associations to mobilize workers, even when the French banned the formation of formal labor unions. By expanding the strike agenda, in the late 1920s these cadres helped convince workers to organize in support of an eight-hour workday, citing a French law that had been in place since 1919, and for overall wage increases (20 percent to 40 percent).[129] They were behind most organized protests in factories, mines, and plantations. In 1926, with some VCP influence, strikes in Nam Định became bigger than before, with thousands of workers involved, which then led to strikes at plantations in the north and south of Vietnam in subsequent years. Starting in 1927, as a result of these large protests, workers were granted Sundays off and some holidays (for workers and officials in the north), ten-hour workdays, and provided with one doctor on-site to attend to workers' health needs at each plantation/factory employing more than three thousand workers.[130]

Labor union activities were curtailed due to the political and economic vicissitudes of the Great Depression and World War II. After a short period of thriving labor union activities in Vietnam between 1937 and 1938, owing to the progressive French Popular Front government under Leon Blum (although the French workers, not Vietnamese workers, were the beneficiaries),[131] the French turned around and suppressed the labor movements and professional organizations in Vietnam when World War II commenced in 1939. Between 1940 and 1945, Vietnam was under the double yoke of France and Japan, simultaneously. Consequently, the labor movement and the VCP went underground from 1940 to 1943. Even then, the party still found ways to remain active. According to Cảnh, the party became involved in non-union activities: "The 'hands' of the communist party existed behind these industrial associations."[132] He elaborated in a second interview six years later:

> There were many ways to get workers together and organize them because the French did not allow us to form labor unions, such as the Vietnamese youth organizations [Việt Nam Cách Mạng Thanh Niên], fellowship associations [hội ái hữu, hội tương tế], industrial associations [công hội], and weddings and funerals associations [hội hiếu hỉ]. The Communist Party organization was behind all these associations to mobilize workers to go on strike.[133]

---

[128] Trịnh Chi, *Questions and Answers*, pp. 15–16.

[129] Ngô Văn Hòa and Dương Kinh Quốc, *Công Nhân Việt Nam Trước Khi Thành Lập Đảng*, p. 331.

[130] Trịnh Chi, *Questions and Answers*, pp. 16–17. However, one doctor for three thousand workers is grossly inadequate.

[131] Jonathan Hoving Los, "The Rise of the Labor Movement in South Vietnam" (master's thesis, University of Texas at Austin, 1975), p. 11; and Hoàng Quốc Việt, *The Trade Union Movement in Vietnam* (Hanoi: Foreign Languages Publishing House, Vietnam Federation of Trade Unions, 1988), pp. 23–24.

[132] Interview with Nguyễn Tiến Cảnh, Nam Định, July and August 2004.

[133] Interview Nguyễn Tiến Cảnh, Nam Định, June 2010.

To be sure, there were other noncommunist political parties, such as the Eastern Capital Non-Tuition School (Đông Kinh Nghĩa Thục), led by Phan Bội Châu, that contributed to labor organizing efforts. But their efforts and influence were short-lived due to inadequate organization and incessant French suppression.[134]

The VCP members in Nam Định's factories reemerged after 1943; many escaped from French and Japanese prisons. After organizing and regrouping, party cadres led workers' uprisings in some key factories, plantations, and mines in historical places (Hà Nội, Nam Định, Hải Phòng, Hòn Gai, Saigon-Chợ Lớn), leading to the seizure of political power from the French in 1945.[135]

During this period, the cadres allied with international labor movements to empower the Vietnamese labor movement. Responding to the International Workers' Day, May Day, 1944, Nam Định workers in weaving and silk plants stopped work and effectively paralyzed the whole production process. More than three hundred workers turned off all the machines in unison and staged a sit-in on the factory floor. Once again, management gave in to workers' requests for higher wages, the abolition of physical punishment, and part-time jobs.[136]

After the successful August 1945 Revolution, the labor unions worked as the "transmission belt" between the party and the workers to mobilize workers for production and defend labor interests. [137] The movement was officially under the leadership of the party in the Democratic Republic of Vietnam. In an effort to develop greater pro-union consciousness, the party held the first National Congress of Trade Unions and renamed the RTUF the Vietnamese Federation of Trade Unions (VFTU) in 1946, under the leadership of Hoàng Quốc Việt, a revolutionary from the North.[138] In 1947, VFTU issued the first comprehensive labor code, which applied to

---

[134] Trần Văn Giàu, *Giai Cấp Công Nhân Việt Nam*, pp. 101–2; Marr, *Vietnamese Tradition on Trial*, pp. 200–1; Interview with Nguyễn Tiến Cảnh, Nam Định, July and August 2004.

[135] Hoàng Quốc Việt, *The Trade Union Movement*, pp. 47–48; Nam Định Textile Combine Party Executive Committee, *Công Ty Dệt Nam Định*, pp. 28–29; Trần Văn Giàu, *Giai Cấp Công Nhân Việt Nam*, pp. 102, 260.

[136] At that time, the Nam Định fiber factory was bombed by the United States and had to close down. Nam Định Textile Combine Party Executive Committee, *Công Ty Dệt Nam Định*, p. 95. According to Trần Văn Giàu, compared to 1943, there were many more (and longer) strikes in 1944, and they spread to a number of provinces nationwide and involved many different types of workers, such as those from button and rug factories in Hải Phòng; lumber, tanning, and footwear operations in Hanoi; wood-working shops and military-uniform mills in Saigon; and rice-processing facilities in Rạch Giá (Mekong Delta), as well as five hundred skilled architectural workers (công nhân kiến trúc) participating in strikes in Saigon. Trần Văn Giàu also pointed out that from the end of 1943 to May 1944, revolutionary units/cells embedded in large factories that were destroyed in 1939 had been re-established in strategic utilities companies in 1944. Trần Văn Giàu, *Giai Cấp Công Nhân Việt Nam, Từ Đảng Cộng Sản Thành Lập Đến Cách Mạng Thành Công: Tập III, 1939–1945* [The Vietnamese Workers' Class, from the Formation of the Communist Party to the Revolution Victory: Volume III, 1939–1945] (Hanoi: Nhà Xuất Bản Sử Học, 1963), pp. 156, 158.

[137] Irene Norlund, "Democracy and Trade Unions in Vietnam: Riding a Honda in Low Gear," *The Copenhagen Journal of Asian Studies* (November 1996): 89. Norlund argues that the "defending labor interests" function of the unions in the Leninist principle of dualism was "reduced" because, ideologically, there could be no contradiction between labor and state management in a workers' state.

[138] *Trade Union Movement* 1988, pp. 7, 9, 48.

both north and south.[139] Then, after the French defeat at Điện Biên Phủ, which led to the agreements of the Geneva Conference in July 1954, many mass workers' protests mobilized thousands of urban and rural people who joined rallies and marches to expedite the French withdrawals from the rest of Vietnam and to denounce the US alliance with the French in the Franco-Vietminh War. In this context, more than two thousand workers in the Nam Định textile factories organized a huge meeting in front of one of the factories, which then turned into a rally and a march that spread through the city of Nam Định and attracted thousands of people there.[140]

With the organization and leadership of party cadres embedded in key French production facilities (factories, mines, and plantations), strikes spread beyond the confines of the factory floor, spilling over onto the streets throughout Vietnam, and were sustained strategically. These protests incorporated long-term goals to sustain the struggle. Marches and rallies lasted longer than before and grew in both scope and scale. To sustain the resistance, the unions advocated for strike funds. On a leaflet, the industrial association cadres in Nam Định Textile Combine advised workers to "raise funds to help all strikers, to stand up, strike and fight for the rights to which they are entitled."[141]

TYPES OF PROTEST IN NAM ĐỊNH TEXTILE COMBINE

To study the following cases, I rely on a variety of Vietnamese materials such as popular poetry, leaflets, and scholarly materials, and find an intermingling of both Polanyi- and Marx-type protests. The workers used "class" language, invoking the injuries or death of workers and violations to the integrity of women workers, to mobilize themselves to stand up and fight for their rights. Even without direct interviews with these workers (this discussion is based on archival materials), I can sense the anguish reflected in their narratives, which might have struck a chord in other workers' hearts.

In 1926, on a petition letter, workers signed as "công nhân xưởng Dệt" (a collective of textile workers), addressing the director of the fiber plant in Nam Định. They saw themselves collectively as textile workers and expressed indignation that a woman worker was beaten brutally and unjustly by a foreman:

> At the 15th hour on 25 August 1926, a female weaver was detained on an alleged charge of stealing.[142] At that time, Ms. Vá happened to pass by that factory, was chased and then brutally beaten by the foreman [đốc công]. She was seriously injured and taken to the hospital. After she had spent several days in the hospital, the doctor dismissed her even though she still needed further treatment. We asked ourselves: could she survive these serious injuries? We are deeply disturbed by these behaviors, and therefore we implore you to

---

[139] Los, "Labor Movement in South Vietnam," p. 14.

[140] Nam Định Textile Combine Party Executive Committee, *Công Ty Dệt Nam Định*, p. 224.

[141] From an archived leaflet in Nam Định Heritage Museum (possibly distributed on July 9, 1929, based on the date given on the leaflet itself), the message addressed to: "Các Anh Chị Em Công Nhân Các Nhà Máy" [To Brothers and Sisters in All Factories] and "Các Anh Chị Em Vô Sản Khắp Mọi Nơi" [To All Proletarians Everywhere]. At the end, this Vietnamese leaflet indicated that it was translated from the French language.

[142] According to workers' archival materials, Vá did not steal; she just happened to pass by at the wrong time.

investigate this mistreatment towards our fellow worker. Also, we are very scared and worried about this supervisor's brutality.[143]

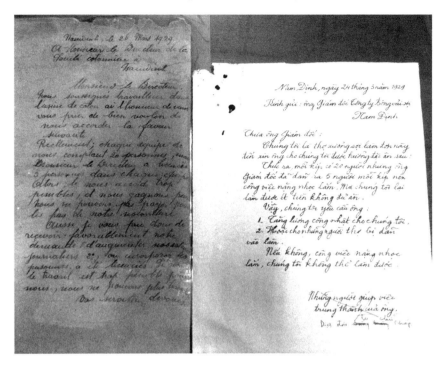

This handwritten petition, a typical example of such a document, was signed by Nam Định fiber workers to protest increasing production quotas (without a livable wage) and to demand a daily wage increase or the rehiring of fifteen laid-off workers. The fiber workers also threatened to stop work due to the excessive pressure. The letter was addressed to the factory owner and signed on March 24, 1929. (Nam Định Textile Combine Museum Archives, author's photo)

Corroborating this 1926 petition, another source stated that, immediately after Nguyễn Thị Vá was denied medical treatment by the French doctor, workers in the fiber factory stopped the machines to protest the French beatings of workers (as a common practice) and demanding compensation for Vá.[144] But their victory was limited. While management had to acquiesce and agreed to pay Vá compensation, they only promised to limit, not stop, the beatings of workers in general.[145]

This shows an intermingling of both Marx- and Polanyi-type protests: the use of collective language is evident in the phrase "our fellow worker," and the concern for the well-being of a fellow woman worker who was beaten brutally is clearly expressed in the petition and another source.

---

[143] Công Nhân Xưởng Dệt, *Bản Dịch Đơn Của Công Nhân Xưởng Dệt* [Translation of the Petition of Workers in the Weaving Plant], signed August 30, 1926, Nam Định Textile Combine Museum Archives.

[144] Nam Định Textile Combine Party Executive Committee, *Công Ty Dệt Nam Định*, p. 31.

[145] Ibid.

In 1928, upon witnessing a French foreman beating up another female worker, both skilled male and semi-skilled female workers sprang into action. This popular poem called upon other workers to stop work through the act of "turning off the engine" and to fight against being treated inhumanely:

Et-Sam hit our coworker,
> kicking her with his shoes,
> seizing and pulling at her hair, while yelling "go"
I was working in room B,
> seeing the brutal abuse, hurriedly I came back to the storage room
> and immediately I turned off the engine.
Everybody was surprised at my act
I then cried out: "the French line-leader hit our fellow worker, we do not know
> whether she is still alive, already dead, or is suffering serious injuries"
All other workers were concerned
> abandoned their machines and went out to check the situation
At the wall a woman worker had collapsed
> Ms. Dan in the Weaving Plant B
We carried her to the stretcher and then to the hospital
Everyone discussed left and right about all possibilities, then came to the
> conclusion: "we are not horses or buffaloes to be beaten like this"
We resolutely determine to organize ourselves
> united as hands and feet in the same body
Two shifts then secretly decided to go on strike
> swearing an oath to be of one mind [to unite and be loyal to the cause]
We swear: never to betray our just cause even when caught
We reassure ourselves: not to worry about one's household
> we will assist striking family members with our salaries
Forty people strong, men and women,
> presented a protest letter to supervisor "Mac-Can" [and]
> collectively demanded the firing of line-leader "Et-Sam" who beat a
> woman worker nearly to death, who is now in the hands of a doctor.
We spoke with one voice, raising our fists, to the management standing there.[146]

In another Nam Định protest in 1928, two shifts of workers in the most important first stage of the fabric-dyeing process stopped their machines, the *máy lờ*, and paralyzed the whole combine for more than a week. They protested the inhumane physical abuse of workers by French supervisors on the factory floor. The workers prevailed and won some small victories: the supervisors promised to raise the wage (although by an insignificant amount), stop beating workers, and reduce the monetary fine (also by a small amount) when disciplining workers. Similar tactics were used in 1929, which again paralyzed the whole textile combine; strikes then spread to other factories in Nam Định and to other industries in Hanoi, as well as Hải Phòng.[147] Moreover, workers won some modest victories, including the

---

[146] *Ca Dao Truyền Miệng Của Công Nhân Kêu Gọi Đấu Tranh Chống Chủ Tây Đánh Thợ* [Oral Popular Poem of Workers Mobilizing Protest against the French Boss Hitting a Co-Worker], 1928. Nam Định Archives.

[147] Trần Văn Giàu, *Giai Cấp Công Nhân Việt Nam*, pp. 472–73.

establishment of child care centers on the premises in factories with more than fifty workers, and the provision of on-site doctors. By this time, some party members were probably embedded in the factories and mines, as noted earlier.

In 1920s Nam Định, a group of workers came together when several of the fellow workers were laid off. These participants were local Nam Định workers—not migrants—who lived with their families in a local neighborhood. While there is no evidence that their solidarity was based on coming from the same native place, a sense of class emerged:

> We brothers and sisters belong to the same work place, enduring life and death together, and had helped each other out many times before. Now that we reached the end of the rope like this, we cannot ignore each other. So, if there is work, then we work together. But if one worker is laid off, then we will all stop work. When management then stops spreading out the work force [*dãn thợ*] we will return to work.[148]

They used the classic "word-of-mouth" method to spread news to each and every worker and effect a work stoppage. Several workers were convinced, but not all were. Then, the following morning, some individuals who had spontaneously come forward to act as labor leaders met up with their fellow workers on the way to work and mobilized them using "class" language:

> To our brothers and sisters, yesterday we had talked to you about the need to stop work and demand management to stop "*dãn thợ*," because if they can force one worker to work just part time, they will convince others to do the same. Now, please listen to us: everyone should go home, stop coming to work, stop operating the machines, and stop connecting the fiber threads [*không nối sợi*], so the French bosses would have to fear us.[149]

While other workers remained silent and hesitant to react, one worker pleaded to return to work because he had a sick father who was waiting for food and medicine at home. The labor organizers responded:

> The French had already taken away your bowl of rice, and had laid off many workers. We belong to the same "torn shirt group" with each other [*cánh áo rách với nhau*], so we have to counsel each other. Please do not return to work now, and if you do, your fellow neighbors [*bà con*] will scold you.[150]

After that, many workers returned home; each spread the word to hundreds of other workers, and the movement snowballed. As a result, no one returned to work, and the factory stood emptied of all but a few workers. Facing such worker unity, by

---

[148] This is a form of temporarization in which workers only have *temporary* part-time, not full-time, jobs. Worse yet, in the context of Vietnam during that era, it is considered a temporary lay-off, during which time workers do not receive any salary, social security, or health benefits. Ngô Văn Hòa and Dương Kinh Quốc, p. 332.

[149] Ibid., p. 332.

[150] Ibid., p. 333. Note: "*cánh áo rách*" is a Vietnamese expression for the working poor.

the afternoon of the same day, the French bosses posted a notice on the factory gate agreeing to workers' demands, thus giving the employees a small victory.

This case shows that workers did not all come to realize their shared interests at the beginning of this process. They all had different family situations, and some wavered about not going to work. But, given limited information, what we can gather is that, after some mobilizing efforts, including community pressure ("your fellow neighbors will scold you"), workers did arrive at some form of consciousness and took collective action at the end of the process. A sense of class emerged based on their belonging to the "torn-shirt group," and they called themselves "brothers and sisters" in the rallies. They articulated a shared predicament of reaching "the end of the rope," and at some point in their struggle, they pointed out their shared circumstances and interests: demanding full-time jobs for all workers, not just part-time jobs. Thus, this case demonstrates that some form of consciousness developed at the time of desperation and the resulting process used an intermingling of Polanyi- and Marx-type protests.

By 1930, the significant protests in Nam Định were inspiring strikes nationwide, and the participants and their actions served to mobilize workers across industries, since the Nam Định Textile Combine had served as an incubator for one of the earliest embedded communist cells.[151] For instance, one of the leaflets distributed in front of the Nam Định fiber plant in 1930 contained this message: "In support of peasant protestors in Thái Bình province who were massacred by the French, fellow workers, please urgently unite with the communist cadres to go on strike and hold a demonstration."[152] Archival materials on the party cells in Nam Định Textile Combine declare that "the red flag and leaflets were found in front of the fiber plant" and "at sunset when workers got off work, they found the red flag raised in the middle of the fiber plant with leaflets spread all around" and "on the night of October 13, policemen doing their routine walk found several leaflets spread in front of the courthouse and a red flag (and leaflets) at the front gate of the Fiber Factory. The leaflets and the red flag were submitted to the security police for investigation."[153]

Once workers were bound by their long-term contracts, they increasingly engaged in open legal protests (*đấu tranh hợp pháp*), using reports and complaints to appeal to colonial French legal mechanisms. They, individually and collectively, signed allegation reports (*đơn tố cáo*) and petitions (*khiếu nại*), and then sent them to colonial French political, police, and legal institutions. These written reports publicly exposed management violations and the French capitalists' failure to abide by the contracts agreed to by both labor and management.[154] Evidence shows that workers used the law and legalistic language to challenge the French legal system. The

---

[151] Nam Định Textile Combine Party Executive Committee, *Công Ty Dệt Nam Định*, p. 25.

[152] *Hỡi Anh Chị Em Thợ Thuyền Binh Lính và Nông Dân* [To Brothers, Sisters, Workers, Soldiers, and Peasants], signed by "The Indochina Communist Party, the translation of a leaflet in French, found in front of the Nam Định Fiber Factory gate on October 20, 1930." Nam Định Archives.

[153] Định Á, *Bắt Được Cờ Đỏ Tại Nhà Máy Sợi* [Found a Red Flag at the Fiber Factory], March 18, 1930; *Tại Nam Định* (At Nam Định), October 14, 1930. Nam Định Archives.

[154] Ngô Văn Hoà and Dương Kinh Quốc, *Công Nhân Việt Nam Trước Khi Thành Lập Đảng*, p. 165.

Vietnamese peasant workers learned "the rules of the game" and fought back, quite early, compared to British factory workers in early nineteenth-century England.[155]

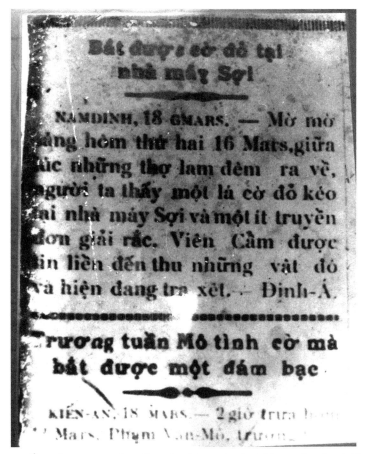

Định Á, *Bắt Được Cờ Đỏ Tại Nhà Máy Sợi* [Found a Red Flag at the Fiber Factory], March 18, 1930. (Nam Định Textile Combine Museum Archives, author's photo)

In a particular case, on May 13, 1936, technical workers in a weaving plant, Thợ Xưởng Dệt, sent a collective petition letter to the director of the fiber plant in Nam Định, threatening to file a lawsuit against the factory management and addressing all forms of labor mistreatment. Workers used legalistic language and legal protocol and demonstrated their understanding of the significance of using evidence to back up their claim in order to contest management practices, and the French system:

---

[155] Thompson said: "The first generation of factory workers were [*sic*] taught by their masters the importance of time; the second generation formed their short-time committees in the ten-hour movement; the third generation struck for overtime or time-and-a-half. They had accepted the categories of their employers and learned to fight back within them. They had learned their lesson, that time is money, only too well." E. P. Thompson, "Time, Work-Discipline, and Industrial Capitalism," *Past and Present* 38 (December 1967): 86.

We were surprised and outraged that Mr. Costa—our supervisor—treated us cruelly to the point that we [could] no longer bear these mistreatments. Workers who arrived to work a little bit late got beaten and kicked out. Passing by an idle spindle, Mr. Costa would slap the tending worker; and to women workers, he would physically abuse them. We demand that the director fire Mr. Costa. If not, we will *file a law suit* against these humiliating behaviors with *complete evidence*.[156]

In this case, workers followed legal protocol: filing a lawsuit and providing evidence. Over time, protests against worker abuses became larger in scope and scale and were reported in local newspapers. The workers used rights-based language in their protests. Translation of a local newspaper report about a strike in a fiber plant in Nam Định Textile Combine on March 31, 1929, shows how workers took up the fight for their rights. In this fight, five thousand workers demanded internationally recognized basic labor rights to preserve their well-being through fair wages, reasonable work hours, overtime compensation, and cost of living increases:

This morning, all fiber workers, including young and old women workers, engaged in a work stoppage to go on strike. All machines were shut down, lifeless, thus making the atmosphere deadly quiet compared to the hustling bustling of factory activities the day before. French soldiers and police guarded with weapons in front of the factory gate. Five strike leaders were imprisoned, and four workers' ID cards were expropriated. The main reasons for this strike included the following workers' fundamental requests: 1. to terminate a French foreman and a Vietnamese line-leader who physically abused the Vietnamese workers inhumanely as a form of punishment; 2. to raise wages since rice prices had gone up; 3. to reduce work hours to less than twelve hours per day (from 6 am to 6 pm) and pay workers for overtime work.[157]

Clearly the third request referred to the eight-hour workday, which had been adopted as a standard in Europe at the end of nineteenth century, and was being demanded by labor representatives in the United States from 1864 (it was the Chicago labor movement's central demand) to 1938, when the New Deal's Fair Labor Standards Act made the eight-hour workday legal throughout the United States.[158] This shows that labor organizing around the globe influenced the movement in Vietnam back then.

The progressive Popular Front government of Leon Blum gave rise to some short-term reforms between 1937 and 1938, including the first meaningful labor code in Vietnam, which offered some protection to workers (such as a forty-hour workweek, an annual paid vacation, collective bargaining via mutual aid associations, protection of women and children, and a regional minimum wage), but

[156] Translation of Petition of Workers in the Weaving Plant sent to the Director of the Fiber Plant at Nam Định. Nam Định Archives; my emphasis.

[157] Translation of a newspaper report of a strike in a fiber plant in the Nam Định textile combine on March 31, 1929. Nam Định Archives.

[158] Ngô Văn Hòa and Dương Kinh Quốc, *Công Nhân Việt Nam Trước Khi Thành Lập Đảng*, p. 331. John B. Jentz, "Eight-Hour Movement," http://www.encyclopedia.chicagohistory.org/pages/417.html, accessed January 7, 2012.

still proscribed the creation of unions.[159] So, seizing on such relative sympathy for labor, on May 1, 1938, workers held demonstrations demanding a labor code that gave them the same rights as their European counterparts, in addition to democracy and independence.[160]

MIGRANT WORKERS IN THE DẦU TIẾNG AND PHÚ RIỀNG RUBBER PLANTATIONS

After World War I, France needed raw materials for consumer products to rebuild its economy and those of other European countries. Additionally, the automobile industry was growing in Europe and the United States, which increased the demand for rubber tires. The French increased their investment in raw rubber, considering rubber expansion (both in acreage and production) a "national strategy."[161] These factors led to the development of new rubber plantations and the expansion of existing plantations in the South (Cochin China).[162] The colonial French government gave French companies—notably four large corporations—the authority to open up massive amounts of land for that purpose.[163] French capitalists and the government profited handsomely from this increasing demand and expansion.

Apparently using the same integration strategy prevalent in the textile industry, the French controlled both inputs and outputs of the tire industry in Indochina. They extracted raw rubber, using some of the rubber in Vietnam for processing into tires and exporting the rest for processing in France. It was a very profitable operation all around: not only did the French use cheap labor from Vietnam to extract raw rubber and then produce tires, but they also sold the final products at much higher prices in Indochina than in Europe.[164]

The demand for rubber workers on these new and expanded tree farms in the South could not be met by the local population. The French rubber companies, frantic to locate new sources of labor, hired Vietnamese recruiters to find and contract with workers from up north to work in the south. These recruiters used deception to convince many desperate and hungry peasants to sign contracts that bound them for at least three years to labor that was to be performed under slavery-like conditions.[165] Demand for labor was high. The four large French rubber companies resorted to various ways to recruit contract workers, from "buying" labor contracts from other

[159] However, Beresford and Nyland realized that, in reality, from 1928, Vietnamese communist cadres—already embedded in textile, coal, and transport industries and plantations—had led the strikes in plantations in the South. Melanie Beresford and Chris Nyland, "The Labour Movement of Vietnam," *Labour History* 75 (November 1998): 60.

[160] Ibid., pp. 59–60.

[161] Another reason for the increase in investment is that French capitalists converted the devalued franc into piasters, which were more stable and tied to silver. Nguyễn Thị Mộng Tuyền, "Công Nhân Cao Su Thủ Dầu Một," p. 231.

[162] Chesneaux, "Stages in the Development," p. 71.

[163] They were: Société des plantations et Pneumatiques Michelin au Vietnam, Compagnie des Terres Rouges, Société indochinoise des plantations d'Hévéas, and Société des Caoutechoues D'extrême-Orient. Nguyễn Thị Mộng Tuyền, "Công Nhân Cao Su Thủ Dầu Một," p. 231.

[164] Hồ Sơn Đài, "Introduction," in *Công Nhân Cao Su Dầu Tiếng*, p. 17.

[165] Nguyễn Thị Mộng Tuyền, "Công Nhân Cao Su Thủ Dầu Một," p. 234; Lê Văn Kim, "Đồn Điền Dầu Tiếng—Xiềng Xích và Đấu Tranh (1917–1945)" [Dầu Tiếng Plantation—Chains and Struggle], in *Công Nhân Cao Su Dầu Tiếng*, p. 29.

companies to direct recruiting efforts in the north (especially Hanoi and Bắc Giang) in order to round up migrant workers to work in the south.[166]

Migrant workers from provinces in the north (Hà Nam, Nam Định, Thái Bình), the north central (Thanh Hóa, Nghệ An, Hà Tĩnh) and central Vietnam (Quảng Trị, Quảng Nam) tended to bond strongly together in groups based on their respective native provinces and villages. These workers constituted about 70 percent of all plantation workers.[167] Workers from the same areas traveled together and stayed together when they arrived at the plantations far away from home. They stood by each other and shared resources when the small amount of advance money they received did not last for long.

In 1917, while World War I was in progress, the Michelin Company developed Dầu Tiếng, the first rubber plantation in Indochina. About seventy kilometers northwest of Saigon, the plantation was situated in Bình Dương province, which has an abundance of "grey" soil, a good condition for the growth of rubber trees. The French had built a vertically integrated operation to maximize their profits: rubber planting and harvesting in Vietnam and manufacturing car and bicycle tires in France. By July 1930, Michelin Company employed almost ten thousand workers.[168] Most were Vietnamese, but there was a small percentage of Hoa and Khmer.[169] From 1917 to 1951, Michelin recruited more than forty-five thousand workers to Dầu Tiếng, of whom more than eleven thousand died, escaped, or joined the anti-French resistance.[170] However, the actual number of people who died in these rubber plantations may have been even higher, since the official records of these operations included only contractual workers, and not the so-called "free workers" (coolies libres) who did not sign any contracts.[171]

Cultural Identity

Through local Vietnamese subcontractors, the French hired the first group of workers for the rubber plantations, most of them poor, local peasants from villages near the Saigon River (such as Định Thành, Gò Dầu, Trảng Bàng, and Củ Chi). Hired as day workers to fell the trees and clear the land, they eventually were employed as permanent rubber workers on this new plantation. Then, starting in 1926, Michelin management, needing more help, began recruiting contract workers from areas in the north and central provinces.

The second group of contract workers were migrant peasants who were landless and hungry, from poor regions of central Vietnam—Thanh Hóa, Quảng Trị, and Quảng Nam.[172] Many poor peasants left their villages after having lost their crops

---

[166] Nguyễn Thị Mộng Tuyền, "Công Nhân Cao Su Thủ Dầu Một," pp. 231–32, 235. About 100,000 people (contract workers and their spouses and children) worked in these plantations in 1930. Melanie Beresford, *National Unification and Economic Development in Vietnam* (New York, NY: St. Martin's Press, 1989), p. 39.

[167] Ngô Văn Hòa and Dương Kinh Quốc, *Công Nhân Việt Nam Trước Khi Thành Lập Đảng,* p. 279.

[168] Ibid., p. 235.

[169] Hồ Sơn Đài, "Introduction," in *Công Nhân Cao Su Dầu Tiếng,* pp. 14–16, 20.

[170] Ibid., p. 17.

[171] Ngô Vĩnh Long, *Before the Revolution: Vietnamese Peasants under the French* (New York, NY: Columbia University Press, 1991), p. 113.

[172] Lê Văn Kim, "Đồn Điền Dầu Tiếng," pp. 26–27.

due to natural disasters or after being evicted from their land or houses due to their failure to pay taxes or debts.[173] In particular, many Quảng Trị peasants often faced poverty due to constant natural disasters—droughts and storms—that destroyed their rice and vegetable crops.[174] Overall, poor peasants from these central provinces, unable to make a living, had either left their villages on their own account, in search of work and food, or followed the call of the Vietnamese recruiters who traveled to these provinces to find workers for the French rubber plantations in the south. These peasants often traveled with others from their native place.[175]

These workers recollected the reasons for their migration and the role of traveling Vietnamese recruiters who established recruitment centers in the north and the central for the French:

> We heard from other villagers in Thanh Hóa that whoever [wanted] to go to the south to work in rubber plantations should talk to Mr. Tám Mì [a Vietnamese recruiter who worked for the French owners] who [would] advance five piasters to spend; life in the south would be much better … We were so hungry … [we] didn't really know what would happen down there … we needed some money [immediately] to survive, and five piasters [was] a large amount at that time. So, that's why a group of us went together to register to work as rubber workers in the south, accepted the five piasters, and waited there for a week until we had enough workers to board a train down south.[176]

These migrant workers stayed together once they arrived at the plantations, similar to the modern-day migration pattern. The vicious cycle of indebtedness started early. A member of the first group of migrant workers from the central region, who arrived in 1926, said:

> Like many people in the central [region], I left my village in order to make a living. After signing a three-year contract, I got several coins [đồng bạc], one set of clothes, and that began a life of selling my labor power as draft animals [kiếp trâu ngựa] in the south. They put hundreds of us in the ship for several days before reaching Saigon. We looked at each other: all ragged! While waiting in Saigon, they opened some gambling to entertain us so we would not be too homesick. But after a while, we lost what little money we had, so we became totally dependent on their daily meals.[177]

These migrant workers tried to make ends meet for self preservation and resented being humiliated by the French owners and their foremen. Upon reaching Dầu Tiếng, they faced a very humiliating welcome, which intensified their

---

[173] Poor peasants had to pay a poll, or head, tax, often known as "body tax," or "grown man tax," which had been established by two eighteenth-century Vietnamese rival polities—the Trịnh and the Nguyễn overlords. Beginning in 1897 in Tonkin, the French increased this tax for all Vietnamese men and created an exemption for all those who worked for them or collaborated with them. Ngô Vĩnh Long, *Before the Revolution*, pp. 62–63.

[174] Nguyễn Thị Mộng Tuyền, "Công Nhân Cao Su Thủ Dầu Một," p. 234.

[175] Ngô Vĩnh Long, *Before the Revolution*, pp. 107-8.

[176] Lê Văn Kim, "Đồn Điền Dầu Tiếng," pp. 26–27.

[177] Ibid., p. 28.

resentment and pushed them toward mass protests. One lamented: "We had to stand in line and wait to be called to get rice. We each got one cup of red rice [about five liters] and dried fish with maggots. Without any containers, we had to use our conical hat or our only one shirt to hold the rice." The French treated the contract workers as prisoners and called them by numbers, not by names:

> Who arrived first had smaller numbers; who arrived later had larger numbers. Everyone had to hang the number sign in front of his or her shirt, and we were not allowed to be called by name. Those who did not remember their numbers would be beaten to death. We contract workers were not different from prisoners, losing our very own names … My name is Nguyễn Cũ, but the French called me "contract worker number 197"; my wife's name is Trần Thị Cang, but the French called her "contract worker number 110."[178]

Each day, these workers earned three coins (*ba cắc bạc*), but most had borrowed money to buy food in advance; so, on payday, they ended up penniless after paying off their debts. This vicious circle was perpetuated over time, intensifying their miseries.[179] Many north and central-region migrant workers stayed in the south after the end of their three-year contracts for various reasons: they had married while in the south—either to a southern woman or a woman from their northern hometowns who had followed them to the plantation—or, by then, they had children who were born in the south. In addition, even though the northern or central parents would have preferred to return to their hometowns at the end of their contracts, they were stuck in the south due to their ongoing indebtedness and, in some cases, illness. At times, their children—some were still teenagers—had to work in the rubber plantations to feed themselves and to help their parents.[180]

When some northern workers in Dầu Tiếng—who had suffered hardships and exploitation at the plantation—reached their limits of endurance, they stuck together and joined the labor movement.[181]

Types of Protest

The process of struggle among the workers in Dầu Tiếng started with everyday forms of individual protests and became more organized when inspired by their neighboring migrant workers in Phú Riềng. In solidarity with Phú Riềng migrant workers, Dầu Tiếng workers spread their organizing efforts and collective actions to other factories in their area (Bình Dương province).[182]

Workers started with individual acts of protest—such as slowdowns, the breaking of bowls and tools, sabotaging rubber trees, pretending to work hard on harvesting the resin when the French foremen were in sight but slowing the harvest when they left, not delivering all the resin that was harvested, and instigating shouting matches with their foremen.[183] Sabotaging young rubber trees by breaking

[178] Ibid., pp. 28–31.
[179] Ibid., p. 35.
[180] Ibid., pp. 35, 44.
[181] Ibid., p. 45.
[182] Ibid., p. 49.
[183] Ibid., pp. 37–38. Nguyễn Thị Mộng Tuyền, "Công Nhân Cao Su Thủ Dầu Một," p. 248.

them or damaging their roots was a form of "disguised resistance," or "hidden transcript,"[184] which could be managed covertly, without the saboteur being caught, and was an effective way to hurt the French commercial interests. The combined individual acts of protest laid the groundwork for impending public resistance.[185] When their neighboring Phú Riềng workers went on strike during Tết (the Vietnamese Lunar New Year) on February 3, 1930, Dầu Tiếng workers were inspired and spread the word about the Phú Riềng labor struggle in preparation for their own public resistance on International Labor Day on May 1, 1930. At that event, almost five thousand Dầu Tiếng workers demanded wage increases and a shorter workday.[186]

As calls for rebellion spread from the neighboring Phú Riềng workers, Dầu Tiếng workers were drawn together to fight for their own rights. On February 10, 1930 (a week after the Phú Riềng strike), labor staged its first open protest against the French, in which hundreds of workers stopped work and congregated at the Dầu Tiếng market—sporadically at first, then, gradually, gaining strength in a large rally. They marched and shouted this slogan: "Soumagnac [the French boss] get out; no more bad rice, no more rotten fish, no more beating." The mercenary soldiers (hired by the French Colonial Force) tried to stop this wave of workers, who continued to march forward and were joined by hundreds of others. Panicking, the soldiers then fired at the rally and killed two migrant workers.

This crisis moment united the workers, who fought resolutely for their common cause. Other members of the crowd immediately carried the deceased to the marketplace (making public this tragedy), covered them with mats, and gathered around the corpses. Then a migrant worker stood up on two chairs piled up next to the two corpses and mobilized his fellow workers to protest against such brutality. He said, using language that referred to class, with an awareness of their shared predicament:

> We worked for the boss for a long time, remained hungry and poor, but the boss still did not raise our wage. We had to eat bad rice and rotten fish, never change. We had endured so many years now and can no longer suffer. We had to come out here to let the boss know, but he ordered his men to fire at workers and did not respond to workers' requests. So, we must not return home; we have to stop work, and demand that the boss compensate for the death of these two workers.[187]

This impassioned speech got an enthusiastic approval from the congregation of workers who had occupied and disrupted the usual activities at the marketplace to mourn the deaths of their fellow workers.

---

[184] Scott defines "hidden transcript" as a critique of power, expressed in anonymity or behind the back of the dominant. It is often expressed in disguised forms such as rumors, gossip, jokes, foot-dragging, evasion, desertion, squatting, and anonymous threats. James C. Scott, *Domination and the Arts of Resistance: Hidden Transcripts* (New Haven, CT, and London: Yale University Press, 1990), pp. xii-xiii.

[185] Ibid., pp. 198–99.

[186] Trần Tử Bình, *The Red Earth: A Vietnamese Memoir of Life on a Colonial Rubber Plantation*, trans. John Spragens, Jr. (Athens, OH: Ohio University Center for International Studies, 1985), pp. 78, 82, 84; Nguyễn Thị Mộng Tuyền, "Công Nhân Cao Su Thủ Dầu Một," p. 253.

[187] Lê Văn Kim, "Đồn Điền Dầu Tiếng," pp. 38–39.

Workers proceeded to use rights-based language, although not quite the language of the law. They rallied by the hundreds at the Dầu Tiếng market to demand their rights (better meals and no beatings). These protesters knew how to negotiate for the proper compensation of their fellow migrant workers [the deceased] and for their own rights, as is evidenced in the following dialogue and demonstrated by subsequent action. They pressed the French management to keep their promise and stayed on course until the very end:

> Management: Mr. and Mrs., you should bury these two corpses and return to work; the big boss already promised to resolve this issue.
> Workers: What did the boss promise?
> Management: Fresh fish, good rice, no beating, and no harassing workers anymore.
> Workers: So, when does he implement this promise?
> Management: The boss said as soon as tomorrow, but you need to stay on the job and not try to escape work.
> Workers: When the boss resolves our requests as promised, we will return to work. Otherwise, we won't, and please do not blame us for what happens.
> Management: Sure, Mr. and Mrs., I will relay the message to the boss.

Only when the boss publicly promised to compensate the surviving relatives of the two deceased workers and to improve the working conditions for the plantation's employees did workers return to their makeshift housing to rest up for work the following day.[188]

After the Dầu Tiếng party cell was formed at the end of 1936, strike agendas became more sophisticated and directly appealed to the law. Workers walked on the streets with banners denouncing the French abuses of their Vietnamese employees, demanding democracy and people's welfare, freedom to form labor unions, proper implementation of the labor laws, higher wages, shorter work hours, and access to social security insurance. In 1937, under pressure from the French Popular Front, the French government sent a French representative to Vietnam to investigate social and labor conditions. Seizing this opportunity, more than five hundred workers and party cadres met him, hoisting banner messages and demanding justice. They also sent the French representative petitions and resolutions requesting decent living arrangements, healthful food, medical facilities, and freedom to form labor unions.[189]

Migrant Workers in Phú Riềng Rubber Plantation

To further expand production, the French built Phú Riềng plantation in Biên Hòa in 1927, ten years after developing the Dầu Tiếng rubber plantation. Phú Riềng's soil—dubbed "red earth" because of its bazan soil[190]—was good for growing rubber

---

[188] Ibid., pp. 39–40.

[189] Ibid., pp. 46–47. The French Popular Front was formed in 1934 by the three political parties in France: the Communist Party, Socialist Party, and Radical Party. It dissolved itself in 1938, facing opposition from the right wing and suffering from the effects of the Great Depression; see http://www.spartacus.schoolnet.co.uk/FRpopular.htm, accessed August 11, 2010.

[190] Bazan soil is dark yellow and red clay, well-suited to long-term and industrial crops, such as coffee and rubber, which thrive in the bazan soil (http://centrofarms.com/Default.aspx?id=9, accessed January 8, 2012). According to Dr. Nguyễn Thị Mùi, there are two main

trees. The plantation also witnessed the bloody struggles of workers against their French bosses. Again, after exhausting the local peasant workforce, the French hired contract workers from the northern and central regions. By February 1930, they had hired almost five thousand workers and, at times, the plantation employed a peak workforce of eight thousand.[191] Once there, migrants were grouped according to the villages from which they came. In 1927, the first group of contract workers arrived, 150 peasants from Hà Nam, who were put into Village No. 2, followed by a second group of 120 peasants from Hà Đông, who were put into Village No. 3.[192]

The memoir of Trần Tử Bình illuminates how the *đồng hương* (native place) factor brought the peasants from some northern provinces together to win their first several struggles before the communist party became truly influential. Trần Tử Bình, from Hà Nam province, grew up as a Catholic and was teaching bible classes while searching for a way to gain independence for Vietnam from the French. In May 1927, he was recruited by a member of the Vietnam Revolutionary Youth League[193] to "proletarianize" himself to enable him to gain workers' trust, a necessary step before being able to "make a revolution to strike down the French." He then signed up as a contract worker to work in Phú Riềng rubber plantation and became a party cadre in 1928.[194]

Cultural Identity

Most Phú Riềng workers were landless peasants from northern provinces—Hà Nam, Nam Định, Thái Bình, and Ninh Bình. Many were illiterate and had been tricked into signing long-term contracts through outrageous tactics: the recruiters (most were Vietnamese) said they had to take workers' pictures to give to the government, which would come to workers' aid if needed. Then after their pictures were taken, workers were asked to make their marks on a piece of paper so they could obtain the pictures later. That piece of paper, however, was a preprinted contract that legally bound them to dangerous work in the rubber plantations.[195]

Evidence shows some camaraderie and a sense of brotherhood among these migrant workers, although they were from different provinces. In June 1927, the first group of peasants—owning not a square inch of land or a coin among them—from the four northern provinces traveled together to the South. This was the first time

---

soil groups in the southeastern region that are consistent with the description of the types of soil at the two rubber plantations: gray soil (covers over 34 percent of the region) and yellow-red soil (covers 44 percent). The yellow-red soil group is heavy with a high silt and humus content. See http://www.fao.org/ag/AGP/AGPC/doc/Counprof/vietnam/vietnam.htm, accessed January 8, 2012. Nguyễn Thị Mùi is a researcher at the Department of Pasture Research and Animal Feed Plant Resources, National Institute of Animal Husbandry, Chèm, Từ Liêm district, Hanoi, Vietnam.

[191] Nguyễn Thị Mộng Tuyền, "Công Nhân Cao Su Thủ Dầu Một," p. 235.

[192] Ibid. The first group of workers, who arrived to clear the land, were put in Village No. 1. They were packed in extremely crowded living quarters with poor sanitary conditions. Source: Trần Tử Bình, p. 23.

[193] Again, the Vietnam Revolutionary Youth League (or Việt Nam Thanh Niên Cách Mạng Đồng Chí Hội) was the predecessor of the Indochina Communist Party, which in turn was the predecessor of the Vietnamese Communist Party.

[194] Trần Tử Bình, *The Red Earth*, pp. 10–13.

[195] Ibid., p. 16.

they had stepped outside their villages; together they waited to board the ship to Saigon, and again they waited together in Saigon for transportation to Phú Riềng, Dầu Tiếng, and other plantations.

The first struggle took place while these recruits were still in the north (the town of Hà Lý) waiting to board a cargo ship in Hải Phòng to Saigon. When the Nam Định and Thái Bình workers realized that a Vietnamese recruiter had skimmed off four piasters (đồng) from each person (each received only six instead of the ten piasters that were promised in the contract), they discussed the loss with the Hà Nam workers, who then went to talk to Trần Tử Bình. Trần Tử Bình said, "We are all in the same situation. If they ask us, we ought to go along and lend them a hand." In response, hundreds of workers from those three villages (Nam Định, Thái Bình, Hà Nam) spontaneously joined forces to protest against bad food and the violations of their contracts.[196] As Trần Tử Bình characterized it:

> It was a struggle, but the truth was that there was no leadership committee and there was no organized rank and file. It was simply a spontaneous struggle by people who had reached the end of their rope, who no longer knew what fear was. My role was only that of spokesman.[197]

Bonding based on native-place identity was important in this first fight. With Trần Tử Bình assigned as their spokesperson, hundreds of these northern migrant workers engaged in shouting and fasting to demand better food and the money that was owed to them. The recruiter finally gave in to this spontaneous struggle by giving them better food and repaying the workers' money. So, workers won their first fight by relying, in part, on their fellow migrant villagers. Moreover, these workers knew how to stage a strike at an opportune moment: Since they had not yet traveled far from home, and Hà Lý town was near their home villages, workers could credibly threaten to return home in waves, so the recruiter had to make amends for his thievery. Thus, place became an important factor in the labor movement in the Phú Riềng case.

Upon their arrival in Saigon, the migrants grew closer during the week of waiting for their paperwork to be processed. They were grouped by hometown and then sent to eight different plantations, including Dầu Tiếng and Phú Riềng.[198] A group of 150 peasants from Hà Nam was sent to Phú Riềng. When they reached their destination, migrant workers from the same home villages were grouped together in makeshift living quarters. The accommodations were arranged like a concentration camp, with rows of barracks in a dozen "villages" (one village for every one kilometer), and fifty fellow villagers were crowded into one barracks—five people to a section of twenty-five square meters.[199] But this concentrated way of living and working together helped cement their solidarity.

---

[196] Ibid.

[197] Ibid., p. 17.

[198] In addition to Dầu Tiếng and Phú Riềng, the other plantations were Lộc Ninh, Minh Thanh, and those with names translated phonetically from their French names: Sa-cam, Sa-cat, Bù Đốp, and Dakia. Nguyễn Thị Mộng Tuyền, "Công Nhân Cao Su Thủ Dầu Một," p. 231.

[199] Ibid., p. 239.

The first three struggles in 1927 evoked a clear awareness of where they came from and the care for their *đồng hương* (natives), whose destinies were joined together in this work-cum-living space:

> We have come here, far from our villages, far from our homes, and we have no close relatives. So we must learn to protect each other … Let's try to take care of each other, wait until the end of the three-year contract, then go back to our families, our villages, and our hometown.[200]

Fellow natives extended their deep sense of care towards those who had perished due to brutal beatings, harsh and dangerous working conditions, and constant hunger. In February 1930, a contract worker from the north (a "coolie Bắc-kỳ" from Hà Nam), in Village No. 9, died, and his fellow workers from Hà Nam wanted to give him a proper burial. The French refused to allow it, citing as a reason that workers must intensify their effort and increase production after Tết (the Vietnamese Lunar New Year). That triggered the first public protest at Phú Riềng, involving more than thirteen hundred workers from two plantation villages, which then erupted into a confrontation with French soldiers. This resulted in casualties for both sides before the French relented.

Use of Law

Phú Riềng workers continued to appeal to the law and used legal language to protect their dignity in struggles subsequent to February 1930. The second fight took place in the cargo ship *Dorier,* where the French ship's master skimped on the provisions given to the migrant workers. Trần Bình led a hunger strike and spoke (French) to the ship's master on behalf of all workers:

> According to our contracts, we are supposed to have enough to eat, meat with our rice, and hot tea to drink. But the galley doesn't give us enough to eat, and there's not enough to drink, either. We ask that you carry out the contract.[201]

For this statement, Bình was shut up in a toilet but the hunger strike continued. Finally, the solidarity of these hundreds of workers forced the French master to release Bình and give all contract workers enough food and drink.[202]

When the cargo ship arrived in Khánh Hội (Saigon), the "overseers" (some were French and some were half Vietnamese–half French) and police treated the workers like "a herd of cattle" and beat them with clubs and canes. When a labor representative was savagely beaten by the overseers and police, the rest of the workers shouted and went on a rampage. That effectively summoned a French inspector, who spoke Vietnamese, to the site. In a condescending voice, he said to those workers: "What's going on? What do you little ones think you are doing?" Trần Tử Bình, as the group's spokesman, stepped forward and cited the law that demanded that workers be treated with dignity: "We 'gentlemen' signed a contract to come down here to work. The contract promised there would be no beatings. Yet

---

[200] Trần Tử Bình, *The Red Earth*, pp. 21, 23.

[201] Ibid., p. 18.

[202] Ibid., p. 19.

they have beaten us 'men.' That is not lawful. If they continue to beat us, we 'men' will take them to court!"[203] Fearful of workers uniting in protest and appealing to the law, the French inspector transferred the two overseers who had beaten the poor workers. So, by confronting the French and appealing to the law, these contract workers reclaimed their status as upright men and as workers who had signed legal contracts with mutually agreed upon terms with the French. Moreover, by invoking the French legal system—the court—these workers effectively put the French on notice that the workers would not stand for abuse of any kind.

The use of law became more prominent as workers progressed along their journey together. After the skirmish at the docks, while waiting to be transported to the rubber plantations, Trần Tử Bình led an effort to negotiate on various clauses of the three-year contract. They focused on essential terms: wages, living quarters, women workers' conditions, medical treatment, food, and the provision of funds to cover expenses for the return journey home.[204]

Their collective action culminated in a major strike in Phú Riềng, started from January 30, 1930 (the first day of the Lunar New Year, the year of the cat), to February 3, 1930 (the fifth day of the new year). This struggle demonstrated the careful planning, organization, and leadership of the Phú Riềng party cell leaders, for five thousand men and women workers participated. After much discussion, the party leaders moderated their plan, deciding to stage a five-day strike instead of taking over the whole Phú Riềng plantation. The revised plan avoided the potential carnage that could have resulted, since the French had by this time sent in eight hundred armed troops to quell a takeover. While all the key communist leaders at Phú Riềng, along with hundreds of workers, were arrested at the end of the strike, the French conceded to a number of strike demands that workers put forth, including that there would be no beatings, no docking of workers' pay, exemption from head taxes, maternity leave for women workers, an eight-hour workday, compensation for workers injured in accidents on the job, and the right to return home after completion of the three-year contract.[205]

When awaiting the Phú Riềng trial after their arrests, hundreds of worker detainees staged a hunger strike to demand decent treatment as political prisoners, not as criminals. The Phú Riềng trial in 1930 was also the first trial of communists, and of Vietnamese workers, based on their *political* struggle (previously, those who were tried for their political activities were mandarins and intellectuals).[206] In that context, these worker and communist prisoners decided to walk out in public with dignity, even though they were wearing only sarongs and shorts (for their shirts had been tattered in the five-day struggle). Hundreds of arrested workers formed up in ranks of four and paraded down Saigon's streets, holding their heads high, singing songs, and shouting slogans. They appealed to the French legal system and argued with the magistrate. This surprised some public onlookers, who uttered: "Wearing sarongs like that, they can engage in politics."[207]

When the case was taken to the appeals court in Saigon, the Phú Riềng workers elevated their struggle to a political level by citing Michelin's violations of the

---

[203] Ibid., p. 20.

[204] Ibid., p. 21.

[205] Ibid., pp. 65, 67, 75–78.

[206] Ibid., p. 81.

[207] Ibid., p. 82.

contract laws, and they appealed to a sense of nationalism in another colonized country. Below is the dialogue between the chief magistrate of the court, a native Indian from Pondichery (a French colony in India), and the Phú Riềng workers' representative:

> The court: "You are guilty of disturbing the peace. Do you understand your crime?"
>
> Bình: "How can I be guilty? Look at me in my rags and tatters and half-starved! The Michelin Company *has not lived up to their contract*. They have shortchanged us on our pay. They have beaten us. It is they who are guilty, not us."
>
> The court: "All right, all right, Michelin is going to take care of the pay and the beatings. But who put you up to this rioting at Phú Riềng?"
>
> Bình: "Who put us up to this? It was the French government that put us up to it! It was Joan of Arc who put us up to it! I ask you, since you are an Indian, do you want India to be independent?" To which the magistrate was stung and his face turned purple.[208]

Evidence from archival and secondary materials shows that the migrant workers who arrived in the South understood, from the beginning, that they should reference the law in their protests. Moreover, Phú Riềng workers appealed to the values of justice and democracy, which were supposed to be upheld by the colonial French legal system, to fight for their rights.

Types of Protest

The party played an important role in the protests at Phú Riềng. Party cadres came to Phú Riềng in 1928 to build the Phú Riềng Party branch and the Red Trade Union in October 1929. Trần Tử Bình, a leader of the protests, became a communist party member in 1929. After that, workers mounted more organized protests against the French, with mixed results.[209] The party's organization and strategies can be detected in the use of more collective language in their subsequent fights. During Tết in 1930, five thousand migrant workers from Hà Nam and the other northern provinces, including three hundred women workers, took control of the whole plantation, which paralyzed production for five days.[210] They raised the red flags.[211] This Tết occupation of the plantation showed great organization and flexible strategies: the workers knew how to attack, advance, and pull back in midstream to avoid brutal bloody retaliation by the French.

Workers' rhetoric indicated an awareness of the strength of collective action and their commitment to the shared interests of the working class. When three hundred legionnaires and five hundred red sash troops[212] arrived at the scene and arrested several alleged strike leaders, hundreds of workers clung to the sides of the trucks,

---

[208] Ibid., p. 82–83.

[209] Ibid., pp. 49, 69; Trần Văn Giàu, *Giai Cấp Công Nhân Việt Nam*, pp. 473–75.

[210] Trần Tử Bình, *The Red Earth*, pp. 71–72.

[211] Chesneaux, "Stages in the Development," p. 73.

[212] These troops came from the historic French Army of Africa: they were indigenous troops from Africa, wearing red sashes around the waist.

declaring: "The masters just said they were good and that we should return to our places, but now the masters are arresting our men. If you want to arrest someone, arrest all the thousands of us. We will all go to prison!" Facing such protest from migrant workers, the French were forced to free the arrested workers.[213] However, the protesters of the five-day struggle in 1930 still lacked experience and could not prevent the infiltration of secret agents who uncovered their plan and resources, as well as arrested their leaders.[214]

When they first arrived on the plantations, angry workers often relied on shouting and staged hunger strikes. But workers learned, through word of mouth, that some disguised forms of resistance (infrapolitics), including desertion, squatting, the decision to deliver less resin than had been harvested, and foot-dragging, could be used quietly without the workers being caught. Forms of sabotage, such as the destruction of rubber saplings, also were used, especially when workers learned that the French capitalists considered the trees to be of higher value than workers themselves.[215] If the French could not identify who had destroyed a young rubber tree's root system, then these "coolies from the north" were in a stronger position to succeed in demanding that the French rectify the laborers' horrific working and living conditions. As such, infrapolitics did probe the boundaries of the permissible, although not without casualties for workers in the long run.

Native-place bonding under such "hell-on-earth" conditions at both the worksite and in living quarters heightened workers' awareness and prompted them to act upon their shared interests. Their collective actions had characteristics of Polanyi's expectation: These migrant workers detested being treated like animals and demanded to be treated with respect, as humans, as was demonstrated in the Dầu Tiếng case. Moreover, shaken up by the deaths and suffering of their fellow villagers, they found their common cause and predicament, firmed up their resolution, and fought back as a collective, consistent with Marx's expectations.

CONCLUSION

In his writing on labor process, Michael Burawoy argues that worker consent to the process is generated at the point of production and not from external values or orientations that workers bring to the factory floor. So, his focus is on how attitudes that emerge at the point of production (internal consciousness)—rather than being acquired outside of work (external consciousness)—shape the relations and activities of the labor process.[216]

But this argument does not explain the case of Vietnam. As workers mingled and toiled in factories and on plantations, what cemented their solidarity were not just experiences inside the workplace, but also social relations that developed outside the work environment. Both types of consciousness (internal and external) are evident in the case of Vietnam. The workers' consciousness, developed at the point of production, was very much engendered and reinforced by the cultural practices and expectations for human decency that they brought to the workplace. For migrant workers, native place acted as the glue that held them together in times of crisis. The

---

[213] Trần Tử Bình, *The Red Earth*, p. 77.

[214] Ibid., p. 84.

[215] Ibid., pp. 42–43.

[216] Michael Burawoy, *Manufacturing Consent*, pp. 135, 156.

site of their collective action and planning was not only on the plantations or in the factories, but also in their makeshift living quarters.

At the very beginning, many workers fought spontaneously as individuals against management, to preserve life, justice, and human decency—especially for women workers—using all forms of protests at their disposal. But the turning point for many individuals who then became involved in organized labor activism involved the deaths and suffering of their fellow villagers, their native sisters and brothers, and, especially, physical abuse inflicted on female and child workers. The brown-shirted peasant workers did not retreat when their fellow villagers were disrespected and oppressed. They rose up against the French. At moments of crisis— according to their own words as recorded in poetry, petitions, and complaints— workers saw themselves as belonging to the working class, that is, to the torn-shirt group, the contract workers, the weaving workers, and collectives of male and female fiber technicians. Then, with more organization, they combined overt actions (e.g., strikes by the thousands in Nam Định and Phú Riềng) with covert types of resistance (such as slowdowns and sabotage).

The analysis of the role of ethnicity must be interwoven with class. Class divisions existed *within* each ethnicity: between the Hoa merchants and the Hoa workers, and between Kinh merchants and Kinh workers. And certainly, class divisions were noted *between* ethnicities: between French managers and Vietnamese workers, and between Hoa supervisors and Kinh workers. Using a divide-and-conquer strategy, the French formed alliances with the merchant class (Hoa and, to some extent, Kinh) and tried to alienate the Kinh from the Hoa. Evidence shows some conflicts *across* class and ethnicity: the Hoa merchant class versus the Kinh workers. But one also witnesses this conflict within the Hoa community, where poor Hoa workers suffered at the hands of Hoa bosses. Available evidence nevertheless shows some forms of worker solidarity across ethnicities against exploitation; it is important to remember the joint forces of Kinh and Hoa workers who participated in both overt and covert resistance against injustice perpetrated upon the workers by the French, Hoa, and Kinh capitalists.

The analysis of the role of workers' skill levels needs to be integrated with a consideration of gender. First, skill differentiation did not divide workers in Vietnam during this era. In fact, workers used their skills to enhance their labor organizing; this was true, for instance, among Nam Định male electricians, mechanics, and drivers who used their freedom of movement within the workplace to communicate with and mobilize other workers of both genders and all skill levels. Moreover, correlating skills with gender and native place shows how strong bonds of sisterhood (the Nam Định Textile Combine "sisters") and brotherhood (the Dầu Tiếng and Phú Riềng migrant men workers) transcended skill differentials. In short, there is no evidence that skilled male workers had a separate agenda based on their own interests that differed from the interests of semi-skilled or unskilled workers, either male or female.[217] Moreover, I found no evidence of a practice that elevated "labor

[217] This makes the Vietnamese case different from that of Shanghai skilled workers in the early twentieth century, before the arrival of the Chinese Communist Party. These skilled Chinese workers had different demands from those of unskilled workers, which divided these different cohorts of employees. Elizabeth Perry, *Shanghai on Strike*, p. 61.

aristocrats" in Vietnam.[218] The blurred division between peasants and industrial workers—the brown-shirted peasant workers—mediated such a potential division.

Was there any form of active consent, or *false* consciousness, by the workers to the arrangements that reproduced their subordination in capitalist production relations? There was no "voluntary servitude" in the manufacturing setting, as young and old, men and women, fought for decent work conditions and human dignity in the Nam Định textile case. Moreover, I found no evidence of *either* thick or thin forms of false consciousness among these employees. First, with regard to the "thick" form of false consciousness—workers' belief in the values of the dominant ideology that justify their subordination—workers did not adopt the French rhetoric that advocated the "civilizing" influence imported by the colonialists to the then-underdeveloped Vietnam. Workers fought against their subordination by both French capitalists and the colonial government, at first with spontaneous protests and later with organized actions in factories and plantations. Workers attempted legalistic appeals to the justice values proclaimed by the colonial power. Second, with regards to the "thin" form of false consciousness—workers' resigned acceptance that the social order in which they live is natural and inevitable—the Dầu Tiếng and Phú Riềng plantations cases show that workers did not believe that their slave-like working and living conditions were "natural and inevitable." Instead, their diverse forms of protest spoke loudly to the contrary: their actions showed that they had faith in challenging an exploitative system to ensure a decent way of living. Some may even have been inspired and influenced by the "motivational power of tradition" of the Nam Định and Hà Nam migrant workers from the early 1920s who protested their workplace conditions *before* the arrival on the scene of the Red Trade Union and the Communist Party.

Evidence shows that an intermingling of Polanyi and Marxist elements underscored these workers' protests. During their actions, workers used explicit language to identify and resist the abuse of workers and the dehumanizing treatment of workers (Polanyi element) and, also, collective language—*"workers' requests"*—that indicated an awareness of belonging to the working class and of their shared interests (Marxist element). Arguably, one could say that such "class" language and clearly articulated political and economic protest agendas were manipulated by the heavy-handed Red Trade Union and the party at least by 1929. But beyond language, these workers challenged French ideological power and their repressive colonial apparatuses—such as the courts, the army, the prisons, the political system, and the media—to secure their rights. They appealed to the rule of law and the use of legalistic language (before and after the arrival of the party) in petitions, resolutions, and court appearances.

---

[218] However, this was a common practice among the Shanghai silk weavers of the same period. Elizabeth Perry, *Challenging the Mandate of Heaven*, pp. 135, 161.

CHAPTER 2

LABOR PROTESTS IN THE REPUBLIC OF VIETNAM (1954–75)

This chapter focuses on the Republic of Vietnam (RVN), south of the seventeenth parallel, commonly called South Vietnam during the period of US intervention (also referred to as "the South"). Already the center of commerce and industry during the colonial French period, the South became the ground upon which the RVN (US-supported) government would set out to develop a capitalist economy.[1]

From the context of a diverse labor movement in the South, I focus on the two famous strikes at the Pin Con Ó (Eagle Battery) factory in 1971 and the Vimytex textile factory (1962–64) in order to examine the significance of cultural identities in workers' protests and labor organizing against management and the RVN state.

I ask the same questions as were posed in Chapter 1: Who were these workers? How did they rely on *cultural identities* (native place, gender, ethnicity, and religion) to bond with each other? How did these ties engender collective action in times of need and desperation? What role did skill levels play in labor mobilization? With regard to *class*, were workers aware of belonging to a working class with shared interests, and, if so, when did they become aware of this? What were their forms of protest, including forms of protest based on knowledge of and use of law?

With respect to those two famous strikes, I offer workers' voices and those of the communist cadres who participated in the strikes. I also give attention to diverse sources of development capital in the South: mainly the Hoa, with the United States, Japan, Taiwan, and South Korea also contributing. This background is important to understand the roles of these contributors in contemporary Vietnam's labor-management relations in the market system since *đổi mới* (renovation).

In addition to class, this chapter analyzes another type of consciousness—social justice consciousness—based on religious beliefs and the ideas made salient by liberation-theology-oriented Catholic priests and lay activists. I offer the voices of these Catholic labor organizers who migrated from the North to the South in 1954 and played a significant role in labor organizing in the South.

How does cultural identity help sustain workers in their protests during this period? Protest is not an easy process. Let's hear from one of the fourteen women

---

[1] During the same period in the Democratic Republic of Vietnam (north of the seventeenth parallel, also referred to as "the North"), the socialist government was developing a command economy, and the trade union was part of the state apparatus. In this model, the enterprise-level union representative was part of state management, and it was the representative's job to ensure delivery of production targets and to take care of workers' welfare needs. Workers participated in the production process and had job security, although workforce discipline was lax. Beresford and Nyland argued that workers relied on "state paternalism" to protect them, thus they were not prepared to function in the market economy which focuses more on efficiency than equity. Melanie Beresford and Chris Nyland. "The Labour Movement of Vietnam," *Labour History* 75 (November 1998): 67–70.

factory workers who participated in the Eagle Battery strike. The women were imprisoned on allegations that they had illegally fomented a thirty-four-day strike in this major factory, the sole battery supplier to the RVN army. The women recorded this history together in a prison diary (*Nhật Ký Trong Tù Của Tập Thể Công Nhân*) that was later featured in a left-leaning Vietnamese Catholic journal. The majority of workers in the factory were women, and almost half were Hoa. This Kinh female worker participated in the struggle from the beginning to the end:

> 18 October 1971. It was late at night. The jail cell was crowded and filled with mosquitoes. The air was hot; no one can close their eyes. My mind wandered. Suddenly I questioned why I am here. I used to be as innocent as other people. Then I had to fight the boss to raise our overtime pay and to pay a bonus for Tết.[2] We were conscious that we had to unite, otherwise we would lose and be laid off. The boss always tried to find ways to break us up. Even so, there were workers who listened to the boss! I went to many meetings, and it took a long time before we [could] form our labor union. I had to invite, beg, and reiterate many times to get our brothers and sisters to participate. It was worth it: due to this participation we were successful "100 percent." This time, I was so happy to see that all the Hoa sisters [*mấy chị Việt gốc Hoa*][3] participated. If I knew Cantonese, I would join them to talk to the boss who would understand [our cause].[4]

In this chapter, I trace the process of struggle these women workers mounted against police brutality, harassment, and unpopular government leaders in order to illuminate the process of discovering a class consciousness. I will also examine forms of protest, including forms of protest based on knowledge of and use of law.

First, let's look at the complex political and historical contexts of Vietnam, steeped in French colonial and US imperialist oppression, as well as the origin of significant amounts of capital from East Asia and Southeast Asia—from, notably, ethnic Chinese—that were invested in the South. One needs to understand this historically rooted foundation to understand the impacts of global sources of capital on a reunified Socialist Republic of Vietnam.

SOUTH VIETNAM STATE POLICIES, CAPITAL, AND THE TEXTILE INDUSTRY

Wartime conditions provided a backdrop for the Eagle Battery strike and other protests in the South. The Geneva Accords of July 1954, reached after the defeat of the French at Điện Biên Phủ, divided Vietnam at the seventeenth parallel with the intent that it would be reunified in 1956 after a general election. But that election never happened. So, in the twenty-one years (1954–75) that spanned the United States–Vietnam war, two separate labor systems developed: a single, general confederation of labor sanctioned by the Marxist-Leninist state of the Democratic

---

[2] This is similar to the common twenty-first century migrant workers' request for the thirteenth-month salary, given as a bonus so that the worker can travel home for the Vietnamese Lunar New Year.

[3] The literal translation is "Vietnamese of Chinese origin."

[4] "Nhật Ký Tập Thể Của Công Nhân" [Diaries of Collective of Workers], *Chọn* 18,7–8 (October 1971): 25–26.

Republic of Vietnam (DRV) and a vibrant labor movement with many trade unions in the Republic of Vietnam (the South).

An estimated 890,000 Vietnamese left the socialist North to resettle in the capitalist South after the adoption of the Geneva Accords.[5] At least two-thirds of those who resettled were Catholics who migrated to the South for fear of religious persecution in the North,[6] and most migrants from Nam Định (the well-known textile town in the North) were Catholic. Among those who migrated were Vietnamese Catholic priests, unionists, and lay people from Nam Định and Hải Phòng; many found themselves involved in the conflicts of owners and workers in the South.[7]

The nationalist motives of President Diệm's government of the RVN shaped the ways in which the Hoa capital functioned in the South. Two specific ordinances drastically curtailed the legal status of Hoa in order to lessen French and Chinese influences over the economy, to curb the dependence of Vietnamese farmers on credit provided by the Hoa, and to encourage Vietnamese entrepreneurship.[8] Ordinance No. 48 of August 21, 1956, declared all Hoa born in Vietnam to be Vietnamese citizens, irrespective of their parents or of their own wishes,[9] and Ordinance No. 53 of September 6, 1956, excluded all foreign nationals from participation in professions known to be controlled by the Hoa.[10]

After the 1963 assassination of President Diệm, the law on Hoa legal status was relaxed: A nationality law in November 1963 gave Hoa the option of choosing Vietnamese or Taiwanese citizenship. Then, from 1964 to 1975, the Hoa were identified in official papers and documents as *người Việt gốc Hoa* (Vietnamese of Chinese origin).[11] In the early 1970s, to circumvent restrictions enacted by the Thiệu-Kỳ government, many Hoa capitalists dispersed their capital not in banks but in small-scale financial commercial outlets. They succeeded in bypassing government monitoring by hiding their money in eighty-nine underground credit outlets (*hệ*

---

[5] Peter Hansen, "The Virgin Heads South: Northern Catholic Refugees in South Vietnam, 1954–1964" (PhD dissertation, Melbourne College of Divinity, 2009), p. 2.

[6] Kevin J. Coy, "Colonel Edward Geary Lansdale and the Saigon Military Mission: The CIA in Vietnam, 1954–1955," *4th Triennial Symposium* (Lubbock, TX: Texas Tech University Vietnam Center, 2002), http://www.vietnam.ttu.edu/vietnamcenter/events/ 2002_Symposium/2002 Papers_files/coy.htm#_ftn32, accessed on July 20, 2009.

[7] Interview with Nguyễn Tiến Cảnh, July 2004 and June 2010, Nam Định, Vietnam.

[8] Trần Khánh, *Vai trò Người Hoa trong nền Kinh tế các nước Đông Nam Á* [The Role of the Hoa in the Economies of Southeast Asian Countries] (Hanoi: Viện Đông Nam Á, 1992); and Lloyd D. Musolf, "Public Enterprise and Development, Perspectives in South Vietnam," *Asian Survey* 3 (August 1963): 357–71.

[9] While 621,000 Hoa declared Chinese nationality in 1955, that number decreased quickly; only three thousand by 1958, and two thousand by 1961, sustained their Chinese citizenship. This included those who held Chinese nationality conferred by Taiwan. Trần Khánh, *The Ethnic Chinese and Economic Development in Vietnam* (Singapore: Institute of Southeast Asian Studies, 1993), p. 29.

[10] Musolf, "Public Enterprise and Development, Perspectives in South Vietnam," p. 363. Such repressive state policies helped shape underground Hoa investment patterns. This pattern foreshadows policy in socialist Vietnam in 1999 that effectively encouraged underground investment (as in the case of Huê Phong leather shoe factory to be discussed in Chapter 6).

[11] After 1975, the socialist state calls them simply "the Hoa."

thống tín dụng chìm), which enabled them to lend money at high interest rates, to sell insurance coverage, and to provide funding/capital for the real estate market.[12]

THE UNITED STATES, THE HOA, AND EAST ASIAN CAPITAL

The United States created a regime that was dependent on foreign capital, and that imported consumer goods, raw materials, and technical expertise from the United States and its East Asian allies—Japan, Taiwan, and South Korea—in the 1960s. Through the Commercial Import Program (CIP), an import subsidization program, the United States controlled the RVN government and its economy by way of imports, aid, and loan mechanisms between 1954 and 1975.[13] Capitalists from the United States and its East Asian allies flooded the South's market with logistical goods and materials in the early 1960s. Statistics showed a high trade deficit: The RVN imported fifty-five times more than it exported.[14] The South exported mainly raw commodities: rubber, rice, and tea topped the export list between 1955 and 1968. In 1960, rice and rubber were the two most important agricultural products; revenue from sales of these commodities comprised 90 percent of all export earnings.[15] The trade deficit was primarily the result of exchanges between the RVN and the United States and its wartime allies. Archival data from the RVN government showed that US capitalists benefited the most from these CIP arrangements, and that Japanese and Taiwanese producers were second and third in line, profiting especially by exporting textile materials and machinery to Vietnam.[16]

The Hoa capital stronghold in Vietnam—already developed under the colonial French—was consolidated under the United States and the RVN regime. Between 1954 and 1975, the Hoa groups controlled key industries—such as those involving rice, textile/garment/shoe, plastics, retail, banking, and construction—that affected the majority of the population in the South.[17] They also controlled small- to medium-

---

[12] Trần Khánh, *Người Hoa Trong Nền Kinh tế Các Nước Đông Nam Á*, p. 237.

[13] "Industrial Development of Vietnam," *Vietnam Information Series 5 September* (Washington, DC: Embassy of Vietnam, 1969); Seth Jacobs, *Cold War Mandarin: Ngo Dinh Diem and the Origins of America's War in Vietnam, 1950–1963* (New York, NY: Rowman & Littlefield Publishers, 2006).

[14] Lê Tấn Lợi, *Vietnamese Exports* (Saigon: The Vietnam Council on Foreign Relations, 1971), p. 3.

[15] Milton C. Taylor, "South Viet-Nam: Lavish Aid, Limited Progress," *Pacific Affairs* 34,3 (Autumn 1961): 242–56, p. 250; Lê Tấn Lợi, *Vietnamese Exports*, pp 9, 13. However, Lợi cautioned that high rice exports were short-lived, primarily between 1955–65; after that, 1966–69, more rice was imported than exported, especially from the United States through the U.S. Food-for-Peace program.

[16] In the scale of imports to Vietnam (1967 to 1970), US products ranked the highest (only a bit lower than Japan's imports in 1968, the year of the Tết Offensive), then came Japan's (except during the period of 1963–65 when Taiwan's imports surpassed Japan's), and then Taiwan's. Interestingly, imports from South Korea were very minimal during this period. See Bùi Quang Minh, *Vietnam Statistical Yearbook, 1970* (Saigon: National Institute of Statistics, Ministry of National Planning and Development, Republic of Vietnam, 1970), pp. 190–91; and Bùi Quang Minh, *Vietnam Statistical Yearbook, 1971* (Saigon: National Institute of Statistics, Ministry of National Planning and Development, Republic of Vietnam, 1971), p. 201; and *Vietnam Statistical Yearbook 1962, 1969*.

[17] Trần Khánh, *The Ethnic Chinese and Economic Development in Vietnam* (Singapore: Institute of Southeast Asian Studies, 1993); and Phan An and Phan Xuân Biên, "Người Hoa trong hoạt động kinh tế của Miền Nam Việt Nam Trước Năm 1975" [The Hoa in the South of Vietnam's Economic Activities before 1975], *Phát Triển Kinh Tế* 12 (October 1991).

scale industry, commerce and services, and finance and banking.[18] Chợ Lớn ("big market") was and continues to be a hub of Người Hoa in Saigon (the former capital of the RVN).

The economic stronghold of the Hoa in Vietnam had already been established by the 1886 Tianjin Commercial Convention, signed between the colonial French and China. In the rice market, this group set the prices for buying and selling, river transports, milling facilities, and credit (which combined usury with trade). Consequently, this group of traders had a near monopoly power over all peasants who had to go through Hoa networks in order to sell their rice. The fact that these peasants could not sell their paddy directly to rice millers and consumers in the cities had "reduced the farmer to a permanent stage of indebtedness."[19] These Hoa capitalists were supported by the powerful network of the Hoa commercial and financial system.

The Hoa chamber of commerce started out small and consisted of groups of relatives who operated in the same, respective trades and industries under French colonial rule. Then this network spread out to include nonrelatives who shared similar commercial interests, such as banking, hotels, rice, and restaurants. This integration created a foundation for capital accumulation and specialization, and it increased the competitiveness of Hoa capital.[20] The resulting chamber's organizational structure was very sophisticated, broadly encompassing, and representative of five key economic sectors (import, export, retail, industrial/manufacturing/handicraft, and banking). It involved about twelve thousand wholesale/retail stores in twenty provinces in the South, and 3,868 commercial and industrial enterprises in the Saigon–Chợ Lớn area.[21] In the RVN, there were ten private banks, of which eight were foreign: three French, two British, and three Hoa (Bank of China, Bank of Communication, Bank of East Asia), and only two were Vietnamese (the Industrial and Commercial Bank of Vietnam and Bank of Vietnam).[22]

Capitalists from the United States, Japan, and Taiwan benefited greatly from the United States–Vietnam War. As close strategic US allies against communist advancement in Vietnam, these capitalists exported raw materials and machinery and sent technical experts and workers to the South of Vietnam during the 1960s. Statistics from the South showed that, among all trade partners, the United States topped the list for exports of food and consumer products (rice, wheat flour, milk

[18] Ngô Quang Định, "Về Thế Mạnh Kinh Tế Của Người Hoa ở Quận 5 và Khu Vực Chợ Lớn Trước Năm 1975" [About the Economic Strength of Ethnic Chinese in District 5 and Cholon Area before 1975], *University of Social Science and Humanities* (n.d.): 22,15.

[19] Bửu Hoàn, "A Study of the Consequences of the Geneva Peace for the Vietnamese Economy," *Far Eastern Economic Review* 25,25 (December 18, 1958): 794, as reprinted and distributed by the American Friends of Vietnam, New York, NY.

[20] Trần Khánh, "Tìm hiểu các tổ chức xã hội và nghiệp đoàn truyền thống của người Hoa ở Việt Nam trong lịch sử" [Understanding Traditional Social Associations and Trade Unions of the Hoa in Vietnam in Historical Perspective], *Tạp chí Dân Tộc Học* [Ethnology Journal] 116 (February 2002): 9–10.

[21] T. M. Kuey, "Người Hoa Ở Miền Nam Việt Nam" [The Hoa in the South of Vietnam] (PhD Dissertation in Literature and Social Science, Sorbonne University, 1968), (Saigon: Bô Quốc Gia Giáo Dục; Ủy Ban Nghiên Cứu Sử Học Và Khoa Học), pp. 144, 150.

[22] Trần Khánh, *The Ethnic Chinese and Economic Development in Vietnam* (Singapore: Institute of Southeast Asian Studies, 1993), p. 60.

and cream, tobacco), raw cotton, fertilizers, machinery (engines, aircraft and parts, textile machines, lorries and trucks) into Vietnam.[23] Second was Japan, which profited through exports of textile materials (cotton yarn, cotton fabrics, synthetic fabrics, silk yarn), food products (fish, sugar), consumer products (motorcycles, bicycles), and industrial products (engines, textile machinery, cement, rubber tires and tubes, paper products).[24] Taiwan ranked third for its exports of construction materials (cement), textiles (cotton yarn, synthetic yarn, cotton fabrics, synthetic fabrics), industrial products (fertilizers, textile and sewing machines), and food and consumer products (sugar, motorcycles and parts).[25] Only a small amount of machinery came from West Germany and Great Britain, which ranked far below Taiwan.

A declassified top-secret document showed how the United States' Agency for International Development (AID) funded irrigation works, agricultural production, and processing development that relied on technical assistance provided by Japanese and Taiwanese, consistent with the trade patterns explained above.[26]

I focus on the textile industry for two reasons. It is one of the most important manufacturing industries in the South, and it clearly demonstrates the shared interests of the two governments (RVN and US) and capitalists from the United States and Taiwan. A study of the textile industry also helps us to understand the scope of cross-border Chinese investments in the "Greater China zone," including Hong Kong, Taiwan, mainland China, and Southeast Asian countries.[27] To sustain these investments, Chinese business firms relied on their ethnic connections (such as social, cultural, language, and personal ties) and networks in their globalization process.[28] The strike cases in textile/garment industries in this chapter demonstrate the close connection between Taiwanese and Hoa investors. In subsequent chapters, there is evidence of cross-border Chinese investments—from Taiwan to China and then to Vietnam, with the Hoa playing an important role—in textile/garment as well as in footwear factories.

---

[23] Bùi Quang Minh, *Yearbook 1971*, pp. 233–35; Bùi Quang Minh, *Yearbook 1970*, pp. 223–28; Bùi Quang Minh, *Yearbook 1969* (Saigon: National Institute of Statistics, Ministry of National Planning and Development, Republic of Vietnam, 1969), pp. 299–302.

[24] Bùi Quang Minh, *Yearbook 1971*, pp. 226–29; Bùi Quang Minh, *Yearbook 1970*, pp. 217–19; Bùi Quang Minh, *Yearbook 1969*, pp. 292–95.

[25] Bùi Quang Minh, *Yearbook 1971*, pp. 230–32; Bùi Quang Minh, *Yearbook 1970*, pp. 220–22; Bùi Quang Minh, *Yearbook 1969*, pp. 296–98.

[26] Top Secret: Section III, *Additional Measures in South Viet Nam*, declassified materials, National Archives and Records Administration (NARA), June 5, 1994. No date for the original top secret memo can be found anywhere on the document. Jay Lovestone Papers, Hoover Institute on War, Revolution, and Peace, Stanford, California. South Korean forces also participated directly in the war as special combat forces, such as the "vicious tiger brigade" (*sư đoàn mãnh hổ*), whose historical legacy had played a role in a labor protest after 1975 (see Chapter 4).

[27] Henry Yeung and Kris Olds, eds., *Globalization of Chinese Business Firms* (New York, NY: St. Martin's Press, 2000), p. 78; Neil Coe, Philip Kelly, and Kris Olds, "Globalization, Transnationalism, and the Asia-Pacific," in *Remaking the Global Economy: Economic-Geographical Perspectives*, ed. Jamie Peck and Henry Wai-chung Yeung (London: Sage Publications, 2003), p. 49; and Farid Harianto, "Business Linkages and Chinese Entrepreneurs in Southeast Asia," in *Culture and Economy: The Shaping of Capitalism in Eastern Asia*, ed. Timothy Brook and Lương Văn Hy (Ann Arbor, MI: University of Michigan Press, 1997), p. 137.

[28] Yeung and Olds, *Globalization of Chinese Business Firms*, p. 98.

This broader context explains the Taiwan–Hoa connection that powerfully influenced the RVN, for Taiwanese investment in Southeast Asia would be dependent on social, cultural, and personal ties that connected the Taiwanese entrepreneurs with the local partners—the Hoa, in the context of Vietnam.[29] Second, this industry background is necessary for understanding the significant textile worker protests in Vimytex—the largest textile mill in the South—discussed subsequently, in this chapter.

The Textile Industry

Textile was the major industry in the RVN, even ahead of the rubber industry in terms of production and employment.[30] But it was heavily dependent on capital and raw materials from the USAID, and its wartime East Asian allies, such as Taiwan, Japan, and Korea. The industry began modestly with a 7,500-spindle spinning plant, outfitted with equipment and built from materials brought down by North Vietnamese migrants in 1954, which were reassembled and put back into operation in Khánh Hội (a Saigon district) in 1958. Most Vietnamese exports of textile and garment products were dependent almost entirely on imported materials, such as raw cotton from the United States, fiber and yarns from Taiwan and Japan, and fabrics and machinery from Japan, consistent with the trade pattern discussed above.[31]

The United States played a key role in the creation of the textile industry in the RVN, an industry marked by heavy dependency on US imports (under the Commercial Import Program, CIP) of machinery, spare parts, raw materials, and technical assistance.[32] Under the United States Operations Mission (USOM), the CIP arrangement, and the Industrial Development Division, the US created the Industrial Development Center (IDC) in 1957 and the Handicraft Development Center in 1958. At least two US consultancy contractors and four US engineering firms were paid by the US government to provide technical assistance and advise on production methods, and to help with implementing loans to twenty-eight private manufacturing firms, including those engaged in textiles. Virtually all textiles and raw materials (cotton, all types of yarn and filament) were imported into the RVN, primarily benefiting US corporations and the RVN government. Since 1966, imports of raw materials were handled under the auspices of the CIP and managed by the Vietnamese government and the USAID. In particular, Vimytex purchased looms using a US$6 million loan from USOM and imported raw materials (cotton, silk, and rayon) from the US under the American farm surplus program.[33]

---

[29] Coe, Kelly, and Olds, "Asia-Pacific," p. 49.

[30] "Industrial Development of Vietnam," pp. 3–4.

[31] Taylor, "South Viet-Nam."

[32] Trần Đức Thanh Phong, *The Textile Industry in Vietnam* (Saigon: The Vietnam Council on Foreign Relations, 1970), pp. 7, 9, 11; Asia Bureau of the Agency for International Development, "Industry: United States Economic Assistance to Viet Nam, 1954–1975," Viet Nam Terminal Report (Washington, DC: Agency for International Development, December 1975), pp. 2, 10, 11–13.

[33] Trần Đức Thanh Phong, *The Textile Industry in Vietnam*, p. 7; Jack Langguth, "A Labor Dispute in Saigon Easing: Appears Resolved by Mill's Concessions to Workers," *New York Times*, October 7, 1964.

Taiwan participated in the United States's special procurement program by supplying materials to Vietnam—estimated at US$150 million in 1967—during the United States–Vietnam war. Based on scant materials, I found that Taiwan exported to the South and also provided an indirect supply of materials to Vietnam via the United States, Japan, and other countries. Chong-se Kim argues that industrial sectors such as cement, iron, and steel played a key role in these arrangements.[34] Moreover, Taiwanese subcontractors for the United States were instrumental in providing technical services and personnel in major industrial projects in the South. I demonstrate the role of Taiwanese material supply and technical assistance in the Vimytex case study below.

The Taiwan–Hoa connections in the textile industry were established back in the 1960s. Networking based on native place was at work here, facilitated by the existence of a common language and culture throughout the Greater China zone, described above. The Hoa capitalists—already established during the French colonial era—controlled the distribution of both imported and domestic woven fabrics via their 350 wholesalers in the Chợ Lớn area of Saigon; they also received support from their chamber of commerce.[35] Hoa investment grew in the 1960s; a number of Hoa entrepreneurs increased production capital, advanced from being traders and middlemen to industrialists, and updated and transformed their businesses into large-scale enterprises with modern equipment well-served by connections with overseas Chinese or to the greater China region.[36]

The common language and cultural practices of the Hoa and Taiwanese influenced the composition of management in some large textile factories, as owners and supervisors preferred promoting colleagues with whom they could interact easily (I examine this issue in greater detail in the case study that follows on the largest textile factory in RVN: Vimytex). At another large textile factory in the South, Vinatexco, the mill manager and technical personnel were Taiwanese. Owners of those factories preferred Taiwanese over Japanese personnel because "they [spoke] the same language spoken by many of Vinatexco's Hoa employees recruited in the Chinese-speaking Chợ Lớn section of Saigon."[37] These Taiwanese engineers then trained female recruits to become skilled technicians, replacing the men who were drafted to fight for the RVN army. The Taiwan-Hoa investment connections in the textile/garment/footwear industries serve as a backbone for many factories that experienced strikes. But first, we need to situate these strikes in a broader context of the vibrant and diverse labor movement in the South.

---

[34] Chong-se Kim, "The Economic Settlement of the Vietnam War: An Analysis of the Economic Impact of a Possible Truce," *International Studies Seoul* (December 1970): 108–9. I found some evidence from an RVN source showing that there had been a triangular trade arrangement—among the United States, Taiwan, and Vietnam ("Industrial Development of Vietnam," 1969), related to the case study of Vimytex, the textile factory in the South discussed below. Such a trade arrangement would have contributed to the RVN's dependence on capital and materials from outside sources (United States and its allies such as Taiwan, Japan, and Korea) to be used in Vietnam. But even with the help of reference librarians at Stanford University, we could not find any further information on the "triangular trade arrangement." We exhausted many sources, including the United States federal registries of commercial treaties, but could not find any more details on this trade arrangement. Author's fieldwork, 2008.

[35] This system had established some major market places for fabrics, such as the Soái Kình Lâm market, in post-1975 reunified Vietnam.

[36] "Industrial Development of Vietnam," 1969.

[37] Trần Đức Thanh Phong, *The Textile Industry in Vietnam*, p. 15.

THE LABOR MOVEMENT IN THE SOUTH

The conditions that prevailed during the United States–Vietnam war—political instability and heavy military and police suppression—had negatively affected the working conditions in the factories in the South and labor's ability to respond. Workers earned low wages in subcontracting employment; they failed to keep up with rising costs of living and were subjected to substandard working conditions in the South. Those conditions included fast machine speeds, accelerated to force workers to work faster; lack of job security due to the prevalent short-term subcontracting work; inadequate social insurance coverage; loss of purchasing power due to the rising costs of living; and unhealthy working conditions, leading to occupational illnesses. The subcontracting system awarded middlemen and recruiters high fees based on a percentage of the salaries earned by workers they had recruited, a practice that led to overzealous and often deceptive recruiting.[38] These conditions show up under each system of government in Vietnam—from the turn of the last century until today—and have been recreated by a variety of production systems, from the colonial French contract system to contemporary global supply chains.

Workers in manufacturing accounted for less than one-third of the total nonfarm labor force, since there were not many large factories with dedicated workforces in Vietnam during the war. The nonfarm labor force in the South totaled 618,000 people, of whom only 200,000 worked in factories.[39] The rest were small retailers, unemployed, or underemployed. Most of the manufacturing workers were women, since most working-class men had been drafted to fight in the war. Textile factories employed about 8,000 workers.[40] In a few large textile factories in the Saigon–Chợ Lớn area, such as Vimytex, Vinatexco, and Đông Á Textile, most of the workers were local Hoa women.[41]

Labor protests escalated in the early 1960s but tapered off later in the decade. Strike statistics from the Saigon Labor Department showed intensification in scope and scale: 227 protests in 1960; 287 protests with 82,000 participants in 1961; 324 with

---

[38] Tiến Khải, ed., Ho Chi Minh City (HCMC) Labor Federation Executive Committee [Ban Chấp Hành Liên Đoàn Lao Động Thành Phố Hồ Chí Minh], *Công Nhân Saigon–Chợ Lớn Trong Sự Nghiệp Giải Phóng Dân Tộc* [Workers in Saigon-Cho Lon and Their Role in National Liberation], (Hanoi: Lao Dong Publisher, 1993), p. 310. According to a *New York Times* article, Vimytex workers (mostly women) earned only 65 cents a day. When they went on strike for better pay and working conditions, the management locked them out from August 8 to August 23, 1964, and later on refused to rehire 190 women (out of 1,950 workers). Jack Langguth, "A Labor Dispute in Saigon Easing."

[39] Tiến Khải, *Công Nhân Saigon–Chợ Lớn*, pp. 309–10. Of those factory workers, a large percentage worked for US contractor firms and military operations. Nguyễn Ngọc Linh, ed., *The Working Man in Vietnam* (Saigon: Vietnam Council on Foreign Relations, 1970), p. 11.

[40] Tiến Khải, *Công Nhân Saigon–Chợ Lớn*, pp. 309–10; Bùi Quang Minh, *Vietnam Statistical Yearbook 1962* (Saigon: Ministry of National Planning and Development, National Institute of Statistics, 1962).

[41] Cao Văn Lượng, *Công Nhân Miền Nam Việt Nam Trong Cuộc Kháng Chiến Chống Mỹ Cứu Nước (1954–75)* [Workers in the South of Vietnam in the Anti-American Resistance to Save the Country (1954–75)] (Hanoi: Nhà Xuất Bản Khoa Học Xã Hội, 1977), pp. 42–43; Tiến Khải, *Công Nhân Saigon–Chợ Lớn*, p. 264; Central Intelligence Agency (CIA) Directorate of Intelligence, *Intelligence Report: The Situation in South Vietnam* (August 15, 1966), pp. 1–3.

103,000 participants in 1962; and 505 with 200,000 participants in 1963. However, the number of strikes decreased between 1965 and 1968 due to improved bilateral dialogues between employers and employees; the decision by owners to raise wages according to rising costs of living; the decisions by workers to moderate their protests, as they were conscious of the difficult situation of RVN; and timely intervention by the RVN labor agencies, which made an effort to consult with and remediate the stakeholders' positions before strikes broke out. The strike statistics are as follows: 28 in 1965, 85 in 1966, 87 in 1967, and 41 in 1968.[42] The agendas of the protestors reflected both economic and political causes: democracy, people's welfare, and anti-suppression of workers.[43]

The United States–Vietnam war framed most protest agendas: All sides mobilized workers using both political and economic goals. This environment created unprecedented alliances between left-leaning Catholics and communists and, to some extent, between Catholics and Buddhists.[44] Such an environment spawned an abundance of labor unions in the South before 1975 that, as a group, reflected the area's political history and the different political organizations that had vied for power and influence in Vietnam: the Vietnamese Communist Party, the French (1940s and early 1950s), and the Americans (1950s, 1960s, and 1970s),[45] as well as the RVN government itself.

In 1956, the RVN government gave workers the right to form labor unions and to strike "under conditions prescribed by law," but proscribed it later when government officials felt threatened by the strikes.[46] But overall, this legal framework allowing independent union structure enabled a vibrant labor movement in the South consisting of many labor unions and trade federations, with both left-wing and right-wing orientations, compared to the one Federation of Trade Union in the North.

Both left-wing and right-wing labor confederations benefited from the law permitting freedom of association—the independent union structure. The right-wing General Confederation of Workers used the law to demand improvement in working

---

[42] Tiến Khải, *Công Nhân Saigon–Chợ Lớn*, pp. 317–18; Bộ Lao Động [The Labor Ministry], *Vài Hoạt Động Quan Trọng: 1965-1969* [Several Important Activities: 1965–1969] (Saigon: Labor Ministry, n.d.), pp. 31–33.

[43] Tiến Khải, *Công Nhân Saigon–Chợ Lớn*, p. 322.

[44] To some extent, progressive Catholics (such as Father Nguyễn Ngọc Lan) and active Buddhists (such as Chân Không/Cao Ngọc Phượng, an activist Buddhist nun) had come together after the immolation of a young Buddhist nun—Nhất Chi Mai—in 1968 to appeal for peace. They signed a petition together to call for an end to the war, which then got them into trouble with the RVN government, which forced them to retract the peace appeal and sign a new petition to condemn the communists. Chân Không (Cao Ngọc Phượng), *Learning True Love: How I Learned and Practiced Social Change in Vietnam* (Berkeley, CA: Parallax Press, 1993), pp. 112–13.

[45] Edmund Wehrle, "No More Pressing Task than Organization in Southeast Asia": The AFL-CIO Approaches the Vietnam War, 1947–1964," *Labor History* 42,3 (August 2001): 277–97; Jonathan Hoving Los, "The Rise of the Labor Movement in South Vietnam" (Master's thesis, University of Texas at Austin, 1975).

[46] Melanie Beresford and Chris Nyland, "Labour Movement of Vietnam." This right, specified in the Constitution of Vietnam, was later proscribed by Decree Number 6, which allowed detention of anyone found to threaten the state. Beresford and Nyland, pp. 63–64.

conditions, to oppose lay-offs, and to protect free trade unions.[47] The Confederation also supported a sort of tripartite negotiation among union representatives, management, and local state officials.[48] The left-wing union also assisted workers in using petitions to demand their rights and organized them to oppose police brutality and even operated undercover to fight for workers' rights (see the Vimytex case, below).

The South recognized six general labor confederations, of which two were large and influential: the General Confederation of Labor (Tổng Liên Đoàn Lao *Động* Việt Nam) and the General Confederation of Workers (Tổng Liên Đoàn Lao *Công* Việt Nam).[49] The first one was alleged to be left-leaning and received support from the North (although this group is not to be confused with the labor confederation of the same name that existed under the Socialist Republic of Vietnam, discussed at length in Chapter 3). The General Confederation of Workers received support from the American Federation of Labor and Congress of Industrial Organizations (AFL-CIO). Together with other independent labor unions, based on types of employment, the total number of trade unions in the South was about six hundred, representing more than 400,000 members.[50] First, I explain the largest general confederation in the South.

General Confederation of Workers (CVT)

The most influential and powerful anti-communist labor union in the South was the General Confederation of Workers, established in 1951.[51] With a membership of

[47] Nguyễn Văn Thư, "Các Nghiệp Đoàn Tại Gia Định," p. 31. Thư was a high-ranking official of Bửu's General Confederation of Workers. He shows an extant list of worker demands from two textile factories (Vinatexco and Vinatefinco) in Gia Định Textile Federation, asking management to enforce policies on complaints related to wages, a social benefits fund, cooperative management, canteen meals, worker dormitories, and doctors and nurses.

[48] Ibid.

[49] In Vietnamese, the only difference in their names is one word: "Động" versus "Công." This confusion had led to mistakes, a few of which can be found even in some internal Vietnamese reports from the RVN government.

[50] Trịnh Quang Quỹ was a senator in the Republic of Vietnam and chairman of the Committee on Labor and Social Affairs. He was also a close assistant to Trần Quốc Bửu, the president of the right-leaning labor union (General Confederation of Workers [the CVT] or Tổng Liên Đoàn Lao Công Việt Nam). This ideological leaning explains his inequitable treatment of these two confederations: only one paragraph on the basic statistics for the left-wing General Confederation of Labor (on which most categories were stated "unknown") versus a whole chapter about the right-wing CVT, which he claimed to be the real representative of Vietnamese labor. Trịnh Quang Quỹ, *Phong trào lao động Việt Nam* [The Labor Movement in Vietnam] (Saigon: n.p., 1970), pp. 34, 38–39, 41; Benedict Tria Kerkvliet, "Workers' Protests in Contemporary Vietnam," in *Vietnam Update Series: Labour in Vietnam*, ed. Anita Chan (Singapore: Institute of Southeast Asian Studies, 2011), p. 172. He came up with a similar estimate of the union membership in the RVN.

[51] Nguyễn Văn Thư, "Các Nghiệp Đoàn Tại Gia Định: Phong Trào Nghiệp Đoàn tại Gia Định; Vài Con Số Chính Yếu và Cách Định Trí" [Trade Unions in Gia Định: The Trade Union Movement in Gia Định; Some Important Statistics and Positionality], *Nghiên Cứu Hành Chánh, Học Viện Quốc Gia Hành Chánh* [Administration Research, National Institute of Administration] 9,9 and 9,10 (September and October 1965), p. 9. However, Trịnh Quang Quỹ provided another date for the founding of the confederation: April 1952. Trịnh Quang Quỹ, *Lao động Việt Nam*, p. 30.

300,000 people in four hundred federations,[52] it represented workers in most economic sectors and many provinces in the South.[53]

Trần Quốc Bửu was the leader of the organization from its inception. Bửu was a complex figure, who maintained shifting alliances with the French and then with the United States. In the 1930s, he participated in anti-French efforts for national independence and eventually was arrested and sent to the Poulo Condore prison (on an island in the South China Sea) in 1940, where he allied with some prominent communist leaders. At the surrender of the Japanese force in August 1945, he joined the resistance against the French but left that force in 1948 to avoid the communist purge against nonparty members who had been involved in the resistance. Under the tutelage of leaders of the French Catholic Trade Union, which primarily protected the interests of French capitalists, in 1952 Bửu founded the Vietnamese Confederation of Catholic Workers. He called it, in French, Confederation Vietnamienne du Travail Catholique (CVTC).[54]

Since Bửu and 90 percent of the CVTC membership were Buddhist and perhaps looking for a broader appeal, in 1964 he dropped the word "Catholic" from the name of his confederation, changing it to, simply, the Vietnamese Confederation of Workers (sometimes referred to by the shorter French acronym, CVT, Confederation Vietnamienne du Travail).[55]

Perhaps the initial goals of Bửu's CVT were noble. As stated in his own words, "We have a labor movement in South Vietnam which is free and independent and which has managed to avoid subversive communist domination on the left and government control on the right";[56] but evidence reveals a more complex picture. Edmund F. Wehrle noted this difficult situation of the CVT, and acknowledged its early success while arguing that "despite enormous strides in a relatively short period, the [then] CVTC remained fragile, caught between the surging Viet Minh and repressive French colonial overlords. Out of necessity, the organization sought outside support."[57] As discussed later, evidence shows that the AFL-CIO, the US government, and the CIA (Central Intelligence Agency) had provided their support to the CVT since the early 1960s. Both claims concerning the character and status of the organization had some ring of truth: In terms of membership and the number of affiliated federations, at least in principle, the CVT represented the largest number of workers in the South, compared to the other confederations. But as declassified CIA documents and other confidential materials became available to the public, they revealed that the CVT had another political motive besides leading an independent labor movement in the South: getting the United States support to "help win the war

---

[52] Nguyễn Thị Sương Kiều, "Hiện Tình Nghiệp Đoàn Công Nhân Tại Viet Nam" (Graduation Thesis, Học Viện Quốc Gia Hành Chánh, 1969), p. 26; Trịnh Quang Quỹ, *Lao động Việt Nam*, p. 34.

[53] Lê Văn Đồng, *Sơ lược về hiện tình các vấn đề lao động ở Việt Nam* [Preliminaries on Current Situations of Labor Issues in Vietnam] (Saigon: Labor Ministry, 1956), pp. 61–75.

[54] Nguyễn Ngọc Linh, *The Working Man in Vietnam*, p. 12.

[55] Ibid., pp. 13, 15.

[56] Trần Quốc Bửu, *The Vietnamese Confederation of Labor (CVT) Speaks to the Free World* (Saigon: Vietnamese Confederation of Labor, Department of Research-Publication-Education, 1966), p. 6.

[57] Edmund F. Wehrle, *Between a River and a Mountain: The AFL-CIO and the Vietnam War* (Ann Arbor, MI: University of Michigan Press, 2005), pp. 39–41.

against the Việt Cộng."[58] Moreover, there were other labor confederations in the South besides the CVT. Their various perspectives, both right- and left-leaning, and workers' voices play important parts in the two case studies discussed below.

When the country was divided at the seventeenth parallel, according to the Geneva Accords in July 1954, conflicts between Bửu's confederation and the North Confederation of Labor came to a head. This led to the closing of the three CVT offices in the North and the evacuation of more than thirty thousand people, mostly Catholics, to Saigon by plane and ship.[59] (More analysis on their settlement can be found in the "Native Place" section in this chapter.) In 1954, CVT members held their first congress with Trần Quốc Bửu as chairman and Bùi Lượng as secretary general.[60] They formed the largest nongovernmental mass membership organization in the South, focusing on workers and peasants in strategic economic sectors. In particular, five federations belonged to the CVT: the Tenant Farmers, Fishermen, Transport Workers, Plantation Workers, and Textile Workers federations.[61] The CVT leadership wanted to shore up forces against the National Liberation Front (NLF) to combat the influence of communist cadres who, historically, were embedded in key sectors such as agriculture, plantations, and factories.[62]

The United States and the AFL-CIO directly financed and supported Bửu's Vietnamese Confederation of Workers, first to train union cadres, rural peasant leaders, cadres for farm cooperatives, and social workers, starting in 1964, and later to perform covert actions for the Commercial Import Program (CIP) and United States Operations Mission (USOM).[63] The political purpose was to gain control of the communist-influenced labor unions in the South that had begun resisting as Bửu politicized and militarized his labor union activities.

Evidence shows inconsistency in Bửu's messages to different audiences. On the one hand, as a leader of an anti-communist labor union, Bửu had close connections to and enjoyed protection from the AFL-CIO, the US government (John F. Kennedy

---

[58] Trần Quốc Bửu, "Confidential Memorandum to the President of the United States of America, May 20, 1964," Jay Lovestone's Collection at Hoover Institution Archives, Stanford University, Stanford, CA, p. 1.

[59] Trần Hữu Quyền, *Báo Cáo Tinh Thần* [The Spiritual Report], from The Third Congress, April 22–24, 1960: Ten-Year Anniversary of the Tổng Liên Đoàn Lao Công Việt Nam (Saigon: CVT, 1960), p. 45.

[60] Trịnh Quang Quỹ, *Lao động Việt Nam*, p. 43.

[61] Nguyễn Ngọc Linh, *The Working Man in Vietnam*, pp. 12, 19; Nguyễn Thị Sương Kiều, "Hiện Tình Nghiệp Đoàn," p. 26.

[62] Beresford and Nyland "The Labour Movement," pp. 60–61; Hoàng Quốc Việt, *The Trade Union Movement in Vietnam* (Hanoi: Foreign Languages Publishing House / Vietnam Federation of Trade Unions, 1988).

[63] Evidence showed that the CVT received US AID support and AFL-CIO sponsorship. Irving Brown, a high-ranking AFL-CIO member, had been working closely with Trần Quốc Bửu since 1964. In 1968, Brown visited Vietnam several times and proposed in March 1968 to support Bửu's 1964 appeal (in writing and in person when Bửu visited the United States). Irving Brown, "Memorandum to George Meany; Subject: South Vietnam, June 1, 1964"; Irving Brown, "Reports," February 6, 1968, and March 26, 1968, in Jay Lovestone's Collection at Hoover Institution Archives, Stanford University; and "Establishing of AID-supported and AFL-CIO-sponsored Institute to Strengthen CVT Participation in Rural and Revolutionary Development," Jay Lovestone's Collection at the Hoover Institution Archives, Stanford University. (NOTE: There is no other bibliographical information available on this document, which includes these sections: background, recommendation, and general guidelines.)

and Lyndon Johnson administrations), and the CIA. He appealed to President Johnson in May 1964 to fund, train, and arm workers so they, too, could engage in paramilitary activities in the countryside against the communists, a plan for which Bửu received support in 1968. In a confidential memorandum to the president of the United States on May 20, 1964, Bửu made a twofold request: (1) for economic aid to provide food and housing for union members, and (2) for political support to create "an almost para-military type of civilian organization to reinforce the armed forces and transform an indifferent and neutral mass of people into an active barrier against the communists in the villages."[64] On the other hand, in a formal publication distributed to the 300,000 members of the CVT in 1966, Bửu claimed to have no political agenda: "What is important is that the CVT has steadfastly declined to engage in partisan political activity, nor has it permitted itself, as a national organization, to become the tail of any one or any group of political parties."[65]

Three months after his appeal to President Johnson, in August 1964, Bửu formed the Action Committee for the Protection of Trade Union Movement (Ủy Ban Hành Động Bảo Vệ Phong Trào Nghiệp Đoàn), which included *"chiến sĩ"* (soldiers) assigned to protect their trade union units. In 1968, he received concrete support from the AFL-CIO and USOM to militarize his trade unions.[66] Being empowered, he denounced communist leadership in the strikes at the two largest textile factories—Vimytex and Vinatexco—and other factories, as well as the political support these workers had received from the communist government in the North and the National Liberation Front in the South.[67]

Bửu's alliance with powerful American organizations and leaders and his inclination to militarize the Vietnamese Confederation of Workers alienated a number of Vietnamese workers, many of whom turned to align themselves with the influential left-wing trade unions in the South. While the CVT had the highest union membership (or density) in terms of RVN-generated statistics, the competing, left-wing unions were effective in utilizing the free trade-union framework to organize workers to demand their rights, as well as to sustain left-wing unions' political agendas.

General Confederation of Labor and Left-Wing Unions

The most prominent left-wing–labor-union confederation was the General Confederation of Labor (Tổng Liên Đoàn Lao Động Việt Nam). Statistics recorded on the General Confederation of Labor were not precise, which may reflect an

---

[64] Trần Quốc Bửu, "Confidential Memorandum to the President of the United States of America, May 20, 1964."

[65] Trần Quốc Bửu, *The Vietnamese Confederation of Labor (CVT) Speaks to the Free World*, p. 12.

[66] In particular, Irving Brown of the AFL-CIO proposed to continue the CVT-AFL-CIO program in Vietnam. That program would involve: community and civil self-defense duties, which must be related to military organization; the organization of trade union elements into units of self-defense that would liaison with military command; underground training and organization, a form of behind-the-lines operation that spies on enemy's plans and infiltrates Vietcong camps such as plantations, fishermen's and farmers' unions, public utilities, power and communications. Brown, "Reports," February 6, 1968 and March 26, 1968.

[67] Trần Quốc Bửu, "Thông Cáo của Hội Đồng Tổng Liên Đoàn Lao Công Việt Nam" [Announcement of the Committee of the General Confederation of Vietnamese Workers], August 30, 1964.

ideological difference between the confederation and the RVN's statistical office. According to RVN official statistics, the confederation was established in 1954 with forty-eight affiliated federations, and its union membership ranged from 25,000 to 50,000 members.[68] Yet another study reported a greater number: 100,000 members.[69]

The second most prominent left-wing federation, the Federation of Trade Unions for the Liberation of South Vietnam (Hội Lao Động Giải Phóng Miền Nam), the FTU, was founded in 1961, subsequent to the public inauguration of the National Liberation Front in December 1960. This federation had a clearly militant agenda. It helped workers set up their own guerrilla, self-defense, and commando brigades in major cities and towns,[70] thus demonstrating a militant orientation equal to that of the right-wing CVT under Bửu (it is not clear which group armed itself first). The FTU's first organized strikes took place in strategic industries, such as electrical power stations, rubber plantations, and docking/shipping ports. These relatively small strikes then led to the two major strikes at Vinatexco and Vimytex that culminated in massive strikes in Saigon after the downfall of the Diệm regime in 1963. All sides took credit for the two-day general strike in Saigon in September 1964.[71]

The RVN government was suspicious of the General Confederation of Labor, believing the confederation to be supportive of the Vietnamese communists (or Việt Cộng). This may have led to an internal leadership rivalry known to all who were involved back then. Both Phan Văn Chí and Bùi Văn Thiện claimed to be the director of the General Confederation of Labor.[72] Trần Văn Hai, the director of police in Saigon, investigated this issue and submitted a report to the head of the Interior Security Ministry (Bộ Nội Vụ) on July 16, 1968:

> Our office knew about this division and [leadership] competition within this confederation. But this confederation continued to operate due to the perseverance of Mr. Phan Văn Chí. We found it suspicious because (1) he had a track record of performing military intelligence for the Việt Cộng during the anti-French resistance, (2) most members in the leadership team [were] of the Hoa ethnicity, and (3) they never condemned the Việt Cộng, but were only critical of the [RVN] government and also wanted peace and an end to war.[73]

Clearly, the government had kept a close eye on the activities of Phan Văn Chí. Hai further noted that the majority of members on the leadership team of this union

---

[68] Trịnh Quang Quỹ, *Lao động Việt Nam*, pp. 38, 41; Another source stated that it was formed in April 1953. Nguyễn Văn Thư, "Nghiệp Đoàn Tại Gia Định," p. 9.

[69] Nguyễn Thị Sương Kiều, "Hiện Tình Nghiệp Đoàn," p. 29.

[70] Tiến Khải, *Công Nhân Saigon–Chợ Lớn*, pp. 301–2. The name "Hội Lao Động Giải Phóng Miền Nam" was subsequently changed to "Liên Hiệp Công Đoàn Giải Phóng Miền Nam" (Federation of Trade Unions for the Liberation of South Vietnam).

[71] Trần Quốc Bửu, *The Vietnamese Confederation of Workers (CVT) Speaks to the Free World*, p. 12; Vietnam Federation of Trade Unions, *1965, A Year of Great Victories for the Workers' Movement in South Vietnam* (Hanoi: Vietnam Federation of Trade Unions, January 1966).

[72] Trịnh Quang Quỹ, *Phong trào lao động Việt Nam*, pp. 41–42.

[73] Trần Văn Hai Report on Phan Văn Chí to the Head of Bộ Nội Vụ on July 16, 1968 [Internal Security Department in Republic of Vietnam], in *Phủ Tổng Thống Đệ Nhị 4161 v/v Tranh Chấp Quyền Lãnh Đạo Tại Tổng Liên Đoàn Lao Công Việt Nam, 1965-8 Archive*, Lưu Trữ Quốc Gia [National Archive] Number 2, Ho Chi Minh City, p. 7.

were of Hoa ethnicity.[74] I will return to this point in considering the case of Eagle Battery factory (in which workers were represented by this union).

In short, the independent union structure had allowed competition between the left-wing and right-wing labor confederations to represent workers, although each was highly partisan and operated based on their own political ideologies. To understand labor organizing and strikes in the South, we need to examine the make-up of its workforce regarding migration, cultural identity, and religion.

CULTURAL IDENTITY

Native Place

As stated earlier, about 860,000 to 1.1 million people from the North migrated to the South in 1954.[75] During the month of July 1954 alone, more than 30,000 people, mostly Catholics (including 22,000 workers and their families, traveling by ship from Hải Phòng, and 8,000 of Bửu's union members and their families, who flew out from Hanoi), migrated from the North to the South, fearing religious persecution under the communists' rule.[76] Most migrants from Nam Định were Catholic.[77]

Upon arriving in Saigon, Bửu's confederation placed all these workers in nine handicraft camps around Saigon. He established the Reception and Resettlement Committee to help them with accommodations and employment while encouraging these refugees to remain anti-communist.[78] By 1960, those who stayed in these camps became weavers and formed textile cooperatives with assistance from the government and Bửu's confederation. In 1964, they formed handicraft workers' unions, which in 1966 became the Federation of Handicraft Weavers (Nghiệp Đoàn Thợ Dệt Thủ Công), an affiliate of the CVT.[79]

Migrants from Hải Phòng (a coastal town in the North)—many of whom were Hoa—brought to the South their disassembled textile machinery, which they promptly put back into operation in Khánh Hội (Saigon). The report of this event is consistent with Cảnh's account about the Hải Phòng textile factory being owned by the Hoa.[80] Many of these migrant workers formed textile cooperatives and subsequently joined the Federation of Handicraft Weavers in the 1960s.[81]

But as the war escalated and the economy became increasingly dependent on aid and imports from the United States and its allies in the late 1960s, small producers—Kinh weavers and Hoa textile producers—found they could not compete with large-scale imports from the United States, Japan, and Taiwan, as explained earlier. Moreover, there were large foreign textile factories built in Saigon in the 1960s. For instance, DACOTEX (Kỹ Nghệ Dệt Đông Á), a textile factory in the South, imported Taiwanese raw cotton and yarns under the triangular trade arrangement that

[74] Ibid.

[75] Kevin J. Coy, "Colonel Edward Geary Lansdale and the Saigon Military Mission."

[76] Trần Hữu Quyền, *Báo Cáo Tinh Thần*, p. 45.

[77] Interview with Nguyễn Tiến Cảnh, July 2004, Nam Định.

[78] Beresford and Nyland, "Labour Movement of Vietnam," p. 63; Trần Hữu Quyền, *Báo Cáo Tinh Thần*, p. 46.

[79] Trần Hữu Quyền, *Báo Cáo Tinh Thần*, pp. 143–44.

[80] Interview with Nguyễn Tiến Cảnh, June 2010, Nam Định.

[81] Trần Hữu Quyền, *Báo Cáo Tinh Thần*, pp. 143–44.

apparently bound Vietnam to Taiwan and the United States, although no documentary evidence can be found on the US federal registries of commercial treaties.[82] Similar production and trade arrangements involving Vietnam are evident in the twenty-first century (chapters 5 and 6).

Ethnicity

Similar to the left-leaning unions, Bửu's CVT tried to win the support of Hoa workers in some strategic industries. From November 8, 1954, non-Kinh workers, especially the Hoa, were allowed to join the unions, and the CVT established a Chợ Lớn communications office with Chinese-speaking representatives who intended to increase union membership by attracting workers from different sectors, especially the textile industry, in addition to the garment, shoe, restaurant, hotel, and printing industries.[83]

The Hoa played many different and significant roles in the labor movements in the South: as workers, capitalists, and embedded communist cadres. Hoa workers dominated vital industries in the RVN—textile, printing, and battery—as well as river-way transportation and three-wheeled taxis. They accounted for a large percentage of the membership of the left-wing union, the General Confederation of Labor.[84]

There is some evidence that Hoa workers forged an alliance with Kinh workers to fight for their common goals—better working and pay conditions—under the influence of embedded communist cadres who had been hired at the factories as regular workers; many of these cadres were themselves Hoa.[85] Like Kinh workers, the Hoa complained about losing their jobs to "foreign" laborers who came to work in the South, many from Taiwan and South Korea. The first real success in organizing Hoa workers occurred in the early 1960s, when large textile firms were built around the Saigon and Chợ Lớn areas. Most of those factories were owned by Hoa capitalists who collaborated with US and Taiwanese investors under the CIP program.[86] As will be shown in the Eagle Battery factory case study, Hoa workers fought alongside Kinh workers, guided by Hoa communist cadres and progressive Catholic labor organizers in this factory.

Many communist cadres were hired by unsuspecting managers to fill both skilled and semi-skilled jobs in factories and on plantations.[87] They worked closely

---

[82] "Industrial Development of Vietnam," 1969, p. 9.

[83] Trần Hữu Quyền, *Báo Cáo Tinh Thần*, pp. 148–49.

[84] Nguyễn Thị Sương Kiều, "Hiện Tình Nghiệp Đoàn," p. 29.

[85] Trần Văn Giàu, *Giai Cấp Công Nhân Việt Nam*; Nam Định Textile Combine Party Executive, *Công Ty Dệt Nam Định*; interviews with Hà Tăng and Lưu Quế, August 2008, Chợ Lớn, Ho Chi Minh City.

[86] Los, "The Rise of the Labor Movement in South Vietnam"; Cao Văn Lượng, *Công Nhân Miền Nam*.

[87] Here are some interesting examples of how to plant party cadres in factories and other enterprises. The underground assisting mobilizing unit (or *Ban Phụ Vận*) selected from among its own cadres when preparing to place them in appropriate units to mobilize other workers. For instance, Nguyệt, a dyeing worker, was planted in Sicovina textile factory; Nhàn, a nurse, was embedded in Grall Hospital to establish a labor union and mobilize the struggle there. My source for this information claimed that subsequent labor movements were strong and successful in both these places. Tiến Khải, *Công Nhân Saigon—Chợ Lớn*, footnote on p. 334.

with Hoa employees who dominated factories in the Saigon–Chợ Lớn area.[88] Hoàng Thị Khánh—a communist revolutionary—told me what was once classified information: the cadres embedded by the Vietnamese Communist Party were not just in the left-wing unions, but also in Bửu's right-wing union. She also confirmed that the common protest agenda at that time was to demand democracy and to protect people's welfare (*dân chủ, dân sinh*).[89] Most strikes embraced this agenda. Then, beginning in 1954, labor leaders began to demand a national election for reunification (which was supposed to take place in 1956, as mandated in the 1954 Geneva Accords), and in the 1960s they intensified the frequency of their strikes, which involved thousands of participants.

Saigon residents joined the general strike to demand welfare and democratic rights, September 22, 1964. This image was part of the public exhibition on the occasion of the eightieth anniversary of the Vietnamese General Confederation of Labor. The original caption in Vietnamese reads: "Nhân Dân Sài Gòn Biểu Tình đòi quyền dân sinh dân chủ, 22 September 1964." (Author's photo)

[88] Tiến Khải, *Công Nhân Saigon–Chợ Lớn,* p. 334.
[89] Interview with Hoàng Thị Khánh, August 2004, Ho Chi Minh City.

Some Hoa communist cadres pointed out the importance of bilingual newspapers to project an image of the party's growing power in the South. As an underground mobilization unit of the party in the South (Ban Công Vận), these Hoa activists secretly printed and disseminated the first underground bilingual newsletter (and, later, newspaper) in some Hoa stronghold districts in Saigon, such as districts 5, 6, and 11. In 1963, the *Liberation Newsletter* (Bản tin Giải Phóng) was printed in two languages: Vietnamese and Chinese, in a secret location in District 6; in 1965, it was renamed the *Workers Newspaper* (Báo Công Nhân). In 1971, it became the *Liberation Newspaper* (Báo Giải Phóng), which published about a thousand issues that were disseminated widely to people of all walks of life in the Saigon–Chợ Lớn area.[90]

Young Catholic Worker Movement and Labor Organizing

As mentioned above, many Catholic priests and labor activists migrated from the North to the South in 1954. I focus here on a perspective not often acknowledged: that of the left-leaning, but non-communist, Catholic priests and labor activists. They distinguished themselves from the Vietnamese communists. The terms that the Catholic priests and Catholic lay activists used to describe themselves were "progressive and left-wing, but not Vietnamese communist" (*tiến bộ, cấp tiến, khuynh tả, không phải Việt Cộng*). Their left-leaning agendas connected a key political goal (democracy, *dân chủ*) with a key socioeconomic goal (people's welfare, *dân sinh*) to mobilize workers. In the interviews with these activists and secondary materials concerning them, they used various terms to describe themselves, most notably *progressive Catholics* (*người công giáo tiến bộ*).[91]

In discussing the Young Catholic Worker movement (more below), Huỳnh Thị Ngọc Tuyết—a researcher at the Sustainable Development Research Institute in the Southern Region (1979–2007)—said, "This movement is progressive, left-wing, not belonging to the Vietnamese communists, but they were allies and did support activities of the Public Mobilization R Department [*ban công vận cục R*] of the Vietnamese communists."[92] Nguyễn Nghị opined, "The Catholic Youth and Worker Movement [Phong trào Thanh Niên Lao Động Công Giáo, PTTNCG] agreed with the vision of communism, and we cooperated with the VC [Việt Cộng] to achieve a common goal: building a just society—which could be a communist society—that includes all classes and religions. The PTTNCG movement believed that communism is the most efficient means to bring about a just society [*xã hội công bằng*]."[93] I will use the terms *progressive* and *left-wing* interchangeably to reflect all these perspectives.

These progressive Catholic priests had reconciled their religious philosophy with communism so that they would be able to coexist with the communists. They tried to conflate their social-justice vision with Marxist ideology, proclaimed in theory by the Party and the Federation of Trade Unions in the North before 1975. At the height of

[90] Bùi Văn Toản, *Đấu Tranh Cánh Mạng của Đồng Bào Hoa Saigon-Thành Phố Hồ Chí Minh* [Revolutionary Struggle of the Hoa in Saigon—Hochiminh City] (Ho Chi Minh City: Nhà Xuất Bản Trẻ, 2005), pp. 180–82.

[91] Trương Bá Cần, "Catholics and Socialism," *Chọn* 21 (October 20, 1974): 7; interview with Nguyễn Thị Thân, September 2008, Ho Chi Minh City.

[92] Interview with Huỳnh Thị Ngọc Tuyết, September 2008, Ho Chi Minh City.

[93] Interview with Nguyễn Nghị, September 2008, Ho Chi Minh City.

the United States–Vietnam war, they found that the slogans and goals they shared with the left-wing labor movement—promoting democracy and people's welfare—were consistent with their social-justice vision and concerns for the working poor.[94]

These clergy cited social justice as a key aspect of shared consciousness that transcended class and religion: People from all walks of life with different religions could appreciate it. This means that they, the progressive Catholics, would work with all classes and non-Catholics: "The key motivation of progressive Catholic priests was to mobilize everyone, including communist cadres, to rebuild a just society that [included] all classes, ethnicities, and religions … because we thought that an unjust society [was] a form of sin and evil."[95]

Progressive priests, operating in the open, increased their level of labor activism and connected with the embedded communist cadres (operating underground). A left-wing Catholic priest, Phan Khắc Từ, was the representative of the lowest rung of the working class in the South—the garbage workers (Đại Diện Lao Công Hốt Rác). He was lovingly referred to as a "garbage priest," a term of endearment for a priest whose life has been dedicated to the working poor. He also published a bimonthly underground periodical under the oppressive RVN regime, called the *Labor Newsletter of the Committee for the Protection of Workers' Rights* (Bản Tin Lao Động: Ủy Ban Bảo Vệ Quyền Lợi Lao Động[96]), to showcase labor activism in many sectors—textile, garment, pharmaceutical—and to present a forum for workers' news and inputs from other labor unions. He signed as the president of the Provisional Executive Council of the Committee for the Protection of Workers' Rights. Thanks to the exposure and influence of this newsletter, while the victories won by pro-labor forces were small, workers received broad-based support from labor unions in other factories and sectors, from labor/human rights committees, from progressive members of the parliament, and from individuals representing all walks of life.[97]

However, Trương Bá Cần (the leader of the Thanh Lao Công [TLC, Young Catholic Worker] movement, discussed below) was honest about the Catholic activists' primary goal: to propagate Catholicism in an environment (*truyền giáo trong môi trường*) by reforming that very environment.[98] At times, the environment could be a factory, a school, or a ward (*xóm*). Given the conditions in these locations, the "Catholic labor soldiers" (*Chiến sĩ lao động công giáo*) realized that they could not "reform an environment in a society that [valued] profit as the basic engine for development, free competition as the ultimate economic principle, [and] controlling the means of production as a private property right, irrespective of related social responsibilities." Therefore, if the movement had to choose between capitalism and socialism, the Catholic labor soldiers who passionately advocated justice (*công bằng*) and brotherhood (*huynh đệ*) had selected socialism.[99]

As the war was raging on, this progressive Catholic movement became more politicized and gravitated toward the underground communists' objective. The

---

[94] Ibid.; and interview with Nguyễn Thị Thân, September 2008, Ho Chi Minh City.

[95] Interview with Nguyễn Nghị, September 2008, Ho Chi Minh City.

[96] This Vietnamese underground publication can be compared to the underground *samizdat*, copied by hand and distributed in the former Soviet Union.

[97] Phan Khắc Từ, *Bản Tin Lao Động: Ủy Ban Bảo Vệ Quyền Lợi Lao Động* [Labor Newsletter: The Committee for the Protection of Workers' Rights] (Saigon), volumes in 1974.

[98] Trương Bá Cần, "Catholics and Socialism," p. 61.

[99] Ibid., p. 62.

Catholic Worker movement (*phong trào Lao Động Công Giáo*) was formed to politicize the TLC movement by selecting socialism instead of capitalism, first, on an individual, implicit, quiet, and sporadic basis in the 1960s, then, on a public, vibrant, and collective basis from 1970 to 1971.[100]

A description of that period by one of the activists who was involved suggests a class conflict: "It is not simply to fight against the bosses/management [*chủ*], but to change society, which necessitated the toppling of the South Vietnamese government that allied with capitalists."[101] By 1971, the discourse justifying collaboration with the communist underground cadres had strengthened:

> If we Catholics were brave enough to unite and fight for equity and social justice, standing in front of the battlefield without fear of anything or anyone, then we would become a sign [*dấu hiệu*] that everyone, especially the poor, the weak, the oppressed … could recognize. And on that front line, we can collaborate with everyone, including the [Vietnamese] communists. It is not surprising that Latin American Catholics can coexist and collaborate with the communists. Catholics and communists are no longer the major problem on that continent. The fundamental objectives are social progress and human development. We need to accomplish these objectives fast, urgently; if not, a lot of blood will spill as predicted by Father Helder Camara.[102]

How did the left-leaning Catholic Youth Worker Movement function in the context of wartime Vietnam?

History of the Catholic Youth Worker Movement

The Catholic Youth Worker Movement was introduced to Vietnam first in the North, in 1947, and then in the South during the partitioning (1954–75), after a number of Catholic priests and TLC activists migrated to the South in 1954.[103] These activists participated in the global Catholic Youth Worker movement, attending conferences in Bangkok (1965) and Lebanon (1969).

Founded in Belgium in 1912, the Young Christian Workers (YCW) movement had spread across Europe and the world by the early 1930s.[104] From 1925 to 1930, the

---

[100] Ibid.

[101] Interview with Nguyễn Nghị, September 2008, Ho Chi Minh City.

[102] Editors of *Chọn*, "Kết Luận" [Conclusion], *Chọn* 6 (February 1971): 80–81. Helder Camara was a Brazilian progressive Catholic priest who wrote *Spiral of Violence* at the time of the United States–Vietnam war. In that book, he argued that the violence of poverty (the structural injustices prevalent in poor countries or the isolated pockets of poverty found in rich countries) is linked to the violence of revolt (ignited when peaceful demands have no effect) and violence of repression (felt when the powerful try to crush demands of the poor). To break this spiral, he appealed to the youth to engage in a movement such as Action for Justice and Peace, and to people of good will to exercise "liberating moral pressure … truth and love" to redress such injustices. Helder Camara, *Spiral of Violence* (London: Sheed and Ward Stagbooks Ltd., 1971), pp. 82–83.

[103] Trương Bá Cần, *Fifty Years Reflection: June 28, 1958 to June 28, 2008* (Hochiminh City: n.p., 2008).

[104] Piya Pangsapa, *Textures of Struggle: The Emergence of Resistance among Garment Workers in Thailand* (Ithaca, NY: ILR/Cornell University Press, 2007), p. 85.

YCW movement began mobilizing and training workers from a number of different countries so that they could join with their compatriots to solve their own labor issues. In Vietnam, where Catholicism was the main Christian denomination, this movement was generally referred to as a proactive Catholic movement (Công Giáo Tiến Hành).[105] In 1947, some progressive Vietnamese Catholic priests in Hải Phòng (the North) adapted YCW's vision to Vietnam's conditions and called it the Phong Trào Thanh Lao Công (TLC) movement, focusing on helping the working poor. These TLC clergy spread this movement to Hanoi and then to Saigon when they migrated to the South in 1954.[106]

Trương Bá Cần was the chaplain of this progressive movement from 1964 to 1975, and during his tenure, in the late 1960s, the spiritual inspiration and influence of Latin American liberation theology were added to strengthen this movement. The TLC action protocols included the three reflective activities of "observing, assessing, and doing" (*xem, xét, làm*) to bring both Catholic and non-Catholic workers together in order to organize them to fight for social justice.[107] These progressive priests wrote and edited a journal, *Chọn*, a monthly publication that provided learning materials for the TLC movement.

Place, Gender, and Progressive Catholics' Activism

The TLC movement shows how affiliation with a native place and religion can empower people. Most of TLC's key members were Catholics who came from the North in 1954. Leadership of the organization's two branches was divided by gender: the Young Female Catholic Worker group was led by a woman, Đặng Thị Thân, and the Young Male Catholic Worker group was led by a man, Nguyễn Tiến Mạo. Most active female members were factory workers from a variety of industries; Thân, for instance, was a textile worker and also a labor organizer. On the other hand, most active male members were teachers, and only a few were workers. The TLC movement had only enough members to enable it to be active in three parishes: Saigon, Xuân Lộc, and Nha Trang. This reality explained the fluid structure and composition of the TLC movement, which consisted of activists, some of whom were not workers. Given these conditions, the organization's membership changed when older female members got married or left the factories.[108]

The TLC was vibrant from 1964 to 1975, focusing on the rights of the working poor. This movement was branded left-wing and was not often supported by the orthodox Vietnamese Catholic Church in the South:

> The TLC movement is the movement of workers so it is considered left-wing [*tả*], if not left leaning [*thiên tả*]. Therefore, it does not often receive support from the Saigon bishop [*giám mục*] or priests who do not care about the poor, and are not concerned about workers. It has been that way in the world and is the same in Vietnam.[109]

---

[105] Trương Bá Cần, *Fifty Years Reflection*, p. 18; Trương Bá Cần, "Catholics and Socialism," p. 61.

[106] Trương Bá Cần, *Fifty Years Reflection*, p. 18.

[107] Interview with Nguyễn Nghị, September 2008.

[108] Ibid.

[109] Trương Bá Cần, *Fifty Years Reflection*, p. 26.

How does a religious identity help bring workers together? How did a progressive religious identity intersect with gender to fortify the struggles of the Kinh and Hoa workers in the factories? I do not intend to generalize in order to categorize the different perspectives within this progressive movement; instead, I will present several perspectives from both men and women in different roles, according to willing and able interviewees and secondary sources.

I focus on the religious identity of the two activists who belonged to the Catholic Youth Worker Movement. Đặng Thị Thân is a Catholic labor organizer who migrated from the North to the South in 1954 and was a textile worker in Nam Hòa textile factory in the 1960s. Nguyễn Nghị was the managing editor of the *ĐD* journal, one of the two journals published by the progressive clergy involved with the TLC. The journal had to exist undercover to avoid state censorship by the RVN regime. The editors changed the name, for example, from *Đối Diện* (facing off), to *Đồng Dao* (singing along), and later to *Đứng Dậy* (rising up), but preserved the initials—ĐD— to alert loyal readers. The resilience and creativity of these progressive clergy members, and their grasp of politics, are demonstrated by their many revisions of the journal's name.

The two activist interviewees argued that, while they supported both Catholic and non-Catholic workers in their protests against management violations (such as in the case of the Eagle Battery struggle), Catholic workers had more chances to bond with each other. On their Sundays off, they got together at each other's houses to socialize and pray together in Bible meetings. At work, the Catholic workers normally gathered together to pray during break or when tragic news reached them.

In a moving interview, Đặng Thị Thân described a turning point that strengthened her consciousness of social justice, an attitude that, for her, focused on people's welfare and democracy. Her voice shook when she recalled that moment:

> I remember when we heard the news of Ms. Lan's death [a sixteen-year-old Catholic female textile worker who was tortured to death by the local police]. We [Catholic workers] stood at the corner of our factory staircase to pray for her. In our subsequent struggle, we received a lot of support from other factories, which gave us money and food. We were fighting for people's welfare and democracy (*dân sinh, dân chủ*) … War is too brutal; our people suffered so much. We desired peace.[110]

The death of their fellow female worker triggered the resolve of these employees to fight for larger and loftier goals for the many—for people's welfare and democracy. The bonding of these Catholic women workers was palpable in Đặng Thị Thân's words. They prayed together at the news of Lan's death. Seeing themselves as sisters and as fellow Catholics brought them together during that oppressive period to fight for peace and justice. At that crisis moment, their collective action was based on indignation against this brutality and the desire to protect life. Moreover, that moment triggered her resolve to go underground as a full-time labor activist, and from there she joined the underground Việt Cộng forces and became a communist.

The following two case studies demonstrate the role of native place, gender, ethnicity, and religion in lived experiences.

---

[110] Interview with Đặng Thị Thân, September 2008.

CASE STUDIES: VIMYTEX TEXTILE AND EAGLE BATTERY PROTESTS

Protests in two factories—Vimytex textile (1962–64) and the Pin Con Ó (Eagle) Battery (1971)—demonstrate the role of cultural identities in the process participants undergo when discovering class consciousness during protests. I analyze how gender, ethnicity, and religion made possible the moments marked by class consciousness, or "class moments," in protests, and in jail as well, thus shaping the forms of resistance arising in these cases.

I rely on both secondary sources and interviews with the labor organizers who agreed to talk to me. In discussing the Eagle Battery case, I used extensive reports from the *Chọn* journal, one of the two progressive Catholic journals in the South.[111] The *Chọn* provided detailed analyses from pro-labor progressive priests, parliamentary representatives, and lawyers who were critical of the RVN government.

This journal showcased workers through their own voices, which were glaringly missing from materials published by the VCP and the RVN government's presses describing these historical events. Since I was unable to interview the workers who were involved directly, which is admittedly a shortcoming, I rely on accounts in prison diaries, in the Eagle Battery case, to interpret the workers' meanings and intentions.[112]

In the Vimytex case, I triangulate different sources to get at workers' perspectives. I cite secondary print sources (originating from both sides of the political struggle) and interviews with some key players at that time. In September 2008, I had a great fortune to interview two Hoa organizers who were embedded as workers in Vimytex in the early 1960s. My interview with Hà Tăng—a Hoa who was an underground labor leader of the Vimytex strikes in 1964—provides firsthand evidence of the underground organizing role of the VCP. As a staunch communist cadre who barely escaped capture several times, Hà Tăng was responsible for mobilizing and leading Hoa activities in the Saigon–Chợ Lớn area. I also interviewed Lưu Quế in September 2008, a Hoa communist cadre who was embedded as a worker at Vimytex in 1962.[113] After being exposed in 1962, she left Vimytex but continued to mobilize workers in other factories. Some South Vietnamese accounts have pointed out that many of these embedded communist cadres directly organized workers' protests in rubber plantations in some southern provinces near the border with Cambodia (such as Phước Long, Long Khánh, Tây Ninh, and Bình Long) in 1964–65.[114]

While I am conscious that reports published by the VCP are bound to be, in part, propaganda, I was moved by the dedication to the cause and the sufferings of these two leaders during the periods when they were operating underground and when they were captured. Narratives about their roles in these well-known protests offer insights into the strategies and tactics they used and the benefits of the independent

---

[111] Compared to the *ĐD* journal, the *Chọn* journal focused on a particular theme and was more theoretically oriented.

[112] "Nhật Ký Tập Thể Của Công Nhân," *Chọn* 18,7–8.

[113] Bùi Văn Toản, *Đồng Bào Hoa Saigon*, pp. 54, 221.

[114] Nguyễn, Quang Quýnh, "Công nhân, nghiệp đoàn và cộng sản" [Workers, Trade Unions, and Communism], *Nghiên Cứu Hành Chánh* (January and February 1965), Saigon, pp. 44–82.

labor union structure—admittedly fragmented in the South—that allowed them to act as workers' representatives to demand changes from the inside.

The Case of Vimytex (1962–64)

I pieced together the puzzle of this case history using a combination of archival materials (from Cornell and Stanford universities), Vietnamese language materials, and interviews with two Hoa labor organizers embedded in the Vimytex factory. Interestingly, these two VCP cadres were able to lead this strike while a right-wing confederation—the CVT—was overseeing the Textile Workers Federation in Saigon–Gia Định.[115]

Vimytex was the largest textile mill in the South, established in 1960, consisting of three main factories that handled all stages of textile production (spinning, weaving, and dyeing/printing) using the most modern textile machinery available at that time.[116] Most of its equipment and materials were imported from the United States, Japan, and Taiwan. The factory employed about 2,400 workers, of whom the majority were Hoa women.[117] The key value added to the Vietnamese economy from such industrial investments is primarily composed of labor wages, which represent a small amount of the income generated through factories. This factory, which later became the Việt Thắng Factory under the Communist government, was located in Linh Trung Ward, Thủ Đức District, Ho Chi Minh City. This preunification labor history is important to understand what happened when this factory became state-owned and then participated in a joint venture with different foreign investors (see Chapter 4).[118]

The name Vimytex reveals the origins of the capital invested in this venture and the connections that functioned between the state and sources of capital. In this case, the venture involved Vietnam (Việt) and the United States (Mỹ) partnering in textiles (tex) manufacturing—hence, Vimytex. The factory was established using US capital and was managed by a Chinese-American textile magnate, referred to simply as Mr. Jen in English-language documents. He received a loan of US$6 million from US-AID or USOM, an alleged CIA-related operation, and worked with the Hoa to manage the factory.[119] The Vietnamese sources confirmed that all management personnel were of Chinese descent and provided specific identification: the top investor was a Chinese American (Nhiệm Hồng Bảo); the second biggest investor was Taiwanese (Tôn Nhơn Khanh); and the third was a Hoa who had migrated from the North to the South in 1954 (Châu Giới Tăng). The organizational and operational structure at Vimytex

---

[115] Ibid., p. 54.

[116] Việt Thắng Factory Newsletter, 2006, http://www.vietthang.com.vn/html/aboutus-1-eng.html, accessed June 2008.

[117] Cao Văn Lượng, *Công Nhân Miền Nam*, p. 66; CIA, *Situation in South Vietnam*, p. I–3. According to Langguth, "A Labor Dispute in Saigon," by 1964 there were only 1,950 workers, mostly young women. This suggests that management discharged workers, perhaps union leaders, over time.

[118] Vimytex was nationalized after 1975 and thereby recast as a state-owned factory, and given an apt name: Việt Thắng (Vietnamese Victory). During *Đổi Mới* (economic renovation), it became a joint-venture, supported in part by South Korean capital, when the FDI policy was signed into law in 1987.

[119] Werhle, *Between a River and a Mountain*; Ngô Quang Định, "Thế Mạnh Kinh Tế Của Người Hoa."

mimicked that of a typical Taiwanese factory,[120] while the management arrangement reflected a connection between Taiwan and the Hoa community in Vietnam, continuing a relationship that dated back to the French colonial era.

Worker protests in Vimytex were marked by the workers' use of law in communicating their demands and by their appeals to the RVN state apparatuses (labor department, unions, and media). Starting in February 1962, Vimytex workers invoked stipulations of the RVN Labor Code and demanded wage increases, collective bargaining contracts, eight- to ten-hour workdays, improvement of work conditions, and fringe benefits, such as paid vacations. When conditions did not improve, the workers went on strike again in August and November 1963.[121] In April 1964, eight hundred Vimytex workers were fired, and then in August more than 1,800 workers lost their full-time jobs when management locked them out. Workers appealed to the Gia Định labor department, but to no avail. RVN soldiers and police suppressed this August 1964 strike brutally, using clubs, guns, and water cannon with such force that hundreds of women strikers fainted or collapsed at the scene. Nineteen strikers were taken away by the police. Only when workers threatened to begin a hunger strike and a few threatened self-immolation did the police release those nineteen strikers. Throughout August 1964, workers took turns rallying in front of the offices of the labor department, the CVT, and Saigon newspapers. All those events created momentum for strikes in other industries that spread throughout the city, and eventually led to the general strike on September 21–22, 1964.[122]

A complex political/ideological context served as the background for this general strike. Bửu's CVT received support from President Nguyễn Khánh's government, which was reacting against the rising influence of the National Liberation Front.[123] Neither the government nor Bửu wanted the strike to take place; the RVN government issued an Emergency Decree to stem these strikes on August 18, 1964. On September 10, 1964, Bửu called an emergency union meeting of CVT's 1,200 members. While union members wanted to put together a resolution in support of the Vimytex workers and to deal with state suppression of union activities, Bửu was ambivalent and hesitant. His hesitation was possibly due to his suspicion that party informants had infiltrated the Vimytex factory. In this meeting, Bửu was reported to have remained quiet and tried to postpone any initiative to intensify pressure against Vimytex management. In the end, he asked, "What if Vimytex management refused to accept workers' demands?" To which union representatives answered, "Then we would engage in a general strike." Some even added, "That's not enough, we need to rally in front of the prime minister's palace and deliver our resolution."[124]

---

[120] Interview with Hà Tăng, August 2008; Bùi Văn Toản, *Đồng Bào Hoa Saigon*, p. 45. Please note that the Vietnamese spellings/pronunciation of these Chinese names are at best approximate. I found different versions of these names. For instance, the Chinese-American owner's name is recorded as both Nhiệm Hồng Bảo and Nghiêm Hồng Pao; the Taiwanese owner's name is referred to as Tôn Nhơn Khanh and Tôn Nhơn Thanh; the Hoa ethnic who lived in Vietnam is identified by two different names, Châu Giới Tăng and Châu Đào Sanh.

[121] Tiến Khải, *Công Nhân Saigon—Chợ Lớn*, p. 319.

[122] Ibid., pp. 320–21, 324–25.

[123] Beresford and Nyland, "Labour Movement of Vietnam," p. 65.

[124] Tiến Khải, *Công Nhân Saigon—Chợ Lớn*, pp. 326–28.

Hoa workers joined a rally in support of the General Strike and Vimytex workers against the exploitative regime of the Saigon government, September 21, 1964. This image was part of the public exhibition on the occasion of the eightieth anniversary of the Vietnamese General Confederation of Labor. The original caption in Vietnamese reads: "Công nhân người Hoa tham gia meeting hưởng ứng cuộc Tổng Đình Công ủng hộ công nhân Vimytex chống chế độ bóc lột của chính quyền Sài gòn, September 21, 1964." (Author's photo)

This general strike received support from people from all walks of life. Moving beyond the wage-hike demand posed in 1963, this general strike focused on *nonwage* benefits, such as an eight-hour workday, paid vacations, cost-of-living allowances, and an increase in the power of union representatives.[125] In August 1964, Vimytex management locked workers out and called in both military and civilian police battalions to disperse and beat up strikers.[126] But though deprived of their wages, these workers held out for three months. How did they prevail? I turn now to discuss how cultural factors played a role in their class moment.

The Hoa Cadres and Labor Leaders

Most Hoa workers from districts 5, 6, and 11 in 1960s Saigon came to work in Thủ Đức district, which was a long distance from their homes. They became essentially migrant workers—staying at the factory dormitories during the week and

---

[125] Beresford and Nyland, "Labour Movement of Vietnam," p. 65.

[126] Cao Văn Lượng, *Công Nhân Miền Nam Việt Nam*, pp. 73–74.

returning home for the weekends.[127] But after the Vimytex strike, the provincial government closed down those worker dormitories for fear that thousands of workers living together might engage in political activities. Moreover, the security police also complained that they could not collect intelligence from worker dormitories because these Hoa workers spoke Chinese.[128] Security police closely monitored workers on a daily basis, in and outside of the workplace, in order to prevent labor organizing. They forbade workers from congregating in groups of more than five people, even after work. They also did not allow workers in one factory department to meet with workers from other factory departments.[129]

Many Hoa labor leaders cum communist agents—some were women—were active in this factory, where the majority of the 2,400 employees were Hoa women, as mentioned earlier. The embedded communist agents (posing as regular workers) formed an underground cell inside Vimytex factory in 1961 consisting of both skilled workers (mostly men) and some less skilled (mostly women). In September 2008, I interviewed two former Hoa cadres who were planted in this factory. Hà Tăng worked as an electrician from 1963 to 1964 until he was exposed during the general strike. Lưu Quế worked at Vimytex as a textile worker from 1961 to 1962, until she was exposed and laid off along with fifty-eight other factory employees. Most workers in this factory were Hoa high-school graduates who spoke several Chinese dialects, but there were a few Kinh workers, too. So, the organizers had to be able to speak several Chinese dialects (such as Cantonese, Mandarin, and Teochew), as well as Vietnamese in order to communicate with this mixed group of workers.[130]

Lưu Quế said:

> I was twenty, and had just finished the tenth grade and passed the exams (math and literature) to work at Vimytex. But at night, I took Vietnamese language lessons as per a request by our leaders in order to function well in the factory. When I was hired to work at Vimytex in 1961, I joined the propaganda group [*lực lượng tuyên truyền*] and worked closely with our leader, comrade Trần Khải Nguyên [a Hoa electrical worker], to develop the first communist cell in the factory.[131] This cell included many young Hoa cadres, less than twenty years old,

[127] There is a discrepancy between the two sources. The RVN source shows workers welcoming the opportunity to stay in these factory dormitories during week days and returning home for the weekends. But interviews with Hà Tăng, the communist labor organizer, tell a different story: workers were forced to stay inside the factory gate and only were allowed to visit home twice a month.

[128] Nguyễn Văn Thư, "Nghiệp Đoàn Tại Gia Định," pp. 36–37.

[129] Cao Văn Lượng, *Công Nhân Miền Nam*, p. 67.

[130] It is interesting that when these Hoa cadres were captured by the RVN security police, they feigned ignorance of the Vietnamese language and denied that they had had any previous contacts with the Vietnamese workers or attempted to mobilize them for the cause. Thus, using this tactic, even under capture, many of the Hoa cadres were able to protect vital intelligence concerning the underground communists' organizing activities. Bùi Văn Toản, *Đồng Bào Hoa Saigon*, p. 196.

[131] The fact that Lưu Quế worked closely with her direct leader, Trần Khải Nguyên—who died in jail in 1967—is consistent with Bùi Văn Toản's overall argument that, during the early stage of forming the first communist cell at Vimytex at the beginning of 1962, most cadres limited their operations and communications with only their direct leaders (Bùi Văn Toản, *Đồng Bào Hoa Saigon*, pp. 54, 72).

who had started their revolutionary career from this very factory. Working as regular workers on the ground, we secretly followed orders to propagandize in order to win support from particular workers for our cause. Most workers in Vimytex were Hoa women, but there were Vietnamese workers as well. We worked with them all. Most were educated [high school] and understood our revolutionary cause. So while the brutal war was raging on, our activism inside the factory was very vibrant. When our activities were exposed, fifty-nine of us were laid off. But our leaders immediately sent other Hoa cadres to replace us in this factory and continue our tasks.

At that point in 1963, since Lưu Quế had not yet been exposed as a communist organizer, she joined another factory employing primarily Hoa workers. This joint-stock factory, Đại Lăng Cô, was established by the French and then bought out by the American, Taiwanese, Hoa, and Vietnamese capitalists. At the time, it was producing rubber tires for bicycles, motorbikes, and cars. In this factory, Lưu Quế formed the first labor union. She joined the Saigon general strike in 1964. Sharing a cultural identity with other Hoa helped her organizing and mobilizing. She said:

> There were several hundred workers here. Most were Hoa, but there were also a few Vietnamese workers. This corporation was owned by a Taiwanese citizen. We had to take turns working all three shifts. Let me tell you, this was hard work: one needed strength to work in this factory. My task was a little bit lighter, working with a small machine. But the worst was that we were not allowed to form a trade union. So, I stepped up and formed a trade union for workers in this factory. When I first started in 1963, there were only several communist cadres. But then we encouraged more Hoa activists to join us here. In our union, we controlled 50 percent of the members [consisting of cadres and sympathizers] and the remaining 50 percent were all types of positions [consisting of staff, such as bus drivers]. When we joined the Saigon general strike in 1964, we were able to recruit the bus driver [a Hoa], who supported our strike and transported workers to the strike location instead of the factory. After participation in this general strike, seven Hoa organizers were killed [several came from this company] … I still remember their names and treasure this document. [She was choked with tears when she pointed out to me a document in the display glass case showing hand-written names in Chinese, dated April 1965, the date when these workers had sacrificed their lives to the cause.]

In 1965, when her anti-government activism was exposed for the second time, Lưu Quế left this rubber factory and went completely underground to join the armed revolutionary unit (*lực lượng vũ trang*) in 1966. Then her task was to visit factories, companies, and poor neighborhoods to mobilize the working poor at large—most were Hoa people—to join the struggle. She recounted how she reached out to all the Hoa communities:

> We had to read, summarize, and memorize the news reported in the bilingual daily newspaper entitled *Giải Phóng* [liberation] in order to explain to all classes of people [meaning rich, poor, and middle class] so that they would support our revolutionary cause. We did not bring [the paper] with us for fear of getting caught with this evidence. We had to speak all three Chinese dialects: Cantonese

(more than 60 percent of District 6 residents spoke this dialect), Mandarin (the middle- and upper-class and intellectuals spoke this dialect), and Teochew (many old Hoa spoke this dialect). We wanted to make sure that we could reach out to all classes of Hoa groups.

Ms. Lưu Quế, representative of the Hoa Executive Committee in Ho Chi Minh City, at the Hoa Revolutionary Heritage House, September 2008. (Author's photo)

In 1967, at age twenty-seven, Lưu Quế was sent to prison together with 341 other Hoa female cadres. They were sent to two prisons in Saigon, and then transferred to the infamous "tiger cage" prison on Côn Đảo Island (formerly known as Poulo Condore, built by the French), where the US-supported RVN government detained these revolutionaries.[132] She was not released until 1974, after the Paris Peace Agreement was signed in 1973. Lưu Quế cried when she reflected about her fellow

---

[132] Interview with Lưu Quế, August 2008; Bùi Văn Toản, *Đồng Bào Hoa Saigon*, p. 221.

Hoa organizers and the young Hoa college student activists she met while serving time in Côn Đảo prison:

> I was in and out of jails very often. But whenever I think about these young [Hoa] female cadres and students, I always cry. I love those young sisters very much; many were only sixteen to nineteen years old. I see them as the Hoa role models that we have to follow [their courage and sacrifice]. They were all very young: many were college students. [She then mentioned several names of these Hoa activists and cadres, and pointed me to the book that recorded their names.] … In jail, we had to accept being tortured but not reveal anything in order to protect our forces. Even with all the brutal torture, we still resumed our strength to practice [group] dancing and singing revolutionary songs … At that time, there were about sixty Hoa women in Côn Đảo prison. Of course, there were also other ethnicities in Vietnam, and the Kinh from the north, the central, and the south [regions of Vietnam].

The Hoa communist cadres embedded in Vimytex played a prominent role in politicizing the strike agendas, using sophisticated strategies and tactics. First, they sustained the efforts of the cadres who fled the factory after being exposed in order to ensure continuity of leadership. When Lưu Quế was laid off from Vimytex in 1962, Hà Tăng continued his activities inside Vimytex until he himself was expelled for his open labor organizing in 1964 (more than a thousand workers were laid off at this time).[133] Then Dư Huệ Liên arrived as one of the four Hoa cadres newly planted in the factory. She was voted in as the vice president of the factory labor union to organize workers. Effectively, from the inside, Dư Huệ Liên continued the work of the cadres who had left.[134] More than forty years later, Dư Huệ Liên recounted her activities in Vimytex:

> With unity, courage, and perseverance, more than two thousand workers there— most were Hoa workers—fought continuously under many banners, such as "against exploitation and suppression," "against harassing female workers," "against termination without cause." In order to combat a growing worker movement there, Vimytex management laid off their whole workforce, stopped production for a period of time, then gradually recruited brand-new workers to work there.[135]

These organizers were able to use their personal skills strategically to win support among the workers and politicize the agenda. The ability to speak multiple languages, such as Vietnamese and various Chinese dialects, proved useful in mobilizing people, both Kinh and Hoa, from all walks of life in the Saigon–Chợ Lớn area. Photos of strikes at Vimytex and Vinatexco show banners with messages

---

[133] Interview with Hà Tăng, September 2008.

[134] Bùi Văn Toản, *Đồng Bào Hoa Saigon*, p. 67.

[135] Minh Nam, "Chuyện bây giờ mới kể về những CN người Hoa" [Stories Just Now Recounted about the Hoa Workers], March 1, 2007, http://suckhoedinhduong.nld.com.vn/181644p0c1010/chuyen-bay-gio-moi-ke-ve-nhung-cn-nguoi-hoa.htm, accessed January 14, 2012.

printed in both languages, Vietnamese and Mandarin.[136] Also, having a technical skill gave cadres the flexibility to roam around the factory. After Lưu Quế had to flee due to her exposure, Hà Tăng was still able to stay behind to build and lead the labor movement. Often, male workers were channeled into skilled technical jobs that gave them invaluable flexibility to mobilize other workers. Employed as an electrician, Hà Tăng seized the opportunity to contact and mobilize workers in support of a concerted strike agenda:

> In Vimytex, as an electrician, I had the opportunity to roam freely around the factory to fix electrical problems and interact with about eighteen hundred workers. Trần Khai Nguyên [the direct leader of Lưu Quế] was also an electrician, who established the first communist cell in this factory. But he got caught and [was] tortured to death in Hoà Hòa military detention center.[137] We led the struggle in Vimytex from 1960 to 1975. [Note that Hà Tăng continued to lead this effort from the outside for more than ten years after he was laid off from Vimytex in 1964.] During the eight struggles at Vimytex [which culminated in the general strike in 1964], in general, we demanded people's welfare [*dân sinh*] and democracy [dân *chủ*]. In particular, our demands included wage increases, improvements in working conditions and meals, and democracy. The last demand was very important because during that time workers were kept inside the factory and [could] only visit home on the weekend twice a month. What's more, workers [could not] go in and out of the factory gate, which was guarded by the police. Surrounding this twenty-acre compound [in which the factory occupied only two acres] were five military posts.[138]

In addition, the organizers made strategic use of the law permitting freedom of association (a defining, recognized aspect of the independent union structure) for infiltrating the factory from the inside, a tactic that was especially important in dealing with the right-wing trade unions, such as Bửu's. Both Hà Tăng and Lưu Quế were elected as union leaders, which enabled them to use collective action to confront government officials even when they were closely watched by the government and the right-wing labor unions, such as Bửu's CVT. Hà Tăng shared with me:

> From when I joined Vimytex in 1960 until I had to flee in 1964, when they terminated [my employment], I was able to form Vimytex Trade Union [Phân Bộ Nghiệp Đoàn Vimytex] under [the auspices of] Bửu's CVT. It was not small: representing several thousands of workers. But later on, I was able to elevate it to Vimytex Workers Trade Federation [Nghiệp Đoàn Công Nhân Vimytex]. While

---

[136] Nghị Đoàn, *Truyền Thống Cách Mạng của Đồng Bào Hoa Ở Thành Phố Hồ Chí Minh Dưới Sự Lãnh Đạo Của Đảng Cộng Sản Việt Nam* [The Revolutionary Tradition of the Hoa in Ho Chi Minh City under the Leadership of the Vietnamese Communist Party] (Ho Chi Minh City: Ho Chi Minh Publisher, 1987), p. 66; Bùi Văn Toản, *Đồng Bào Hoa Saigon*, pp. 34, 68, 86. Also, some of these photos can be found at the Museum of Câu Lạc Bộ Kháng Chiến Người Hoa [the Hoa Revolutionaries Club] in District 5, Chợ Lớn, Ho Chi Minh City.

[137] Bùi Văn Toản, *Đồng Bào Hoa Saigon*, p. 54.

[138] When I asked why workers were confined to the factory area, Hà Tăng said that they wanted to: 1) control and suppress factory workers; and 2) monitor and protect the nearby rubber plantations from the Vietnamese communists' activities and infiltration.

still under Bửu's CVT, I took advantage of his confederation's influence to fight, while Bửu wanted to pressure the federations belonging to his confederation to make compromises and accept management's terms. That was the reason for the tense negotiation in early September 1964 leading up to the general strike in Saigon on September 21–22, 1964. Consequently, Bửu had to convene an urgent meeting with his general secretary, the Chinese-American and Hoa owners of Vimytex, and myself as the workers' representative (I was elected by the workers). This difficult negotiation lasted for the whole week in the headquarters of the Ministry of Labor. Moreover, strengthened by thousands of Vimytex workers who elected me as their union representative, I carried out the daring feat of meeting face-to-face with the Thủ Đức district chief [*quận trưởng*] to convince him to avoid using violence against striking workers. That was a big risk for me because the secret police [could have imprisoned] me right then and there. But they did not do it!

Hà Tăng's successful infiltration of the CVT, a major anti-communist labor union, is consistent with Beresford's critical assessment that the CVT leadership did not have full support of its membership.[139]

The death of or injuries to a fellow worker often sparked workers' collective action, in a response that, as we have seen, was also common during the colonial French period. In November 1963, a Hoa woman worker, Huỳnh Mỹ Tiên, returned to work three days late (no reason is given in the source). Management laid her off, admonished her, and humiliated her by not giving her the rice ration card to which she was entitled. Anguished, she returned to the worker dormitory and committed suicide. There is no doubt that workers were greatly distressed about her death, and organizers were prepared to channel some of this grief and rage into action. The active mobilizing effort of the four-member VCP cell in this factory—including Hà Tăng—triggered a struggle that lasted eighteen days and nights, as the protestors demanded compensation for Huỳnh Mỹ Tiên's family and other rights for workers. They succeeded in having five of their seven demands met.[140] Again, only a half year after Tiên's death, in June 1964, management announced the lay off of yet another female worker in the fiber department, claiming that she was unable to keep up with the daily work quota due to poor health. Management may have been testing the workers' will, or perhaps they simply intended to replace "problematic" workers with compliant and healthy workers for their operations. In response, the party cell organized workers to give management a list of demands, including the rehiring of the worker who had been threatened with dismissal, and the provision of better health care for workers, to sustain them. To press for these concessions, workers engaged in a slowdown and performed at only 50 percent of their productivity. They won one of their demands: management withdrew its lay-off decision and rehired the woman worker.[141]

---

[139] Beresford and Nyland, "Labour Movement of Vietnam," p. 66.

[140] The two demands that management refused to satisfy concerned a 30 percent wage increase and reduction in work speed-up (or lowering the daily work quota). Bùi Văn Toản, *Đồng Bào Hoa Saigon*, pp. 54–55, 59.

[141] Ibid., p. 60.

These strategies resulted in longer strikes and some victories for workers. Victories were much more difficult to achieve in the Vinatexco textile strike, however, which lasted from December 1963 to January 1964.[142]

Class Moments in 1964 Saigon

In the events leading to the general strike in Saigon in 1964, a "class moment" occurred when the Hoa workers not only supported each other but also allied with the Kinh workers. Archival materials show that Hoa workers in the Vinatexco textile factory (another factory employing mostly Hoa workers) hoisted their Chinese banner side-by-side with the Vietnamese banner to protest against the suppression of Vimytex workers.[143]

Communist organizers elevated the strike agendas from focusing on basic economic demands to focusing on political rights in order to mobilize not only factory workers but also the general public, including college students in Saigon. Hà Tăng recounted his experiences:

---

[142] The case of Vinatexco (December 1963 to January 1964) set the stage for the major strike in Vimytex. Chinese leaflets and local support played important roles. Wartime Saigon was rife with constant political unrests and military coups. The one-month strike in Vinatexco with 1,600 workers—most were local ethnic Chinese—received widespread local support. Workers faced police brutality and attacks from the forces mustered by the RVN state. On December 28, 1963, about sixteen hundred Vinatexco strikers occupied the whole factory and put forth a six-point resolution, which demanded wage increases, improvements in working conditions, and decent meals on the factory floor. They received broad-based support from local residents, students, peasants in Bà Quẹo province (near Saigon), and from the families of workers who lived nearby. The strong military force sent by the Nguyễn Khánh government in the South— one battalion (*tiểu đoàn*) with eighteen armored vehicles, thirty jeeps, five fire trucks, and three ambulances—stormed the front gate to scatter and subdue the strikers. Equally determined local supporters, especially students, blocked and prevented them from entering the factory. Then the military resorted to bayonets and tear gas, killed two workers, and injured several dozen others. One should note the political and global nature of this struggle. Throughout this ordeal, workers received strong and sustained public support from leftist organizations, including the revolutionary media from the North (Radio Liberation and Radio Hanoi) and international labor unions, including the French General Confederation of Labor. The strikers achieved victory on January 19, 1964, as the management agreed to some concessions: a 6–8 percent pay raise, and the reopening of the factory and rehiring of all strikers. See HCMC Labor Federation Executive Committee, *Công Nhân Saigon–Chợ Lớn Trong Sự Nghiệp Giải Phóng Dân Tộc,* pp. 319, 322–23. Labor unions from both sides of the spectrum had two goals, political and economic: to promote their own ideologies and fight for workers' rights. The left-leaning strikers were against the right-wing Bửu's Confederation—no doubt influenced by planted VCP cadres in the factory. In addition, these strikers were committed to press their economic demands for practical improvements, such as higher wages and better working conditions. Other workers who were inclined to be more conservative, and allied to Bửu's union, responded by calling attention to the underground role of Communist cadres in fomenting the strike. In this way, they revealed the intention of the RVN government and the right-wing labor unions to "unmask communists." Nguyễn Quang Quýnh, "Công Nhân, Nghiệp Đoàn Và Cộng Sản" [Workers, Trade Unions and Communism], *Nghiên Cứu Hành Chánh* [Journal of the Association for Administrative Studies], January and February 1965: 44– 82. Moreover, according to Quýnh, this was a wildcat strike because workers went on strike before completing the conflict resolution and remediation process. Thus, this strike violated Stipulation Number 378 of the RVN Labor Code (pp. 52–56, 64).

[143] Ibid., p. 54; Bùi Văn Toản, *Đồng Bào Hoa Saigon,* p. 68.

In 1964, we elevated the strike demands to include political demands such as democracy for the people, and protesting against the involuntary national draft, which affected poor people mostly, and against the confiscation of property of local residents, including those of the Hoa residents, to finance the war. So, with this broader agenda, we occupied the headquarters of the CVT, using it as our cannon firing command [*pháo đài*], calling for support not just of Vimytex workers, but also the media, which reported on the participation of the working poor in Saigon and peasants from surrounding provinces. Vimytex workers also supported the movement of the Saigon College Student Union/Association [Tổng Hội Sinh Viên Saigon].

Vimytex workers staged a rally in front of the CVT headquarters, an event that helped lead up to the two-day general strike in September 1964.[144] The workers appealed to the RVN-government-supported media to broadcast their messages; this plea attracted overwhelming local support. They also received cooperation from strategic industries—such as transportation (buses, taxis, trucks, and trains), utilities (electricity, water, gas), consumer products (shoes, rubber, plastics, cigarettes), and port and hotel workers—which engaged in sympathetic strikes and paralyzed Saigon for two days. Moreover, workers received broad-based support from their own families (most were local), Buddhists, Catholics, university students, and transportation workers through donations and the delivering of food and drinks.[145] Also, residents in predominantly Hoa communities, such as in Chợ Lớn and District 11, sent food and drinks to workers, both Hoa and Kinh, who struggled in this factory in Thủ Đức.[146]

These intensified efforts culminated in a massive general strike on September 21 and 22, 1964, in which thirty thousand participants completely paralyzed the Saigon–Chợ Lớn area, which was without water, electricity, or buses due to the shut-down.[147] But Bửu also took advantage of this victory, claiming that this forty-eight-hour general strike led to a May Day parade in 1966, for which he took credit.[148]

From this strike, workers won the following concessions from management: the right to free association (but activities had to be on union premises); reinstatement of registration for some unions that had participated in the protest; unconditional rehiring of Vimytex strikers with twelve-day advance notice; disciplining of a local state official (vice mayor of Gia Định) who had suppressed workers; and an agreement that management would not harass strike participants.[149] In particular, management acquiesced to these specific requests and agreed that they would: (1) hold the boss responsible for Huỳnh Mỹ Tiên's death and properly compensate her family; (2) pay a monthly salary (for twenty-six workdays/month) instead of offering daily pay; (3) allow workers one day off per week and the freedom to return home weekly, rather than requiring them to stay in the worker dormitories for two

---

[144] This is the same location that has housed the current Vietnamese General Confederation of Labor since 1975.

[145] Los, "Labor Movement in South Vietnam"; Tiến Khải, *Công Nhân Saigon–Chợ Lớn*, pp. 329–30.

[146] Bùi Văn Toản, *Đồng Bào Hoa Saigon*, p. 58.

[147] Tiến Khải, *Công Nhân Saigon–Chợ Lớn*, p. 331.

[148] Trần Quốc Bửu, *Vietnamese Confederation of Labor*, p. 12.

[149] Tiến Khải, *Công Nhân Saigon–Chợ Lớn*, p. 331.

weeks and only visit home on their free weekends;[150] (4) pay double wages for work carried out at night and triple for work done on Sundays; (5) impose no fine nor take revenge on workers [Note: this implied that the company could not retaliate against workers who participated in strikes]; (6) improve factory meals; and (7) compensate workers for the time they were on strike.[151]

Types of Protest and Use of Law

Workers were anguished about the tragedies that had befallen their fellow Hoa workers, notably by Tiên's death and the dismissal of other employees from their jobs. During these crisis moments, both Hoa and Kinh workers identified themselves as being in the same class and joined by a common cause, that is, their commitment to win compensation for their fellow workers and insure their rights and benefits. This agenda combines commitments to both Polanyi's human rights and Marx's labor rights.

The embedded Hoa cadres took advantage of the independent labor union structure and rule of law to the extent permitted by the RVN regime to organize workers and carry out their political agenda.[152] For instance, Hà Tăng acted as one of the elected worker representatives while simultaneously working underground as an embedded cadre. He and four other worker representatives (of whom two were embedded Communist Party cadres) participated in a four-way negotiation, on September 10, 1964, with representatives from the Saigon Department of Labor, the CVT, and the Chinese-American owner of the textile factory. In this meeting, the employees' representatives gained support from other Hoa workers in textile and other factories owned by the Hoa, such as Vinatexco, Intertexco, Đông Á, Chấn Á, and Visyfasa.[153] Declassified CIA materials showed that the CIA knew of "Communist-inspired labor strife in the plant," which suggests they suspected the role of those embedded cadres. But management had to abide by the legal framework and could not lay off these leaders without apparent reason.[154]

Workers also appealed to state institutions and the rule of law. They requested that the labor department in Gia Định (the Vimytex factory was located in this legal jurisdiction) demand that management resume production and rehire laid-off strikers. They appealed to the Gò Vấp labor court and sent complaints about labor violations to the local newspapers. Prepared for a protracted struggle, they divided into small groups, took turns protesting, and delivered petition letters to all involved—the management, the Ministry of Labor, the CVT, and the media—to expose their hardships, management oppression, and police brutality.[155] Moreover, in Hà Tăng's official meetings with his opponents (Bửu and the Thủ Đức district chief), he was able to use the labor union's legal framework to negotiate with them

---

[150] According to some accounts, these workers were locked inside the factory and surrounded by gates guarded by security police. Bùi Văn Toản, *Đồng Bào Hoa Saigon*, pp. 54–55, 58.

[151] Ibid. Interview with Hà Tăng, September 2008.

[152] Ironically, the benefits of trade union freedom and the right to hold union meetings, for which Bửu had fought, facilitated activities directed against him. Trần Quốc Bửu, *Vietnamese Confederation of Labor*, p. 12.

[153] Bùi Văn Toản, *Đồng Bào Hoa Saigon*, p. 56; Interview with Hà Tăng, September 2008.

[154] CIA, *Situation in South Vietnam*, pp. 1–3; and Bùi Văn Toản, *Đồng Bào Hoa Saigon*, p. 61.

[155] Tiến Khải, *Công Nhân Saigon—Chợ Lớn*, pp. 324–25.

from a position of strength to empower the strikers he represented. In short, both labor organizers and workers used the law and appealed to the media in Saigon to gain support and coverage.[156]

The next case study shows that while the party cadres mobilized inside the factory, progressive Catholic priests and lay labor activists were active *outside* the factory.

Pin Con Ó Battery (Vidopin) Factory Strikes (1971)

The Eagle Battery factory (Hãng Pin con Ó), or Vidopin (as its acronym), is situated in the predominantly Hoa Chợ Lớn area. Its workers' protests in 1971 highlight the significance of gender in labor activism and, to some extent, ethnicity, as well as the role of religion in labor organizing and protests. Using workers' diaries, I was able to trace their lived experiences through various stages of collective consciousness. First relying on their cultural identities, then through the ebbs and flows of this struggle, they discovered class consciousness while in jail fighting for their rights and dignity. I will show how the left-wing Catholic priests in the TLC movement appealed to the RVN rule of law to protect workers and promote social justice.

The Eagle Battery factory, established in 1951, employed 650 workers; most were local Hoa women, residents in the Saigon-Chợ Lớn area, and most were Buddhists (both Kinh and Hoa and of both genders).[157] The Hoa played different roles in this factory—as workers, owner, managers, labor union leaders, and protesters. Workers went on strike twice in 1971, and received an outpouring support from their families, friends, and sympathizers from all walks of life.

Their union representation was complex. In 1970, workers joined two competing trade unions belonging to two opposing confederations.[158] The union that led the strike was the Trade Union of Workers in the Far East Battery Company (Nghiệp Đoàn Công Nhân Công ty Pin Viễn Đông), led by two Hoa women: Tô Sang (president) and Trương Bá Huê (general secretary); the union belonged to Phan Văn Chí's left-leaning Confederation of Labor. This trade union represented 65 percent of the factory total workforce (422 out of about 650 workers). The competing union was the Trade Union of Workers of the Vietnamese Battery Company (Nghiệp Đoàn Công Nhân Hãng Pin Việt Nam), led by Tô Thanh Tuyền and belonging to Bửu's CVT. While this union represented a much smaller number of workers, the close connection between Tô Thanh Tuyền and Lê Văn Y (the factory administrative director)—both were union leaders of the then-defunct Bus Workers Trade Union, also under the CVT—led to Tuyền taking sides with the management against the striking union.[159]

[156] Ibid., pp. 322–23.

[157] In this period, most able-bodied men were drafted to serve in the RVN army. Nguyễn Quang Quýnh, *Quyển 1: Những Vấn Đề Lao Động* [Book No. 1: Labor Issues] (Saigon: Lửa Thiêng, 1974), p. 118.

[158] Ibid., pp. 118–19.

[159] Lê Văn Đồng, *Sơ Lược Về Hiện Tình Các Vấn Đề Lao Động ở Việt Nam* [Preliminaries on Current Situations of Labor Issues in Vietnam] (Saigon: Labor Ministry, 1956), p. 61; Nguyễn Quang Quýnh, *Vấn Đề Lao Động*, p. 131.

The close relationships among the governments of RVN and the United States, and the Hoa managers and its investors, demonstrate deep-rooted connections between the government and the capitalists. With US approval, this Eagle Battery factory was the sole supplier of flashlight batteries for the general public in South Vietnam (for more than twenty years) and for the South Vietnamese army (in 1970 and 1971). Both the owner and manager were Hoa: Quách Nhạn—the general president—was a Hoa tycoon (born in China in 1916 and living in Vietnam); Vương Khải Hồng was the plant manager. Quách Nhạn owned other companies in Hoa-controlled economic/commercial areas, such as factories that produced garment accessories (zippers), processed foods (such as dried noodles), carton boxes, tins, and plastics. The Kinh management team included Lê Văn Y (the administration director) and Lê Kim Ngọc Tuyết (the operation manager), who was the wife of Vương Khải Hồng.[160] But it was the personal connection with President Nguyễn Văn Thiệu's wife—who owned 60 percent of the company shares—that explained why the government used all of its repressive apparatuses to suppress this strike. The economic profit and monopoly power for the Hoa owner was great: Being the only approved supplier of batteries for the RVN military, he received the government bid, which resulted in ten times the normal profit margin.[161]

The two waves of protest that shook this battery factory—in March 1971 and in October 1971—need to be contextualized relative to the larger labor movement in Saigon (and its vicinities), where strikes were staged by both Hoa and Kinh workers in textile, garment, and battery factories.[162] In both waves, there is clear evidence for bonding among participants based on gender, which became a basis for Kinh and Hoa workers to take collective action on the street and in the prison. While the sense of cross-ethnic solidarity was clear from the Kinh workers' perspectives, expressed in their diaries, I cannot ascertain the Hoa workers' reactions and opinions since I did not have a chance to interview them nor did I have access to their firsthand accounts. However, from the labor organizers' perspective, the sense of cross-ethnic solidarity was clear, given the accounts of the mixed Hoa and Kinh labor union team at this factory.

From March 8 to March 31, 1971, the Hoa and Kinh union representatives—Trương Bá Huệ and Tô Sang (both were Hoa) and Trần Lượng (Kinh)—led a twenty-three-day strike.[163] The union leaders and the Hoa workers used their shared Chinese dialect (Cantonese) to communicate and negotiate with the Hoa management, as described in the October 18, 1971, prison diary quotation at the beginning of this

---

[160] Nguyễn Quang Quýnh, *Vấn Đề Lao Động*, p. 118.

[161] Hồ Ngọc Nhuận, "Tại Sao Chính Quyền Can Thiệp?" [Why the Government Intervened?], *Chọn* (Lê Văn Duyệt, Saigon, 1971), p. 51.

[162] Đồng bào người Hoa ở Sài Gòn đấu tranh chống Mỹ–Ngụy [The Hoa in Saigon Fought against the Americans and the South Vietnamese Army], in *Chung Một Bóng Cờ Và Lịch Sử Sài Gòn—Chợ Lớn Kháng Chiến 1945–1975* (corporate authors) (Hà Nội: Chính trị Quốc gia Press, 1995), www.hochiminhcity.gov.vn/left/gioi_thieu/lich_su_van_hoa/lich_su/tp_chung_nhan_cua_dong_chay_ls/khang_chien_chong_my/nguoihoa.htm?left_menu=1, accessed July 2008.

[163] Based on sources from the socialist government, back in the early 1950s some Hoa communist cadres already had been planted in this factory and in other small-scale occupational unions, as was true at Vimytex. Momentum from their victory then spread to other factories that made consumer and food products. The first Eagle Battery factory strike in 1955 demanded basic labor rights such as an eight-hour day, female workers' rights, no employment of child labor, no wage deductions for illness absences, health coverage for on-the-job accidents, and no layoffs. Bùi Văn Toản, *Đồng Bào Hoa Saigon*, pp. 32–33.

chapter.[164] As a result of the strike, workers won the thirteenth-month bonus for the Vietnamese Lunar New Year and overtime compensation. But, in retaliation, management prosecuted union and strike leaders, who received four- to six-month sentences for locking management inside the factory.[165] In August 1971, workers initiated a formal legal complaint (*đơn khởi tố*), filed with the Saigon Labor Department. They had four demands: (1) a 30 percent wage increase for all workers; (2) equal wages for women and men workers; (3) maintenance of the tradition of providing semi-yearly scholarships for workers' children; and (4) provision of safety masks for workers in the "black powder room" (*phòng bột đen*) to mitigate their inhalation of toxic gases, and monthly special allowances for preventative care.[166]

While the role of Hoa activists was prominent during the first wave of protests, the progressive Catholic priests and lay activists were key to the second wave, which lasted longer: a thirty-four-day strike from October to November 1971. At this point, with those three union leaders being laid off in October 1971 (altogether, seventeen union members were laid off), workers had to prove that they could sustain the struggle by themselves, only with assistance from the progressive Catholic priests and youth activists.[167]

On November 11, 1971, the police force finally stopped this strike and imprisoned fourteen female workers and seven organizers: three Catholic Youth members from the TLC, three priests—including Trương Bá Cần and Phan Khắc Từ—and one labor union cadre from the central office of the left-wing labor confederation.[168] The court ruling announced in December 1971 showed that the protestors had secured at least a partial victory, in principle, for workers. The court acknowledged that this was a collective struggle between workers and management at Vidopin and recommended the following: (1) Vidopin should raise workers' income by 30 percent of their basic wages instead of by 30 percent of the cost-of-living increase; (2) Vidopin management should rehire laid-off workers; and (3) Vidopin should reject all other worker demands. Several attempts by the Labor Investigation Office in December 1971 to pressure Vidopin management into implementing the court ruling failed. Vidopin management refused to rehire the workers who had been dismissed. At this point, only forty workers persisted with picketing in front of the Saigon Labor Department (most other workers had returned to work, since they could not survive without income). The only concession that the Saigon Labor Department was able to gain from Vidopin management was payment equivalent to unemployment benefits to the laid-off workers (depending on their

---

[164] "Nhật Ký Tập Thể Của Công Nhân," pp. 25–26.

[165] Vũ Xuân Hiểu, "Tường Thuật Vụ Tranh Chấp Giữa Công Nhân và Chủ Nhân Hãng Pin Con Ó" [Report of the Conflict between Workers and the Owner of the Eagle Battery Factory], *Chọn Special Issue*: *Một Bài Học Cho Công Nhân Và Nghiệp Đoàn: Vụ Pin Con Ó* [A Lesson for Workers and Trade Unions: The Case of the Eagle Battery Factory] (Saigon: Lê Văn Duyệt, 1971), pp. 20–21.

[166] Ibid., p. 12; and Nguyễn Quang Quýnh, *Vấn Đề Lao Động*, pp. 119–20.

[167] Nguyễn Quang Quýnh, *Vấn Đề Lao Động*, pp. 121, 123.

[168] Vũ Xuân Hiểu, "Tường Thuật Vụ Tranh Chấp," p. 20. Another source, writing from the perspective of the RVN government, stated that only thirteen women workers were imprisoned, and the three Catholic Youth members were university students. Nguyễn Quang Quýnh, *Vấn Đề Lao Động*, p. 126.

years of service), plus a fifteen-day bonus for Tết.[169] These former strikers were not rehired, however.

The most devastating setback for workers was that management successfully fired those core workers who had led the struggle. Those workers filed a class action suit against management for wrongful layoffs, but the Saigon Labor Court dismissed the suit on the grounds that the Court could hear only individual labor conflict cases, not a collective labor–management conflict case such as this one.[170]

The failure of the Eagle Battery protest was not so much that the two unions sabotaged each other,[171] but, perhaps, that the self-interest of the smaller union, led by Tô Thanh Tuyền (who belonged to Bửu's CVT), motivated its leaders to try to increase their organization's strength at the expense of workers due to the failure of the larger union, led by Phan Văn Chí.[172] As discussed earlier, the ideology-based–internal-leadership conflict in Phan Văn Chí's confederation had robbed him of the legitimacy necessary to carry out effective bargaining throughout this struggle.

Unfortunately, workers were defeated in the end. But how did they persist in their struggle for so long? Cultural identity was a key factor in strengthening their collective resolve.

Gender Identity and Police Brutality

Narratives of the fourteen women workers who were jailed for alleged illegal labor organizing and protests showcase how they found strength in and supported each other as fellow female workers. One can sense the solidarity between the Kinh and the Hoa female workers, and their shared appreciation for each other, as portrayed in the diary entry at the beginning of this chapter. Workers demanded improvements in basic working conditions: wage increases to keep up with inflation; equal pay for female workers doing the same jobs as men; and protection against toxic materials used in making batteries, which could cause tuberculosis and gynecological problems.[173] Their prison diaries lay bare their anger toward management–government entrenched interests and the brutality of the police forces mustered to oppose their collective action. To respect the full spirit of these activists' words, I have translated verbatim, in the quote below, the derogatory terms used in this one diary entry to characterize management, the police, and government officials and their families.

These women workers literally relied on other women workers standing next to them in the line of fire. The worker who penned the October 18, 1971, diary entry cited at the opening of this chapter continued with the following passage, which expresses her deep resentment of the brutal police forces:

---

[169] The fifteen-day payment resulted from negotiations between the Saigon Labor Department and Vidopin management, and was instituted in place of the common thirteen-month (thirty-day) *Tết* bonus awarded to hardworking employees. Nguyễn Quang Quýnh, *Vấn Đề Lao Động*, p. 129.

[170] Ibid., pp. 128–29.

[171] Tiến Khải, *Công Nhân Saigon–Chợ Lớn*, pp. 275–76.

[172] Nguyễn Quang Quýnh, *Vấn Đề Lao Động*, pp. 132–33.

[173] Vũ Xuân Hiểu, "Tường Thuật Vụ Tranh Chấp," p. 11.

We have to consider several policemen, especially the mean Captain Trần Công Hoàn. This guy beat us up like dogs. Strange. At first, we did not know the effects of tear gas so we just stood firm when they threw it at us. Only when crying as if our grandmothers had just died, did we get to know its effect. At that point, several people yelled out: "Bad guys, *hung thần*, are coming, run, run sisters!" Then I felt so hot, soaked with sweat, and became dizzy; I grabbed hold of a woman next to me and fell down on the street, unconscious.[174]

These women participated intimately in each other's lives—in jail, at work, and at home. Outside of work, they spent time with each other at social gatherings: visiting each other's houses, joking with each other, and singing together to lift their spirits during hard times. This social networking based on gender gave workers vital support against the pressures that many female labor activists faced: challenges from their own parents, who wanted them to live more conventional lives, get married, have children, and not engage in labor activism. One striker was supported by her fellow women strikers when she complained about being "slapped" by her mother for having participated in the strike.[175]

These activists received broad-based support from other labor unions, the press, and the local communities, including the Buddhist nuns (*ni sư*), who came to give them food and spiritual comfort:

Many fellow labor unions had come to help us, two to three times. The press also helped. In addition, many people had come to bring rice, fish sauce, and other food items for those of us who were temporarily staying at the TLC center. Many nuns, whose names we did not know, came all the way from Thủ Đức to visit us. *We sisters* are so very moved by their kindness. Gradually, we sisters became less pessimistic. Perhaps most people are on our side, except for those mentioned above [management], the police, and the government, of course.[176]

The "we sisters" language is significant in their narrative. But how did this process foment a form of consciousness? The strikers' own words describe that arduous personal journey.

Ebbs and Flows of Class Consciousness

The case of Eagle Battery factory demonstrates the significance of the various stages in the process of fomenting a class consciousness. As the accused strikers spent time in jail together, their awareness of gender and class became heightened: the "we women workers" language—which was not evident in the October entries—

---

[174] "Nhật Ký Tập Thể Của Công Nhân," entry on October 18, 1971, p. 26.

[175] Ibid., p. 36. It is important to understand the context of this "slapping." Judging from the report, this punishment should be interpreted not as physical abuse, but as the desperate action of a single poor mother to protect her family. This striker admitted that she knew her mother loved her and her younger brother, the only two people left in her mother's life. But while she understood the reason why her mother tried to prevent her from joining various protests with her fellow women workers, she compared her case with those of her three fellow strikers whose mothers had not only permitted, but also supported, her friends time and time again when they ventured out to take part in the strike.

[176] Ibid., p. 33. My emphasis.

became prominent in the December entries. These women workers were conscious that capitalists and their allies were attempting to manipulate, divide, and conquer them. They identified with each other as fellow female workers and cared for the well-being and dignity of each other. Broad-based religious support from the Buddhists and the Catholics also empowered them in their struggle.

The women suffered from brutal police practices, not only physical but also psychological, that tried to demean them, weaken their commitment, and ridicule their cause. The war-time context colored these struggles, and the police, most of whom in the South were anti-communist, penalized workers for participating in this struggle:

> On October 19, 1971. I can never forget the flirtatious and drunken voice of the police chief, Trần Công Hoàn, who was beating me up, threatening and maligning me at the same time: "Why don't you just accept whatever management paid you? Why do you even dare to protest?" Then he slapped me violently on the face, "For your livelihood? (slap) Are you a communist (slap)?" My anger rose up, I could hardly breathe. Normally I can cry easily, but today, my tears disappeared and were replaced by visceral anger and a sense of hopelessness. After beating me to a pulp, he used a piece of wood to beat up Mr. Trần L., who was the age of his father or uncle, to get his statement. I had to turn away because I no longer had the courage to witness such inhumane brutality. At which point, tears were streaming down my face unexpectedly. After beating us both to a pulp, he threatened: "You all have to stop fomenting strikes illegally."[177]

The individuals who participated in these struggles together and faced this sort of treatment tended to evolve, becoming more class conscious over time, as their diaries make clear:

> On December 30, 1971. But the most unscrupulous thing that the Department of Labor [Sở Lao Động] did was to create doubt and division *among us workers*. They dared to say that some of our sisters, in private meetings with the boss, had begged for money. We had been on strike for several months now; our families needed money; we needed money; those statements were true. But since we have already sacrificed for several months, there is no reason for us now to kowtow to such a mean and manipulating boss as Mr. Lê Văn Y. But the most painful thing that angered us is that they dared to allege that Ms. H.—who is the most loyal and committed union member from beginning to end—kowtowed to the boss that way. Suspicious eyes were directed at Ms. H., which humiliated her and made her cry, and because of that, the Department of Labor and the boss had succeeded to some extent. But over time the misunderstanding was resolved; our love for each other during several months of fighting side-by-side had gotten rid of all doubts and suspicion. *Capital is still capital; the state is still the state. The state and capital are one. But we women workers have found our love for each other stronger than ever.* That night we stayed in jail together. Many police cars were sent there for reinforcement. Many local people came by to bring us flowers. The jail

[177] Ibid., pp. 26–27.

guards locked the door, but several Buddhist nuns [*ni sư*] stayed to spend the night with us sisters. We are so moved by that gesture.[178]

It took time to build class consciousness. In the workers' own words, they arrived at the decision to take collective action by themselves, *without* the labor unions' leadership or embedded VCP cadres' guidance (they were already in jail by this stage). It is clear from these reports that the women perceived each other as sisters at the beginning of their imprisonment, even when they recognized their fellow inmates' different ethnicities, Kinh and Hoa.[179] But toward the end of this struggle, over a month later, a sense of class consciousness ("among us workers") arose that was deeply intertwined with gender ("we women workers"). This demonstrates that, as the women workers went through a challenging and protracted struggle, they arrived at a sense of class consciousness—it is unclear how long it lasted—that led them, in moments of crisis, to be in solidarity with their fellow women workers. This evolution in attitude is consistent with Thompson's argument that workers become conscious of their class identity at the end—not the beginning—of their struggle against some forms of exploitation. In this case, over time, workers developed a sense of class outside the realm of VCP influence in moments of crisis, engendered by the bonding of sisterhood and, to some extent, ethnicity.

One of the progressive priests praised the workers' consciousness of their conditions and how they were proactive in setting out to improve them. Nguyễn Nghị even compared them with the underground communist cadres and found them to be relatively more advanced in their responses to injustice:

> Workers, conscious of real-life conditions, were even more progressive and advanced than the committee of communist cadres who were in charge of mobilizing intellectuals [Ban Trí Vận],[180] who only learned theories but lacked lived experiences in social realities [*lý thuyết, chưa sống qua thực trạng xã hội*].[181]

Young Catholic Workers' Activism and the Law

The embedded cadres, the progressive priests, and the TLC activists made use of the law to organize workers. Workers started with a formal legal complaint filed with the Saigon Labor Department in August 1971 and appealed to the legal institutions of the RVN regime, such as the Saigon Labor Court and the Labor Investigation Office. Even when their efforts went nowhere, given the tepid responses of these institutions and their failure to implement the court ruling, these activists proved that they understood the potential power of the rule of law.

The TLC activists defended workers' rights by confronting the repressive state apparatuses, such as the Ministry of Labor, Ministry of Communication, Ministry of

---

[178] Ibid., p. 38. My emphasis. These strikers not only spent time in jail. Many had also sold their personal belongings, such as rings and earrings, when the strike fund ran out in order to continue funding their protracted struggle. Ibid., p. 32.

[179] Ibid., pp. 25–26.

[180] They were commonly known as well-trained underground communist cadres in the South.

[181] Interview with Nguyễn Nghị, September 2008.

Justice, and the police (civil and military), as well as the state ideological organs/institutions, such as TV, radio, and newspapers. For instance, on November 8, 1971, two priests, including Trương Bá Cần, cited the right to strike to the local police in order to protect strikers: "The police can only intervene when there is violence."[182] On November 13, 1971, some TLC activists provided protest banners to workers who were new to these public acts of resistance and inexperienced; they nervously staged the protest in front of the Saigon parliament. These activists confronted the police by citing the laws that allowed workers to strike. One TLC representative protested when the organization's banner was confiscated by the police: "This is the house of people's representatives. We have the right to be here and to voice our aspirations." And they appealed to the vice president of the Senate, who came out of the parliament house to investigate the commotion and introduced himself to the strikers. A male TLC representative addressed him:

> First, we'd like to inform you and to protest the thieving behavior of the police here. We only had a banner presenting our requests, but they snatched it away from us. Please, Mr. Senator, we brothers only want to present to you the truth about the Eagle Battery case.[183]

Cutting them off in the middle of a sentence, the senator refused to listen to their cause, and commanded them to go home and write and submit a petition letter. Then a female TLC representative spoke up:

> Please listen to us, Senator, at least please just listen to us to understand the suffering of the people, of the workers. Up until now, the Senator has been listening to the government, the management, but never before have you listened to us, workers.[184]

Convinced by this group effort, the senator granted them a ten-minute hearing to present their case inside the parliament building. But after just a few minutes of their presentation, the senator got up and left without referring them to another senator who might listen to their concerns. This evidence confirmed the TLC representatives' complaint: the failure of government officials to listen to workers' concerns and aspirations.

Another form of protest involved publically exposing a close alliance between the government and the capitalists and their complicity in the infliction of suffering and injustice on workers. Hồ Ngọc Nhuận, a progressive House representative in Saigon, wrote an article in *Chọn*'s special issue on the Eagle Battery case, in which he asked a rhetorical question to introduce his argument: "Why [did] the government assist the owner in breaking the workers' strike, by mobilizing the huge state apparatus from the Ministry of Information, to the police department, to the Ministry of Justice?"[185] He pointed to the entrenched interests of the government and capitalists, and spoke of the symbiosis linking the factory's management team (a Hoa

---

[182] Vũ Xuân Hiểu, "Tường Thuật Vụ Tranh Chấp," p. 19.

[183] Ibid., p. 20; "Nhật Ký Tập Thể Của Công Nhân," p. 31.

[184] Ibid., pp. 31–32.

[185] Hồ Ngọc Nhuận, "Tại Sao Chính Quyền Can Thiệp?" [Why the Government Intervened?], *Chọn Special Issue*, 1971, p. 40.

husband, a Kinh wife) with President Thiệu's wife: "They were close friends of the First Lady ... they donated a large sum of money to the public hospital Vì Dân [For the People]. So, taking advantage of such high-powered support from the government, the bosses became obstinate, looked down on workers, and cared less about public opinion."[186]

The TLC activists relied on their liberation theology to facilitate this legal process and elevate the sophistication of their forms of protests: the use of petition and rule of law. But again, one has to analyze this whole struggle remembering that it took place in a wartime context, which would have intensified the passionate desire for peace and social justice that sparked labor activism. Phan Khắc Từ—the progressive priest who lived among the garbage workers—reflected this sentiment succinctly in his newsletter, *Labor Newsletter: The Committee for the Protection of Workers' Rights*. In the February 1975 issue (published two months before the fall of Saigon), he included this short poem, entitled "Diagnosing the Illness," written by a Buddhist nun, Huỳnh Liên, who was hospitalized in Saigon with other nuns. The poem evinces an alliance between the two religions regarding aspirations for peace and social justice.

> This illness is quite common in people,
> And it can only be cured by Peace.
> In protests, we ran long distances
> Fainted, but when back on our feet, we move forward.[187]

CONCLUSION

Gender and religion play important roles in people's development of class consciousness during protests. In the particular historical context of wartime South Vietnam, religion—the religious identity of the workers and the commitment of left-wing priests and lay Catholic activists—significantly influenced labor activists and striking workers. Overall, the narratives of the labor activists who were interviewed, who organized workers in many factories in the South, suggest that gender, ethnic, and religious factors were interconnected as forces that served to unite and educate activists and workers.

The process of bonding based on ethnicity is complex and needs further research. Evidence shows a deep bonding between the Hoa labor organizers and the Hoa workers, judging from the interviews related to two cases. While the class and ethnicity consciousness of the two Hoa labor organizers whom I interviewed were crystal clear, the same is not as clear for the Hoa workers. For that, we need another study to examine whether such workers felt themselves united based on their Hoa identity.

Workers came together in dire circumstances, and transcended their ethnic differences: in prison, on the street, and in front of the factory gate. When it came to

---

[186] Ibid., p. 51.

[187] Huỳnh Liên and other Buddhist nuns handed two poems to Phan Khắc Từ when he and members of the Committee for the Protection of Workers' Rights visited them in the hospital. While there was no explanation for why the nuns were hospitalized, the second poem suggests that they were injured while protesting against the war. Phan Khắc Từ, "Trang Thơ Tranh Đấu" [Resistance Poetry Page], *Bản Tin Lao Động: Ủy Ban Bảo Vệ Quyền Lợi Lao Động* [Labor Newsletter: The Committee for the Protection of Workers' Rights], February 1975, p. 24.

the harassment of female factory employees, Kinh and Hoa female workers became more resolute when they faced police brutality (as evidenced by the collective workers' diaries in the Vidopin case), or marched side by side to protest "against harassment of female workers" (the Vimytex case). These acts of solidarity raised the consciousness of the general public concerning the general plight of female factory employees.

The process leading to class consciousness was arduous: it was full of ebbs and flows. An awareness of class came relatively later as the workers established a sense of solidarity. Early in their activism, Kinh and Hoa workers identified with each other as sisters (while acknowledging their different ethnicities). But as these protestors grew closer while struggling together for the same goals, they realized their class identity as workers. As seen in the Eagle Battery case, the process of arriving at class consciousness was not at all linear. In stages corresponding to their increasing engagement with public protests, these workers moved from a culture-based "comfort zone" (both inside and outside of the factories) to relating to each other as sisters in the line of fire. But they had their moments of self-doubt, and experienced anguish and frustration when they were under siege during the struggle. As those women workers struggled or stayed in jail together over a period of time, their narratives began to reveal a "we women workers" spirit, culminating in a sense of class consciousness. Again, the jelling of this class consciousness occurred at the latter stages of their struggle.

Judging from available evidence, we can conclude that the social justice consciousness of progressive priests and lay people supported both Catholic and non-Catholic workers of different ethnicities.[188] These Catholic activists had worked out a rationale to reconcile their social justice vision with Marxist ideology, and they coexisted with many underground Communist cadres, in a similar manner to the three labor organizers whom I interviewed.[189] In short, when one combined different types of consciousness (class and social justice) with an existing cultural bond, a sense of resoluteness emerged, as seen in the workers' prison diaries and interviews with the Hoa and Kinh labor leaders/organizers.

---

[188] However, in reviewing labor experiences in the United States, I am conscious of how ethnicity and religious practices can divide, rather than unite, workers. While there are many external factors that affect the success or failure of efforts to organize diverse groups of workers, the cases of early twentieth-century strikes called in support of common causes, such as the eight-hour day and higher wages, in Paterson, NJ, Lawrence, MA, and Passaic, NJ, show how different immigrant ethnic groups and their respective religious orientations could hinder labor mobilization and union activities. For instance, the church-based loyalties of Polish and Slovak workers were in conflict with the more leftist orientation of Hungarian workers. In addition, the Irish and French Canadian Roman Catholic workers refused to join the strikes, while Franco-Belgian, Lithuanian, German, and Italian workers, as well as Jewish workers from many countries, were more receptive to radical leadership. Many of these left-wing supporters had organized their community life outside of their church or synagogue. David J. Goldberg, *A Tale Of Three Cities: Labor Organization and Protest in Paterson, Passaic, and Lawrence, 1916–1921* (New Brunswick, NJ: Rutgers University Press, 1989), pp. 206–7.

[189] Disillusioned after 1975, many of these progressive priests and lay people have retreated to advocate for social and humanitarian causes, and they no longer practice the type of social-justice activism they had before 1975.

War, Capitalism, and the Law

One must not forget that a war was being waged throughout Vietnam during this period. The twin goals of peace and economic justice, rendered even more desirable by the workers' experiences with and suffering from the war, spurred on labor activism. That activism began spontaneously and independently, facilitated in part by cultural bonds, and then grew to become a more organized effort with the assistance of on-the-ground progressive Catholic activists and underground VCP cadres, fighting for human rights and labor rights. I found an intermingling of Polanyi- and Marx-type collective actions carried out by both Hoa and Kinh workers in pursuit of their shared interests.

In many cases, the deaths or injuries of their fellow workers affected them emotionally and awakened their consciousness and anger, compelling them to fight resolutely for the well-being of their fellow workers and the preservation of their lives. In different situations, these workers reached the point of no return after having witnessed the death of a young Catholic worker, the suicide of a young Hoa worker, the lay-offs of many Hoa strikers, the beatings of workers and union leaders in jail, and the brutality of the soldiers and police dispatched against strikers. Their fight for human dignity is reminiscent of the rubber-plantation-worker protests discussed in Chapter 1.

Both sides of the ideological spectrum—the left-wing and right-wing labor confederations and their supporters—benefited from the law permitting freedom of association. Both referred to the law when demanding basic labor rights and nonwage benefits, and while asserting the legality of the independent labor union structure. The left-wing Young Catholic Worker activists and progressive priests appealed to the rule of law (especially laws protecting the right to strike *and* laws shielding strikers) established by the RVN state in order to confront the police, to protect strikers, and to appeal to Saigon representatives about rampant labor violations and police brutality. The right-wing CVT claimed to use the law to improve working conditions and to protect the independent free trade union structure.

Moreover, these cases also demonstrate entrenched interests of the state and of the capitalists. They show how the state's actions and inaction benefited both local and global capitalists. This explains the RVN state's failure to enforce the court ruling on behalf of workers in the Eagle Battery case. In addition, blatant economic interests shared between the state (RVN and the United States) and the capitalists ignited workers' indignation—as seen in the Eagle Battery case.

Finally, during this period, the Kinh and the Hoa workers did not exhibit either "thick" or "thin" forms of false consciousness.[190] Workers did not agree that the social order in which they lived was "natural and inevitable," as would be true if they had adopted the thin form of false consciousness. While not always successful, they defied exploitation and control by the state and the capitalists, as shown in the case studies. The Vimytex protests leading to the general strike in 1964 in Saigon demonstrated how these workers persisted and triumphed through the ups and downs of their struggle, successfully paralyzed the whole city, and gained some modest victories. In cases when they did appeal to the local labor courts and the

---

[190] James Scott, *Domination and the Arts of Resistance: Hidden Transcripts* (New Haven, CT, and London: Yale University Press, 1990), p. 72.

Saigon parliament, they did not consent to those ideological state institutions (as they would have if burdened by a thick form of false consciousness), but instead demanded proper implementation of the law, such as the right to strike and the right that guarantees protection of strikers.

Overall, workers were resourceful in their protests. In their own voices, they expressed their anger and resistance in many forms and communicated through many sources: letters, petitions, strike banners, denouncements, journals, *samizdat*, poetry, work slowdowns, leaflets, singing and even making jokes in the darkest hours of their struggles to sustain themselves.

CHAPTER 3

STATE INSTITUTIONS AND THE LEGAL FRAMEWORK: THEIR INFLUENCE ON LABOR–MANAGEMENT RELATIONS SINCE *ĐỔI MỚI* (1986 TO PRESENT)

With the end of the United States–Vietnam war in 1975, a reunified Socialist Republic of Vietnam was faced with integrating the capitalist-oriented legacy of the South with the very different economic culture of the socialist North. Since this merger, Vietnam has undergone tremendous political and economic transformations that have brought the country to its present position in the global economic system, a process intensified during the *Đổi Mới* (renovation)—or market reform—era that began in 1986. In this chapter, I focus on the formation of the legal framework that has been established throughout *Đổi Mới* and pay attention to the laws and policies on labor–management relations developed before and after Vietnam joined the World Trade Organization (WTO). I also identify and explain the roles of the key state ideological apparatuses, such as the Ministry of Labor, Invalids, and Social Affairs (MOLISA); the Vietnamese General Confederation of Labor (VGCL); and the VGCL-controlled labor newspapers. MOLISA and VGCL play key roles in formulating and implementing policies based on laws and executive directives. The labor newspapers play a complex role: They not only report on the ramifications of these laws to the general public, but have been proactive—when permitted by the state—in providing various forums in the papers for workers to express their discontent, to ask questions, and to fight for their rights and interests in general.

First, I examine a broad historical context and the rise of the rule of law in Vietnam, a development that has underpinned workers' organizing and resisting efforts beginning in the 1990s.

MARKET SOCIALISM AND THE RULE OF LAW

Between national reunification in 1975 and the present, Vietnam underwent three major, economically significant periods. During the earliest period (1975–80), Vietnam expanded its original command economy—where the state controls all economic sectors, makes all decisions on the use of resources and production organization based on national and social objectives, and oversees the division of labor and the distribution of foodstuffs and manufacturing products to the whole population—to include the former Republic of Vietnam (RVN). Between 1980 and 1985, the government resorted to the so-called "hybrid transitional model," which was characterized by concessions to market-oriented transactions that were beyond government officials' control; yet, at the same time, the government tried to preserve the original pre-1975 Democratic Republic of Vietnam (DRV) Soviet-style central planning model. Since 1986, Vietnam has transitioned to the market system that is currently integrating the nation into the global capitalist economy.

The politico-economic conditions in a unified Vietnam, during the 1975–80 period, were very different from those that had characterized both the DRV and the free-market RVN. This central planning model aimed for "rapid industrialization with collectivization of agriculture and strong central control of the economy."[1] The state expropriated the private property of Kinh and Hoa merchants, and of capitalists in the South. But this model soon faced growing structural problems and exacerbated food and consumer-goods shortages. Those problems led to the flow of goods into the informal market throughout the country and to "fence-breaking," a literal translation of the Vietnamese phrase "*phá rào*," which means, in a figurative sense, circumventing state regulations in productive activities and commercial exchange. People would supplement their incomes through informal means, such as barter (for example, by exchanging fertilizer for access to a rice paddy or bicycles for pigs) and reselling whatever goods can be purchased at state stores at higher (black market) prices. Moreover, many government offices and state agencies engaged in corrupt behavior by selling their rations of consumer goods (including large quantities of gasoline) in the informal market for a profit. Overall, these activities led to growing gaps between official and market prices.[2] In addition to those bottom-up people's initiatives, there were other events that led to this system's failure in 1978 and 1979, such as Vietnam's military intervention in Cambodia and the US trade embargo, as well as natural disasters that caused bad harvests. In response, the Sixth Plenum of the Central Committee in 1979 began to initiate economic reforms.[3]

After the 1979–80 crisis, the state attempted to re-centralize the economy and halt economic liberalization by introducing the hybrid transitional model (intended both to placate citizens and to reinstitute aspects of the socialist DRV model). The state articulated its position at the 1982 Fifth Party Congress.[4] This period was characterized by a limited role for central planning and rolled-back market reforms, with strict controls on import–export activities, and strict controls on prices and

---

[1] Adam Fforde and Stefan de Vylder, *From Plan to Market: The Economic Transition in Vietnam* (Boulder, CO: Westview Press, 1996), p. 12.

[2] Angie Trần and David Smith, "Cautious Reformers and Fence Breakers: Vietnam's Economic Transition in Comparative Perspective," *Humboldt Journal of Social Relations* 24,1–2 (1998): 63–64.

[3] Fforde and de Vylder, *From Plan to Market*, p. 13. A note about the tensions between Cambodia and Vietnam is needed to explain the Hoa ethnic expulsion issue. The root of conflicts between Vietnam and Cambodia dates back to territory occupation in the eighteenth and nineteenth centuries, which escalated and led to bloodshed between them. The Khmer Rouge attacked and slaughtered Vietnamese civilians along the border in 1977, and Vietnam responded by invading Cambodia in December 1978. During that time, while Vietnam aligned closely with the then Soviet Union, China had been backing the Phnom Penh regime and mounted a retaliatory attack on Vietnam in February 1979 and began a long campaign with the approval of the United States. William S. Turley, *The Second Indochina War: A Concise Political and Military History* (Lanham, MD: Rowman & Littlefield Publishers, 2009), p. 258. Within that broad political context, the exodus of Hoa and Kinh refugees from Vietnam accelerated in 1978 and 1979; these refugees were known as "boat people." At the peak of the exodus, hundreds of thousands of Hoa resettled in Hong Kong and mainland China. Tom Lam, "The Exodus of Hoa Refugees from Vietnam and their Settlement in Guangxi: China's Refugee Settlement Strategies," *Journal of Refugee Studies* 13,4 (2000): 374–75.

[4] For details about this economic period, see Fforde and de Vylder, *From Plan to Market*, pp. 13–14.

distribution, in accord with the DRV model. But this rolling back led to another cycle of fence-breaking in 1983, with many people trying to circumvent state regulations on free-market activities.[5] In the years that followed, the government's economic policies—including decisions to print more money and allow state budget deficits to grow—failed to reestablish economic control and led to rising inflation in 1984 and 1985. There are complicated reasons for the failure of the 1985 wage and price reforms, but the fundamental problems included the incompatibility of the socialist and market systems; the deep-rooted, conflicting interests of society's different stakeholders; and the widespread dependence on the state subsidy system.[6]

These cycles of policies and reforms culminated in the Sixth Party Congress (1986–95), which legalized the pursuit of private interests in the free market system and fence-breaking activities, in addition to the pursuit of public interests. Essentially, the state recognized the shortcomings of the old model and from then on legislated new policies that were no longer short-term retreats but fundamental changes intended to move the country towards a market economy.[7] Moreover, the 1989 disintegration of the Soviet Bloc and the collapse of the Eastern European market (whose members were Vietnam's major trading partners) led to dwindling aid, loans, and commerce from those sources. Facing such difficulties, Vietnam opened itself to other markets—especially Japan, countries in the Association of Southeast Asian Nations (ASEAN), and the European Union (EU)—circumventing the US trade embargo (1975–94), which curtailed Western capital investment in Vietnam.[8] Since 1989, the state has called itself a "market economy with socialist orientation" (*Kinh tế thị trường, Định hướng xã hội chủ nghĩa*).

The twenty-year US trade embargo ended when the Clinton administration lifted it in 1994 and established diplomatic relations with Vietnam in 1995. As a result, the United States and its Western allies began investing anew in Vietnamese enterprises. Even during the embargo, major investments were already being made by East and Southeast Asian countries—Singapore, Korea, Taiwan, Hong Kong—and China. Today, US investment pales in the face of the financial commitment made by these Asian nations and their ethnic communities abroad. Trade between Vietnam and China increased when the two countries normalized their relations in November 1991, after Vietnam's withdrawal from Cambodia in 1989.

The socialist state has used the law—in terms of the constitution, legislation, decrees, directives, and circulars—as an instrument of governance and a source of legitimacy. While the ruling party still issues decrees, the majority of Vietnam's legal framework now consists of laws, the result of the government's intensified effort to integrate into the global neoliberal system.

A snapshot of the structure of the labor force in all types of Vietnamese enterprises shows the rising role of the domestic private sector, following that of the foreign-direct investment (FDI) sector, and the decreasing role of the state-owned

---

[5] Trần and Smith, "Cautious Reformers and Fence Breakers," pp. 68–69.

[6] Ibid., p. 70. For instance, there were conflicts of interest among state officials who controlled the national budget (including government salaries), but who also received wages from it (and whose purchasing power would shrink if inflation went uncontrolled). State factory managers wanted the best of both a free market system (for profits) and a government-subsidy program (for purchasing raw materials, and for price supports for consumer goods).

[7] Fforde and de Vylder, *From Plan to Market*, p. 14.

[8] Trần and Smith, "Cautious Reformers and Fence Breakers," p. 78.

sector. Labor-intensive and low-tech manufacturing enterprises still employ most workers, a great proportion of whom are migrant workers. In 2009, about 8.9 million people worked in all types of enterprises, of which 59 percent worked in the domestic private sector, 21.52 percent in FDI, and 19.45 percent in state enterprises.[9] Of these workers, about 4.1 million people worked in manufacturing enterprises.[10] Together apparel/garment, leather shoe, and textile products industries employed about 38 percent (or 1.57 million) of the total workers in manufacturing enterprises.[11] Throughout the book, I will focus on these three largest, labor-intensive industries, which continue to employ a high percentage of manufacturing workers.

Since 2002, when the state started to privatize state-owned enterprises (SOEs) in the whole economy and the military, the percentage of workers in state-owned enterprises has been shrinking. The public sector went from employing 59 percent of workers in 2000 to only 19.45 percent of workers in 2009.[12] The state calls this process "equitization" (*cổ phần hóa*), an ideologically correct way to express the transfer of public assets to the private sector in a socialist country. In principle, state managers would determine the values of these SOEs and then sell shares to, presumably, workers and other investors, creating joint-stock companies in the private sector.

In the process, the boundaries between state and nonstate sectors in Vietnam became blurred. The domestic private sector has almost doubled between 2000 and 2009: it employed 29.4 percent (of total workers in enterprises) in 2000 and 59 percent in 2009.[13] But the diverse subcategories of the domestic private sector involve various forms of state-owned capital. These consist of collective, private, limited-partnership arrangements, as well as joint-stock companies functioning with and without state capital.[14] Between 2000 and 2009, the FDI sector—including 100 percent of foreign capital and joint-venture capital—doubled its share of the workforce: the proportion of workers employed by this sector increased from 11.5 percent in 2000 to 21.5 percent in 2009.[15]

The boundaries between domestic private and FDI sectors also have become blurred. The FDI statistics do not take into account various types of underground investment, of the kind involving foreign owners who register their ventures as domestic factories. Thus, some foreign investment is included in the domestic private sector's data. I will return to this topic in chapters 6 and 7.

---

[9] General Statistics Office, *Statistical Yearbook of Vietnam 2010* (Hanoi: Statistical Publishing House, 2011), p. 190.

[10] *Statistical Yearbook of Vietnam 2010* also provides a higher figure for workers—all those fifteen years old or older—in the general manufacturing sector in 2009: 6.5 million. This implies that about 2.4 million people may have worked in small workshops in home-based situations, not in manufacturing enterprises. Ibid., pp. 100, 191.

[11] Ibid., p. 191.

[12] General Statistics Office, *Statistical Yearbook of Vietnam* 2006 (Hanoi: Statistical Publishing House, 2007), p. 127; *Statistical Yearbook of Vietnam 2010*, p. 190.

[13] Ibid. *Statistical Yearbook 2006*, p. 127; *Statistical Yearbook 2010*, p. 190.

[14] Ibid.

[15] Ibid.; and *Statistical Yearbook 2008* (Hanoi: Statistical Publishing House, 2009), p. 130.

THE MINISTRY OF LABOR AND THE LABOR UNIONS

The Ministry of Labor, Invalids, and Social Affairs (MOLISA) advises the Vietnamese state on labor–management negotiations. In April 2009, the prime minister formed the Center for the Development of Industrial Relations, led by a high-ranking, experienced official from MOLISA, Nguyễn Mạnh Cường. This center is consistent with the state's focus on the rule of law; it is intended to support negotiations before, during, and after labor–management conflicts erupt.

In an interview with a journalist, Nguyễn Mạnh Cường explained that this new institution provides state support for labor–management relations, in particular industrial negotiations in a market economy based on the rule of law, in an effort to avoid conflicts. He stressed the importance of finding a balance in the distribution of any enterprise's profits between labor and management, because balance would bring stability and mutual benefits for both sides. He warned that conflicts and strikes will erupt when this balance is missing. He explained that such balance is based on two foundations—law and negotiations: the rights (*quyền*) of both sides being regulated by law and the contention over interests/benefits (*lợi ích*) being resolved through negotiations.[16] The labor unions have been utilizing these very tenets when negotiating with management and signing collective bargaining agreements (CBAs) that achieved higher-than-minimum benefits for workers. I will elaborate on this issue below.

The Labor Code and Chapter 14

The Vietnamese Labor Code, which was ratified in June 1994 and became effective in January 1995, is quite progressive; it encompasses all the work and pay conditions, nonwage benefits, and special stipulations for women workers as well as the right to strike (Chapter 14).[17] According to the labor code, management has to contribute 15 percent of the total wages paid by their enterprise to social insurance and 2 percent to health insurance, and workers were to contribute 6 percent to social insurance. Many violations have resulted from the fact that management often does not calculate their contributions based on higher take-home salaries, which tend to include a lot of overtime pay, but on lower base minimum wage salaries, resulting in underfunded benefits (social insurance and health care) for workers.

MOLISA has played a key role in drafting the Labor Code. Over the years, the Labor Code has come under scrutiny by the parliament, a process complicated by increasing inputs from local labor unions and pressure from the owners of capital. The latest proposed revision of the Labor Code has been delayed, perhaps due to the conflicts resulting from diverse stakeholders' interests concerning key contentious areas such as strikes, labor representation in factories where employees lack union representation, wages, and work hours. The original deadline for the final drafting phase and ratification was November 2010, but the ratification process was delayed

---

[16] Phạm Hồ, "Chuyển 'hậu đình công' sang 'tiền tranh chấp'" [Moving from 'Post-strike' to 'Pre-conflict' Negotiations], *Người Lao Động* (April 3, 2009), http://nld.com.vn/20090 403125216500p0c1010/chuyen-hau-dinh-cong-sang-tien-tranh-chap.htm, accessed November 2012.

[17] For an analysis of the implications of the strike law, please see Angie Ngọc Trần, "Alternatives to the 'Race to the Bottom' in Vietnam: Minimum Wage Strikes and Their Aftermath," *Labor Studies Journal* 32,4 (December 2007): 430–51.

until June 2012, when the Labor Code was ratified without many changes to Chapter 14 (on strikes), as discussed below.

Tremendous conflicts surfaced in the process of drafting the proposal. The title of a newspaper article, written by an experienced journalist, Dương Minh Đức, says it all: "Completely Destroyed Proposal!" (Nát Bấy Dự Thảo!). In particular, Proposal No. 3 (Dự Thảo 3) includes seventeen chapters with 271 amendments on often-cited items such as labor contracts, collective bargaining agreements, training, wages, work hours and rest, work safety, stipulations for women workers and underage workers, social security, union membership, and strikes. But it also includes two items that reflect management's interests: "labor discipline and labor responsibility on management property."[18]

Labor unions at all levels (including the export processing zones [EPZs] and industrial zones), MOLISA (central and local), the ILO (International Labor Organization), and management representatives, such as the Vietnamese Textile and Apparel Association (VITAS) and the American Chamber of Commerce (AmCham), participated in drafting the proposal and lobbied for some key revisions. For instance, Amendment No. 50, on special worker representation (chủ thể đặc biệt), allows upper-level labor unions to intervene directly in factory-level labor union negotiations, thus recognizing the general weakness of workplace labor unions, whose representatives are employed by management and, therefore, face conflicts of interest in their representation of workers.[19] Moreover, the level of unionization in factories, as of March 2010, was low: only 20 percent of workers in domestic private factories and 40 percent in FDI factories were protected by unions.[20] An alliance of management representatives tried to influence the proposal's mandate concerning overtime work. Both VITAS and AmCham strongly supported the elimination of restrictions limiting annual overtime hours. But this was met with strong opposition from officials in the Department of Labor in Bà Rịa-Vũng Tàu province and Trương Lâm Danh, who was vice president of the Ho Chi Minh City Labor Federation. Danh showed proof of increasing workplace accidents resulting from overworked employees' fatigue: in 2009 there were 102 workplace accidents due to excessive overtime fatigue, resulting in the deaths of 103 workers.[21]

As might be expected, the most discussed topic was Chapter 14 (Resolution of Labor Disputes) of the proposal. Participants generally lamented that a lot of work had been put into revising this chapter, but that the revised procedure still did not address the Vietnamese realities. AmCham has been pressuring the top Vietnamese leadership to curb labor strikes and to advocate for the interests of management. With regard to the proposed amendments to the Labor Code, AmCham sent a formal position letter on July 18, 2011, to the National Labor Relations Committee (NLRC), the prime minister, MOLISA, the VGCL, the VCCI (Vietnamese Chamber of Commerce and Industry), three other ministries, and other interested agencies; in

---

[18] Dương Minh Đức, "'Nát Bấy' Dự Thảo!" [Completely Destroyed Proposal!], *Lao Động* 68, March 27, 2010, http://www.laodong.com.vn/Utilities/PrintView.aspx?ID=178942, accessed June 2010. This seasoned journalist advocates for workers' right to strike for three basic human necessities: food, clothing, and shelter.

[19] Interview with Phạm Ngọc Đoàn, July 2006, Ho Chi Minh City.

[20] The 2008 statistics were: 67 percent joined the unions in FDI enterprises, and 36 percent joined in domestic private factories. Communication with Trần Văn Lý, November 2009. So the union-membership figures for March 2010 are lower than those for 2008.

[21] Dương Minh Đức, "'Nát Bấy' Dự Thảo!"

addition, AmCham hosted the National Employers' Conference 2011 on industrial relations and Labor Code revision. Regarding Chapter 14, AmCham has requested "a temporary lockout ... without previous notice to the authority if the employer deems the situation dangerous for staff or corporate assets" and recommended that the district level people's committee issue a "stop order" to unions and striking workers if a particular work stoppage does not follow procedures. Overall, they blamed the workers and the government for "illegal strikes," which they claimed were because: 1) the government had established complicated procedures for strikes that workers did not understand; 2) local governments do nothing to stop "illegal" strikes; 3) workers don't know the difference between rights and benefits.[22]

While it is constructive for these companies to recommend a streamlined timeline for a collective labor dispute resolution process involving local stakeholders, nowhere in either the formal letter or the AmCham Statement (presented at the National Employers Conference 2011) did the VITAS and AmCham acknowledge management's mistreatment of employees as the main cause for most strikes. According to Nguyễn Thị Thanh Mai, the Head of Division for Labor Supervision in Foreign Enterprises, MOLISA: "About 90 percent of spontaneous strikes were caused by employers' violating labor legislation, out of which 80 percent involved wages and fringe benefits."[23]

The distinction between "rights" and "interests" was again open for lively discussion in 2011, which then led to the ratification in June 2012.[24] Proposal No. 3

---

[22] AmCham, "Letter to National Labour Relations Committee (NLRC) and other interested agencies re proposed amendments to Labour Code w Attachment (Eng)," July 18, 2011, http://www.amchamvietnam.com/download/1525, accessed September 19, 2012; "National Employers Conference 2011–Labour Code Revision (AmCham Statement) on Industrial Relations and Labour Code Revision," Melia Hanoi Hotel, October 24, 2011, http://www.amchamvietnam.com/5063, accessed June 2012.

[23] Nguyễn Thị Thanh Mai, "Labor Disputes in HCM City: Resolutions and Recommendations," the Head of Division for Labors Supervision in Foreign Enterprises, Department of Labor, Invalids, and Social Affairs, at http://www.amcham vietnam.com/1239, accessed June 2012.

[24] In my 2007 article "Alternatives to the 'Race to the Bottom' in Vietnam," I pointed out the vibrant and nuanced Vietnamese policymakers' debates showing two perspectives: 1) the pro-worker perspectives of the outspoken delegates in strike-prone provinces who argued for the inseparability of rights and interests, and 2) the perspectives of people who compromised with the FDI community by allowing workers to strike only when the violations relate to interests, not to rights (pp. 444, 450). Ben Kerkvliet concurs with this complex situation in his 2011 chapter "Workers' Protests in Contemporary Vietnam," in *Labour in Vietnam*, ed. Anita Chan(Singapore: Institute of Southeast Asian Studies, 2011), pp. 180, 182, 198 (endnote 112). Writing from an industrial-relations perspective, Clarke and coauthors have criticized both MOLISA—for failing to enforce labor legislation—and, more scathingly, the VGCL, for failing to represent workers at the workplace level and for failing to lead their strikes. These authors argued that labor strikes have grown from demanding basic workers' rights to protecting their interests/benefits. Simon Clarke, Chang-Hee Lee, and Đỗ Quỳnh Chi, "From Rights to Interests: The Challenge of Industrial Relations in Vietnam," *Journal of Industrial Relations* 49,4 (2007): 545–68. While I agree with Clarke and his coauthors' general argument about the VGCL's organizational and structural weaknesses, I find their argument ignores the powerful and very influential pressure from the FDI community—AmCham in particular—which managed to sway this whole strike debate to favor *their* interests. I also found that Clarke's argument ignores the dissonant perspectives found within the state (such as the delegates' debates on the strike law mentioned above). The state is not monolithic. Clarke's general argument also fails to recognize the differences between the central VGCL's tendencies and the activities of the more proactive city- and district-level labor unions, as well as the dynamic

argued that "interests" requests (such as for health and social security benefits) were higher than "rights," and that strikes were allowed only when management had failed to fulfill the agreed-upon interests. By comparison, violations concerning "rights"—as stipulated in the Labor Code—should be settled in labor courts.

In June 2012, the Labor Code revision—including Chapter 14, on strikes—was ratified. While the November 2006 revision and the current version maintain the distinction between rights and interests with two separate protocols, four points of difference stand out that place greater control of labor–management relations and disputes in the centralized state and labor unions, while significantly weakening the workers' role in the whole process of strike resolution.[25]

First, for both protocols, there is no longer a role for "*Hội đồng hoà giải lao động cơ sở*" (enterprise-level labor mediation committee) elected by both the workers' collective and management. Instead, a labor arbitrator (*hòa giải viên lao động*), appointed by local DOLISA (Department of Labor, Invalids, and Social Affairs) departments, is given the task of mediating the strikes for both rights-based and interests-based conflicts.

Second, in non-unionized factories, there is no longer a role for "*Đại diện tập thể lao động*" (representatives of the workers' collective) who formerly could organize and lead the strikes; the only stipulation was that they needed to inform the ward/district/city level labor unions of their plans. In the 2012 revision, the upper-level unions (*Tổ chức công đoàn cấp trên*) are tasked to organize and lead the strikes "according to suggestions of the workers." These changes undermine the workers' role allowed by the 2006 version, which gave a strategic role to representatives of the workers' collective and enterprise-level labor mediation committee in both the organizing and leadership of strikes.

Third, the role of the people's committee chairperson at the city/province level is more prominent in the 2012 revision of the code, in that s/he would appoint members of the important labor arbitration committee (*Hội đồng trọng tài lao động*)—composed of seven representatives led by the local state labor department (DOLISA), and joined by the city-level unions and management. While this arbitration committee would mediate the interests-based conflicts, the people's committee chairperson and the people's courts would have the final ruling on the rights-based conflicts.

Fourth, only a simple majority—over 50 percent of the number of workers consulted, compared to 75 percent in the 2006 version—is needed for the union leaders to declare a strike.

Over the six years that have passed since the 2006 revision, the state has acceded to the lobbyists of the foreign-direct investment community to minimize the role of

labor media, as these organizations try hard to respond in a timely manner to workers' strikes. While these efforts are not always successful because of various constraints, it is important to note that the VGCL is not monolithic either, and that it has shown varying levels of effectiveness in responding to the needs of workers. Angie Ngọc Trần, "The Third Sleeve: Emerging Labor Newspapers and the Response of Labor Unions and the State to Workers' Resistance in Vietnam," *Labor Studies Journal* 32,3 (September 2007): 268, 271, 275.

[25] Bộ Luật Lao Động [The Labor Code], 10/2012/QH13, http://thuvienphapluat.vn/van-ban/Lao-dong-Tien-luong/Bo-Luat-lao-dong-2012-142187.aspx, accessed July 2012, Stipulation numbers: 198, 199, 203, 204, 210, 212, 213; Luật Sửa Đổi, Bổ Sung Một Số Điều Của Bộ Luật Lao Động Của Quốc Hội Khoá XI, Kỳ Họp Thứ 10 [The Revision of Some Stipulations of the Labor Code, Parliament Session 11, Meeting No. 10], 74/2006/QH11, November 29, 2006, Stipulation numbers: 162–164, 168–170, 172, 174.

workers in both rights-based and interests-based conflicts. At the same time, the state has centralized its control by granting an unrivaled, powerful role to the VGCL in organizing and leading strikes, even in non-unionized factories. It remains to be seen if this latest revision in practice—which undermines workers' direct inputs to the strike process and resolution—will hinder workers from negotiating for better pay and improved working conditions.

At the time of writing, the reality shows that most violations concern basic labor rights, which are closely connected with workers' interests (as discussed below). In addition, the local labor and people's courts, and some of the local people's committees, have implemented the laws in arbitrary ways, thereby failing to protect workers consistently, while also neglecting to force management to pay workers' back wages and basic entitlements (such as social and health insurance).

FROM RED TRADE UNION TO VIETNAMESE GENERAL CONFEDERATION OF LABOR

To understand the interactions among labor, capital, and the state in reunified Vietnam, one needs to review the history of the labor unions. This history is closely connected to that of the Vietnamese Communist Party. The Red Trade Union (RTU)—formed in 1930 by a network of persons engaged in labor organizing in a number of major industrial enterprises, factories, and textile mills under colonial French rule—acted as a guerrilla base to sabotage key French industries.[26] From this original union the Vietnamese Federation of Trade Unions (VFTU) was formed in 1946, which later was largely responsible for organizing workers (in the North) to participate in the resistance against US intervention in the late 1960s and early 1970s. Then, in the context of renewal, openness, and democracy, in 1988 the VFTU was transformed into the Vietnamese General Confederation of Labor (VGCL) "to ensure their independent character in terms of organization … to voice ideas of their own, not opinions borrowed from the party committees or from management."[27] Of course, to be characterized as having an "independent character" is a paradox for the VGCL, which still is ensconced in the state structure. But VGCL activities at the local level have demonstrated that both local labor unions and the labor newspapers have had much more leeway and flexibility, since 1988, in cracking open a space for protecting and promoting workers' rights and interests, especially during the minimum wage strike in 2005–06.[28] At times, they have even publicly criticized the pro-FDI governmental policies and their consequences. Evidence for this point will be discussed in subsequent chapters.

---

[26] Eva Hansson, "Trade Unions and Đổi Mới: The Changing Role of Trade Unions in the Era of Economic Liberalization in Vietnam," *Politics of Development Group* (Stockholm: Stockholm University, Department of Political Science, 1995); Hoàng Quốc Việt, *The Trade Union Movement in Vietnam* (Hanoi: Foreign Languages Publishing House, Vietnam Federation of Trade Unions, 1988); and Đỗ Quang Hưng, *Công Hội Đỏ Việt Nam* [The Vietnamese Red Trade Union] (Hanoi: Nhà Xuất Bản Lao Động, 2004).

[27] Irene Norlund, "Democracy and Trade Unions in Vietnam: Riding a Honda in Low Gear," *The Copenhagen Journal of Asian Studies* (November 1996): 90. This openness was in no doubt influenced by Gorbachev, who came to power in the former Soviet Union in 1984 and introduced the policy of "openness" (*glasnost*) and "restructuring" (*perestroika*).

[28] The level of autonomy enjoyed by local unions and newspapers was inconsistent and then curtailed after Vietnam joined the World Trade Organization in 2007. I will return to this point in Chapter 7.

Under a command economy (1954–75, in the North, and 1975–86, in the reunified Socialist Republic of Vietnam), labor and management (mostly state-owned enterprises) were assumed to have the same interests: they were expected to meet the Vietnamese Communist Party (VCP) directives. Thus, the trade unions served the one-way, top-down transmission between the party and the workers, a system in which the unions made sure that workers met the party's directives (production quotas and smooth transitioning into market-based mechanisms).[29]

Both Irene Norlund and Melanie Beresford have argued that, before the influx of foreign capital began in 1988, few conflicts occurred in state-owned enterprises, and workers had some control over the production process and access to enterprise resources, which made it possible for workers to "moonlight" to improve their personal incomes.[30] According to these writers, state-owned enterprises have contributed adequately to social security and workers' health benefits funds, a fact that still distinguishes most state factories from nonstate factories. Beresford has pointed out that, under the centrally planned system, trade unions did not primarily defend workers' interests against management—or the state—and workers' annual congresses did not exercise management rights over the enterprises, nor did workers have much control over the economic policies that shaped their lives. But she also notes that workers had some say on how products were made.[31] As imperfect as the general situation was, Vietnamese workers were more involved in the labor process before 1988, according to these authors, compared to what they are subjected to under the neoliberal subcontracting system.

The VGCL Structure

Labor unions in Vietnam are well organized by administrative area (city, district, workplace levels), by industry (such as textile/garment/footwear, commerce, railroads), and by state corporations—privatized former state-owned enterprises that now report directly to the VGCL. This study focuses on the three-tiered labor unions of the administrative area because within these areas, labor, capital, and the state interact with each other most extensively.

Labor unions at the workplace level are the weakest link in this hierarchy. Most union representatives at the factory level are employees, who are themselves paid by management; thus, they have conflicts of interest and are not effective in representing workers at the negotiating table. However, with help from the city and district unions, where staff members have more experience and expertise in collective bargaining, workers have been able to make inroads when seeking to protect their rights and interests.

Labor Unions in Export Processing Zones: The Case of HEPZA Labor Union

After the promulgation of the law promoting foreign investment in Vietnam in 1987, foreign investment in Vietnam increased rapidly. But these projects faced difficulties because of inadequate infrastructure, an inefficient bureaucracy in charge

---

[29] Norlund, "Democracy and Trade Unions in Vietnam," p. 89.

[30] Ibid.; and Melanie Beresford and Chris Nyland, "The Labour Movement of Vietnam," *Labour History* 75 (November, 1998), pp. 70–71.

[31] Beresford and Nyland, "The Labour Movement of Vietnam," pp. 69–70.

of granting investment licenses, and the difficulties of actually implementing these projects. So, in October 1991, the government established the export processing zone,[32] and then, in November 1991, Tân Thuận EPZ, the first EPZ in Vietnam, was established. A year later, Linh Trung I and II EPZs were established.

In 1996, the prime minister established the Ho Chi Minh City EPZs Authority (HEPZA) to manage EPZs and industrial zones (IZs), which encompass both foreign and domestic companies producing for domestic and export markets; the decision to set up this umbrella organization, HEPZA, was prompted by the "one-stop service" principle.[33] It created a powerful structure: HEPZA is authorized to issue investment licenses for all projects with investment capital up to US$40 million in the EPZs and up to US$10 million in the IZs.

Since October 2000, the HCMC (Ho Chi Minh City) People's Committee has played a key role in HEPZA: managing human resources, planning, and finance.[34] Of the 124 EPZs and IZs nationwide, HEPZA manages three huge EPZs (Tân Thuận, Linh Trung I, and Linh Trung II). These were the sites of some major worker-initiated protests that resulted in 40 percent minimum-wage increases in 2006, as well as subsequent increases in 2008 and 2009. I will elaborate on these strikes in chapters 5 and 6.

HEPZA continues to expand. With sixteen existing zones (three EPZs, thirteen IZs) already established, its master plan for 1996–2020 includes twenty-one new zones (including two EPZs, eighteen IZs, one high-tech zone) with a total area of 8,540 hectares. Overall, HEPZA manages more than nine hundred enterprises employing 170,000 workers.[35] An interesting recent development to address workers' discontent is the creation of a Questions–Answers forum on HEPZA's main website, to which workers can send questions and concerns and receive answers from HEPZA's personnel office.[36] This innovation shows HEPZA's intention to prevent potential workers' strikes.

Most FDI companies in HEPZA are owned by Taiwan, Japan, South Korea, Hong Kong, the United States, and Singapore. They manufacture a wide range of products and provide a range of services representing such industries as textile/garment/footwear, electronics/information technology, pharmaceuticals and chemicals (such

---

[32] Nghị Định Của Chủ Tịch Hội Đồng Bộ Trưởng Số 322-HĐBT Ngày 18-10-1991 Ban Hành Quy Chế Khu Chế Xuất [Decision No. 322/HDBT of the Chair of the Ministerial Committee on Export Processing Zone Regulations], October 1991, http://thuvienphapluat.vn/archive/Nghi-dinh/Nghi-dinh-322-HDBT-Quy-che-Khu-che-xuat-vb38198t11.aspx, accessed July 2010.

[33] Directors of the management boards—appointed by the Chair of the Ministerial Committee based on the recommendation of the National Committee on Cooperation and Investment, and the chair of the people's committee of the province/city hosting the EPZ—can grant investment licenses, control their implementation, and manage their activities in each zone. Ibid., Stipulations 57–64.

[34] Quyết Định Của Thủ Tướng Chính Phủ Số 100/2000/QĐ-TTg Ngày 17 Tháng 8 Năm 2000 Về Việc Chuyển Giao Ban Quản Lý Khu Công Nghiệp Cấp Tỉnh Trực Thuộc Uỷ Ban Nhân Dân Tỉnh, Thành Phố Trực Thuộc Trung Ương [Prime Minister's Decision No. 100, August 17, 2000 to transfer EPZ management to the people's committee of that province/city], http://thuvienphapluat.vn/van-ban/Bo-may-hanh-chinh/Quyet-dinh-100-2000-QD-TTg-chuyen-giao-Ban-quan-ly-khu-cong-nghiep-cap-tinh-thuoc-Uy-ban-nhan-dan-tinh-thanh-pho/46698/noi-dung.aspx?tab=7, accessed July 2010.

[35] http://www.amchamvietnam.com/company/883/detail, accessed August 17, 2010.

[36] http://www.hepza.hochiminhcity.gov.vn/web/guest/kcn_kcx-tphcm/gioi-thieu-chung, accessed June 1, 2012.

as plastics, rubber), construction and building materials, household products, food processing, machinery and wood products, consultancy services (related to trading, finance, accounting, intellectual property, technology, hotel/tourism, real estate), and auxiliary services for industrial production.[37]

To deal with the labor–management issues of factories belonging to HEPZA, the VGCL formed a special type of labor union, called the HEPZA Labor Union, which is parallel, in the bureaucratic hierarchy, to the district labor-union level. This special labor union reports directly to its higher-level labor union, the HCMC Labor Federation, and it represents all enterprise-level labor unions within HEPZA.[38] In principle, an FDI factory must facilitate the formation of an enterprise labor union within six months after the establishment of an enterprise in an EPZ or industrial zone. This is one of the progressive features of the Vietnamese Labor Code that is sometimes absent or not as strong in the labor codes of other developing countries.[39] Workers in these FDI companies are expected to join HEPZA enterprise labor unions, which report directly to the HEPZA Labor Union. However, while the VGCL labor union structure and membership requirements are progressive, they still struggle with enforcement.

Union Membership and New Challenges

Resolutions made in the Tenth Congress of the VGCL in November 2008 for a five-year plan of action (2008–13) focus on addressing some key weaknesses in the labor union's membership (or union density), effectiveness in conflict resolution, gender representation, and worker participation. Out of their eight goals, several stand out: 1) increase the membership by 1.5 million people and establish additional workplace labor unions; 2) provide training (technical, bargaining) to 100 percent of union representatives; 3) increase the number of collective bargaining agreements at the sector/industry level (such as the textile and garment industries); 4) increase the percentage of women in union leadership to at least 30 percent; (5) and increase the number of annual worker/employee/public servant congresses in both state and nonstate sectors.[40]

---

[37] http://www.hepza.gov.vn/web/guest/39, accessed June 1, 2012; and http://www.hbahochiminh.com/danhsachthanhvien.php?Page=1, accessed June 1, 2012.

[38] Fulltime HEPZA Labor Union representatives and staff, including the director of the HEPZA Labor Union, are on the payroll of the HCMC Labor Federation.

[39] An example would be the Philippine Economic Zone Authority (PEZA). While organizing workers in Philippine special economic zones is not officially prohibited (as it was under the Marcos "no union, no strike" policy of the early 1980s), workers in the EPZ factories there face overt and covert actions used by the management—such as intimidation, bribery attempts, physical isolation, and dismissal—to discourage trade union activity in many EPZ factories. "Trade Union World Briefing," *International Confederation of Free Trade Unions*, 2005. http://www.icftu.org/www/PDF/LMSDossier8-05YouthEN.pdf, accessed July 19, 2012. However, some other studies have found that women workers in the Philippine EPZs were able to organize amid many difficulties and challenges. They worked in different forms of unions: unionized companies (with or without a collective bargaining agreement), independent unions, labor–management councils, and worker's associations. "The International Textile Garments and Leather Workers Federation," *ILO* (Manila, December 2003), at www.itglwf.org/docs/EPZStudy.doc, accessed July 19, 2012.

[40] Vietnamese General Confederation of Labor, June 4, 2009, Goals from Resolutions Made in the Tenth Congress of the VGCL in November 2008, Five-year Plan of Action (2008–13);

Since the adoption of the five-year plan, union membership has increased, but many challenges remain, some have intensified, and new ones have arisen. As of May 2012, the total VGCL membership is 7.7 million, of which union members in the state sector accounted for 51 percent (3.9 million). Union members in the nonstate sector accounted for 49 percent (3.8 million), and 45 percent of those nonstate-sector union members work in the FDI sector (1.7 million).[41] Union members in the state sector represent a wide range of occupations: most of them are state public servants—such as teachers, researchers, administrators, and health workers—and union members in state-owned enterprises.

The 2009 statistics break down as follows: 3.7 million union members in the state sector, of whom 2.4 million were state public servants, and only 1.3 million were employees in state-owned enterprises.[42] Given the transformation of state-owned enterprises to equitized companies, and comparing the 2009 with the 2011 statistics, we can assert that, over time, the number of union members employed in domestic private factories has steadily increased in proportion to the number working in state-owned enterprises.

A relatively new challenge facing the VGCL is to organize workers engaged in different types of retailing in the growing private sector.[43] Traditionally, most local retailers are small and not unionized (there are no official union statistics). But large-scale retailers, such as chain supermarkets, have grown quickly in metropolitan areas, with about 400 supermarkets, 60 commercial centers, and 200 convenience stores. Their projected sales could in some years reach more than US$50 billion. Organizing workers in the retail industry has been very difficult, partly because labor union organizers have not had much experience in this service-oriented sector. For FDI retailers, their union members belonged to the provincial or city labor unions (*liên đoàn lao động tỉnh*), where organizing effectiveness varies.

Newspapers

Scholars have argued that local media content in Vietnam is dictated by the state, which sets and follows a Marxist-Leninist ideology and maintains organizational control. These authors have focused mainly on the top-down control of media content, which is governed to insure it reflects a Marxist-Leninist ideology and broadcasts positive reports of the party-state, the military, people's committees, and mass organizations (such as the Fatherland Front and the VGCL).[44] But I have found that the effects of the state's control over the media move in two directions in Vietnam, and that the central government's authority has not simply empowered the state by sapping the power of the citizenry, for the Vietnamese media has given

---

interview with Châu Nhật Bình, June 2009, Hanoi; and S. A., "Bế mạc Hội nghị BCH TLĐ: Nỗ lực hơn nữa để chăm lo cho đoàn viên" [Concluding the Conference of the VGCL Executive Committee: Try Harder to Serve the Members], *Người Lao Động*, July 13, 2012, http://www.congdoanvn.org.vn/details.asp?l=1&c=22&m=5951, accessed June 2012.

[41] Email communications with Trần Văn Lý, Director of the Organizing Department, Vietnamese General Confederation of Labor, October 30, 2012.

[42] Correspondence with Trần Văn Lý, June 2010, based on the *VGCL Union Membership Statistics*, through to November 20, 2009.

[43] Interview with Châu Nhật Bình, June 2010, Hanoi.

[44] Russell Heng, "Media in Vietnam and the Structure of its Management," in *Mass Media in Vietnam*, ed. David Marr (Canberra: Australian National University, 1998).

greater voice to the factory worker than is apparent in the traditional structure of communist systems. So, when discussing the role of the media, I will refer to the two most important daily labor newspapers—or the labor press, for short—that cover labor–management relations issues extensively: the *Người Lao Động* (the Laborer, the official forum of HCMC Labor Federation, and one of the most popular and dynamic pro-labor newspapers in Vietnam), and the *Lao Động* (the Labor, the media arm of the central office of the VGCL based in Hanoi).

Other forums in Vietnam also offer workers spaces in which to voice their discontent, although not in as focused a manner as in those two labor newspapers. Other Vietnamese newspapers offer daily or weekly coverage and analyses of labor issues. Most post online versions of their stories that are accessible worldwide; those newspapers accessible online include *Nhân Dân* (People), *Tuổi Trẻ, Công Đoàn* (Labor Union), *Pháp Luật* (Law), *Viet Nam News*, VCCI Forum, VnNet, VnExpress Net, Tinnhanh, and so on. Moreover, the labor unions oversee two weekly TV programs on workers and labor union issues, as well as maintaining the VGCL official website.[45]

Both *Người Lao Động* and *Lao Động* have their own news bureaus and journalists to cover news and developments in both the North and the South, and both have complete online coverage. Workers can send their complaint letters into either one of these periodicals, come to the newspaper offices to seek help, or call the offices (many newspapers offer twenty-four-hour hotlines) and journalists to inform the paper about impending strikes. Investigative journalists rush to cover these unfolding conflicts. Once workers' grievances are exposed through these public forums, whereby perpetrators are put on the spot, all stakeholders often come together to address the workers' concerns. I will demonstrate these dynamics in subsequent chapters. Since most strikes erupt in the South, I focus more on coverage by *Người Lao Động*. This newspaper's reporting has created public forums and facilitated conditions that pushed the central labor unions and the state to respond to workers' spontaneous organizing and strikes in different types of factories (FDI, state-owned, and domestic private).

The *Người Lao Động* and the *Lao Động*, while still very much ensconced *within* the state and labor-union structure, have been using connections and knowledge inside the system to expose conflicts within the state structure and to mediate among competing state interests with respect to labor organizing vis-a-vis foreign capital. The journalists try to maintain a balance between serving their main constituencies—workers—and responding to the political agendas of the party, the state, and the labor unions. In subsequent chapters, I will analyze how these newspapers have been walking a fine line that divides what they are permitted to report from what they may not when circumscribed by the party-state.

LAWS ON DOMESTIC INVESTMENT ('99), INVESTMENT ('05), AND ENTERPRISES ('05)

Louis Althusser developed a theoretical framework to explain the hegemony of the state and how the state uses ideology by way of policies and laws to perpetuate production relations and to control people. The state creates social subjects and controls them using certain policies, and it expects citizens to comply with these laws

---

[45] Interview with Trần Văn Lý, August 2006, Hanoi.

that have been set by both repressive and ideological state apparatuses.[46] In the context of Vietnamese industrial and labor relations, the state uses policies/laws to create and govern different categories of labor and capital. In this section, I discuss how the state differentiates among and controls people using laws that distinguish between rural/migrant workers versus urban/local workers; Kinh versus non-Kinh citizens (especially as related to the Hoa); workers in FDI factories versus workers in domestic factories; and redundant (state workers who have been laid-off when state-owned factories have been privatized) versus regular workers.

In three consecutive years (1986–88), the Vietnamese state made an effort to lay a foundation to attract foreign-direct investment into Vietnam. The Sixth Party Congress in 1986 instituted economic "market" reforms that recognized private interests and prioritized food production, consumer goods, and export expansion instead of heavy industry. In 1987, a law on FDI was passed to approve the introduction of foreign-owned factories in Vietnam. In 1988, three state decisions further unleashed a proliferation of private firms.[47] Also, in 1990, the state amended the law on FDI to include all other forms of FDI, such as joint-ventures, joint-stocks, and business cooperation contracts.

The present state's use of citizenship/ethnicity to control both capital and labor predates 1975. For instance, in the 1960s and early 1970s, prohibitive laws in the Republic of Vietnam restricting Hoa investment prompted the Hoa managers of underground credit outlets to charge high interest rates for seed money, land investment, and speculation.[48] Then the reunified Vietnamese state used the expulsion of the Hoa to break their lending network, which had controlled investment throughout Vietnam. But two decades later, the Socialist Republic of Vietnam's Law to Encourage Domestic Investment (*Luật Khuyến Khích Đầu Tư Trong Nước*) resulted in various forms of underground investment, establishing enterprises with officially registered owners who were not the actual owners. I will discuss this in Chapter 6.

The Law to Encourage Domestic Investment—ratified by the parliament in 1998 and effective as of 1999—aimed at attracting investment from overseas Vietnamese. Its implementation followed the lifting of the US trade embargo in 1995, which further opened the door to foreign investment. But, in fact, an increase in investment in Vietnam by overseas Vietnamese and ethnic Chinese (from East Asian countries) had started in 1989, when the collapse of the former Soviet Bloc ended the Council of

---

[46] Repressive state apparatuses consist of the courts, police, and prisons. Ideological state apparatuses (ISA) consist of legal ISA, trade unions, communications, schools, cultural ISA, families, the political system, and churches. Louis Althusser, "Ideology and Ideological State Apparatuses," in *Lenin and Philosophy, and Other Essays*, trans. Ben Brewster (New York, NY, and London: Monthly Review Press, 1970), pp. 143–45, 170–73, 181; R. Resch, *Althusser and the Renewal of Marxist Social Theory* (Berkeley, CA: University of California Press, 1992).

[47] Prime Minister's Decisions 27CP, 28CP, 29CP, cited in Trần and Smith, "Cautious Reformers and Fence Breakers," p. 91. By 1992, the private sector was already vibrant, with over 3,200 small, domestic, private textile and garment factories, established mostly in the South. By 1995, the FDI sector had grown, with fifty joint-ventures (between domestic and foreign partners) and sixty-eight wholly foreign-owned factories in the textile and garment industries, compared to less than ten FDI factories before 1991. Angie Ngọc Trần, "Through the Eye of the Needle: Vietnamese Textile and Garment Industries Rejoining the Global Economy," *Crossroads: An Interdisciplinary Journal of Southeast Asian Studies* 10,2 (1997): 92.

[48] Trần Khánh, *Vai trò Người Hoa trong nền Kinh tế các nước Đông Nam Á* [The Role of the Hoa in the Economies of Southeast Asian Countries] (Hanoi: Viễn Đông Nam Á, 1992), p. 237.

Mutual Economic Assistance's economic aid and Soviet commercial relations with Vietnam. To cope with this loss of trade with the communist bloc, the state attempted to encourage the now-offshore investors by favoring those who claimed to have a Vietnamese identity.

The key determination of which investors would be favored hinged on the citizenship issue: how to define "overseas Vietnamese" (*Người Việt Nam định cư ở nước ngoài*) and Vietnamese origin (*nguồn gốc Việt Nam*). The law defined these vaguely as "Vietnamese nationals and/or having Vietnamese origins, who stay, work, and make a living in other countries for a long time." There is no clear definition or criterion to determine a person's "Vietnamese origin," with respect to whether that individual was born in Vietnam or had resided there for a particular period of time. This vagueness had enabled many state ministries and agencies to have a final say on the decisions about whether certain individuals qualified as "overseas Vietnamese" or as having "Vietnamese origins," a situation that had implications for underground investment.

Financial benefits to "Vietnamese nationals" were generous between 1999 and 2005. In addition to the fact that these investors could offer lower minimum wages to their workers because they were engaged in the domestic sector, the key benefits had to do with land. Land-use fees (*tiền sử dụng đất*) for these new businesses were to be reduced 50 percent for Type A projects (located in urban and suburban areas and involving investments in forestry, physical infrastructure, education, training, health, ethnic cultures, exports, fisheries, scientific research, technology transfer and upgrades, legal counsel, intellectual property rights, and protection of the environment and eco-systems). Land-use fees for Type B initiatives—that is, projects that invested in poor provinces and rural districts in mountainous and remote areas where most ethnic minorities live—were reduced 75 percent. Land taxes could be waived 100 percent or reduced by 50 percent for periods of seven to fifteen years. Moreover, revenue taxes could be waived 100 percent or reduced by as much as 50 percent for several years. Import taxes could be waived for certain products (that were or are not yet produced in Vietnam). Also, the tax on profit repatriation was also very low: 5 percent.[49]

To receive all those privileges enjoyed by the native Vietnamese, one must show proof of having been born in Vietnam or of having lived and worked in Vietnam for a period of time (although no minimum number of years was stated). This stipulation is especially geared at the Hoa, the ethnic Chinese group that has a long history in Vietnam, residing and raising families there, and having the capital to invest in various enterprises. Importantly, one also must obtain a certificate of "*nguồn gốc Việt Nam*" from the Ministry of External Affairs (Bộ Ngoại Vụ) ("external" since this determination involves "external factors" [*yếu tố nước ngoài*]). At least four ministries have gained power in implementing various aspects of this policy: the Ministry of Foreign Relations and the Ministry of External Affairs, which handle paperwork and grant certificates of "Vietnamese origin," the Ministry of Planning

---

[49] *Nghị Định Chính Phủ*, 51/1999/NĐ-CP Ngày 08 Tháng 7 Năm 1999 Quy Định Chi Tiết Thi Hành Luật Khuyến Khích Đầu Tư Trong Nước (Sửa Đổi) Số 03/1998/Qh10 [Prime Minister's Decree 51/1999/NĐ-CP on details on the implementation of the Law to Encourage Domestic Investment (revised)], Section 17 and Appendix A and B, http://thuvienphapluat.vn/van-ban/Dau-tu/Nghi-dinh-51-1999-ND-CP-huong-dan-thi-hanh-Luat-Khuyen-khich-dau-tu-trong-nuoc-sua-doi-so-03-1998-QH10/ 45440/noi-dung.aspx?tab=7, accessed July 2010.

and Investment (MPI) for business licenses, and the Ministry of Justice for overseeing all these transactions.

The requirements that Vietnam fulfilled in order to join the World Trade Organization in 2006 clearly encouraged its bureaucrats and lawmakers to develop a legal framework that would facilitate Vietnam's integration into the global market system. For instance, the Investment Law (*Luật Đầu Tư*) has replaced the Law to Encourage Domestic Investment; it was signed into law in November 2005 and went into effect in July 2006. In thirty-two pages and ten chapters, the law defines all forms of investment (foreign and domestic), responsible parties, and their rights and responsibilities. The law indicates some important tendencies, for instance, that the state would take control in prioritizing large infrastructural projects with foreign partners,[50] paying attention to the rights and responsibilities of investors. The law also attends to workers' rights, by mandating compliance with labor law and the protection of workers' legal rights and benefits, provision of insurance, respect for workers' honor and integrity, and protection of workers' rights to establish and join social political organizations.[51] Furthermore, it requires investors to comply with the laws to protect the environment. Some stipulations in Chapter VI of the Investment Law outline the penalties that will be incurred by investors who violate the law after they receive their business licenses; these penalties include measures such as withdrawing the licenses or terminating the operations of the violators.[52]

Following the trend of centralizing state control, the state introduced another important law in 2005: the Enterprises Law (*Luật Doanh Nghiệp*), which also went into effect in July 2006. This law centralized state control over all types of factory ownership in a market system. It oversaw an expanding private sector and a shrinking state sector. It replaced all previous laws on enterprises, including the 1996 and 2000 Foreign-Direct Investment Law, the 1999 Enterprise Law, and the 2003 State-Owned Enterprises Law. In ninety-one pages, the 2005 Enterprises Law spelled out definitions of the origins of capital (*quốc tịch của doanh nghiệp*); types of ownership, including state-owned enterprises, which include those enterprises for which the state owns more than 50 percent of the legal capital; and guidelines for assessing the value of contributing capital (*tài sản góp vốn*).[53] The law had separate sections to define the rights and responsibilities of all types of enterprises. It stated specifically that within four years of the implementation of this law (by 2009), all state-owned enterprises would have to be transformed to either limited or joint-stock companies.[54] Currently, most private companies are listed as limited companies, whereas most equitized/privatized state enterprises are defined as joint-stock

---

[50] *Luật Đầu Tư* No. 59/2005/QH11, Quốc Hội Nước Cộng Hoà Xã Hội Chủ Nghĩa Việt Nam Khoá XI, kỳ họp thứ 8, November 29, 2005 [Investment Law, Vietnamese Parliament, Session 11, Meeting No. 8], http://thuvienphapluat.vn/van-ban/Doanh-nghiep/Luat-dau-tu-2005-59-2005-QH11/6916/noi-dung.aspx, accessed July 2010, Chapter I, p. 3; Chapter IV, pp. 10–11.

[51] Ibid., Chapter III, pp. 96–97.

[52] Ibid., Chapter VI, pp. 23–24.

[53] *Luật Doanh Nghiệp*, 60/2005/QH11, Quốc Hội Nước Cộng Hoà Xã Hội Chủ Nghĩa Việt Nam, Khoá XI, kỳ họp thứ 8 (Từ ngày 18 tháng 10 đến ngày 29 tháng 11 năm 2005) [Enterprise Law, Parliament Session No. 11, Meeting No. 8], http://thuvienphapluat.vn/van-ban/Doanh-nghiep/Luat-Doanh-nghiep-2005-60-2005-QH11/7019/noi-dung.aspx?tab=7, accessed July 2010, pp. 2-4, 14–15, 89.

[54] Ibid., p. 89.

companies.[55] I will discuss the laws that affect state and migrant workers later. But now, given this legal framework for investment, who are the key investors in the global supply chain?

Capital Owners in the Global Supply Chain, 1986–2012

The influx of foreign capitalist investment into Vietnam creates a dilemma for the state trying to maintain its legitimacy as a government based on a socialist ideology, while integrating into the neoliberal global market system. This ideological split has turned management-labor relations under socialism into competing forces within the government. In this section, I examine different types of capital ownership in contemporary Vietnam, with attention to historical legacies of both socialist and capitalist regimes in Vietnam.

Foreign capitalists saw an opportunity to situate Vietnam in the global supply chain in their "race to the bottom," especially since the *Đổi Mới* market reforms. As the Eastern European communist bloc—the backbone of Vietnam's economic support before *Đổi Mới*—collapsed, many Vietnamese students/researchers and workers in the former Soviet Union and its satellites stayed behind to develop markets in these reemerging European nations.[56] They placed garment orders with producers and subcontractors in Vietnam to cut costs. Moreover, as relations between Vietnam and the United States warmed up, East Asian investors—the wartime allies of the United States—also increased their investment in Vietnam.

I start with some definitions for the statistical data on investment in Vietnam's context. Legal capital (*vốn điều lệ*) is the minimum required level of capital set by the Vietnamese state for projects that investors wish to initiate in a particular sector. Of course, investors can put in more than what is legally required for projects in that sector. Registered capital (*vốn đăng ký*) is a plan or a promise to invest; it has to involve at least the legally required amount of capital, but, in reality, the investment plan does not always come to fruition. Implemented/disbursed capital (*vốn thực hiện/vốn giải ngân*) is the money that is actually disbursed to carry out the proposed investment. Often, there is a gap between registered and disbursed capital.[57] Unfortunately, data for disbursed capital are not always available for analysis.

---

[55] Email correspondence with Lan Hương, September 2008, Ho Chi Minh City.

[56] I conducted a case study on an eastern European network by interviewing two entrepreneurs (on different occasions, from 2002 to 2006): One was an expatriate from the former Soviet Bloc and the other was a local weaver in a HCMC district. In this case, I found harmonious labor–management relations when owners and workers shared the same native place and practiced occupational traditions (for weaving), and when the owners had control over both production and distribution processes with attention to workers' rights. A more in-depth follow-up study on this topic would provide an interesting case on how cultural identities and linkages with local domestic suppliers could result in positive labor–management relations. For an excellent analysis of the expansion and contraction of foreign trade and aid with the Soviet Bloc and the history of Vietnamese guest workers in the former Soviet Union and Eastern Europe, see Melanie Beresford and Đặng Phong, *Economic Transition in Vietnam: Trade and Aid in the Demise of a Centrally Planned Economy* (Cheltenham and Northampton, MA: Edward Elgar, 2000).

[57] There are several reasons that help to explain the gaps between registered and disbursed capital: time is needed to carry out a project, so all funds are not needed up front; bureaucratic agencies demand fees; corruption has been a part of doing business in Vietnam; lastly, there are problems with the FDI owners themselves. Interview with Nguyễn Thùy Hương, Ministry of Planning and Investment, July 2007, Hanoi.

The top three areas of FDI registration in 2009 were in manufacturing (US$2.97 billion in 245 projects), construction (US$487 million in 74 projects), and mining and quarrying (US$397 million in 6 projects).[58] Investment in manufacturing (1988–2008) involved the lowest amount of registered capital, and projects in this sector were lowest in implementation rate: 27 percent. I will return to this point when discussing the "cicada factory" (or the fleeing owners) phenomenon in Vietnam in future chapters.

Through the end of 2008, East Asian investors—such as Taiwan, South Korea, Malaysia, Japan, and Singapore—often topped the list of foreign-direct investors in Vietnam,[59] but this pattern has been changing. In 2009, the United States rose to the top, and the top five countries that had the highest number of FDI licenses granted in Vietnam were: the United States, the Cayman Islands, Samoa, South Korea, and Taiwan.[60] For the first six months of 2012, the top three were: Japan (65 percent of total FDI), British Virgin Islands (7.6 percent), and South Korea (7.5 percent).[61] Still, one has to use caution when considering these statistics, because they may underestimate the real magnitude of investment by failing to account for underground ventures. Interestingly, as of July 2012, the geographical concentration of foreign-direct investment coincides with the hotspots for strikes, with Ho Chi Minh City no longer in the top three. In 2012, the three cities that have seen the most strikes are Bình Dương (accounted for 28 percent), Đồng Nai (14.8 percent) and Hải Phòng (14.6 percent).[62]

---

[58] General Statistics Office, *Statistical Handbook of Vietnam 2009* (Hanoi: Statistical Publishing House, 2010), Table 42, p. 66, http://www.gso.gov.vn/default_en.aspx?tabid=515&idmid=5&ItemID=9633. Meanwhile, in 2009, FDI in health and social work ($8.3 million) and education and training ($28.9 million) were the lowest. See ibid., Table 42, p. 67. Updated FDI statistics for the first six months of 2012 show that manufacturing still tops the list (63 percent, US$4 billion), along with real estate (24.7 percent, US$1.57 billion), and retail sales (3.3 percent, US$207.7 million); this shows how deeply Vietnam has become entrenched in the global economic trends that focus on real estate and consumption. MPI, "Tình hình đầu tư trực tiếp nước ngoài 6 tháng năm 2012" [FDI Status in the First Six Months of 2012], July 2, 2012, http://fia.mpi. gov.vn/News.aspx?ctl=newsdetail&aID=1153, accessed July 2012.

[59] MPI, "Đầu tư trực tiếp nước ngoài vào Việt Nam năm 2009" [Direct Foreign Investment in Vietnam in 2009], http://fia.mpi.gov.vn/Default.aspx?ctl=Article2&TabID=4&mID=265&aID=877, accessed July 2010.

[60] General Statistics Office, *Statistical Handbook of Vietnam 2009*, Table 43, p. 68. According to the Ministry of Planning and Investment, up to October 2007, investments from the United States and Japan have returned to where they left off in the late 1970s, especially in oil, and in high-tech and information technology (IT) industries. United States investment in Vietnam has been increasing, especially via third countries: Intel did not invest directly from the United States, but through Hong Kong. So, if one counts investment from subsidiaries in a third country, the United States' investment would rank fifth (over US$3 billion). Moreover, the rippling effect of the one-billion USD Intel investment in Vietnam has spread to giant multinationals such as Cannon, Panasonic, and Ritech. Other Japanese multinationals have also entered Vietnam: Brothers, Terumo (making medical products), and Robotech. MPI-FDI Department, "20 Năm Đầu tư nước ngoài tại Việt Nam (1988–2007)" [Twenty Years of FDI in Vietnam (1988-2007)], pp. 10–11, http:// fia.mpi.gov.vn/Default.aspx?ctl=Article2&TabID=4&mID=237&aID=507, accessed August 2010. Furthermore, the investment by Intel added to the existing presence of some small-scale multinationals under the leadership of Vietnamese Americans who returned to Vietnam over a decade ago to oversee production. Interview with Jocelyn Tran, October 2003, Ho Chi Minh City.

[61] MPI, "Tình hình đầu tư trực tiếp nước ngoài 6 tháng năm 2012."

[62] Ibid.

In terms of breakdown by type of FDI, most foreign-direct investment continues to be 100 percent foreign-owned, which has been true since the inception of such projects in 1988, when the FDI law went into effect. According to statistics for the first six months of 2012, wholly owned FDI enterprises accounted for 65 percent of total registered capital; joint-ventures constituted 27 percent; the three other types of contracts (including the Build-Operate-Transfer Contract [BOT Contract], the Build-Transfer-Operate Contract [BTO Contract], and the Build-Transfer Contract [BT Contract]), which are signed between the Vietnamese government and investors, made up 3 percent,[63] and other forms of business contract cooperation made up 5 percent of the total.[64]

The many levels of hierarchies in manufacturing and subcontracting evident in the global supply chain, while varying by industry, follow similar structural patterns. Workers are at the bottom of the global supply chain, in both the foreign contract factories and those of Vietnamese subcontractors. At the top of the textile/garment/shoe chains are the corporate buyers, both brand-owned corporations (such as Levi-Strauss or Nike) that market to general retailers, and retailers with lines that are exclusively store-linked (such as Walmart or Payless Shoe Source). These American and European corporate buyers place orders with their suppliers, most likely from East Asia, who have operations in Vietnam.[65]

Most suppliers in Vietnam are in the FDI sector. These enterprises are mostly owned and managed by Taiwanese or South Koreans, who have established long-term relationships with the foreign corporate buyers or brands.[66] They take orders and produce goods according to designs and sizes provided by the brands. These suppliers are medium to large in size, employing from several hundred workers to more than 65,000 workers in Pou Yuen, a Taiwanese-owned Adidas supplier located in Bình Tân, a suburban district in Ho Chi Minh City. This is one of the largest shoe

---

[63] Ibid. The statistical details are in the appendix of this source, however, data are not broken down for each of these three types of contracts, and there are no further details. In general, in a BOT contract, after the project is built, the investor can generate income and profits from this project for a specified period of time. After that term is over, the investor transfers the project to the Vietnamese state. In a BTO contract, after the project is built/completed, the investor transfers it to the state, which then permits the investor to operate the enterprise for a specified period of time to recuperate his or her investment and generate profits. In a BT contract, after the completion of that project, the investor transfers it to the state, which would permit the investor to engage in another project to recuperate his or her investment and generate profits, or the state would pay the investor according to the agreement stipulated in the BT contract. Investment Law, p. 3. On November 27, 2009, the Government issued Decree 108/2009/NĐ-CP governing investment under these forms: BOT Contract, BTO Contract, and BT Contract, http://luatviet.hubpages.com/hub/New-regulation-on-BOT-BTO-and-BT-forms-of-investment, accessed May 2012.

[64] These forms include: financial cooperation contracts, joint-stock companies, and mother-subsidiary contracts. Appendix of MPI, "Tình hình đầu tư trực tiếp nước ngoài 6 tháng năm 2012."

[65] Angie Ngọc Trần, "Corporate Social Responsibility in Socialist Vietnam: Implementation, Challenges, and Local Solutions," in *Labour in Vietnam*, ed. Anita Chan (Singapore: Institute of Southeast Asian Studies, 2011), p. 134.

[66] Hong-Zen Wang and H. H. Michael Hsiao, "Ethnic Resources or Capitalist Logic? Taiwanese Investment and Chinese Temporary Migrants in Vietnam," paper presented at the "Symposium on Experiences and Challenges of Economic Development in Southeast and East Asia," October 17–18, 2000, PROSEA (Program for Southeast Asia Area Studies) and the Institute of Economics, Academia Sinica, Taipei, Taiwan, August 2001, p. 18.

factories in Vietnam and was the site of a strike by thousands of workers in June 2011, as discussed in Chapter 5.[67] As business relationships developed over time, the brands—such as Nike—have been placing orders directly with many large Vietnamese (apparel and footwear) factories, in economic and industrial zones as well as export processing zones throughout Vietnam.[68]

Many Vietnamese subcontractors fill orders for the larger FDI contract factories (or suppliers) in peak seasons to enable the contract factories to meet their delivery schedules. These Vietnamese factories are legal in that they register with the Vietnamese government and pay taxes, but they may not be licensed directly by those foreign brands to produce for them (therefore, they are brand-unlicensed). Hence, these companies may be engaged in labor violations but be invisible to NGO-based or international private monitors (such as the Fair Labor Association [FLA] and Global Standards) that oversee labor standards or establish international codes of conduct for management.[69] Overall, such monitors provide insufficient data as to the extent of violations that actually occur.

Relationships between the suppliers and the brand-name companies are ambiguous, creating a murky situation that each has used to its advantage when deciding to turn a blind eye to workers' requests.[70] On the one hand, most brand-name companies transfer the day-to-day production responsibilities to their suppliers, but they promise that they will fulfill certain ethical obligations—via codes of conduct—in communication with consumers in industrialized countries, and also promise that they can terminate contracts with noncompliant suppliers. On the other hand, most large suppliers/contract factories are themselves multi-national corporations, which, like their corporate buyers, are divorced from the processes that produce their goods, and are interested only in their bottom line.

These global suppliers (or contract factories) can be constrained by their own mother companies (in their home country) or by the brands. They have to consult with the brands for guidance and direction in case of conflict with labor. But they also take advantage of this ambiguity to stall the negotiations; they often cite the need to obtain approvals from their superiors, which could be the brand companies, the supplier's headquarters, or both.[71]

The next set of laws marked one of the blueprints of the neo-liberal agenda in Vietnam: the equitization of state-owned enterprises and implications for state workers.

EQUITIZATION (PRIVATIZATION) LAWS (2002–13)

The state planned to complete the equitization process by 2010, but at the time of writing, the process still had not been completed.[72] According to Prime Minister

---

[67] http://protectvietworkers.wordpress.com/2011/07/12/huge-strike-by-some-90000-pouyen-shoe- workers-some-strike-leaders-arrested/, accessed November 2011.

[68] Nike 2012 Export Factory List, http://nikeinc.com/pages/manufacturing-map (click "View/Export Factory List"), accessed November 3, 2012.

[69] Trần, "Corporate Social Responsibility in Socialist Vietnam," pp. 134, 137.

[70] Ibid., pp. 141–42.

[71] Ibid.

[72] The Ministry of Finance has announced its 2011–15 plan to equitize 899 state enterprises, of which 367 will be equitized by selling shares; the rest (532) are expected to be privatized in

Nguyễn Tấn Dũng, certain industries, such as defense, would remain state owned. State capital had been distributed in three different types of enterprises: joint-stock companies, limited liabilities, including the one-member companies (which could include companies for which the state was the sole owner, with limited liabilities), and joint-ventures (owned by both the state and a private entity). To start the process, the state had to establish the value of its own assets, such as factories and business ventures. This first step has been challenging, and the pace has been slow because it is difficult to establish value for an enterprise that is operating at a loss. In such cases, shares in the assets were sold to workers—presumably at discounted prices—and to the public. State managers and private investors ended up buying most of the workers' shares, which were sold by the workers at low prices because they needed the money. I will return to this "selling young rice" (or short sales) practice in Chapter 4.

The emerging pattern does not benefit workers. Under the new types of ownership, labor protections are diminished, and there is less oversight from the VGCL and the MOLISA following this equitization process. Most state workers are considered "redundant" (*lao động dôi dư*) and are laid-off, while managers have been able to keep their jobs. Overall, the state and the military still control large state-owned enterprises. As of August 2008, the remaining 1,824 state-owned enterprises were in monopolist public utilities and military and defense industries.[73]

The rhetoric used to describe this equitization process sounds benevolent but vague: "rearrangement of SOEs" (*Sắp xếp lại công ty nhà nước*). The Committee to Renew State Enterprises (Ban Đổi Mới Doanh Nghiệp), the state outfit to oversee this operation, includes representatives from state and labor unions. Overall, the committee reflects the state's intentional efforts to strengthen its own legitimacy by using legalistic means to shift to a market economy without incurring too many losses; it has retained the power to sell off unprofitable enterprises while holding control of profitable ones. The trend is to invite more foreign investors to buy shares of these former SOEs-turned-joint-stock companies. Still, the laws are complex and confusing. They consist of two sets: one set applies to the state enterprises themselves;[74] the other concerns the benefits and compensation owed to state

---

various ways, including transfers, sales, bankruptcies, dissolutions, and conversions to limited liability companies. T. Phương, "Sẽ cổ phần hóa 93 doanh nghiệp Nhà nước," [Will Privatize 93 State-Owned Enterprises" (in 2012)], *Người Lao Động*, June 24, 2012, http://nld.com.vn/2012062410   1732603   p0c1014/se-co-phan-hoa-93-doanh-nghiep-nha-nuoc.htm, accessed November 2012.

[73] Lê Đăng Doanh, "Equitization of State-Owned Enterprises: Crucial Test for Vietnam's Reform Process and the Role of SCIC," Institute of Southeast Asian Studies Conference on "Emergence of Vietnam as a Middle Income Country: Opportunities, Constraints, and Regional Implications," Singapore, October 30–31, 2008, p. 7.

[74] Nghị Định 109/2007/NĐ-CP on June 26, 2007, Về Chuyển Doanh Nghiệp 100% Vốn Nhà Nước Thành Công Ty Cổ Phần [Decree 109/2007/NĐ-CP about Transforming 100%-State-Owned Enterprises to Joint-Stock Companies]; Nghị Định 187/2004/NĐ-CP Ngày 16 Tháng 11 Năm 2004 Về Việc Chuyển Công Ty Nhà Nước Thành Công Ty Cổ Phần [Decree on transforming state corporations to joint-stock companies], http://thuvienphapluat.vn/van-ban/Doanh-nghiep/Nghi-dinh-187-2004-ND-CP-chuyen-cong-ty-nha-nuoc-thanh-cong-ty-co-phan/52554/noi-dung.aspx, accessed June 2011; Nghị Định 64/2002/NĐ-CP Ngày 19 Tháng 6 Năm 2002 Về Việc Chuyển Doanh Nghiệp Nhà Nước Thành Công Ty Cổ Phần [Decree on transforming state enterprises to joint-stock companies], http://thuvienphapluat.vn/van-ban/Doanh-nghiep/Nghi-dinh-64-2002-ND-CP-chuyen-doanh-nghiep-nha-nuoc-thanh-cong-ty-co-phan/49622/noi-dung.aspx, accessed June 2011.

workers who are laid-off.[75] MOLISA and the Ministry of Finance are responsible for overseeing the implementation of the whole process.[76]

The state has classified long-time state workers based on several factors: types of labor contract (with or without time limits); retirement age (sixty for men, fifty-five for women); social insurance benefits (old enough to retire but not having enough social insurance coverage to survive); and the award of a one-time severance pay of 5VND million (about US$313, using 16,000VND to US$1).[77] Most state workers were over fifty years old when the enterprises in which they had been employed were privatized, and their chances of getting other jobs were grim. Older workers had different sets of skills than were required by most of today's factories. Younger workers (in particular, females between eighteen and twenty-five) possessed skills that were in general more up-to-date. In 2008, many of the older workers were still waiting for their severance pay and living very hard lives.[78]

In principle, within the first year after being fired or forced to take early retirement (*nghỉ hưu sớm*), the former state workers were entitled to two sources of compensation: the first was from their own state-owned factory, and the second was from the Fund to Assist Redundant Workers (*Quỹ hỗ trợ lao động dôi dư*), jointly managed by the World Bank (and other international donors) and the Ministry of Finance.[79] But compensation for workers whose jobs had been terminated went from bad to worse. Decree 110 (2007) cut compensation to laid-off state workers and put all control into the hands of the remaining state corporations. As of 2012, no more severance payments (of the one-time 5VND million) are offered to newly laid-off workers, and the processes involved in their termination and the provision of unemployment compensation are not overseen by MOLISA. If the local departments of MOLISA (such as Dân's Wages and Salaries office) are not engaged in overseeing and insuring workers' compensation, workers are once again at the mercy of the ebb-and-flow of this equitization process.

Sparse information is available about the status of this process. As of August 2008, 5,041 state enterprises had been "transformed" in various ways. Seventy-five percent of these equitized factories had been local state-owned enterprises, various ministries, and state-owned conglomerates (*Tổng Công Ty*); 15 percent had either

---

[75] These workers were classified as "redundant workers" or "lao động dôi dư." Nghị Định 41/2002/NĐ-CP Về Chính Sách Đối Với Lao Động Dôi Dư Do Sắp Xếp Lại Doanh Nghiệp Nhà Nước [Decree 41/2002/NĐ-CP About Policy for Redundant Workers Due to the Rearrangement of State-Owned Enterprises]; Nghị Định 155/2004/NĐ-CP Sửa Đổi, Bổ Sung Một số Điều Của Nghị Định Số 41/2002/NĐ-CP Ngày 11 Tháng 4 Năm 2002 Của Chính Phủ Về Chính Sách Đối Với Lao Động Dôi Dư Do Sắp Xếp Lại Doanh Nghiệp Nhà Nước [Corrections and Supplements to Decree 41/2002/NĐ-CP about Policy for Redundant Workers Due to the Rearrangement of State-Owned Enterprises]; and Nghị Định 110/2007/NĐ-CP Về Chính Sách Đối Với Người Lao Động Dôi Dư Do Sắp Xếp Lại Công Ty Nhà Nước [Decree 110/2007/NĐ-CP about Policy for Redundant Workers Due to the Rearrangement of State-Owned Companies], accessed June 2011.

[76] Nghị Định 41/2002/NĐ-CP, "Chính Sách Đối Với Lao Động Dôi Dư."

[77] Ibid.

[78] Nam Dương and Phạm Hồ, Người Lao Động, "Mỏi mòn chờ trợ cấp sau cổ phần hóa" [Desperately Waiting for Compensation after Equitization] http://nld.com.vn/239342P1010C1012/moi-mon-cho-tro-cap-sau-co-phan-hoa.htm; September 15, 2008.

[79] Decrees 41, 64, 155, 110, 187, 109.

been dissolved or had declared bankruptcy. The third group comprised state-owned factories that were merged, leased, sold, or handed over without payment.[80]

Vinatex—a state-owned corporation—oversaw 52 textile and 122 garment factories by 1997.[81] The history of Vinatex's management of the textile industry shows tensions between two contending development ideologies. The resolution of these tensions resulted in the ascendancy of garment assembly by low-paid workers for export.[82] This development coincided with a substantial increase in foreign-direct investment in the textile and garment industries, especially in factories that assembled imported inputs into pieces of apparel as part of a multi-level subcontracting system, a system that primarily benefited foreign corporate buyers, while workers received only 4 percent of the total retail price for cutting, making, and packaging garment products.[83]

By the end of 2007, 90 percent of Vinatex member firms had been equitized; presumably, by the end of 2008, shares of the rest should have been sold. Provincial/city people's committees oversaw the equitization of local state-owned textile and garment factories.[84] In 2011, throughout Vietnam, Vinatex was overseeing sixty textile-and-garment equitized members, as well as a training center, industrial and fashion colleges, a trade/export promotion center, a fashion design institute, one medical center, and the Center for Overseas Labor Cooperatio. Although most are joint-stock companies (or joint-ventures), the state maintained control by owning the majority shares of Vinatex's big textile factories, such as Phong Phú (52 percent of its total value), Viet Tien (60 percent of its total value), and countless one-member companies.[85]

---

[80] Lê Đăng Doanh, "Equitization of State-Owned Enterprises," p. 13.

[81] Vinatex.com, 2009, accessed in August 2010.

[82] I argued in another study that to increase value-added and to promote the use of domestically made inputs, the Vietnamese textile and garment industries should develop backward linkages—such as textile and accessories industries and machinery—to provide inputs for and support of garment production. The Vinatex's position was consistent with that argument: it demanded state investment in the textile industry as part of Vietnam's industrial policies back in the late 1990s. Unfortunately, that industrial policy lost state support when the contending development ideology—led by World Bank's affiliated groups—gained influence in Vietnam and argued against backward linkage development on the basis of "lack of comparative advantage" in Vietnam. Melanie Beresford and Angie Ngọc Trần, *Reaching for the Dream: Challenges of Sustainable Development in Vietnam* (Copenhagen: Nordic Institute for Asian Studies Press, 2004), pp. 136, 138–39. In a follow-up study, I found that despite rapid growth in exports, market-oriented integration into the global supply chain limited Vietnam to low value-added activities and exposed firms and consigned workers to volatile fluctuations in demand, thus causing substandard working conditions and a vicious circle of underdevelopment and poverty. See Angie Ngọc Trần, "Vietnamese Textile and Garment Industry in the Global Supply Chain: State Strategies and Workers' Responses," *International Journal of Institutions and Economies* 4,3 (2012): 123–50.

[83] Angie Ngọc Trần, "Global Subcontracting and Women Workers in Comparative Perspective," in *Globalization and Third World Socialism: Cuba and Vietnam*, ed. Claes Brundenius and John Weeks (Houndmills, Basingstoke, Hampshire: Palgrave Macmillan, 2001), p. 220. Angie Ngọc Trần, "Through the Eye of the Needle: Vietnamese Textile and Garment Industries Rejoining the Global Economy," *Crossroads: An Interdisciplinary Journal of Southeast Asian Studies* 10,2 (1997): 92, 98–99, 102.

[84] The list of Vinatex member firms/factories can be found at: http://www.vfabric.com/textile/Vinatexmembers.htm, accessed in January 2012.

[85] Interview with Phạm Minh Hương, August 8, 2011, Ho Chi Minh City.

THE HOUSEHOLD REGISTRATION (*HỘ KHẨU*) POLICY (2005–12)

Hộ khẩu (permanent household registration) law controls and limits migration—primarily from rural to urban areas, driven by the migrant's ambition to live and work at the (usually urban) destination—and dictates conditions that give privileges to urban residents over rural/migrant workers. The Vietnamese state consciously adjusts this policy based on the demand for labor in the export processing zones and industrial zones in and around cities.

A rich literature on the similar Chinese *hukou* system warrants a future comparative study on the impacts of this policy on migrant workers in China and in Vietnam.[86] My findings show that in both cases (*hộ khẩu* and *hukou*), these policies perpetuate local–migrant inequality. Glaring disparities exist between local residents and migrant workers in terms of opportunities for housing, jobs, childcare, utilities, and education for upward mobility. In Vietnam, resources available in a person's birthplace (such as a network of relatives) continue to provide support for those workers who need childcare, either in the cities or back in the hometowns or villages. Local governments and labor unions have gained some flexibility to implement and modify the *hộ khẩu* policy. In particular, intervention by the HCMC Labor Federation and the Ho Chi Minh City utilities company in May 2009 won a case on the workers' behalf; from then on, migrant workers could pay for electricity at the lower local-residents' rates. Findings from this study can serve as a foundation for subsequent studies to compare and contrast the power and flexibility of Vietnamese local governments and labor unions with the power and flexibility of equivalent entities in China.

Under Decree 51-CP-2005, a migrant worker faced many obstacles to obtain a temporary residency permit (KT3), which still granted fewer privileges than those enjoyed by permanent residents. In principle, the residency law (Luật Cư Trú) states that migrant workers have to satisfy only the following conditions: register with the local government within thirty days of arrival and, if renting a room, obtain a rental agreement/documentation from the landlord or owner.[87] Within three working days from the day of receipt of those documents the head of the local security police must issue the KT3 card to the migrant worker, who is then allowed to reside and work at that registered location for an unlimited time. In reality, however, in addition to having to submit a certified rental agreement (as proof of residence), migrant workers must meet two additional conditions that are beyond their control: proof of

---

[86] Since the 1980s, a more flexible Chinese *hukou* policy has been adopted, but it still differentiates opportunity structures for the Chinese population on the basis of spatial hierarchy and foreign capital: urban above rural, well-developed above less-developed cities. It privileges capitalists (such as investors, property buyers) over migrant workers, and urban residents over migrant workers in the two-tiered residential registration system. The so-called temporary residential permit (similar to Vietnam's KT3) is available only to those who have legitimate jobs or businesses in the city. On the other hand, investors in corporate settings in the special economic zones could obtain the blue stamp or blue cards. Tiejun Cheng and Mark Selden, "The Origins and Social Consequences of China's Hukou System," *The China Quarterly* 139 (September 1994): 644–68.

[87] Đỗ Viết Hải, "Điều kiện và thủ tục làm KT3" [Conditions and Procedure to Obtain KT3], June 2, 2012, Đoàn Luật Sư Thành Phố Hà Nội [The Lawyers Syndicate in Hanoi City], http://danluat.thuvienphapluat.vn/dieu-kien-va-thu-tuc-lam-kt3-69863.aspx#190854, accessed November 2012.

stable employment and a long-term labor contract. Consequently, this has created additional barriers for migrant workers and their families to obtain KT3 permits.[88]

Fortunately, signs of some improvement have developed since July 2007. If a worker has a job and owns or rents a place to stay, he or she is granted a temporary permit unrestricted by any time limit. Moreover, a migrant worker no longer needs to have a labor contract to obtain the KT3. With possession of the KT3, a migrant worker can vote and even own a house in the city to which he or she has migrated. In addition, if the person has a specific job skill needed by the city, he or she can obtain permanent residency.[89] However, in reality, migrant workers are too poor to afford private housing and still have to struggle with childcare and rental and utilities costs once they have moved to a city. Regarding these most basic needs, permanent residents still have advantages over KT3 holders, as they are guaranteed spaces in schools for their children and in most cities are charged lower utilities costs.[90]

According to Prime Minister Decision 276/2006, migrant workers can pay the lower electricity rates that local residents pay if four workers—comprising one household—have temporary cards (KT3) and rental contracts of at least twelve months. All four workers have to bring their rental contracts to the office of the people's committee of their ward to complete and sign the paperwork. But these conditions were virtually impossible for a number of migrant workers—especially at the height of the global economic crisis—because most such workers could not afford to take a day off to complete the paperwork and risk losing their meager bonus, which requires perfect attendance. Moreover, according to Huỳnh Trí Dũng (head of the Finance Department of the HCMC Utility Company), to sell electricity directly to workers requires such a policy and coordination among local governments, the Vietnamese Chamber of Commerce, and the district labor unions, a difficult task to accomplish.[91]

In Chapters 5 and 6, I will assess the implementation and the impacts of the *hộ khẩu* policy on migrant workers and their families, focusing on housing, utilities, childcare, and the children's education.

MINIMUM WAGES IN THE FDI AND DOMESTIC SECTORS (2006, 2008–12)

The state legislates two systems of minimum wage in Vietnam: one system applies to all domestic enterprises and public service; the other applies to the foreign-direct investment sector. The state officials have divided the country into zones; each has a different minimum-wage rate. These zones are applicable to both the FDI and the domestic sectors. (These Vietnamese zones are similar to Ong's "zones of development" or "graduated zone of sovereignty," whereby the state creates and controls zones inhabited by different populations that are given different

[88] Interview with Dr. Huỳnh Thị Ngọc Tuyết, Ho Chi Minh City, January 2013.

[89] Correspondence with Lê Định Quy, June 2009, Ho Chi Minh City.

[90] Hoàng Lan, "Người Nước Ngoài Được Cấp Sổ Hồng, Sổ Đỏ Trong 30 Ngày" [Foreign Citizens Can Obtain the Red Cards within Thirty Days], VNExpress.net, June 8, 2009, http://www.vnexpress.net/GL/Kinh-doanh/Bat-Dong-san/2009/06/3BA0FE33/?q=1, accessed June 15, 2009.

[91] Nam Dương and Hồng Đào, "Công Nhân ở Trọ Được Mua Điện Trực Tiếp Của Điện Lực" [Migrant Worker Renters Can Buy Electricity Directly from the Utility Company], *Người Lao Động*, October 9, 2008, http://nld.com.vn/242024P0C1010/cong-nhan-o-tro-duoc-mua-dien-truc-tiep-cua-dien-luc.htm, accessed June 2009.

privileges.[92]) Vietnam's zones are not based on geographical area, but on factory clusters around metropolitan and high-growth areas. Zone 1 includes primarily metropolitan areas: the downtown districts of Hanoi and Ho Chi Minh City; Zone 2 includes semi-metropolitan areas outside of Hanoi and Ho Chi Minh City and other industrial, commercial, or oil-rich cities. The Prime Minister Decree No. 98, effective in January 2010, split the original Zone 3 into two zones: the new Zone 3[93] and Zone 4 (primarily rural and mountainous areas). Dividing the country into four zones like this, the state can dictate higher (zones 1 and 2) and lower (zone 3 and 4) wage rates, thus maintaining a strong hand in governing labor–management relations.

While the zone-based minimum wage differentiation is not the cause of the rural-urban divide in Vietnam, it exacerbates the gap and creates an incentive for (mostly foreign) investors to expand their operations in zones 3 and 4. This differentiation disadvantages rural workers, who have to pay rising costs of living yet receive the lowest pay. Studies have shown that the estimated cost of living in the rural areas has been increasing and catching up with that of the urban areas. The national average monthly income of an urban dweller was about twice that of a rural resident in 2008: 2.1 million VND versus 1.1 million VND.[94] The cost of living in a typical urban area was also about twice (1.94 times) that of a rural area in 2008. However, the cost-of-living gap between urban and rural seems to be getting smaller over time (it was 2.1 times in 2002–04 versus 1.94 in 2008[95]), which means it may be becoming more expensive to live in rural areas than before because minimum wages there are not rising at the same rate as the cost of living.

Public opinion has also supported increasing the minimum wage levels for workers in non-metro and mountainous areas (Zone 3 and 4). In response to a newspaper article published on November 3, 2009, about the 2009 four-tiered minimum wage structure, two readers posted online their criticisms of this minimum wage policy, which they argued would penalize workers in poor areas disproportionately, compared to residents in metropolitan areas. One reader posted a comment on November 3, 2009: "Why are there different minimum wage levels in these four regions, while the prices of electricity, gasoline, rice, and other necessities are equally high in these regions?" The other posted a comment on January 11, 2010: "Why wage differentiation based on regions? It is precisely the mountainous, remote, and poor regions, with higher costs of living than in commercial centers, that

---

[92] Aihwa Ong, *Neoliberalism as Exception: Mutations in Citizenship and Sovereignty* (Durham, NC, and London: Duke University Press, 2006), pp. 7, 78–79.

[93] According to Decree No. 98-2009-NĐ-CP, Zone 3 includes the rest of the districts of the major cities listed in Zone 2, and other cities and provinces. http://thuvienphapluat.vn/van-ban/Doanh-nghiep/Nghi-dinh-98-2009-ND-CP-quy-dinh-muc-luong-toi-thieu-vung-lao-dong-Viet-Nam-lam-viec-cho-doanh-nghiep-co-von-dau-tu-nuoc-ngoai-96929.aspx, accessed November 2009.

[94] Note that the highest average income gap separates residents of the eastern region of the South (Đông Nam Bộ) from residents in the northern mountainous region; those in Đông Nam Bộ earn 2.6 times more than residents in northern mountainous region. General Statistics Office, *Một Số Kết Quả Chủ Yếu Từ Khảo Sát Mức Sống Hộ Dân Cư Năm 2010* [Key Findings from the Vietnam Household Living Standards Survey in 2010 (VHLSS)], June 2011, pp. 2–4, http://www.gso.gov.vn/default_en.aspx?tabid=515&idmid=5&ItemID=12426, accessed July 2011.

[95] Ibid.

suffer from lower minimum wages. Isn't that ironic to [pay] lower wages in mountainous areas?"[96]

Minimum Wage in the FDI Sector

The waves of worker-led–minimum-wage strikes that occurred in late 2005 and early 2006 won a significant victory—a 40 percent increase in the minimum wage in FDI companies. The ensuing systematic annual cost-of-living increases in the minimum wage are applied to both the FDI and the domestic sectors.[97] The strikes took place in the factories of three East Asian shoe and garment suppliers for Nike and Adidas in the Linh Trung I EPZ in Ho Chi Minh City. I will discuss in detail in Chapter 5 how worker-led strikes in a large FDI shoe factory in Ho Chi Minh City sparked this wave of strikes.

The 2006 victory effectively raised the minimum wage in the FDI sector after it had been frozen for seven years (1999–2005) at 625,950VND.[98] This momentum led to more rounds of minimum wage increases and inflation adjustment (in 2006, 2008, 2009, 2011, 2012; see Table 3.1). Since 2009, every November, the state has announced minimum wage increases for both the FDI and domestic sectors that were to take effect on January 1 of the *following* year. In 2011, in response to subsequent workers' struggles for a livable wage, the state put into effect the cost-of-living adjustment three months earlier than in previous years, starting on October 1, 2011 (instead of January 1, 2012), and lasting until December 31, 2012.[99]

Workers not only fought for higher minimum wages and inflation-rate adjustments, but also for the higher payout of social benefits—such as social insurance and health insurance—which are supposed to be calculated on base pay. Thus, the higher the wages now, the higher future retirement and unemployment benefits will be.

The Vietnamese social services system uses a formula that calculates benefits based on wage tables, with steps, scales, and coefficients to reflect different skill levels, experience, and years of service.

The labor press has provided timely, de facto, legal guidelines to facilitate proper implementation of these important minimum-wage laws that affect millions of workers and their families. Regarding the increase in 2011, only seven working days after the announcement of the 2011 minimum-wage increases in both the FDI and domestic private sectors, the *Người Lao Động* newspaper published an important

---

[96] Thái An, "Từ 1-1-2010: Tăng lương tối thiểu nội thành TPHCM và Hà Nội lên 980.000 đồng/tháng" [From January 1, 2010: Raising the Minimum Wage in HCMC and Hanoi to 980,000 VND per Month], *Người Lao Động*, http://nld.com.vn/20091103123525575P0C1002/tu-112010-tang-luong-toi-thieu.htm, November 3, 2009.

[97] Trần, "Alternatives to the 'Race to the Bottom' in Vietnam," p. 437.

[98] Ibid., p. 446. In terms of USD, the minimum wage was actually decreasing from US$45 to less than US$40, from 1996 to 2005.

[99] Nghị định số 70/2011/NĐ-CP của Thủ tướng Chính phủ: Quy Định Mức Lương Tối Thiểu Vùng Đối Với Người Lao Động Làm Việc ở Công Ty, Doanh Nghiệp, Hợp Tác Xã, Tổ Hợp Tác, Trang Trại, Hộ Gia Đình, Cá Nhân Và Các Cơ Quan, Tổ Chức Có Thuê Mướn Lao Động [Decree 70/2011/NĐ-CP: Stipulation on the Regional Minimum Wage For Employees/Workers in Factories, Enterprises, Cooperatives, Cooperative Groups, Farms, Household Units, Individuals and Agencies, Organizations that Hire Workers], http://www.chinhphu.vn/portal/page/portal/chinhphu/hethongvanban?class_id=1&mode=detail&document_id=151322, accessed July 2010.

article to explain the key features of these two new laws. In this article, the head of the Wages and Salaries Department of the HCMC DOLISA, Nguyễn Thị Dân, distinguished between the two effective dates for the minimum wage hike: January 1, 2011, and July 1, 2011. She articulated that *all workers* in the FDI sector would get a raise starting January 1, 2011, and that there would be *another* raise for workers in the four rural districts—Củ Chi, Hóc Môn, Bình Chánh, Nhà Bè (the strike-prone districts bordering the Ho Chi Minh City urban center)—on July 1, 2011.[100]

Table 3.1: Minimum Wage (VND) in the FDI Sector[101]
(Stipulated by Laws for these Zones)

Decrees/Announcements	Zone 1	Zone 2	Zone 3	Zone 4
Decree 03/2006/NĐ-CP (effective February 1, 2006)	870,000	790,000	710,000	Not applicable
Decree 168/2007/NĐ-CP (effective January 2008, as inflation adjustment)	1,000,000	900,000	800,000	Not applicable
January 2009	1.2 million	1 million	920,000	Not applicable
Decree 98-NĐ-CP (effective January 1, 2010)*	1.34 (1.7)* million	1.19 (1.6)* million	1.04 (1.5)* million	1.00 (1.3)* million
Decree 107/2010/NĐ-CP (effective January 1, 2011)	1.55 million	1.35 million	1.17 million	1.10 million
Decree 70/2011/NĐ-CP (effective October 1, 2011, to December 31, 2012)	2.00 million	1.78 million	1.55 million	1.40 million

* The CBA-stipulated wages are in parentheses. This pilot CBA in the Vietnamese Textile and Garment Industry (VTGI) was signed on April 26, 2010.

Zone 1: All districts in the downtown areas of Hanoi and Ho Chi Minh City
Zone 2: Suburbs of Hanoi and Ho Chi Minh City and downtown areas of other key industrial, commercial, or oil-rich cities (such as Hải Phòng, Hạ Long, Vũng Tàu, Đồng Nai and Bình Dương provinces, and Thủ Dầu Một)
Zone 3: Areas defined by Decree 98-NĐ-CP, January 1, 2010 (as explained in the text)
Zone 4: Effective since January 2010 (as explained in the text)

---

[100] Hoàng Hà, "Đồng loạt điều chỉnh lương tối thiểu từ ngày 1-1-2011" [Uniformly Adjusting the Minimum Wage from January 1, 2011], *Người Lao Động*. November 9, 2010, http://nld.com.vn/20101109015453591P0C1010/dong-loat-dieu-chinh-luong-toi-thieu-tu-ngay-112011.htm, accessed November 10, 2010.

[101] Sources: Mai Đức Chính and Nam Dương, *Người Lao Động*, January 25, 2008; *Nam Dương*, "Lương tối thiểu không phải là lương căn bản" [Minimum Wage Is Not a Basic Wage], *Người Lao Động*, January 22, 2008, http://nld.com.vn/213304P1010C1012/luong-toi-thieu-khong-phai-la-luong-can-ban.htm, accessed November 2010; Nguyễn Hữu Vinh, Policy Paper, Harvard Asian Program, Fulbright Vietnam; 98/2009/NĐ-CP, October 30, 2009; Hoàng Hà, "Uniformly Adjusting the Minimum Wage"; http://thuvienphapluat.vn/van-ban/Lao-dong-Tien-luong/70-2011-ND-CP/128163/noi-dung.aspx, accessed August 27, 2011; http://vietnamtextile.org/ChiTietTinTuc.aspx?MaTinTuc =3041&Matheloai=5, accessed August 27, 2011; Jan Jung-Min Sunoo, Chang Hee Lee, and Đỗ Quỳnh Chi, *Vietnam: A Foreign Manager's HR Survival Guide* (Hanoi: International Labour Organization, 2009), p. 36.

This 2011 minimum wage increase in the FDI sector led to 10 percent to 16 percent increases in these four zones, intended to alleviate the deleterious effects of the high inflation that had raised rent and food prices in urban centers like Ho Chi Minh City and hurt, especially, migrant workers.[102]

To what extent do these inflation-adjusted minimum wages provide a livable wage to workers? The answer is not at all: workers, especially migrants, still cannot make ends meet. Given the recent minimum-wage levels, effective from October 2011 to December 2012, while it costs twice as much to live in metropolitan areas (roughly, Zone 1) than in non-metropolitan areas (roughly, Zone 4), the minimum wage in Zone 1 is only 1.4 times that of Zone 4.[103] Worse yet, the costs of living in rural areas have been increasing while the state-sanctioned minimum wage for those areas continues to be low, as discussed earlier.

So, this wage-differential policy demonstrates that the state encourages foreign investment by keeping labor costs low (and *not* commensurate with rising costs of living), especially in rural and mountainous areas. That explains why many EPZs and industrial zones have spread to poorer areas throughout Vietnam.

Minimum Wage in the State and Domestic Private Sectors

The minimum-wage strikes also engendered one positive spillover effect: the state has been forced to reconcile the disparity between the minimum wages in the FDI and those in the domestic sectors (state and nonstate) by 2011, as planned.[104] But according to Michael Karadjis, on average, the majority of workers in the state sector are paid more than that sector's established minimum wage—and their salaries rise at a faster rate than those in the FDI sector—plus these workers receive better social and health benefits, enjoy greater job security, and are not so intensely pressured to maintain a fast production pace.[105]

With mounting pressure from the domestic sectors, the state has been raising the minimum wages for the state and domestic private sectors, effective in May of each year (Table 3.2), thereby closing the wage-disparity gap relative to the FDI sector. Starting on May 1, 2009, the state raised the minimum monthly wage to 650,000 VND (about US$40) for state workers and public servants (including members of the

---

[102] Tùng-Nhàn- Nga-Anh, "Giá tăng, đời sống càng căng," *Người Lao Động*, November 15, 2010, http://nld.com.vn/20101114101649841P0C1010/gia-tang-doi-song-cang-cang.htm. Moreover, another article reported that an average annual inflation rate of 9 percent to 10 percent has also affected the personal income tax: the household tax deduction of 4 million VND per person was grossly inadequate, especially for migrant workers. The tax deduction/exemption should be at least 6–8 million VND per person. Nam Dương, "Khổ Với Thuế Thu Nhập Cá Nhân: Mới ban hành đã lạc hậu" [Suffering with Personal Income Tax: Already Obsolete When First Implemented], *Người Lao Động*, November 4, 2010, http://nld.com.vn/20101103103011314   P0C1010/moi-ban-hanh-da-lac-hau.htm,   accessed November 2010.

[103] These are estimates only because the official indicators of cost-of-living are categorized into six regions, not exactly the four minimum wage zones. These six regions are: Red River delta; northern mountainous; north central and coastal central; central highlands; eastern southern; and Mekong delta. General Statistics Office, *VHLSS*, pp. 2–4.

[104] Jan Jung-Min Sunoo, Chang Hee Lee, and Đỗ Quỳnh Chi, *Vietnam: A Foreign Manager's HR Survival Guide* (Hanoi: International Labour Organization, 2009), pp. 36–37.

[105] Michael Karadjis, "State Enterprise Workers: 'Masters' or 'Commodities'?" in *Labour in Vietnam*, p. 55.

armed forces, state agencies, and sociopolitical organizations). It also raised these workers' pensions and social insurance.[106] On May 1, 2012, the state again raised the minimum monthly wage in the domestic sector, from 830,000 VND to 1,050,000 VND (a 26.5 percent increase), and as of July 1, 2013, will raise it further to 1,150,000 VND.[107] While the government has been carrying out its annual minimum wage increases in the domestic sector, Vietnamese citizens' postings in newspapers' comments section express frustration about the rising cost of living that is outpacing the minimum wage increases, thus making it not a livable wage.[108]

Table 3.2: Minimum Wage (VND) in the Domestic Sector (Stipulated by Laws for these Zones)

Decrees/Announcements	Zone 1	Zone 2	Zone 3	Zone 4
108/2010/NĐ-CP (effective January 1, 2011)	1.35 million	1.20 million	1.05 million	830,000
97/2009/NĐ-CP (effective May 1, 2010)	980,000	880,000	810,000	730,000

Source: Hoàng Hà, November 9, 2010; 97/2009/NĐ-CP

Again, neither the state nor management voluntarily raised the minimum wages. It took workers' direct actions to bring about those changes. I now turn to the overall picture of strikes and the reasons for them.

STRIKES

Nationwide, strike statistics show that reported labor–management conflicts occurred mostly in the foreign-direct investment sector, while increasing in the domestic private sector and diminishing in the state sector since the equitization process went into full swing in 2002 (Figure 3.1, below). Compared to strike agendas in history, modern-day strikes in Vietnam have been mainly worker led and focused on achieving economic justice, not mounted for political reasons (in support of democracy, for example). As we have seen, under French colonial rule in the late 1920s, workers followed a combined *political and economic* strike agenda—for democracy and livelihoods (*dân chủ, dân sinh*)—put forth by the Kinh and the Hoa protestors. Then, in the Republic of Vietnam period (1954–75), as noted in Chapter 2,

[106] Nghị Định Quy Định Mức Lương Tối Thiểu Chung [Decree stipulating the minimum wage (in the state sector)], http://thuvienphapluat.vn/van-ban/Lao-dong-Tien-luong/Nghi-dinh-33-2009-ND-CP-muc-luong-toi-thieu-chung/86858/noi-dung.aspx, accessed June 2011.

[107] T. Hà, "Lương tối thiểu công chức lên 1,05 triệu đồng" [Minimum Wage for Public Servants Increased to 1,05 million VND], *Người Lao Động*, http://nld.com.vn/20111020060747110p0c1002/luong-toi-thieu-cong-chuc-len-105-trieu-dong.htm, October 20, 2011, accessed November 2012; Nguyễn Duy, "Lương tối thiểu chung tăng lên 1.150.000 đồng từ 1-7-2013" [General Minimum Wage (for Domestic Sector) Increased to 1,150,000 VND from July 1, 2013], *Người Lao Động*, http://nld.com.vn/20121031103851629p0c1002/luong-toi-thieu-chung-tang-len-1150000-dong-tu-172013.htm, October 31, 2012, accessed November 2012.

[108] *Người Lao Động*, readers' comments sections, http://nld.com.vn/20111020060747110p0c1002/luong-toi-thieu-cong-chuc-len-105-trieu-dong.htm, October 20, 2011, accessed November 2012; and http://nld.com.vn/20121031103851629p0c1002/luong-toi-thieu-chung-tang-len-1150000-dong-tu-172013.htm, October 31, 2012, accessed November 2012.

strikers adopted a similar, yet more pronounced, combined agenda in the protests sparked by garment workers, leading to the general strike that brought Saigon to a standstill.

On the other hand, the three spikes in labor resistance over the last decade (2006, 2007, and 2008) were primarily motivated by economic causes, regarding minimum-wage and costs-of-living increases. The spike in 2006 was related to the first minimum-wage-strike wave, which forced the state to legislate and FDI factory owners to comply with the 40 percent minimum-wage increase after the minimum wage had been frozen for seven years. The spike in 2007 occurred when workers demanded increases in wages to compensate for spiraling inflation, leading to Prime Minister Decision 168/2007 as an adjustment for inflation, effective in January 2008. The 2008 spike was in reaction to FDI factories refusing to implement the inflation-adjusted decision or failing to implement the adjustment properly. The sharp drop in 2009 in both the FDI and Vietnamese domestic sectors had to do with the global economic crisis. But in 2010, the frequency of strikes went up again in both the FDI and domestic private sectors, and down in the SOE sector (Figure 3.1). The increasing number of strikes in the domestic private sector coincides with the fact that this sector now includes various forms of equitized (former) state enterprises. Former state-owned factory workers tend to be more accustomed to labor rights and entitlements, thus more potentially vocal and active when these rights and benefits are taken away or diminished.

Figure 3.1: Nationwide Strikes by Type of Capital Ownership (1995–2010)

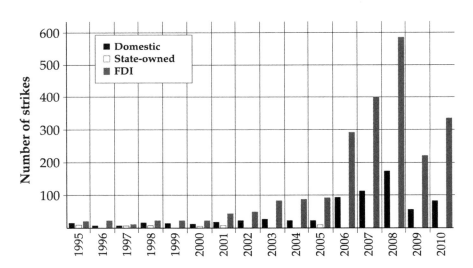

Source: Vietnamese General Confederation of Labor (VGCL), July 2010; Trần Văn Lý (VGCL), October 2011.[109]

---

[109] In 2009, there were 310 strikes reported, of which 239 (77 percent) occurred in FDI factories, 67 (22 percent) in domestic private factories, and 4 (1 percent) in SOEs. Internal report, Vietnamese General Labor Federation of Labor (VGCL), Report on Strikes, July 2010. In 2011, there were 978 strikes nationwide. Nguyễn Quyết, "Giảm đình công, tăng an sinh xã hội" [Reducing Strikes, Increasing Social Security], Người Lao Động, February 22, 2012,

Migrant workers' long hours to meet production quotas meant taking breaks at their machines. (2008, photo courtesy of a Freetrend worker)

According to Trần Văn Lý, since 2008 and 2009, the state and the VGCL have categorized these protests as "work stoppages" not "strikes." The official reason was that most of these protests did not follow the legal strike protocol (which includes a key role for the workplace unions, whose representatives must lead the remediation process, obtain more than 50 percent of workers' agreement to strike, and forward such a decision to the management for remediation, according to Chapter 14 of the Labor Code) and were considered "illegal," or "wildcat strikes." Therefore, the Vietnamese courts have not considered any of the grievances raised with regard to these strikes.[110] Trần Văn Lý further mentioned that the International Labor Organization (ILO) also considers them work stoppages instead of strikes.[111] But I think the unspoken reason for this designation may have to do with the VGCL's ongoing structural weakness—the inability of workplace unions to lead the strikes according to the legal stipulations—and the state's undeterred goal of attracting foreign-direct investment.

---

http://nld.com.vn/20120222095732102p0c1010/giam-dinh-cong-tang-an-sinh-xa-hoi.htm, accessed March 2012.

[110] Correspondence with Trần Văn Lý, July 2010.

[111] The HCMC Labor Federation used the same language in its report on the first six months of 2012. The HCMC Labor Federation, "Báo Cáo: Tình hình công nhân, viên chức, lao động và hoạt động Công đoàn Thành phố 6 tháng đầu năm 2012; Phương hướng hoạt động 6 tháng cuối năm 2012" [Report: Situation of Workers and Public Employees, and Activities of HCMC Labor Federation in the First Six Months of 2012; Directions for Activities in the Last Six Months of 2012], June 25, 2012.

Strikes in Vietnam were largely a consequence of dissatisfaction arising from low wages, long working hours, inadequate overtime compensation, high daily productivity targets, high fines levied as disciplinary actions, inadequate benefits (with regard to social security, health and unemployment insurance, paid leave, meals at work), harmful and dangerous work environments, and inadequate labor contracts.[112] In FDI factories, workers' complaints also concerned physical and verbal abuse by foreign managers and experts. Concrete evidence of the conditions that led to these common reasons for strikes will be offered in subsequent chapters.

Additionally, strikes often occur in the period around Tết, when workers demand the thirteenth-month pay bonus. This common request for a bonus is due to overall low wages and also workers' expectation that they will continue to be offered the entitlement they received under the socialist system. The importance placed on the Tết bonus is rooted in cultural practices and priorities. To be able to afford a bus ticket as soon as they go on sale[113] and to also purchase gifts for their families, workers rely on the Tết bonus (in addition to any accumulated overtime pay earned by working long hours). Workers also need a reasonable amount of time off to travel home for Tết, especially those who live in faraway northern and central regions. Workers told me that, on average, they need at least seven to ten days of vacation in order to take the bus home and return to work.[114] When migrant workers find it difficult or impossible to return home for Tết, they are motivated to rise up to demand these entitlements.

At the time of writing, while wage and wage-related issues continue to be the main causes of most strikes, new issues have begun to emerge that show the inseparability of "rights" and "interests" when wages are insufficient, that is, when workers are not receiving a "living wage."[115] Workers have complained about receiving inadequate benefits (or, sometimes, no benefits at all), such as social security, health and unemployment insurance, and annual sick leave, and they have often called attention to poor working conditions. Increasingly, workers have been complaining about the need to receive a livable/living wage, which is higher than the government-set–minimum-wage levels. Due to overall low wages and high costs of living, workers over the last few years have increasingly demanded more allowances (*trợ cấp*) to enable them to make ends meet. Internally circulated reports from the HCMC Labor Federation in 2010, 2011, and the first six months of 2012, showed that workers spoke repeatedly about "difficult lives" and asked for "improving meals at work, and allowances" in addition to "increasing wages/piece rates." Moreover, two emerging issues at the time of writing are (1) management has failed to raise wages periodically according to the published steps legislating proper

---

[112] Ibid. See also HCMC Labor Federation, "Tình hình Thành phố 6 tháng đầu năm 2012."

[113] Interview with Đường, July 2004, Vũng Tàu.

[114] Interview with Đông from Nam Định (a northern province), August 2002. Interview with Bình from Quảng Nam (a central province), August 2007.

[115] HCMC Labor Federation, cited in Thùy Linh, "Ngập ngừng … tăng lương tối thiểu" [Haltingly … Raising the Minimum Wage], *Người Lao Động*, September 20, 2010, http://nld.com.vn/20100919105149803P1010C1012/ngap-ngung-tang-luong-toi-thieu.htm, accessed September 26, 2010. For more analysis on rights and interests, see Trần, "Alternatives to the 'Race to the Bottom' in Vietnam."

wage increases, registered with the local labor department, and (2) management has failed to deduct personal income tax appropriately.[116]

Management, predictably, has judged these matters from a different perspective. Managers of FDI contract factories (Tier 2) pointed out that they had to come up with "non-wage allowances" to supplement nonlivable wages for workers. The brand-name corporations (Tier 1)—the ones that placed orders with FDI suppliers—have been very savvy about basing the low subcontracting price on a firm legal ground— the government-set–minimum wage—so these corporations tend not to approve "nonwage allowances" for workers, even when those increases account for a very small percentage of the subcontracting price paid to the suppliers.

However, there were some bright spots. Many owners/managers have agreed to add the stipulated raises to the workers' basic salary, which made the raise permanent and meant that workers would get appropriate increases in their benefits.

During the period from 2010 to 2012, strikes spread beyond the textile/garment/footwear industries, although most strikes still took place in these highly labor-intensive factories. Beginning in 2010, more strikes emerged from electronics factories and other industries, and most of them occurred in Japanese electronics factories.[117] Workers complained about: 1) A toxic work environment, 2) management's verbal abuse of Vietnamese workers, 3) interethnic conflict between Japanese bosses and Vietnamese workers, and 4) hard working conditions for pregnant workers. There also have been more strikes in Vietnamese- and American-owned factories during recent years.[118]

Starting in 2010, the VGCL publishes strikes categorized by reasons for the actions. In that year, 111 strikes were related to rights; 81 to interests; and 232 were related to a combination of the two.[119] The fact that relatively more strikes were linked to demands for basic labor rights and interests—wages and nonwage benefits—reveals a continuing problem with management. For the whole country in 2010, for strikes against companies in which managers had not complied with the labor law of Vietnam, 128 of the strikes involved managers from Taiwan, and 109 of the strikes involved managers from Korea.[120] An in-depth analysis of the reasons for these trends follows in Chapter 5.

---

[116] Ibid.; HCMC Labor Federation, "Báo Cáo: Tình hình công nhân, viên chức, lao động và hoạt động Công đoàn Thành phố 6 tháng đầu năm 2012" [Report: Situation of Workers and Public Employees, and Activities of HCMC Labor Federation in the First Six Months of 2012]; *The HCMC Labor Federation Reports on Strikes* in 2010 and 2011. Information about personal income tax deductions was extremely sketchy from the HCMC Labor Federation's report on the first six months of 2012.

[117] Communication with Trần Văn Lý; The VGCL Report on Strikes, 2011; the HCMC Labor Federation Report on Strikes, 2011.

[118] The HCMC Labor Federation Reports on Strikes, 2010 and 2011.

[119] The VGCL Report on Strikes, 2011. These statistics and reports indicate the VGCL's increasing awareness and acknowledgment of the different types of labor grievances and the inseparability of rights and interests, especially when the wages are not livable for most migrant workers.

[120] In 2010 nationwide, there were twenty-six strikes in Japanese factories, and seventy-six broke out in other FDI factories. Ibid.

OVERALL TREND OF STRIKES IN HO CHI MINH CITY

Statistics show that, before 2010, most strikes occurred in Ho Chi Minh City—a hot spot for labor–management conflicts—and Hanoi.[121] However, since that time, strike activity has increased in rural or "growth" areas outside of Ho Chi Minh City and Hanoi, where FDI factories have moved away from the established EPZs and IZs to take advantage of lower minimum wage levels. For instance, strikes spread to Đà Nẵng (central) in 2005, Thăng Long (the North) in 2008, Trà Vinh (the Mekong region) in February 2010, and Thanh Hoá (north central) in October 2010.[122]

Table 3.3: Protests in Ho Chi Minh City (1995 to November 2011) by Type of Capital Ownership

Year	State-owned (%)	Domestic Private (%)	FDI (%)	Total Number of Protests
1995–96	33	44	22	36
1997	15	37	48	46
1998	16	37	47	38
1999	10	65	26	31
2000	15	50	35	34
2001	19	50	31	32
2002	6	56	39	36
2003	2	57	42	60
2004	No SOE	38	62	47
2005	No SOE	38	62	50
2006	6 (7 joint-stocks)	49	45	113
2007	No SOE	40	60	108
2008	1 (2 SOEs)	31	68	200
2009	No SOE	58	42	78
2010	specific data unavailable	specific data unavailable	50	70
2011	specific data unavailable	specific data unavailable	58	189

Sources for Table 3.3: HCMC Labor Federation (1995–July 2010); HCMC Labor Federation (2011), Report on 2011 Labor Union Campaigns and Activities and Roadmap for 2012; Trần Văn Lý (VGCL), October 2011.
Note: All percentages are shares per ownership type relative to the total number of protests in each year.

---

[121] In Ho Chi Minh City, 81 percent in 2008, and, with a lull during the global economic crisis, 68 percent in 2009. Thùy Linh, "Ngập ngừng ... tăng lương tối thiểu."

[122] Dương Minh, "Đình công ... chuyển vùng!" [Strikes ... Changing Places!], *Người Lao Động*, May 30, 2005, http://nld.com.vn/119362P1010C1012/dinh-cong-chuyen-vung.htm, accessed July 10, 2009; N.Quyết, "Vụ đình công kéo dài tại KCN Thăng Long: Lãnh đạo TP Hà Nội đề nghị DN tăng thu nhập cho NLĐ" [Strike Extended at Thăng Long Industrial Zone: Hanoi Leaders Suggested Management to Increase Wages for Workers], *Người Lao Động*, June 12, 2008, http://nld.com.vn/228163P1010C1012/lanh-dao-tp-ha-noi-de-nghi-dn-tang-thu-nhap-cho-nld.htm, accessed July 2009; BBC-Vietnamese section (no author), "Một vạn công nhân đình công ở Trà Vinh," February 2, 2010, http://www.bbc.co.uk/vietnamese/vietnam/2010/02/100202_labour_strike.shtml, accessed November 2, 2010.

Data on protests in Ho Chi Minh City show more conflicts in the domestic-private sector, compared to the shrinking state sector. Protests in the state sector proper decreased after 2001, but reemerged in 2006 in joint-stock companies. Starting with 2007 data, privatized state-owned enterprises have been included in the domestic-private sector statisics (Table 3.3, above).

In 2010, compared with the other two major provinces with many large EPZs and industrial zones, there were fewer strikes in Ho Chi Minh City (67), while Bình Dương province had 127, Đồng Nai had 140, and the rest of the country had 90 strikes.[123] According to the HCMC Labor Federation reports in 2010 and 2011, most strikes in Ho Chi Minh City took place in Taiwanese-owned factories (ten reported cases in 2010 and twenty-seven cases in 2011). Next in line were strikes in Korean- and Japanese-owned factories during these two years. However, increasingly, more strikes in Vietnamese-owned factories than in previous years were recorded by the HCMC Labor Federation (sixteen reported cases in 2011).[124]

As the state increasingly relies on rule of law since its ascension to the WTO in 2006, it has passed new policies that directly affect state-labor-capital relations.

LAWS ON LABOR–MANAGEMENT RELATIONS (2008, 2009, 2010)

As the introduction of more foreign-direct investment companies and the equitization process have undermined the iron-fisted control of the socialist command system, the cracks in the structure have caused the state to act to shore up its own stability. Direct intervention by the VCP—such as Directive 22—and the high-level labor unions (at city and national levels) in labor–management conflicts demonstrate the state's intention to sustain their power and legitimacy, especially when they choose to rule *by* law (arbitrary discretion). Furthermore, new policies have emerged to address one of the most common causes of strike: the lack of social and unemployment insurance protection for workers.

The VCP-Mandated Directive

The VCP-Mandated Directive (*Chỉ Thị*) 22, issued in June 2008 by the Central Committee, demonstrated the Party's control and leadership in all facets of labor–management relations and its intention to cope with rampant "cicada" behaviors—the tendency of certain foreign investors to abandon their factories after they had been operating for a relatively short time—that had been spreading to provinces and rural districts. The top Party leaders showed serious concerns about outbursts of labor unrest, and their directive showed that they planned to make an effort to insure stable labor–management relations. The VCP has been mobilizing all of its apparatuses to participate in this effort, including the Communist Youth group (Đoàn Thanh Niên), the Women's Union (Hội Phụ Nữ), and the media.

The directive also focused directly on the role of the media, to which it devoted a paragraph, stating:

> The media should organize well the propagation of the VCP viewpoints and
> positions on global economic integration and FDI promotion, in order to reflect

---

[123] The VGCL Report on Strikes, 2011.

[124] The HCMC Labor Federation Reports on Strikes, 2010 and 2011.

accurately and objectively the accomplishments, as well as work-in-progress. It should avoid one-sided reporting, which can create disadvantageous reactions in labor relations and public opinions.[125]

Local labor unions and people's committees had been pushing for some strategies to strengthen the workplace labor unions, the weakest link in the VGCL structure. Improving collective bargaining agreements at the factory level was and is seen as crucial. The local state officials—the HCMC People's Committee and the HCMC Labor Federation—understood the tactics of "cicada" factories on the ground and needed pragmatic ways to implement Directive 22. For instance, in June 2008 Madame Huỳnh Thị Nhân—former vice minister of MOLISA, now deputy general secretary of Ho Chi Minh City (a high-ranking Communist Party position)—and Mai Đức Chính (now vice president of the VGCL) initiated the "Four Reals" (*Bốn Thật*) Directive to overcome the union's weaknesses in collective bargaining and to support workplace labor unions.[126]

The Four Reals Directive attempts to address deficiencies at the negotiating table. First, it promotes "real counterparts" (*đối tác*) who can make decisions, not empty promises. Second, it promotes "real negotiations" (*đàm phán*) that are "full, serious, and respectful discussions … Neither side should be a 'rubber stamp' for the other." Third, the document asserts that "real issues" (*nội dung*) are "burning issues for both workers and employers" based on the particular conditions, time, and situation in each factory. Fourth, the "reals" call for "real implementation" (*thi hành*): "Once a CBA is signed, it is a legal business document that should be widely upheld and enforced."[127] Of course, it remains to be seen how these guidelines are implemented, but they seem to address common, exploitative practices of "cicada" factories. I present case studies on these practices in subsequent chapters.

Collective Bargaining Agreements (CBAs)

To counteract management misuse of the labor contract, which was supposed to be signed by the employee upon hiring (although this was not always the case, since management did not consistently offer contracts to new workers) and which could differ from individual to individual and factory to factory, the use of standardized contracts, known as collective bargaining agreements, negotiated for each industry, was proposed. A pilot CBA in the textile and garment industries was signed in April 2010 (Thỏa Ước Lao Động Tập Thể Ngành Dệt May) between Lê Quốc Ân (the president of the Vietnamese Textile/Garment Association-VITAS) and Nguyễn Tùng Vân (the president of VITAS Labor Unions).[128]

---

[125] Ban Bí thư Trung Ương, *Chỉ Thị 22 Về Xây Dựng Quan Hệ Lao Động Hài Hoà, ổn Định, Tiến Bộ Trong Doanh Nghiệp* [Central Committee of the Communist Party of Vietnam, Directive No. 22-CT/TW of the Central Committee of the Party: On the Development of Harmonious, Stable, and Progressive Labor Relations In Enterprises], Hanoi, June 5, 2008, Paragraph No. 7, 2, http://amchamvietnam.com/3451, accessed July 2009.

[126] Personal communications with Journalist B, September 2008; Sunoo et al., *Foreign Manager's HR Survival Guide*, pp. 47–48.

[127] Sunoo et al., *Foreign Manager's HR Survival Guide*, pp. 47–48.

[128] Thanh Vân, "'Mức Sàn' Quyền Lợi Công Nhân Dệt May" [The Floor-level of Garment/Textile Workers' Rights and Interests], *Người Lao Động*, June 24, 2010, http://nld.com.vn/20100623100136446P1010C1012/muc-san-quyen-loi-cong-nhan-det-may.htm;   accessed   July

In principle, the focus in the discussions regarding CBAs has been on the two most contentious areas: *wages* and *benefits*. With respect to wages, this model CBA requested minimum wages higher than the most recent increase in minimum wages: a 27 percent to 44 percent increase in the four zones, based on the respective costs of living in those zones.[129] Moreover, workers could get at least 7 percent more if their work was designated as heavy/hard, dangerous, or toxic. Also, workers who were certified as having completed a vocational class would be entitled to receive at least 10 percent higher than the minimum wage in their zone.

With respect to benefits, the CBA requested three that are commonly offered: an increase in allowances for meals within a shift (each meal should be worth at last VND 5,000 per worker/day) to ensure the provision of meals sufficiently nutritious to help sustain workers' health; the thirteenth-month salary (very important for migrant workers who need money to send home); and other bonuses, such as those given at Tết or for exceptional performance. Of course, there is one important limitation for workers: they cannot go on strike if management upholds the agreed-upon CBA terms. In cases where strikes do break out, both VITAS and its labor unions must send representatives to work with management and relevant state officials to resolve the conflict in a timely manner. However, given the newness of the pilot CBA, it remains to be seen how these terms are actually implemented. At the time of writing, in HCMC, there has been an increase in the number of CBAs signed that offer workers benefits beyond those stipulated by the basic Labor Code. For instance, the District 1 Labor Federation claimed that 51 percent of enterprises in the private sector in its district (452 out of 888) had signed CBAs. Of the signed CBAs, 82.5 percent (373 out of 452) won more benefits for workers than what employers are required to provide by the Labor Code. These extra benefits include: a 40–44 hour work week; three-day parental leave for male workers to help their wives after childbirth; and management's purchase of round-the-clock accident insurance for workers.[130]

"Action Teams" and Direct Intervention in Factory-Level Conflicts

To implement an initiative passed by the Tenth Congress of the VGCL, the VGCL has been allowing high-level union members to intervene directly in the workplace in labor–management conflicts at the factory level, as well as to negotiate and sign CBAs. In such instances, as part of the "action teams" (*đoàn công tác*), the

---

2010. This collaboration involved some conflict and tension, for both the VGCL and the VCCI had questioned whether VITAS and VITAS Labor Unions truly represented management and workers, respectively. Lệ Thủy—Nam Dương, "Quyết Định 1846 Của Bộ LĐ-TB-XH Về Thí Điểm Ký Thỏa Ước Lao Động Tập Thể Ngành Dệt May VN: Quá nhiều sai sót" [Decision 1846 of MOLISA on the Pilot Collective Bargaining Agreement in the Vietnamese Textile and Garment Industries: Too Many Mistakes], February 24, 2009, http://nld.com.vn/2009022401325466 P0C1012/qua-nhieu-sai-sot.htm, accessed July 2009.

[129] The CBA rates for the four zones, in comparison with the respective minimum wages in FDI factories, are: VND 1.7 million per person/month in Zone 1 (27 percent increase from the FDI minimum wage in this zone); VND 1.6 million in Zone 2 (34 percent increase); VND 1.5 million in Zone 3 (44 percent increase), and VND 1.3 million in Zone 4 (30 percent increase). Thanh Vân, "'Mức Sàn' Quyền Lợi Công Nhân Dệt May."

[130] Hồng Đào, "Không có thỏa ước sao chép luật" [There are No CBAs that (just) Copy the Law], *Người Lao Động*, October 31, 2012, http://nld.com.vn/20121031092633689p0c1010/khong-co-thoa-uoc-sao-chep-luat.htm, accessed November 2012.

district or city union officials come to the factories to resolve the unfolding conflict.[131] The team includes representatives from the people's committees, representatives from the appropriate district labor federation,[132] and representatives from the Ho Chi Minh City Labor Federation.[133] The initial results have been mixed. For instance, according to data on protests from the HCMC Labor Federation, in 2009, the action teams were involved directly in twenty cases out of seventy-eight (26 percent). Of the twenty, four cases were related to managers/owners who engaged in "cicada" practices, or who fled Vietnam, completely, or relocated their factories or operations to other locations in Vietnam or remained at large in Vietnam.[134]

During the first six months of 2010, in thirteen out of thirty-five cases (37 percent), those teams came down to negotiate directly with management. Compared to 26 percent in 2009, this shows some growth in their involvement. In particular, these teams achieved some concrete resolutions in nine cases in which management agreed to raise wages as part of the basic salary. In various cases, management agreed to pay wages on time; to compensate overtime work properly; to reduce excessive overtime; to improve the work environment; to allow annual leave; to pay workers for the day or days they spent on strike; to provide some allowances, such as improved meal quality, payment of workers' monthly rental, and some bonus if a a person worked all twenty-six days in a month; and to rehire workers who had lost their jobs due to wrongful layoffs. In one case, management promised to comply with all the requests reiterated by the action team. In four cases, the managers refused to meet with the team, closed down the factory, and delayed making a decision, saying that they were waiting to receive guidance/instructions from their board of directors on production goals (a common excuse, which shows ambiguous relations between brand-name corporations and their local suppliers). In one case, management argued that they could only negotiate with the industrial zone management, and only when that failed would they accept help from the team.[135]

Social Insurance and Unemployment Insurance Policies

Employees' contributions to their social insurance benefits are deducted monthly from their paychecks. Management is supposed to withhold workers' social insurance contributions and also contribute the company's designated share to the city social-insurance office (*sở bảo hiểm xã hội*) for the duration of the workers' employment. In principle, if both sides (labor and management) contributed adequately, workers would be eligible for five types of assistance, depending on that person's circumstance: support during times of illness, maternity benefits, compensation for on-the-job accidents and occupational illnesses, a retirement pension, and death benefits.[136]

---

[131] It would be called: "*Đoàn công tác quận*" in urban areas, and "*Đoàn công tác huyện*" in rural areas.

[132] This is called "*liên đoàn lao động quận/huyện.*"

[133] This is called "*liên đoàn lao động thành phố.*"

[134] The HCMC Labor Federation Report on Strikes, 1995 to July 2010.

[135] Ibid.

[136] Luật Bảo Hiểm Xã Hội [Social Insurance Law], Section 4 and Chapter III, http://thuvienphapluat.vn/van-ban/Bao-hiem/Luat-bao-hiem-xa-hoi-2006-71-2006-QH11-12985.aspx, accessed November 2012.

Yet, often management does not contribute adequately to the state funds. For example, a company may calculate its contributions to the insurance pool based on workers' lower base pay instead of on gross wages, which tend to be higher than base pay because they often include a sizable amount of overtime work, or the company may fail to contribute for the full duration of a particular worker's employment. Strategies such as these frequently deprive workers of adequate social insurance benefits. The city social-insurance office manages this fund and responds to workers' requests for the benefits to which they are entitled when they end their employment, either through job termination or voluntary resignation.[137]

Within the first six months of 2010 in Ho Chi Minh City, about 1.5 million workers participated in the social-insurance program (this level of participation constituted about 40 percent of the goal/plan). About 4.2 million people joined the health insurance plan (a 45 percent increase from the previous period, in 2009). By mid-2010, the HCMC Social Insurance Office had accepted and provided social-insurance benefits for 67,000 workers: a total of about VND 500 billion. However, the real problem remains long-term debts of delinquent factories totaling more than VND 50 billion. To cope with this perennial problem, the HCMC Social Insurance Office and the HCMC Labor Federation intend to expose to the general public the companies that have been past due in their contributions for more than three months. They also plan to file lawsuits against the nine factories the owners of which either fled Vietnam and/or expropriated workers' contributions to the social-insurance fund.[138]

The unemployment insurance policy, started in January 2009, requires that the state contribute 1 percent of the wage funds to match managements' and workers' equivalent contributions. Employees and management have to meet other conditions, too, in order for workers to receive unemployment benefits. Workers must have contributed to the unemployment insurance fund for at least twelve months before they can claim funds for themselves, and they must register for unemployment benefits within seven days of being unemployed. In addition, within a fifteen-day window, employers must show proof of termination of the labor contract and submit (*chốt sổ*) the employee's social security record to show that the employee has contributed to the unemployment insurance fund for at least one year. The policy tries to address one of the most blatant ongoing violations and could provide a long-overdue protection for workers. Starting in January 2010, eligible workers enjoyed some unemployment insurance. At the time of writing, in Ho Chi Minh City, out of 25,000 people who applied for unemployment benefits, only 15,000 people actually received some benefits. For those who applied, the most urgent problem is that most employers are not completing and submitting workers' social security records within the fifteen-day window, so many workers end up disqualified from receiving unemployment insurance benefits.[139]

---

[137] Correspondence with Journalist B, June 2009.

[138] Dương Minh Đức, "Bảo hiểm xã hội TPHCM tiếp tục kiện 9 DN chiếm đoạt tiền" [HCMC Social Insurance Office Continued to Sue the Nine Companies for Expropriating Money], *Lao Động*, June 16, 2010, http://www.laodong.com.vn/Utilities/PrintView.aspx?ID=188410, accessed July 1, 2010.

[139] Correspondence with Journalist B, June 2010, Ho Chi Minh City.

CONCLUSION

The state has used policies and laws to create and govern different categories of labor, but has demonstrated an inability or reluctance to control capital. Various laws successfully pit workers against each other: local resident workers versus migrant workers; laid-off state workers versus workers employed in the domestic private or FDI factories; and FDI workers versus workers in domestic factories. By providing different benefits packages to different types of workers, state apparatuses such as MOLISA, the VGCL, and local people's committees have exerted control over workers, but never completely.

The party-state is not monolithic; internal state contradictions are reflected in conflicts among its apparatuses. Since *Đổi Mới*, such divisions have caused an ebb-and-flow effect on the state's control over capital–labor relations. At the time of writing, these divisions have been revealed, for instance, in the parliamentary debates leading to the delay and the 2012 ratification of the revised Labor Code with its most-anticipated Chapter 14. As revealed in the strike protocols of this revised chapter, the state has implemented more top-down government control through its central labor union (the VGCL), and granted a much weaker role to workers who seek to fight for their rights through independent labor organizing and worker-led "wildcat" strikes.

The VGCL is not monolithic, either, as can be seen by the activities of labor unions at the city and district levels and their alliance with the labor press, such as the *Người Lao Động* and the *Lao Động* newspapers. But the labor press walks a fine line and tends to shift its tone in response to conditions, sometimes championing migrant workers' rights—support from these newspapers was key to the victory of the worker-led minimum wage strikes in 2005–06—but then downplaying labor struggles when the party-state feels threatened by workers' growing strength. As apparatuses of the party-state, both the VGCL and the labor press are still circumscribed by and responsive to the political agendas of the party-state, which, at the time of writing, has acted unambiguously to maintain its strong control over all facets of labor-management relations.

Global players have influenced the party-state's policies in fundamental ways. The ILO and the United States play powerful roles in many facets of labor-management relations (such as drafting and revising of the Labor Code, creating the Center for the Development of Industrial Relations, and implementing state-management-labor dialogues—rather than strikes—to improve their relations). There are also substantial lobbying efforts on behalf of the management interests of both Vietnamese business associations (VITAS and VCCI) and of global capitalists (including the powerful AmCham and the chambers of commerce of the top investors in Vietnam, such as Korea, Taiwan and Japan).

Compared to labor activism in the Republic of Vietnam, workers' agency after 1975 is circumscribed and channeled to secure only basic economic labor rights, not to implement a particular political agenda; before 1975, both of these comprehensive goals were significant factors in guiding and motivating workers' protests. But workers engaged in factories under various types of ownership, since 1975, are not uniformly victimized. They use these very laws to claim their entitlements—as part of the socialist contract with workers—and to fight for their rights and benefits as stipulated in their labor contracts, individually or collectively.

CHAPTER 4

STATE WORKER AGENCY IN STATE-OWNED AND EQUITIZED ENTERPRISES

Many Vietnamese workers grew up listening to socialist propaganda and ideals; no private ownership was allowed, and the state was supposed to manage the means of production (such as labor, factories, land, and other resources). But Vietnam's integration into the global, neoliberal market system necessitated the transformation of state-owned enterprises into enterprises that were, to varying degrees, privately owned. To be sure, the state still controls the economy, although through the use of different means.

The transformation of state-owned enterprises (SOEs) to varying levels of private ownership has used private (including foreign) and state capital to turn these enterprises into joint-stock companies, joint ventures, and one-member companies (the state as the one owner with limited liabilities), starting in 2002. As would be true of private enterprises in a market system, these companies aim to maximize profits. This chapter shows how, in their own words and actions, state workers responded to this transformation, making use of their cultural resources, socialist ideology, historical legacy, and rule of law to fight for their rights as workers in these enterprises that once had been entirely owned by the state but have evolved to become hybrids of a sort.

In these cases, I examine relevant factors of cultural identity and the meaning of class and socialist legacy to state workers. I pay special attention to state workers' knowledge and use of the law in their mobilization in the neoliberal era. Protests in the state sector—broadly defined as consisting of various types of companies with state investment, such as 100-percent state-owned, joint-stock companies, joint-ventures with foreign investors, and one-member companies with the state as the sole owner—exist, but most have not been reported in the state media. This chapter fills in that gap by showing forms or instruments of worker protest in different types of companies under full or partial state ownership.

As explained in Chapter 3, the state began divesting itself of thousands of the factories that it had run for decades. As a result, many state workers lost their jobs and employment benefits. The first phase of state-owned-enterprise (SOE) reform, 1992–2000, resulted in 900,000 state workers being laid off, which reduced the SOE workforce from 2.5 to 1.6 million workers. By 2005, an additional 400,000 workers were laid off.[1] Women accounted for 75 percent of the total number of retrenched

---

[1] Mark Evans and Bùi Đức Hải, "Embedding Neoliberalism through Statecraft: The Case of Market Reform in Vietnam," in *Internalizing Globalization: The Rise of Neoliberalism and the*

workers, and most of these women were low-skill clothing-industry workers with low levels of education. Times were also tough for those workers who were retained or found new work in non-state sectors because, even though post-equitization wages were higher than wages prior to SOE reform, the cost of living was now also higher and still increasing. Consequently, workers' living standards drastically declined. In surveying one hundred equitized SOEs and interviewing the workers in those companies, a study found that more than 50 percent of all retrenched workers had received only half of the compensation due to them. In this sample, for those who found employment after being laid off, most had found new work in low-paying jobs or were self-employed.[2]

In general, those who have been able to find new employment have had to cope with the change in purpose—from serving the people through state factories to serving the bottom line of new corporate owners who place orders with their suppliers in Vietnam (which could be foreign-owned or Vietnamese factories).

For sources of data concerning the condition of workers during this transition, I rely on two internally circulated materials: the HCMC (Ho Chi Minh City) Labor Federation report (1995–2009) and a sampling of thirty-nine worker complaint letters and petitions; some of these complaints had been resolved by the time I reviewed the letters. My focus will be on the state-sector workers in the reports and their protests up to 2011. These are the most recent reports I was able to obtain.

I found that while most complaints by state workers in the broadly defined state sector (as defined above) were generated by those employed in the manufacturing industries, complaints also spread to other sectors of the economy, such as banking, healthcare, education, mechanics, and construction. Manufacturing workers in state-owned factories face labor violations similar to those faced by workers in foreign-direct investment factories (analyzed in Chapter 5) and domestic-private and underground enterprises (explained in Chapter 6) manufacturing for the global supply chains. However, unlike many domestic-private and FDI factories, most state enterprises have contributed adequately to workers' social and health insurance funds.

In 2001, at the beginning of the privatization process, worker complaints focused on basic labor rights that were being ignored by the actors in the global supply chains. These complaints cited lack of work due to reduction in work orders (caused by the global economic crisis); the employer's failure to pay back wages and other basic pay issues (unclear combination of hourly pay and piece rates); excessive overtime work (due to high daily productivity quotas and very low piece rates); substandard work conditions involving poor on-the-job safety, low-quality meals at work with insufficient nutrition to sustain workers, and limited toilet time; the abusive attitudes and actions of foreign experts (verbal and physical abuses); the employer's deduction of the workers' wages if mistakes were made (regardless of who caused them); and labor contract issues regarding apprenticeship pay. Moreover, due to nonlivable wages, workers increasingly relied on overtime work— a common phenomenon in factories producing for the global market—and nonwage allowances to make ends meet; these allowances often took the form of bonuses and meals at work for those workers engaged in overtime work. Employees worked very

---

Decline of National Varieties of Capitalism, ed. Susanne Soederberg, Georg Menz, and Philip Cerny (Hampshire: Palgrave Macmillan, 2006), pp. 230, 233.

[2] Ibid., pp. 233–34.

hard to earn the "hard-working" bonus *(tiền chuyên cần)*, or attendance bonus, given for those who showed up on the job all twenty-six days per month. The attendance bonus was called the Tết bonus, or the thirteenth-month pay, and had been part of the "entitlements" of the socialist era.

Table 4.1. Protests in State-Owned Companies in Ho Chi Minh City (1995–2011)

Year	Total Number of Protests in HCMC (in State and Nonstate Enterprises)	Protests in SOEs in HCMC (as Percentage of Total Number of Protests in HCMC)
1995–96	36	33%
1997	46	15%
1998	38	16%
1999	31	10%
2000	34	15%
2001	32	19%
2002	36	6%
2003	60	2%
2004	47	No SOE protests
2005	50	No SOE protests
2006	113	(6%: joint-stock-owned company protest)
2007	108	No SOE protests
2008	200	1%*
2009	78	No SOE protests
2010	70	No data
2011	189	No data

Sources: HCMC Labor Federation (1995 to July 2010); HCMC Labor Federation (2011), Report on 2011 Labor Union Campaigns and Activities and Roadmap for 2012; Trần Văn Lý, October 2011.

Note: All percentages are the shares of protests in state-owned enterprises relative to all protests in all sectors in Ho Chi Minh City each year.

* Please note that this includes only two SOE protests. These two cases are Việt Thắng Jeans Limited and Industrial Chemicals in the South. I discuss the Việt Thắng Jeans Limited case at the end of this chapter.

Almost one-third of these thirty-nine complaint letters came from workers in equitized SOEs. Reviewing these letters, it becomes clear that many of the workers whose jobs in state-owned factories were terminated—"redundant workers" *(lao động dôi dư)*, as the state euphemistically called them—did not receive severance allowances, overtime pay, unemployment, social insurance, or health benefits. But in letters to the editor, complaints, and newspaper interviews, workers showed how they bonded and what resources they applied to their fight for rights and entitlements.

Table 4.1 shows a declining trend of labor conflict—all forms of protest including strikes—in the state sector from 1995 to 2011. Statistically, the HCMC Labor Federation shows a decrease in protests in SOEs: from 33 percent to 2 percent (these are shares of protests in SOEs as part of the total number of protests in Ho Chi Minh City each year) between 1995 and 2003. Then, after 2003, there were protests in "equitized" or joint-stock companies. This increase corresponded with the implementation of the Equitization Laws, with sections that applied to laid-off state workers taking effect in 2002, 2004, and 2007. In 2006, there were seven strikes in joint-stock companies and, in 2008, two protests in SOEs. There were no reported strikes in SOEs in 2007, 2009, 2010, and 2011. But this does not mean that there were no protests in the state sector; it may mean that protests in the state sector were not reported or that they were reported in internally circulated documents to which I had no access.

However, to see beyond these descriptive statistics, one needs to analyze the qualitative data from the labor press. In a small window of time permitted by the state, the *Người Lao Động* and the *Lao Động* published sharp criticism of how these equitization policies benefited state managers but failed to compensate laid-off state workers. I turn next to the voices of state workers.

State Workers: Local and Migrant Before the Equitization Process

Laborers in state-owned factories used more subtle forms of protest than did workers in open strikes in nonstate sectors. Workers sent petitions and complaint letters to state and union officials at different levels of the bureaucracy and to labor newspapers. These open protest letters—"pen protests"—exposed an increase in labor violations in the 100-percent state-owned enterprises before the equitization process. Even back then, SOEs already served the expanding Vietnamese private-sector manufacturing network for corporate buyers in the global supply chains. First, I present some worker narratives from the North in two letters I received in 1999: one complaint letter and one petition. Then I show findings from my interviews with migrant state workers in the South in 2002.

Pen Protests in State Garment Factories in the North (1999)

In 1999, when the state opened the country further to the capitalist world, manufacturing for the global supply chains, with their low wages and poor working conditions, was already a fact of life. Some state workers in the North—including some from military-owned garment factories (where military uniforms were made, as well as other apparel)—submitted petitions and complaint letters to state institutions as well as state media. These petitions and letters got some attention from the state Labor Union Program–Vietnam TV (Ban Chuyên Mục Công Đoàn-Đài Truyền Hình Việt Nam) and Radio Vietnam. The workers' complaints were not only about the severe treatment of the line leaders toward workers, intensification that could be traced to global production pressures, but the workers also expressed their expectations that the communist cadre plant managers would defend them more effectively and their perception that these managers had failed to stand up for them.

Workers expected their VCP (Vietnamese Communist Party) managers to act consistently with their pro-labor claims. A complaint letter written by a group of workers in the North addressed the VCP members directly. Two themes emerged from this narrative: 1) the expectation that Party members should care about workers' welfare; and 2) the perception that older (female) workers had acted like sisters to younger migrant workers by attempting to protect their rights and benefits as stipulated in the labor contract.

> Most of the female workers were quite young and had little work experience; they came from far away, poor villages such as Thanh Hóa, Hà Giang, and Tuyên Quang. Most just got up to the sixth or seventh grades, hence they were not aware of workers' rights and benefits in terms of a labor contract, health and social insurance, and vacation time. *But the main thing we wanted to mention here is that members in our management are Party members who we thought should be thoughtful and respectful in their communications with us* and should clearly understand our rights stipulated in the Labor Code. But, to the contrary, they did not seem to care about workers' welfare, as long as they could use their power to make sure that workers completely obey them.[3]

As the basis of their reasoning, workers appealed to ideological state apparatuses, whose staff members they expected to enforce the law—the Labor Code. In making this appeal, they complied with the laws and reproduced the socialist ideology, but they did it in pursuit of their own interests and well-being, first and foremost, not those of the party state. They knew their rights and expected to be treated with respect; they pointed out the identity of their immediate supervisors by name, *Đảng viên cộng sản* (Communist Party members), and described how they misused their power to treat workers badly, thus failing in their designated responsibilities.

Military-owned factories that were manufacturing for the global supply chains participated in labor exploitation, too, an ironic development given that the Vietnamese military's implied purpose had been to defend workers.[4] Workers were indignant about the exploitation prevalent as a result of international trade and protested to remind the state and its officials that, according to the social contract that had framed the workers' state in which they grew up, they were not supposed to be treated this way. In the workers' own words, their protests were against labor commodification in subcontract work (a Polanyi-type protest). They expected that the social contract would be respected, especially in military factories, which were supposed to be more attuned to socialist ideology.

The protest of workers employed at a military-uniform garment factory in 1999 demonstrated those sentiments. Twenty-six workers from that state-owned garment factory in Hanoi signed several petitions collectively and sent them to state legal institutions in Hanoi, including Viện Kiểm Sát Nhân Dân (Hanoi People's Oversight Committee), Toà Án Nhân Dân (People's Court), and Cơ Quan Thanh Tra (State Investigation Agency) to expose the excessive pressure that was being imposed on workers by management intent on meeting delivery dates for subcontract work, and the unbearable working conditions, especially during peak season (May to October):

---

[3] My emphasis. From a complaint letter written by some garment workers in the North in 1999 (there is no information on the complete date) that was sent to two state-owned media sources: the Labor Union Program–Vietnam TV and Radio Vietnam.

[4] I thank the participants in the ARI (Asia Research Institute) Vietnam Workshop, October 2008, who raised inquiries about the meaning of protests in military-owned factories. Angie Ngọc Trần, presentation, "Mobilized Workers vs. Morphing Capital: Unlocking the Global Supply Chain in Vietnam," at ARI, National University of Singapore, October 17, 2008.

We have worked continuously from May 15, 1999, to the present [Note: the letter is dated July 6, 1999, so they worked seven weeks straight with continuous overtime] without any Sunday off for sixteen hours per day, from 6:30 AM to 10:30 PM. This strenuous workload was precisely the reason why many workers couldn't stand it any longer; many passed out right at their sewing machines. Working at the machine every hour and every minute for such long hours, for sure the quality of finished garment products off the assembly line did not always meet the management's expectations. So at that time, the management verbally abused and hurt the integrity of workers. For example, *Ms. HTH, the manager of Factory Number 4 and a Party member, considered us "uneducated" folks*; she often shouted at us when we made mistakes and temporarily kicked us out of the factory [as a form of discipline]. There are many other forms of repression that we can't recount here. And our [workplace] labor union representatives also acquiesced like the rest of us![5]

The sentiments expressed in this correspondence show that these state workers expected Communist Party managers to respect them and to behave virtuously in accord with socialist ideals. Melinda Tria Kerkvliet encountered the same kinds of reactions and expectations when interviewing retired workers in a state-owned Hanoi tobacco factory in 1997. She found that workers did want to preserve the idealistic image of their virtuous factory and union leaders, and they expected to be shown respect as workers in return.[6]

More than a year after the petition, in November 2000, this very same state garment company was awarded three prestigious national awards, including the "Heroes of the People's Army Award" (*Anh hùng lực lượng võ trang nhân dân*) for "ensuring order, safety, and political security in the factory premise."[7] The other awards were for economic performance (production, export, quality) and social achievement (population control/family planning). These awards failed to acknowledge the extent to which the workers' social contract with the state had been violated and superseded by a labor contract with the exploitative global supply chains.

Migrant State Workers in the Việt Thắng Factory in the South (2002)

What is the meaning of "native place" for migrant workers who worked in a large state textile combine in the South? I focus on Việt Thắng Textile combine in Thủ Đức District in the northeast of Ho Chi Minh City, which employed about 4,500 workers, most of whom were women. In August 2002, I interviewed two migrant

---

[5] My emphasis. A petition letter, signed on July 6, 1999, by twenty-six workers in a state-owned garment factory in the North, was sent to the Labor Union Program–Vietnam TV and Radio Vietnam.

[6] Other themes in her paper include: 1) the factory's responsibility toward workers concerning housing, childcare, children's schooling, healthcare, and subsidized meals; 2) the workers' conviction that unions must truly protect their interests because union representatives were workers themselves; and 3) recognition of complex working-class relations and the need to balance harmonious relationships among workers. Melinda Tria Kerkvliet, "Life Stories of Retired Workers In Hanoi," proceeding for the EUROVIET III Bi-Annual Conference, July 2–4, 1997, Amsterdam.

[7] n.a., *Tạp Chí Công Nghiệp Việt Nam* 23 (2000): 4.

women workers in this factory: Mai from a Nam Định village (in the North; her husband also came from the North) and Loan from Trà Vinh (a Mekong Delta province in the South).

In this factory, Mai was part of the 15 to 20 percent of the workforce that migrated from the North, most of whom were from rural provinces; the rest of the workforce comprised local workers and migrants from the nearby Mekong Delta provinces.

At the time of the interview, Mai had already worked for twenty-two years at Dệt Việt Thắng (since 1980) after being trained as a fiber technician at the Nam Định textile vocational school. She supervised fifty to sixty workers in her unit within an eight-hundred-worker fiber division in Việt Thắng. I talked with her in her spacious and well-ventilated housing unit (sixty square meters), allocated by factory management. Although by this time the socialist subsidy era of the mid-1980s had passed, the government still subsidized part of housing expenses for workers. So, Mai had to pay only for her utilities. She told me:

> I met my husband here at Dệt Việt Thắng, working in the same fiber division. He is from Hải Phòng and was trained at Bách Khoa University in Hanoi [Note: This was (and is) the most prestigious polytechnic university in the country, training engineers, professors, and other professionals]. He worked in the machinery-repair section. We got married and have two children. Our daughter was born in 1982 and our son in 1984.[8]

The state provided technical training and sent workers—women and men—to their job destinations. Once they had reached their destinations, these migrant workers divided work among themselves just as they learned to do in school in the North:

> Most workers in my unit were women. Our jobs were to spread the raw cotton, compress/graft it, and spin it onto spindles. We three women from Nam Định took care of these three tasks. We were trained in the same technical school in Nam Định, and are of the same age group, so we get along very well [*cánh mình làm việc thuận lợi lắm*]. After being trained in that school, we worked together when we arrived here. One woman spread the cotton; I grafted it; and the other woman spun it. Three women, three stages, the tasks are considered done! Also, the factory management was very supportive: They gave the three of us full authority to design and operate these three tasks.[9]

Cultural identity bonding—being women and coming from the same hometown—smoothed their working conditions. Mai happily shared how she met her female classmates:

> I was only twenty when I went to the South. I was very nervous because I did not know anyone in the South. My classmates went back to their villages for summer break after we were done with our classes. Then individually we went back to school to find out where we were being sent to work. [Note: The state policy at the time was to train technicians; after the training, they were assigned

---

[8] Interview with Mai, August 2002, Thủ Đức District, Ho Chi Minh City.
[9] Ibid.

to work in various factories according to the needs at that time]. Then several days after I arrived here, I was so surprised and very happy to see my two classmates [who also just arrived] because we studied together in Nam Định and now worked together here. That is a big advantage [*thuận lợi lắm*].[10]

At the beginning, there were some tensions between migrant workers from the North and their fellow workers from the South. Most of these tensions were due to different cultural practices and inaccurate perceptions and stereotypes, such as that Southern workers are lazy and Northern workers are stingy. But as these women worked side-by-side and socialized with each other, they came to tolerate their differences and learned to respect each other's cultural practices. Mai said:

> I think that at the beginning there were some tensions. But gradually as we focused on our work, we did not interfere with each other's way of life [*không va chạm*], so we can moderate [*dung hòa*] our positions. At first we did not understand each other [our ways of life], but as we worked together for some time, we began to understand each other more and feel closer to each other [*gần gũi*].[11]

I witnessed a sense of togetherness among these migrant workers, although they had originated from different native places. When I talked to Mai, Loan—a migrant worker from a southern province who lived in a nearby factory housing unit—was listening in on our conversation. She was a friendly neighbor of Mai's and often came over for a visit in the evening. She was happy to talk to me as soon as I finished my conversation with Mai. Loan did not see conflicts among migrant workers in her garment factory and said matter-of-factly: "I have not seen any conflicts between migrant workers from the North and from the South. In this factory of over four hundred workers working in nine assembly lines, I have not seen any protests or strikes yet."

I found out that Loan had been working in the Việt Thắng garment factory (another unit of the Việt Thắng combine) for over a year at the time of our interview. She assembled kimonos for a Japanese corporate buyer and jeans for an American buyer; both buyers supplied their own fabrics and accessories to be assembled by Vietnamese workers.

Workers tend to pool resources and rely on kinship to cope with difficulties while living away from home. Loan said:

> I am from Trà Vinh [a coastal province in the Mekong Delta region, about two hundred kilometers from Ho Chi Minh City]. I only studied up to the ninth grade because my family is poor. My sister is also working in this garment factory. My aunt owns a house near here, and she only works around the house. But we do not stay with her because we want to be close to the factory, so the two of us rent a unit here.[12]

---

[10] Ibid.

[11] Ibid.

[12] Interview with Loan, August 2002, Thủ Đức District, Ho Chi Minh City.

Migrant workers perceive that employment in a factory away from home is only temporary; most expect to return home with money saved for their parents and for their future plans back in their hometowns, not in big cities. Loan shared:

> I only want to try it out here for several years, and will come home to be with my mother because she is home alone. Plus, we have a fruit orchard—*nhãn* [longan] and *na* [a type of custard apple]—so I need to come home to help my mother harvest the fruits. For now, I've been saving up and am sending money home for my mother during national holidays. I plan to open a tailoring shop at home.

Evidence shows that native place and gender gave these migrant workers some comfort and made their work life tolerable and even fun at times. But how did workers fare in joint-stock companies or former state-owned enterprises in the equitization process?

EQUITIZATION POLICIES AND IMPACTS ON WORKERS (AFTER 2002)

Not much has been written about the implementation and impact of the equitization process. I focus on the works of several scholars, internally circulated reports, newspaper accounts, and workers' narratives to investigate how this process affects laid-off state workers.

The state had missed several deadlines to complete the equitization process of all state-owned enterprises, first, in 2005 and then again in July 2010. "No, they—once again—did not meet the deadline of July 2010 to reform and equitize the remaining SOEs. They simply [turned] them into companies with limited liabilities with one owner as the state."[13] This means that the state has to sustain 100 percent of the equity in the many companies that were not transformed into jointly owned enterprises.[14] In such a situation, there is no real change in state ownership.

Workers were classified according to four categories—retained, retrained, redundant, and those bound for early retirement. Different entitlements were associated with each category. Other factors in this classification scheme included types of labor contract (temporary or permanent); retirement age (sixty for men; fifty-five for women); and social insurance coverage based on age. As of 2008, about 240,000 redundant (laid off) state workers received some compensation.[15] Almost half a million (428,000) in 1,340 equitized SOEs in fifty-three provinces could buy preferential shares (explained below).[16] But this "redundant" classification was detrimental to state workers; in many cases, these state workers who had been dismissed from their jobs needed retraining to gain the skills needed to produce for the global supply chains, as in any restructuring economy.

According to Decree 41, within the first year after employees are laid-off or forced into early retirement (*nghỉ hưu sớm*), they are entitled to receive a one-time

[13] Correspondence with Lê Đăng Doanh, July 4, 2010.

[14] Lê Đăng Doanh, "Equitization of State-Owned Enterprises: Crucial Test for Vietnam's Reform Process and the Role of SCIC," paper presented at the Institute of Southeast Asian Studies conference on "The Emergence of Vietnam as a Middle Income Country: Opportunities, Constraints, and Regional Implications," October 30–31, 2008, p. 4.

[15] An exact number of laid-off state workers is unavailable; *Lê Đăng Doanh*, p. 7.

[16] Ibid., p. 11.

severance payment of up to VND 5 million (about US$313).[17] But there were delays in determining the status of many state workers who lost their jobs, as well as delays in the equitization process itself, that lasted far past the first year following an employee's dismissal from his or her job; as a result, many workers never received their severance pay. There were some key reasons for the delays in the process of evaluating each state-owned company slated for equitization.[18] First, this process was complex and lengthy: on average, a state-owned enterprise needed 270 to 330 working days for the equitization process. The state managers needed to evaluate the assets of each SOE, the value of the land, the value of its trademark, and the amount of outstanding debts. Furthermore, many of these state managers did not have incentives to abandon the privileges they had been enjoying in the SOEs. And since most of the listed SOEs in the securities market in Vietnam had been showing big losses, the managers delayed the process of restructuring these SOEs. Moreover, the delay was also due to state managers' failure to take into account a sufficient market value for the land and land-use rights in their evaluations of SOEs. This led to tremendous losses for the state and, significantly, for state workers, since a high percentage of state shares was sold to private investors, not workers. There were cases in which the new private owners of property formerly owned by the state then used part of the spacious leased land to operate in real estate.[19]

Workers were disadvantaged by this whole process. Ideologically, the state promoted the idea that workers be co-owners of the enterprises at which they had been working almost all their lives. In principle, they were supposed to get low-interest rate credit provided by state-owned commercial banks for five years. However, this was not the case in practice, a fact that was exposed by the newspapers discussed below. So, on average, workers owned only 11 to 15 percent of the total shares in most equitized SOEs, because they did not have much money to buy shares. So, as minority shareholders, they did not have much influence on the decision-making process. Worse yet, in 2007, the price of shares in the securities market was about 300 to 500 percent higher than their nominal value; thus, most workers could not buy their entitled shares. Moreover, to cope with high inflation, many workers exercised "short sales" of their shares. According to a survey by the VGCL (Vietnamese General Confederation of Labor), about 17 percent of workers had sold their shares to private investors (60,331 out of 356,648), leading to private investors reaching the status of majority shareholders.[20] We will revisit this issue from the labor union's perspective.

Compensation for laid-off workers has gone from bad to worse over time. In 2007, Decree 110 cut compensation to laid-off state workers and put all the control in the hands of state corporations. Since 2007, there is no more severance pay (VND 5 million) and no oversight from MOLISA (Ministry of Labor, Invalids, and Social Affairs). Without MOLISA's central regulation on workers' compensation, workers are once again at the mercy of the ebb and flow of this process. But the labor press rushed to the rescue.

---

[17] Back in 2002, this money came from two sources: workers' state factories and the Fund to Assist Redundant Workers (Quỹ Hỗ Trợ Lao Động Dôi Dư) jointly managed by the World Bank (and other international donors) and the Ministry of Finance (Decrees 41, 109, 110, 155).

[18] Lê Đăng Doanh, "Equitization of State-Owned Enterprises," pp. 3, 6.

[19] Ibid., pp. 9–10.

[20] Ibid., pp. 11–12.

Labor Newspapers' Coverage and Labor Unions' Response

The labor press has sought to expose the plight of workers by reporting on their protests and critiquing the social consequences of equitization laws in order to protect laid-off state employees. Both the *Người Lao Động* and the *Lao Động* newspapers have been very critical of these problems and brought them to public awareness. In 2007, the *Người Lao Động* published a series of four articles entitled "Cổ Phần Hóa: Đừng Để Người Lao Động Trắng Tay" (Equitization: Do Not Leave Workers Empty-Handed). These articles were critical of the social consequences of equitization laws, which gave rise to forced retirement, vulnerability on the part of laid-off state workers, and the unequal benefits that accrued to the new owners of these equitized enterprises, most of whom were state managers. Moreover, these articles also tried to influence legislation to ensure that new laws (being drafted then) would respect and protect the rights of workers dismissed from companies that had formerly been state-owned enterprises.[21]

In 2008, some journalists investigated how laid-off state workers had been languishing, waiting for their severance pay and living very hard lives.[22] Most former state workers were over fifty years old; their chances of getting other jobs were grim, since they had been trained in sets of skills while working under the socialist production system that were no longer relevant or useful in the new factories. Now, modern-day subcontracting factories require new sets of skills (although low skills are sufficient for mostly assembly work); most prefer and hire young workers—especially females between the ages of eighteen and twenty-five—who can withstand fluctuating job availabilities and handle overtime pressure in peak seasons to produce for the global supply chains.

These investigative reports detail those workers' situations: 374 laid-off workers from Nam Á Shoe joint-stock company in Phú Nhuận district had been waiting from 2004 to the time the article was published, in 2008, for their one-time severance pay (about VND 2.4 million per person, or about US$160, which was only half of the original $313) from the Fund to Assist Redundant Workers (managed by the Ministry of Finance). Worse yet, at the time the article was published, 124 workers from Leather Garment 30-4 joint-stock company had been waiting since 2002 to receive that payment. According to a worker from Leather Garment 30-4 who had been laid

---

[21] Phạm Hồ and Nam Dương, "Cổ phần hóa: Đừng để người lao động trắng tay/Nước lên thuyền lên" [Equitizing State Enterprises: Do not Leave Workers Empty-handed/Rising Water Raises all Boats], *Người Lao Động*, http://www.nld.com.vn/tintuc/cong-doan/184129.asp, March 26, 2007; Phạm Hồ and Nam Dương, "Cổ phần hóa: Đừng để người lao động trắng tay/Mặt trái cổ phần hóa" [Equitizing State Enterprises: Do not Leave Workers Empty-handed/The Negative Side of Equitization], *Người Lao Động*, http://www.nld.com.vn/tools/print.asp?news_id=184345, March 29, 2007; Lệ Thủy, "Cổ Phần Hóa Doanh Nghiệp: Đừng Để Người Lao Động Trắng Tay: Yếu tố bền vững trong chính sách lao động bị xem nhẹ" [Equitizing State Enterprises: Do not Leave Workers Empty-handed/Sustainable Aspect in Labor Policy has been Ignored], *Người Lao Động*, April 2, 2007, http://nld.com.vn/184870P0C1010/yeu-to-ben-vung-trong-chinh-sach-lao-dong-bi-xem-nhe.htm; Nguyễn Quyết, "Cổ phần hóa doanh nghiệp: Đừng để người lao động trắng tay/Bán cổ phần là tăng nguy cơ mất việc!" [Equitizing State Enterprises: Do not Leave Workers Empty-handed/Selling Shares Leads to Losing Jobs], *Người Lao Động*, http://www.nld.com.vn/tools/print.asp?news_id=185087, April 5, 2007.

[22] Nam Dương and Phạm Hồ, "Mỏi Mòn Chờ Trợ Cấp Sau Cổ Phần Hóa" [Desperately Waiting For Compensation after Equitization], http://nld.com.vn/239342P1010C1012/moi-mon-cho-tro-cap-sau-co-phan-hoa.htm, September 15, 2008.

off in 2004 and only received half of the one-time severance pay that was due, the remaining 50 percent of the payment proved to be elusive and kept getting even smaller due to the rising cost of living in the big cities: "Compared to 2004, this amount became much smaller. Perhaps to other people, the amount of VND 1.2 million [was] not big. But to us, those who no longer [had] any steady income: This amount [was] not small." On the other hand, one of the personnel managers of this company lamented that, "Many times when laid-off workers complained to us, we had to remain silent because we ourselves [didn't] even know when we would receive money from the Fund to Assist Redundant Workers to pay them."[23]

Most of these state workers were local people, and they had worked for those state-owned enterprises for many years (some had been employed by the same company for more than twenty years). At the time of the article, in 2008, many workers had waited from four to six years but still had not received their severance pay in full.[24] They suffered when responsibility for their compensation, and blame for failure to deliver it, were shifted from factory management to state management.

The newspapers also exposed how workers engaged in the "short sale" of their shares, or *"bán lúa non"* (selling young rice), phenomenon. After purchasing the shares on credit with high interest rates, most workers succumbed to the pressure—imposed either by other powerful shareholders or by the simple necessity to survive—to sell their shares at low prices to both private investors and state managers.[25] The state continues to exert strong control over these privatized SOEs: in 2008, the state's shares in many equitized SOEs remained very high, in part because of an unspoken rule that "the state's share of capital has to be 51 percent [of the total project]," which would maintain state control over the respective enterprises.[26]

Đặng Ngọc Tùng, the president of the VGCL, recognized the consequences of this infamous "selling young rice" problem:

> As of now, many SOEs—with advantages in location, land, and facilities—have been able to raise their share prices tremendously when they went public in the open stock market. Consequently, while workers were able to buy shares at lower prices, either they had no money to buy those shares or had to "sell young rice" to those big investors, including state owners/managers. Therefore, after the shares were listed on the open stock market, a few people had become billionaires while the majority of poor workers remained poor.[27]

---

[23] Ibid.

[24] Ibid.

[25] Lệ Thủy, "Yếu tố bền vững trong chính sách lao động bị xem nhẹ"; Lê Đăng Doanh, "Equitization of State-Owned Enterprises," p. 12.

[26] Lê Đăng Doanh, "Equitization of State-Owned Enterprises," p. 8; and Ngọc Lan, "Cổ phần hóa DNNN vẫn lúng túng" [Equitized state-owned enterprises still stuck in a quagmire], *Saigon Times*, July 14, 2008, http://www.thesaigontimes.vn/Home/doanhnghiep/phapluat/7469/.

[27] Đặng Ngọc Tùng, cited in Lệ Thủy, "Yếu tố bền vững trong chính sách lao động bị xem nhẹ."

An enterprise-level labor-union leader (on left, in white short-sleeve shirt) of an equitized cotton/textile company led this protest. The strike message on the left banner reads: "Request the management board to restore production according to the resolution of Workers' Congress on February 19, 2009." The strike message on the right reads: "Request that Mr. Tạ Xuân Thọ [the former director of this company] pay back wages to the workers from August 2008 to the present." (Photo by journalist Trần Nam Dương, March 3, 2009, then with *Người Lao Động*)

The labor unions have also been advocating on behalf of state workers, but their influence has been limited. In 2005, during a global labor union conference in Vietnam, some Vietnamese enterprise-level labor union chairpersons in equitized SOEs in the North openly alerted the top leaders of the VGCL to the diminishing role of Vietnamese workplace labor unions in these joint-stock companies in the post-equitization era, *"hậu cổ phần hóa."*[28] In frank language, they offered several valuable insights. First, the workplace labor unions can no longer participate in the decision-making process in production and profit-sharing schemes in ways they did before. Second, the workers' congress (*đại hội công nhân viên chức* or *hội nghị công nhân lao động*), in which workers can participate in decision-making processes concerned with production and profit-sharing, was eliminated by the equitization process in most cases. Third, most cash-rich investors, mostly state managers, were able to buy more shares and, thus, served on the respective boards of directors, accentuating the deep divide between owners and laborers. These patterns are consistent with Lê's finding: Not only did the state fail to empower state workers as co-owners, but the voices of workers became weaker over time. Fourth, given these conditions, the state should legislate policy to distinguish boards of directors from chief executive officers, because most of those directors had their own private factories and would tend to

---

[28] Quang Chính, "Hậu cổ phần hoá các doanh nghiệp nhà nước: Vai trò công đoàn dần bị vô hiệu hoá" [Post-Equitization of state-owned enterprises: The role of labor unions became ineffective], *Lao Động*, November 12, 2005 (no URL for this article).

secure the best contract orders for their own enterprises, leaving the "crumbs" for the joint-stock companies.[29]

But most workers did not play the role of victim. I now turn to workers' voices, which demonstrate their knowledge of the complex equitization laws they cited to claim their rights and entitlements.

Workers at an equitized bio-chemical company protesting against the decision made at the mother company (Vietnam National Chemical Group) to stop production meet with the Department of Labor, Invalids, and Social Affairs head of District 9, HCMC. (Photo by Trần Nam Dương, October 5, 2010, then with *Người Lao Động*)

STATE WORKERS IN EQUITIZED, JOINT-STOCK COMPANIES

State workers' loss of employment was the key human consequence of the equitization process. Most redundant workers did not receive the one-time severance payment due to them upon dismissal. Some workers even complained about being coerced into resigning with and releasing the state enterprise where they had been employed of any claims before they could receive any financial assistance.[30]

"Workers were uncertain about their future" is the common theme I heard from various sources. This sense of uncertainty is echoed in FDI- and domestic-private factories. Workers were in the dark about the likelihood that they might be laid off and how that would affect their livelihoods; they did not know whether their factories were to be closed, relocated, privatized, or merged with other "equitized"

---

[29] Lê Đăng Doanh, "Equitization of State-Owned Enterprises," pp. 14–15; Phạm Hồ and Nam Dương, "Mặt trái cổ phần hóa"; T. Hà, "Các DN sau cổ phần hóa đều phát triển tốt" [After equitization, enterprises progressed well], http://nld.com.vn/111992P0C1002/cac-dn-sau-co-phan-hoa-deu-phat-trien-tot.htm, February 22, 2005; Phạm Hồ and Nam Dương, "Nước lên thuyền lên"; Quang Chính, "Vai trò công đoàn dần bị vô hiệu hoá."

[30] The HCMC Labor Federation Report on Strikes, 1995–July 2010; and the Thirty-Nine-Letter Sample (worker complaint letters and petitions submitted to newspapers in the South in 2005 and 2006).

SOEs. There were cases in which the workers' labor contracts were vague or confusing in the items that concerned pay and benefits such as unemployment and social insurance.

The HCMC Labor Federation reports on protests in Ho Chi Minh City show a decrease in the number of protests in the state sector from 1995 to 2003 (after that, the equitization process took effect, and the strike data for SOEs became very spotty; see Table 3.3). Due to the equitization process, protests appear to have shifted to joint-stock companies or one-member (the state as the owner) companies with limited responsibilities, as former state workers have come to be employed in these enterprises. Out of the eight cases documented in these reports, six involved individuals who were speaking of their personal situations, looking for remedies through legal means; some revealed the harsh working conditions of and difficulties faced by women workers. The other two cases involved collective actions that clearly focused on the law in their use of legal language and their appeal to state authorities.

The Tầu Cuốc Joint-Stock Company Case (2006)

The Tầu Cuốc Joint-Stock Company, which provides river-bottom dredging and construction services, is located in District 7 in Ho Chi Minh City. According to the HCMC website, this company was established in 1970 and focused on construction, transportation, water, and dredging projects.[31] On April 15, 2006, one hundred local workers protested the lay-off of 351 of their fellow workers:

> The company [or its state management] slowed the progress of equitization that directly affected workers. Management did not establish the reserve fund of VND 14 billion for workers, and did not hold the *annual workers' congress* for five years. This company had not yet implemented Prime Minister Decree 41/2002, but had already laid off 351 of *our fellow workers*. We [the remaining workers] appealed to the Minister of Agriculture and Rural Development to save these 351 workers because they did not receive their compensation as stipulated in Prime Minister Decree 41.[32]

When the state delegation came down to investigate this strike, its members first asked workers to "take down the strike banner" and then explained the "redundancy" policy. They told those who had been fired to return to the factory four days later (on April 19) to collect three months' worth of minimum-wage pay, but no workers were rehired.[33] Then the state officials from the Ministry of

---

[31] I found another Tầu Cuốc in Hưng Yên (the North) by searching the Internet. I emailed the company on July 1, 2010, to inquire about their address, activities, and workers, but received no answer. Information from the Hưng Yên website shows that the Tầu Cuốc Joint-Stock Company is part of a huge state conglomerate: Vinacorp. Vinacorp has member companies in almost all sectors of the economy. These sectors include industry, manufacturing, services, retailing, education, banking, finance, insurance, pharmaceuticals and hospital supplies, publications, tourism, real estate, oil, gas, chemicals, mining, forestry, raw materials, cars, beverages, seafood, accessories, entertainment and toys, household accessories, garments, cigarettes, steel, paper, air plane supplies, and electronics. http://www.vinacorp.vn/stock/otc-tcxd/ctcp-tau-cuoc-va-xay-dung/tin-tuc, accessed July 1, 2010.

[32] My emphasis. The HCMC Labor Federation Report on Strikes, 1995–July 2010.

[33] This was the minimum wage for state and domestic-private workers, which was even lower than that for workers in foreign-direct investment enterprises.

Agriculture and Rural Development promised to investigate the responsibility of the director of this company. In their own voices, these local workers showed a sense of solidarity based on their knowledge of the equitization law and the state's responsibility to carry it out in a timely manner so the workers could receive their severance pay. The protesters evoked the "socialist contract" by complaining that the management (or state managers) had not convened the annual workers' congress for five years. Thus, workers reminded the state of a form of workplace democracy that they used to enjoy during the now bygone socialist years. Moreover, they used collective class language—referring to 351 of their "fellow workers"—to protest the state's failure to implement the policy properly.

Sagoda Leather Shoe Case (2006)

A local worker from a leather shoe joint-stock company in Gò Vấp District sent a letter to a newspaper in the South to expose many problems with the equitization process, as well as problems employees faced doing subcontract work for the global supply chains. She stated her name and address at the beginning of the letter dated April 2006. After she had worked at the shoe company from 2004 to 2005, her resignation was accepted by the company president. Still, she did not receive adequate benefits:

> Fifty percent of the severance pay should be paid by the factory and the other half by the state.[34] I asked Mr. Dũng [the vice president] from what state agency and when would I receive my one-time severance pay, to which he said the HCMC office of the Ministry of Labor [MOLISA] would pay, that files are only processed periodically, and when my file arrived, I would be notified. But from my understanding about this very issue, the HCMC office of the Ministry of Finance [MOF] had already issued a policy requesting that the factory pay laid-off workers all of their severance pay in one lump sum. [The assumption here is that MOLISA was to reimburse the factory subsequently, once it caught up with its backlogs of files.] The factory [management] had received the MOF directive [stated above], but did not implement it. *Perhaps when the factory became a joint-stock company, the managers no longer felt obligated to the state, and the state directives and guidance sent down to the factory became a nonissue to management?* There were cases when workers, after being laid off [and out of work] one to two years, called the personnel office to ask about their severance pay, to which they always got the response that money had not yet arrived. But when those workers wrote complaint letters to the Voice of the People in HCMC radio station [Đài Tiếng Nói Nhân Dân Thành Phố Ho Chi Minh], they were called up to the factory to receive their severance pay almost immediately.[35]

Two themes are prominent in her letter. First, she expected that the factory's management would meet the obligations inherent in an inferred "socialist contract." With a sense of irony, she reminded this joint-stock company of its obligations toward workers. Second, she showed her knowledge of the law, especially the policy about paying severance pay in one lump sum. Her message also pointed to the

---

[34] This is the exact stipulation of Decrees 41 and 64.
[35] My emphasis. The Thirty-Nine-Letter Sample.

effectiveness of the state media: only when workers complained to the Voice of the People in Ho Chi Minh City radio station did the factory management act promptly to fulfill its obligations. This is similar to the practices of FDI management discussed in Chapter 5.

Bình An Brick Factory Case (2005–06)

Another case took place in a brick factory in Bình Dương province. Twelve (out of nineteen) local workers—including five women—who had been fired after working in the company for fourteen years signed a petition letter to complain about management's violation of rules concerning layoffs. This factory belonged to a state-owned construction corporation in Ho Chi Minh City. These workers submitted the letter first to the Center for Legal Assistance of the HCMC Labor Federation (Trung Tâm Tư Vấn Pháp Luật Liên Đoàn Lao Động Thành Phố Hồ Chí Minh), and four other groups: the Wage Monitoring Department of DOLISA (Department of Labor, Invalids, and Social Affairs), the HCMC Labor Federation, and two newspapers in Ho Chi Minh City. This factory employed thirty-three workers, of whom nineteen were classified as redundant. Knowing the law intimately, these workers cited Article No. 17 of the Labor Code, which clearly articulates the rights of laid-off workers and the responsibilities of their employers, in case of a "restructuring of the business or the change of technology."[36] In 2006, these workers were coerced into resigning with and releasing the then state-owned enterprise of any claims before they could receive any severance allowances and other assistance, such as retraining and other job opportunities, to which they were entitled.

To protest, twelve workers signed with their full names on a handwritten petition and demonstrated how their collective action was based on knowledge of the Labor Code and of their entitlements:

On July 1, 2005, management told us the lay-off decision, without offering any compensation of wages and severance pay, except for a contribution of 15 percent of the basic salary to our social insurance funds. After that they received our complaint letters; still they did not resolve the issues collectively. Instead, they called each of us to the personnel office, first threatening us, then trying to buy us off by saying that if any of us had any financial difficulties, then the company could advance some money to us, under the condition that we sign a letter relinquishing all of our rights to petition for our entitlements. So who is correct, in the name of the law: their action or our petition?[37]

This letter expresses a clear understanding that the authors were acting collectively, with a sense of class power. None of the twelve workers, all of whom signed their full names on a handwritten petition, concealed his or her identity. This shows that they were confident and not afraid to be penalized by management.

[36] This includes duly notifying the local labor union of the impending lay-offs, posting a public list of the employees who will be dismissed (taking into consideration skills and family situations), and providing severance allowances, as well as job retraining, job opportunities, low-interest loans, and other financial support so that the laid-off workers can find work. The Labor Code of the Socialist Republic of Vietnam www.dncustoms.gov.vn/web_English/english/luat_pl/LABOR-CODE.htm, accessed June 21, 2009.

[37] The Thirty-Nine-Letter Sample.

Moreover, this worker collective clearly reminded the state leaders to implement the law properly and expected them to take action. After enumerating all the violations in chronological order, these local workers ended with a rhetorical question: "So, is it not true that the company had violated Article 17 of the Labor Code? We sincerely hope to obtain assistance from all levels of state leadership."

The Machine Assembly and Construction 45-4 Company Case (2005)

A local female worker in the Machine Assembly and Construction 45-4 Company, a state-owned company, in Đồng Nai province, wrote to a newspaper in the South in 2005 to complain about being wrongfully fired from her job. She specifically asked for legal guidance to bring this state company to the labor court and the people's court in Đồng Nai. According to her account, the company had laid her off, reclassifying her as a redundant worker, while she was on sick leave during and following major ovarian surgery, and had failed to give her the severance pay that was due. She brought her case to her workplace labor-union representative but did not get support from him, for he agreed with the management's decision. As a last resort, she sent a long letter to a newspaper, starting with "To the labor newspaper for the rights of the laborers," and challenged the legality of the management's unilateral decision. She cited the difficulties of trying, as a woman, to find another job:

> I felt like the floor was falling beneath me, and [I] am extremely depressed because I lost my job when I just returned home from the hospital and was not yet recovered from the operation. *It is very difficult for a woman to find a job elsewhere.* I don't know how I'm going to make a living.[38]

She cited the laws that govern her rights and entitlement. First, she documented that, according to social security policy, she was legally entitled to a forty-five-day recovery leave after undergoing the surgery. Second, she reviewed the details of Decree No. 41/CP outlining her rights, and then she appealed to the Department of Labor, Invalids, and Social Affairs (DOLISA) in Đồng Nai province. She wrote:

> The decision to lay me off is premature because they did not give me proper advance notice according to the law; moreover, I just returned home from the hospital and am still recovering, so I'd like to continue working for a short time to stabilize my life while also looking for another job, but the management stuck to their decision … I had to find another job to make a living. After many requests to the management for my severance pay according to Decree No. 41 (*according to Decree No. 41/CP, the company director would determine the layoff based on redundancy and settle the severance package for the laid-off workers within fifteen days*) the company still did not give me my severance pay, and created many problems for me.[39]

She attached a response from the general president of this company, who informed her that he had received her letter from the DOLISA office in Đồng Nai.

---

[38] Ibid., my emphasis.

[39] Ibid., emphasis is in the original letter.

But the content of the management letter had mixed messages for her: It acknowledged her complaints and reprimanded the director of the machinery division who wrongfully dismissed her. Still, the letter did not confirm that she would immediately be given her severance pay, for the management letter vaguely promised: "At present, the company is following the protocols to calculate the severance package for redundant workers according to Decree 41/2002/CP ... When that process is complete, we will inform the redundant workers accordingly." She ended her letter with a line clearly stating her expectations, given her understanding of the rights of all workers in similar situations: "I hope that the newspaper, as a genuine forum for those of us who are workers, will help us achieve our workers' rights according to the Labor Code of the Socialist Republic of Vietnam."

While I have no way of knowing the outcome of this case, this woman worker's voice clearly delineates the vulnerabilities of female workers in a state-owned factory, workers whose livelihoods are deeply and negatively affected by this "equitization" process. In fighting for her self-preservation as a female worker, desperately searching for a living, this woman sought out all levels of the state organization within her reach—the workplace labor-union representative, the Đồng Nai DOLISA, the state media, the labor court, and the people's court—requesting legal guidance on how to demand her rights and entitlements properly. This former state worker clearly expected the socialist state to uphold the law, not just for herself, but for all workers, as indicated on the heading of her letter: "To the labor newspaper for the rights of the laborers."

The Bến Nghé Port Case (2006)

A local wharf worker in Bến Nghé port in Ho Chi Minh City—a former state-owned enterprise turned into a one-member company with limited liability—wrote to a newspaper in the South in 2006 to expose the dangerous working conditions at the worksite. He described vividly four accidents that had occurred over several years that had caused death or dismemberment of wharf workers dealing with huge containers. Workers repeatedly complained about the unsafe conditions and the fatigue that resulted when they had to work long hours, at times twenty-four hours without a break, even when another shift was scheduled for the following day:

> These tragic accidents were happening continuously [and were] red alerts about the lack of work safety in the wharf. These accidents were unavoidable when work intensity was extremely high and work hours were very long. Container drivers worked the twenty-four-hour shift, then rested one day, and then back to the twenty-four-hour shift. No human being could be fully awake to withstand such a work pattern ... When the ship arrived, workers had to work from thirty-six to forty hours continuously ... which amounted to more than three hundred hours of overtime work per year. This is clearly in violation of the maximum two hundred hours of annual overtime work sanctioned by the Labor Code. Still the Bến Nghé port management remained silent and refused to explain or compensate our losses. So, we would invite the newspaper [reporters] to come to the wharf to see with their own eyes about our work conditions, to investigate the real wages that we received—not as high as claimed by the management and

as published in the newspaper—and to get responses from the wharf management for us.[40]

This worker exposed the dangerous working conditions that affected the lives and well-being of *all* his fellow wharf workers, not just his own. He understood and appealed to the overtime stipulation in the Labor Code. He also understood the evidence-based protocol of the law, which he demonstrated by inviting the journalists to come to the port and investigate conditions "with their own eyes." Like other state workers, he expected the state media to be able to trigger the response from management and the relevant state authorities, prompting them to intervene on the behalf of those laboring at the wharf.

The next three cases concerned complaints and inquiries from local workers about labor contracts, salary, and social and retirement benefits. All of these cases involved employees who had worked for many years in state-owned enterprises that were then transformed into joint-stock companies. The references to law and legal entitlements are clear in these three cases.

The X32 Shoe and Garment Factory Case (2005)

In Vietnam, when the name of a factory starts with the letter *X*, it means that the military owns it. Historically, these factories manufactured military uniforms, but since the market reform in 1986, they have expanded in scope and now produce items that fulfill any commercial orders that come their way. In this case, a local female worker in Ho Chi Minh City wrote to a newspaper in the South in 2005 to complain about not receiving social insurance benefits from the military-owned X32 Shoe and Garment Factory–Logistics Central (Công Ty Giày May X32 Tổng Cục Hậu Cần) after her resignation. She had worked at the factory for ten years and should have received social insurance benefits based on the labor contract that she had signed with this company. She complained:

> About the social insurance benefit, I had worked there for ten years but had neither received any sum of money nor any notification [about receiving social security benefit] from any state agency or unit. I know that under the labor contract that I signed, I am entitled to receive social security benefits and other nonwage allowances [she implied that benefits she was seeking were available to her in the socialist era]. Where and how can I complain about this?[41]

Unfortunately, there is no information available about the outcome of this case; however, it is clear that this worker knew about the law and demanded her entitlements.

The Construction Corporation No. 4 Case (2006)

A local female worker was employed for more than twenty years in a joint-stock company in Bình Triệu (in Ho Chi Minh City) that belonged to state-owned

---

[40] From the Thirty-Nine-Letter Sample.

[41] Ibid.

construction corporation No. 4 (Tổng Công Ty Xây Dựng Số 4).[42] In 2006, she wrote to a newspaper in the South to complain about not receiving her proper layoff subsidy and to ask for advice.[43] She had been forced to resign due to ill health before she was fully vested with regard to full retirement. Moreover, she claimed that the layoff subsidy should be based on the relatively *higher* salary she was earning when she resigned in 2004, not on her lower starting salary. She demonstrated her understanding of the law by showing her calculation of the expected benefit, which points to a discrepancy of almost VND 300,000 per month, not a small amount for poor workers. Again, no information is available about the outcome of this case, but it is clear that this worker knew about her entitlement and expected to receive the correct subsidy. She also expected the state media to provide legal counsel so she could pursue the case.

The Case of an Unnamed State-Owned Enterprise (c. 2006)

A male worker sent a letter from Cần Thơ (a province in the Mekong Delta region) to a newspaper in the South, specifically addressing its policy section. He complained about not having received a permanent labor contract after fourteen years of working in a state-owned enterprise (he did not mention the name of the company) and questioned the legality of being expected, and so effectively required, to work without a long-term contract and the implications:

> So, the fact that this company continued to give me temporary short-term contracts (three to six months at a time), is it consistent with the government policies? Is it consistent with certain articles in the Labor Code? Who is right, and who is wrong? Also, the fact that I only received temporary, renewable contracts, how will that affect my social insurance benefits when I retire? I always completed all the tasks very well and thus received many recognition awards, from the city government to the company management, for my good work ethic but, still, without a permanent contract. In sum, I'd like to find out about the differences between temporary and permanent contracts and their implications for my rights and responsibilities in the present and future. I am anxiously waiting for your legal guidance and response to these questions so I can have peace of mind.[44]

In addition to his clear references to the law and legal entitlements, this worker also reminded the state that job security was part of the socialist contract. His line of argument calls for a sense of justice: on the one hand, he did his fair share and received many recognition awards from the local state for his strong work ethic; on the other hand, he expected that the state would, in return, fulfill its responsibility by providing him with job security.

All eight cases described here demonstrate that workers knew the labor laws and their corresponding rights and legal entitlements. They cited the legal details

---

[42] According to the naming practices in Vietnam, if the name of an enterprise includes a number, or a calendar date for a historic event, it often means the company is state owned.

[43] From the Thirty-Nine-Letter Sample.

[44] Ibid. See also: Bùi Đức Hải, "Labor Issues in Equitized Enterprises" (Southern Institute of Social Sciences, 2004, unpublished), which confirms an increase in short-term labor contracts.

accurately regarding redundancy packages, severance pay, termination, labor contract, and social insurance benefits, among many other issues. Also, they used rhetoric referring to class in their letters—either individually or collectively—and expected state managers and leaders to act in accord with socialist ideals. Their complaint letters and petitions show how they appealed to the state media and expected it to help them demand proper enforcement of the labor laws.

VIỆT THẮNG STATE WORKERS AND A HISTORICAL LEGACY (1964–2010)

Việt Thắng was a state-owned factory that went through transformations spanning more than four decades under three different political and economic systems: the Republic of Vietnam (1954–75), socialist Vietnam (1975 to 1986), and a market-oriented system (after 1986). In the 1960s, Việt Thắng was known as Vimytex, the company discussed in Chapter 2, and was supported by investment from the United States, Taiwan, and Japan. After 1975, the state converted it to Việt Thắng (Vietnamese Victory) Textile, a 100 percent state-owned enterprise producing both textile and garment products. In the early 1990s, the company contributed funds to form two joint ventures, one with South Korean capital (Choong Nam-Việt Thắng), and one with Russian capital (Việt Thắng-Vicoluch). Additionally, during the equitization process of 2005 and 2006, Việt Thắng Textile itself was divided into three parts in District 9, Ho Chi Minh City: a joint-stock garment factory (Việt Thắng Garment), a joint-stock accessories factory (Bình An factory), and a state-owned textile company (Việt Thắng Textile Limited).[45]

In November 2006, right after Vietnam's ascension to the World Trade Organization, Việt Thắng Textile underwent the equitization process to form joint-stock companies by selling its legal capital of VND 140 billion (or US$8.75 million) as shares to interested stakeholders.[46] This is an example of a short sale from a workers' perspective. The state and capitalists had tremendous power over workers in this process; their combined shares constituted about 81 percent of legal capital in the venture, with the state holding the lion's share under a joint-stock arrangement (after equitization). The state held 52 percent of the stock, public bidders 20 percent, and strategic investors 9 percent, while workers held just 19 percent. In principle, workers had been offered a 40 percent discount on the share prices, but, in reality, workers were too poor to part with their money, so they borrowed at high interest rates to purchase the low-priced stock. Most workers ended up selling their shares short—a demonstration of the "selling young rice" phenomenon discussed earlier—mostly to factory managers. Consequently, management ended up owning most of this enterprise.

---

[45] In Vietnamese, they are, Công ty cổ phần May Việt Thắng, Công Ty Cổ Phần Nguyên Phụ Liệu Dệt May Bình An, Công Ty Trách Nhiệm Hữu Hạn Nhà Nước Dệt Việt Thắng, respectively, http://www.tuoitre.com.vn, Dệt Việt Thắng chuyển thành Công ty cổ phần, December 18, 2006; BIDV Securities Co., Ltd., *Bản Công Bố Thông Tin: Bán Đấu Giá Cổ Phần Lần Đầu; Công Ty Trách Nhiệm Hữu Hạn Nhà Nước Một Thành Viên Dệt Việt Thắng* (Ho Chi Minh City: November 20, 2006).

[46] T.V.N., "Dệt Việt Thắng chuyển thành Công ty cổ phần," *Tuổi Trẻ*, December 18, 2006, http://tuoitre.vn/Kinh-te/178372/Det-Viet-Thang-chuyen-thanh-Cong-ty-co-phan.html. Meanwhile, the three unnamed strategic investors received a 20 percent discount on the share price. BIDV Securities Co., Ltd., *Một Thành Viên Dệt Việt Thắng*, p. 15.

Two protest cases involving Việt Thắng joint ventures are significant in our discussion. One of the earliest strikes in reunified Vietnam took place at Choong Nam-Việt Thắng and showed the importance of cultural identities and the workers' use of socialist ideology, as well as their historical knowledge and recognition that the wartime alliance between the RVN government and South Korea was relevant to their case. In addition, a later protest in Việt Thắng-Vicoluch underscored how workers made use of the law and invoked socialist expectations to fight for their rights.

Choong Nam-Việt Thắng (1993)

Choong Nam-Việt Thắng was established in 1992, the first joint venture between South Korea and Vietnam; Vietnam provided facilities and workers, while Korea supplied raw materials and marketing outlets. Choong Nam-Việt Thắng workers were very diverse, as the company employed both local and migrant workers throughout its history. This Korean-Vietnam joint venture employed six hundred workers, consisting of three working-class generations: (a) the oldest generation (in their fifties and sixties in 1992) were the older Thủ Đức natives, as well as migrants who had come from the North in 1954, after experiencing French colonial rule, and resettled in the South at the time of the 1954 partition; (b) the second generation (in their thirties and forties) had grown up in Thủ Đức during the Vietnam–United States war but had never experienced French rule; (c) the youngest generation (in their teens and twenties) were mostly migrant female workers who had come from the northern, the central, and Mekong areas in the 1990s; they had known only the reunification and the Đổi Mới period.[47]

As part of the socialist contract and expectations, workers received bonuses for Tết, the Vietnamese Lunar New Year, and other nonwage allowances, such as paid vacations in guesthouses owned by the VGCL and visits from union representatives for celebrations (such as weddings), illnesses, or a death in the family. (While the union representatives often brought small gifts for the workers, the monetary value was just one factor. The gesture of care and concern comforted workers during hard times, and thus was equivalent to a nonwage benefit.) However, Choong Nam-Việt Thắng's Korean management refused to pay workers this expected bonus. They also used the "divide-and-conquer" policy to break labor solidarity; the Vietnamese line leaders were paid four to five times more than regular workers. According to Suhong Chae, the Korean manager's refusal to pay the Tết bonus was not so much due to economic calculations—the Korean management actually could afford it, since it was not a large amount—but was an ideological issue, because the manager would not accept the communist practice of offering workers a bonus in their capitalist factory.[48]

The older migrants, who left the North in 1954, bonded with the workshop labor union representative. This older generation of workers was enraged and wanted to stop work when they discovered that they were being denied the Tết bonus. But Vinh—the enterprise union chairman at this joint venture—was hesitant at first. He

---

[47] Suhong Chae, "Spinning Work and Weaving Life: The Politics of Production in a Capitalistic Multinational Textile Factory in Vietnam" (PhD dissertation, City University of New York, 2003), pp. 30, 66–67.

[48] Ibid., pp. 81–82.

tried to negotiate with management, but to no avail. Then he obtained a "no-strike" decision from the labor unions at Thủ Đức District, with the agreement that, if he, Vinh, did not follow this decision, he would be disciplined and fired from his post. The reservations of local labor unions and state officials may have to do with the pro-FDI tendency back then, in addition to the state's paranoia about religious protests, since this conflict occurred during Christmas.[49] But under pressure from the workers, Vinh approved the work stoppage. This action won him the workers' approval and support.

The 1993 "hot Christmas" strike at Choong Nam-Việt Thắng was significant because it took place before strikes were sanctioned in the Labor Code, which was ratified in 1994. This protest also showed how the 1954 migrants from the North and the workshop labor union representative—all of whom belonged to the oldest generation or the second generation of workers at the plant, as Chae explains—politicized the strike agenda.[50] They used a historically informed strategy based on the socialist government's resentment of the historical alliance that had bound South Vietnam and South Korea during the Vietnam–United States War, as well as playing on the state's paranoia about organized religious protests.

Two days before Christmas, on December 23, 1993, Vinh staged a sit-down of six hundred workers, claiming that some management team members—who had served in the notorious South Korean "vicious tiger brigade" (Sư Đoàn Mãnh Hổ)—had instructed the workers to wear stripes on their uniform that resembled the former South Vietnamese flag pattern—three red stripes on a yellow band. In reality, the colors of these armbands simply denoted different skill levels: one stripe for assembly-line workers, two for line managers, and three for higher-level management.[51] But in protest, workers used this coincidence to evoke the image of old war-time enemies of the Democratic Republic of Vietnam in order to win the support of the Vietnamese socialist government in power at the time.

Their verbal protest message played on this historical sentiment: "The former South Korean veterans in Vietnam [sided] with the South Vietnamese regime [and now have] humiliated the Vietnamese workers." There was also a sense of class inherent in the protest rhetoric, invoking an historic "enemy of the state": Korean capitalists versus Vietnamese workers. The sensitive timing of their work stoppage also triggered state paranoia, for the government always feared organized protests near major religious holidays. The workers began their one-day, sit-down strike on December 23, 1993, in front of this joint-venture factory, an action that sent the South Korean general director, or the "vicious tiger," to hide in his office. At that time, Hoàng Thị Khánh—the chairperson of the HCMC Labor Federation and member of the Central Communist Party—intervened to appease both sides. The strike ended in a modest victory for the workers: half a month's wages would be given to each employee as a bonus, but this still did not equal the whole thirteenth-month bonus that had often been awarded in state factories. But this concession came with other compromises to placate workers, for example, some workers were assigned to manage the cafeteria and low- to mid-level managers were replaced by Vietnamese (although Koreans still handled the most important positions in budgeting and accounting).

[49] Interview with Bùi Đức Hải, August 2007, Ho Chi Minh City.
[50] Ibid.
[51] Chae, "Spinning Work and Weaving Life," pp. 96–97.

Việt Thắng-Vicoluch Joint Venture (2006)

According to the HCMC Labor Federation 2006 report, 250 workers (out of 980 total workers at the factory) went on strike on May 18, 2006, in a Vietnam-Russia joint venture (Việt Thắng–Vicoluch) that produced jackets for Western brand names. The Vietnamese ownership of this joint venture belonged to the state-owned enterprise Việt Thắng. Most of these workers were local. In their protest, they made several requests:

> We recommend that we be paid according to Prime Minister Decree No. 3 without losing other nonwage allowances.[52] The director and the head accountant have to recalculate the low piece rates and are *not allowed to look down upon laborers* [không được xem thường người lao động]. They also need to raise our annual wages based on seniority.[53]

This case shows that workers were knowledgeable about the law that would benefit them. They knew that they should be paid the higher minimum wage (which would give them a 40 percent increase) required in foreign-direct investment companies. But as of May 2006, three months after the February 1 implementation date of Decree No. 3, it took a workers' collective action to have the law implemented properly.

As stated in this unpublished report, the management of this joint venture agreed to pay workers the FDI minimum wage, which is higher than the minimum wage in the state sector. This means that even when they worked on the piece-rate system, they were still guaranteed the minimum wage. Moreover, they would receive the entitlements they had previously been offered under the socialist contract. No employee would be assigned more than sixteen hours per week of overtime work, and there would be no overtime work on Sundays; regarding bonuses, they would receive the thirteenth-month's pay if they had worked all twelve months of that year. Their severance pay and raises would be based on published rankings in a wage table, and they would get work credits for the days during which they went on strike. Together, this package deal—if implemented properly—would outmatch the concessions offered to employees in FDI and domestic-private factories.

Three points emerge from this case. Again, the workers successfully cited the law to demand their rights, they invoked a sense of class, and they were keen to remind the state that it must fulfill its socialist contract with the workers. They reminded the socialist state that it—and management—must not condescend to Vietnamese laborers. These 250 workers engaged in a collective action, during which they pointed out that, since they worked for a joint venture, they were entitled to receive the higher FDI minimum wage.

There is no evidence from this brief report that these (former) state workers were migrants. Therefore, native place does not appear to be central in their labor organizing. But their expectations of continuing to receive the quintessential benefits of the bygone socialist system are clear. They explicitly asked for the thirteenth-

---

[52] Indeed, the workers referred to Decree 03/2006/NĐ-CP, which raised the minimum wage levels by 40 percent, effective February 1, 2006, in FDI companies.

[53] My emphasis. The HCMC Labor Federation Report on Strikes, 1995–July 2010.

month bonus and demanded the respect and responsibilities state workers used to be given, such as participation in the production process and in decisions concerning the distribution of incomes.

Việt Thắng Jeans Limited Company (2007, 2008)

The Việt Thắng combine developed yet another state-owned company, the Việt Thắng Jeans Limited Company. Established in 2005, it assembled, washed, and dyed eight thousand pairs of jeans per day. Since 2005, its factory has repeatedly dumped polluted water into the nearby Rạch Chiếc River in Ho Chi Minh City and ignored warnings from the local government.[54] It has violated both environmental and labor laws.

In September 2008 and again in December 2008, the HCMC Environmental Agency issued a warning that this company had exceeded by five to ten times the restrictions on disposal of wastewater, as well as violating other environmental policies. In June 2009, Việt Thắng Jeans Limited was still polluting, so the HCMC People's Committee issued a fine of VND 81 million (or about US$5,400). By July 2009, the HCMC Environmental Agency found that this company was still failing to comply with the law and that it was not treating its polluted water properly.[55]

Labor relations in this factory had been rocky since 2007. A female worker had complained publicly on the Người Lao Động in May 2007 about management intimidation, arguing that she had been transferred from one job to another, as punishment for her activism. In her complaint, she represented other workers to demand proper labor contracts and management contributions to social security and health funds. The state management's response claimed that this woman "did not get along well with other workers [on the job], so we had to transfer her to another factory."[56] Unfortunately, it is difficult to verify these competing claims by labor and management without actually interviewing the parties involved. The situation is complicated by a gap in the forums published by these newspapers: while it is good that workers' complaints are exposed publicly, it is difficult to know the final settlement or to verify the claims.

In January 2008, 140 garment workers at Việt Thắng Jeans Limited engaged in a four-day work stoppage to complain that their minimum wage had not been raised, their bonuses were not being made public, and they had to work excessive overtime on Sundays. According to the HCMC Labor Federation 2008 report, a brief one-liner describing the outcome of this protest tells us that "there was successful resolution within the factory." Then, following that collective action, in March 2008, a female worker was laid off because she turned off the machine while the factory

---

[54] Việt Dũng, "Phạt gần 81 triệu đồng một công ty gây ô nhiễm," *VTC News*, http://www.tin247.com/phat_gan_81_trieu_dong_mot_cong_ty_gay_o_nhiem-16-21453192.html, July 14, 2009, accessed July 2010.

[55] http://vietnamnet.vn/xahoi/doisong/2009/08/863020/, accessed July 1, 2010. This link was no longer active in 2012.

[56] Tư Vấn Pháp Luật Lao Động (Labor Law Counsel Section), "Bị điều chuyển công việc nhiều lần" [Being Transferred to Different Jobs Many Times], *Người Lao Động*, http://nld.com.vn/190 909P1010C1012/bi-dieu-chuyen-cong-viec-nhieu-lan.htm, May 31, 2007.

management was assessing collective workers' requests to raise wages.[57] Apparently, this worker was penalized for participating in a work stoppage that supported the January 2008 collective workers' request.

In sum, workers in this company appealed to the laws on minimum wage and overtime work, as well as nonwage allowances, such as bonuses, to improve their conditions. Unfortunately, I cannot find any information on native place and other cultural factors to analyze their impacts on labor mobilizing.

CONCLUSION

Historical legacy matters. In the various manifestations of state capital—whether fully or partly state-owned enterprises—workers have carried the socialist ideology with them, into the workplace, along with their expectations that the socialist contract would be honored, even as Vietnam has become fully ensconced in the global capitalist system. When the older workers flexed their historical knowledge and appealed to the socialist values they had been taught (as in the 1993 sit-down strike at Choong Nam-Việt Thắng), they won some concessions from management. Such successful workers' protests against flexible capital offer hope, contrary to concerns raised by Harvey and other scholars who have argued that fragmented place-bound identity renders workers less inclined to engage in collective action.[58]

Cultural factors played important roles in bringing migrant workers together in temporary housing away from home. Interacting in the Việt Thắng worker-housing area in Ho Chi Minh City, women migrant workers from the North (Hanoi, Nam Định, Hà Giang, Tuyên Quang), the Central region (Thanh Hóa), and the South (Trà Vinh) reinforced their solidarity. Older female workers looked out for younger workers, regarding them as sisters. Such acts of recognition and care inform workers' collective action.

Class consciousness emerged when workers organized and undertook a collective action (for instance, at Choong Nam-Việt Thắng and Việt Thắng-Vicoluch) or signed petition letters to express their frustration and discontent (as happened at the Bình An brick factory and in the penned protests of women workers in Hanoi in 1999). Even when they wrote their complaint letters as individuals, focusing on their own situations, they dared to raise people's consciousness about the hardships and dangerous working conditions facing their fellow workers generally (as demonstrated in the Bến Nghé wharf workers' case).

Clearly, workers did not agree that dangerous working conditions were "natural and inevitable." But it is harder to tell whether these former state workers truly believed in the socialist values they cited or if they were just using the tools of the state (by way of complaint letters, legal counsel from the state media, and appeals to state legal institutions and agencies) to fight against the unfair practices of their employers. Thus, it is relatively difficult to determine whether or not these employees were subject to a "thick" version of false consciousness.

The state workers utilized many forms of protest, showing an intermingling of Marxist and Polanyi-type protests. Open protest letters and petitions reminded the

---

[57] Vĩnh Tùng and Nam Dương, "Khi Công Nhân 'Quậy'" [When Workers Made Waves], *Người Lao Động*, http://nld.com.vn/216837P0C1010/khi-cong-nhan-quay.htm, March 3, 2008.

[58] David Harvey, *The Condition of Postmodernity: An Enquiry into the Origins of Cultural Change* (Cambridge, MA, and Oxford: Blackwell, 1990).

state to live up to its socialist vision and to respect worker rights, especially at the point of production. From this space, where humans are often reduced to commodities, workers reminded the state and new non-state management to respect them as people. While not perfect, at least such respect was acknowledged in the socialist era. Failure to give respect, in the eyes of workers, would cause the state to "lose" its legitimacy. These actions recall Anagnost's analysis of a Chinese villager (who reminded his Party state-manager to recognize the villager's entitlements) and Lee's analysis of Chinese state workers' protests.[59]

While worker protests were open—in the cases discussed above, the protests did not constitute a "hidden transcript of critical dissent"[60]—the media did not report them for the general public, except in a few cases, when short dialogues between journalists and state managers were reported in the controlled environment sanctioned by the state.[61] In short, it is evident that the state keeps the lid tightly shut and only allows some openness when publicity of a certain kind fits the state's political agenda.

But workers have been politically savvy in coping with the state. They used state apparatuses to demand their rights and entitlements. They appealed to these government offices, trusting the state would not send in a police force to "discipline" state workers when they used the law and appealed to state legal institutions and agencies, such as the People's Oversight Committee, People's Court, Labor Court, and State Investigation Agency.

Even with such agency, however, many workers and local residents have continued to suffer from the weak implementation and enforcement of labor laws. This is consistent with Mark Sidel's argument about how the gap between textual intent and implementation of labor laws creates contradictory effects and does not protect labor rights.[62] One example is the state's failure to implement Decree No. 41/CP, which mandated that workers laid-off from state enterprises be duly compensated. But hundreds of thousands of state workers who were terminated from their jobs in equitized SOEs received little or no compensation, although clearly they were owed severance pay according to the law.

While there are very few public reports of legal violations or protests in SOEs, there are almost daily reports of strikes in FDI enterprises and, increasingly, in domestic-private factories. The next chapter investigates the reasons for that phenomenon and analyzes how factors such as cultural identity, historical legacy, and the law empower workers who fight for their rights in FDI factories.

---

[59] Ann Anagnost, *National Past-Times: Narrative, Representation, and Power in Modern China* (Durham, NC: Duke University Press, 1997); Ching Kwan Lee, *Against the Law: Labor Protests in China's Rustbelt and Sunbelt* (Berkeley, CA: University of California Press, 2007).

[60] James C. Scott, *Domination and the Arts of Resistance: Hidden Transcripts* (New Haven, CT, and London: Yale University Press, 1990), p. 198.

[61] One example of such an interaction was reported on May 31, 2007, in the Labor Law Counsel Section of the newspaper *Người Lao Động*, "Bị điều chuyển công việc nhiều lần" [Being Transferred to Different Tasks/Jobs Many Times].

[62] Mark Sidel, *Law and Society in Vietnam: The Transition from Socialism in Comparative Perspective* (Cambridge: Cambridge University Press, 2008), pp. 92, 116, 118.

CHAPTER 5

LABOR ORGANIZING AND PROTESTS IN FOREIGN-DIRECT INVESTMENT FACTORIES

In this chapter, I investigate the reasons for the almost daily strikes, as reported by the media, in Vietnamese foreign-direct investment (FDI) enterprises—and, increasingly, in domestic-private factories. I examine Thompson's argument (as discussed in the Introduction and Chapter 1) that workers do not necessarily begin their struggle with a class consciousness; rather, through their common experiences and struggles, these workers come to recognize their common interests and those of management. From that awareness, workers begin to see themselves as members of a class (class consciousness). In Vietnam, migrant workers' real-life experiences are influenced by their cultural identities, historical legacies, shared working and living conditions, and their expectations of fairness under the rule of law, all of which contribute to their fight for their rights in FDI factories.

In 2010, out of 424 strikes nationwide, 339 strikes broke out in FDI enterprises, of which 128 strikes (38 percent) occurred in Taiwanese-owned factories, 109 (32 percent) in Korean-owned factories, 26 (8 percent) in Japanese-owned factories, and 76 (22 percent) in other FDI factories.[1] The same trend was observed in Ho Chi Minh City. Most strikes there took place in Taiwanese-owned factories (10 reported cases in 2010 and 27 cases in 2011). Strikes also broke out in Korean- and Japanese-owned factories in that city during 2010 and 2011.[2]

Many of these strikes were organized because the managers of the respective enterprises did not comply with Vietnam's labor laws. In particular, from 2010 to 2012, most strikes in HCMC factories continued to revolve around wage issues, such as low wages, late wage payments, inadequate overtime compensation (with excessive overtime demanded on weekends and holidays during peak subcontracting seasons), low piece rates, high daily productivity targets, the imposition of monetary fines as disciplinary actions, unclear labor contracts and apprenticeship periods, and inadequate benefits (social security, health and unemployment insurance), which were based on calculations that did not take into account money earned through overtime. Other labor-standards issues cited by the workers involved lack of transparency with regard to salary and raises (a number of factories did not publish their salary-rank tables); inadequate annual sick leave; and substandard work environments.[3]

---

[1] Communication with Trần Văn Lý, member of the presidium, and director, International Department of the Vietnam General Confederation of Labor (VGCL), October 2011.

[2] *The HCMC Labor Federation Report on Strikes*, 1995–July 2010 and 2011.

[3] Wage-related issues were also causes of strikes in Ho Chi Minh City in 2008 and 2009, according to the HCMC Labor Federation, cited in Thùy Linh, "Ngập ngừng … tăng lương tối

Inflation could serve as an indirect reason for strikes, since it exacerbated the problems faced by low-income factory workers, yet even with the inflation-adjusted minimum wages in FDI contract factories, workers would still struggle to make ends meet.[4] For this reason, increasingly, workers have demanded a living wage. These conditions have been recognized by Đặng Ngọc Tùng, the president of the VGCL (Vietnam General Confederation of Labor), who said in May 2012 that the current level of inflation-adjusted–minimum wages meets only 60 percent of the bare necessities for workers' livelihood. He went on to criticize the state: "The state has to listen more closely, because, inadvertently, this state-sanctioned minimum wage had violated Stipulation No. 92, Section 1, of the Proposed Labor Code Revision, which states that the minimum wage has to ensure the basic *livelihood* of workers."[5] Consistently, many workers have demanded more allowances (*trợ cấp*) to cope with high costs of living. They repeatedly complained about "difficult lives" and asked for "improving meals at work, and allowances" in addition to "increasing wages/piece rates."[6]

According to HEPZA (Ho Chi Minh City Export Processing Zones Authority), low wages and bad working conditions have given rise to labor shortages in EPZs (export processing zones) and IZs (industrial zones) in urban areas such as Ho Chi Minh City. In May 2010, many enterprises in those areas needed workers—on the order of 37,000 workers, combined—primarily in textile and garment, footwear, and seafood processing sectors.[7] Faced with "nonlivable" earnings, many workers had abandoned working in EPZs and IPs and had switched to non-manufacturing work, or returned to their hometowns to do farm-related work or factory work there (many FDI enterprises had expanded their factories into non-metropolitan areas in order to take advantage of even lower minimum wages in these zones).[8]

This chapter tackles these questions: who are the workers in those FDI factories producing for the global supply chains and concentrated in export processing and

---

thiểu" [Haltingly … raising the minimum wage], *Người Lao Động*, http://nld.com.vn/2010091 9105149803P1010C1012/ngap-ngung-tang-luong-toi-thieu.htm, September 20, 2010, accessed September 26, 2010.

[4] Nguyễn Tấn Định—Vice Director of HEPZA Management Department—cited in Thùy Linh, "Ngập ngừng … tăng lương tối thiểu."

[5] My emphasis. Interestingly, Đặng Ngọc Tùng was referring to the concept of livable wages for workers. Nguyễn Quyết, "Quốc Hội Thảo Luận Dự Án Bộ Luật Lao Động Sửa Đổi: Lương Tối Thiểu Phải Sát Thực Tế Cuộc Sống" [The parliament discussed the Labor Code proposed revision: Minimum wage must accommodate the real costs of living], May 24, 2012, http://nld.com.vn/20120524124132940p0c1010/luong-toi-thieu-phai-sat-thuc-te-cuoc-song. htm, accessed May 2012.

[6] *HCMC Labor Federation Report on Strikes, 2010*; *HCMC Labor Federation Report on Strikes, 2011*. (Both were published in Ho Chi Minh City by the HCMC Labor Federation and circulated internally only.)

[7] "Firms in HCM City IPs, EPZs Lack 37,000 Workers," *Business Times*, http://vietnambusi ness.asia/firms-in-hcm-city-ips-epzs-lack-37000-workers/, May 27, 2010; accessed February 22, 2012.

[8] According to the vice chair of the management department of HEPZA, based on a survey of more than one thousand factories in HEPZA, the average wage for factory work is even lower than that of construction work and harvesting. So, such nonlivable wages gave rise to labor fluctuations; workers moved from one factory to another in search of higher wages, however small the increment, and therefore no new workers were added to HEPZA's labor force. Thùy Linh, "Ngập ngừng … tăng lương tối thiểu."

industrial zones in Vietnam? What are relevant cultural identity factors that empower their agency and connect them to one another while they are living in "factory towns," such as Linh Trung and Đồng Nai in the South? How do the workers use these common cultural identities as a foundation for action in times of extreme crisis that make "class moments" possible? What types of protests have been mounted when workers have responded to unbearable working conditions in FDI factories?

Let's focus on how these migrant workers relied on their cultural identities to bond with each other. Then we'll look at the origins (or cultural identity) of some contract factory owners from East Asia and Southeast Asia. We will hear worker voices through their protest letters, petitions, interviews, and even graffiti strike messages on the women's lavatory walls, as they carry on the fight for their rights and benefits.

CULTURAL IDENTITY: NATIVE PLACE, GENDER, RELIGIOUS RITUALS

This section describes the cultural ties that bring workers together in both social and work settings that constitute their common experiences, as informed by Thompson. In 2008, more than 85 percent of factory workers in the EPZs, IZs, and joint ventures nationwide in Vietnam were young females between eighteen and thirty years old.[9] In 2009, during the global financial crisis, only 75 percent of migrant workers in Ho Chi Minh City were women, and in Hanoi the number was 70 percent.[10] Many came from rural provinces. For migrant workers, native place is central to their networking and their protests, but the effects of this factor—a shared place of origin—are complicated by other cultural identity factors such as gender and religion. By 2011, the top three cities that received the highest number of migrants were in the South: Bình Dương (65 percent of the city's total population), Đồng Nai (31 percent), and Ho Chi Minh City (25 percent).[11]

Native Place and Migrant Workers

Tradition has motivational power to engage workers in collective action.[12] Workers coming from places with a revolutionary past tend to participate in or lead

---

[9] Bùi Thị Thanh Hà, *Công Nhân Công Nghiệp Trong Các Doanh Nghiệp Liên Doanh ở Nước Ta Thời Kỳ Đổi Mới* [Industrial Workers in Joint-Ventures in Vietnam in Renovation Era] (Hanoi: Social Science Publishing House, 2003); Trần Xuân Cầu, "Sức Ép Của Lao Động Nhập Cư Trong Các Khu Công Nghiệp Và Chính Sách Đối Với Họ" [The Pressure of Migrant Workers in Industrial Zones and Migrant Labor Policy], Đại học Kinh tế Quốc Dân (National Economics University), http://www.vienkinhte.hochiminhcity.gov.vn/xemtin.asp?idcha=1679&cap=3&id=4301, August 22, 2008, accessed June 2009.

[10] Thảo Lan, "Tác động của khủng hoảng tài chính đối với công nhân nữ nhập cư và nguy cơ mua bán người" [Effects Of Global Financial Crisis on Female Migrant Workers and the Dangers of Human Trafficking], September 8, 2009, http://www.molisa.gov.vn/news/detail/tabid/75/newsid/49916/seo/Tac-dong-cua-khung-hoang-tai-chinh-doi-voi-cong-nhan-nu-nhap-cu-va-nguy-co-mua-ban-nguoi/language/vi-VN/Default.aspx, accessed November 2012.

[11] General Statistics Office, *Statistical Yearbook of Vietnam, 2011* (Hanoi: Statistical Publishing House, 2012), p. 93.

[12] David Harvey, *The Condition of Postmodernity: An Enquiry into the Origins of Cultural Change* (Cambridge, MA, and Oxford: Blackwell, 1990), pp. 16–17, 302–3.

protests even when they face uncertainty and risk being severely penalized in foreign-owned enterprises. Many migrant workers from revolutionary places—Nam Định, Thái Bình, Củ Chi, Hóc Môn—have carried on the "fighting spirit" and relied on the strength of their place-based identity to mobilize their fellow workers to protest.

Migrant workers rely on cultural networking to support them as they seek and find work far away from home. Many individuals who become migrant workers have to pay local or company recruiters to secure jobs in the cities; many of these individuals seeking work use their families' savings or incur debt to get the job. Then they travel with friends or spouses and rent a living space near the EPZ, industrial zone, or district where FDI contract factories and local subcontractors are located. After securing a job and a place to stay, they bring other relatives and friends to live in the same units and work with them in the same factories.[13]

There are several statistics for the total numbers of EPZs and IZs from different reports.[14] At the time of writing, the most updated statistics came from an interview with Bùi Quang Vinh, the Minister of Planning and Investment, who reported that there are 267 EPZs and IZs.[15] These EPZs and IZs are spread out in four key economic zones: the North, the Central, the southern region, and the Mekong Delta region, with the last two zones accounting for the lion's share of the number of EPZs and IZs.[16] Interestingly, at the time of writing, Long An Province tops the list with the highest number of EPZs and IZs (34), surpassing Đồng Nai Province (31), Bình Dương Province (25), and Ho Chi Minh City (19).[17]

According to Bùi Quang Vinh, those 267 EPZs and IZs are responsible for around 40 percent of total FDI companies registered in Vietnam, with the top investors coming from East Asia—Taiwan, Korea, Singapore, Japan, and Malaysia.[18] As of 2012, these zones employed more than 1.6 million workers throughout Vietnam.[19] More than 700,000 workers (of whom 70 percent are migrant rural workers) have been employed in the EPZs and IZs in Ho Chi Minh City, Bình

---

[13] Nghiêm Liên Hương, "Work Culture, Gender, and Class In Vietnam: Ethnographies of Three Garment Workshops in Hanoi" (PhD dissertation, University of Amsterdam, 2006), pp. 234–35.

[14] There are 284 EPZs and IZs, according to Vietnam Industrial Parks Investment Promotion, under the umbrella of the Indochina International Consulting Co., LTD., http://viipip.com/homeen/?module=listip, accessed June 6, 2012; 260 industrial zones and export processing zones from the "Guidebook on Business and Investment In Vietnam" by the Embassy of Socialist Republic of Vietnam to the Federal Republic of Germany, published in Berlin in 2011; and 159 IZs and EPZs from "An Investment Guide to Vietnam" by the Canadian Trade Commissioner Service (TCS), December 2011.

[15] "Zones Playing an Active Role," Vietnam Investment Review, February 13, 2012, http://www.vir.com.vn/news/investlink/zones-playing-an-active-role.html, accessed May 2012.

[16] According to the Vietnam Industrial Parks Investment Promotion, out of 284 total EPZs and IZs, 189 are in the southern zone and Mekong Delta, whereas 55 are in the North, and 40 in the Central zones.

[17] Ibid.

[18] Ministry of Planning and Investment, "Accumulated Inflow of FDI by the End of 2010," cited in "Guidebook on Business and Investment In Vietnam," pp. 11, 13.

[19] "Zones Playing An Active Role," *Vietnam Investment Review.*

Dương, and Đồng Nai.[20] Most of these migrant workers come from rural areas of the Mekong Delta, the Red River Delta, and north central Vietnam. Most of the workers are young, from twenty to thirty-five years of age. Female migrant workers accounted for the majority of the migrant workforce, as discussed above; most were hired to work in factories producing textiles, garments, and shoes. Most of the workers have little education; about 60 percent of migrant workers in the zones in Ho Chi Minh City, Bình Dương, and Đồng Nai completed up to eight years of schooling. As they live far from home, their main goal is to make enough money to live on and send remittances home. Consistent with other sources discussed in Chapter 3, Trần Xuân Cầu provides evidence that migrant workers generally have to pay more than local workers to cover their living expenses (rent, utilities, child care, education), costs that absorb 80 to 90 percent of their income. This leaves a small amount either to send home or to save for emergency purposes.[21]

Most young migrant workers come from poor and rural provinces throughout Vietnam, especially Hà Tây, Vĩnh Phúc, Bắc Giang, Đà Nẵng, Quảng Nam, Quảng Bình, Phan Thiết, Long An, Tiền Giang, Kiên Giang, Nam Định, Thái Bình, and An Giang.[22] When these migrants arrive in the region where they will work, most of them congregate in concentrated worker housing areas, called *"làng"* (the proverbial village), which become their home away from home.[23] These *làng* are near or within the confines of the two largest export processing zones in Ho Chi Minh City—Tân Thuận and Linh Trung. The Tân Thuận EPZ—the first one established in Vietnam, in 2000—employs local workers from Ho Chi Minh City, along with migrant workers from the Mekong Delta, and other southern provinces (such as Tiền Giang and Kiên Giang).[24] In the Linh Trung EPZ (in another district of Ho Chi Minh City), on the other hand, most workers came from poor northern provinces (such as Thái Bình, Nam Định, Thanh Hóa, and Nghệ An) and central provinces (Quảng Nam and Quảng Bình).[25] Some of these northern provinces, such as Thái Bình and Nam Định, have a notably revolutionary past, and migrants originating from those regions have been influenced by that legacy. Linh Trung EPZ is the site of many well-known strikes, such as the migrant-workers-led strikes in 2005–06 at Freetrend (a 100 percent Taiwanese-owned shoe factory) that resulted in a 40 percent minimum-wage increase at the beginning of 2006. Some factories in this strike-prone EPZ had been

---

[20] VietNamNet Bridge, "Fewer Rural Workers Can Return For Tet," May 27, 2010, http://english.vietnamnet.vn/en/society/17999/fewer-rural-workers-can-return-for-tet.html, accessed February 21, 2012.

[21] Trần Xuân Cầu, "Sức Ép Của Lao Động Nhập Cư," pp. 1–3.

[22] Huỳnh Thị Ngọc Tuyết, "Báo Cáo Kết Quả Cuộc Khảo Sát Về 'Phòng Chống Mua Bán Phụ Nữ—Trẻ Em' và 'Tăng Cường Trách Nhiệm Xã Hội'" [Findings of the Survey on the Trafficking of Women and Children and Strengthening Social Responsibility] (Ho Chi Minh City: Gò Vấp District People's Committee, ActionAid Vietnam [Southern Office], and Development Assistance Project, 2005); Hà Dịu, "Nhọc Nhằn Đời Lao Động Nhập Cư" [Hardships of the Life of Migrant Workers], May 1, 2008, http://www.Vietnamnet. vn/service/ printversion.vnn?article_id=1057357, accessed June 8, 2009; and Trần Xuân Cầu, "Sức Ép Của Lao Động Nhập Cư."

[23] Interview with Journalist D, June 2008, Ho Chi Minh City.

[24] Interview with Journalist C, June 2008; correspondence with Nguyễn Thùy Hương, 2007, Hanoi; Ministry of Planning and Investment, "Report to the Prime Minister on Strikes in Đồng Nai, Bình Dương, Thành Phố Hồ Chí Minh," 2004.

[25] Interview with Journalist D, June 2008, Ho Chi Minh City.

hesitant to hire workers from certain volatile, northern provinces because of their fighting spirit.[26]

Migrant workers watch a wedding video in their rental unit in Linh Trung Export Processing Zone, August 2006. (Author's photo)

Migrant workers possess different levels of education and skills; these differences play out in the two major EPZs in Ho Chi Minh City. In the Tân Thuận EPZ, most workers had a high school education and were working at relatively high skilled jobs in electronics, whereas many Linh Trung workers had not finished high school—most had only finished eighth grade—and they were employed in a variety of comparatively low skilled jobs in textile, garment, and shoe factories.[27]

Working and Living Conditions of Migrant Workers

Most migrant workers employed in FDI and domestic-owned factories in Vietnam since Đổi Mới (late 1980s) had to work overtime to make up for the low piece rates. Staggering inflation in 2008 exacerbated their predicament and necessitated even more overtime work; many worked continuously from 7:30 PM to 5:00 AM the next morning, rested for three hours, then returned to work at 8:00 AM.

---

[26] Interview with Journalist A, June 2008, Ho Chi Minh City.

[27] Ibid.

Even working at that intensity, on average, the employees earned only about VND 1.3 to 1.5 million, or less than US$100, per month. But that level of income is not sufficient for a person living in Ho Chi Minh City, so many of the workers ended up going on strike to fight for a living wage.[28]

In 2010, the minimum monthly wage levels in four zones, in Vietnamese *đồng* (VND), were set at: 1.34 million in Zone 1; 1.19 million in Zone 2; 1.04 million in Zone 3, and 1.0 million in Zone 4. But according to Trần Đăng Thanh—an official of the Vietnamese Textile and Garment Association—incomes set at these levels do not constitute livable wages. Therefore, the pilot garment collective bargaining agreement proposed and signed in 2010 stipulates that workers must be ensured they will receive a livable wage that is based on the actual costs of living in the four areas, as estimated by the General Statistical Office: 1.7 million in Zone 1; 1.6 million in Zone 2; 1.5 million in Zone 3; and 1.3 million in Zone 4.[29] MOLISA (Ministry of Labor, Invalids, and Social Affairs) proposed slightly lower wage levels for foreign-direct investment enterprises, set to range from 1.5 million (Zone 1) to 1.1 million (Zone 4).[30]

Aspirations, Upward Mobility, and Library-for-Workers Campaign

Most migrant workers in Vietnam consider factory work in big cities to be only temporary. They see it as a stepping stone, a way to save money, learn some skills, move up the job ladder before returning home to raise their families and open their own shops in their native region. They are willing to endure for several years working in low-paid, low-skilled, and often dead-end jobs to achieve their goals. During that time, they live together in squalid, "sardine-packed" conditions so that they can save some money to send home to help their families, to serve as seed money for marriage, or to invest in small-scale businesses after they leave factory work.[31] Most of my interviewees lived together with their kin or with acquaintances from their native village.

Many of those who travel away from home to find jobs are women. Women workers enjoy having some financial independence to help themselves and their families. This aspiration is not new: it was an important factor for female migrant workers centuries ago in many countries.[32] I met Liễu, a migrant worker from Phan

---

[28] Nam Dương, "Hơn 100 CN ngừng việc vì tăng ca quá sức" [Over One Hundred Workers Went on Strike Due to Excessive Overtime Work], *Người Lao Động*, May 18, 2008, http://nld.com.vn/ 225178P0C1010/hon-100-cn-ngung-viec-vi-tang-ca-qua-suc.htm, accessed July 2009.

[29] Thanh Vân, "Mức sàn" quyền lợi công nhân dệt may," *Người Lao Động*, June 24, 2010, http://nld.com.vn/20100623100136446P1010C1012/muc-san-quyen-loi-cong-nhan-det-may. htm, accessed July 2010.

[30] Thùy Linh, "Ngập ngừng … tăng lương tối thiểu."

[31] Bùi Thị Thanh Hà, *Công Nhân Công Nghiệp*, p. 53.

[32] Two examples demonstrate this point. Naila Kabeer provides an excellent and nuanced study on Bangladeshi garment workers who enjoyed formal employment (as opposed to informal employment, which would have subjected them to even worse abuses) because it gave them some financial independence to strengthen their bargaining power at home. Naila Kabeer, "Globalization, Labor Standards, and Women's Rights: Dilemmas of Collective (In)action in an Interdependent World," *Feminist Economics,* March 10, 2004: 3–35. In the 1830s and 1840s, the American "mill girls"—a mixed group of working-class and middle-class women—came from the surrounding farms and villages of New England to work in cotton

Thiết province—a coastal town in central Vietnam where fisheries are an important means of livelihood—who worked in several FDI factories in Ho Chi Minh City, first at Huê Phong (in a factory that produced leather shoes), then at a garment factory jointly owned by Vietnamese and Taiwanese.[33] She lived with other migrant workers from her hometown. She expressed her aspirations clearly:

> In my case, it is to make a living. My family financial situation was OK, but I liked to go [to work in the factory] because I did not have a job back home. I asked for my mother's permission to open a tailor shop but she declined because I was still too young. But I did not like the idea of relying on my mother for pocket money, so I volunteered to go to work in the South. The employment office in Phan Thiết province advertised that migrant workers would make VND 450,000 per month, so I calculated that at least I could save and send home for my mother about VND 200,000 per month [after deducting all living and housing expenses]. So that's the reason why I went to work in the city.

Later, Liễu shared information about her family's financial situation, which was not very good. Her parents owned a small boat for near-shore fishing, which, in the late 1990s, was sufficient to provide for a family of seven (parents and five children). But things got difficult in 2002. Liễu explained:

> Now it is more difficult because our boat is small so we can only fish near shore. Other households have bigger boats, so they can fish in large quantities offshore. We can't compete with that, and that caused some trouble for us. So, I saved up money and sent home about VND 600,000 every three months. I am the only one working in the city; my four siblings stay at home with my parents.

In Liễu's case, financial necessity and independence are strong, both for herself and for her family. Even so, her original intention was not to find factory work, but to open a tailor shop at home so she could work and support herself independently. This strong woman went on to participate in several protests for the workers' rights and interests in the joint-venture factory.[34]

The position of contemporary Vietnamese women workers in factories producing for the global supply chains is more restricted than that of the 1830s

---

mills in Lowell, Massachusetts, and lived in boarding houses near the mills. JoAnne Weisman Deitch, ed., *The Lowell Mill Girls: Life in the Factory* (Lowell, MA: Discovery Enterprises, Ltd., 1991), pp. 10–11. For a short time (four to five years), those Lowell mill girls joined the factory life for some financial stability or independence, and to assist their families with remittances that helped pay farm mortgages or the costs of their brothers' college education. Interestingly, almost two centuries later, modern-day Vietnamese women migrant workers engaged in practices very similar to those engaged in by the Lowell mill girls. These mill girls did not work for long in this factory town due to the poor working conditions—dust, lint, and accidents on the line—and the long work hours that were controlled by the factory bells. These conditions were similar to those faced by the Vietnamese workers in the French-owned Nam Định textile combine discussed in Chapter 1.

[33] Interview with Liễu, August 2002, Ho Chi Minh City.

[34] More details can be found in Angie Ngọc Trần, "Sewing for the Global Economy: Thread of Resistance in Vietnamese Textile and Garment Industries," in *Critical Globalization Studies*, ed. William Robinson and Richard Appelbaum (New York, NY and London: Routledge, 2005), pp. 379–92.

Lowell mill workers, for those New England women at least had access to many cultural and educational resources.[35] In today's neoliberal world, the Vietnamese workers toiling on the assembly lines of factories owned by foreign investors have much less free time and resources to improve themselves, with respect to both skills and additional education. The refrain I heard from workers and read in newspaper accounts is that they barely have enough time to sleep, rest, and get ready for another work day. Here is the lament of a young female worker in the Đồng Nai industrial zone, as reported in a local newspaper:

> Every morning, I have to report to the factory at 6:30 AM. Once there, my face is glued to the sewing machine, working until noon without any break. After a thirty-minute break to eat lunch, rice has not yet settled down in my stomach, I have to return to the sewing machine until early evening. At this point, if I were to go home, then at the end of the month I would only receive over VND 600,000. So, I often decide to work overtime until 8:00 or 9:00 PM before I leave the factory. When I get home, I barely have time to wash, clean, and collapse in bed to sleep in order to continue working [the next day].[36]

But they do not deprive themselves of simple fun in their daily lives. Whenever possible, they hang out to chat, shop, cook, walk, ride bicycles, and watch TV or videos together. And they don't give up the love for reading. Fortunately, the *Người Lao Động* journalists who contributed to the newspaper's daily "Rights and Responsibilities" page stepped in to enrich workers' lives in a meaningful way. They mobilized a "library-for-workers" campaign and got books, newspapers, and magazines donated by local bookstores and Ho Chi Minh City residents. From December 2006 to January 2007, they successfully delivered more than sixty-two "libraries-for-workers" (*tủ sách công nhân*) to both state-owned factories and some large FDI factories,[37] including three factories in Linh Trung II EPZ that sparked the 2005 minimum-wage strikes: Freetrend, Kollan, and Hugo.[38]

Most workers with whom I spoke greatly appreciated these reading materials because, before the libraries were introduced, they had access to very few forms of entertainment. Photos of workers reading during break times were published in the labor newspapers to give momentum to this program. The photos showed that

---

[35] Many Lowell mill women workers—certainly not all—took advantage of what the city's life offered, advantages that were not available in their home farms and villages. In the evenings and on Sundays, they checked out books from the libraries, attended lectures, shows, and concerts, and had their writings published in the local magazines, including criticisms of working conditions in the mill. The *Lowell Offering* magazine exposed those criticisms and union activism. Deitch, *The Lowell Mill Girls*, p. 14.

[36] Nhóm phóng viên Chính Trị-Công Đoàn, "Làm công khổ lắm!" [Work for Hire is Atrocious!], *Người Lao Động*, August 29, 2007, http://www.nld.com.vn/200603P0C1010/lam-cong-kho-lam-.htm, accessed June 2009; G. H, "Nhọc nhằn' lao động nhập cư" [Arduous Work of Migrant Workers], *Lao Động*, December 4, 2006, http://www.laodong.com.vn/Utilities/PrintView.aspx?ID=13668, accessed June 2009.

[37] Minh Nam—Hồng Đào, "Sách lại về với công nhân" [Books have Returned to Workers], *Người Lao Động*, January 28, 2007. http://nld.com.vn/178827P0C1010/sach-lai-ve-voi-cong-nhan.htm, accessed July 2008.

[38] Hồng Đào, "Đã tặng 22 tủ sách công nhân" [Already Donated 22 Book Cases (with books) for Workers], *Người Lao Động*, December 29, 2006, http://nld.com.vn/175709P0C1010/da-tang-22-tu-sach-cong-nhan.htm, accessed May 2007.

workers are thirsty for knowledge and entertainment, for their eyes were glued to the pages as they ate or rested.[39] The "library-for-workers" idea spread to some worker dormitories in districts in which proactive labor unions provided employees with this reading entertainment after work.

Impacts of Household Registration (Hộ Khẩu) Policy on Migrant Workers

Migrant workers face three substantial financial challenges: paying for housing, electricity, and child care. While both migrant and local workers receive the same minimum wage according to the level of their job, migrant workers' lives are much more difficult and their expenses higher, due in part to various restrictions imposed by the household registration policy (*Hộ khẩu*). The lack of affordable housing for migrant workers in big cities such as Ho Chi Minh City and Hanoi, and the negative impacts of the household registration policy, were exposed by the media as early as 2005.[40] Even when these workers can afford to purchase a house in the city, it is virtually impossible for them. Decree 51/CP stated that those who lack *Hộ khẩu* registration in the city are classified in the KT3 category (*Giấy đăng ký tạm trú*)—a category for temporary city residents—which does not allow their names to be registered on house (or land) deeds. On a rare occasion when a migrant worker can afford to buy a house or land, the worker has to register a local person's name on the deed. This practice tends to cause problems, for when conflicts erupt between the person who paid for the property and the person registered as owner of the property, the migrant is likely to lose his or her home or land.[41] So most migrant workers resort to renting rooms from local homeowners (first renting out extra rooms in their houses, then building guest houses to seize this source of rent income). In my fieldwork, I witnessed situations in which four to six workers lived together in dilapidated, unsanitary, and very small rental units. Some large factories

---

[39] Hồng Đào, "Những điều mới mẻ từ sách" [New Insights from Books], *Người Lao Động*, April 23, 2007, http://nld.com.vn/187096P1010C1011/nhung-dieu-moi-me-tu-sach.htm, accessed May 2007; Nhóm phóng viên Chính Trị—Công Đoàn, "Sách đã về với công nhân" [Books have Reached Workers], *Người Lao Động*, December 17, 2006, http://nld.com.vn/174398P0C1002/sach-da-ve-voi-cong-nhan.htm, and Chương Trình, "Tủ Sách Công Nhân: Sách về nhân đôi niềm vui!" [The Book-drive Program for Workers: Arriving Books Double the Happiness!], December 30, 2006, http://nld.com.vn/175813P0C1010/sach-ve-nhan-doi-niem-vui.htm, accessed March 2007.

[40] Nguyên Thủy, "Lao động nhập cư tại TP.HCM phải có "sổ lao động" [Migrant Workers in Ho Chi Minh City Must Have "Labor Booklet"], *Việt Báo*, June 24, 2005, http://vietbao.vn/Xa-hoi/Lao-dong-nhap-cu-tai-TP-HCM-phai-co-so-lao-dong/45159 503/157/, accessed June 8, 2009; Tuổi Trẻ (cited as the author), "Hộ Khẩu KT3, Công Dân Thiệt Đủ Đường" [KT3 Household Registration Policy, Migrant Workers got Shortchanged in Every Way], May 8, 2005, http://dantri.com.vn/c20/s20-54015/ho-khau-kt3-cong-dan-thiet-du-duong.htm, accessed June 8, 2009; Đoàn Loan, "Hơn 19.000 người nhập cư sẽ được cấp thẻ công dân" [Over 19,000 Migrant Workers will be Issued Citizenship Cards], http://www.vnexpress.net/GL/Xa-hoi/2006/06/3B9EA8C3/ June 7, 2006, accessed June 8, 2009; Nhóm phóng viên Chính Trị-Công Đoàn, "Làm công khổ lắm!" [Work for Hire is Atrocious!]; V. Hùng, "Bình Dương: 268.800 CNVC-LĐ có nhu cầu nhà ở xã hội" [Bình Dương: 268,800 workers-employees have social needs for housing], *Người Lao Động*, April 11, 2009, http://www.nld.com.vn/20090411125455697P0C1051/268800-cnvcld-co-nhu-cau-nha-o-xa-hoi.htm, accessed June 8, 2009; and Hà Dịu, "Nhọc Nhằn Đời Lao Động Nhập Cư" [Hardships of the Life of Migrant Workers].

[41] Tuổi Trẻ, "Hộ Khẩu KT3."

(such as the Huê Phong factory) rent out rooms to workers within the confines of their gated facilities; some factory managers use these restricted accommodations to monitor, control, and curtail workers' activities.[42]

Until recently, migrant workers have paid more than local residents for utilities, such as electricity, which could run very high in the hot and humid climate. As migrants, they cannot buy utilities directly from the city company but must depend on the meters of the local homeowners. Many unscrupulous local homeowners have taken advantage of this situation and charged these vulnerable workers higher fees, because the migrants had no other option.[43] To fight this treatment, migrant workers exposed this gouging practice to the labor press and local labor unions, prompting reports that triggered intervention by local authorities. After many newspaper reports exposing the disadvantages migrant workers faced with regard to housing, electricity, and child care, the HCMC Labor Federation mandated in May 2009 that migrant workers could pay for electricity at the same low rate enjoyed by local residents.[44] Progress of this kind has been facilitated, in large part, by the proactive *Người Lao Động* newspaper.

---

[42] Some factories rented out dormitory rooms at affordable rates. But they had restrictions that resulted in low occupancy rates; most of those temporary dormitories were less than 50 percent occupied. The rents varied: Tân Bình Industrial Zone (VND 123,000 per person per month plus VND 30,000 electricity); Tân Tạo Industrial Zone (VND 180,000 per person per month plus official rates for utilities); Tân Thuận Industrial Zone (VND 90,000 to 170,000 per person per month); Nissei-Linh Trung EPZ housing (each worker had to pay only VND 20,000 for electricity and water, but only 36 percent of rooms were occupied). The main reason for low occupancy was that these places had curfews (10:00 PM in most places) and no visitation rights. In the words of one female worker, "I have to present my ID card to the security guard every time I come in and out of this dormitory. I felt like [I was] going to an army base [mainly due to curfew and visitation policies]. Worse yet, when my friends come to visit me, they were not allowed to enter. So, I had to move out to have more freedom." According to another female worker, "My parents often visit me and stay with me for several days, but this dormitory did not allow them to do that, so I moved out." On the other hand, Nissei management explained: "To prevent thefts and chaos, we [did] not allow workers to invite anyone to their rooms. Workers who [couldn't] comply with this policy [could] move out, and receive VND 70,000 per person per month." Hồng Đào, "Công nhân không 'mặn' nhà lưu trú" [Workers are not Welcoming Dormitories], *Người Lao Động*, May 4, 2009, http://nld.com.vn/20090503085942700P0C1010/cong-nhan-khong-man-nha-luu-tru.htm, accessed June 2009. Another interpretation of this gated community monitoring could be that the local state administrators, labor unions, and management wanted to detect and preempt any sign of workers' protests or strikes.

[43] For instance, using the justification that the minimum wage had increased in January 2009, some local homeowners raised the rents (VND 350,000 to 400,000 per person/month) and electricity costs (VND 3,500 per kWh) and water (VND 10,000 per m3). Hồng Đào, "Đối Mặt Với Tăng Giá" [Facing Rising Costs], *Người Lao Động*, April 13, 2009, http://nld.com.vn/20090412095249576P0C1010/doi-mat-voi-tang-gia.htm, accessed May 2009. This made life even more miserable for migrant workers.

[44] Consistent implementation has been the challenge. In 2009, only a small percentage of migrant workers received such equal treatment. Not all districts implemented this policy properly; monitoring and disciplinary actions were proposed to curb violations. The newspaper article specifically mentioned the people's committee of a ward in Tân Bình District (in Ho Chi Minh City) that failed to carry out this policy even though the administrators had received proper information from a state official at the district level. The HCMC Labor Federation planned to monitor and audit local rental units, and impose a fine (VND 3–5 million) against homeowners who sold electricity to migrant workers at high rates. Nam Dương, "Quyết liệt đưa điện đúng giá đến CN" [Resolutely Charging Workers Correct Electricity Costs], *Người Lao Động*, May 7, 2009, http://www.nld.com.vn/200905 06112236709

Migrant workers have also faced problems finding affordable child care. Child care is crucial, because most likely both parents have to work long hours—regular and overtime—without nearby family support. The demand for reliable child care is high, and the supply low. In only one industrial zone in Ho Chi Minh City, Tân Tạo, where 70 percent of the 20,000 workers were women, about three thousand women workers were unable to find affordable child care. The reason had to do with a shortage of several thousand kindergarten teachers per year in Ho Chi Minh City.[45] For those who lack *hộ khẩu* in the city, access to affordable child care support and other social services is very limited. Local parents have priority over migrant workers: each public preschool has to set aside a certain number of seats for the children of local residents, and thus space is limited for migrants' children, even when the migrants have proper KT3 cards, as discussed in Chapter 3.[46]

Last but not least, migrant workers have much less access to affordable public education for themselves and for their children. Without the KT3 cards (unavailable to those who lack a steady job or a "permanent" local address), workers cannot borrow money to take vocational classes after work to improve their conditions.[47] Their children are forced to attend overcrowded public schools (if space is available at all), because the workers cannot afford the cost of private schools. Many workers

P0C1010/quyet-liet-dua-dien-dung-gia-den-cn.htm, accessed May 2009. But the "First Six Months of 2012" report by the HCMC Labor Federation showed that the unions' effort had achieved some positive outcomes on behalf of workers' social welfare in the HCMC area: 90 percent of the local homeowner renters had promised not to raise rent until the end of 2012 and to charge correct electricity prices to 1.1 million migrant workers. Moreover, the unions also ensured that 1,637 local childcare centers did not raise the tuition fees to care for 166,954 children of migrant workers. HCMC Labor Federation, "Báo Cáo: Tình hình công nhân, viên chức, lao động và hoạt động Công đoàn Thành phố 6 tháng đầu năm 2012; Phương hướng hoạt động 6 tháng cuối năm 2012" [Report: Situation of Workers and Public Employees, and Activities of HCMC Labor Federation in the First Six Months of 2012; Directions for Activities in the Last Six Months of 2012], June 25, 2012.

[45] Dân Trí, "HCM City: Low Salaries Prompt Kindergarten Teachers to Give up Jobs," May 27, 2008. http://english.vietnamnet.vn/education/2008/05/785163/, accessed June 2008.

[46] For instance, a decent preschool built right next to Tân Tạo Industrial Zone in Bình Tân District gave priority to local residents' children in enrollment. The school provided good child care, meals, and lessons for children from twenty-five months to three years old, with affordable tuition: around VND 500,000 per month, with three meals included. This arrangement was perfect for workers, who could drop children off in the morning before work and pick them up after work. When parents had to work overtime, their children could stay in the center until 6:00 PM without any extra fee. However, without the temporary card (KT3), their children would not be admitted. A female worker complained: "When I heard about this wonderful and affordable preschool, I immediately came to inquire in hopes of enrolling my child, but they asked for a KT3 registration card. As a migrant worker without a permanent rental place, I did not yet have a KT3 card, therefore I had to bring my child to a private preschool that cost me over VND 700,000 per month." With food, uniforms, and learning materials added to the tuition, these poor migrant parents would have to pay up to almost VND 1 million per month to enroll a single child. This monthly child-care cost almost equaled the monthly wage of an FDI worker. Phạm Hồ and Hồng Đào, "Con công nhân với nguy cơ thất học" [Children of Workers with Inadequate-Education Peril], *Người Lao Động*, September 24, 2008, http://nld.com.vn/240431P1010C1012/con-cong-nhan-voi-nguy-co-that-hoc.htm, accessed September 2008; Hồng Đào, "Trường mầm non cho con công nhân" [Preschools for Workers' Children], *Người Lao Động*, September 7, 2008 [hardcopy].

[47] Phạm Hồ, "Doanh nghiệp giấu khó, công nhân khốn khổ" [Enterprises Hide their Problems, Workers Bear the Brunt], *Người Lao Động*, March 27, 2009, http://nld.com.vn/2009032610 349806P0C1010/doanh-nghiep-giau-kho-cong-nhan-khon-kho.htm, accessed April 2009.

have had to send the children back to their hometowns or villages, where the grandparents take care of them. Such parents may then worry about the safety and care of those children, especially if elderly grandparents are unable to provide proper oversight or the schools are deficient. When sending the children home is not an option, for there are no grandparents to care for them, then finding childcare and accessible schools for their children are difficult challenges for most migrant workers who have to work overtime. Many workers have had to let their children stay inside the school yard until they can be picked up after work, or play outside of their rental units during the day (the parents would lock the house for fear of theft), or sleep at a neighbor's house when both parents have to work overtime.[48]

Facing all these challenges, how do migrant workers manage and what makes them pull together? What are the roles of native place and gender? The workers themselves answer these questions.

Place and Gender

The following stories of several migrant female and male workers, chosen from among the many reports I heard in interviews over the years, show how the cultural resources they bring to the workplace enlighten their lives in rental units and in their occasional trips home. These cases demonstrate the multifaceted nature of workers' lives, as they aspire to financial independence and upward mobility and rely on their native-place networking. Many of them traveled to Ho Chi Minh City together, stayed together, and came home for short visits together during national holidays. They also exuded a sense of sisterhood and brotherhood during good and bad times.

I interviewed several migrant women workers from Nam Định and Quảng Nam in 2002 and 2004 at their rental units. I met and talked with two women, Nhung and Thoa, several times in 2004. Nhung was a leader of spontaneous protests. She had come from Nam Định to work in Shilla Bags, a 100 percent South Korean–owned factory making many types of bags. She lived with her husband and three brothers-in-law from Nam Định in a tiny apartment (one living room, one kitchen, one bathroom, one bedroom in the attic) rented from a local resident in Bình Chánh district. They each contributed VND 100,000 to pay the monthly rent of VND 500,000, not including water and electricity costs. The young son of Nhung and her husband stayed with his grandparents in Nam Định so the parents could work in Ho Chi Minh City. Nhung said that she missed her son a great deal, and Tết—the Vietnamese Lunar New Year—was the only time that she could afford to go home to visit him and her own parents.

Thoa was a timid, frail, and soft-spoken young woman. Having migrated from Nam Định, she lived with her aunt and other relatives from Nam Định in a small rental unit nearby. She clearly looked up to Nhung, calling her "*chị*" (elder sister). Thoa worked at Top One, a Taiwanese garment factory. She participated in a food boycott; I will describe both women's roles in the Food-Water Boycott later in this chapter.

---

[48] Phạm Hồ and Hồng Đào, "Nhọc Nhằn Đưa Con Đến Lớp" [Taking Children to School, Arduously], *Người Lao Động*, September 25, 2008, http://nld.com.vn/240554P0C1010/nhoc-nhan-dua-con-den-lop.htm, accessed September 2008. Migrant workers are temporary—not career—employees, but many still work and live in the cities for years, trying to improve their lives and the lives of their children.

Their shared links to native place bonded them. During holiday seasons, such as Tết, they traveled home together by bus:

> We took ten days off to come home and celebrate Tết with our parents. We paid VND 600,000 one-way for the bus trip home, which normally takes two full days of traveling. Then the bus dropped off workers whose families live in downtown Nam Định, then the rest of us in various locations. After the holiday, we would take the bus back to the factory together.[49]

Migrant workers tend to help out their friends who came from their native place by referring them to their bosses, or, if they are in supervisory positions, hiring these newcomers in the departments in which they work. Nhung established a rapport with a line supervisor, also a migrant woman worker from Vinh, a northern province, who hired mostly northern migrant workers to work in a Taiwanese-owned factory she supervised. Relying on this connection, Nhung successfully convinced her supervisor to negotiate with the Taiwanese boss to improve the meals and sanitary conditions for all workers. But such mid-level Vietnamese supervisors are also employees who have their own interests and are in an unequal power relationship with management. Thus, these Vietnamese supervisors or line leaders are often entangled in conflicts-of-interest and have to make compromises—even with their native fellow workers—to ensure their own job protection and advancement. On substantial issues such as work hours, Nhung's supervisor sided with management, perhaps to advance her own financial interests. Nhung complained to me, "My [female] boss allied with the Taiwanese boss and gave us workers a hard time. She never approved any workers' requests to take a day or two off, even when we had family emergencies."[50]

Male workers, too, found support from bonding with other male workers coming from the same hometowns. There is evidence for place and brotherhood networking. Đông was from a peasant family in Nam Định. He used to work in the fields to help his family on their small family plot. When it became very difficult to earn even VND 500,000 per month working on their land, he traveled to Ho Chi Minh City with his male friends from Nam Định. When speaking to me, he mentioned them using terms of endearment and of brotherhood: *bạn bè anh em* (friends and brothers). In 1995, he and seventy other Nam Định residents traveled south, and many started working together at a South Korean–owned bag factory (making purses and backpacks).[51] He learned his sewing and stitching skills on the job by assisting other garment workers, and then became a garment worker himself, making about VND 900,000 per month at the time of the interview in 2002.

There were gender differences with respect to sending money home. Unlike Liễu and many other women workers who saved and sent money home for their families, men workers seemed to have a harder time saving money, especially given their

---

[49] Ibid.

[50] Interview with Nhung in July and August 2004, Ho Chi Minh City.

[51] Đông explained, in addition, that in the early 1990s the Nam Định textile combine went bankrupt due to corrupt officials who squandered state money. Then, in 1995, the state essentially salvaged the company, covered the losses, rented out some facilities, and converted the rest into a state corporation. The local state officials then appointed an entirely new group of managers.

purchases of coffee and cigarettes, which provided some comfort after a long, grueling workday. When asked if he had money to send home, Đông lamented:

> Our parents did not expect much from those of us who came to work down here. Our monthly wage [was] very low, plus we had to pay the rent, food, and utilities. So when other friends asked us to go for coffees and cigarettes as entertainment, we quickly ran out of money. No money was left even before the end of the month.[52]

Religious and Occupational Rituals and Stereotypes

In addition to bonding with each other as sisters and brothers, the migrant workers also connected through religious and occupational practices. Maintaining these practices could enrich their lives and strengthen their ties in good and bad times. Many of the workers from Nam Định were Catholic. Nhung told me about an informal network of their friends from the North, with whom she and her family hung out every night. On Sundays they attended a local Catholic church together near their rental units.

Both Nhung and Thoa shared with me the motivational power of occupational rituals among seamstresses that created a strong bond, in both foreign-direct investment and domestic factories. These migrant workers observed the *giỗ tổ thợ may* (day of the sewing saint), a ceremony to venerate their occupation's saint in whichever ways that they could. For instance, members of the Nam Định group in Gò Vấp would pool their money (VND 5,000 per person) to prepare a big tray of food: a boiled chicken, rice, and fruit offerings. The line leader would stand in front, with workers in tow, all burning incense to pay respect to the saint, and then they would share a meal together. Another practice is for workers to use the bonuses of the whole assembly line to pay for all expenses for this ritual.[53]

Workers originating from different regions of Vietnam certainly have their own perceptions and cultural stereotypes, which they tend to perpetuate, but I found no evidence that these stereotypes divided workers from one another in "class moments." For instance, workers from the central region had a general reputation for working hard and persevering at the job (*miền trung cam chịu*). Migrant workers from the central region tended to ally more with northern migrants than with workers from the South (both locals and migrants from rural southern provinces). Liễu, a female migrant worker from Phan Thiết province (in the central region), reiterated a persistent, shared perception of workers from the Mekong Delta as people who are unwilling to work hard and who desire a comfortable lifestyle, as reflected in their "white skin and long hair." Yet labor organizers with whom I spoke refuted many of these stereotypes of employees from the southern provinces, as I discuss below, using workers' own words.

EAST ASIAN AND SOUTHEAST ASIAN CAPITALISTS

Many of the workers with whom I spoke were employed in companies at least partially owned by East Asian and Southeast Asian capitalists—ethnic Chinese, in

---

[52] This is one explanation for the cycle of debt suffered by many migrant workers.

[53] Interview with Thoa, July 2002, Ho Chi Minh City.

particular. Many of these contemporary companies are engaged in manufacturing for the global supply chains in labor-intensive industries, the sector that still employs the highest number of nonfarm workers in Vietnam.

After the reunification of Vietnam in 1975, the government imposed its socialist, central-planning model over the whole country, and cracked down on the free market in the South, in general, with measures that sought to control the Hoa merchant community, notably in Chợ Lớn.[54] But within twenty years, ethnic Hoa had reemerged not just as merchants, but as industrialists in the South. I will examine the concentration of the Hoa capital in several key districts in Ho Chi Minh City: districts 5, 6, 10, and 11.

By the time I interviewed migrant workers in Ho Chi Minh City, East Asian and Southeast Asian capitalists had returned to manufacturing, especially in the textile, garment, and footwear industries.[55] Ethnic Chinese investors from the greater China zone—Taiwan, mainland China, and Hong Kong—together with the Hoa capitalists in Vietnam, resumed their commercial and manufacturing strongholds in sectors that had existed since colonial times: the textile and garment, shoe, food processing, plastics, and banking industries and import–export activities.[56] Since 2006, Taiwanese investors have operated some two to three thousand factories in Vietnam, most concentrated in Ho Chi Minh City and the surrounding provinces.[57] The United States, Japan, South Korea, and Singapore investors also returned since *Đổi Mới*; many companies have invested in heavy and high-tech industries, as discussed in Chapter 3.

As suppliers for brand-name products in the twenty-first century, East Asian capitalists, and Taiwanese capitalists in particular, followed a pattern of developing their subsidiaries in China in the mid-1980s by using the relatively cheap supply of labor and tapping the huge market there. When faced with rising labor costs, high taxation, and increased regulation in China, many of these companies relocated their operations to lower wage countries, such as Vietnam, where conditions had improved thanks to *Đổi Mới* and the resurgence of the market system in the early 1990s.[58] Taiwanese overseas investment in apparel and shoes follows this pattern closely. Hong-Zen Wang and H. H. Michael Hsiao have argued that, similar to Western multinationals, Taiwanese multinational companies relocated their manufacturing operations to cheaper labor countries—notably, from China to

---

[54] Adam Fforde and Stefan De Vylder, *From Plan to Market: The Economic Transition in Vietnam* (Boulder, CO: Westview Press, 1996), p. 128.

[55] Ministry of Industry and Commerce (with data from Vietnamese Textile Corporation—Vinatex), "Thu Hút Đầu Tư Nước Ngoài Vào Dệt May—Những Chuyển Động Tích Cực" [Attracting Foreign Investment in Textile and Garment Industries—Some Positive Developments], February 21, 2008, http://www.tinthuongmai.vn/IWINews.aspx?Catalog ID=1987&ID=67319, accessed May 2008.

[56] Trần Khánh, *The Ethnic Chinese and Economic Development in Vietnam* (Singapore: Institute of Southeast Asian Studies, 1993), p. 107.

[57] Anita Chan, "Strikes in Vietnam and China in Taiwanese-Owned Factories: Diverging Industrial Relations Patterns, in *Vietnam Update Series: Labour in Vietnam* (Singapore: Institute of Southeast Asian Studies, 2011), p. 213.

[58] Interview conducted by David Smith and Angie Ngọc Trần with Jung Won-Joon, KOTRA (Korea Trade-Investment Promotion Agency) official, October 14, 2003, at KOTRA Office Daeha complex at Daewoo Hotel, Hanoi; and Keith Bradsher, "Investors Seek Asian Options to Costly China," *New York Times*, June 18, 2008.

Vietnam—in the 1990s.[59] Taiwanese capitalists hired Chinese professionals who had worked for Taiwanese companies in China as midlevel managers to supervise their Vietnamese factories. These Chinese professionals have the social capital necessary for such positions, as they use a common language with their Taiwanese owners/managers, such as Mandarin, possess a Taiwanese education, and demonstrate a way of thinking and management style dedicated to maximizing profits: "These Chinese managers are also very good in enforcing the rules set by Taiwanese managers' order."[60] This strategy perpetuates the patterns of the Greater China Zone investment. I found this practice evident in many of my visits to factories: skilled mainland Chinese technicians and engineers, trained by the Taiwanese in mainland China, rotated in for several months to work in Taiwanese-owned factories in Vietnam, and then returned to China. I will discuss this pattern more fully in relation to the Huê Phong Leather Shoe factory case study in Chapter 6. Many companies did not register as Taiwanese-owned, but as Vietnamese-owned, so they could evade government regulations imposed on FDI factories, such as restrictions on sales in the domestic market and the requirement that FDI factories pay their employees a higher minimum wage than do non-FDI factories.[61]

STRIKES IN FDI FACTORIES

The conditions that typify foreign-direct investment factories, defined in part by the alienation of foreign managers from Vietnamese employees, predictably incited workers' dissatisfaction and led to strikes. Yet one can say that the first two rounds of minimum wage strikes in Vietnam (at the end of 2005, and in 2007) were effectively directed against the state, not the factories, because state policies had frozen the minimum wage for seven years (1999–2005) and the state macro-economic policies had given rise to the crippling two-digit inflation starting in 2007, making workers' lives miserable. But the third round of strikes in 2008 was directly against FDI companies that had delayed paying workers inflation-adjusted minimum wages. Overall, it is politically "safe" for the workers to strike in foreign-owned—rather than state-owned—factories, and, in this context, the workers did win on two counts: 1) they won approval of a policy that raised the minimum wage; and 2) they insured that a mandatory annual inflation adjustment would be reflected in the "new" minimum wage (the revised annual minimum wage takes effect at the beginning of January). Still, these victories are not enough to guarantee the workers would be able to earn a fair living. As argued bluntly by Phạm Ngọc Tùng, the president of the VGCL in May 2012, even the annual-inflation-adjusted minimum wage only covers 60 percent of workers' basic necessities.[62]

---

[59] Hong-Zen Wang and H. H. Michael Hsiao, "Ethnic Resources or Capitalist Logic? Taiwanese Investment and Chinese Temporary Migrants in Vietnam," paper presented at the "Symposium on Experiences and Challenges of Economic Development in Southeast and East Asia," October 17–18, 2000, PROSEA (Program for Southeast Asia Area Studies) and the Institute of Economics, Academia Sinica, Taipei, Taiwan, August 2001, pp. 6, 8, 18, 19.

[60] Ibid., pp. 15–17.

[61] Ibid., pp. 9, 15, 17–18.

[62] Nguyễn Quyết, "Quốc Hội Thảo Luận Dự Án Bộ Luật Lao Động Sửa Đổi: Lương Tối Thiểu Phải Sát Thực Tế Cuộc Sống" [The Parliament Discussed Labor Code Proposed Revision: Minimum Wage had to Accommodate Real Costs of Living], *Người Lao Động*, May 24, 2012,

Consequently, workers need to work overtime in order to earn the remaining 40 percent to make ends meet. This reality explains the vicious cycle endured by workers, who are paid a non-living wage, which they supplement with excessive overtime work, while receiving inadequate social/health/unemployment benefits. The sad facts about the need to work overtime due to non-living wages, "*lương không đủ sống*," are conveyed in an article about workers in Pou Yuen, a huge subsidiary of the Taiwanese-owned Pou Chen Group, which employs over ninety thousand workers producing footwear for Adidas.[63] Talking to two Người Lao Động journalists at the factory gate, workers confided that they never work just eight hours per day, but usually put in twelve hours, in order to make a living. Many pregnant workers in this factory, up to the eighth month of pregnancy, are desperate enough to work overtime regularly, even knowing that it will negatively affect their babies.

Three Rounds of Minimum Wage Strikes

The first round of strikes in the new millennium started at the end of 2005 in protest again the minimum wage in the FDI sector, which had been frozen at VND 625,950 for seven years, as noted above. In response to worker-initiated protests that shut down factories in Ho Chi Minh City export processing zone, the state raised minimum wages by 40 percent, effective at the beginning of 2006. The labor newspapers played a key role in publicizing these strikes. They had pressured both the HCMC Labor Federation and MOLISA to come together and push for the prime minister's decree.[64]

The second round was triggered by high inflation in 2007 and 2008 (19 percent in March 2008 and 25 percent in May 2008), which raised food prices by as much as 30 percent, and housing rentals by 20 percent.[65] This pattern of inflation—exacerbated by the household registration policy—had a greater impact on migrant workers than on city workers, because migrants had to pay higher nonresident prices for necessities such as rent, utilities, child care, and education for themselves and their children. This wave of spontaneous labor strikes took place in 2007. To respond to

---

http://nld.com.vn/20120524124132940p0c1010/luong-toi-thieu-phai-sat-thuc-te-cuoc-song.htm, accessed June 2012.

[63] Phan Anh and Hồng Nhung, "Kiệt sức vì làm thêm" [Exhausted because of Overtime Work], *Người Lao Động*, December 09, 2011, http://nld.com.vn/20111209103658773 p0c1010/kiet-suc-vi-lam-them.htm, accessed December 2011.

[64] Angie Ngọc Trần, "Alternatives to the 'Race to the Bottom' in Vietnam: Minimum Wage Strikes and Their Aftermath," *Labor Studies Journal* 32,4, (December 2007): 439–40.

[65] Dương Minh Đức 2008, "Qua hàng loạt vụ đình công ở TP.Hồ Chí Minh: Lương, thưởng chưa tương xứng với công lao động" [After Waves of Strikes in HCMC: Wages and Bonuses not Commensurate with Workers' Effort], *Lao Động*, January 14, 2008, http://laodong.vn/Home/congdoan/tranhchapld/2008/1/72907.laodong; accessed July 1, 2010; Nhóm phóng viên Chính Trị—Công Đoàn, "Đơn Độc trong cơn bão giá: trong vòng vây giá cả" [Lonely in the Price Storm: Under Siege of Prices], *Người Lao Động*, November 6, 2007, http://nld.com.vn/206761P0C1010/trong-vong-vay-gia-ca.htm; "Chống Chọi trong cơn bão giá: mới nửa tháng đã hết vèo tiền lương" [Coping with the Price Storm: Wages Gone/Spent in Half a Month], *Người Lao Động* November 7, 2007, http://nld.com.vn/206856 P0C1010/moi-nua-thang-da-het-veo-tien-luong.htm; "Chống Chọi trong cơn bão giá: làm thêm, bỏ nghề" [Coping with the Price Storm: Working Overtime, Abandoning (Nonlivable) Jobs], *Người Lao Động*, November 8, 2007, http://nld.com.vn/206917P1010C1012/lam-them-bo-nghe.htm, accessed July 12, 2009; and Hồng Đào, "Đối Mặt Với Tăng Giá."

those protests, the state instituted a cost-of-living adjustment of 13 percent to the base minimum wage in FDI companies, which went into effect on January 1, 2008.

The third round of strikes took place in January 2008, after many FDI companies had delayed paying these inflation-adjusted minimum wages mandated by the state.[66] This led to the state's announcement at the end of 2008 that it would institute another round of minimum-wage increases (10 to 20 percent) for the FDI sector effective in January 2009, addressing both inflation and the global economic crisis.[67] In sum, as a result of these series of protests, the state initiated a systematic minimum-wage increase intended to appease workers and not surprise management. They would announce the new minimum wage increases in October or November of each year, and these increases would then take effect on January 1 of the following year. Thus far, the state has implemented this policy in a timely manner.[68]

However, the three- and four-tiered minimum wage policy (with tiers based on the respective zones in which the factories are located) continues to privilege local urban workers at the expense of migrant workers. Moreover, the household registration policy works hand-in-hand with the minimum wage policies to control migration and sustain rural–urban inequality. Drawn to relatively high wages in urban areas, migrant workers from poorer areas desperately need registration cards if they wish to have access to affordable basic necessities equivalent to those local residents enjoy.

But this situation has been changing. Apparently, the four-tiered–minimum-wage policy (three-tiered before January 2010) has prompted East Asian foreign-direct investment to spread to rural districts throughout the country to take advantage of the comparatively low minimum-wage levels in those regions. Still, the main offices of these foreign-direct-investment companies continue to be located in big cities, such as Ho Chi Minh City and Hanoi, locations that enable management representatives to continue their lobbying efforts and to enjoy modern urban comforts. Since 2005, FDI factories have expanded beyond Ho Chi Minh City and Hanoi, and established sites in emerging industrial provinces (such as Đồng Nai, Bình Dương, Vũng Tàu, Tây Ninh, Long An, Bến Tre, Đồng Tháp, Cần Thơ, Đà Nẵng, Quảng Ngãi, Hưng Yên, Vĩnh Phúc, Bắc Giang) nationwide, in regions where provincial governments have laid out the red carpet to attract foreign investment. These pro-investment policies also demonstrate the Vietnamese state's power and flexibility to grant privileges and protections to certain groups of people—foreign investors in this case—for their investment in these export processing and industrial zones (as described by Aiwa Ong and discussed in the Introduction). However, from the Vietnamese perspective, it is precisely in these provinces where we witness

---

[66] Nam Dương, "Lương tối thiểu không phải là lương căn bản" [Minimum Wage is not a Basic Wage], *Người Lao Động*, January 22, 2008, http://nld.com.vn/213304P1010C1012/luong-toi-thieu-khong-phai-la-luong-can-ban.htm; "Doanh nghiệp phải điều chỉnh lương cho tất cả NLĐ" [Enterprises Have to Adjust Wages for all Workers], *Người Lao Động*, January 25, 2008, http://nld.com.vn/213621P0C1010/doanh-nghiep-phai-dieu-chinh-luong-cho-tat-ca-nld.htm, accessed January 2008.

[67] E. Lee Sunoo and Đỗ Quỳnh Chi, *Vietnam: A Foreign Manager's HR Survival Guide* (Hanoi: International Labour Organization, 2009), pp. 36–37.

[68] For the 2012 minimum wage increase, the state instituted the raise three months earlier than it had in previous years, making it effective from October 1, 2011, instead of January 1, 2012 (see Chapter 3).

increasing labor discontent and unrest due to management's labor violations.[69] The relatively recent strikes at Mỹ Phong, a Taiwanese-owned leather shoe factory, took place in Trà Vinh in the Mekong Delta region (recently designated as the fourth economic zone), where the minimum-wage level is lower than that in Ho Chi Minh City. The strikes were set off by some common grievances: that workers were given no Tết bonus; that steep fines were imposed when workers had to take some days off to attend to their family emergencies; and that women workers had been verbally abused by a Taiwanese specialist on the management team, among other complaints. This factory had been expanding production capacities in its two branches in Trà Vinh, hiring more than eleven thousand workers, and building a new factory in nearby Vĩnh Long province.[70]

Nationwide Strikes against Foreign Capital Ownership

Most strikes reported from 2005 through 2010 occurred in factories involving foreign capital and management from Taiwan, South Korea, and Hong Kong, with Taiwan and South Korea often topping the list (Figure 5.1). The spike in strikes in 2006 corresponded to the waves of minimum-wage-strikes initiated by FDI factory workers in Linh Trung I EPZ, and the higher spike in 2007 corresponded to worker-led protests to push FDI factories to implement the 2006 minimum-wage increase, which took effect in February 2006. The spike in 2008 corresponded to worker protests against management, spurred by dissatisfaction that management had failed to implement the inflation-adjusted–minimum-wage increases, which took effect in January 2008. There were fewer strikes in 2009 compared to 2008—only 310 cases, of which 239 cases erupted in FDI factories (77 percent)—due to low orders from brand-name corporations (which reduced the pressure to produce and work long hours), a decrease in business that resulted from the global financial crisis. While FDI factories accounted for the highest share of strikes, there is no breakdown by country origin of FDI in 2009.

In 2010, nationwide, there was a total of 424 strikes; most occurred in the southern economic zone: Đồng Nai (140 strikes) and Bình Dương (127 strikes) provinces.[71] Of the total strikes nationwide, 339 strikes (around 80 percent) occurred in FDI factories. Most of these 339 strikes erupted in the factories that involved capital originating from three East Asian countries: 38 percent (128) of strikes in the FDI sector erupted in Taiwanese factories; 32 percent (109), in Korean factories; 8 percent (26), in Japanese factories; and the rest were in other FDI factories. The case studies of protests below further illustrate the labor-management relations in those Taiwanese and Korean factories.

---

[69] Dương Minh, "Đình công … chuyển vùng!" [Strikes … Moving to Different Places!], *Người Lao Động*, May 30, 2005, http://nld.com.vn/119362P1010C1012/dinh-cong-chuyen-vung.htm, accessed July 10, 2009.

[70] BBC-Vietnamese section (no author), "Một vạn công nhân đình công ở Trà Vinh" [Ten Thousand Workers Went on Strike in Trà Vinh], http://www.bbc.co.uk/vietnamese/vietnam/2010/02/100202_labour_strike.shtml, accessed November 2, 2010.

[71] Communication with Trần Văn Lý, October 2011.

Nationwide strikes more than doubled in 2011: there were 978 strikes.[72] While breakdown data by region and by type of investment were not available when I wrote this, official statements and messages from Prime Minister Nguyễn Tấn Dũng show that he sided with workers over management, but he stressed the rule of law and the leadership role of the VGCL in strike resolution. Regarding a meeting with the VGCL leadership on February 22, 2012, in Hanoi, he said: "If working in the factories directly, I also support strikes because many factories failed to treat workers properly. We need to resolve the conflicts according to the law." He suggested that the VGCL cooperate with MOLISA and the Ministry of Public Security (or Ministry of the Interior) (*Bộ Công An*) to "actively expose and fight [*đấu tranh*] with the capitalists [*chủ sử dụng lao động*].[73]

Figure 5.1: Nationwide Strikes in Factories Funded by East Asian Capital and Other Foreign-Direct Investment (1995–2010)

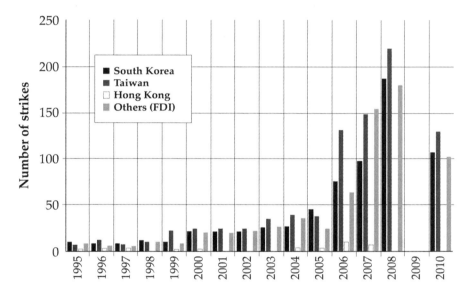

Source: Vietnamese General Labor Federation of Labor (VGCL), July 2010; Trần Văn Lý, VGCL, October 2011.

In 2011, the employment situation was very bleak for workers, with thousands of them—in construction and transportation, and in EPZs and IZs—unable to find work that offered a living wage. Migrant workers, especially in the EPZs and IZs, have continued to encounter the same problems that have troubled them for years: nonlivable wages reduced by high inflation, high costs of housing and utilities (much higher than stipulated by law), and a woefully inadequate supply of worker dormitories (only 9 out of 110 registered public housing projects throughout Vietnam have materialized and are in use). Meanwhile, management in a number of these

---

[72] Nguyễn Quyết, "Giảm đình công, tăng an sinh xã hội" [Reducing Strikes, Increasing Social Security], *Người Lao Động*, February 22, 2012, http://nld.com.vn/20120222095732102p0c1010/giam-dinh-cong-tang-an-sinh-xa-hoi.htm, accessed March 2012.

[73] Ibid.

factories continues to violate the law egregiously by appropriating workers' contributions to social, health, and unemployment insurance. By the end of 2011, the staggering social security debt incurred by management was VND 5,800 billion, or around US$277 million (using the exchange rate of US$1 = VND 21,000).[74]

Table 5.1: Protests in FDI Companies in Ho Chi Minh City (1995–2011)

Year	FDI Factories (%)	Total Number of Protests in Ho Chi Minh City
1995–96	22	36
1997	48	46
1998	47	38
1999	26	31
2000	35	34
2001	31	32
2002	39	36
2003	42	60
2004	62	47
2005	62	50
2006	45	113
2007	60	108
2008	68	200
2009	42	78
2010	50	70
2011	58	189

Sources: HCMC Labor Federation (1995–July 2010), HCMC Labor Union for EPZs and IZs (2010, 2011). Note: All percentages are shares of protests in FDI factories relative to the total number of protests in all sectors in Ho Chi Minh City annually.

Table 5.1 shows protests in FDI factories in Ho Chi Minh City. The global economic crisis in 2009 reduced the relative number of strikes during that year to a level similar to those experienced *before* the 2005–08 minimum-wage and inflation strike waves.

Concerning the strikes in FDI factories in 2011, it is important also to consider perspectives that critique the responses of the VGCL and the Vietnamese state. According to the Committee to Protect Vietnamese Workers (CPVW), a member of Free Viet Labor Federation, from June 21 to 28, 2011, thousands of Pou Yuen Vietnam factory workers in Bình Chánh District, Ho Chi Minh City, went on strike to demand a pay raise of VND 500,000 per month. To answer this demand, management promised to add VND 300,000 to their basic wage plus VND 200,000 for

---

[74] Ibid.

supplemental payments (which are *not* benefit bearing). However, CPVW argued that, even with this compromise, the practical implementation was unclear and potentially ineffective because management had broken its promises before. Moreover, CPVW claimed that dozens of strike leaders had been arrested by the Vietnamese authorities, and some were laid off by factory management.[75] Another critical source confirmed this: The Hong Kong–based Students and Scholars against Corporate Misbehavior (SACOM)—cited in Chinaworker.info—claimed that around twenty Vietnamese workers had been arrested in connection with this strike.[76] There is no information from the Vietnamese official sources, or Adidas, or the Pou Chen Group (Pou Yuen's Taiwanese industrial holding company) about this strike and its settlement.

CASE STUDIES OF WORKERS' PROTESTS

As we have seen, the influx of East and Southeast Asian investment in textile, garment, and shoe factories in Vietnam coincided with a substantial number of strikes and protest activities, and it is important to examine what factors of cultural identity played a key role in labor organizing in these factories. How did workers, empowered by their cultural ties, trigger and encourage "class moments" when they "[commenced] to struggle around common issues" of rights and interests?[77] How did they protest against the commodification of their labor to regain their own human dignity? How did they fight against capitalist exploitation and use the law to demand their rights and entitlements? The following eight cases illuminate the protests that took place in the most troubled sectors: six occurred in textile/garment and shoe factories; two involved the service sector (building maintenance and security).

Hoàn Cầu Migrant Workers: A Sit-In that Raised the Piece Rates

I interviewed a twenty-seven-year-old migrant worker, Đông, in 2002, in Gò Vấp district. He worked in Hoàn Cầu, a handbag factory owned by a Korean company and led by a Vietnamese woman president, who oversaw the production process and personnel issues. The company subcontracted for a United States corporate buyer, making backpacks and other types of bags. Đông was from Nam Định and stayed with his hometown friends, whom he considered his "friends and brothers" [*bạn bè anh em*], in a rental unit in Gò Vấp. They were peasants who had come from a few Nam Định villages, hoping to improve their income by coming to work in Ho Chi Minh City. But the cost of living in Ho Chi Minh City dashed their dream:

> There were seventy of us from Nam Định who [had come] here to work since 1995, about the same number of men and women. Making VND 600,000 or 700,000 per month back in our villages is difficult. It is difficult to make a living in our village so we went to Saigon [Ho Chi Minh City] together. But here we

---

[75] http://protectvietworkers.wordpress.com/2011/07/12/huge-strike-by-some-90000-poyen-shoe-workers-some-strike-leaders-arrested/, accessed June 2012.

[76] http://chinaworker.info/en/content/news/1511/, accessed June 2012.

[77] E. P. Thompson, "Eighteenth-Century English Society: Class struggle without Class?," *Social History* 3 (1978): 133–65.

found that our salary is not that much higher, [our wages] only barely covered the costs of living, you know, for young men like us.

Like most other migrant workers, these men and women often got together to come back to their villages (*về quê*) to celebrate Tết. This factory owner—similar to most other owners—only gave workers seven to ten days for their Tết vacation. This is often not enough time, especially for migrant workers whose hometowns are in faraway northern or central provinces. If they failed to return to work on time, they would be fired, lose most of their wages, and receive only part of their social security benefits, even though they attempted repeatedly to collect them. In that context, the migrants bonded as brothers, as Đông described:

> We [needed] to visit our families [*thăm gia đình*]. But the factory only gave us seven or ten days. The distance was so far away, so how can we make this short vacation and return to the factory on time? Therefore, I quit in 2000 after spending several months in Nam Định [he was rehired by this same factory several months after that]. Between 1995 and 2000, I only came home once. I only wrote letters home. No money to call home. Only when I was able to borrow several hundreds *đồng* [Vietnamese currency] from my "brothers" [*anh em bạn bè*], I called home. Otherwise, most of the time, I wrote letters to my family.

When asked about his family situation, he shared with me:

> My parents are still in Nam Định on a small piece of land, about two to three *sào* [one sào is 360 square meters]. I have three siblings who are here in Saigon. The only one in Nam Định was married. My dream [was] to return to Nam Định, *về quê*, after I [made] some money here. Land is very expensive here, and we are only workers. We spend most of our salaries, so how can we have any future to settle down here? My parents work on the land, and barely make enough money for their daily needs. They never [asked] us to send money home. In fact, sometimes, they even sent candies and cookies [*kẹo bánh*] from our hometown to us in Saigon!

During the conversation, he mentioned a sit-in that took place in 1998 when he and his fellow workers received an order for a product that was difficult to make, and yet the piece rate was very low. The whole plant went on strike: six assembly lines with forty workers each, all 240 migrant workers (most were from the North of Vietnam), participated in this sit-in. He told me how the protest occurred:

> There [were] six assembly lines per plant (four women's lines and two men's lines), and each had two line leaders (12 leaders, total). When the shift started, the line leaders [*chuyền trưởng*] met with the workers and told them that with such low piece rates workers could not survive; then they forwarded our request to the management office [*văn phòng quản trị*]. There were twelve line leaders: leaders and assistants [*chuyền trưởng, chuyền phó*], both male and female also from the North, overseeing six assembly lines. After receiving a negative response from management, we had to go on strike. First, we sat quietly in front of our machines for thirty minutes, and then we started to talk, making a lot of noise. In several minutes, the Vietnamese president of that handbag factory came

down to tell us, "If you sympathize with me, please stay and work. If not, you can leave." [After] which all of us left. So, the sit-in lasted about an hour. After two days, the president sent people looking for us to tell us that she would give each assembly line [with forty people each] VND 2 million more per month. Then we all returned to work.

When I asked about his participation in the protest, he said:

Yes, I did join the sit-in because everyone in the whole plant went on strike. But we went home with uncertainty, not knowing what would happen the following day, not knowing if we would receive a raise in the piece rate or not. We [male] workers were a bit worried about losing our jobs, but I was not very worried. This is because our skills [in sewing handbags] were quite high by that time [*tay nghề cao*]: we could always get [sewing] jobs elsewhere because there were many factories needing workers then, and we could work on different tasks.

While the sit-in lasted only one hour inside the factory, the whole strike lasted two days, both inside and outside of the factory. When I asked whether the raise was permanent and divided equally among the workers, his response implied that there was a pay differential based on skills: "There were times when the seamstresses [females and males] received higher pay than the assistants [*thợ phụ*]: VND 2,000 [for the former] and VND 1,000 to 1,500 [for the assistants], per piece. This raise became permanent after this 1998 sit-in and there were no more strikes after that."

When I asked whether such a raise was reasonable, he explained:

To them [management], paying VND 2 million per assembly line per month [did] not make any dent in their pocketbooks. I know that there were some Korean factories [100 percent Korean-owned] where salaries [were] higher because there were no intermediaries, and the owners paid workers directly. When there were rush orders, workers were asked to sign a form if we agreed to work overtime. That was voluntary, and not forced, work. But this whole process [was] very messy. For example, the piece rate might not start very low: say VND 10,000, but when it reached the workers, each worker would only get VND 7,000 to 8,000. The problem [was] that the piece rates traveled through too many people and offices that handled [the money].

Clearly, the workers questioned why they did not receive the full piece rates, only partial rates, due to many deductions.

These migrant workers treated each other as brothers who attended to fundamental—at times, mundane—needs while living away from home. They lent each other money to call home in Nam Định or to buy cigarettes during their work breaks to relieve stress. Đông constantly referred to "*bạn bè anh em*" (friends and brothers) throughout my conversation with him. When mobilized by their line leaders—who were migrant workers themselves—the workers rose up together to demand higher piece rates and joined the sit-in with their brothers. Together, they won a small victory: a permanent increase in the piece rate. But still they were worried about their future, since they had only acquired limited skills, primarily for sewing, after years of working there.

These workers were conscious of the nationality factor and the corresponding power differential based on the hierarchy of the global supply chains. They knew who had the ultimate power in this handbag factory and adjusted their expectations accordingly. They understood how the origins and situations of the Korean factory owner and his staff affected their working conditions. The owner was a Korean capitalist who only visited the factory once or twice per year. The Korean technical officers who frequented the assembly lines to correct manufacturing mistakes and to provide technical guidance and supervision often pushed workers for on-time and rush deliveries dictated by the corporate buyers/MNCs, even to the extent of excessive overtime work. Such a work pattern is the hallmark of global flexible production at the expense of workers' well-being. Workers also knew the limited power of the Vietnamese president of the factory: she only oversaw the manufacturing process and had very little control over how products were made and profits distributed. This case confirms a systemic problem in thousands of "wildcat" strikes that have occurred in Vietnam since 1996: workers—the line leaders, in this case—organized and led this protest, though according to the Labor Code, representatives of the union should have organized and led this strike. But the union leaders were little help.

In 2008, the situation got worse in this factory, and all 174 workers went on strike for one day in November 2008. They exposed the fact that the owner had fled to France, claiming losses, without having paid workers for months and having defaulted on bank loans. After that, workers got some relief. The bank and local government officials sold the factory property and used that money to pay workers their back wages. However, these employees did not receive the unemployment and social security benefits due to them.[78]

Shilla Bags and Top One Workers: Boycott against Rotten Food, Bad Water

Protests do not always take place on the factory floor. In the following two cases, they began in the cafeteria. Meals are very important for factory employees who work continuously to meet the daily quotas, need adequate nutrition to endure the long work day, and often sit at their tasks long into the night, working overtime. Most factories sell food to workers in the company cafeteria and provide a free meal if overtime work is needed. To save money, some managers or outside catering contractors purchase rice and vegetables of poor quality—so poor that it is often insect-infested or rotten. Since it is inedible, the workers who depend upon the food for sustenance during their shifts often return to their machines hungry, distracted, and without the energy to complete their regular shifts and, all too often, overtime shifts as well. Dehydration is also a factor. Thus, bad food becomes a safety issue, and the lack of edible food and clean water becomes a health issue.

We have already met Nhung and Thoa. As noted above, Nhung worked at Shilla Bags, a Korean-owned bag factory. Here, management forced workers to buy cafeteria food that was spoiled. Nhung described how the older women workers led a spontaneous collective action in a class moment in 2004:

> There [was] no enterprise-level labor union here. But the female leaders led the strike. When the female assistant in the accessories department informed us

---

[78] *HCMC Labor Federation Report on Strikes in 2008.*

about contaminated food in the cafeteria, we decided not to eat it. We sat at different tables from the younger workers [*đàn em*]. As soon as we broke all the wooden chopsticks on the table as a sign of protest, the younger workers followed suit. *We all stood up and yelled out "bad food."* No one dared to continue eating because they would be blamed for not participating in this eating stoppage. Within an hour, the full management team came down to talk to us. Since there was no enterprise-level labor union here, each assembly line sent one representative to talk to the management team, who then said "sorry" and promised to improve the meals.[79]

When workers all stood up together, they participated in a class moment and won a small victory: management allowed them to buy food from outside vendors in addition to cafeteria food. But the class moment began because of the decision of the female leaders to act, a decision that stemmed from cultural-identity bonding based on gender, sisterhood, and native place.

Nhung told me that the drinking water in this factory was not potable. At the beginning, many workers got sick when they drank the company's cold water. It turned out that the cold water was not boiled; it was just stored in the clean water tank. In the hot working environment of the factory—very steamy in a tropical country—most workers would prefer cold water, but this eventually made them sick. So workers ended up bringing their own water to the factory.

Seeing no improvement after having made many suggestions to the line leaders, on August 1, 2004, several workers went to the *Người Lao Động* newspaper office to report these problems. Several days later, an article appeared in this newspaper to expose not only the problems with bad food and water, but other persistent problems as well. These included a lack of healthcare services (workers paid for their own doctor's visits, even when they had already paid for health insurance), the imposition of (unpaid) "vacation" time when there were no work orders, and the fact that workers were prevented from having direct contact with foreign corporate buyers or brand-name representatives who visited the factory to inspect the working conditions. The reporter for *Người Lao Động* also uncovered evidence that certain managers had verbally and physically abused workers.[80]

Earlier on, several workers wrote as a collective to the Labor Law Consultancy Section to complain about being forced to work overtime excessively, including on Sundays, and having to endure constant verbal abuse from the Korean technical staff. This complaint had triggered a formal, public response from Nguyễn Minh Hà, the chief financial officer of Shilla Bags:[81]

> We acknowledge that recently we requested overtime work in order to deliver products on time. When requesting overtime, we did give advance notice to the

---

[79] My emphasis. Interview with Nhung, 2004, Ho Chi Minh City.

[80] Phạm Nguyễn, "Những hành xử làm xấu quan hệ lao động. Thô bạo với người lao động—Ai xử?" [Bad (Management) Practices Damaged Labor Relations: Abuses to Workers—Who Judges (these Behaviors)?], *Người Lao Động*, August 5, 2004, http://nld.com.vn/97529 P1010C1012/tho-bao-voi-nguoi-lao-dong-ai-xu.htm, accessed July 2010.

[81] Tư Vấn Pháp Luật [Labor Law Consultancy Section], "Hạn chế tăng ca, chấn chỉnh nhân viên kỹ thuật" [Minimizing Overtime Work, Disciplining Technical Personnel], *Lao Động*, June 29, 2004, http://nld.com.vn/94556P1010C1013/han-che-tang-ca-chan-chinh-nhan-vien-ky-thuat.htm, accessed on July 14, 2010.

workers and paid overtime compensation according to the law. But we will try to reorganize our production schedule to limit overtime work. After hearing workers' complaints about problems with our health staff, we had laid off some of those employees. About the problems with the foreign technical staff and plant manager who verbally abused [*la mắng*] workers, we will investigate these complaints and rectify them promptly.

Nhung informed me later that this degree of public exposure had successfully forced management to fix problems that were noted. So, workers' collective action and their appeal to the law section of the labor newspaper were effective in getting attention from the key stakeholders.

In the process of struggling to improve their condition, workers invoked the image of draft animals—such as water buffaloes, oxen, horses—and made it clear they resented being treated as such. They urged their co-workers to stand up for themselves and join the strike. Thoa worked in Top One, a Taiwanese garment factory supplying clothing products for various markets, including the United States. Thoa looked up to Nhung, as her older sister, for advice on basic labor rights such as clean food and water, and the boycott at the Shilla Bags factory inspired Top One workers, such as Thoa, to stand up for their rights. She was teary-eyed when she recounted the lunch boycott to me:

> There were seven hundred workers assembling clothes on eleven assembly lines for the US market. Most are migrant workers from the Mekong Delta region, the North and the Central. There was no enterprise labor union in this factory. My co-workers and I boycotted the lunch sold by the factory cafeteria when we found worms in the soup and other dishes. *We workers are human beings, not dogs and cats*, so we deserve to have clean and decent meals, not contaminated food like this![82]

That lunch boycott did grab the attention of management at Top One, causing them to switch to a better food provider.

While these two migrant workers were employed in different factories, when they were off work, settled back in their rental units, they compared notes on protest tactics in their factories, their daily activities, and the trips they had taken together, to Nam Định, for Tết. No rigid boundaries separate work and home in labor organizing. Each woman experienced some brief class moments in her respective protest when each fought separately for workers' common goals: decent food and clean water. They also fought against being treated as less than human beings, and demanded basic rights at work.

In these cases, bonding as sisters and connecting to their native place played important roles in labor organizing: younger Nam Định workers looked up to the experienced "elder sister" workers (*đàn chị*) for advice on their rights and benefits, such as clean food and potable water, proper treatment by foreign managers, overtime compensation, and reasonable numbers of overtime hours.

---

[82] My emphasis. Interview with Thoa, July 2004, Ho Chi Minh City.

Freetrend Migrant Workers: Handwriting on the Wall

I had the good fortune to see evidence of workers' expressions of anger toward management and their call for direct action: photos of graffiti messages on toilet stall walls. I cannot determine or assert directly that cultural identities influenced these creative and "underground" graffiti worker-authors. I can only interpret the meaning these graffiti messages conveyed to me. The reference to "rights" in these writings may refer to the right to go on strike, which had been sanctioned since 1996, or the rights and benefits stipulated in the Labor Code. But in either case, the messages on these walls strongly declare that workers know that the law enables their collective action and empowers their struggle to demand their rights and entitlements.

Graffiti: "Go on strike!" August 2008. Photo courtesy of Minh and Bình (pseudonyms), Freetrend workers.

In August 2008, I met Minh and Bình—both women from Quảng Nam—who rented rooms in Gò Vấp district in Ho Chi Minh City, a hub for migrant workers. They worked at Freetrend, a 100 percent Taiwanese-owned shoe factory in Linh Trung EPZ. The women confirmed that most workers in Linh Trung EPZ came from poor provinces in the North (Nam Định, Thái Bình, Thanh Hóa, Nghệ An) and the central region (Quảng Nam, Quảng Bình).

In her Quảng Nam dialect, Bình shared how she enjoyed helping other migrant workers, even when she lived in poverty herself: "I always want to help other migrant workers. Everyday, either at home or at work, I do some small things to help them … sometimes giving them a flower, a newspaper … It is the smile on their faces that makes me feel so happy." But life was not easy inside the factory. Both women gave me several photos that they had taken of handwritten strike slogans drawn on the walls of the women's toilet. Some of the graffiti looked recent; some was faded, as if written far in the past. These old and new strike messages may have come from different strike waves at Freetrend: the December 2005 minimum-wage strike or the 2008 inflation-adjustment strike.

Graffiti: "Everyone let's demand the rights and benefits for ourselves: go on strike!" August 2008. Photo courtesy of Minh and Bình (pseudonyms), Freetrend workers.

Both women workers told me that most migrant workers at Freetrend knew who wrote these slogans but did not tell anyone, and most workers were effectively mobilized and stirred to action by these messages. Apparently, migrant workers knew about this underground labor organizing and engaged in it while protecting their underground labor organizers—who were also workers.

Bình took pictures of graffiti from the women's lavatory in one of several departments (*xưởng*) at Freetrend. She told me that there are a lot more strike messages—clearer and newer than the ones she had given me—in the lavatories of other departments, but her hectic work schedule and inter-department security system did not allow her to go to those places to take photos.

The photos she offered me captured the following strike slogans recorded as graffiti:

– Wage like this, how can we live? Everyone, let us go on strike [*Lương thế này làm sao sống được, Mọi người hãy đình công*]
– All of us have to strike [*Tất cả chúng ta phải đình công*]
– Let's go on strike; we have to strike [*Hãy đình công, phải đình công thôi*]
– Everyone, let's demand the rights and benefits for ourselves: go on strike! [*Mọi người hãy đòi quyền lợi cho chính mình: Đình Công*]

The underground labor organizers' messages appealed to a sense of belonging to the working class. Those leaders knew that strength comes from collective action, and used words such as "we," "everyone," "all of us," and "ourselves."

But the more legalistic, rights-and-benefits-based language also emerges here. I see several ways to interpret these messages. The "Everyone, let's demand the rights and benefits for ourselves: go on strike!" graffiti (see photo, previous page), refers to the workers' right to strike that is sanctioned in Chapter 14 of the 1996 Labor Code. The "Wage like this, how can we live? Everyone, let us go on strike" slogan that Bình found in 2008 was consistent with the workers' demand that management at the factory comply with the 2008 minimum wages hike mandated for all FDI factories by the state. Moreover, this slogan also hinted at the need to earn a *living* wage that is higher than the minimum wage, as discussed in Chapter 3.

Kollan Migrant Workers: The Strike Next Door

On December 28, 2005, four thousand workers went on strike at the Kollan factory, which was located right next door to the Freetrend plant. The interactions between the workers at these adjacent factories recall the 1930 case I discussed earlier, involving protests that spread from Phú Riềng to Dầu Tiếng, the two rubber plantations about seventy kilometers apart from each other.

 Kollan, a 100 percent Hong Kong–owned company, made garment products to export to the United States. Most Kollan workers were migrants who came from poor provinces in the North and the central region, and at this time of year, most hoped to return home for the Tết holiday (*về quê ăn Tết*). For this, they needed bonus money to buy bus tickets, as well as money for presents for their families. When they saw that the "workers next door" in Freetrend had gone on strike during the critical pre-Tết period, the Kollan workers followed suit.

In August 2006, I interviewed a male migrant worker, Hưng, from Bình Định, a poor province in the central region, who worked as a garment worker (a stitcher) on an assembly line at Kollan. This was one of the three FDI factories in Linh Trung I EPZ that sparked the minimum-wage-strike waves at the end of 2005 and the beginning of 2006.

Hưng had been working at Kollan for five years, but, like most other migrant workers who aspired to shift to other careers, he had not originally planned to work in the factory for long: "As to my plan for the future … I take it one day at a time." In my short conversation with him, Hưng confirmed that he and his fellow workers had gone on strike to demand a minimum wage increase at the beginning of 2006, about a month before Tết:

> Tết was coming very soon, but there was no wage increase. So I joined the strike; we stopped work for almost one month and got paid for this period. We saw that other workers had gone on strike right "next door" [Freetrend], so we went on strike ourselves. *No one led us. We spread information about this strike, and prevented workers from coming inside to work.* We did not do [anything violent]. A lot of workers participated in the strike. I'm not sure [how many], perhaps the whole factory, probably thousands. I don't remember the percentages of women and men. But most workers were women, over 70 percent. When the strike broke out, some labor union representatives came down to our factory. But, hmm … I don't know about our workplace labor union [he laughed]. Well, I did join the union and [paid] VND 5,000 every month as union fee [about US$0.30]. But still, I don't know who is our workplace labor union representative [*công đoàn cơ sở*].[83]

Hưng's narrative conveyed the solidarity of migrant workers pursuing their common goal: securing a wage increase so they could go home for the Lunar New Year holiday—Tết. But it also indicates the ineffective (or utterly useless) role played by his labor union, which may explain why he twice mentioned that he did not know his workplace union representative. Thousands of migrant workers participated in a

---

[83] My emphasis. Interview with Hưng, July 2006, Ho Chi Minh City.

class moment, demanding a minimum-wage increase in an FDI factory, a fundamental legal change that affected not only FDI factories, but also, subsequently, domestic factories. They got their hard-won victory: "After we went on strike for almost a month, the management finally agreed to pay the increased minimum wage for FDI [workers]. Now the working conditions are somewhat better." In addition, they won another small victory, for they were paid for the month that they went on strike. With regard to forms of protest, they used the popular informal tactic—word of mouth—and steered clear of violence.

Quảng Việt Workers and the Củ Chi Revolutionary Past

Quảng Việt is a 100-percent Taiwanese-owned contract factory making Nike shoes and sports apparel in the Củ Chi district. During the Vietnam–United States war, the Củ Chi district was called "steely land" (or "*đất thép*"), and it was an important base for the National Liberation Front of Vietnam. The Củ Chi Tunnel wartime memorial stands witness to the region's anti-American past. Now, in the twenty-first century, following that revolutionary past, Củ Chi remains one of the places in South Vietnam with the highest number of worker protests against labor violations.[84] In this district, both local and migrant workers have had to face the exploitative practices of modern-day global capitalists in foreign-owned factories.

Quảng Việt in Củ Chi district was one of the thirty-four official Nike subcontracting or direct contracting factories nationwide during the time of my interview in 2004. It began its operation in 1997, quickly expanded in 2004, and came to employ over 6,500 workers.[85] In 2004, about 70 percent of Quảng Việt workers were Củ Chi residents, and the rest were migrant workers from the North and Central. Over 90 percent were women.[86]

In July 2004, I interviewed DC, a senior member of the Taiwanese management, who was responsible for managing the factory, paying social insurance and utilities, purchasing raw materials, and ensuring factory security. This factory's hiring tactic was to recruit migrant workers from northern and central regions without providing job security. But given that 70 percent of the workforce came from Củ Chi, that hiring tactic was not successful.

According to DC, most workers were not offered permanent labor contracts; instead, they received primarily seasonal and renewable one-to-three year contracts based on "good performance." But the key requirement for contract renewal was that workers acquiesce to work overtime. Only after the third contract renewal would workers become permanent employees. DC had this to say about these workers: "Củ Chi workers are tough. They have bad manners and are against management. They can be violent and threatening at times. But that seems to be their custom—their revolutionary tradition."

Quảng Việt engaged in vertical integration to maximize control and profits, and it benefited from capital networks of Taiwanese multinational enterprises that supported each other to maximize profits. Quảng Việt's accumulation of profits and mobility are shown by the way Taiwanese capitalists operate in both China and

---

[84] *HCMC Labor Federation Report on Strikes in 2008*, p. 16.

[85] As reported in the International Textile, Garment, and Leather Workers Federation (ITGLWF) 2009 report. This ITGLWF document lists contract factories for Nike as of 2008.

[86] Correspondence with Journalist D, July 2010, Ho Chi Minh City.

Vietnam.[87] DC shuttles between China and Vietnam to oversee production facilities on both sides of the border. Quảng Việt also purchased fabrics from Formosa Taffeta Vietnam, a Taiwanese company that produced taffeta—a high-end woven fabric— and other fabric types in Vietnam to manufacture apparel for Nike.[88] This certainly saved them transportation costs.

DC oversaw all activities of the enterprise labor union by controlling its budget, approving union activities, and paying the enterprise labor-union representatives. With their salaries fully paid by the Taiwanese management, the Vietnamese labor-union officials in Quảng Việt were coopted and weak in representing workers' interests. On average, management allocated US$700, twice a year, to the union for their activities supporting workers. The rest of the union's budget, contributed by workers, was very small and mainly used for social purposes, such as in cases of sickness, or for weddings, and funerals. DC mentioned proudly several times that Quảng Việt respected the Labor Code and instituted the suggestion box as a way for workers to voice their opinions. He also mentioned that workers waited for his return from China to resolve their problems.

These financial arrangements and the manager's comments speak volumes about who has real power in Quảng Việt's labor-management relations. The suggestion box practice was designed to appease workers rather than grant them real influence. And it obviously did not satisfy them. In 2004, about six thousand Quảng Việt workers went on strike to demand overtime compensation and adequate company contributions to their social insurance and healthcare funds. This protest triggered solidarity strikes carried out by other migrant workers employed in nearby contract factories in Củ Chi that were owned and managed by East Asian capitalists. This case demonstrates that the motivational power of tradition informed workers' collective action in this historic district, with its resistance legacy, even in the face of capital mobility and the fluctuations that characterize flexible global production.[89]

Workers demonstrated that they understood the labor law by appealing to the state media to aid them in their fight for their legal rights. Class rhetoric was apparent in the two petitions (Đơn Khiếu Nại) signed by a collective of workers in Quảng Việt, one addressed to the *Người Lao Động* newspaper, in general, and the other to the Labor Law Consultancy Section of the *Người Lao Động* newspaper.[90] In 2006, management tried to lay workers off, claiming that the increased minimum wage made it necessary to reduce their workforce (giảm biên chế).

In the first petition to the *Người Lao Động* newspaper (dated January 23, 2006), the workers signed as the "collective of brother and sister workers in Quảng Việt Plant No. III" (tập thể anh chị em công nhân Quảng Việt Xưởng III):

---

[87] Anita Chan and Hong-Zen Wang, "The Impact of the State on Workers' Conditions: Comparing Taiwanese Factories in China and Vietnam," *Pacific Affairs* 77 (2004): 4.

[88] Interview with Dương Thị Anh Thy, Formosa Taffeta Vietnam Co., Ltd., Import–Export Section, Saigon Tower, Ho Chi Minh City, October 28, 2003.

[89] This Vietnamese reality contradicts David Harvey's caution about the eroding role of "the flux and ephemerality of flexible accumulation" on place-bound identity and on workers' attachment to a place well-known for its revolutionary tradition. Here, it appears that the workers have been keeping up with the fighting tradition of historic Củ Chi district.

[90] The Thirty-Nine Worker Complaint Letters and Petitions (submitted to newspapers in the South in 2005 and 2006).

When the management lays off workers, according to the Labor Code, workers should be compensated one-month's salary for every year that they worked for this company. But the management only paid half-a-month's salary for each year we worked. When we fought back to demand our rights, the foremen told us that if we [were] too vocal, we would get nothing. When the president called for a meeting with the workers, *we struggled very hard for our rights*. But then the management called in the security to take us out. Was the president right or wrong [in doing that]? Note that our labor contract [was] without a time clause [*không xác định thời hạn*].[91] On January 2, 2006, the president stood in front of forty-four laid-off workers and promised that, in addition to the Tết and seniority bonuses, he would also give us four-months' salary. But they did not fulfill their promises—the factory had already hired new workers to replace us. Now we had no jobs, and the company refused to pay our compensations. We [hoped] the newspaper [would] intervene to protect the rights of workers.

In this first petition, workers used class-based and rights-based language and appealed to the law (the Labor Code), while exposing management's failure to fulfill its promises. In protesting for their well-being, they exposed management's bad treatment of its employees, exemplified by the use of threats and of brute force ("calling in the security to take us out"), and the decision to sack workers without compensation.

The class rhetoric reappears in the second petition (dated January 24, 2006), with an added emphasis on the petitioners' knowledge of the law. Again, workers signed the petition collectively as "the brother and sister garment workers of Quảng Việt" [*anh chị em công nhân may Quảng Việt*]. They reiterated most of the points they had raised in the first petition and added more on the legal details:

While still negotiating and not reaching any resolution with the workers, the management had already confiscated our ID cards. Is that right or wrong? On January 21, 2006, we were told that the layoff was caused by workforce downsizing, but that it was not yet finalized because workers had not agreed [to receive only half-a-month severance pay, instead of one month, for each year they worked at the factory]. Then on January 23, 2006, the president informed us that this is not a case of workforce downsizing, but it is a forty-five-day notification to end our labor contracts. Is it right or wrong? In the afternoon of January 23, 2006, the personnel director called a meeting to tell us that it is because the Vietnamese government raised the minimum wage from VND 560,000 to 790,000 that they were not able to pay us. So, according to the labor law, is that right or wrong? The president said that they followed Articles 38 and 41 of the Labor Code. Is that accurate? We workers really need the newspaper to intervene so that we can stabilize our lives.

The rhetorical question, "Is that right or wrong?" that recurs throughout this petition does not indicate that workers did not know their rights. In each case, they know that management has violated the law. They used public exposure to inform others about these labor violations and to seek legal guidance and remedies.

---

[91] This is the Vietnamese version of a permanent contract, which suggests that the workers have job security. My emphasis.

Class-based rhetoric and appeal to the law are evident in both petitions. Workers continuously identified themselves as belonging to the working class, with words such as, "brother and sister garment workers, we workers." While I find no direct evidence from available sources on the significance of native place in labor organizing and protests in this case, the fact that most of the workforce were Củ Chi residents is suggestive. More research is needed to determine the significance of native place to *local* workers, especially in a place with a revolutionary past such as this district. As noted by management, "Củ Chi workers are tough."[92]

Another struggle in March 2008 showed an emphasis on collective action and the law. More than one thousand Quảng Việt workers went on a one-day strike to demand increases in food and gasoline subsidies (inflation had increased the cost-of-living by 30 percent), new uniforms, minimum-wage hikes—Decree 168 on minimum wage, in effect since January 2008, had stipulated a 14 percent increase for factories in Zone 2, which included the suburbs of Ho Chi Minh City—and an additional 8 percent annual-wage increase. Workers won *most* of their agenda: an increase in food and gasoline subsidies, a 14 percent increase in the minimum wage, and a 5 percent annual-wage increase.[93]

Viva-Blast Prezioso Workers versus European Bosses

Not all complaints against foreign-direct investment enterprises during these years were focused on East Asian-owned and East Asian-managed factories. A European joint-venture, formerly named Prezioso, later Viva-Blast, was involved in a labor dispute in 2005.[94] In June 2005, the local workers in Prezioso, a French company that specialized in building maintenance and fabrication, mobilized in a way that showed a clear awareness of their ethnicity and an indignation against being treated without dignity and decency. The workers sent a typed Accusation Letter (*Đơn Tố Cáo*), signed collectively as a "group of former and current workers at Viva-Blast Prezioso company," to the Hochiminh City Export Processing Zones Authority (HEPZA) labor unions and three influential local newspapers: *Tuổi Trẻ, Thanh Niên,* and *Người Lao Động*. In this letter, the workers exposed serious management labor-law violations: The company allowed workers for five years to work without a contract when the law required that workers be offered a contract upon hiring; it made no contribution to social insurance funds; and it did not give advance notice of layoffs.

Workers expressed humiliation at being treated by the general director and his son without respect for Vietnamese culture. The workplace labor union resigned in protest against this mistreatment. Workers claimed that they were being stripped of their uniforms as soon as they were laid off and were wrongfully accused of stealing a camera from a foreign guest who visited the factory. They suspected the guest may have lost the camera elsewhere.

---

[92] Interview with DC, July 2004, Ho Chi Minh City.

[93] *HCMC Labor Federation Report on Strikes in 2008*, p. 7.

[94] This company advertised specific services, such as painting, floor coating, waterproofing, fireproofing, blasting, insulation, heat tracing, rubber lining, scaffolding, building maintenance, on/offshore maintenance, electrical work, construction and steel fabrication, and coating inspection. http://www.vivablast.com/index2.html, accessed July 10, 2009.

Workers made clear that they belonged to the working class, and they distinguished their national identity from that of their bosses. Moreover, they ended the letter by indicting the behavior of management and calling for direct intervention by the media and the labor unions:

> We, *người lao động Việt Nam* [Vietnamese workers], urgently request the local media and labor unions to come down to the factory directly so you can witness with your own eyes to investigate and verify what we have claimed to be labor violations. As workers with "short necks and little voices" [*thấp cổ, bé họng*], we cannot continue fighting when enterprise labor unions no longer exist. Our union representatives resigned in disgust. The general director and his son are both very rich, but the more affluent they are, the more they look down on the Vietnamese labor. They gave themselves the power of laying-off workers who allegedly did not please them, even though that *type of termination is not sanctioned by the labor law*. Why don't they know that the *source of their own wealth comes from the sweat and hard work of Vietnamese labor*?[95]

Clearly, the authors of this document were very conscious of their nationality and class. The document manifested this class consciousness by noting that the general director and his son were rich and looked down on Vietnamese labor. Also, the workers appealed to the law—for example, the lay-off stipulation in the Labor Code, "termination not warranted by the labor law"—through the appropriate state authorities, from which they received a public response five months later. An article in *Người Lao Động*, published on December 1, 2005, reported that the Labor Investigation Office of the HCMC Labor Federation had ordered the HEPZA labor unions to visit the Viva-Blast factory to investigate the claims so that the labor federation could take appropriate action. While I could not find any reported results, this shows how workers' collective action had caught the attention of the local media, led to the public exposure of the violations, and triggered local state intervention, a first step toward rectifying this situation.

CICADA FACTORIES

The so-called "cicada" factories have plagued Vietnamese labor unions and workers for decades. They earned their name based on the perception that modern global capitalists morph and relocate like the protean cicada. Many factory owners, acting as predators, have abandoned their factories and, in many cases, also liquidated all factory machinery to turn the factories into "empty shells"—similar to the cicada's shedding its skin and flying away—in order to escape responsibilities to workers, such as back pay and benefits.[96]

---

[95] My emphasis. This letter does not indicate their citizenship, but possibly it is French, as the nationality of the company itself.

[96] "Workers' Republic," a sixty-minute 2010 documentary, chronicles an important (and increasingly rare) sit-down-strike victory in the United States. Upon learning that the Republic Windows and Doors factory in Chicago, IL, was going to be shut down in December 2008 without providing workers either the sixty-day notice or sixty-day pay required of management by the federal WARN Act, and witnessing management's attempts to remove the factory machinery, more than two hundred workers stood guard and occupied the factory day and night for nearly a week to stop this cicada-like practice. Workers ended up winning

Not just FDI factories, but also private-domestic factories, have engaged in similar cicada behaviors and incurred social insurance debts.[97] Investors from South Korea have topped the list of violators, followed by "joint-ventures with Vietnam," followed by Taiwanese investors. Private-domestic factories and joint-ventures involving partnerships between Vietnamese and foreign capitalists have also owed social insurance, although less frequently than East Asian FDI factories. The nationality of the investor and the source of capital is only one factor of many that should be considered when examining why there are more reported strikes in Taiwanese and South Korean factories. Since 2004, more violations by domestic-private factories have been seen, such as in Hiệp Hưng Shoes, Hừng Sáng, Minh Phụng, Limited Garment Nhật Tân, Limited Thụy Bang, and Shoe Gia Định.[98]

As of 2012, both FDI and domestic factories continue to demonstrate cicada-like behavior. In a recent instance, the Taiwanese president of Magnicon factory in District 12 in Ho Chi Minh City escaped owing about VND 1 billion in back wages to hundreds of workers for several months of overtime work (eighty hours per month) that had been ordered to meet urgent delivery deadlines. Angered by losing their hard-earned income, workers seized the factory and demanded that its chief remaining assets, the machinery, be liquidated in order to pay their wages. Only then did the local government intervene. But local state and union officials discovered a common practice among these cicada factories: many factory owners rent their machinery rather than purchasing it, and that equipment is promptly reclaimed by the owner-lessor as soon as the factory owners abandon the site. Therefore,

---

US$1.75 million in severance pay, back wages, and benefits, but only 75 of the original 240 workers were rehired by Serious Materials, which by then had bought the closed factory. In February 2012 workers again occupied this same factory when Serious Materials management announced that it planned to close the plant effective immediately. After a one-day negotiation session with management, workers won a reprieve: the plant would remain open for ninety days while Serious Materials management and workers attempted to find new ownership, including the possibility of converting it to a worker-owned cooperative. To save this factory, two dozen longtime employees formed a cooperative—New Era Windows—and tried to raise funds to buy the equipment. On July 4, 2012, New Era was told that its offer of $1.2 million was insufficient, and that liquidation was imminent. See http://workersrepublic. tv/index.php?option=com_content&view=article&id=49&Itemid=27, accessed November 2012; Jane Slaughter, "UE Occupies Chicago Window Plant Again, and Wins Reprieve," February 24, 2012, http://labornotes.org/2012/02/ue-occupies-chicago-window-plant-again-and-wins-reprieve, accessed January 2013; and Laura Flanders, "Workers vs. Investors: Chicago Window Factory in Danger of Liquidation," July 4, 2012, www.thenation.com/blog/168727/workers-vs-investors-famous-windows-factory-danger-liquidation, accessed January 2013. In March 2013, the factory reopened with a small workforce and under new management. As per a transaction announced on September 17, 2012, it became Republic Holdings Corporation, which operates as a subsidiary of New Era Windows, LLC and The Working World. See "Company Overview of Republic Holdings Corporation," Bloomberg Businessweek, March 17, 2013, http://investing.businessweek.com/research/stocks/private/snapshot.asp?priv capId=4392048, accessed March 17, 2013. In May 2013, New Era workers finally "cut the ribbon on their own cooperatively run business." See Laura Flanders, "New Era for Labor: Creative Defiance from the Factory to the Street," May 20, 2013, http://truth-out.org/news/item/16470-new-era-for-labor-creative-defiance-from-the-factory-to-the-street, accessed May 22, 2013.

[97] Appendix D: List of Companies with Social Insurance Debts in 2007–08.

[98] Khánh Bình, "Trốn, né đóng bảo hiểm xã hội: Chưa có thuốc đặc trị" [Evading and Avoiding Paying Social Insurance (for Workers): Still Lacking Special Solution], *Saigon Giải Phóng*, July 2004, http://www.sggp.org.vn/xahoi/nam2004/thang7/6991/, accessed July 2006.

liquidation is often not a solution to obtain money to pay workers' arrears and benefits.

Trương Lâm Danh, the then vice president of the HCMC Labor Federation, had openly complained about the silence and ineptitude of local state agencies—especially the labor court at the HCMC level—and how this ineptitude affected the workers:

> The situation at Magnicon factory is not unique, and certainly not the first time in Ho Chi Minh City. However, the seriously delayed intervention and lack of commitment by local government continue to hurt workers' rights and benefits. Coming up soon [at the time of this quote], the HCMC Labor Federation will recommend to the HCMC People's Committee that it find concrete solutions and actions to resolve these cases in a simpler and speedier manner to protect workers' rights.[99]

At the end of this newspaper article, some readers posted messages expressing their indignation at this practice, and two even suggested that the Ministry of Planning and Investment (MPI) request that the management of any factory submit a mandatory deposit (such as an amount equivalent to six-months' labor wages) before the enterprise would be granted a business license.

Haimin Workers and Hóc Môn's Revolutionary Past

Hóc Môn literally means "corner of taro." This whole area was home to the revolutionary "*mười tám thôn vườn trầu*," or "eighteen betel leaves villages": an anti-French headquarters that initiated the 1885 uprising against the French and their underlings. After the Indochina Communist Party was formed in 1930, this region became a hideout for communist leaders and their secret documents.

Haimin Vietnam, located in Hóc Môn, is one of the factories that engaged in "footloose," cicada practices.[100] This is a 100 percent Korean-owned computerized embroidery factory, employing several hundred workers; it had no enterprise labor unions. It received its operational licenses through the MPI in 1994 and produced for some time in Ho Chi Minh City, but from the year 2000 on, several succeeding Haimin presidents, all South Koreans, fled Vietnam, leaving thousands of workers stranded without salaries, social insurance, or health coverage and with unused vacation time and severance allowances. Workers continued at their jobs even after the presidents had fled, relying on management's promise to pay their arrears.

When I tried to contact the Haimin Vietnam company during my fieldwork in September 2008, no one could be found at the closed facility. The registered

---

[99] Vĩnh Tùng, "Vẫn không "xử" được chủ DN bỏ trốn!" [Still Cannot Sue these Escaping Owners], *Người Lao Động*, February 23, 2011, http://nld.com.vn/20110223090551376 p1010c1011/van-khong-xu-duoc-chu-dn-bo-tron.htm, accessed March 2011.

[100] There were other companies—FDI and private domestic—engaged in similar cicada behaviors, which also incurred social insurance debts (Appendix D). However, investors from East Asian FDI companies top the list of violators. Private-domestic factories and joint-ventures with other foreign investors also owed social insurance, although less frequently than those East Asian FDI factories. Of course there are law-abiding East Asian companies, and law-*avoiding* domestic Vietnamese or state-owned factories. Khánh Bình, "Trốn, né đóng bảo hiểm xã hội."

president, Yang Soo-Min, had fled to South Korea and transferred all corporate responsibilities (including showing up to labor courts) to the vice president, Sin Sung Man. This is consistent with behavior workers have criticized in such comments as "small boss referred to big boss and vice versa." Local authorities later found out that the company had leased their machinery from another Korean company. So with the cicada owner leaving a "shell" of a rented facility and leased machinery, there was not much collateral, if anything at all, left to pay wage arrears and other benefits to workers. Other creditors often had the first chance to recoup what they could, so most workers in these cicada factories ended up losing their wages, social insurance, and health benefits.

Haimin workers guard the closed factory to prevent management from moving the machinery, May 2009. (Photo courtesy of *Người Lao Động* journalist Vĩnh Tùng)

Workers' Response at Haimin Vietnam

About half of the Haimin workers were Hóc Môn residents; the rest were migrant workers who came from all regions of Vietnam.[101] From available information, there is no evidence that native place played a significant role in labor organizing in this case. But class moments materialized in different forms. Workers stood guard in front of the factory for months to prevent management from moving machinery and property from the building. They had no enterprise-level labor union, so all of their collective actions were spontaneous and organized by themselves. They knew that factory machinery and equipment—if owned by the factory owner—could be used to pay workers' back wages and social security benefits. However, as noted above, Haimin management had leased their embroidery machinery so, when

---

[101] Correspondence with Journalist D, July 2010, Ho Chi Minh City.

its management fled Vietnam, the rental company that owned the equipment successfully challenged the local court and was able to retrieve all of its rental machines.

Workers were proactive in contacting journalists. A workers' collective complaint letter addressed to *Người Lao Động* newspaper in February 2006 exposed labor violations and frustration with the Korean management as well as the Vietnamese authorities who had failed to respond to the workers' complaints. There is no signature on this handwritten letter, but it was clearly written by a person representing a collective of workers. The writer used the words "fellow brother and sister workers" (*anh chị em công nhân*) many times throughout the letter:

> Recently I read the newspaper and saw that you published news about this embroidery factory. I am very happy because your newspaper dares to tell the truth. For a long time now, *I saw many Haimin workers quit their jobs and lodge their cases in court, but no one listened to them.* Now, I have some more to share with you in hopes that your newspaper will help *our fellow sisters and brothers.* For workers who quit their jobs before Tết—from November 2005 to February 2006—none of these workers received any of their hard-earned wages. From January 2006, Haimin no longer deducted social insurance from our salaries, but they never mentioned the social insurance funds that they had deducted in previous years, and when we workers would receive those benefits. The Korean male bosses were very irresponsible. In the meeting, when we asked the big boss, the big boss said that he'd talk to the small boss; but when we met with the small boss, the small boss said that he needed to consult with the big boss. So, the two of them played the ping-pong game with us. *We workers* are very sad and disappointed because these bosses promised, and then promised some more, but never delivered on their promises to us. So, not only did we not receive social insurance benefits, we did not receive any remaining money, which is equivalent to our unclaimed vacation benefits from 2004 to 2006. We asked that *the newspaper speak up on our behalf and call on the appropriate state authority* [*cấp có thẩm quyền*] *to investigate* [this factory] and resolve these violations.[102]

This letter shows an intermingling of Marxist and Polanyi-type protests. The writer constantly appeals to the journalists to help "fellow brother and sister workers." This worker also shows an awareness of the nationality of the bosses: that they are Korean.

Workers were frustrated about the delayed and weak state response that prolonged their sufferings. When the FDI management gave them the runaround and did not pay their salaries and benefits, the workers resorted to all means at their disposal: guarding the factory to prevent management from moving machinery and property from the building, filing lawsuits with the court, and sending letters to the *Người Lao Động* as a last resort, asking the newspaper to intervene on workers' behalf and to expose this issue to state authorities.

The author of the complaint letter reminded the press and the state of the infamous 2005 strike in Huê Phong shoe factory (see Chapters 6 and 7), when frustrated workers destroyed some machinery. The writer stressed that workers wanted a peaceful resolution:

---

[102] My emphasis.

We cannot wait until something happens before authority steps in to help. Do you remember the worker strike at Huê Phong Shoe factory in 2005? Workers were desperate and rose up to strike; they smashed and destroyed some company's property before some authority stepped in to resolve the issue. Many [Huê Phong] workers went on strike due to low wages, late wage payment, inappropriate monthly wage deductions, inadequate social insurance contributions … But back to the Haimin case, we recommend that all levels of state authorities discipline Haimin management sternly for their violations, and that they pay in full all of their obligations—social insurance, severance pay—to both existing and laid-off workers [which have accumulated] in the last several years.

During this whole struggle, both the *Người Lao Động* and the *Lao Động* newspapers covered the Haimin workers' story through the publication of more than twenty articles from October 29, 2005, to November 1, 2006. This joint effort led to some state actions and a resolution for laid-off workers, announced in the twentieth article on December 8, 2006. Then, on May 11, 2007, the newspaper reported resolute actions that had been initiated by the Hóc Môn District Labor Union, in coordination with the HCMC Labor Federation and state bureaucracies from MOLISA and MPI. The authorities had locked up the factory to prevent the loss of machinery and other property and arranged for the sale of the remaining factory property to pay some of the workers' back pay. But the story does not end here. In Chapter 7, I will follow this story to its bitter end, in 2009, when the state ultimately failed to protect the workers' interests.

The Case of the C & N Security Service Company

This case shows how a local worker, starting off with little knowledge of the Labor Code, became more knowledgeable of the law through his struggle with management and used the law to challenge the wrongful actions of a foreign-owned company. A laid-off security guard—who worked for C & N Security Service Company, a limited responsibility company in the Linh Trung Export Processing Zone—sent a petition letter and his six-month's labor contract (attached as evidence) to the labor union office of the HCMC Export Processing Zone Authority (HEPZA) in 2005. He complained that he had been wrongfully fired from his job, without proper justification, *before* the end of his labor contract (he was terminated three months early). When he did not receive a satisfactory response from either the company personnel official or the union representative, he then sent the same letter and his labor contract to a newspaper in the South.

He diligently checked the legal justifications management used to explain why he had been laid off, and pointed out that neither of the reasons applied to him and so did not justify his termination. Moreover, he announced the nationality of the company vice president (*phó tổng giám đốc*) at the beginning of his letter:

I worked as a security guard for this C & N Company in Linh Trung EPZ with Mr. MBC—a Filipino citizen—as the company vice president, on a six-month contract (starting in March and ending in August). I performed well all my responsibilities without any violations. But in May, I received a phone call from

Ms. Tuyết (the head of the personnel office of this company), who laid me off because the company wanted professional guards, not amateurs like me. I did not know the Labor Code at the beginning, but after thinking it through with my family helping, I called Ms. Tuyết again to inquire about the reason for the lay-off, and was given a specific article in the Labor Code, Article 38 (Part d), which does not apply to my case at all.[103] After many conversations with Ms. Tuyết [in my attempt to reach] a reasonable resolution, she maintained the [original] allegation. This company also violated another term in the contract: they are supposed to provide each worker two uniforms, but I got none since I signed my labor contract … How can a pretty good size foreign company like this one not fulfill its agreements stated on the labor contract? So, in June 2005, I sent my petition to the labor union office in HEPZA, and Ms. Nga—a HEPZA union representative—explained to me that Ms. Tuyết had used the wrong article in the Labor Code to lay me off. Ms. Nga insisted that Ms. Tuyết should have used Article 17, Section 1.[104] Still, I don't see the relevance: this case was not about business restructuring or technology change. This case was about how the management did not honor the terms of the contract and its corresponding benefits. Up to now, there is still no resolution to my wrongful termination. If any company is allowed to invoke Article 17, Section 1 of the Labor Code [to terminate workers], then *it is not just me personally but other Vietnamese citizens [công dân Việt Nam] in general would be terminated indiscriminately by the owner*. I hope that the newspaper promptly resolves this issue and explains this case clearly.[105]

This worker used the law to appeal to the proper state agencies: first, the labor union in HEPZA, where he worked, then the newspaper. Also, by calling out the citizenship of the capital owner, he made public the violations of this foreign company as well as raising the shared interests of other Vietnamese workers.

CONCLUSION

In the neoliberal era, since the Vietnamese state announced that it planned to develop an economy that would be "market-oriented with a socialist orientation," workers have faced a series of problems in their interactions with non-Vietnamese factory owners and managers. Workers have repeatedly mobilized not only to complain about labor-law violations, but also to seek redress for those violations.

---

[103] Article 38 (Part d) says: "An employer shall have the right to terminate unilaterally a labour contract in the following circumstances: … (d) The employer is forced to reduce production and employment after trying all measures to recover from a natural disaster, a fire, or another event of force majeure as stipulated by the Government." So, based on this stipulation, this worker is absolutely correct: There was no natural disaster, no fire, no "force majeure as stipulated by the Government" that would justify his termination. In this case, it was the management's wish to change security guards, not any government's stipulation.

[104] Article 17, Section 1, is about layoff due to the restructuring of the business or the change in technology; it says that the employer has the responsibility to retrain a worker in order to employ him/her in a new job.

[105] My emphasis.

The Irony of Cultural Identity

In factories where migrant workers were in the majority, networking based on native place, gender, religion, and economic situation fostered a sense of sisterhood and brotherhood at workers' housing units, at the work place, and at protests. However, an alliance between management and the state proved able to use a sense of native place to divide workers. While migrant workers rely on their social networks to support each other in settings that constitute the totality of their existence—living, playing, and working—the state and capitalist enterprises also manipulate this very social networking for their shared interests (i.e., to monitor and control worker dissent and resistance). Chapter 7 elaborates on how the state and management operate in workplace environments and worker rental communities to achieve their goals.

Class and False Consciousness

Cultural ties brought workers together in both social *and* productive relations in labor struggles. The Vietnamese case studies add workers' cultural bonding—employees relate to each other as fellow villagers, sisters, and brothers—to the process of developing a class consciousness found in collective class moments. This finding is consistent with Thompson's argument that workers come together first in their common experiences for shared interests, and then discover class consciousness at the end of their struggle.

Workers did not resign themselves to labor violations as "natural and inevitable" or participate in "voluntary servitude"; they did not, in short, demonstrate false consciousness by consenting to the dominant ideology, capitalist power, or state policies. Rather, they fought back in various ways. However, their struggles tended to be short-lived. After they won some immediate rights-based concessions from management on wage and nonwage allowances, most returned to work to make a living. Moreover, workers often appealed to state apparatuses, such as labor newspapers and labor unions, within the framework of the law. To some extent, these compromises might be interpreted as forms of consent to state policies, but when workers appealed to state apparatuses by using the rule of law, they did so to fight for their rights and interests, *not* those of the state.

Types of Protest and Use of Law

Similar to workers in the state sector and Nam Định workers a century earlier under French colonial rule, Vietnamese employees of FDI factories used a combination of Polanyi and Marxist language and the rule of law in their protests. They used Polanyi rhetoric to oppose being treated inhumanely, using such terms as "buffalos" and "draft animals," "dogs and cats," and "commodities" to describe how management perceived or treated its employees. In moments of collective action or crisis, they used Marxist class language, such as "collective of workers," and positioned themselves as "we" and "us" versus management. They saw themselves as members of the working class who shared a common purpose.

Workers cited relevant laws and appealed to the state ideological apparatuses— the labor press and labor unions—for their entitlements and rights. Each of the two key labor newspapers supported and protected the other and together flexed their public-influence muscles to raise awareness and pressure the appropriate authorities to act according to the law. In turn, state officials tended to intervene only after full-blown news articles were published that featured repeated workers' complaints and poignant photos, as well as interviews with legal experts and labor union officials. For example, thanks to the *Người Lao Động* journalists' faithful reports on the negative consequences of the *hộ khẩu* policy on migrant workers, local state and labor unions intervened and helped to insure that migrant workers would be charged the same (low) rent and electricity rates as local residents. Ideologically, there is no contradiction at work in a socialist state when workers rise up against "exploitative capitalists." So, the state permitted the media to report on workers' protests against foreign-owned companies, but it forbade coverage of protests against enterprises in the morphing state sector. As if in a test of courage, the sympathetic labor press printed pro-labor articles until they were censored. At other times, they were less combative and quietly waited out the period of silence dictated by the state.

Flexible resistance takes on many different and creative forms. Workers used all mechanisms at their disposal to fight, albeit for short-term victories. Workers are very creative about using different sites and forms to evade management suppression and state monitoring: protest letters and petitions, sit-ins, food–water protests, and graffiti. Apparently, secretive strike messages on the wall in Freetrend contributed to the direct action by thousands of workers there and in neighboring factories, resulting in the historic 2006 minimum-wage increases in the FDI sector and subsequent rounds of wage-related protests. These actions led to a significant turning point in Vietnamese labor relations. Following these acts of resistance, the government decided to implement an annual minimum-wage increase, and the gap between minimum wages in the FDI and state/domestic sectors has been shrinking.

Workers also revealed that their resentment over unfair income distribution is heightened when management is of a different nationality. In FDI factories, workers were conscious of their nationality and stressed the unfairness of the distribution of income and wealth between management and labor. They made this distinction in their public protest letters and verbal complaints.

This chapter has shown that workers in formal FDI factories analyzed their conditions, their alliances based on cultural ties and the use of the law, and their relationships to management in a variety of ways, some of which strengthened their consciousness of themselves as members of a working class. The next chapter looks into how workers dealt with violations in domestic–private factories, in large-scale underground foreign investment enterprises, and in different forms of underground foreign investment in small-scale factories.

CHAPTER 6

WORKERS' ACTIVISM IN VIETNAMESE PRIVATE AND UNDERGROUND FOREIGN-INVESTMENT FACTORIES

The growth of the domestic-private sector in Vietnam has been accompanied by an increase in labor discontent since 2006. The private sector now includes not only domestic-private factories, but also equitized, state-owned factories—many are joint-stock companies, joint-ventures, or one-member state corporations (the state as the one owner with limited liabilities). Labor discontent arises in all of these types of factories, with actions ranging from strikes initiated in sympathy with the 2006 minimum-wage worker protests in the FDI sector, to entitlement strikes led by dissatisfied and disillusioned state workers who were laid off when their factories were equitized and who never received their rightful compensation.

Labor protests also developed in Vietnamese-owned private factories and in those foreign-owned factories that claimed to be owned by Vietnamese nationals in order to gain tax breaks and other advantages offered by the state only to ethnic Vietnamese owners. Such underground investment (*đầu tư chui*) factories are also known as "shadow-foreign enterprises."[1] These are cases in which owners/investors are not Vietnamese, but they operate the factories in the background and appoint Vietnamese persons as titular heads in order to receive privileges enjoyed by Vietnamese owners.

I will first present the overall trends of protest in the private sector, and then focus on five protest cases in domestic-private factories. I also look at underground-investment factories, highlighting a well-known case through the first-hand accounts of two young labor organizers, and will conclude with the stories of written protests in two other underground-investment cases.

OVERALL TRENDS OF PROTESTS IN PRIVATE-DOMESTIC FACTORIES

The increase in protests in the growing domestic-private factories in Ho Chi Minh City (1995–2011) puts the share of protests in the private sector in Ho Chi Minh City at a higher percentage than the share of private protests nationwide (see Table 6.1 and Chapter 3). In particular, the share of protests in Ho Chi Minh City's domestic-private factories, relative to the total number of protests in the city, was between 37 percent and 44 percent between 1995 and 1998 (compared to only 27–35

---

[1] "Underground investment" is the literal translation of the Vietnamese expression describing this practice. Jee Young Kim used "shadow-foreign enterprises" in "How Does Enterprise Ownership Matter? Labor Conditions in Fashion and Footwear Factories in Southern Vietnam," in *Vietnam Update Series: Labour in Vietnam*, ed. Anita Chan (Singapore: Institute of Southeast Asian Studies, 2011).

percent *nationwide* in the same period). But that share increased to between 50 percent and 65 percent during the 1999–2003 period (compared to only 24–33 percent *nationwide* in the same period). The 1999 and 2003 peaks coincided with the rise of equitized state-owned enterprises.

The rise in the percentage of protests in the domestic-private sector—now including equitized state-owned enterprises—suggests that there were problems with the equitization process, which presented a new set of problems for workers. State workers—the ones who were not laid off—had become "private" workers with less protection and fewer social benefits than before. According to a 2006 study that interviewed workers in one hundred equitized state-owned enterprises, overall working conditions in the then newly equitized state-owned enterprises were less than satisfactory: the wages may have increased, but costs of living were also higher; meanwhile, welfare entitlements had decreased for these workers.[2] This study also found particular concerns: 1) a decline in the number of workers with permanent contracts; 2) an increase in the work-hours per day; 3) fluctuating dividend income from shares; 4) the erosion of social welfare entitlements, such as bonuses; and 5) poor vocational training for workers. A worker, cited in this study, provided a reality check on the government's expectation that workers would become shareholders in these businesses: "The policy is fair but unrealistic and unattractive to workers because almost all employees are poor and cannot afford to purchase shares, no matter how much of a discount is given."[3]

The total numbers of protests in Ho Chi Minh City began to rise in 2003, ranging from 113 in 2006 to 200 in 2008. In 2006, protests in domestic-private factories made up nearly half of total protests (49 percent) in Ho Chi Minh City; in 2009, they constituted 58 percent.[4] Labor discontent in the domestic-private sector in Ho Chi Minh City had become as serious as the pervasive discontent in the often maligned FDI sector. As shown in Table 3.3, in 2010 and 2011, protests in FDI-owned factories accounted for at least 50 percent of the total strikes in Ho Chi Minh City.

The rise in protests in domestic-private factories during 2006 and 2007 could have been related to two occurrences. First, workers in private factories carried out sympathetic strikes corresponding to protests in FDI factories demanding minimum-wage hikes (2006) and an inflation adjustment in wages (2007); the private-factory workers wanted this minimum-wage increase to apply to their domestic-private factories as well as to FDI factories. Second, in 2007, Decree 110 discontinued all compensation to laid-off state workers—including the one-time severance pay. This decree stripped MOLISA (Ministry of Labor, Invalids, and Social Affairs) of its power to oversee the equitization process and ensure the distribution of compensation to workers. Since then, state corporations were at liberty to dismiss workers without compensation, and this exacerbated the discontent of those employees who lost their jobs. For those fortunate enough to keep their jobs in equitized SOEs, they had to protest in a new environment—the domestic-private-

[2] Mark Evans and Bùi Đức Hải, "Embedding Neoliberalism through Statecraft: The Case of Market Reform in Vietnam," in *Internalizing Globalization: The Rise of Neoliberalism and the Decline of National Varieties of Capitalism*, ed. Susanne Soederberg, Georg Menz, and Philip Cerny (Hampshire, England: Palgrave Macmillan, 2006), pp. 233–35.

[3] Ibid., p. 235.

[4] The two comparable statistics at the national level—shares of domestic-private protests in total strikes nationwide—are: 25 percent in 2006 and 22 percent in 2009.

sector—about which they had little knowledge and experience. This reality is confirmed in Evans's and Bùi's study, which found that the majority of workers in these equitized SOEs did not understand the conditions of their new jobs, the nature of shareholding, the operation of financial markets, and the responsibilities of shareholders. The majority of these workers were in the clothing/textile industries and had low skills and low levels of education.[5]

In 2009, the share of protests in domestic-private factories in Ho Chi Minh City increased to 58 percent of the total number of labor protests in the city, the highest for this sector between 1995 and 2011 (except for 1999, although there were only thirty-one total protests in Ho Chi Minh City then). This trend is consistent with the national 2008 protest spike discussed in Chapter 3, when workers protested against FDI managers who refused (or failed) to implement the inflation-adjusted–minimum-wage increase.

**Table 6.1: Protests in Private-Domestic Factories
in Ho Chi Minh City (1995 to 2011)**

Year	Percentage of Protests in Ho Chi Minh City Domestic-Private Sector	Total Number of Protests (in all sectors in Ho Chi Minh City)
1995–1996	44 %	36
1997	37 %	46
1998	37 %	38
1999	65 %	31
2000	50 %	34
2001	50 %	32
2002	56 %	36
2003	57 %	60
2004	38 %	47
2005	38 %	50
2006	49 %	113
2007	40 %	108
2008	31 %	200
2009	58 %	78
2010	specific data unavailable	70
2011	specific data unavailable	189

Sources: HCMC Labor Federation (1995–July 2010); HCMC Labor Federation (2011), Report on 2011 Labor Union Campaigns and Activities and Roadmap for 2012.

While nationwide the rate of strikes seems to have slowed down after 2008, perhaps due to the overall effects of the global economic crisis, workers in private factories in Ho Chi Minh City still used this form of protest. In 2009, 58 percent ot the total number of strikes in Ho Chi Minh City took place in domestic-private factories, which was much higher than the nationwide proportion of 22 percent.[6]

---

[5] Evans and Bùi Đức Hải, "Market Reform in Vietnam," p. 233.

[6] Nationally, there were 67 strikes in the domestic-private sector out of 310 total strikes in 2009.

There are two interpretations for this trend: 1) workers in "underground" factories (such as the Huê Phong case) demanded to be recognized as FDI workers in order to be paid according to the higher minimum-wage levels required in FDI factories; and 2) former state workers who were rehired in privatized joint-venture factories demanded to be paid the higher FDI minimum wage (see the Việt Thắng-Vicoluch case).[7] This may explain the rise in protests in Ho Chi Minh City private factories in 2009.

The reasons for protests in the domestic-private sector are similar to those in the FDI sector: low pay, excessive overtime, inadequate social insurance, insufficient health and unemployment benefits,[8] inadequate bonuses, and other violations to workers' rights and interests.[9] The top complaints involved violations of labor laws, such as those dealing with labor contracts, severance pay, early retirement, and end-of-contract benefits. Also, workers protested against management's failure to pay its full share of the state-managed social insurance and health funds; in some cases, no contributions were made at all.

PROTESTS IN VIETNAMESE PRIVATE FACTORIES

The following five cases highlight protests in various Vietnamese industries—shoe, textile, garment, tire, and security—that represent a range of labor-management issues. In these cases, I examine the role of cultural identities and resources, a sense of class, and forms of protest, as well as the employees' use of the law.

Minh Nghệ Leather Shoe Workers

A group of local workers in Minh Nghệ[10]—a factory in Thủ Đức district producing men's and women's leather shoes—sent a handwritten letter in February 2006 to the newspaper, *Người Lao Động*. In it, they exposed violations to the Labor Code and other laws and signed the document "collective of workers" (*tập thể công nhân*). These local workers had worked in this factory for many years. They began their letter with an uppercase title to enunciate the message, *"PLEASE LISTEN TO OUR CALL FOR HELP,"* and proceeded to cite specific violations of the labor law, especially excessive overtime and unfair treatment:

---

[7] Correspondence with Journalist B, Ho Chi Minh City, October 2010.

[8] Similar to the nationwide trend, management calculates workers' benefits based on the non-livable minimum wage, not on the higher, real take-home pay, which includes overtime pay. This is a common practice. Workers end up receiving relatively low social insurance, and limited health and unemployment benefits, due to this calculation by management.

[9] HCMC Labor Federation, "Báo Cáo Tình Hình Tranh Chấp Lao Động Tập Thể [Report on the Situation in Collective Labor Conflicts], every year from 1995 (1995 and 1996 in the same report) to 2011; HCMC Labor Federation, "Báo Cáo: Tình hình công nhân, viên chức, lao động và hoạt động Công đoàn Thành phố 6 tháng đầu năm 2012; Phương hướng hoạt động 6 tháng cuối năm 2012" [Report: Situation of Workers and Public Employees, and Activities of HCMC Labor Federation in the First Six Months of 2012; Directions for Activities in the Last Six Months of 2012], June 25, 2012.

[10] http://vietnam.panpages.com/listings/vn19894. This factory, known under the English name Minh Nghe Trading and Industrial Co., Ltd., is part of the Vietnam Leather Footwear Export and Import Consortium (http://vietnamexportsimports.com/import-export/vietnam-products/l-m-n-o-products/leather-footwear.html?start=200, accessed March 2012).

Our most urgent concern [*bức xúc*] is about work hours. First, every day we worked at least nine hours, but only got paid for eight hours, not counting overtime. Second is about overtime work. We are all familiar with the saying: "Minh Nghệ, the two wretched words: low wages and excessive overtime." After almost four years of working, we were never let off work on time at 5 PM (except Sundays). On overtime days, we have our meal at 5 PM then go right back to work at 5:30 PM. Overtime work until 8 PM is considered early, until 9 PM is normal, and until 10 PM or 11 PM is for rush orders (workers who work in the "outside sole" assembly line have to work overnight most likely). Six weeks like that, continuously; there were many times when we had to work two consecutive Sundays. We know that "work more, eat more" [*làm nhiều, ăn nhiều*], but how can we swallow food under such intense working conditions? Counting overtime work, we have to work from twelve to fourteen hours/day from Mondays to Saturdays (on Sundays we work "only" nine hours/day). It seems as if we are completely isolated from the outside world. The third concern is about pay, our supervisor's attitude, and our lunch. When receiving our salary, we felt as if we just received charity money [*tiền bố thí*]: no envelope, no accounting of our work hours including overtime ... so we don't know how our salary is calculated. The supervisor's attitude (toward us) is beyond reproach: making mistakes is synonymous with being scolded and humiliated. We are here to work, *not to sell our human values* [*bán nhân phẩm*]. If we made mistakes, why not use the labor code to judge us? And about our lunches, we used to call it "prison meals" [*bữa cơm tù*]: no table to sit down, just a tree trunk, a cement embankment, or an alley to sit down. Each has to pay VND 3,500 for our meal; the meal that has more style than substance ... We are anxiously waiting, night and day, for relevant state officials' intervention to bring justice to us.[11]

These workers expressed indignation regarding the level of work intensity and the requirement that they work continuous overtime, which effectively alienated them from the rest of society. They felt "completely isolated from the outside world." They wanted to be respected: "We are here to work, not to sell our human values." They fought as a "collective of workers" for their shared interests in work hours, overtime, wages, and lunches. Similar to state workers, they, too, wanted the state to intervene to bring them justice and dignity. This is a successful case: *Người Lao Động* journalists listened to their plight, published their complaints, and successfully prompted the district state authorities to intervene. Then the president of this company promised publicly in the newspaper to reduce overtime and compensate workers adequately.[12]

An Electrical Worker at Thời Ích Rubber

Thời Ích is a 100 percent Taiwanese-owned company that operates a large tire factory in the Tây Ninh Industrial Zone (outside of Ho Chi Minh City), which was

---

[11] My emphasis.

[12] Vĩnh Tùng, "Báo động tình trạng nợ lương công nhân" [Alert about the Situation of Owing Workers' Wages], *Người Lao Động,* April 26, 2006, http://nld.com.vn/149183p0c1010/bao-dong-tinh-trang-no-luong-cong-nhan.htm, accessed July 2006.

established in 2000 with eight hundred workers.[13] On its glossy English website, the focus is to sell; the site advertises all types of tires for various moving vehicles and showcases three quality certifications—International Standards Organization (ISO-9001), the United States Department of Transportation, and the European Economic Community.[14] Clearly, this factory has produced tires for export to the United States and European markets. But the Vietnamese website focuses on hiring Vietnamese employees in order to expand its retail sales and distribution offices to provinces in the North.[15]

The complaint letter reproduced here shows how workers and their relatives appealed to the law and expressed their concerns for other workers in the same situation. A man wrote an email to inquire about a law involving benefits on behalf of his brother, who worked in the electrical department of the tire factory. This worker's brother wrote:

> According to the law, after a worker stopped work for seven days, s/he should have received all benefits and supplements within thirty days. I called the personnel office to explain this to them, and they found out that they made a mistake. Still they did not apologize. But more than thirty days had passed, and my brother still had not received anything … I know about the law, so I can help my brother to petition [for redress], but other workers, not knowing the law, will be at a disadvantage, for their hard work will not be appreciated in the end due to this [management's] negligence.

This case speaks to the benefits of knowing the law.[16] This worker's brother appealed to a very specific law: supplementary benefits were to be given to workers within thirty days after a labor contract had ended. He also showed concern for other workers' interests: "other workers, not knowing the law, will be at a disadvantage."

A Đông Á Garment and Textile Worker

A local worker from Đông Á Garment and Textile factory[17] in Ho Chi Minh City tried to follow up on her complaint about the failure of this company to remit any severance allowance to her even after her repeated complaints. As mentioned by this worker, the follow-up was published in the *Người Lao Động* newspaper in July 2005. But several months later, the company still had not complied. She signed her own name, but made an appeal on behalf of all workers in this company:

[13] http://muaban.net/ha-noi/raovat/chi-tiet/7462018/cong-ty-tnhh-cao-su-thoi-ich-br-good time-rubber-co-ltd-br-nha.html, accessed March 2012.

[14] http://www.goodtimegroup.com.tw/aboutus.html, accessed March 2012.

[15] http://muaban.net/ha-noi/raovat/chi-tiet/7462018/cong-ty-tnhh-cao-su-thoi-ich-br-good time-rubber-co-ltd-br-nha.html, accessed March 2012.

[16] In some ways, this case is similar to the case of Phú Riềng rubber plantation workers, who appealed to the colonial French law in their 1930 trial.

[17] This is a joint-stock company (Công Ty Cổ Phần Dệt May Đông Á) that manufactures and trades garment and clothing products, http://www.vietnamimportexportnews.com/garment/16034-dong-a-garment-textile-co.html, accessed in March 2012.

Even after the *Người Lao Động* had reported my complaint [in] the July 2005 issue, still this company did not follow the labor law. As of now [August 2005], I still have not received my severance allowance based on the new [higher] salary level. Personally, I am very disappointed that this company still does not follow the Labor Code properly, even after being reminded publicly by the media that represents workers' voices. Therefore, I implore the newspaper to look into this issue and intervene in a timely manner, because as of now, I still have not received any severance pay. For my own benefits and the *collective benefits of all workers* [*tập thể công nhân*] in this company, please investigate closely the *implementation of current labor laws* in this company for the rights of the Workers [*sic*].[18]

Registering her complaint even more strongly than did the brother of the Thời Ích rubber factory employee, this worker not only shows faith in the law, but also appeals to the state media—the newspaper—to investigate and intervene in the enforcement of the law. This worker focused on her entitled severance allowance, which should have been based on her new salary level, and she also used a collective language, referring to "collective benefits of all workers," as if that would strengthen her case. Overall, this case focuses on rigorous law enforcement, rather than a struggle with the opposing class.

A Sơn Kim Garment Worker

This case highlights one of the most common complaints in the garment industry: excessive overtime work. A local worker from a private garment factory in Ho Chi Minh City sent a desperate letter to the *Người Lao Động* newspaper, asking for help after being turned down by the enterprise-level union representative and the personnel office. He had been demoted from a quality-control position to a job working on the assembly line under the (false) pretext that his health was poor and the condition made him unsuited for a quality-control position. However, he claimed that the real reason for the demotion was his inability to work overtime one day due to a family emergency. Here is his account:

According to a *worker's thinking* like mine, using the "ill health" reason to demote me is not logical because: 1. My day-off was approved by the plant supervisor, and it was not because of a health reason; 2. If they demoted me because I could not stay to work overtime [when asked to do so] at the last minute, then it is against the Labor Code of the Socialist Republic of Vietnam, which says that two hundred hours are the maximum overtime hours per year. At that point in time [about July 2005], I had already worked more than two hundred overtime hours. Therefore, I can refuse to work overtime, but, really, there was no advance notice for overtime work on July 19, 2005, and I couldn't find anyone to take my mother to the doctor's office; 3. According to the above reasons, from a worker's perspective, I think this demotion is illogical, and I respectfully ask: on what basis did they transfer me from the quality-control position to assembly-line sewing [the bottom job]? Ms. TR [the foreperson in his department] said this in a letter to her boss: "Based on Mr. H's [the worker's name] report, I'd like to ask

---

[18] My emphasis.

the management to give him one more chance. If/when overtime is needed, Mr. H will try to make a better arrangement to work overtime; if he still violates [factory procedure], he will accept all punishment [*trừng phạt*] from the management." I completely disagree with her because *we are living in a socialist country, not in a regime where people can exploit people.* So when Ms. TR used the word "punishment" when I don't work overtime, I don't know what she thinks she is that she can judge and punish [workers] like that.[19]

This Sơn Kim worker used class language to invoke the socialist contract and the law. He was very conscious of his class, demonstrated by his use of the words "a worker's thinking" several times to remind the socialist state about the exploitative nature of the market system ("we are living in a socialist country, not in a regime where people can exploit people"). He understood the overtime section of the Labor Code very well, as is clear from his assertion that employees cannot be required to put in more than two hundred hours of overtime annually. He also understood the evidence-based legal protocol and provided the "Healthy and Fit for Work" certificate, his foreperson's handwritten note, and the "Personal [*sic*] Action Form." He appealed to two state apparatuses—the labor unions and the labor newspaper—to support him in his efforts to make sure the law restricting mandatory overtime was enforced and workers were protected from the exploitation of the market system.

A Công Ty Dịch Vụ Bảo Vệ Việt Nam (Vietnam Security Guard Services) Worker

On a flashy website with photos of well-clad security guards wearing dark glasses, featuring a rolling column of quoted accolades from various companies, this company in Ho Chi Minh City offers all forms of security-guard services for private property, events, conferences, and VIPs, as well as providing escorts and money carriers.[20] The company promises the world to their potential customers: "VNSS always puts customer interest [at] the top of our priority [list]. People are considered the decisive factor. Our company's motto is: virtue, health and professionalism." It also claims to have adopted a quality management system through recruitment, training, education, compensation, and career development.

The complaint letter submitted by an employee contradicts these boasts regarding the company's principled mission and motto. The contrast between the company promises made to its customers and the reality and working conditions of its workers—the guards—is stark. A local worker from this company, bypassing the unresponsive enterprise labor union, reminded the state of the socialist contract with the people. In his letter, he exposed a series of sustained violations to the labor contract and repeatedly mentioned the need to relay his complaints to the "ears" (*chuyển tới tai*) of the state authorities. In a handwritten letter to a local newspaper in the South, he claimed to be representing all of his fellow guards, "*đại diện nhân viên bảo vệ,*" but said that he did not sign his name for fear of retribution:

This company also violated other stipulations of the Labor Code and labor contract. But no state agency was aware of these violations ... We got paid less

---

[19] My emphasis.

[20] http://www.baovevietnam-vnss.com/, accessed March 2012. My emphasis.

than what was stated on the labor contract without any explanation ... The company did not contribute to our social insurance and health funds even when the workers contributed their shares, so when we were laid off, we had no social and health benefits; we often received our pay almost one month late, or were paid in small installments. How can we pay our expenses and save under that condition? *Our enterprise labor unions did not even have a kind word for us when we had accidents or fell ill* ... This company also violated other articles in the Labor Code, which are stated on the labor contract, yet no state office is aware of these violations. Now, being extremely frustrated by the violations to our labor contract, I had to write this letter to implore the newspaper to report and to relay our message to *the "ears" of the state authorities.*[21]

This worker used state apparatuses—the labor unions and their labor newspaper—to call on the state authorities to enforce the law. He expected the workplace union representatives to treat workers with compassion, an expectation similar to that of the state workers in the North, as noted earlier. He expected the state to do its job properly in both monitoring and enforcing the law, which he understood and invoked as a right. He acted on behalf of his fellow workers and implicitly reminded the state of its socialist contract: "Our enterprise labor unions did not even have a kind word for us when we had accidents or fell ill."

During the bygone socialist days, workplace labor unions often performed social functions, such as visiting and giving small gifts to workers who suffered from accidents or illnesses, or were facing the death anniversaries of family members, weddings, or funerals. Those gestures of kindness—even when they involved little money—lifted workers' spirits. Later, with the market system in place, these small benefits were lost.

In sum, the Minh Nghệ leather shoe worker invoked worker's dignity, implored state authorities to intervene for justice, and supported collective class action; the Thời Ích rubber factory worker's brother appealed to the law; the Đông Á garment worker used collective language to appeal to part of the state apparatus (the labor newspaper) to facilitate state enforcement of the law; the Sơn Kim garment worker used class language to invoke the socialist contract and appealed to state apparatuses (the labor unions and labor newspaper) to enforce the overtime law and protect workers from market exploitation; the security-guard services worker reminded the state of its socialist contract and used a state apparatus (the newspaper) to remind state authorities of their responsibility to enforce the laws properly.

Workers stressed the need to be treated with respect and dignity. Many used class-based language and engaged in class action for broadly defined workers' rights. In most of these cases (four out of five), workers cited specific protections in the labor code and used legalistic language and protocols. Interestingly, workers appealed to the state, requesting that it intervene in labor-management disputes, in two ways: one, by reminding the state of the implicit socialist contract it had established with the workers (the Sơn Kim case: "we are living in a socialist country, not in a regime where people can exploit people") and, two, by reminding the state and its representatives—the labor unions and the labor newspapers—to enforce the law and to restore justice, as we heard in the Minh Nghệ case, "We are anxiously waiting, night and day, for relevant state officials' intervention to bring justice to us,"

---

[21] My emphasis.

and in the security-guard services case, "I … implore the newspaper to report and relay our message to the 'ears' of the state authorities."

Next, I turn to three forms of underground investment, or "*Đầu tư chui*," and examine how workers responded to "shadow" foreign-investment enterprises in the domestic-private sector. But first, who are these capitalists and where do these workers come from?

THE CASE OF THE HUÊ PHONG LEATHER SHOE FACTORY

Evidence shows that the 1999 Law to Encourage Domestic Investment and the two systems of minimum wage—lower for domestic and higher for FDI factories—may have created perverse incentive for underground practices. The 1999 law offered tax breaks, extended low land rents, and allowed profit repatriation to encourage overseas Vietnamese to return home and invest in Vietnam. As long as the investors obtained proper certification (confirming they were of Vietnamese descent), their investment was legitimized, even when the source of money was from non-Vietnamese citizens.

I examine three cases to demonstrate how underground investment practices circumvented the laws at the expense of workers: one case is based on firsthand interviews with two Vietnamese labor organizers (the case of Huê Phong, a Taiwanese-owned-and-managed factory registered as a Vietnamese company), and I describe two protests against factories that used Vietnamese nationals as "fronts" for the true foreign-born owners.

Significance of Place: Gò Vấp District and Thái Bình and Kiên Giang Provinces

To understand the Huê Phong case, we need to understand the living situations of migrant workers. Three social spaces—Gò Vấp district and Thái Bình and Kiên Giang provinces—were significant in showing how human relations, influenced by cultural identities, can propel people toward collective action that is greater than themselves. Gò Vấp district, or *quận nội thành*—within Ho Chi Minh City—has long been the meeting place for migrant workers who live together, work together, and go on strike in times of oppression. This district is home to thousands of migrant workers, most of whom have come from the Central and Mekong Delta regions, and the North.[22]

The 2005 fine-grained study sponsored by ActionAid and the People's Committee of Gò Vấp district surveyed three hundred migrant workers, of whom one hundred worked in garment and shoe factories, manufacturing for export, in three wards of this district. About 90 percent of the whole sample (of three hundred people) were migrant workers from poor northern regions such as Thái Bình, Thanh Hóa, and Nam Định provinces.[23] A team of local researchers conducted both in-depth interviews and focus-group discussions with ninety-nine workers in five garment and shoe factories subcontracting for foreign buyers. One of these five

---

[22] Huỳnh Thị Ngọc Tuyết, "Báo Cáo Kết Quả Cuộc Khảo Sát Về 'Phòng Chống Mua Bán Phụ Nữ—Trẻ Em' và 'Tăng Cường Trách Nhiệm Xã Hội" [Findings of the Survey on the Prevention of the Trafficking of Women and Children and Strengthening Social Responsibility] (Ho Chi Minh City: Go Vap District People's Committee, ActionAid Vietnam [Southern Office], and Development Assistance Project, 2005), p. 3.

[23] Ibid., pp. 4–5.

factories was the Huê Phong leather shoe factory, which employed many migrant workers from Thái Bình. These researchers also interviewed management representatives from the five factories and five rental owners (*chủ nhà trọ*) to understand their perspectives on the employees' working and living conditions.

Workers originating from the same hometowns or villages (or *người đồng hương*) tended to stay in the same rental units where they were able to support each other.[24] They shared rooms and meals together, in fluid subgroups based on gender, shared familial relations, village origins, or being old schoolmates. Many migrant workers from Thái Bình, Thanh Hóa, and Nam Định provinces either had left their hometowns together, migrating as a group to stay together in their new residences, or, if they moved south at different times, relied on the ones who had settled in the cities first to help out fellow villagers who came later. The first group would find jobs and a place to stay for the next group of migrants. To save rent money, most would stay together in households of four to five people. At the time of this 2005 study, most of the renters interviewed worked in the same few factories, such as the garment factories and Huê Phong shoe factory mentioned above. This native-place bonding was more pronounced among women migrant workers. Together, native-place and gender bonding strengthened the sense of community and organization among the workers who stayed in these temporary rental places.

The ActionAid study found evidence of widespread, poor working conditions characterized by excessive overtime with low pay and little potential for future advancement or improvement. Overtime was one of the key concerns of those interviewed. It was excessive, continuous, and non-voluntary. Many workers complained:

> We have a saying, "going to work with no return," because we leave at dawn when it is still dark, not knowing when we will return home. Working until 9 PM is a common thing; sometimes it is until midnight, even until 2 AM the following day, but then we have to return to work at 7 AM. With rush orders, we had to work overnight and the following morning until noon … We often do not see the sun.[25]

Management and employees view overtime work from very different perspectives.[26] According to a manager interviewed for the study, "Workers like to work overtime to make more money. Besides, they would have nothing to do when they return to their rental places early. Also, if everyone came back at the same time, the rental place, often shared by many, would become overcrowded and hot." But most of the interviewees contradicted this condescending summary of their lives and offered a more nuanced position. On the one hand, they wanted to work overtime to complement the low piece-rates and low wages. On the other hand, they clearly articulated these conditions for working overtime: 1) there must be a limit on the number of overtime hours required per day; 2) there must be a limit on the number of days involving overtime per week; 3) employees must have the opportunity to take a break for a few hours between shifts (for example, some workers wanted a break between the third shift and the next shift so they could rest before returning to

---

[24] Ibid., pp. 2, 8, 24.
[25] Ibid., p. 10.
[26] Ibid., pp. 12–13.

work);[27] 4) the factory must offer adequate hourly overtime compensation; 5) there must be transparency in the calculations of overtime hours, in the calculations of the quota (or pieces) to be completed during overtime, and in public information about take-home money from overtime work; and (6) management must provide non-wage benefits such as extra meals and breaks during overtime work.

After working under such sustained pressure, many interviewees came home exhausted and barely had enough time for personal hygiene, to eat and sleep to get ready for the following workday. They lamented: "There is nothing for our future; we live day by day; murky future, we work all day but have no clue about our future; our life has no meaning." Over the one-day weekend—when there was no overtime work—the women had a very limited cultural life. Often they spent time together, reading the newspapers, watching television, or walking around the rental areas or in nearby shopping malls. They had no money to attend cultural and social events or to take even a brief vacation outside of the little world in which they lived. The factories did not provide them with any form of entertainment to reward their hard work. Most of the women workers interviewed said that they spent their weekends washing clothes, cooking, and sleeping to "gain strength for another week of hard labor."[28]

These migrant workers understood the strength of unity and the power of collective action even without labor union support. One said, "When we got so angry, we wanted to go on strike. But when you go on strike, everyone has to do it; if only several workers did it, they would get crushed." Another one said, "Yes, I had participated in a strike because we were forced to work during this past Tết; we'd win if all workers in the factory went on strike; otherwise, if workers fought individually, then for sure we would lose." Some were disillusioned with enterprise-level labor unions. One woman said, "When I wanted to speak up in a union meeting, the shop-floor union steward advised us to think twice because we are only workers so we have to accept [the working conditions]. Therefore, I was stopped even before I could begin to speak."[29]

While native place and gender were the binding forces uniting the migrants' community, low pay and unbearable work conditions triggered collective action in moments of crisis. Gò Vấp district became the "incubator" for strikes, a place where workers bonded with each other in good and bad times.

Even under such gloomy conditions, many migrant workers had a purpose: they considered these low-paying, low-skilled jobs as stepping stones to advancement and support for themselves and their extended families.[30] Most used these jobs to help their parents, to pay debts (for long-term illness, bad harvests, or natural disasters), and save seed money for better careers. Most planned to return home after saving up some money, a difficult goal to achieve, given their low wages. Only a few wanted to stay in the cities. They aspired to change their life prospects (*khát vọng đổi đời*) with upward mobility. These expectations also were socially constructed based on gender: males were more interested in technical fields (such as mechanics,

---

[27] In fact, this reasonable request to prevent tragic accidents due to fatigue—for any type of manual labor—is stipulated in the Labor Code, No. 106, 109, 110 (in Chapter 7 of the Labor Code).

[28] Huỳnh Tuyết, "Phòng Chống Mua Bán Phụ Nữ—Trẻ Em," p. 9.

[29] Ibid., p. 24.

[30] Ibid.

electrical work, and electronic repair) while females were interested in beauty fields (hair and make-up).[31] Overall, they did not see these dead-end factory jobs as "natural and inevitable" (a form of false consciousness), but wanted to advance in their positions and better their lives.

Identity of Huê Phong Factory Owner

Huê Phong was established and registered in 1992 as a domestic leather shoe factory in Gò Vấp district that manufactured shoe and garment products for export. This was (and is) a Taiwanese-owned-and-managed company registered as a domestic enterprise under the name of an ethnic Hoa—Tô Gia Đương—who acted as its legal frontman and apparent owner (*pháp nhân*). It once employed more than ten thousand workers, mostly migrants, but after thirteen years of frequent strikes, as of 2008, its numbers were down to only 4,600 workers.[32] Appendix C shows the chronology of protests in Huê Phong factory and intervention from the *Người Lao Động* and local state officials between 1992 and 2008.

Huê Phong workers, striking over wage and bonus issues, converse with management, March 13, 2008. (Photo courtesy of *Người Lao Động* journalist Vĩnh Tùng)

---

[31] Ibid., pp. 24–25.

[32] Interview with Journalist C and Journalist D, April 2008, Ho Chi Minh City.

Huê Phong is a supplier factory; it takes orders from foreign corporate buyers, then coordinates production and oversees the Vietnamese workers who assemble leather shoes for many United States and European retail companies. Huê Phong ships the final products directly to the buyers' destinations.[33] Đào, a staff member in the accounting office whom I interviewed in 2006, showed me a list of the names of some corporate buyers whose accounts she had worked on, including three big customers from Canada, Japan, and the United States and some smaller corporate buyers from Europe (Germany, Britain, Austria, Hungary, Poland, and the Czech Republic). These corporate buyers distributed the shoes to popular shoe chains in the United States and Europe.

This factory had been granted the privileges and advantages accorded to a domestic factory based on the 1999 Vietnamese Law on Domestic Investment. The identity of Tô Gia Đương, the supposed "Vietnamese" president of Huê Phong, still remains veiled in a cloud of secrecy. What is unambiguous is that Tô had been able to secure a certificate of "being born in Vietnam" from the local external affairs department (*Sở Ngoại Vụ*) in Ho Chi Minh City to operate Huê Phong. He then obtained a business license/permit from the Ministry of Planning and Investment to run the shoe manufacturing and export activities.[34] His birthplace is still a mystery. According to Phạm Ngọc Đoàn, the Gò Vấp labor-union president, Tô was born in Hải Phòng, a port in the North of Vietnam, and skillfully took advantage of the 1999 law:

> It's very difficult to catch Huê Phong because it knows how to evade the law, and takes advantage of the Vietnamese policy on attracting FDI. The head of the board of directors is a Hoa who was born in Hải Phòng. So this is consistent with Vietnamese law promoting 'Vietnamese nationals' to return to and invest in Vietnam.[35]

As of 2010, Tô Gia Đương was still listed as the legal representative (*Người đại diện pháp lý*) of this limited responsibility company on a public website.[36]

Why do the real owners of Huê Phong continue to remain out of the spotlight and manage the factory from "underground," even when the 2005 Enterprises Law no longer allows special privileges for "Vietnamese national" investors? First, the salary savings for them is sizable: pay for workers in domestic factories is about VND 350,000 per month, as opposed to VND 630,000 per month for workers in FDI factories, due to the state's fixing of the minimum wage in the FDI sector between 1999 and 2005. Second, the company saves by making relatively smaller contributions to social insurance and health insurance funds for workers, using the

---

[33] Interview with Đào in 2006, Ho Chi Minh City.

[34] Conversations with Journalists A, B, C, D, E, and G between 2006 and 2008, Ho Chi Minh City.

[35] Interview with Phạm Ngọc Đoàn, Gò Vấp District, July 2006. Another version says that he was born in Saigon and left Vietnam in 1978 during the infamous "*nạn kiều,*" a policy that evicted the Hoa when Vietnam and China entered the border war. This version of the story was repeated to me in a conversation in 2006 with a Taiwanese researcher who had access to Huê Phong management and the facility. Tô came back to Vietnam in 1990 to take advantage of the pro-FDI law, well before the Law on Domestic Investment was implemented in 1999.

[36] http://baomuabanraovat.com/raovat/100826/cong-ty-giay-da-hue-phong-tnhh, accessed March 2012.

low wage base to calculate management's share. Third, they may continue to benefit from low land rent and tax exemptions.

Globally, this case connects the greater China investment zone (Taiwan, mainland China, and the Hoa in Vietnam) to consumption in the United States and other countries. It also confirms the "national home base" concept, which suggests that the upper-level managers of multinational corporations maintain their cultural, social (with ethnicity and kinship networks), political, and economic characteristics even though they have expanded their operations worldwide.[37] This concept explains the behaviors and practices of Taiwanese corporations in Vietnam, such as Huê Phong, which maintains ties with China, hires Chinese professionals (from mainland China) to work in Vietnam, and thereby reconfirms the employees' (generally distrustful) impressions of the thinking and practice of Taiwanese management, as discussed in Chapter 3.[38]

Huê Phong's connection to mainland China was revealed recently. For years, Huê Phong had been listed in the directory of Mekong Research (an industrial market research services company) as "Huê Phong Footwear Co. Ltd., HUFOCO (Everglory Footwear Co. Ltd.)," manufacturing "leather and leatherette products, footwear soles, [and] packages" for European and US markets.[39] This factory's direct relationship to China becomes clearer if one searches further, to discover a slightly different name, Everglory International, a sportswear manufacturer located in Nanjing, which sells its products to huge American big-box stores such as Walmart and Kohl's. In the late 2000s, there was evidence that Everglory International relocated its factory from China to Vietnam.[40]

In recent years, the three-way connection among Huê Phong, the Taiwanese office, and Chinese experts has been established. Most prominent is the presence of Chinese experts on the assembly line and the use of the Chinese language in all production and management aspects of this factory. All the line-leaders and technical staff came from China.[41] This fact is consistent with the relocation of the Everglory International factory from China to Vietnam and Wang's and Hsiao's findings that Chinese experts from mainland China underwent a "Taiwanese experience," a period of training in Taiwan, to teach them to oversee a Vietnamese assembly line.[42]

Đào, the staff member in accounting whom I interviewed, confirmed the real owners. She showed me part of a memo from a discarded printout written in

---

[37] Jamie Peck and Henry Wai-chung Yeung, eds., *Remaking the Global Economy: Economic-Geographical Perspectives* (London, Delhi: Sage Publications, 2003), p. 41.

[38] Also in Hong-Zen Wang and H. H. Michael Hsiao, "Ethnic Resources or Capitalist Logic? Taiwanese Investment and Chinese Temporary Migrants in Vietnam," paper presented at the "Symposium on Experiences and Challenges of Economic Development in Southeast and East Asia," October 17–18, 2000, sponsored by PROSEA (Program for Southeast Asia Area Studies) and the Institute of Economics, Academia Sinica, Taipei, Taiwan, August 2001.

[39] Hue Phong Footwear Co. Ltd. (HUFOCO; Everglory Footwear Company Ltd.), http://www.mekongsources.com/Industry7.htm, accessed December 2012.

[40] Keith Bradsher, "Investors Seek Asian Options to Costly China," *New York Times* June 18, 2008.

[41] In the late 1990s, the Taiwanese technical specialists—not Chinese experts—managed Huê Phong's factory floor, as pointed out by the HCMC Labor Federation (and discussed in the "Conflicts among State Apparatuses" section, below).

[42] Wang and Hsiao, "Taiwanese Investment and Chinese Temporary Migrants in Vietnam."

Mandarin demonstrating the direct connection between Huê Phong and the Taiwanese office: all production activities—purchasing, business planning, quality control, managing, particular production stages—were linked to a purchasing office in Taiwan.

In the aftermath of the 2006 minimum-wage strike, all FDI factories were supposed to raise the minimum wage for their workers. When Huê Phong failed to raise the monthly minimum rate by 40 percent, as mandated by the 2006 Minimum Wage Law, workers protested and demanded to be paid the FDI wage. They knew Huê Phong was a foreign-direct-investment company, but the company was (and still is) registered as a domestic factory to take advantage of the lower wages permitted for workers employed in Vietnamese-owned factories.

But what factors make possible labor mobilizing in migrant workers' rented living quarters? How did these factors lead to those "class moments" during which thousands of migrant workers came together in Huê Phong factory to demand their rights?

Identity of Workers: Kiên Giang and Thái Bình Migrants

In this section, I explore the significance and complexity of place bonding by analyzing in-depth interviews with two organizers who became close friends in Kiên Giang—a fishing province near the southernmost tip of Vietnam—and followed each other to work in Ho Chi Minh City. Follow-up interviews revealed that one of these two organizers—the Huê Phong employee—was originally from Thái Bình (a poor province in the North). She mobilized from the inside and connected with Huê Phong workers. Most of them were also from Thái Bình.

I met and interviewed Nga and Đào in their rental unit in Gò Vấp in August and September 2006. In different ways, they had organized Huê Phong workers earlier that year. Again, they had been friends before they arrived in Ho Chi Minh City. Nga is a Kiên Giang native. Đào—originally from Thái Bình—migrated with her aunt and uncle to find work in Kiên Giang (her relatives still lived there at the time of the interview). These two young women attended three years of high school together in Kiên Giang. After high school, they left for Ho Chi Minh City and together rented a place to stay. This enduring friendship saw them through good and bad times in this big city.

I had the opportunity to get to know these women and observed their activities at their rental unit several times. Although they had been born in different villages, the women enjoyed a friendship linked to their years in Kiên Giang, a place they both called their "hometown." Đào secured employment at Huê Phong through the recommendation of other Thái Bình workers at that factory. She confirmed the identity of the real owner of this factory:

> I worked at the "red house" [*nhà đỏ*], a place for management. There I worked with the Chinese people, so I had to learn how to speak Mandarin. The Taiwanese boss was gentle and nice. His office was on the top floor. He stayed with his wife in their living quarters also up on the top floor.

Đào told me that all contracts and communications to workers were bilingual, written or spoken in both Vietnamese and Chinese. In our interviews, she showed me some language lessons (that she took) and memos; all were in Chinese. Most Huê

Phong workers were required to learn Chinese in order to communicate with the Chinese experts overseeing the assembly line. Like other workers, Đào was required to take a language class. She told me that she could speak and read some Mandarin and was thus able to understand the work orders.

The story of the other organizer, Nga—a diminutive and wiry woman—is complex and introduces the class-consciousness factor to this phenomenal effort. She wanted to become a college student and had been taking some computer classes when we talked. Nga came from a relatively well-to-do family of communist party members. After 1975, her family was doing well financially, with investment in a shrimp-farming business. But the drinking and infidelity problems of her father led to the disintegration of the family and the downfall of their shrimp-farming business. Still, her mother paid VND 900,000 per month to send Nga and her youngest brother to Ho Chi Minh City, where Nga attended a vocational college and her brother went to an elementary school. Nga had two other younger brothers at home who helped their mother with the family business.

On their only day off—a Sunday—Nga and Đào invited me to join them for lunch in their one-room rental unit. It was in this social space that I learned how they organized the strike. We sat on the tile floor to have a simple yet delicious lunch with ground dried shrimp from Kiên Giang, fresh coconut juice, and fish sauce over rice noodles. While we were having lunch, Nga's five-year old brother—who stayed with the women—played happily with Đào and called her "*chị*" (sister). Over lunch, they shared with me their life stories and accounts of their activism. After lunch, we walked around to visit the working-class neighborhood where most units were rented to Huê Phong migrant workers. These two women organizers had mobilized workers in several dozen of rental units in early 2006. But how did the Kiên Giang *and* Thái Bình bonding enable the courageous actions of a Huê Phong worker and a class-conscious vocational student?

Significance of Place in Labor Organizing in 2006 Protests

These two women played key roles in labor organizing and mobilizing in the show-down that successfully forced Huê Phong management to comply with the 40 percent minimum-wage increase in the FDI sector, effective in February 2006. Nga—the vocational student—organized workers from outside the factory and convinced them to participate in two important meetings inside the factory. Đào organized factory workers from the inside as a Huê Phong employee. Đào had been earning about VND 1,200,000 per month (about US$75) as an assistant in the factory's management office for several years. Every month, she put aside money (about VND 1,000,000) in order to send one large sum annually to her parents, who worked their small plot of rice paddies in Thái Bình.

In evening conversations in their shared apartment, Đào informed Nga about the details of Huê Phong's labor violations and substandard working conditions. Both women were very excited to describe to me their sufferings, struggle, and triumph. They took turns telling me about how management promised changes but did not follow through on their promises; they laid bare the fact that these empty promises were meant to appease both workers and the labor unions. They lamented that six years of labor organizing (by other labor activists) had passed (2000 to 2006), but workers still suffered from the same problems: bad food, low wages, and excessive and forced overtime.

Nga described the strategies used by management to quiet the workers' anger and prevent further protests, and added that management hired "scabs" to replace activist employees and squelch protests. This was her argument when she went around the neighborhood to mobilize workers:

> Huê Phong management always used the time strategy of *"câu giờ"* [fishing time, or dragging their feet]. In the meetings, they promised many things. If they promised ten things, they only carried out 40 to 50 percent of what they promised one week later. The important thing was that workers' anger got cooled down [*nguội đi*] and workers did not come to be organized and united in support of a strike as they were before.[43] If one thousand workers went on strike, the remaining nine thousand workers could not work. But if there were some workers coming in to work, other workers would follow suit and come in to work also. Only one week after they had made promises to appease the strikers, management immediately changed their message: They would pay for only four hours per day for the four strike days, instead of four complete work days. But in reality, the situation was even worse. Most workers only worked two hours because management closed the factory right after workers went on strike. Consequently, Đào got paid only 1.5 days because all workers were sent home after the strike broke out.

Moreover, Đào complained about a whole host of violations at Huê Phong, which also occurred in other FDI factories:

> We protested bad and rotten food, low wages, and too much overtime. They fed us food like feeding pigs; it had a bad taste, and was not enough nutrition because when we had to work overtime, we needed a lot of energy. After only five years [of working here], our health deteriorated tremendously, and then we found out that the *management did not contribute adequate money to the social insurance funds* for us.[44]

With such division of labor, these two women played important roles in the four-day strike beginning on February 13, 2006. Working inside as a Huê Phong worker, Đào acted as a lookout and a union informer. Motivated by her sustained commitment, Đào quietly assisted Nga in her labor mobilizing efforts. Working from the outside, Nga mobilized more than one thousand Huê Phong workers to come to two meetings, with management in the factory, to expose ongoing labor violations and to reach a resolution with management.

Đào explained to me how the 2006 strike broke out at Huê Phong from the inside, carried out mostly by Thái Bình workers:

> The men workers were doing the [critical] finishing step of putting in the outside soles [*đế dưới hoàn thành*] when they stopped work. This was a strategic stage because without its completion, management could not deliver the final

---

[43] There had been many earlier protests that took place before these women joined the 2006 strike (see Chronology in Appendix C). These previous strikes are important because they set the stage for later strikes.

[44] My emphasis.

products. Often it was the men who led the work stoppage. They got angry, slammed on the table, and stood up, and female workers followed suit. But this time, it was one experienced female worker in that finishing step [who triggered the protest]; she got angry and mobilized the other men in her unit to stop working. She worked there for eight years. These were the experienced workers who had been employed since the factory opened; only seven or eight of them were still there. First the stoppage spread to (mostly) male workers in the same unit, and then to all workers, males and females, in the whole factory, who joined in the work stoppage and chanted: "*No wage increase, no work.*"

At home that evening, Đào alerted Nga about this work stoppage, which propelled Nga into direct action. When I asked Nga how she mobilized one thousand Huê Phong workers to attend the two meetings with management inside the factory, the two friends took turns responding. Nga fired away with pride: "I did it by myself" ["*mình ên,*" she said, using a southern expression]. "Then when I asked the workplace union representatives to join me, they declined to help." Đào chimed in: "Yeah, they [the workplace union representatives] were very weak. All they wanted was to collect union dues of VND 5,000 on the tenth of each month. And this was mainly for the social fund: illnesses, death in the families, weddings, maternity presents, etc."

Nga continued:

So, I went by myself to those rental units near the factory. Everywhere when I saw Huê Phong uniforms being hung to dry either inside or outside of the rooms, I knocked on the door and told the workers: "You need to go to the meeting this afternoon at 2 PM. Come a little bit earlier so we can plan before the meeting. You need to go to defend workers' rights [*quyền lợi công nhân*]; we need to go together to have one voice [*tiếng nói chung*]; please do not engage in violence [*đừng bạo động*]." However, some workers told me, "You are a vocational student; why did you meddle into this issue [*xía mồm*]?" Nevertheless, gradually, I was able to convince about one thousand workers to come to these two meetings. [She relied on word-of-mouth to gather this number of people.] I completely lost my voice after doing this. Those who went to the meetings were passionate [about the workers' plight]; those who did not were just waiting for low-hanging fruits to fall [*nằm chờ sung rụng*].[45]

Clearly, not all workers were responsive to Nga's mission. Many challenged her because she was not a Huê Phong worker, and a number of employees must have dreaded joining a movement that promised to trigger retaliation from both the state and the factory owner. This fear was well-founded. Since 2003, the local state and unions have established so-called "social opinions" and "workers-self-managed" units as their surveillance tools to monitor labor activism in factories and in workers' rental units. I discuss the impacts of these two entities in Chapter 7. But even given such threats, Nga charged ahead to convince workers to resist and attend the meetings. Her "no violence" message explicitly asked those involved to avoid repeating the violence that took place in the June 2005 strike at Huê Phong (see Chronology in Appendix C). Thanks to this wise strategy, no violence erupted in the

---

[45] My emphasis.

February 2006 strike, and the two meetings with workers resulted in a resolution among the three key stakeholders: management, local state officials, and district-labor-unions officials—a small victory for workers!

Still the challenge remained: How could Nga get inside the factory so she could witness the meetings herself? Đào again turned out to be a good ally, for she lent her uniform and ID badge to Nga so she could enter the factory *twice*. Like many factories in the EPZs or industrial zones, Huê Phong has an imposing gate, with several men standing guard twenty-four hours a day, seven days a week. Nga told me that she was very nervous when entering the gate, keeping quiet and pretending to be one of the thousands of workers reporting to work. She succeeded twice. Once inside, Nga remained quiet in both meetings, both because she feared that trying to speak up would reveal her non-worker status and because she had completely lost her voice while trying to mobilize hundreds of workers earlier.

Both women recounted the sequence of events in the meetings with excitement. First, the workplace union representatives outlined the conflict; then the company president and their lawyer presented their side; then the Gò Vấp district labor unions (in the hierarchy, these are above the workplace unions) and an official from the Department of Labor in Ho Chi Minh City, Nguyễn Thị Dân, presented their analyses; then, finally, workers expressed their indignation about the violations.

When asked how workers participated in those meetings alongside the labor-union representatives at both levels—district and workplace—Nga responded with pride and showed an awareness of the nationality of workers:

> In the meeting, workers spoke from the heart [*tâm huyết*]. Many said: "We poured in all of our energy and passion to our work, but our salary is only VND 1.2 million, working from 6:30 AM to 8 PM." Many workers who spoke up to demand the rights and benefits due to workers received loud applause from other workers. I'm really proud that *Vietnamese* workers are very articulate and calm. I myself don't have that skill, but I'm good at calling workers to come to the meetings and applauding them to lift up their spirit [*ủng hộ tinh thần*]. There were a lot of labor union leaders at higher levels who came down to the factory, including the Gò Vấp district labor unions. But these union leaders talked in circles, we did not hear any concrete details. Specifically, we were anxious to hear an answer to this basic question, "Will our salaries be raised or not?"[46]

The outcomes of this struggle, however, were mixed, due to the strategies adopted by the factory's managers, which were meant to buy them time and appease the employees. In a formal statement dated February 16, 2006, Huê Phong management announced the implementation dates of the five items agreed to with the state and labor-unions officials in Gò Vấp district and Ho Chi Minh City.[47] The resolution minutes show these five agreements: 1) the deadline to adjust wages to a higher level is February 28, 2006; 2) a new labor contract based on the new wage level would be signed by March 20, 2006, at the latest; 3) strikers would get paid 100

---

[46] My emphasis.

[47] Tô Gia Đương, "Thông Báo, Ủy Ban Nhân Dân Thạch Phố Hồ Chí Minh, Công Ty Tránh Nhiệm Hữu Hạn [limited responsibility company], Giày Da Huê Phong" [Announcement, Ho Chi Minh City People's Committee, Limited Responsibility Company, Huê Phong Leather Shoes], Số TB-HP-06, February 16, 2006.

percent of their basic salary for their four-day strike; 4) Huê Phong would contribute to the social insurance funds based on the new, higher salary level starting February 1, 2006; and 5) in cooperation with local state and union officials, Huê Phong would organize a class session on the Labor Code for workers.

Workers won two long-overdue corrections: 1) that the wage table would be "transparent," available for all to review, and 2) that the steps workers must undergo to gain pay raises would be simplified, a revision long requested by the HCMC Department of Labor. The new wage table has seven steps, each leading to a comparatively larger raise (with increases of approximately VND 40,000 to 50,000 [US \$2.67 to 3.33]), as opposed to the old table, which had thirty-eight steps (with increases of only VND 10,000 [about US\$ 0.67] between steps).[48] However, while Huê Phong promised to pay VND 880,000 per month (VND 10,000 more than the minimum wage), it did not reveal the daily production quotas (based on a combination of three levels of productivity and technical skills), nor did the factory's management post the meanings of those three levels for workers, the state, and union officials to review.[49] Thus, many of Huê Phong's promises were mere "dangling carrots," especially since the daily quota requirements were not transparent.

After years of protests, in 2007, management finally agreed to pay the mandatory social insurance to workers, VND 5.2 billion, based on a slightly higher base salary, VND 560,000 per month (which was still lower than the FDI monthly minimum wage of VND 870,000; see Table 3.1), instead of the domestic minimum-wage level of VND 330,000.

Ethnicity and Class Consciousness

Workers involved in the 2006 protest at Huê Phong clearly distinguished between the ethnicities of the capitalist owner and managers, and of the workers. This awareness emerges when workers deal with foreign bosses, both in underground resistance efforts (Huê Phong case) and in officially sanctioned protests (such as the FDI factory cases discussed in Chapter 5). When recounting the two meetings with management inside Huê Phong factory, Nga described with pride the Vietnamese workers who clearly expressed their indignation. Nga and Đào also had alerted relevant state officials about Huê Phong management's repeated failure to contribute adequately to social insurance and health funds for workers based on their higher actual take-home salaries. Đào expressed these concerns to me, conjecturing about the long-term effects of Huê Phong's labor practices and wondering to what extent the Taiwanese bosses actually profited from Vietnamese workers' losses:

> Often five years of working under such bad conditions are the maximum
> for most of the ten thousand workers here. Consequently, not having any
> vocational school experiences, no other job skills, chances are some of them

---

[48] Tô Gia Đương, "Quy Chế Trả Lương (Áp dụng cho công nhân trực tiếp sản xuất)" [Wage Regulations (Application to Direct Production Workers)], Công Ty Trách Nhiệm Hữu Hạn, Giày Da Huê Phong, February 16, 2006.

[49] Công Ty Trách Nhiệm Hữu Hạn, Giày Da Huê Phong, "Thang Bảng Lương Công Nhân" [Huê Phong Wage Table], February 16, 2006.

may turn into small-time criminals … *In the long run, Vietnam will have to absorb all these long-term social problems; meanwhile the Taiwanese owners bring all the profits back to their country.*[50]

I found evidence of strong class consciousness in Nga, less so in Đào. When I asked how Nga understood the rough life of workers, not being a worker herself, and how she became so determined to fight for their rights, she responded matter-of-factly that she had engaged in manual labor:

> When my family fell apart and was heavily in debt, I worked for richer families, unshelling, deveining, and cleaning shrimp all day long knee-deep in the water. Out of that experience, I came to understand the hardship of workers because I worked as one.

That experience led her to empathize with the plight of laborers and to engage spontaneously in organizing and mobilizing. In other words, she developed a class consciousness at the end of a *previous* process (triggered by her family situation) and carried it over to the Huê Phong struggle, a manufacturing setting. In 2009, I heard from some confidential and reliable sources that Nga had been detained by the local police when she and other workers stood in front of Huê Phong gate to distribute some flyers about Huê Phong's social-insurance violations. She was released after several days in jail. But this incident reflected a broader intention of the state, for the government showed no tolerance toward publicly engaged, independent labor organizers for fear that these activities were linked to pro-democracy efforts staged by political dissidents. State suppression was often carried out in the name of industrial peace and national security.

These two organizers showed me that they had a nuanced understanding of the various ways in which place bonding can assist workers' collective action. Evidence shows that the Kiên Giang bonding played a key role in leading Đào to assist Nga in labor organizing. In short, these two organizers told me that they did not bond with one another as workers but, rather, as two friends who had shared a childhood together. By comparison, the Thái Bình bonding facilitated Đào's successful drive to mobilize her native-place migrant friends working in the factory to join the struggle. Class consciousness also contributed to the struggle, as the awareness that Nga developed previously while cleaning shrimp seemed to prepare and propel her into this fight for manufacturing workers' rights.

Types of Protest and Use of Law

The two women, Nga and Đào, resorted to many forms of protest available to workers, both formal and informal, to unite and mobilize one thousand employees. First, familiarity with the employees' working-class neighborhood was a big advantage. They both knocked on the doors of the units that had Huê Phong uniforms hung on the clothes-drying racks to ask the renters to come to the meetings. Second, before coming to the meetings, they asked workers to stand up when it came their turn to speak. At the two meetings, as some workers got up and spoke as individual employees, not leaders, Nga remained silent to protect her identity. This

---

[50] My emphasis.

tactic was used to protect the identity of the strike leaders (a tactic somewhat similar to that used by the anonymous writers of the strike messages in the women's lavatory in Freetrend factory). Thus, "hidden transcripts,"or protests enacted in anonymity behind management's back, were used by these organizers.

When I asked about the identities of the inside-the-factory strike leaders, Đào said that most workers know and protect them:

> People from the outside and management did not know who the leaders were because when individual workers stood up, they spoke as regular employees. There were times when they all stood up in unison. Of course the workers themselves do know, but they did not reveal that [in order to protect their leader(s)].

It was important to shield underground strike leaders from discovery, whether by the state or management, because these non-union labor leaders would be in trouble if caught. Chapter 14 of the Labor Code, the chapter on strikes, still does not recognize any leadership other than the state-sanctioned VGCL. As discussed in Chapter 3, after many lively debates in the parliament (a house divided by various factions within the state), in June 2012, the Labor Code revision—including Chapter 14—was ratified. In this latest revision, a strike organized and led by anyone other than the upper-level unions (including ward/district/city levels) is considered a wildcat action, or "illegal." If those non-union leaders were found to be organizing workers, the leaders would lose their jobs and be imprisoned. In sum, non-union strike leaders are penalized by both the factory owner/manager and the state.

In addition, these women had knowledge of and skill in using the law. They clearly understood the disadvantages posed by a system that granted a higher minimum wage to workers in foreign-owned factories than for workers in Vietnamese-owned factories. In addition, both Nga and Đào pointed out the long-term consequences of management's failure to contribute to workers' social and health funds. I was impressed with Nga, who showed great understanding of the social insurance law and cited concrete statistics:

> The real salary of workers was about VND 410,000 per month, and many had worked [at Huê Phong] from eight to eleven years. But management only contributed about half of the workers' years of service [four years' worth] to the social insurance fund, using a lower base: VND 330,000 per month for all skill levels. In sum, the cheating [in contributions to the social insurance fund] is not only that they consider just half the number of years worked, but also that they based the payment on the lowest wage level, not the higher take-home pay, and [compute based on] the same wage rate for different skill levels. Thus, management had been profiting billions of VND per year at the expense of workers.

The labor organizers at the factory turned to some state officials and journalists whom they trusted to give advice and for news coverage to publicize their quests for rights and benefits. Workers' direct action got the ball rolling. They first notified the labor press, which put all stakeholders on notice by publishing the workers' complaints in the next day's newspaper. Many local state officials and journalists were informed of the impending strike and came out to the strike scene to deal with or witness the situation.

At the strike scene, these dedicated officials and some journalists met with Nga and other workers who had arrived at the factory gate. The officials gave the organizers some legal advice about holding peaceful meetings inside the factory, and avoiding violence, in order to gain resolution for their grievances. These pro-labor state officials advised workers to appeal to the rule of law for their rights. Once inside the meeting, these same officials led the negotiations with management.

Both women expressed their trust in and listened to the advice of the state officials who worked closely with them and were genuinely sympathetic to the workers' plight.

Nga said to me: "When the HCMC Labor Federation and the Gò Vấp district labor unions arrived at the strike scene, we told them that we would wait for signals from "Cô Dân" [Aunt Dân],[51] because we trust her and don't really trust the enterprise labor unions." When I asked for the reasons, Đào said:

> We don't trust our enterprise labor-union representatives because when we submitted our complaints detailing how management repeatedly violated labor rights, they threw our petitions into the trash can. Then when we went on strike, they disappeared. Also, not all of us know about the Gò Vấp district labor unions.

Conflicts among State Apparatuses

Evidence shows that the state is not monolithic, especially at the local level. I found that state officials at the Gò Vấp district and the HCMC Labor Federation responded to labor-capital conflicts at Huê Phong differently. In 1997, migrant workers at Huê Phong staged the first (reported) strike, five years after its establishment. The Gò Vấp People's Committee (district level) did report the first strike, but the committee was vague about the nationality of the owner, reporting that "a strike erupted because one *foreign* technical specialist disciplined workers by forcing them to stand under a tropical sun for an hour."[52] On the other hand, the HCMC Labor Federation pointed out the nationality of the real investors who had money in this factory and provided more details about the cause of strike: "The *Taiwanese* technical specialists forced workers to work overtime and allowed no break time. Both sides came to a resolution. One hundred workers participated in a work stoppage for half a day on April 3, 1997."[53]

The difference between the positions of these two state organizations reemerged three years later when more than 2,500 workers went on strike over similar problems with the foreign specialists at Huê Phong on September 12 and 13, 2000. This time, DOLISA (Department of Labor, Invalids, and Social Affairs) in Gò Vấp ignored the

---

[51] Nguyễn Thị Dân is the head of the Wage/Salary Department of the HCMC DOLISA (Department of Labor, Invalids, and Social Affairs).

[52] Gò Vấp People's Committee Conference, "Hội Thảo Tranh Chấp Lao Động: Nguyên Nhân và Giải Pháp" [Conference on Labor Strikes: Causes and Solutions], June 27, 2003. My emphasis.

[53] HCMC Labor Federation, "Tranh Chấp Lao Động Tập Thể" [Collective Worker Struggle/Conflict], 1997; my emphasis.

nationality of Huê Phong's owner and failed to mention the nationality of the "foreign technical specialists":

> The company management did not clarify to the workers the charge and responsibility of the foreign technical specialists [*chuyên gia kỹ thuật nước ngoài*] and had allowed them to intervene "too deeply" into management decisions in the cafeteria and dormitories … This had inadvertently created tension and psychological oppression [*ức chế tâm lý*] for the workers.[54]

On the other hand, the HCMC Labor Federation clearly pointed out the real reasons for the 2000 strike—low wages, no overtime pay, and financial discipline—and, again, explicitly noted the nationality of the foreign specialists:

> [This happened] … due to conflicts with the manager of the collective cafeteria. But the root cause was about the low monthly wage, about VND 230,000 per worker. For many workers, after deducting food expenses and fines [this is one of the key complaints], their take-home monthly salary was only VND 180,000 per person. Also, management requested a lot of overtime work, but did not pay overtime compensation properly. Management disciplined workers by *deducting from their wages*; *meals between shifts were rotten*. The treatment by the Taiwanese specialists [*chuyên gia người Đài Loan*] of the workers was not good: [the Taiwanese threatened] unilateral job termination [*tùy tiện đuổi việc*][and] workers were expelled from the worker dormitory without any reason.[55]

The HCMC Labor Federation showcased specific workers' requests in their union forum to help their cases. First, its report stated that there should be *no* monetary fines imposed on workers' already low salaries, and any money that management had deducted from employees' salaries must be refunded; second, overtime work should be minimized, and, if overtime were performed, proper compensation would be mandatory; and, third, the quality of the meals between shifts must be improved. The HCMC Labor Federation noted that after the strike in 2000, a multi-stakeholder meeting was held to try to resolve the conflict. In attendance at the meeting were representatives of the Gò Vấp district Labor Union, the HCMC Labor Federation, the Department of Labor in Ho Chi Minh City (DOLISA), the local police, and Huê Phong management. As a result of the meeting, workers agreed to return to work on September 14, 2000.

In another conference with Huê Phong management in 2003, the Gò Vấp People's Committee showcased the perspective of the factory's managers. As reflected in the report of the conference, Huê Phong management knew how to curry favor from the committee by using socialist rhetoric (such as "production management *cadres*") instead of the bureaucratic language (such as "supervisor" or "manager"). The managers were savvy in using a very conciliatory tone to appease the local government and to acknowledge the "thousands of workers" it employed

---

[54] Tham luận của Phòng Lao Động—Thương Binh Xã Hội Quận Gò Vấp [Proceedings of Gò Vấp DOLISA], "Tình hình tranh chấp lao động trên địa bàn quận Gò Vấp từ năm 2000 đến tháng 6/2003" [The Strike Situation in the Gò Vấp Vicinity from 2000 to June 2003], Gò Vấp People's Committee Conference, p. 5.

[55] My emphasis.

and management's labor violations. In fact, these violations were consistent with accusations made by the HCMC Labor Federation.[56]

As shown, the actions of state officials are triggered by the different priorities guiding various state ministries: The state is not monolithic. Some state offices are pro-capital in the name of "job creation." As mentioned before, the local office of the Ministry of External Affairs had granted Huê Phong the "Vietnamese origin" certificate; the local office of the Ministry of Planning and Investment continued to renew the company's business license even after a decade of ongoing violations.

However, other state apparatuses played a countervailing role on the workers' behalf. During my fieldwork, I interacted with many caring and dedicated state and union officials and newspaper journalists who had won the trust of workers and labor organizers in strike-prone districts. Some committed state officials in the DOLISA in Ho Chi Minh City worked closely with labor union representatives and journalists to resolve labor-management conflicts. Nguyễn Thị Dân, the highly respected head of the Wage Department of DOLISA in Ho Chi Minh City, has maintained a record of commitment to the workers' interests in labor-management disputes, and she intervened directly in repeated strikes at Huê Phong. She was often quoted in the labor press, offering her legal and expert advice, and she led periodic workshops on the labor code and workers' rights and responsibilities in factories in HEPZA and Gò Vấp district. She was on site during the minimum-wage strikes in 2005 and 2006 to help labor unions negotiate with foreign management.[57]

Local officials had to maintain a difficult balancing act. When I asked Nguyễn Thị Dân why workers trusted her, she said, "Working with the wage issues, I deeply understand their concerns and demands. Also, it has to do with the balanced way in which I presented both sides of the issues, from worker and management perspectives, so they trusted me." She offered some workshops about negotiations in HEPZA. Dân, along with others, had convinced Huê Phong strikers to abstain from the vandalism that had erupted in previous strikes: "If you were to destroy these

---

[56] Huê Phong management said, "No one can claim 'eating rice every day and not dropping a grain on the ground.' As to our case, having employed thousands of workers, we had problems that caused workers' discontent on issues such as 1) some production management cadres [*cán bộ quản lý trực tiếp sản xuất*] engaged in verbally abusive behaviors, such as humiliating and yelling at workers; 2) when workers violated the labor protocol of the factory, they were disciplined and denied their bonuses. Also, workers living in the dorms had to stand in line for a long time for their evening meals … These conditions led to the strike in September 2000. This strike was very costly to us, both in monetary terms and reputation … Since then, we've made the following changes and improvements: 1) we established worker opinions boxes in the cafeteria, dorms, and meeting rooms, and the workplace labor unions opened them [and reviewed the opinions] in the Saturday meetings between management and (enterprise-level) labor union representatives. We then classified these comments and requests into several categories: response-now and need-clarification, et cetera. We announced these categories in the company weekly newsletter each Wednesday. Therefore, communication between labor and management was improved, and workers' reasonable requests were addressed in a timely manner. [Note: that claim is far different from what actually happened on the ground.] We firmly disciplined production cadres who verbally abused and humiliated workers. We paid workers on time and in full, and if mistakes were found, we fixed them promptly." Công Ty Trách Nhiệm Hữu Hạn, Giày Da Huê Phong, "Báo cáo nguyên nhân và cách xử lý đình công" [Report on the Causes and Ways to Resolve Strikes], in Gò Vấp People's Committee Conference, "Hội Thảo Tranh Chấp Lao Động" [Conference on Labor Strikes], June 14, 2003.

[57] Interviews with Nguyễn Thị Dân, Ho Chi Minh City, August 2006.

machines, you would be destroying Vietnamese property, which would incur high costs to the Vietnamese, not management."[58] The strikers heeded her advice.

With this dedication to good labor-management relations and a deep understanding of the connection between wage/salary and social-insurance benefits, Dân won a long-overdue concession from Huê Phong. She announced that the HCMC People's Committee had agreed with her office to request that Huê Phong pay its outstanding debt to the HCMC social security office by July 1, 2007. Finally, together, the local state officials, local unions, labor newspaper journalists, and workers had won a long-overdue victory. After more than a decade of protests and media exposure, on July 18, 2007, Huê Phong paid its debt of US$325,000 to the HCMC social security office.[59]

Union officials at the national level who followed this case closely shared their wisdom. According to Châu Nhật Bình, deputy director, International Department of the VGCL, that estimated debt grossly underestimated the real social security and health benefits owed to migrant workers. In reality, it was virtually impossible to locate the workers and give them back their arrears and benefits: thousands of affected workers had found other jobs and/or returned to their home villages. A well-seasoned journalist of the *Người Lao Động*, Phạm Hồ, agreed with this assessment for an additional reason. He argued that the social security calculation leading to this VND 5.2 billion debt was based on the *smaller* base salary (using the lower minimum wage level for domestic workers), which did not take into account common allowances, such as special compensation for working with toxic materials—the chemicals used in treating leather for the shoes—and extra pay for perfect attendance (paid to an employee for working all twenty-six workdays in a month).[60]

In December 2011, concerned with ongoing violations of the laws mandating that employers contribute designated amounts to their workers' social insurance funds, the Investigation Office of the HCMC Department of Labor investigated 1,662 factories that were not in compliance.[61] It became clear that the fines leveled against enterprises guilty of repeated violations were too low, with an upper limit set at 30 million VND (or about USD $1500), so that it was common for companies to pay the token monetary fines and continue to shirk their social insurance obligations.[62] The management of Huê Phong chose to follow that path.[63] Therefore, the Investigation

---

[58] Interviews with Nguyễn Thị Dân, Ho Chi Minh City, August 2007.

[59] Phạm Hồ, "Công ty Huê Phong–TPHCM: Trả dứt 5,2 tỉ đồng nợ BHXH" [Huê Phong Company: Paid Off the 5.2 billions VND Debt to Social Insurance (for Workers)], *Người Lao Động*, July 18, 2007, http://nld.com.vn/195890p1010c1012/tra-dut-52-ti-dong-no-bhxh.htm, accessed July 2008.

[60] Phạm Hồ, "Công ty Huê Phong nợ 5,2 tỉ đồng BHXH" [Huê Phong Company: Owing 5.2 billions VND Debt to Social Insurance], *Người Lao Động*, January 4, 2007, http://nld.com.vn/176268p0c1010/cong-ty-hue-phong-no-52-ti-dong-bhxh.htm, accessed July 2007.

[61] K. An, "Kiến nghị nâng mức phạt BHXH lên 500 triệu đồng" [Proposal to Raise the Social Insurance Fine to 500 Millions VND], *Người Lao Động*, December 22, 2011, http://nld.com.vn/20111222105552667p0c1010/kien-nghi-nang-muc-phat-bhxh-len-500-trieu -dong.htm, accessed December 2011.

[62] Lê Thủy, "Chỉ dọa suông, DN xem thường!" [Only Verbal Reprimand, Companies Ignore (the Fine)], *Người Lao Động*, December 3, 2007, http://nld.com.vn/208989P0C1010/chi-doa-suong-dn-xem-thuong.htm, accessed June 2008.

[63] Conversation with Châu Nhật Bình, April, 14, 2008, Hanoi.

Office recommended steeper fines be levied, amounting to 20 percent of the amount of a company's social insurance debt, up to 500 million VND (or about USD $25,000). But, at the time of writing, the situation is getting worse, for the fine is still low and so has little effect as a deterrent.[64]

District labor unions were also very familiar with Huê Phong's labor violations and tactics because they were located near the Huê Phong factory, in the Gò Vấp district. In particular, the Gò Vấp district labor union leader spoke to me of Huê Phong's practice of "taking money from one pocket and putting in the other." This common Vietnamese expression alludes to the fact that workers received *no net gain* through their labor. For instance, they would receive a tiny wage increase, but a cut in other allowances. Having closely monitored Huê Phong factory for years, Phạm Ngọc Đoàn, the head of Gò Vấp district labor union, revealed that another common tactic used by management to hinder the investigations was to prevent his union staff from entering the factory. He said that Huê Phong often made the excuse that the presence of the union representatives would interfere with their busy production schedule (at the command of their corporate buyers) and interrupt the work flow, but that management often sought his union's help in times of conflict with the workers:

> When I wanted to meet Huê Phong labor unions, the management closed up the gate [*bế quan toả cảng*] with an excuse that they were very busy with the orders during work hours. So, we could only meet at the Gò Vấp labor unions office. But when there are any potential labor protests/strikes, Huê Phong management would contact me immediately.[65]

Significance of the 2008 Strike at Huê Phong

Labor discontent at Huê Phong continued well into 2008, and no one could foresee an end to the ongoing conflict. The two-week strike in 2008 by four thousand workers marked one of the longest strikes in Vietnam since 1994. When the Huê Phong factory failed to raise wages (and the corresponding overtime payments) and allowances (especially on improving the quality of the meals for workers), according to the inflation-adjusted rates (effective starting March 13, 2008), four thousand workers stayed off the job for more than two weeks.[66] As before, Huê Phong vowed in March to make good on their obligations in a timely manner; but on payday, on April 9, when workers found that their salary had not changed and the meal quality continued to be bad, they became angry and took action because, once again, Huê

---

[64] B. Nghi, "Nợ BHXH, BHYT hơn 8.000 tỉ đồng," [Over 8,000 Billion VND Owed to Social and Health Insurance], *Người Lao Động*, March 19, 2012, http://nld.com.vn/20120319095139988 p0c1010/no-bhxh-bhyt-hon-8000-ti-dong.htm, accessed March 2012; K. An, "Kiến nghị nâng mức phạt BHXH lên 500 triệu đồng."

[65] Interview with Phạm Ngọc Đoàn, Ho Chi Minh City, August 2006.

[66] Yến Trinh and Quốc Thanh, "Đình công tại công ty Huê Phong (TP.HCM): Cần can thiệp mạnh!" [Strike at Huê Phong company (HCMC): Need to Intervene Forcefully], *Tuổi Trẻ*, April 26, 2008, http://tuoitre.vn/Chinh-tri-Xa-hoi/252763/Dinh-cong-tai-cong-ty-Hue-Phong-TPHCM-Can-can-thiep-manh.html, accessed March 2012.

Phong had failed to fulfill its promise.[67] So, on April 12, more than three hundred workers in the cutting/pressing department started the strike and went around the factory to mobilize fellow employees in other departments. In the fog of activism, some radical workers "threatened to beat up" reluctant fellow workers if they chose not to strike. Security forces were called in to prevent this from happening. While there was no destruction of factory machines, there were some minor casualties: A pregnant worker was slightly injured in this turmoil, and some workers had broken a security guard's camera when he tried to take photos of the unfolding strike.[68]

On April 13, alarmed by the severity of this strike, the state interdepartmental team came to resolve the labor-management conflict. On this occasion, workers presented the three reasons for their strike:[69] 1) inequitable social security contributions from management and from workers. (Huê Phong contributed to the HCMC social security fund based only on wages of VND 330,000 per month, whereas workers' contributions were based on the then official minimum wage [VND 540,000]); 2) increased quotas and productivity demanded by management without adequate compensation given to employees. This problem related to the labor fluctuation problem; after the Vietnamese Lunar New Year, many migrant workers (from the North and the South) did not return to work, but the daily quota for the whole assembly line remained the same, thus putting an unbearable burden on each of the remaining workers; 3) the productivity allowance (designed to create incentive for workers to work harder and faster) and other small allowances (such as a perfect attendance bonus) were inadequate and *not* included in the total of their take-home salary (which was used to compute other vital benefits). Once again, workers demonstrated that they knew their legal entitlements and fought for them.

After two weeks of striking, on April 26, the three branches of officials in Gò Vấp district—the people's committee, DOLISA, and the district labor union—intervened directly to address the root causes of this conflict and resolve it. The DOLISA official noted how Huê Phong had been using a feeble justification for ignoring workers' requests—the owners claimed that they had to seek opinion and approval of the workers' requests from the multinational corporate buyers (or brands) the factory supplied. In addition, DOLISA and the district labor union officials argued that Huê Phong had skillfully transferred the responsibility to resolve labor-management conflicts to local Vietnamese state offices. According to these officials, "[The] company representative had intentionally allowed the strike to last this long to pressure local state offices to stabilize the local condition on their behalf. Now, their responsibility to workers has become that of the state management offices."[70] This point was echoed by Phạm Ngọc Đoàn, the Gò Vấp district labor union director:

---

[67] Hà Dịu, "Công nhân Huê Phong lại đình công" [Huê Phong Workers Went on Strike Again], "http://www.tin247.com/cong_nhan_hue_phong_lai_dinh_cong-1-5492.html and http://vietnamnet.vn/xahoi/2008/04/777989, accessed March 2012.

[68] Ibid.

[69] M. Hương and Q. Lâm, "Vụ đình công tại Công ty Huê Phong (quận Gò Vấp, TPHCM)—Lan rộng toàn công ty" [Strike at Huê Phong Company [Gò Vấp District, HCMC]—Spread to the Whole Company], April 13, 2008, http://www.baomoi.com/Home/LaoDong/www.sggp.org.vn/Vu-dinh-cong-tai-Cong-ty-Hue-Phong-quan-Go-Vap-TPHCM--Lan-rong-toan-cong-ty/15 39152.epi, accessed March 2012.

[70] Yến Trinh and Quốc Thanh, "Cần can thiệp mạnh!"

"When facing an impending strike, Huê Phong management often called on our labor union staff to come down and help resolve the conflict."[71]

On April 27, 2008, Huê Phong announced an ultimatum to workers. From April 28 onward, if workers stopped work for five consecutive days without reason, the management would cancel its contracts with those employees.[72] Then, on April 28, the security guard tried to convince about twenty workers to return to work. These workers immediately protested and incited hundreds of fellow workers to stop the machine and join the strike. While no violence was committed during this round of protests, about one thousand workers remained working until the end of that shift. But among the hundreds of workers who walked out of the factory, about two hundred resigned for fear of retribution from the management. These two hundred workers did receive all of their entitlements soon after their resignation.[73] The conflict had become too public for Huê Phong to ignore.

Overall, workers gained some short-term victories, and Huê Phong was put on notice, publicly, regarding their treatment of workers and violations of the labor code. Accepting an agreement effective from August 2008, the factory's management agreed to pay workers supplements that would be part of the base salary. Each worker would receive between VND 100,000 and VND 250,000 per month (averaging about 12 US cents).[74] Since 2008, there have not been many reports of labor discontent in Huê Phong. The one relatively recent piece of evidence I found indicated that Huê Phong had tacitly accepted that it was an FDI factory and complied with the higher minimum wage for Vietnamese workers required of an FDI factory. Huê Phong's 2011 advertisement—aimed to recruit students from Ngọc Phước Vocational School in Ho Chi Minh City—offered *close* to the state-sanctioned minimum wage for workers employed in an FDI factory in Zone 1: VND 1.55 million per month, or VND 100,000 short of the proper amount, which is VND 1.65 million.[75] Still, this pay increase constitutes a victory for workers that should be recognized. Without their sustained sixteen-year struggle (1992–2008) with Huê Phong management, this younger generation of workers at Ngọc Phước Vocational School would not have enjoyed the FDI wage to which they are entitled.

PROTEST LETTERS AGAINST UNDERGROUND INVESTMENT

What are some other forms of underground investment in Vietnam? How did workers react to those practices? What cultural resources united them, and what forms of protest did they adopt? To find answers to those questions, I interviewed

---

[71] Interview with Phạm Ngọc Đoàn, August 2008, Ho Chi Minh City.

[72] Vĩnh Tùng, "Công ty Huê Phong ra "tối hậu thư" [Huê Phong Company Issued an Ultimatum], *Người Lao Động*, April 27, 2008, http://nld.com.vn/222826P0C1010/cong-ty-hue-phong-ra-toi-hau-thu.htm, accessed June 2008.

[73] Trang Công Đoàn, "Công ty TNHH giày da Huê Phong—TPHCM: Gần 200 công nhân xin thôi việc" [Huê Phong Shoe Factory: About Two Hundred Workers Resigned], *Lao Động*, April 28, 2008, http://laodong.com.vn/Home/Cong-ty-TNHH-giay-da-Hue-Phong--TPHCM-Gan-200-cong-nhan-xin-thoi-viec/20084/86547.laodong, accessed July 2008.

[74] Ibid.

[75] This school advertises two-to-five year vocational training programs for assistance in various professional fields for students with high school degrees. See http://www.ngocphuoc.edu.vn/index.php/san-giao-dch-vic-lam/vic-lam-them-cho-hc-sinh/37-thong-bao-tuyn-dng-cong-ty-giay-hue-phong.html, accessed March 2012.

state officials and journalists and, also, turned to workers' voices. In this section, I examine thirty-nine worker complaint letters and petitions, and address examples of underground investment in two small enterprises in Ho Chi Minh City.

These complaints were related to the consequences of the 1999 Law on Domestic Investment and the 2006 minimum-wage increase. By examining the letters and interviewing Vietnamese researchers, labor activists, and several journalists, I gained insight into various manifestations of underground capital, most often involving small- to medium-sized factories.[76]

An interview with a seasoned Vietnamese entrepreneur in 2008 informed me about how and why small businesses in Vietnam engaged in underground investment.[77] Khanh told me that before the lifting of the United States trade embargo in 1995, foreign investors often used Vietnamese personnel as figureheads in small companies, which acted as "incubators" or test cases in their plans, so they can learn about Vietnam's complex political, economic, and legal environment and to test the market for several years before they decide to invest on a long-term basis. Then, as more foreign-direct investment companies poured into Vietnam after the normalization of relations with the United States in 1995 and, most notably, after the bilateral trade agreement with the United States in 2002, many investors gained confidence and formed larger factories with a knowledge of how to operate in the Vietnamese investment and legal environments.

In addition to those interviews, I used the workers' letters, not to make generalizations, but to understand some types of underground investment, about which the letters revealed much. In this sampling of letters and petitions, 13 percent (five cases out of thirty-nine) were written by workers employed in the "underground" category. Most workers in those five cases were conscious of the nationality of the alleged underground investors and raised complaints about that. Their key complaint had to do with the consequence of the two-tiered–minimum-wage system in which the Vietnamese employers were able to pay workers less than the owners of FDI companies were required to pay (see Chapter 3).

As noted above, these conditions gave rise to a common practice of using a "Vietnamese figurehead" for such factories. Foreign investors would hire a Vietnamese person, who often served as president, officially, while the real foreign owners served as vice presidents or vice directors and made the major decisions. The foreign owners benefited by paying workers the lower domestic minimum wage and the corresponding lower social and health benefits mandated for enterprises owned by Vietnamese. Workers knew about these practices and exposed the citizenship status (of the foreign bosses and of the workers themselves) to demand a *higher* minimum wage, with the attendant higher social insurance, health and unemployment benefits.

There is evidence of some connection between commerce and conjugal relationships (as an unintended consequence of the 1999 Law on Domestic Investment). In the textile and garment, construction, and plastics industries, some investors (many were from Taiwan, the Philippines, and South Korea) began to work with their Vietnamese assistants or interpreters who acted as the "front"—presidents

---

[76] Phan An, Hà Tăng, Hùynh Đệ, September 2008; interviews, Journalist C and Journalist D, Ho Chi Minh City, September 2007.

[77] Interview with Khanh, Ho Chi Minh City and Singapore, September and October 2008.

of their companies—to take advantage of the 1999 law.[78] In some cases, some of these investors ended up marrying their Vietnamese interpreters and assistants. While the foreign husbands inherited domestic privileges, thanks to their Vietnamese spouses—as they gained the right to offer lower wages to their domestic workers, pay cheaper land rent, and get easier access to buying or building houses—the Vietnamese workers employed by these persons were thereby shortchanged. This differential was getting smaller, but is still salient in 2012.

Thanh Loan Thi Ltd. (TLT)

In 2006, a local worker sent a complaint letter to a newspaper in Ho Chi Minh City. He worked at Thanh Loan Thi Ltd., where he fixed cameras and amplifiers. This worker began his letter with his full name and contact information; he then wrote: "Together with several brothers [direct translation of "*anh em*"] working in this TLT Company Ltd, I want to present the following issues." Then at the end, he signed his full name with the phrase "representing a number of workers at TLT Company." He complained that the company did not give workers labor contracts, that workers were treated inequitably depending on their status (relatives vs. non-relatives of the management), and that conditions were dangerous.

The worker pointedly exposed the nationalities and the roles played by all involved. In this case, a Vietnamese father and his daughter served as president and vice president of the company, respectively, but the real power and control were in the hands of the daughter's Taiwanese husband and his Taiwanese staff:

> We worked at this limited responsibility TLT Company with Mr. NVD as the president and Ms. NTLT as vice president (the daughter of Mr. NVD). Our job was to fix camera systems, speaker phones, and internal communications switchboards. In principle, our salary level was to be negotiated jointly, then after two months of probation, we signed a labor contract. But for most of us brothers [*anh em chúng tôi*], those who worked here two to three years, and those who had just joined here one year ago, none was offered a labor contract to sign … Most long-term workers were relatives of this [family]. Our jobs were dangerous because we needed to climb up high. Recently, due to low wages, high gasoline prices, and the need to travel to different workplaces, we signed a petition to demand a wage increase. After that, the president asked who was the leader to reprimand. First, the leader was sent to fix things in faraway locations continuously; other participants were fined for the smallest mistakes. (Their intention was to pressure us to resign so that they wouldn't have to pay severance) … In my case, I was just laid off for several days; I worked there for over one year, but without any labor contract. More importantly, because Ms. NTLT—the vice president—has a Taiwanese husband, *everything was controlled and managed by his Taiwanese staff*. And Ms. NTLT did not even finish the third grade. I wanted to pose a question: is it a labor violation that this company did not offer labor contracts to [its] workers (after passing the probationary period)? Why is the real number of workers not the same as the number of workers

---

[78] Ibid.

whose salaries are on the books? We sincerely wish that the newspaper speaks up on our behalf.[79]

This worker used class language (we, brothers) to expose legal violations related to underground practices and push for better enforcement of the law. He expressed a sense of caring for his fellow male workers who had endured dangerous working conditions. His words evoke a sense of gender bonding: "[For] most of us brothers [*anh em chúng tôi*], those who worked here two to three years, and those who had just joined here one year ago, none was offered a labor contract to sign." He also demonstrated an understanding of the relevant laws and sought justice for the illegal practices, which he attributed, implicitly, to the influence of the Taiwanese husband of the vice president, whose nationality he mentioned explicitly.

Phú Sĩ Washing and Ironing Services

The case shows not only migrant workers' consciousness of the nationality issue, but also their awareness of belonging to the working class. They appealed to the law and sought legal remedies. Thirty angry migrant workers from the North who worked at a private dry cleaning and laundry facility in Ho Chi Minh City signed a complaint letter to expose wrongdoings at this business venture. They started the letter and signed it as a collective: "*Tập thể công nhân Phú Sĩ*" (the collective of Phú Sĩ workers).[80] Right at the beginning of their letter, they pointed out the citizenship of the real owner and went on to expose many other violations:

We are the collective of thirty workers at Phú Sĩ Washing and Ironing Services … Mr. NDB [pseudonym] is a Vietnamese expatriate who lived in Japan, the real investor. He hired a Vietnamese, Mr. NDT [pseudonym], to be the president. But in reality, Mr. NDT is just a façade. All of the company affairs are controlled by Mr. NDB and his young girlfriend (who is the age of his youngest daughter). He forced us to work twelve hours per day without any overtime pay. We had no labor contracts, no social insurance, and no health benefits. Worse yet, [the owner] established two accounting systems to avoid taxes, not to mention the goods that he smuggled from overseas and stored on the company's premises … In addition to violating the laws, he and his young girlfriend verbally abused us and related to us as their slaves, not their workers. They took advantage of our "weak points" [*điểm yếu*] as migrant workers from the North working in the South: we had no relatives in Ho Chi Minh City, and thus we had to depend on our jobs in his factory. We were forced to work until we dropped (*làm việc cật lực*); if we declined, we would be laid off. For example, another worker had worked for Mr. NDB for over ten years, but when he was terminated, he received absolutely no lay-off compensation. We implore the relevant authorities to intervene promptly in order to demand the labor rights of our collective

---

[79] From the Thirty-Nine Worker Complaint Letters and Petitions (submitted to newspapers in the South in 2005 and 2006); my emphasis.

[80] Phú Sĩ is "Fuji" in Vietnamese. The name itself reveals the Japanese connection of the real owner.

workers here. We ask to be anonymous to be safe and to avoid intimidation [by management].[81]

Native-place bonding among migrant workers from the North is a central and explicit focus in this case, while in cases with local workers, reference to native place is generally implicit, unstated, or not a factor. These migrant workers used class rhetoric: "collective of thirty workers at Phú Sĩ company" to appeal to the law with respect to the company's failure to provide labor contracts, social insurance, and health benefits. The workers exposed the underground practices of this company by exposing the citizenship of the owner and management's duplicitous double-accounting systems, intended to hide the true revenues of the company and thereby reduce taxes.

Conclusion

Underground investment has created an array of problems in many privately owned enterprises of various sizes in Vietnam, as demonstrated through firsthand interviews and from the letters and petitions of workers. Clearly, there are more abuses in these shadow-foreign factories than in formal foreign-direct investment factories.[82] While there is no doubt that horrible working conditions and dismal pay triggered their collective action, native-place bonding brought these migrant workers together in the first place, in a manner that resembles the experiences and actions of workers employed in foreign-direct investment factories (Chapter 5).

Insights from this chapter show some nuances of native-place bonding in labor organizing. Đào—the Thái Bình migrant worker—adopted Kiên Giang as her second home, and networked with both Kiên Giang and Thái Bình friends, outside and inside her workplace, respectively. However, for local (non-migrant) workers, place bonding is not mentioned explicitly in their organizing efforts, complaint letters, or petitions. Local workers commute to work and return home after work and thus, for the most part, do not interact with migrant workers in their rental units. More research is needed to ascertain different expressions of native-place bonding for local workers.

The role of ethnicity has taken on a global dimension in the *Đổi Mới* era. In their protests, workers exposed the industry practice of using Vietnamese figureheads to conceal the nationalities of the true factory owners. This was true in the well-known Huê Phong case (Taiwanese owner) and in protests at smaller companies with Vietnamese figureheads, such as in the case of Thanh Loan Thi Ltd. (Taiwanese investor) and Phú Sĩ (the owner was an overseas Vietnamese who had lived in Japan). Workers were indignant because they knew the law and could see that they were being shortchanged by this strategy of deception, which prevented them from claiming the higher FDI wages and corresponding benefits.

This chapter confirms that workers who participated in either overt protests or quieter forms of protest (such as sending their collective petition letters to local newspapers) were not burdened by false consciousness. However, it remains unclear

---

[81] The Thirty-Nine-Letter Sample; my emphasis.

[82] This is consistent with Kim's findings that "shadow-foreign enterprises" were worse in almost all aspects of labor conditions. Jee Young Kim, "How Does Enterprise Ownership Matter?" p. 303.

whether the non-participants could be said to have a "false consciousness" of their situation. To what extent do these "wait-for-low-hanging-fruit opportunists" (a phrase coined by activist Nga) have false consciousness? Without the opportunity to interview them directly, I can only conjecture based on what I know about their working conditions. These non-involved workers may have had a credible fear of management harassment or layoffs, or they may have found that their deep desire to rest up and prepare for another long work day took priority over participation in active resistance, which a number of them may have considered futile in any case. Under that assumption, it is not necessarily true that they consider violations in labor laws and, in particular, working conditions, as "natural and inevitable." Rather, fear or health issues may have affected these workers' conscious decisions to preserve their energies so they could function, for their own interests, in the conditions that incited the protests.

Private workers—similar to state workers—valued their own labor, cared for their fellow workers, and were concerned about the long-term impacts of the global market system. I noted the class-based Marxist language expressed in their petition letters, language that frequently appealed to the socialist contract: "We are living in a socialist country, not in a regime where people can exploit people." I also registered the fact that these workers showed a sense of human dignity and decency, as described by Polanyi: "We are here to work, not to sell our human values." In most cases, workers demonstrated that they understood the law, and alerted state and union authorities about management violations.

These workers were assisted by labor organizers, labor journalists, and some local state officials who recognized and warned about the deleterious long-term effects of the global market system. Inadequate social insurance and health benefits affected not only the elderly, but also the younger workers and their offspring. Interestingly, external organizers, such as Nga, used "hidden transcripts" to mobilize workers in their rental units (sighting Huê Phong uniforms as a cue) and to infiltrate the Huê Phong factory to cheer them on from the inside.

Finally, given the evidence in this chapter, underground foreign investment in Vietnamese factories had two important effects on workers. First, it heightened workers' awareness of their cultural and legal assets, and strengthened the importance of solidarity. Second, it propelled workers to expose the nationalities of these factories' real owners in order that workers might claim their full rights and benefits.

CHAPTER 7

INTERNAL STATE CONTRADICTIONS, WORKERS, AND THE RULE OF LAW

Workers' knowledge and use of law with respect to organizing and protesting, already noted in previous chapters, became especially prominent after *Đổi Mới* (1986). But given the constraints on the rule of law as practiced in Vietnam, how much organizing and protesting are workers allowed?

How does the party–state's arbitrary powers affect the ability of workers to redress their grievances through the court system? What dilemmas does the labor press face in trying to deliver on the twin goals of opening up a space for workers' rights and being the official forum for the labor unions and the state? At the same time, how do the journalists use the law to protect themselves and to assist workers in dealing with the state's legal system?

In this chapter, I first analyze the social consequences of some major laws affecting workers that were introduced since *Đổi Mới*, with attention to an increase in state and labor-union surveillance of workers' potential labor organizing, and the complex role of native-place bonding. Second, I examine how the labor press, in its reporting, deals with the dilemma of representing workers' rights, unions' positions, and the state's needs—and the mechanisms the media use to protect themselves. Finally, I summarize the various ways workers used labor law depending on the sector in which they were protesting: state, foreign-owned, and domestic-private.

SOCIAL CONSEQUENCES OF STATE CONTRADICTIONS

In Vietnam, the state centralizes control over *both* labor and capital, and it grants exceptions to accommodate global corporations' demands, consistent with Ong's "neoliberalism as exception."[1] The state's legal structure facilitates the application of the market economy throughout the nation. The 2005 Enterprise Law oversees all types of capital (FDI, private, and equitized state) and ended the incentives offered in the 1999 Law on Domestic Investment. Moreover, the Vietnamese state maintains control over all facets of labor-management relations to ensure the labor peace and flexibility necessary for on-time delivery of goods for the global supply chain. But the state often—though not always—does permit the labor newspapers and local labor unions to report on predatory capitalist practices.

By law, factories in the EPZs and industrial zones are required to establish labor unions. However imperfect in its enforcement of labor laws, the state requires labor-union representatives on the factory floor to monitor labor-management relations *for the state's own interest*. As discussed in Chapter 3, the Ho Chi Minh City Export Processing Zone (HEPZA), created by the state, does not simply yield to global

---

[1] Aihwa Ong, *Neoliberalism as Exception: Mutations in Citizenship and Sovereignty* (Durham, NC, and London: Duke University Press, 2006), pp. 7, 78–79.

capital demands. Since 2003, the state has created two closely related communities—social-opinion cells (on factory premises in EPZs and industrial zones) and workers' self-management cells in their rental units—in order to obtain timely information about worker discontent and to preempt their potential protests. Below, I will discuss the development of these two types of cells.

The Vietnamese state and its apparatuses are not monolithic, but, rather, full of internal paradoxes and contentions. While some state apparatuses support workers, others turn a blind eye to management's violations of the law. Nguyễn-võ Thu-hương eloquently argues about the "freedom and unfreedom pair," that is, the split personality of the ruling party, which benefits itself and the neoliberal global economy while it controls and suppresses the most vulnerable of workers—the sex workers in Vietnam. She argues that the state used intervention in prostitution to expand their surveillance activities "to protect the rest of the population" for their legitimation and for the benefit of enterprise managers. Thus, she shows a contradictory role of the state: on the one hand, they perform seemingly legitimate functions: public health officials' attention to health threats posed by prostitutes, and public security police's efforts to "fight crime and ensure social order." On the other hand, the intensifying surveillance of sex workers and officials' decision "to incarcerate prostitutes to rehabilitate them" do not truly help or empower these most vulnerable workers and fail to make the "clients" accountable to their demands for these sex services.[2] Overall, I find that the state's web of control and its internal contradictions also apply to labor-management relations in Vietnam. To demonstrate these contradictions, I analyze three laws that have had negative social consequences for the working class: the minimum wage law, the household registration (*hộ khẩu*) law, and the 1999 Law to Encourage Domestic Investment, with attention to the long-lasting effects that persisted even after these policies were changed as a result of worker protests.

Minimum-wage Policy

The successful, worker-initiated minimum-wage strike (December 2005–January 2006) was actually aimed against the state, not FDI factories, for the strikers were protesting against the state's decision to freeze the minimum wage in the FDI sector for seven years (1999–2005). This strike victory is significant for workers because they forced the state to institutionalize annual adjustments, beginning in 2007, to the minimum wage based on the (rising) cost of living. Additionally, this law had the positive spillover effect of bridging the minimum-wage gap between workers in the FDI and domestic sectors, thus spreading benefits to the entire Vietnamese workforce, not just those in the FDI sector. Once the 2006 minimum-wage law was in place, workers were able to hold the state accountable to the rule of law, and for proper implementation and provision of the corresponding social benefits. Further worker strikes after this initial victory then led to annual adjustments corresponding to the rising cost of living. But the urban–rural wage disparity remains; workers in urban areas still earn more than workers in rural, mountainous, and remote provinces, even though some evidence suggests that the cost of living in rural areas

---

[2] Nguyễn-võ Thu-hương, *The Ironies of Freedom: Sex, Culture, and Neoliberal Governance in Vietnam* (Seattle, WA, and London: University of Washington Press, 2008), p. 246–47; and email correspondence with Nguyễn-võ Thu-hương, January 28, 2013.

has been increasing.[3] Overall, these long-term victories resulted from the direct actions of workers, journalists, and local state and union officials, especially in the two strike-prone districts of Hóc Môn and Củ Chi.

The Household Registration (Hộ Khẩu) Policy

The household registration (*hộ khẩu*) policy works hand–in-hand with the minimum wage law to control migration and to perpetuate rural–urban inequality. Drawn to high wages in urban areas, migrant workers from poor areas provide a "reserve army of the unemployed" (or surplus labor) who need local-resident registration cards to take advantage of the low rates available to residents for basic necessities such as utilities, housing, child care, and education.

The lowest minimum wage is allowed in Zone 3 (and Zone 4 since 2010), a rule that has motivated FDI investors to expand their production facilities to those rural areas in order to exploit the low-cost labor. An example is Mỹ Phong, an FDI factory where leather shoes, all types of bags, and imitation-leather products are manufactured. The company employs more than twelve thousand factory workers in Trà Vinh, a province in the Mekong Delta region, 200 kilometers (about 125 miles) southwest of Ho Chi Minh City.[4] In 2008, this FDI factory paid workers the then minimum wage for Zone 3, which had the lowest legally mandated wage in the country. Mỹ Phong management paid workers VND 850,000 per month, but, after the state-mandated minimum-wage increase, the company cut back on its productivity bonus of VND 40,000 per month. As a result, the typical worker's wage dropped to around VND 800,000 per month. Dissatisfaction over wages led more than two thousand workers to participate in a strike in January 2008.[5]

Foreign investors have also expanded into far-flung poor places in the North, such as Vĩnh Phúc province, promising to create jobs for local workers. But many of these plans never materialized and, because of this, local peasants were left landless and jobless—as the following case demonstrates.[6] In 2007, Hồng Hải, a Taiwanese-owned corporation and registered investor in the proposed Bá Thiện Industrial Zone, planned to build the facilities for this new zone on land that had been occupied by rice paddies in a rural district in Vĩnh Phúc province. At that time, around seven hundred peasants from 201 households yielded two plentiful harvests per year on this land. They were promised employment as factory workers, and forced by an

---

[3] While I found no direct empirical evidence, the gaps in the cost of living between rural and urban areas seemed to be getting smaller, albeit at a very slow rate. In 2006–08, the cost of living was 2.03 times greater in urban areas than rural areas; in 2004–06, it was 2.06 times greater. General Statistics Office, *Một Số Kết Quả Chủ Yếu Từ Khảo Sát Mức Sống Hộ Dân Cư Năm 2010* [Key Findings from the Vietnam Household Living Standards Survey in 2010 (*VHLSS*)], June 2011, pp. 2–4, http://www.gso.gov.vn/default_en.aspx?tabid=515&idmid=5&ItemID=12426, accessed July 2011.

[4] See http://www.xuctientravinh.com.vn/DoanhNghiep/CacDoanhnghiep/Doanhnghiepnuocngoai/TabId/182/ArticleId/114/2011/2/8/cong-ty-tnhh-giay-da-my-phong.aspx, accessed March 2012.

[5] http://www.tin247.com/hon_2000_cong_nhan_da_giay_dinh_cong-15-83789.html, accessed March 2012.

[6] Hoành Anh and Văn Nguyễn, "Chỉ có gió và cỏ: Tan giấc mơ công nhân" [Only Wind and (Wild) Grass: Gone with the Dream of Being Workers], February 29, 2012, http://nongnghiep.vn/nongnghiepvn/72/149/150/91008/Tan-giac-mo-cong-nhan-.aspx, accessed March 2012.

aggressive campaign launched by Hồng Hải and local government officials to sell their paddy fields at a very low price; some peasants were even forced to donate their lands to the project. Consequently, they lost their livelihoods and had to wait to be employed as factory workers. But five years later, nothing had been built on this big swath of barren land, and these poor peasants had already spent what little money they had gotten from selling their land and from doing odd jobs. They were living in poverty, in conditions worse than before. Ironically, over time they returned to what they knew best, farming, and planted in any available public land near the failed industrial zone. These peasants lodged their complaints with local government officials, but to no avail—they were given the runaround because officials who had been involved in this forced sale of land had been transferred to other provinces and no one accepted responsibility for the peasants' plight. In general, poor peasants suffer the most when they lose their land to industrial expansion, and some poor villages have learned from that lesson and successfully fought to keep their land.

Law to Encourage Domestic Investment (1999) and Investment Law (2005)

The law to encourage investment from overseas Vietnamese gave rise to "underground" investment in some factories, such as the case of Huê Phong. But the Investment Law (2005), which replaced the law to encourage domestic investment, has not prevented the cicada-type practices of some foreign capitalists (such as the Haimin case) and domestic-private factories (described in Chapter 6). At the time of writing, cicada violations are still a pressing problem, due in part to state inaction and weak law enforcement.

Overall, the social consequences of underground investment and cicada-type practices are grave. This widespread practice perpetuates the bifurcation of local and migrant workers and the vicious cycle of poverty into the next generation, among the children of migrant workers. Faced with nonlivable wages, poor housing, expensive utilities, and unaffordable child care and education, many workers have left their children behind to be raised by grandparents in their hometowns and have migrated to EPZs and industrial zones hundreds of kilometers away. Most often these workers' children do not obtain adequate education, a disadvantage that ultimately consigns them to employment in unskilled, low-paying, and dead-end jobs.

The combined effects of these policies perpetuate a class of working poor that produces goods for the global economy. A newspaper article has summed up this vicious cycle: the four-tiered minimum-wage policy leads to the payment of low piece-rates in supplier factories, which leads to employers' relatively low contributions to social security and benefits, which then gives rise to a growing class of relatively insecure Vietnamese working poor.[7] With such a working class at its disposal, factory owners have what they want—downward pressure on labor costs. The state's reluctance to enforce the law regarding employers' contributions to social insurance and health care funds for workers helps sustain this downward pressure. Overall, multinational companies stand to gain from this cycle; they successfully transfer all the employer's mandated responsibilities for migrant workers (such as management's responsibility to comply with governmental requirements concerning

[7] Thùy Linh, "Ngập ngừng … tăng lương tối thiểu" [Haltingly … Raising the Minimum Wage], *Người Lao Động*, September 20, 2010 http://nld.com.vn/20100919105149803P1010 C1012/ngap-ngung-tang-luong-toi-thieu.htm, accessed September 2010.

wages, working conditions, benefits, and insurance) to their suppliers, while taking advantage of very low labor costs.

State Surveillance: Social-Opinion and Worker-Self-Management Cells

There are two types of "cells," which, in this context, act as nuclei for migrant workers' day-to-day activities in factories and in their rental units.[8] The outcomes from these two types of cells have been mixed, reflecting their complex realities. On the one hand, cells benefit the state and the unions in pre-empting strikes and ensuring labor peace, a development that tends to benefit management and may stifle justified protests, thereby functioning to the detriment of workers; on the other hand, the cells empower local authorities to act in a timely manner to prevent or stop the hollowing out of factories and the vanishing of assets, actions that clearly benefit workers.

As migrant workers have often used their social spaces as incubators of spontaneous labor organizing, local labor unions and state officials have increased their surveillance to monitor and reign in such activities. In 2003, the unions formed two types of "cells" with the officially stated purpose of "securing an understanding of workers' innermost feelings and aspirations" (*nắm chắc tâm tư, nguyện vọng công nhân*) to help management "resolve workers' anxieties and build harmonious labor relations."[9] But the unstated additional purpose of these cells was to make it easier for officials to monitor incipient labor actions and protests.

While social-opinion cells (*tổ dư luận xã hội*) operate on the factory floor, worker-self-management cells (*tổ công nhân tự quản*) operate in the workers' residences. Both the state and the unions have been proactive in monitoring workers' discontent, and especially the whereabouts of activist workers, to prevent and preempt potential labor unrest.

The Vietnamese General Confederation of Labor (VGCL) drafted guidelines to form these cells in worker rental units.[10] In March 2012, the VGCL made an official announcement, effective from 2011 to 2015, directing all levels of the labor union to establish worker-self-management cells in their rental units.[11] Organizationally, the four key members of a worker-self-management cell are the cell leader (*tổ trưởng*) or the local homeowner (who rents out rooms to migrant workers); a worker representative (*tổ phó*), who acts as the cell's second-in-command; a labor union representative (most likely from that ward or district); and a local police officer.

---

[8] Broadly defined, communist cells operate in any areas where there are at least a few members or candidate members of the Communist Party. Their stated activities include: door-to-door agitation, party studies, press work, and literature distribution, as well as intelligence-gathering and communications. http://www.marxists.org/history/international/comintern/3rd-congress/organisation/guidelines.htm, accessed June 2012.

[9] Khánh Chi, "Nắm chắc nguyện vọng công nhân" [Understanding Workers' Aspirations], September 5, 2011, http://nld.com.vn/20110905094917453p0c1010/nam-chac-nguyen-vong-cong-nhan.htm, accessed October 2011.

[10] Khánh Chi, "Nắm bắt tâm tư, nguyện vọng CN tổ tự quản" [Securing the Innermost Feelings and Aspirations of Workers in Self-Management Cells], *Người Lao Động*, September 28, 2010, http://nld.com.vn/20100928021218209P0C1010/nam-bat-tam-tu-nguyen-vong-cn-to-tu-quan.htm, accessed November 2010.

[11] K. Linh, "Tập trung thành lập tổ CN tự quản" [Focusing on Forming Worker-self-Management Cells], *Người Lao Động*, March 21, 2012, http://nld.com.vn/20120321092351508p0c1010/tap-trung-thanh-lap-to-cn-tu-quan.htm, accessed April 2012.

Local district authorities where the rental units are located control these cells, functioning through a structure that parallels the administrative apparatus established for EPZ labor union representatives and party members who control the social-opinions cells.

Representatives of Thủ Đức District Labor Federation met with a worker self-management cell at Vạn Thành Garment Factory in November 2012 to learn about workers' living and working conditions. (Photo courtesy of *Người Lao Động* journalist Vĩnh Tùng)

This model has been growing, especially in districts with high concentrations of migrant workers, which are known as hot spots of strike activities, such as Hóc Môn, Bình Chánh, Thủ Đức, and District 7 (which includes the Tân Thuận EPZ).[12] In October 2010, the labor unions and local police in Gò Vấp district formed thirty-three worker-self-management units in workers' rental apartments, monitoring more than thirteen hundred migrant workers.[13] Since 2011, they have begun to monitor even more workers. State and union officials in two historically "revolutionary" districts, Hóc Môn and Củ Chi, established hundreds of worker-self-management cells involving thousands of migrant workers. The intention is clear: The state wants to

[12] Khánh Chi and Quốc Hải, "Tổ công nhân tự quản: Vì môi trường sống lành mạnh cho công nhân nhập cư" [Worker-self-Management Cells: Toward Better Living Conditions for Migrant Workers], *Người Lao Động*, July 13, 2006, http://nld.com.vn/157536P0C1010/vi-moi-truong-song-lanh-manh-cho-cong-nhan-nhap-cu.htm, accessed July 2008.

[13] K. An, "Quận Gò Vấp—TPHCM: 21.508 công nhân mua điện đúng giá" [Gò Vấp District—HCMC: 21,508 (Migrant) Workers Bought Electricity at the Right Price], *Người Lao Động*, October 13, 2010, http://nld.com.vn/20101012111539418P0C1010/21508-cong-nhan-mua-dien-dung-gia.htm, accessed November 2010.

control the activities of migrant workers who have been or may be active in labor organizing and strikes. By September 2011, more than four thousand workers were participating in 187 worker cells in Hóc Môn. Also in 2011, the Củ Chi district labor union claimed to have established seventy worker-self-management cells with about five thousand workers joining.[14] These models have expanded to the North; for example, ten worker-self-management cells were established in Sóc Sơn district in Hanoi by the district labor union, security police, and people's committee.[15]

Overall, based on incidents reported in state-sanctioned newspapers, I found that the main purpose of these cells is for the local state officials to obtain timely and accurate intelligence about conditions of labor relations on the factory floor. What they do with this intelligence is mixed: sometimes it is used to help workers (such as stopping the hollowing-out behavior of a fleeing factory owner); sometimes the effect on workers is ambiguous, such as when the intelligence is used to resolve conflict in the name of "labor peace," a code word for strike suppression, which tends to benefit management.

For instance, Hóc Môn district union officials receive timely information and monthly reports from these worker cells about workers' feelings regarding the impact of policies on their work and their lives.[16] A union official said that they received worker complaints about the Vina Duke factory from the social-opinion cell much faster than from the enterprise-level labor union.[17] Within fifteen minutes of receiving the report from the social-opinion cell, district union officials showed up at Vina Duke to hold a dialogue with management in order to resolve the conflict and prevent an impending strike![18]

These cells also inform officials so they can respond quickly to "cicada" managers fleeing their factories. In August 2010, twenty workers at Haekwang Vina (a 100-percent Korean-owned factory) called officials to alert them to the fact that the factory's owner was about to leave the country. Local officials responded quickly and immediately confiscated the factory's property and machinery to help pay workers' benefits. They also successfully pressured one corporate buyer associated with the factory to pay workers' back wages. Similar sequences of events occurred in other foreign-owned factories, such as Mido, and Thanh Phong Vina, where timely state and union intervention helped retrieve some of the workers' back wages and benefits from fleeing owners.[19]

---

[14] K. Linh, "5000 CN tham gia tổ tự quản" [5000 Workers Participated in Self-Management Cells], August 25, 2011, http://nld.com.vn/20110825093058187p0c1010/5000-cn-tham-gia-to-tu-quan.htm and Khánh Chi, "Nắm chắc nguyện vọng công nhân."

[15] Đ. Minh, "Hà Nội thí điểm ra mắt tổ công nhân tự quản" [Hà Nội Presented Piloted Worker-self-Management Cells], July 04, 2011, http://nld.com.vn/20110704092339621p 1010c1011/ha-noi-thi-diem-ra-mat-to-cong-nhan-tu-quan.htm, accessed July 2011.

[16] Khánh Chi, "Nắm chắc nguyện vọng công nhân."

[17] http://panjiva.com/Vina-Duke-Co-Ltd/1308426; http://www.importgenius.com/suppliers/vina-duke-co-ltd; http://panjiva.com/Vina-Duke-Co-Ltd/3709667, accessed March 2012.

[18] Khánh Chi, "Nắm chắc nguyện vọng công nhân."

[19] Ibid.

THE WORKINGS OF WORKER CELLS

Worker cells serve many functions. Monitoring worker activities outside of work—in their living quarters or rental units—is one key function. Through the information gathered from these cells, concerning poor working conditions and employees' discontents, the state and labor unions can preempt potential workers' activities, including strikes, by "reducing the heat" (*hạ nhiệt*), or level of anger, through various methods, such as selectively enforcing wage regulations to appease workers. Surveillance can also uncover activist leaders who would otherwise be unknown, and it can keep the state informed about the first stirrings of unsanctioned labor activities and pro-democracy insurgencies. The housing owners work with district security police and local people's committees in running worker cells. They distribute leaflets about relevant laws to workers and keep an eye on security and sanitation in their neighborhood.

On the other hand, to some extent, these cells provide social-support functions that used to be offered by enterprise-level unions during the former socialist era and are now absent in the market system. For instance, some cells provide workers with support during emergencies and personal financial crises. The cell may lend money to pay a worker's hospital bills after an on-the-job accident,[20] to pay expenses for a loved one who has just passed away, to underwrite the cost of a bike for transportation to work, or to assist a worker's needy parents.[21] The cells also provide some forms of cultural entertainment and enrichment not otherwise available to the workers: books, film nights, and musical performances. According to one worker, a sense of a "blue-collar community" (*cộng đồng áo xanh*) was formed through his self-management cell: "Before [this unit was formed], after work everyone return[ed] to their own rooms. But when we have this self-managed unit, we learn to take care of each other and not [be] individualistic as before."[22] During the Vietnamese Lunar New Year, the cells organized year-end parties and home visits and gave small gifts to migrant workers who did not have money to go home for the holiday. For many migrant workers who couldn't go home for Tết, these caring and kind gestures touched their hearts.[23]

A SOCIAL-OPINION CELL AND THE COMPLEXITY OF NATIVE PLACE

The state and labor unions understand the significance of native place (*yếu tố đồng hương*) in labor organizing and protests, and they want to control its power. The state formed social-opinion cells in two strategic EPZs—Linh Trung and Tân Thuận—the sites that sparked the key minimum-wage strikes that started at the end of 2005. Since 2006, state officials and local factory managers have recruited some migrant workers with good interpersonal skills to participate in these social cells. Their job is to gather information from other workers, especially those who migrated

---

[20] In a sense, this particular cell had effectively taken over the factory's responsibility to pay the hospital bills since the worker's accident took place on the job.

[21] Khánh Chi and Quốc Hải, "Vì môi trường sống lành mạnh cho công nhân nhập cư" [For the Healthy Living Environment of Migrant Workers].

[22] Nguyễn Quốc Anh, a worker at Đông Á Textile company, cited in ibid.

[23] Khánh Chi, "Tết vui ở các tổ CN tự quản" [Lunar New Year Celebration for Workers in Worker-self-Management Cells], January 31, 2011, http://nld.com.vn/20110131121726423 p1010c1011/tet-vui-o-cac-to-cn-tu-quan.htm; K. Linh, "5000 CN tham gia tổ tự quản."

from the informer's native place, to register worker discontent and potential protests, and then inform the state.

To understand the inner workings of a social-opinion cell, I interviewed Trọng (a pseudonym) several times and observed his interactions with other migrant workers at his rental place. I was introduced to Trọng, who was the vice president of a social-opinion cell in Tân Thuận EPZ in 2008, by a journalist who also came from the same native place, Tiền Giang. This cell consisted of five people: Trọng, his brother (also a worker), two other workers, and the cell's president. Trọng, as a candidate member of the Vietnamese Communist Party, had been nominated to this position by the Communist Party members in HEPZA and by members of its labor unions, who worked closely with him to guide his activities. When asked why he was chosen, he responded with great pride, "Because I stand out."

The information he shared not only confirms the strong hold of the Party in labor-management relations but also the state-capital alliance designed to preempt potential labor protests. The participation of some FDI companies in this social-opinion cell indicated that they shared interests with the state:

> There were 110 companies in Tân Thuận EPZ, of which only twenty companies joined [the social-opinion cell]. About sixty people [were] in the cell, but only about twenty went to the meetings regularly. After Tân Thuận, other EPZs (Tân Tạo and Linh Trung) followed suit in forming these cells. We [met] every Sunday, the off-work day, in the meeting room of HEPZA near the gate. Occasionally, we changed the locations of the meetings (gathering in places such as union-owned vacation facilities and public beaches) to attract more participants. In these meetings, workers raised a lot of concerns about pregnant workers' paid breaks, overtime compensation, forced Sunday work, laid-off enterprise-level union representatives, and toxic [exposure] compensation (in addition to salaries). We also [learned] about the labor laws in these meetings. *In the meeting, most women spoke up and many served in a leadership role.* About twenty FDI companies participated in this project; most [were] from Japan and Taiwan. We did conduct a survey about the need for dormitories for workers [*khu nhà lưu trú*].[24]

When asked if there were any responses to his survey findings (his survey noted, for instance, that members of his cell had stressed the need for affordable housing), he said: "When I reported this information to the higher-ups, I did not check to see if they had acted on my reports. But I [noticed] that they only announced what they actually implemented, not the other issues."

Clearly this information-gathering opportunity can be interpreted in several ways. As with the worker-self-management cells, there are pros and cons to this type of cell. On the negative side, potential labor leaders and activists were exposed through their participation, making them subject to potential harassment and suppression. The state and foreign management could get to know what workers thought and planned to do and learn which employees were the most vocal and active, and they could impede workers' actions. On the positive side, workers learned about labor laws through their involvement in social-opinion cells and could express their needs (such as for dormitories for migrant workers) directly to the EPZ

---

[24] Interview with Trọng, Ho Chi Minh City, August 2008; my emphasis.

Party and labor-union officials and management; there were opportunities to improve situations. Unfortunately, there was no evidence of follow-up with regard to implementation of these recommendations.

On another occasion, when Trọng was about to receive an award from the HCMC Youth Group, I asked why he joined this cell. He answered matter-of-factly:

> I don't get paid for this job. I want to learn more about the labor laws. The Youth Group does not have any code to protect workers; meanwhile the VGCL has its own law to protect workers' rights and interests. I would like to understand workers' sentiments [*tâm tư tình cảm*], their anxieties, and so forth. If there are any potential strikes or issues about management oppression, I have to report these to the labor unions in HEPZA in an objective manner. Of course, I also have to report this information to the Party member in the HEPZA labor unions. If I know workers are preparing a strike, I will talk to workers about their rights, interests, and penalties based on the strike law. *I will advise them not to act in an extreme manner because their salaries come from the company's profits.*[25]

When asked what he would do with such important information and which side he would choose when determining his own allegiance, Trọng said, "Oh, I don't report this impending strike to management, just to the HEPZA labor unions. If I were to choose, of course, I'd be more on the side of workers." But this statement contradicts his earlier advice to workers "not to act in an extreme manner because [worker] salaries come from the company's profits," which, when he spoke those words to me, had a "threatening" tone toward workers.

Trọng was honest and open about his future ambitions and his desire to hone his skills in "spying and espionage":

> I was chosen because I have good speaking skills and people believe in me. But I want to learn more about this espionage field [*tình báo*]: walking between two sides. I want to study overseas to learn new things, new skills, and new experiences. I want to finish my schooling here [he was learning English at a local school at night] and return to Tiền Giang to teach elementary school. In addition, I want to continue writing short stories.

Trọng clearly relied on his fellow natives to obtain the information he sought. He made it clear that he tended to rely on men and women who, like him, had migrated from Tiền Giang, so that "native place" was a key factor for him to gather information about that particular worker neighborhood. When he introduced me to a Tiền Giang woman worker next door, who was feeding her child, she was very friendly to us. While we talked, a migrant worker from his home village called him on his mobile phone to get his advice on some personal issues. When I asked Trọng how he gathered "opinions" from this community, he responded confidently:

> This rental complex has thirty rooms; the owner was from the North, therefore, most workers here came from the North. There were only four rooms rented out to Tiền Giang workers. When I need information, I only need to go to these four households to talk to people from my hometown. [As a common practice, many

---

[25] My emphasis.

migrant workers may share the same room to save rent money. Therefore, four "households" could possibly represent about fourteen to sixteen people.] The other workers from the North often closed their doors after work and did not talk to other people.[26]

What is problematic in this case is the moral dilemma that Trọng did not seem to consider: sensitive information confided to him by fellow Tiền Giang natives could come back to haunt them. While it may not have been the intention of Trọng to hurt his fellow Tiền Giang friends, given such gross power differences between state-capital and workers, this information tended to benefit the state and capitalists more than workers.

The net effect of these cells seems to have empowered the state and investors more than workers. Focusing on workers' rights and the laws in these meetings tended to neutralize this "spying" activity by making it seem harmless and even useful to workers. While workers can empower themselves by learning about their labor rights and responsibilities through these small organizations, the state *and* management benefit even more than do the workers by extracting valuable and timely information from workers to control and prevent their labor organizing.

Here we encounter the complexity of the "native place" factor. Migrant workers network and empower themselves based on their sharing a common birthplace. This one case shows that an informer can rely on the trust of one's fellow natives to obtain information about other workers in the same rental area. This vital intelligence was then forwarded to the state and the unions.

DILEMMAS OF THE LABOR NEWSPAPERS

David Koh made a cogent argument about the important role of the state media in Vietnamese state-society relations. According to Koh, while the Vietnamese media is controlled by the party-state, the media regularly (and either subtly or not so subtly) "turns up its nose at the state."[27] Throughout this book, we have witnessed the important role of labor newspapers, a particular type of state media, in labor-management-state relations.

Both the *Người Lao Động* and the *Lao Động*, the labor-union newspapers, won some important battles. First was the successful campaign in Ho Chi Minh City to secure residents' low electric rates for migrant workers. Migrants had been paying a nonresident rate because of the household registration policy, a cost that was hard for them to afford, given their limited salaries. Pressure from the *Người Lao Động* newspaper empowered the HCMC Labor Federation, in May 2009, to rule that migrant workers would pay for electricity at the same low rate enjoyed by local residents.

The second victory developed from the timely publication of articles that served as legal guidelines (*văn bản dưới luật*, literally translated as "below-the-law legal documents") for workers, since they effectively provided step-by-step instructions

---

[26] This is a common practice, since sleep and rest are vital for employees who must work the following day.

[27] David Koh, "Law, Ethics, and Political Legitimacy," in *Vietnam's New Order: International Perspectives on the State and Reform in Vietnam*, ed. Stéphanie Balme and Mark Sidel (New York, NY: Palgrave: 2007), p. 233.

explaining how to implement new laws. As such, these newspapers' articles addressed one of the key weaknesses identified by Nguyễn Quốc Việt in the Introduction: the lack of direction from the state to guide the implementation of a new law.[28] In the case of the 2006 minimum-wage strike, the labor press cracked open some space to expose labor discontent and succeeded in pressuring all sides to come to the negotiating table, which resulted in a 40 percent increase in the minimum wage in the FDI sector. Then, together with local state, and union officials, the press expedited the implementation just days after the state's announcement, ensuring immediate relief for workers. The strikes in Freetrend, Kollan, and Hugo in 2006 provide ample evidence here. Domestic workers benefited from these strikes as well: the state was forced to raise the minimum wage annually in the state and domestic sectors, commencing in May 2009. This chain of events hastened the convergence between minimum wages in FDI and domestic-private sectors, which the state previously had determined would converge by 2012.

In the case of the 2011 minimum wage increases, as soon as the state made the announcement that these would be approved, *Người Lao Động* journalists published an exposé to prevent business owners from evading the law. That article explained important details, such as the effective dates of the two-step increases in the 2011 minimum wage law and the specific districts that would be affected (see Chapter 3). In short, the newspapers' reports helped bridge the gap between legal intention and implementation (as discussed in the Introduction).

By playing key roles in aiding workers to achieve victory in early 2006 minimum wage strikes, the labor newspapers championed labor rights, thus implicitly confronting the state. But this sense of autonomy was short-lived.

After Vietnam's admittance to the World Trade Organization in 2007, the leash on labor newspapers was tightened. Since 2007, the labor press—still ensconced *within* the state structure—has been circumspect in its attempts to represent workers' rights while responding to the political agenda of the state and labor unions. The labor press cites its own role as the official forum of the VGCL to evoke the strength of collectivity, to provide a place where workers' complaints may be aired, and to appeal to the rule of law. But after 2007, labor coverage did not regain the intensity it had in 2006. Since then, the influence of the labor press has been limited by the state. Due to the government's increased surveillance and paranoia over pro-democracy movements, the labor press quickly retreated to being a mere state apparatus, with little independence, walking a fine line by adding management perspectives to pro-labor-union activities and reporting on the surveillance activities of the worker-self-management and social-opinion cells.

David Koh talks about the idea of "state disaggregation," noting that the state has different motivations that operate in different contexts and with different results.[29] He argues that state capacity in Vietnam is a function of not only legality, power, and authority, but also ethics or norms concerning interpersonal relations and society–individual relations. The state can choose whether to implement certain laws depending on how it weighs "social and public consequences." Indeed, it suppresses newspaper coverage of sensitive issues, as shown below.

---

[28] Nguyễn Quốc Việt, "Explaining the Transition to the Rule of Law in Vietnam: The Role of Informal Institutions and the Delegation of Powers to Independent Courts" (PhD dissertation, Kassel University, 2006), http://kobra.bibliothek.uni-kassel.de/bitstream/urn:nbn:de:hebis:34-2006070313842/1/VietDiss-final.pdf, pp. 72–73, accessed August 6, 2012.

[29] Koh, "Law, Ethics, and Political Legitimacy," pp. 218–19.

Labor-press coverage demonstrates the difficult balancing act necessary to placate the state's paranoia and meet its calculations. The media can showcase with big headlines labor protests in Taiwanese- and South Korean–owned factories, because this coverage is politically consistent with the implicit socialist ideology about exploitative capitalists. Also, the fraud perpetrated by owners of "cicada" factories is the type of issue that touches on general social concerns, yet this type of coverage does not challenge the state's power or integrity, and therefore it is permitted. So, at the time of writing, both *Người Lao Động* and *Lao Động* continue to expose ongoing workers' predicaments, especially workers' losses resulting from the typically irresponsible cicada-type practices described in Chapter 5.

When confronted by issues that were critical of the state, however, how did labor journalists protect themselves from retribution that could result from bold and brave reportage? They wrote collectively and used various resources to sustain their efforts, mainly, evidence-based analysis citing relevant laws and legal protocol to assist workers and to protect themselves. When publishing politically sensitive articles, some *Người Lao Động* journalists relied on strength in numbers, and used the collective byline "A Group of Political and Labor Union Journalists" (*Nhóm Phóng Viên Chính Trị—Công Đoàn*) to protect themselves from attacks by state agencies whose inaction or incompetence were being exposed by the newspaper. However, even with such collective authorship, journalists were still criticized harshly, including by others within their work units. I was fortunate to learn from confidential sources about one incident in 2007 when some brave *Người Lao Động* journalists were internally reprimanded for criticizing the state for failing to offer sufficient help to migrant workers coping with spiraling inflation. Publishing three articles on three consecutive days in 2007 (November 6, 7, and 8) on the *Người Lao Động*'s Labor Unions Page (Công Đoàn), these journalists criticized the state's promises to provide "rent-free worker dormitories, price stability, and [a] worker benefits fund" as "theory-based only," as talk without action.[30] The journalists charged that state officials turned a blind eye toward workers' sufferings, so workers had to fend for themselves. In particular, the November 6 article, "Lonely in the Price Storm: Besieged by High Prices," revealed migrant workers' need for price stabilization and equitable rates because their wages were not adjusted for inflation. The November 7 article, "Coping with the Price Storm: The Wages are Gone after Two Weeks," explained how quickly wages disappeared even when workers spent very little money on food. The November 8 article, "Coping with the Price Storm: Working Overtime, Leaving Jobs," explained employees' constant need to work overtime due to very low piece-rates, and how that condition led to work-related health problems, which in turn required workers to take on additional work to pay medical bills and to make ends meet.

---

[30] The three articles that appeared on the Labor Unions Page (Công Đoàn) are: Nhóm phóng viên CT-CĐ, "Đơn Độc trong cơn bão giá: trong vòng vây giá cả" [Lonely in the Price Storm: Besieged by High Prices], November 6, 2007, *Người Lao Động* http://nld.com.vn/ 206761P0C1010/trong-vong-vay-gia-ca.htm, accessed October 2012; "Chống Chọi trong cơn bão giá: mới nửa tháng đã hết vèo tiền lương" [Coping with the Price Storm: The Wages are Gone after Two Weeks], November 7, 2007, http://nld.com.vn/206856P0C1010/moi-nua-thang-da-het-veo-tien-luong.htm, accessed October 2012; "Chống Chọi trong cơn bão giá: làm thêm, bỏ nghề" [Coping with the Price Storm: Working Overtime, Leaving Jobs], November 8, 2007, http://nld.com.vn/206917P1010C1012/lam-them-bo-nghe.htm, accessed July 2009.

But there are limits to these newspapers' criticisms and complaints about the state. Notably, after Vietnam's accession to the WTO in 2007, the papers did not report on protests in the state sector. Since November 2006, few articles on protests in state-owned factories or labor violations in equitized state-owned factories (most are joint-stock companies) have been printed. Also, the newspapers have published no reports of the two labor organizations established in October 2006—United Workers–Farmers Association and Independent Trade Union of Vietnam—and the imprisonment of several self-proclaimed labor activists who were members of those organizations.[31]

Journalists' Use of Law

The labor press and local state and union officials had been keeping up with the laws and relying on them to mitigate state-capital alliances and state *inaction* and to fight on the workers' behalf. The journalists equipped themselves with legal knowledge; some even obtained law degrees so that they could be more effective in using the law to assist workers and to protect themselves while in the line of duty. The outcomes were mixed: the journalists publicly reported many of management's violations, but won only modest victories for workers. As demonstrated below, journalists eventually reached the end of their rope, so to speak, because even when they cited all the relevant laws related to capitalists' repeated violations, the state still failed to implement the law or punish the capitalists to protect the employees.

The journalists cited appropriate laws to defend workers' rights and interests in their reports and their position articles in the labor press. For instance, to protect the rights of state workers who had been laid off due to the equitization process, the journalists revealed that the 2002 Fund to Assist Redundant Workers failed to distribute the past-due severance pay owed to workers who had been laid off, as mandated by the equitization laws (see Chapter 4). For workers in FDI factories, journalists exposed the inconsistencies in the people's court system's decisions that benefited owners/managers at the expense of their employees, and they cited the 2006 Law on Social Insurance that—if invoked—could protect workers (see Chapter 5). For workers in various domestic-private companies, the journalists cited the negative consequences of the 1999 Law on Domestic Investment, the necessity of the social insurance law, the 2009 Law on Unemployment Insurance, and various articles in the Labor Code (see Chapter 6) to help workers strengthen their cases. In these reports, the reporters presented concrete evidence regarding the costs to workers and the hollowing out of the state budget.

Some local state officials urged that Decree No. 02/CP/2003 be used to freeze the bank accounts of cicada-type factory owners or underground owners (such as the owners of Huê Phong), and proposed that the state could withdraw money from those accounts to pay workers' social insurance benefits.[32] For instance, based on this decree, which allows the Social Insurance Office to direct the State Bank to deduct money directly from the violator's account to cover its social insurance obligations

---

[31] Human Rights Watch, "World Report Chapter: Vietnam, 2009," http://www.hrw.org/en/world-report/2009/vietnam, accessed June 2010.

[32] "Công ty Kwang Nam xin miễn 2,4 tỷ đồng nợ BHXH" [Kwang Nam Company Asked to be Exempted from Its 2.4 billion VND Social Insurance Debt], September 21, 2004 http://vietnamnet.vn/xahoi/laodong/2004/09/261765/, accessed June 2010.

and late fees in full,[33] Bùi Đức Tráng, the vice president of the Social Insurance Office in Ho Chi Minh City, proposed to freeze Huê Phong's bank account and to use that money to pay the factory's debt to workers and the state. Some labor journalists cited the 2005 Investment Law, which includes specific stipulations that allow the Ministry of Planning and Investment to withdraw business licenses should the investors fail to perform according to the terms of their licenses.[34] Below are three examples of internal state conflicts and journalists' reliance on the law for their own protection: one describes the underground case of Huê Phong, and the other two involve factories whose owners fled the country and left their employees stranded and bereft.

Huê Phong Leather Shoe Factory

The labor press played an active role in forcing state officials at various levels to be accountable for their actions or *in*action. Starting off with an important article entitled "Monitoring then Left as Is," Lệ Thủy, a senior chief editor of the Unions Page of the *Người Lao Động*, sharply criticized the investigation team (with representatives from local state and labor unions offices)—which had resumed their operations in December 2004 after four years of inaction—for failing to impose disciplinary measures on these companies in response to their violations (e.g., underground investments, which shortchanged workers' wages and benefits, as described in Chapter 6).[35] The common complaint had been that the punishment was too lenient, so perpetrators would opt to pay the small fine and go on breaking the law rather than changing their practices. Such practice is called "*giơ cao, đánh khẽ*," which can be translated as "raising the hand high but striking gently." Essentially, this article prodded relevant state officials to discipline Huê Phong appropriately. Then, in the aftermath of Thủy's article, on the tenth anniversary of Huê Phong's establishment (1995–2005), the *Người Lao Động* followed up with a series of critical articles to reopen and assess this case. The collective effort was designed to push local state offices to discipline Huê Phong for its continuing labor violations. In June 2005, an article entitled "Strange Tale at Huê Phong" clearly exposed the negative consequences of the 1999 Law on Domestic Investment and cited evidence regarding substantial costs to workers and state budget that had resulted from the deceptions orchestrated by the factory's management:[36]

> In Gò Vấp district, everyone knows Huê Phong is a foreign-owned factory operating in an "underground" manner, using a Vietnamese front to avoid the laws. But over ten years have passed, and everyone just leaves it alone. Consequently, both the state and the laborers suffered. For instance, the factory

---

[33]Vietnamnet, "Công ty Kwang Nam xin miễn 2,4 tỷ đồng nợ BHXH."

[34] http://www.business.gov.vn/assets/4affd5880fd94ef183de7d615c5a887c.pdf, accessed March 2012.

[35] Lệ Thủy, "Vẫn chưa có giải pháp hạn chế tranh chấp, đình công!" [Still No Solution to Minimize Conflicts and Strikes!], *Người Lao Động*, December 16, 2004, http://nld.com.vn/107177P1010C1012/van-chua-co-giai-phap-han-che-tranh-chap-dinh-cong-.htm, accessed June 2006.

[36] Phạm Nguyễn, "Sổ tay: 'Chuyện lạ' ở Huê Phong" ["Notebook: 'Strange Tale' at Huê Phong"], June 6, 2005, http://nld.com.vn/119833P0C1010/chuyen-la-o-hue-phong.htm, accessed June 2006.

employed ten thousand workers but only registered and contributed to the social insurance funds for seven thousand workers at VND 400,000 per person per month. So, roughly, every month, this company profited at least VND 519 million due to different obligations of "Huê Phong with domestic capital" and "Huê Phong with foreign investment." If one multiplies this number by ten years, it becomes a huge figure … Moreover, many workers' rights and benefits were lost, such as wages, bonuses, social insurance and health benefits, and compensation for accidents on the factory floor.[37]

The state investigation team finally began to take action after more critical articles were published. In July 2005, the article "Re-opened the File on Underground Investment at Huê Phong" reviewed this case in depth. On August 1, 2005, the HCMC People's Committee redirected its Inter-departmental Investigation Team (Đoàn Kiểm Tra Liên Ngành) to investigate all aspects of Huê Phong. On October 18, 2005, this investigation team announced its findings to Huê Phong's management, which essentially reiterated the well-known facts. The report said,

Huê Phong registered and went into operation in 1992 as a company with domestic capital. However, after years of its operation, there is clear evidence that this is a foreign-owned company operating underground [đầu tư chui]. Recently, some Taiwanese investors have openly appeared to manage and operate the factory. Therefore, one of the investigatory goals is to make official [the factory's] real ownership in order to determine appropriate disciplinary actions. From the evidence we have collected, it appears the commercial relationships between Huê Phong and other individuals and organizations are extremely complex, and it shows that this factory is not an independent business venture.[38]

Instead of signing individual names, the journalists reported under the "A Group of Journalists of the Rights and Responsibilities Page" (Nhóm Phóng Viên Quyền và Nghĩa Vụ) banner since writing as a group shielded them from reprisals to some extent. They elaborated on how the financial investment of the four founders (Tô Gia Đường, listed in this article as Taiwanese, and three ethnic Chinese men) was not reported on any company documentation, nor on the company's public financial statement. Their actual investment is less than the amount they registered with the government, and the founders falsified the real amounts of their financial investment in their accounting books.

The journalists also listed serious labor violations, such as Huê Phong's failure to contribute to workers' social insurance benefits and its assignment of excessive overtime work (seven hundred hours per year, on average, which clearly surpassed the two to three hundred hours/year limit on required overtime permitted in the

---

[37] Ibid.

[38] Nhóm Phóng Viên Trang Quyền và Nghĩa vụ [A Group of Journalists of the Rights and Responsibilities Page], "Công ty Huê Phong: Vi Phạm Nghiêm Trọng Pháp Luật Lao Động [Huê Phong Company: Seriously Violated Labor Law], *Người Lao Động*, October 18, 2005, http://nld.com.vn/130198P1010C1012/cong-ty-hue-phong-vi-pham-nghiem-trong-phap-luat-lao-dong.htm, accessed June 2006.

Labor Code).[39] The modest worker-led victory in 2006 discussed above (see also Appendix C) signifies that Huê Phong tacitly admitted a well-known fact: it was a foreign-owned factory, operating underground.

Less than two years later, on January 4, 2007, Phạm Hồ, under his own byline, wrote an article directly criticizing the alliance between the Gò Vấp People's Committee and Huê Phong. In his analysis, he relied on the 2006 Law on Social Insurance that required contributions from both owners and workers. His article was entitled "Huê Phong Company Owed VND 5.2 Billion to Social Insurance Funds," and it included a blunt paragraph heading: "Gò Vấp District People's Committee 'Rescued' Huê Phong." He criticized this local people's committee for not only turning a blind eye to Huê Phong's egregious failure to contribute to social insurance funds, but also for its request that the HCMC People's Committee "forgive" Huê Phong's social insurance debt (about US$325,000). He argued that the benefits of more than six thousand workers would be obliterated if the HCMC People's Committee were to erase this debt. He went on to prove that the real loss to workers and state social insurance funds far exceeded VND 5.2 billion when one considered all of the ways this factory had violated the labor code in its calculation of its own social insurance obligations—for instance, by using the lower minimum wage level appropriate for domestic (not FDI) workers, by failing to take into account nonwage allowances, and by failing to contribute to the employees' benefits funds for the whole duration of the labor contracts signed with workers.[40]

Phạm Hồ's argument is consistent with the findings of a senior researcher, Huỳnh Thị Ngọc Tuyết, who said, "The insurance costs continued to be deducted from workers' salaries so they would not be suspicious that management was not contributing their portion of the contribution."[41] But that article (and others) put Phạm Hồ in trouble with the high-ranking party members of the newspaper, and resulted in internal reprimands. Phạm Hồ also cited Decree 2/CP/2003, which was supported by some state officials in HCMC's department of labor and the social insurance office. This is just one of many examples showing how journalists investigated and exposed illegal labor practices even though they were under a credible threat of reprisals, especially when they criticized the state-capital alliance (such as the alliance between the Gò Vấp People's Committee and Huê Phong's management, in this case), and relied on the law to protect themselves. In general, while the forms of reprisals experienced by these journalists were not overt job losses, the effects were punitive: being transferred to editing positions—no longer the cutting-edge investigative journalistic functions that reported on labor activism and strikes—or to administrative positions; losing opportunities for promotion; and facing barriers to travel overseas for conferences.[42]

---

[39] Ibid. Overtime is high during crunch delivery time in high seasons, but underemployment is prevalent during low seasons.

[40] Phạm Hồ, "Công ty Huê Phong nợ 5,2 tỉ đồng BHXH" [Huê Phong Company Owed 5.2 Billion VND to Social Insurance Funds], *Người Lao Động*, January 4, 2007, http://nld.com.vn/176268p0c1010/cong-ty-hue-phong-no-52-ti-dong-bhxh.htm, accessed June 2007.

[41] Interview with Huỳnh thị Ngọc Tuyết, Ho Chi Minh City, July 2005.

[42] Interviews with journalists C, D, and E in each year from 2009–2013 in Ho Chi Minh City.

Huê Phong was just one of many cases that the labor press exposed. I now turn to a newspaper's exposé of an infamous cicada-type factory, which showcases the weakness of the rule of law in Vietnam, leading to ineffective law enforcement.

Haimin Embroidery Factory

The labor union's media arm is often aided by workers' direct action. At the Haimin embroidery factory, when it became obvious that the owners were planning to abscond from Vietnam without paying their debts, workers engaged in direct action by guarding the factory gate to prevent the Korean managers from moving machinery and property from the building. Workers had been sending collective complaint letters to the labor press (Chapter 5), which triggered direct intervention by the newspapers and local labor unions but did not result in compensation for the workers. Three different people's courts—in Ho Chi Minh City and in Hóc Môn and Tân Phú districts—failed to secure back wages and benefits for workers, but resolved a lawsuit to the benefit of a company creditor of the now-defunct Haimin factory. Kexim, the company that rented the embroidery machinery to Haimin, had appealed to Hóc Môn district state officials in 2007 to retrieve its twelve machines from the factory, and successfully did so in July 2009.[43]

In response to workers' direct action, the *Người Lao Động* journalists were very vocal and critical of the state's inaction and lack of accountability, especially at the city level. Most articles started with the facts and ended with rhetorical questions criticizing city and district state authorities who had failed to discipline the perpetrators of such repeated offenses. For instance, in the perspective column (*Góc Nhìn*), Lệ Thủy criticized the HCMC government, the city-level authority, for its lack of action in response to requests by district-level (Hóc Môn) officials to discipline Haimin's management. She wrote, "This is not the first time that Hóc Môn authorities called the HCMC authorities to dispatch a city-level auditing team to finalize the Haimin case. But it appears as if this case is not yet in their sights, so as of now, these [city] agencies are still motionless."[44]

Not willing to accept the feeble response of the authorities, Lệ Thủy continued to push for some concrete action and ended her editorial with a rhetorical question: "Again, the Haimin situation is not better. Why was there no one responsible for this? And appropriate authorities only folded their arms, sat there, and watched [*bó tay ngồi nhìn*]?"[45]

Vĩnh Tùng—another seasoned *Người Lao Động* journalist—openly criticized the inaction of HCMC officials and called out specific state offices for their failure to respond to workers' repeated complaints concerning the Haimin factory and others:

---

[43] Vĩnh Tùng, "Giải quyết tình trạng 'vô chủ' tại Công ty Haimin VN" [Resolving the Ownerless Situation at Haimin Vietnam Company], *Người Lao Động*, May 11, 2007, http://www.nld.com.vn/tintuc/cong-doan/188853.asp, accessed July 2007; Vĩnh Tùng and T. Nhàn, "Công ty bị kê biên tài sản, công nhân điêu đứng," *Người Lao Động*, July 31, 2009, http://nld.com.vn/20090731024824763P0C1010/cong-ty-bi-ke-bien-tai-san-cong-nhan-dieu-dung.htm, accessed July 2010.

[44] Lệ Thủy, "Xin đừng bó tay ngồi nhìn!" [Please Do Not Just Sit There, Fold Your Arms and Watch!], *Người Lao Động*, March 14, 2006, http://nld.com.vn/145024P1010C1012/xin-dung-bo-tay-ngoi-nhin.htm, accessed June 2006.

[45] Ibid.

The *Người Lao Động* had alerted [state officials] repeatedly about these factories closing their gates, discontinuing their operation, which resulted in workers losing all their benefits. The point we want to stress here is the *irresponsibility of those factories [owners] and the lack of concern on the part of local state authorities.* When conflicts erupted, workers, especially in FDI factories, had sent many petitions and complaints to seek help everywhere; local district/ward labor unions had also requested the *city authorities* to intervene and investigate proper implementation of the Labor Code in those factories. But in return was an inexplicable silence. Workers in these factories had been waiting for answers from the city offices of the Ministry of Planning and Investment (MPI), the MOLISA [Ministry of Labor, Invalids, and Social Affairs], and the HCMC Labor Investigation board.[46]

In this case, *Người Lao Động* journalists reported the direct intervention of two active labor unions, the Hóc Môn district union and the HCMC Labor Federation. The Hóc Môn District Labor Union did intervene to represent the workers in their negotiations with those members of the management team who were still available. The HCMC Labor Federation joined in later to support the Hóc Môn District Labor Union. Together, they alerted local state agencies (the MPI and MOLISA). For instance, Lê Văn Vũ, the Hóc Môn District Labor Union representative (a full-time union cadre at the district level), even advised workers on how to bring a lawsuit against the Haimin company.[47] I had a chance to interview Lê Văn Vũ in January 2011 and was able to confirm all of his actions on workers' behalf.

This article went on to say that Lê Văn Vũ had gone searching for former Haimin workers. This was a difficult task, since most had dispersed, and were either working elsewhere or had returned to their hometowns. When he found two former Haimin migrant workers engaged in other jobs and living in nearby rental units, he came to see them after work hours to guide them through the necessary steps in the arduous legal process of filing a lawsuit to claim their back wages and social security benefits. Trần Thị Lệ, the one former Haimin employee who worked closely with Vũ in this lawsuit all the way through to the finish (the other worker had given up on the suit), expressed her appreciation for his sacrifice and dedication: "Many times when we had to work overtime, Mr. Vũ patiently waited in our rental unit until late at night for our return, so that he [could] guide us [in] how to file this lawsuit for our rights. There were times when we were ready to give up; Mr. Vũ gave us timely encouragement and spiritual support [*tình cảm*] for us to go on."[48]

This case demonstrates how conflicts among state apparatuses and their arbitrary discretion led to weak law enforcement and an inefficient court system. Workers and the local labor unions were sent to three different people's courts, only to face the time-limitation statute at the end of this three-year legal runaround. Evidence shows that the HCMC People's Court (*Toà Án Nhân Dân Thành Phố*) had sided with business and management at the expense of the workers. First, the Hóc

---

[46] Vĩnh Tùng, "Báo động tình trạng nợ lương công nhân" [Alerting about Back Wages Owed to Workers], *Người Lao Động*, April 26, 2006, http://nld.com.vn/149183p0c1010/bao-dong-tinh-trang-no-luong-cong-nhan.htm, accessed July 2006, my emphasis.

[47] Vĩnh Tùng, "Người thân" [A Close Friend], *Người Lao Động*, February 16, 2010, http://nld.com.vn/20100128095442468P0C1010/nguoi-than.htm, accessed July 2010.

[48] Ibid.

Môn District Labor Union and the two workers they represented filed a lawsuit in November 2006 with the HCMC People's Court, which transferred it back to the Hóc Môn People's Court, located in Hóc Môn district, which was assumed to be the proper jurisdiction for a case involving this factory. After four months of waiting, the Hóc Môn People's Court transferred the case to the Tân Phú People's Court because the Haimin main office was registered in Tân Phú district. But at this point, the Tân Phú People's Court requested that the Hóc Môn District Labor Union withdraw its name from the case because the case involved an individual labor-capital conflict and the union was not the plaintiff. The Hóc Môn District Labor Union continued to support the two workers, who filed their legal claim for social security benefits with the Tân Phú People's Court. But after two months, in March 2009, the Tân Phú People's Court decided to return the case to the HCMC People's Court, stating as the reason, "Mr. Yang Soo Min, the legal representative of Haimin, is a foreigner who did not register his residency at Tân Phú district." At this point, after three years of legal confusion, only Trần Thị Lệ remained as a plaintiff. On March 17, 2009, when the HCMC People's Court closed her case due to the time-limitation statute, Lệ cried out loud, "This is the end [of hope]!" and declared that she had lost everything pursuing this legal process.[49] Throughout this three-year ordeal, Lê Văn Vũ faithfully represented these two workers, although to no avail.

The only recourse that workers had then was the promise of the HCMC Labor Federation to continue fighting for justice. Trương Lâm Danh, the then-deputy of the HCMC Labor Federation,[50] pointed out the pro-capitalist orientation of the HCMC People's Court and vowed to fight on:

> The ruling of the HCMC People's Court concerning the Haimin Vietnam Limited case, once again, shows a lack of consistency among the various court levels in resolving labor dispute cases. *While the HCMC People's Court did not accept [the] workers' lawsuit, they did resolve the lawsuit filed by Kexim Company*—another creditor of Haimin Vietnam—and this ruling had been implemented. The HCMC Labor Federation will appeal to the HCMC People's Committee as well as the HCMC People's Court about this decision, so that workers will not lose all of their rights.[51]

Ironically, all the "people's courts" not only failed to protect labor rights, but discreetly and effectively served capitalist interests. For example, the HCMC People's Court granted Kexim Company the return of its twelve machines, thereby protecting this company's property rights at the expense of workers' rights.

State officials could have utilized two other existing laws to stem repeated labor violations. As noted above, Decree 02/CP/2003 permits the social insurance office to freeze the violator's account and take money directly from that account to pay debts owed to employees.[52] Also, the Ministry of Planning and Investment can cancel the

---

[49] Vĩnh Tùng, "Gian nan khởi kiện, rốt cuộc trắng tay" [Struggling with the Law Suit, Empty-handed at the End], *Người Lao Động*, August 5, 2009, http://nld.com.vn/ 2009080411409640P0C1010/gian-nan-khoi-kien-rot-cuoc-trang-tay.htm, accessed July 2010.

[50] As of 2012, Trương Lâm Danh was replaced by Nguyễn Việt Cường as the vice president of HCMC Labor Federation.

[51] Vĩnh Tùng, "Gian nan khởi kiện, rốt cuộc trắng tay."

[52] http://vanban.chinhphu.vn/portal/page/portal/chinhphu/hethongvanban?class_id= 1&_ page=1&mode=detail&document_id=14142, accessed March 2012.

business licenses of violators.[53] Sadly, the state utilized neither of these legal actions to rectify the injustice.

A senior journalist of the *Lao Động* newspaper, Dương Minh Đức, bluntly explained the key reason for the state's lackluster defense of the workers in an article concerning another cicada-type factory, Kwang Nam, the foreign owner of which also left thousands of workers stranded:

> According to many sources of information, some officials (whose names I was not allowed to mention) who were not concerned about workers' rights had a strange viewpoint: "*being too tough will negatively affect FDI.*" However, a majority of state officials had come to a consensus that attracting FDI [companies] such as Kwang Nam would only hurt the Vietnamese society! But such [a] pro-FDI viewpoint had pressured local officials to turn a blind eye to those violations and not withdraw the business licenses of those violating factories.[54]

Đức asserts here that the contradictory goals and benefits of being pro-labor *and* pro-capital prevented officials from using their legal muscle to discipline the owners of those factories that had cheated their employees. Moreover, the article suggests that the pressures from and lobbying efforts of the FDI sector—via the power of their chambers of commerce, which often have direct access to and influence over the prime minister—influence the implementation of the law.

Anjin Shoe Factory: Two-Year Legal Delay

Anjin was a 100-percent Korean-owned factory. When it went out of business, it owed thousands of workers their social security contributions. In October 2008, Eun Ho Kang, Anjin's Korean owner, publicly stated her intention to declare bankruptcy so that she could liquidate her machinery in order to pay her workers. Then the HCMC Social Security Office filed a lawsuit against Anjin because it owed this office VND 4.4 billion (as of 2008; see Appendix D) and requested that the HCMC People's Court grant Anjin its bankruptcy status so that the Social Security Office could secure Anjin's money to pay workers. The HCMC People's Court accepted the case on November 12, 2008, but took no action until May 21, 2009, when it formed a team to manage and liquidate Anjin's machinery and property.[55] This team further delayed action until September 2010, almost *two years* after the HCMC Social Security Office

---

[53]   http://www.business.gov.vn/assets/4affd5880fd94ef183de7d615c5a887c.pdf, accessed March 2012.

[54] Dương Minh Đức, "Sẽ cưỡng chế, phát mại tài sản các DN nợ BHXH" [Will Impose the Liquidation of the Property of the Companies that Owed Workers' Social Insurance], *Lao Động* April 3, 2008, http://www.laodong.com.vn/Utilities/PrintView.aspx?ID=82930, accessed July 2008. This was an act of courage on the part of this investigative journalist who effectively exposed the state–capital alliance and media censorship when he mentioned that *he himself* was prohibited from revealing the names of those officials. The "local state officials" are presumably associated with the social insurance office, the state bank, and the HCMC departments of the Ministry of Planning and Investment, as well as the Ministry of Finance. Kwang Nam, a Korean-owned factory, owed social insurance contributions to the tune of VND 2.8 billions as of 2007, making it the third highest violator on the list (Appendix D).

[55] Kim Chi, "Kê biên tài sản Công ty Anjin" [Registering the Property of Anjin Company], *Người Lao Động*, September 9, 2010, http://nld.com.vn/20100908102245541P1010C1012/ke-bien-tai-san-cong-ty-anin.htm, accessed September 2010.

requested bankruptcy status for Anjin to secure money for workers. This two-year legal delay caused "the evaporation of property," and thousands of workers ended up losing all of their benefits.[56]

The owner of the facility that housed the shoe-manufacturing machines had sold the machines that were still in good condition to recover the rent owed, and left behind the rusted machines that could only be sold for spare parts. A former worker lamented, "When this factory owed us our social security contributions, we already lost a lot. We had hoped that the legal authorities would promptly execute the bankruptcy process so that we [could] get a small fraction of our lost benefits. At this rate, we lost everything!"[57]

Again, this case points to the arbitrary power of the HCMC People's Court, which minimized the property owner's loss, but, sadly, maximized the loss to thousands of workers.

WORKERS AND THE RULE OF LAW SINCE *ĐỔI MỚI*

Workers' resistance strategies in Vietnam are circumscribed due to the weakness of the rule of law and arbitrary power of the executive and legal state branches. The workers and their closest allies—the newspapers and the local labor unions—can move the state and local officials only to a certain point. As discussed in the examples above, when cases are struck down or delayed by the courts, the workers are left with very few avenues for moving forward.

Throughout one hundred years of labor history, Vietnamese workers have always appealed to the legal systems and state institutions that governed them to demand justice and the right to strike, and for better treatment and respect. For example, during the French colonial era, workers appealed to contract laws and the first progressive labor code introduced in 1937–38. In the 1960s and early 1970s, in the Republic of Vietnam, workers invoked laws regarding free trade unions, the right to strike, and protections for strikers.

State Workers

State workers used the state media as an important vehicle for protest to combat violations committed by different types of capital investors, including the state. Workers fought against state-owned enterprises that did not follow the law. As shown in the workers' protest letters (Chapter 4), laid-off state workers in former state-owned enterprises (which had become joint-stock companies) sought legal remedies. They reminded the state of both social contracts and legal contracts by filing petitions, complaint letters, and lawsuits citing appropriate laws and the Labor Code. Their broad repertoire of actions, which included protests and strikes, resembles the actions and methods employed by state workers in China.[58]

---

[56] Nam Dương, "Mỏi mòn chờ phá sản" [Desperately Waiting for the Bankruptcy (Clause)], *Người Lao Động*, September 6, 2010 http://nld.com.vn/20100905111058438P1010C1012/moi-mon-cho-pha-san.htm, accessed October 2010.

[57] Ibid.

[58] Ching Kwan Lee, *Against the Law: Labor Protests in China's Rustbelt and Sunbelt* (Berkeley, CA: University of California Press, 2007), pp. 11, 202–3. Vietnamese state workers' demand to restore traditional entitlements is similar to one of the demands of Chinese state workers (see Lee, *Against the Law*, 121).

As noted earlier, workers have resorted to a combination of Polanyi- and Marxist-type rhetoric in their protests. Based on sparse materials available concerning written protests in the North, I found relatively more Marxist, class-based rhetoric used before 2002 (the year marking the official onset of the equitization process) than after, rhetoric demanding basic rights as well as traditional entitlements. In the "pen" protests in 1999, female state workers in the North used Marxist rhetoric and appealed to state agencies by sending signed petitions to state legal institutions, such as the labor courts, and letters to state TV labor-union programs. Also, as shown in the early 1993 Choong Nam–Việt Thắng strike (which took place before strikes were legalized in 1995), state workers used socialist ideology and historical knowledge of the United States–Vietnam war to score a partial victory, winning half of the thirteenth-month bonus they had often received when they were employed in state-owned factories.

Then, in their protest letters after 2002, as the equitization of state-owned factories began, workers used more legalistic rhetoric, but at times combined it with socialist social-contract rhetoric.[59] For instance, one hundred (mostly male) workers demanded their compensation rights and rights available under the workers' congress law (the right to have union meetings at least annually). Female workers invoked gender stipulations in the Labor Code and other entitlements, such as their entitlement to severance pay and social and health insurance.

As discussed in Chapter 4, in 2006, 250 male workers in a Vietnamese–Russian joint venture used Marxist rhetoric *and* cited the law to demand higher minimum wages—because they were no longer employed in a state-owned factory—and other entitlements. In another protest in 2006, workers at the Việt Thắng–Vicoluch joint venture enterprise demonstrated how they understood the law and won their rights: a higher FDI minimum wage, in addition to other wage and nonwage allowances. In 2008, 140 garment workers at the Việt Thắng Jeans Limited Company stopped work for four days to complain about the factory's failure to honor and provide basic workers' entitlements (minimum wage, bonuses, and a limit to overtime work) and won "some resolution within the factory" (unfortunately, only limited information is available on this case).

In worker letters and petitions, there is a sense of trust in the effectiveness of the labor newspapers and the legal guidance provided by the newspapers and the labor unions to expose workers' plight to the public. However, the cynical tone in these letters/petitions ("*to the eyes and ears of state authorities*") reveals state workers' frustration with the legal system and their awareness that gaining satisfaction through the courts is unlikely.[60] In some cases, the newspapers did forward state workers' complaints and won some relief for workers by demanding a response from management and proper government offices; but in many other cases, there is no evidence that workers' complaints went far.

FDI Workers

Workers showed their understanding of the Labor Code and the minimum-wage law for FDI factories, and used them to their advantage. One example is the 2005

---

[59] Arguably, this strategy could empower state workers, who can use the state's own rhetoric regarding "a market economy with socialist orientation" when arguing their case.

[60] For some comparable situations in China, see: Lee, *Against the Law*, p. 116.

minimum-wage strike, which gave rise to the 2006 minimum-wage increase and subsequent annual minimum-wage increases in the FDI sector, which also raised the minimum wage in the domestic sector so that the gap between the FDI and domestic sectors decreased.

The workers cited specific laws and management's obligations to its employees in their protest letters to demand workers' rights and entitlements. The Freetrend women's lavatory slogans, and the protest letters composed by the Quảng Việt, Viva-Blast Prezioso, and Haimin workers, are especially potent examples of this strategy. In the case involving the Haimin embroidery factory, employees filed lawsuits in various courts and received support from the Hóc Môn District Labor Union representative along the way. They wrote letters to the Labor Law Consultancy Section of the *Người Lao Động* newspaper; employees at the Shilla Bags, Huê Phong, and Quảng Việt factories all contacted *Người Lao Động*.

These strikes were covered by the labor press, which broadcast news of the workers' struggles; the labor press's reports, in turn, triggered other state apparatuses (local labor unions and state offices) to intervene. Sometimes there were short-term victories, but on many occasions, there were losses, since often the capital owners had already fled Vietnam or were still at large. Also, as discussed earlier, the courts could raise barriers and prevent workers from realizing their rights.

But there are limits to the rule of law. By operating according to the rule of law, workers legitimize state power. The state, in turn, uses the rule of law to govern both labor and capital, but its tendency to wield power arbitrarily means that many of these significant laws are not implemented consistently. The labor newspapers and labor unions could expose all the workers' grievances and use strong language against incompetent state agencies and the legal system, but the grievances might only fall on deaf ears. In most cases, workers suffered all the losses and injustices, while capital owners fled with their profits and sometimes even retrieved their property.

The three FDI cases (Haimin, Anjin, and Huê Phong) analyzed above demonstrate the weakness of the rule of law and point to the weakness of the executive branch (the Gò Vấp People's Committee, in Huê Phong's case) and the judiciary (the HCMC People's Court, in the Haimin and Anjin cases). These cases also show the efforts and dedication—unfortunately futile—of the members of the district and city labor unions, who often registered strong complaints about the shortcomings of the legal system and resolved to fight on even after repeated disappointments. The final outcome of the Vietnamese labor unions' efforts on workers' behalf remains to be seen.

Domestic Private Workers

Workers in domestic-private factories demonstrated their knowledge of the law in most of the cases discussed above and exposed the illegal practices of underground foreign owners.[61] These workers alerted the state and union authorities about management violations regarding pay, social and health benefits, severance

---

[61] In the case of Minh Nghệ workers (from the Thirty-Nine-Letter Sample of worker complaint letters and petitions submitted to newspapers in the South in 2005 and 2006), while they did not cite the law explicitly, they appealed to and expected state authorities to intervene to restore justice and dignity for them.

allowances, maximum overtime hours, and labor contracts, as we saw in the Đông Á, Sơn Kim, and Dịch Vụ Bảo Vệ cases. They publicized the importance of knowing the Labor Code, in the Thời Ích case, and they exposed tax evasion and inadequate contribution to social and health funds in protests involving the Huê Phong, Thanh Loan Thi Ltd., and Phú Sĩ Washing and Ironing factories.

In the written protests organized by employees in private-domestic factories (2005–06), the workers used both legalistic and Marxist rhetoric to appeal to state authorities and institutions. Workers appealed to both socialist social and legal contracts to restore the entitlements they used to receive and reestablish justice in the workplace. They called for state intervention in labor-management disputes in two ways: by reminding the state of the implicit socialist contracts that bound the government to defend the interests of the workers (recall in the Sơn Kim case, "We are living in a socialist country, not in a regime where people can exploit people") and by reminding the state and its apparatuses—the labor unions and the labor newspapers—to enforce the law and to restore justice for workers (recall in the Minh Nghệ case, "We are anxiously waiting, night and day, for relevant state officials' intervention to bring justice to us"; and in the Dịch Vụ Bảo Vệ case, "I … implore the *Người Lao Động* to report and relay our message to the 'ears' of the state authorities").

In private Vietnamese factories manufacturing for Western markets, workers' voices indicated that Vietnamese labor laws were decent, but their implementation was substandard. When no response from state offices was forthcoming, workers utilized the Labor Code and other state ideological apparatuses, such as the labor unions and the labor press. They trusted in and appealed to the labor press, even when other state agencies failed them.

Workers' complaint letters published in the *Người Lao Động* newspaper had launched the journalists to investigate another long-standing case. Journalist Nam Dương found that H-M Vina enterprise (a 100-percent Korean-owned knit sweaters company) did not sign labor contracts or pay benefits to 130 workers for seven years without being caught by the district authorities. Effectively, such proactive workers and journalists shed light on these violations and requested local state authorities to face up to their responsibilities and be accountable for their (in)actions.[62]

But there were limits to the workers' deployment of the law. Their resistance strategies were circumscribed time and again. Workers could appeal to various state agencies and the labor courts when FDI factories failed to act in accordance with the law, but they had no further recourse when state agencies turned a blind eye to their grievances. Even with sustained support from local labor unions, court delays have made legal cases uphill battles that become unaffordable for most migrant workers, who have neither time nor resources to withstand such long cases. In the Haimin case, the three-year circuitous legal procedures resulted in case dismissal due to the statute of limitations. In the Anjin case, the almost two-year court delay resulted in the hollowing out of factory property and rusted machines. In both cases, thousands of workers suffered from losses of pay and benefits.

---

[62] "H-M Vina" (sometimes it is spelled "H&M Vina" in the *Người Lao Động*) is the complete name of this factory, not an acronym or pseudonym. Nam Dương, "7 năm phạm luật, quận - phường không hay?!" [Seven years of legal violations without district and ward's knowledge], *Người Lao Động*, October 21, 2010, http://nld.com.vn/20101020104450127p0c1010/7-nam-pham-luat-quan-phuong-khong-hay.htm, accessed November 2012.

In general, workers have no legal recourse if the state apparatuses do not take up their cases. Not all the petition letters found their way to the newspaper pages, and most workers do not have the resources, time, or energy to pursue their rights without guidance and legal assistance.

Labor Legal Assistance Centers

In recent years there has been some cause for hope: labor legal assistance centers established jointly by some local labor unions and international NGOs, such as Oxfam in Vietnam. These centers provide free-of-charge legal assistance to poor migrant workers to empower them in labor–management negotiations.[63] The centers are strategically located in strike-prone areas in the South—Ho Chi Minh City, Đồng Nai, Bình Dương provinces. This model shows an emergence of the proactive role of global civil society actors in working with local stakeholders in Vietnam. The success of each center depends very much on the support of local government and labor unions.

The first and most active and efficient legal center has been located in Đồng Nai province since 2005.[64] It has received both financial and technical support from Oxfam-Vietnam and Oxfam Belgium Solidarity in collaboration with the Đồng Nai Labor Federation. The full-time staff members have been providing not only free (and accommodating to workers' schedules) legal assistance to both workers and enterprise-level union representatives, but also educational resources (such as books, newspapers and magazines, and Internet access), job information, and cultural activities. As of December 2012, this local–global collaboration has been providing many rounds of legal workshops in three support centers for workers: Biên Hòa city, Nhơn Trạch district, and, the newest center, Trảng Bom district, which hosted four rounds of workshop in 2012.

---

[63] For the legal assistance center in Đồng Nai province, see: Thanh Thúy, "Đại hội thi đua yêu nước tỉnh Đồng Nai lần IV—2010, Trung tâm tư vấn pháp luật Liên đoàn Lao động tỉnh: Địa chỉ tin cậy của người lao động" [The 4th Patriotic Campaign in Đồng Nai Province in 2010; Legal Assistance Center of the Province Labor Unions: A Trustworthy Address for Workers], *Báo Đồng Nai*, September 1, 2010, http://www.baodongnai.com.vn/chinhtri/doanthe/201009/dai-hoi-thi-dua-yeu-nuoc-tinh-dong-Nai-lan-iV-2010Trung-tam-tu-van-phap-luat-Lien-doan-Lao-dong-tinh-dia-chi-tin-cay-cua-nguoi-lao-dong-2069086/, accessed July 2012; Hằng—Phước, "Lợi ích từ mô hình 'Điểm hỗ trợ công nhân'" [Benefits from the Model "Support Center for Workers"], June 18, 2012, www.dnrtv.org.vn/news/tin-dia-phuong/phong-su/2087/loi-ich-tu-mo-hinh-diem-ho-tro-cong-nhan, accessed July 2012. For the legal assistance center in Ho Chi Minh City, see: www.sotuphap.hochiminhcity.gov.vn/to-chuc-hanh-nghe-cc/Lists/Posts/Post.aspx?List=083510bd-ad39-4456-867f-91341c25f78f&ID=13, accessed July 2012; and Tr. Hoàng, "Ra mắt Văn phòng Luật sư Công đoàn" [Opening the Lawyers' Office of HCMC Labor Federation], *Người Lao Động*, December 2, 2010, http://nld.com.vn/20101201115959323P1010C1012/ra-mat-van-phong-luat-su-cong-doan.htm, accessed December 2010. For the legal services in Bình Dương province, see: http://www.binhduong.gov.vn/vn/sobannganh_detail.php?id=136&idcat=16&idcat2=3, accessed July 2012.

[64] Huỳnh Thị Ngọc Tuyết, Nguyễn Thị Minh Châu, Vũ Ngọc Hà, "Increasing Access to Information and Legal Assistance to Migrant Workers in Đồng Nai Province," Project Midterm Report [Dự Án Tăng Cường Tiếp Cận Thông Tin Và Tư Vấn Pháp Luật Cho Người Lao Động Nhập Cư Của Tỉnh Đồng Nai], Legal Assistance Center of the Đồng Nai Labor Federation and Institute of Sustainable Development in Southern Region, August 2012, pp. 10, 13, 35.

In December 2010, the HCMC Labor Federation opened a legal assistance center in Ho Chi Minh City to provide free legal counsel and representation for workers and the labor unions. The impact of the HCMC legal assistance center on workers' struggles there was not as dynamic as that of Đồng Nai province. Furthermore, legal support provided to workers in Bình Dương province has been the least robust. Bình Dương lacks a full-time, union-run legal assistance center. Instead, workers must seek legal counsel from the justice department (*sở tư pháp*) governed by the people's committee of Bình Dương province. At the time of writing, Bình Dương's legal services primarily assist the general public, not the specialized legal needs of migrant workers.

CONCLUSION

Contemporary Vietnam's government is not monolithic and has surrendered some authority over the last two decades as a result of reforms, yet it has not lost its grip on power. It has successfully endorsed legal and judicial structures to function in the neoliberal market system since the late 1990s. Unfortunately, its implementation of the laws has been arbitrary and inconsistent. The state has not been willing to subject itself to the rule of law, functioning as if "law is not above the state but rather emanates from the state."[65] But the state does pay attention to "social and public consequences"[66] in choosing whether to implement certain laws and ignore others.

Both descriptions help to explain labor–management–state relations in Vietnam. The 2005–06 minimum-wage strike by hundreds of thousands of workers in the South provides an example of how the state calculates the "social and public consequences" of its actions. This open struggle was essentially mounted against a state policy that had frozen the minimum wage over the previous seven years. But the strike took place in foreign-owned factories—the protestors did not target the regime—and the workers' agenda was consistent with the state's professed socialist values.

Moreover, these events played out during a period when the Vietnamese state was on the world stage—right before it was admitted to the WTO—so it was of great "public consequence" for the government to demonstrate its tolerance of labor dissent and "independent" media coverage. We witnessed a period of newspapers' frank and open critiques of irresponsible state apparatuses that failed to respond to workers' demands. The workers' victory not only challenged the state's power without triggering any repressive action from the government, but also brought about annual systematic inflation-based raises in minimum wage levels in both FDI and domestic sectors. However, even with an established legal system in place, the courts did little to expose and penalize owners who cheated their workers and deceived the state.

The situation for workers changed after Vietnam joined the WTO. When subsequent worker-led strikes in 2008 gained momentum and became more widespread, the state grew concerned for its power. Since 2008, the state has circumscribed labor resistance efforts and labor newspapers' reportage. Local state

---

[65] John Gillespie, "Understanding Legality in Vietnam," in *Vietnam's New Order*, ed. Balme and Sidel, p. 143.

[66] Koh, "Law, Ethics, and Political Legitimacy."

and union officials heightened surveillance by using already existing worker-self-management and social-opinion cells in order to monitor, control, prevent, and preempt various forms of worker protest. Furthermore, the state and the police suppressed protests that opposed the confiscation and appropriation of lands owned by poor peasants for use by industry and commerce, and quelled workers' demands for democracy and the establishment of independent labor unions.[67]

In Trà Vinh, a coastal province in the Mekong Delta region, the state incarcerated three young labor activists (a man and a woman from Bình Dương province and a man from Đồng Nai province) on charges that they had incited workers from the Mỹ Phong leather shoe/bag factory to go on strike in early 2010; the suspects were also charged with disseminating more than four thousand anti-government flyers.[68] These activists were accused of "disrupting order to overthrow the government of Vietnam" in collaboration with the "Committee to Protect Vietnamese Workers," operating from Poland.

Official state media coverage of these disruptions at Mỹ Phong factory was limited, while external coverage portrayed a more complete picture of this struggle. Two articles from the BBC (the Vietnamese Section) described how more than ten thousand Mỹ Phong workers sustained a strike from January 30 to February 2, 2010, in protest against often-cited management violations: the lack of a Tết bonus, steep fines imposed when workers had to take days off to attend to family emergencies, and the verbal abuse of women workers.[69] During the October 2010 trial of the three activists accused of fomenting resistance in Mỹ Phong, they were not allowed to speak in order to defend themselves; two were sentenced to seven years each in prison, and the other to nine years.[70] The official state media did not broadcast news about this trial or the sentencing. Instead, the media published only brief articles about how ten thousand workers had returned to work after one-week of not working in February 2010 upon receiving promises by management to address their concerns on wages and bonuses.[71]

Incidents such as these confirm that the contemporary Vietnamese state has demonstrated a heightened sense of paranoia and sought continued and strong control over labor activities. But emerging cross-border solidarity among global

[67] This is not unlike China's ruthless crackdowns on Chinese workers' protests as soon as they turned toward organized political dissent. Lee, *Against the Law*, p. 122.

[68] T. Đ., "Trà Vinh: Xét xử vụ án phá rối an ninh" [Trà Vinh: Ruling on the Case of Disrupting Security], *Lao Động,* October 27, 2010, http://www.laodong.com.vn/Tin-Tuc/Xet-xu-vu-an-pha-roi-an-ninh/18156, accessed July 2012; X. Thạnh, "Phá rối an ninh, 3 người nhận 23 năm tù" [Disrupting Security, 3 People Received a (total of) 23-Year Prison Term], *Người Lao Động,* October 27, 2010, http://nld.com.vn/20101027013519810P0C1019/pha-roi-an-ninh-3-nguoi-nhan-23-nam-tu.htm, accessed June 2011.

[69] BBC–Vietnamese section [no author], "Một vạn công nhân đình công ở Trà Vinh" [10,000 Workers Went on Strike in Trà Vinh], February 2, 2010, http://www.bbc.co.uk/vietnamese/vietnam/2010/02/100202_labour_strike.shtml, accessed November 2010.

[70] X. Thạnh, "Phá rối an ninh, 3 người nhận 23 năm tù"; BBC–Vietnamese section [no author], "Phản ứng sau phiên xử ba nhà hoạt động trẻ" [Reactions after the Trial of the Three Young Activists], October 2010, http://www.bbc.co.uk/vietnamese/mobile/vietnam/2010/10/101027_activist_trial_reax.shtml?page=all#page2, accessed November 2010.

[71] Hữu Trãi, "Hơn 10.000 công nhân Công ty Giày da Mỹ Phong trở lại làm việc" [Over 10,000 Mỹ Phong Leather Shoe Factory Workers Had Returned to Work], February 4, 2010, http://tuoitre.vn/Chinh-tri-Xa-hoi/362648/Hon-10000-cong-nhan-Cong-ty-Giay-da-My-Phong-tro-lai-lam-viec.html, accessed November 2010.

NGOs and local stakeholders to empower workers provides a reason for hope. Labor legal assistance centers give advice and empower workers who are attempting to protect their rights and interests. While just a small project at present, these centers offer primarily migrant workers a way to establish their legal claims by using the party-state's own legal mechanisms and directing the state to accept its responsibilities to protect labor in its battles for respect and dignity.

CHAPTER 8

CONCLUSION

This book investigates how social relations, influenced by cultural identities, can propel people toward collective action that is greater than themselves. In particular, let us return to the questions raised in the Introduction:

1. What is the significance of cultural identity factors with respect to Vietnamese workers, and how did these factors coalesce to foster the development of social ties in different historical contexts (during the French colonial rule, in the Republic and the Democratic Republic of Vietnam, and in the Socialist Republic of Vietnam)?

2. To what extent did the workers' nexus of cultural identity and social ties enable labor mobilization and make possible "moments of class consciousness" in times of crisis and desperation?

3. What are the *types of protest* that workers used to demand their rights, entitlements, and human dignity at particular historical moments?

Evidence from this book supports the theoretical framework that there is a cultural identity-based underpinning to labor resistance. By analyzing the totality of migrant workers' experiences in Vietnam, including those of individuals on the shop floor and in the dormitories where they lived, and the historical legacy workers inherit, a clearer picture develops of how cultural factors play important roles in enabling moments of class consciousness.

The "red thread" running through more than one hundred years of labor resistance and woven into the fabric of social life is reinforced by cultural identity—native-place, gender, ethnicity, and religion—that enabled such labor mobilizing and resistance in moments of crisis. From the comfort afforded by these aspects of cultural identity, class consciousness emerged during what I call "class moments." During these times of struggle, workers engaged in flexible types of resistance, including Polanyi resistance, Marxist resistance, and the use of law to demand not only their rights and entitlements, but also respect for their human dignity.

There are some unambiguous findings from the thirty-three protest cases (see Appendix B for a summary of these cases). Based on native-place bonding, migrant workers came together in both good times and times of struggle with fellow workers from the same birthplace. However, native place does not seem to play a role for local and commuter workers who did not explicitly remark about it. In many cases, workers tended to gather strength among workers of their own gender.

The split between Marx- and Polanyi-type protests that one might expect—that state workers would use Marx-type protests and private workers would rely on Polanyi-type protests—did not necessarily hold true. While state workers did use relatively more Marx-type rhetoric and actions (in ten out of eleven cases), they also used Polanyi-type resistance (three out of eleven cases). But the most interesting finding involves private workers—the growing section of the labor force in Vietnam—who utilized nearly equally *both* Marx-type (fifteen out of seventeen) and Polanyi-type (twelve out of seventeen) rhetoric and actions. Workers in all types of factories enacted the historical legacy of fighting for their rights as workers who demand respect and a living wage.

When each crisis passed, workers returned to their daily lives in their social communities, whether those communities were situated in their native places or in temporary housing away from home. Further research is needed to examine whether the class-consciousness experience changed the way these workers identified themselves once the crisis was over, and whether class consciousness, lingering on after "class moments" that involved collective action, remained an active part of the worker's agency, or whether this awareness returned to dormancy, to be called upon when the next crisis occurs.

Ninety-one percent of the workers used the law (in thirty of thirty-three cases), citing legal statutes in their arguments for labor justice. State and private workers fought for entitlements they had once received under the socialist system, and wanted those benefits restored. For the remaining three cases, workers either did not use the law or did not state it explicitly. While the state uses the law to govern labor–capital relations in the neoliberal era, workers and their allies (the labor newspapers and local unions) also use the law to crack open more space for their rights and benefits. In the twenty-first century, both state and nonstate workers have used legalistic language and appealed to legal remedies as their first line of offense and defense, in addition to using class-based language.

THE SIGNIFICANCE OF CULTURAL IDENTITY

To be sure, not all elements of cultural identity are central in every protest. Workers utilize what cultural resources are available to them at any particular moment. Native place is central for migrant workers, but it is not explicitly a part of the organizing or collective action for local workers. Similarly, ethnicity and religion play a role in some particular historical moments, but not in all.

For local workers, we can hypothesize that the sense of "native place" may take on various expressions, and be found in the workers' local community and through neighborhood support. There is some evidence that local support was significant in the Eagle Battery and the Vimytex cases. And the effectiveness of a general strike, such as the one in 1964 Saigon, also demonstrates the ability of those engaged in resistance to communicate through local networks.

Gender plays an important role in bringing workers together—women bond as sisters *and* men as brothers—both for local workers and for migrants toiling far away from home. There is also evidence of cross-ethnic gender solidarity present among the Hoa women workers and the Kinh women workers, who suffered the same exploitation and hardships and fought alongside one another (see the Eagle Battery and Vimytex factory cases).

In my analysis, I have linked ethnicity with gender and class to explain how Kinh workers organized and networked with Hoa workers, especially female workers (Chapter 2). Similar to their Kinh counterparts, the Hoa have always bonded together in their *đồng bang* (or similar kinship association), such as Phúc Kiến (Fukien) and Quảng Châu (Cantonese). To eliminate the misconception that all Hoa are "merchants" or "capitalists," I have introduced the perspectives of Hoa workers and labor organizers who fought alongside the Kinh workers in those struggles. Based on archival materials and interviews with two Hoa Communist cadres, Chapter 2 revealed how Hoa and Kinh workers, union organizers, and Communist cadres supported each other in their struggles in major factories in Saigon and Chợ Lớn ("big market") against the local managers and their supporters in the RVN and the United States governments.

In the *Đổi Mới* era, the issue of nationality—rather than ethnicity—is significant. We have seen that workers identified and publicized, insofar as they were able, the nationalities of the real capital owners in cases that involved "underground" factories purporting to be owned by Vietnamese, but which were, in fact, owned by foreign investors (such as Huê Phong, ThanhLoanThi Ltd., and Phú Sĩ), and that they exposed the labor violations in some foreign-direct investment factories (such as Quảng Việt, Haimin, Viva-Blast, and C & N).

Skill differences, based on socially constructed gender-based divisions of labor, historically have not divided workers engaged in a wide range of enterprises, from colonial French factories to modern-day global assembly lines. In the colonial French era, gender-based divisions of labor gave skilled male workers higher pay than less-skilled women workers. But the Vietnamese used this differentiation to their advantage: it gave some men flexibility to move about the factory, and thus increased their opportunities to organize all labor. One example can be seen in the actions of the night-shift male electricians at the Nam Định Textile Combine who distributed flyers to semi-skilled female weavers (Chapter 1). There was no evidence of an "aristocracy" (or hierarchy) of labor—divisions based on skill and level of organization. But the situation is more ambiguous in modern-day protests on the global assembly line, which requires primarily low skills, with the labor leaders and organizers operating mostly underground to prevent state and management suppression.

Historical legacy, tradition, and knowledge play important roles in facilitating migrant workers' protests with regard to state-foreign–joint ventures (the "hot Christmas" case in Choong Nam-Việt Thắng) or foreign-direct-investment factories (consider the Nam Định workers in the Shilla Bags and Top One cases). The Choong Nam-Việt Thắng workers' armband sit-down strike (Chapter 4) showed how elder workers used historical knowledge and evoked socialist ideology to obtain a modest victory. The two young Nam Định women workers led and participated in food-and-water boycotts that won better meals and potable water for the employees (Chapter 5). Workers today in strike-prone districts famous for their historical revolutionary activism (Củ Chi and Hóc Môn) fought (and continue to fight) against labor violations in many FDI factories (Chapter 5) and in "underground" factories (Chapter 6).

These struggles won only short-term economic gains, but they show that the workers' localized fight against foreign capital was not fragmented as a result of mobile capital and flexible accumulation, as David Harvey has cautioned in his portrait of the "postmodern" condition.[1] Moreover, as argued in those chapters, workers do have the "motivational power of tradition" in their protests in the modern-day market system.

[1] David Harvey, *The Condition of Postmodernity: An Enquiry into the Origins of Cultural Change* (Cambridge, MA, and Oxford: Blackwell, 1990).

On Consciousness

Conventional Marxist analyses of the labor process, worker consent, consciousness, and class struggle tend to focus on the point of production, ignoring the environment, social relationships, and conditions outside of work. As such, these analyses are incomplete and do not provide an adequate explanation for the collective actions of migrant workers—the majority of the Vietnamese manufacturing workforce.

To come full circle to the argument I made in Chapter 1 on Vietnamese worker protests under the colonial French, the conditions outside of work, such as cultural ties and practices, are as important as (if not more so than) conditions at the point of production, which lead to such worker responses as protests.[2] Migrant workers bring to the workplace their cultural resources that reflect connections to the histories of their native place. For migrant workers, there is a blurred boundary between work and home, so the internal–external distinction does not make sense in this context. In many cases, they migrate with their hometown friends and relatives, labor together in the factory, and share temporary living quarters, where together they compare notes about labor violations and injustices on the factory floor and discuss what needs to be done to restore justice. With this porous border between home and work, externally derived consciousness very much empowers internal consciousness to foment collective actions in critical times—class moments—as evidenced in Chapters 5 and 6.

In his 1985 study, Burawoy argues that workers cooperated in their own subordination (through their own complicity) due to their uncertainty about the outcomes of their work, such as outcomes from the piece-work and piece-rate system.[3] He contends that workers blamed themselves for mistakes made during the production process and did not think of alternative ways of organizing production.[4] Instead, they were absorbed and overwhelmed by daily work responsibilities and by differences in types of tasks, machinery, and supplementary wages and bonuses. Vietnamese workers, too, were caught up in the piece-rate system, which implicitly imposes overtime work, and acceded to those conditions in order to make ends meet (and to keep their jobs). But when comparing notes with their fellow migrant workers in their rental units late at night, these social gatherings help to raise consciousness, by way of sharing legal counsel on their rights and incubating labor organizing. Also, while it is true that most Vietnamese strikes did not change the capitalist production relations in the global supply chains, the workers successfully challenged the state and won some permanent changes that have benefited

---

[2] This is different from Burawoy's focus on conditions at the point of production, rather than those outside of the labor process. Michael Burawoy, *Manufacturing Consent: Changes in the Labor Process under Monopoly Capitalism* (Chicago, IL, and London: The University of Chicago Press, 1979), p. 156. However, Burawoy did acknowledge that we need to compare the responses of workers in a capitalist society with those in different political economic regimes (such as in Vietnam).

[3] Ibid., pp. 171–73.

[4] Michael Burawoy, *Politics of Production: Factory Regimes under Capitalism and Socialism* (Thetford, Norfolk: Verso, 1985). "In this way they were sucked into participating in their own brutalization." p. 172.

employees in both the foreign-direct-investment and domestic sectors (for instance, institutionalizing annual adjustments of the minimum wage tied to inflation rates).

Types of Consciousness: Not Just Class-Based

This book argues that different types of consciousness (as well as distinctions in class) exist among the workers, and that these types have not been adequately analyzed in labor studies. Neither Trần Văn Giàu nor E. P. Thompson recognized religion as a form of consciousness that could transcend class and ethnicity to mobilize people from all walks of life on behalf of the working poor. Religion, as part of cultural identity, played a role in labor organizing and protests during the Vietnam–United States war (1954–75). Catholic priests and lay people—many of whom had migrated from the North to the South at the time of the partitioning of the country in 1954—fomented *social-justice consciousness* in the Republic of Vietnam via the Young Catholic Worker movement and liberation theology.[5]

On behalf of the working poor, this group mobilized people from all walks of life, including workers, priests, lay people, students, Saigon parliamentary representatives, and lawyers. These progressive priests and lay people promoted broad-based social justice as a form of consciousness that fought for democracy (*dân chủ*) and people's welfare (*dân sinh*).[6] Under that banner, these progressive Catholics coexisted with the communist cadres who were planted in many factories in the RVN, working in concert to organize workers of all faiths to fight for social justice. However, it is important to note that significant historical conditions at that time— the urgent desire for peace and social justice that would end a brutal war—had helped foment alliances among these strange bedfellows.

Native-place bonding was important to this progressive religious movement, which centered on a resettled Vietnamese Catholic population, mostly from northern provinces such as Nam Định and Hà Nam, where high concentrations of Catholics had lived before the 1954 partition. So, the labor organizing carried out by these groups demonstrates how workers' cultural *and* religious identities made possible class moments that became important in their fight for their rights and human dignity.

Members of this religious progressive movement were able to rationalize its coexistence with Marxist ideology and its coordination with communist cadres embedded in factories in the South. The desire for social justice and for an end to the people's suffering, the wartime destruction, and police brutality at the height of the Vietnam-United States war had brought both left-leaning activists and clergy together based on their shared interests.[7]

---

[5] This progressive Vietnamese Catholic movement predated and then paralleled the evolution of the spiritually inspiring Latin American liberation theology movement, which supported labor activism during the war. "Kết Luận" [Conclusion], *Chọn* 6 (February 1971): 80–81. Also, see Vũ Xuân Hiểu, "Tường Thuật Vụ Tranh Chấp Giữa Công Nhân và Chủ Nhân Hãng Pin Con Ó" [Report of the Conflict between Workers and the Owner of the Eagle Battery Factory], *Chọn Special Issue: Một Bài Học Cho Công Nhân Và Nghiệp Đoàn: Vụ Pin Con Ó* [A Lesson for Workers and Trade Unions: The Case of the Eagle Battery Factory] (Saigon: Lê Văn Duyệt, 1971), p. 16.

[6] Trương Bá Cần, *Fifty Years Reflection: June 28, 1958 to June 28, 2008* (Ho Chi Minh City: n.p., 2008).

[7] In the context of Vietnamese labor organizing during the brutal Vietnam–United States war, the division had more to do with the ideological orientations within the Catholic Church in

Ample evidence shows the significance of the development of class consciousness throughout more than one hundred years of labor history in Vietnam. At times of crisis, the ties created by cultural identity brought workers together in "class moments" during which they became aware of belonging to the one working class and of their shared interests. What triggered those class moments—in times of crisis or desperation—was concern for the well-being and integrity of their fellow workers. Workers jumped into the fray because they could not allow, for example, fellow workers from their hometowns to be cheated by the Vietnamese recruiters (Phú Riềng rubber plantation case in the 1920s), their sisters from Nam Định to be beaten by the French line-leaders (1920s), or their fellow Catholic workers to be tortured by the Saigon military police (1960s). Then in 1971, fourteen female workers of different ethnicities (Kinh and Hoa) relied on sisterhood to protect each other from police brutality before, during, and after sharing jail time in Saigon. As described, through a quotation, in the "Prison Diaries of a Collective of Workers,"[8] the women workers' strong bond fostered a strong class consciousness: "Capital is still capital; the state is still the state. The state and capital are one. But we women workers found our love for each other more than ever."

Process of Consciousness

To what extent does class consciousness always develop during times of struggle, and to what extent is it created at the end of a struggle? Does the workers' class identity survive and persist after the struggle is over? In his reexamination of the argument he first made in 1978, E. P. Thompson became less deterministic about this class-consciousness formation process: "Class consciousness arises in different times and places, but never in just the same way"[9] and "No model can give us what ought to be the 'true' class formation for a certain 'stage' of process."[10] While this is a less deterministic argument than his earlier one, I still find a "teleological element" in Thompson's formulation; he still assumes that class consciousness tends to be achieved at the end of the process of struggle.[11]

In the case of Vietnam, poor working conditions by themselves do not explain how workers act collectively in moments of crisis. It is cultural bonding in workers' everyday activities that unites and prepares them for some forms of collective action. The turning points, as discussed throughout the book, were worker fatalities and the

---

Vietnam rather than differences between religions: the right-wing, anti-Communist clergy, and the progressive Catholic priests inspired by the Latin American–based liberation theology (see Chapter 2). Christopher Kauffman, "Politics, Programs, and Protests: Catholic Relief Services in Vietnam, 1954–1975," *The Catholic Historical Review* 91,2 (April 2005).

[8] Chọn, "Nhật Ký Trong Tù Của Tập Thể Công Nhân" [Prison Diaries of a Collective of Workers], 18,7 and 18,8 (October 1971).

[9] E. P. Thompson, "The Making of Class," in *Class*, ed. Patrick Joyce (Oxford and New York, NY: Oxford University Press, 1995), p. 131.

[10] Ibid., p. 137.

[11] Ira Katznelson points out that Thompson's conception of class is a "junction term," which lies at the intersection of structure and process, social being and social consciousness. She argues that "Thompson makes the movement from class structure to class action too certain a passage." Joyce, *Class*, p. 148. I agree with Katznelson about this teleological element of Thompson's formulation. Ira Katznelson, "Levels of Class Formation," in *Class*, ed. Patrick Joyce (Oxford and New York, NY: Oxford University Press, 1995), p. 148.

infliction of pain and humiliation on workers. Also, not earning even a living wage and not receiving adequate benefits propelled many workers to action for economic justice. Therefore, it is the combination of both factors—native place bonding and unbearable working conditions—that enables these class moments when workers act for a common cause. But this combined effect does not ensure that workers end up with class consciousness at the end of their struggle. The process of arriving at class consciousness is not linear and not preordained to emerge during a "last stage" or at the end of a process.

There were distinctions made and divisions maintained along ethnic (Kinh and Hoa) and religious (Catholic and Buddhist) lines in the 1960s and early 1970s. But as these workers struggled, stayed in jail, and suffered from police brutality together, they became aware of their shared grievances and identified themselves as members of a class distinct from management. During that process, they transcended their different cultural identities and fought as a group based on their shared interests and objectives.

The Language and Duration of "Class Moments"

As workers struggled together, the "we workers" language became more prominent, appealing to Vietnam's stated but eroding socialist ideology. Workers in both state and private factories referred to themselves and signed petitions and protest letters as *"công nhân"* ("industrial workers," a category energetically promoted by the state, by which the government aims to modernize and industrialize Vietnam), *tập thể người lao động* (collective of workers), or *anh chị em công nhân* (brother and sister workers). Laid-off workers in privatized state-owned factories (whose stories were reported by the labor journalists and in workers' own writings) reminded the state of its obligations to state workers: it must pay the mandated severance and early retirement compensations.

How long class moments are sustained after a class struggle reaches its conclusion remains to be seen. There is no guarantee that class consciousness would persist after workers leave a strike scene and return to their "normal" lives, in the factories or back to their hometowns or villages to build their families. What we know unambiguously is that during protests, class moments were in strong evidence in workers' letters, petitions, and graffiti messages, as well as in the labor journalists' reports. But, before we can assume a linear process of class consciousness, we need to interview these "strike veterans" to find out how they identify themselves in post-struggle situations.

ON FALSE CONSCIOUSNESS AND MANUFACTURING CONSENT

Not all workers arrived at consciousness during "class moments," but they did not succumb to "false consciousness," either. Most workers consider low-skilled, low-paying, and dead-end assembly jobs as temporary and do not stay in these jobs for more than several years. Such workers typically left their villages with big dreams, planning to send remittances to their families, to learn new skills to move up the employment ladder, to learn skills to prepare themselves for better jobs back in their home villages, and to save money to start a family wherever their futures led them. A number took advantage of their factory jobs. Some of the women I interviewed said that they learned new skills on the jobs, such as accounting and facility in the Chinese language, skills they could use to advance their careers, either in the same factories or elsewhere. Some labor organizers and strike leaders (like Nga in the Huê Phong case) stayed in the cities to work and lead the protests in various venues.

Workers whom I interviewed, as well as Vietnamese workers from the past hundred years, whom I studied, were not resigned to the social order in which they lived and did not regard it as being "natural or inevitable."[12] There is no evidence that they were partially blinded by false consciousness (in the "thin" version). Workers fought against slave-like conditions in the Dầu Tiếng and Phú Riềng rubber plantations under the colonial French; against the state–capitalist alliance and police brutality in the Eagle Battery case and Vimytex protests in the Republic of Vietnam; against the post-reform state when it failed to pay the one-time severance to laid-off state workers and other entitlements that state workers had received during the socialist era; against foreign capitalists, demanding that they pay the minimum wage and benefits stipulated in the legal contracts; and against underground foreign capital owners who ignored the higher FDI minimum wage and related benefits.

While workers consent to work on the factory floor within the minimum-wage and piece-rate structure, they do not work to reproduce "voluntary servitude,"[13] nor do they submit to the dictates of the labor process. To the workers, it is a matter of survival, a short-term sacrifice for a better future. They are not fooled by the "semblance of independence with [the] piece-rates" system;[14] many clearly point out that low wages are caused by low piece-rates that are based on the low minimum-wage requirement. So they fought and won government's commitment to the annual minimum-wage increase (for cost-of-living adjustments) in both the FDI and domestic sectors, and, as a result, the disparities between those sectors, insofar as wages are concerned, have been shrinking. In short, both FDI and domestic sector workers were *not* complicit in the subordination process.

Workers were and still are not resigned to the idea that their current working and living conditions were natural and inevitable. The thousands of strikes that have erupted since 1995, when they were first sanctioned, speak volumes about worker defiance. Workers confronted the "new owners" who now consist of foreign and domestic owners, as well as state managers (in equitized state-owned enterprises) in Vietnam's market socialism. Workers reminded these "new owners" to respect them and treat them fairly.

However, by appealing to the rule of law in those different eras, workers showed that they recognized the state and its apparatuses, such as the labor unions and the newspapers, in particular historical moments. To some extent, workers legitimized them. In doing so, the workers did not demand an alternative relationship with the state and its apparatuses, but accepted the one in force at the time. But they requested better treatment, such as a living wage that would keep up with crippling inflation. After all, workers struggled for their shared interests—not the state's—to sustain themselves for another day, another fight.

Are Vietnamese workers acting with false consciousness in their protests by using the rule of law as a weapon? Are they thereby legitimizing the state's existence

---

[12] James C. Scott, *Domination and the Arts of Resistance: Hidden Transcripts* (New Haven, CT, and London: Yale University Press, 1990).

[13] Burawoy, *Manufacturing Consent*, pp. 80–81.

[14] Burawoy, *Politics of Production*, p. 171.

and its power over them? The answers, based on this research, are complex and telling. Over the years, workers in Vietnam have used *all* of the strategies and tactics, including raising the legal flag and both Marx-type and Polanyi-type protests, that would help them to reach the goals of securing a living wage and the social and health benefits to which they were legally entitled. But workers' intentions are not to legitimize the state when they use the rule of law as a weapon. Rather, they use the state's legal framework to gain leverage for better working and living conditions. Is this false consciousness? I think not.

FLEXIBLE RESISTANCE IN VIETNAM

Flexible resistance in Vietnam encompasses an intermingling of Polanyi- and Marx-type protests and the use of law to confront both capitalist accumulation (achieved through the exploitation of workers and the appropriation of peasants' land) and state control. The Vietnamese workers are not "locked" into one way of protesting, but use a wide array of tools at their disposal: the labor code, the labor press, the labor unions, and relevant local and central authorities. What transpires on the ground, according to the workers' own descriptions, are flexible protests against "cicada" capital enterprises, which then trigger a chain of responses from the state ideological apparatuses. The workers' methods are diverse. They include strikes involving thousands, protest messages, graffiti sketched on lavatory walls, letters to newspaper editors, and petitions and complaints to the labor press, state media, and relevant authorities.

Workers used many forms of public and hidden resistance over the past century. They destroyed the young saplings in the colonial French rubber plantations, published and distributed *samizdat* (written by progressive Catholic priests and lay people in the RVN regimes), and petitioned and faced the court to demand legal entitlements in contemporary socialist Vietnam.

During opportune moments, workers broke the silence and moved from hidden transcript to open resistance.[15] Freetrend workers secretly wrote graffiti on the walls of women's lavatories; these acts led to open protests in the form of strikes joined by the thousands who demanded raises in the minimum wage, a victory that subsequently benefited workers in both the FDI and domestic sectors. The workers have been speaking loudly and clearly that their lives were not supposed to be this way in a workers' state; they are not willing to act as victims of any kind of capital, including state capital.

Workers even feigned ignorance to protect their labor organizers and/or protest leaders, most of whom operated in the shadows, underground, at their own risk. Resisting "below the line," some disguised leaders, such as the two Kiên Giang female friends, organized Huê Phong workers against management's illegal practices.[16] Their direct resistance successfully created an autonomous space in which workers could fight for their rights. But some FDI workers were suspicious of external organizers who came to mobilize them (such as in the Huê Phong case).

This was a real and justified fear, since the state intensified its overt surveillance efforts in the twenty-first century to suppress labor discontent by creating two types

---

[15] Scott, *Domination and the Arts of Resistance*, p. 206–7. He argues that at such moment of crossing the threshold to open resistance, a politically charged occasion will take place.

[16] Ibid., p. 198.

of cell systems: worker-self-management cells and social opinion cells, in the EPZs and worker rental units, especially in strike-prone districts. The state's intention has been to obtain information and monitor migrant workers' organizing activities in order to preempt the potential protests that it fears are being instigated by anti-communist forces outside of Vietnam. While I believe that the workers I interviewed knew the identities of their leaders and organizers, they never divulged that information to me; I totally respect their wise decision.

Unlike C. K. Lee's bifurcation, in which state workers fight for a social contract and migrant workers for a legal contract,[17] state *and* nonstate workers in Vietnam used both types of protests, especially after 1999 and the onset of equitization/privatization of the state sector, which resulted in a porous border between these two sectors.

In almost all written protests (disseminated by both state and nonstate workers), one sees *both* types of struggle: Polanyi and Marxist. When 250 state workers in a joint venture supported by Russian capital (the Việt Thắng-Vicoluch case) rose up collectively to fight for the wages and nonwage allowances they had received prior to the company's transformation, they cited the relevant laws and demanded respect from state officials. Thus they fought for their entitlements by citing both legal and socialist social contracts.[18] Also, class consciousness was not "muted" among Vietnamese migrant workers.[19] When workers in a domestic private shoe factory sent a handwritten petition signed as a "collective of workers" to complain about illegally excessive overtime, they identified themselves as members of a working class. In doing so, they demonstrated not only an understanding of one of the most relevant items in the labor code, but also expressed indignation at being treated as less than human beings.

Vietnamese workers evoke socialist ideology to remind the state to live up to its promise. This ideology effectively grants the state power to proclaim and act in the name of the workers.[20] In the late 1990s, the protest rhetoric of state workers in 100-percent-state-owned enterprises was more class based, expressing a sense of disillusionment with their own government's move away from the socialist ideology. State workers specifically called out some Party members who treated workers without respect after these Party members effectively joined the management teams overseeing production for the global capitalist economy.

State workers, well-versed in socialist rhetoric and conscious of the power of relevant state apparatuses, appealed to the labor press and labor courts, asking them to defend the very socialist values the state espoused. Workers wanted the state to restore nonwage allowances and benefits distributed in the bygone socialist era.

---

[17] C. K. Lee, *Against the Law: Labor Protests in China's Rustbelt and Sunbelt* (Berkeley, CA: University of California Press, 2007), pp. 10–11.

[18] Lee argued how Chinese state workers engaged in protests primarily for socialist social contract. Ibid., p. 71.

[19] Lee argues that migrant workers in China rarely see themselves as part of the working class but as peasants instead. Ibid., p. 195.

[20] This is similar to an argument made by Ann Anagnost, who analyzed a newspaper story about a Chinese villager who wanted to be recognized in a state competition as a member of a "law abiding household." Through his action, he effectively said this to the party secretary: "I have played your game up to this point, recognize me now—or forever lose this opportunity to use me to make visible your power." Ann Anagnost, *National Past-Times: Narrative, Representation, and Power in Modern China* (Durham, NC: Duke University Press: 1997), p. 114.

Those who were laid off during the equitization process appealed to the law to get their severance pay and compensation. But relatively young nonstate workers, who have little or no direct experience of living in a socialist regime, have also invoked socialist ideology in their various forms of struggle, as cited in this book. They reminded the state of its socialist social contract: "We are living in a socialist country, not in a regime where people exploit people," said a young worker from a private garment factory.

In the neoliberal era, flexible resistance occurs more often in public forums. As the state continues to give lip service to the rule of law, workers have complained in labor newspapers' columns about the very laws that aim at dividing them: migrant from local workers; workers in FDI factories from workers in domestic factories; and state laid-off workers from non-state workers.[21]

Many newspapers' articles have exposed how the household registration policy privileges urban residents over rural/migrant workers, and how the multi-tiered minimum wage policy divides labor not only by type of workers—FDI versus domestic workers—but also by location of factories—metropolitan versus rural areas. Together with the HCMC Labor Federation and the labor journalists, workers won a small victory: starting in May 2009, migrant workers could pay the same lower utilities rates as local residents.

CONCLUSION AND FUTURE RESEARCH

The Vietnamese state is caught in persistent contradictions with respect to the labor scene. It uses socialist pro-labor rhetoric but engages in labor suppression at times; it uses *the law* as an instrument of governance/legitimacy to integrate itself further into the global neoliberal system, yet it still claims to uphold its socialist values. The "fluctuating" modus operandi of the state, which generally exercises firm control over labor–management relations, is due to the fact that the state still wants to use its socialist pro-labor legacy to claim legitimacy in the name of workers. Therefore, at least in the cases involving economically motivated strikes, the state has not overtly suppressed labor protests when workers appealed to such ideologies. But the state has been cracking down ruthlessly on protesters when agents of the government judge that the workers' resistance was politically motivated.

With regard to future research, more comparative studies would engender a better understanding of the workers' plight and of their struggles in order to help improve the lives of these hard-working citizens of the world. Such comparative studies need to be contextualized in the globalization process. One important topic would be the effects of global labor migration—beyond rural–urban migration—on workers' lives and the lives of their families and communities. Another topic could be how local stakeholders negotiate with global enterprises and international non-governmental organizations (such as Oxfam Belgium Solidarity) and to what extent the locals internalize the implicit and explicit ideologies of these organizations. It will be important also to gain insight into the perspectives of (local and global) migrant workers who have returned to their hometowns or villages in order to gain a deeper understanding about the relationship between global forces and local responses, and workers' sense of class consciousness.

---

[21] See Louis Althusser's argument as discussed in Chapter 3.

It is important to understand the totality of workers' lives in order to understand how they organize and fight. Vietnamese workers are not victims of neoliberal, flexible accumulation in Vietnam. While toiling under exploitative working conditions, they do stand up for their dignity and better conditions, using whatever tools they have at their disposal to secure local and cultural support, obtain legal remedies, and avoid state suppression. Their journey has been one of ebbs and flows, but they have never failed to take up the challenge throughout over one hundred years of labor history.

I conclude with a worker's voice, two stanzas from a poem written by a female worker in Tân Bình district (Ho Chi Minh City), submitted to the *Người Lao Động* in January 2009. It evokes a sense of solidarity and pride, for the workers identify themselves as "blue-uniformed workers" (*công nhân áo xanh*), toiling and uniting on the assembly line:

The Workers and the Color of their Uniforms (Công Nhân Và Màu Áo)

No matter how many assembly steps there are
Assembling clothes or shoes
Cutting fabrics or applying glues
We are all blue-uniformed workers
Working in the same factory

A giant hand
Linking hands, joining forces
Building up this factory
Uniting wholeheartedly
Blending in our blue uniforms …

Appendix A

Glossary of Terms and Acronyms

AmCham: American Chamber of Commerce

CBA: Collective Bargaining Agreement

COMECON: Council for Mutual Economic Assistance (CMEA), an organization established in 1949 to facilitate economic development of the former Soviet bloc

CVT: *see CVTC*

CVTC: Confederation Vietnamienne du Travail Catholique (Vietnamese Confederation of Catholic Workers), founded in 1952; renamed Confederation Vietnamienne du Travail (CVT, Vietnamese Confederation of Workers) in 1964

DOLISA: Department of Labor, Invalids, and Social Affairs

DRV: Democratic Republic of Vietnam

EPZ: export processing zone

FDI: foreign direct investment

HCMC: Ho Chi Minh City

HCMCLF: Ho Chi Minh City Labor Federation

HEPZA: Ho Chi Minh City Export Processing Zones Authority

ILO: International Labor Organization

IZ: industrial zone

KT3: temporary residency permit

Lao Động: *Labor* newspaper

MOEA: Ministry of External Affairs

MOF: Ministry of Finance

MNC: multinational corporation

MOLISA: Ministry of Labor, Invalids, and Social Affairs

MPI: Ministry of Planning and Investment

Người Lao Động: *Laborer* newspaper

RTUF: Red Trade Union Federation

RVN: Republic of Vietnam

SOE: state-owned enterprise

TLC: Thanh Lao Công (Vietnamese Young Catholic Worker movement)

VCCI: Vietnamese Chamber of Commerce and Industry

VFTU: Vietnamese Federation of Trade Unions

VGCL: Vietnamese General Confederation of Labor (after 1975 under the Socialist Republic of Vietnam)

VINATEX: Vietnam National Textile and Garment Corporation Group

VCP: Vietnamese Communist Party

VITAS: Vietnam Textile and Apparel Association

APPENDIX B

THIRTY-THREE CASES CLASSIFIED BY PROTEST TYPE (BASED ON ARCHIVAL MATERIAL, 39-LETTER SAMPLE, AND WORKERS' INTERVIEWS)

Cases (year; status)	Marx/ Socialist	Polanyi	Use of Law	Chapter
Nam Định Textile (from 1926)	yes	yes	yes	1
Dầu Tiếng (from 1930)	yes	yes	yes	1
Phú Riềng (from 1927)	yes	yes	Yes	1
Vimytex (from 1962)	yes	yes	yes	2
Eagle Battery (1971)	yes	yes	yes	2
Tầu Cuốc joint-stock (2006)	yes, socialist contract	no	yes	4
Sagoda leather shoe (2005)	yes, socialist contract	no	yes	4
Bình An brick factory (2006)	yes	no	yes	4
Machine Assembly & Construction (2005)	yes, socialist contract	yes	yes	4
Bến Nghé Port (2006)	yes	yes	yes	4
X32 shoe, (military-owned) (2005)	implicit, socialist contract	no	yes	4

Cases (year; status)	Marx/ Socialist	Polanyi	Use of Law	Chapter
Construction Corp. No. 4 (2004)	no	unclear, too brief, not enough evidence	yes	4
Unnamed SOE (2005)	yes, socialist contract	implicit	yes	4
Choongnam-Việt Thắng (1993)	yes, socialist contract	no	no	4
Việt Thắng–Vicoluch (2006)	yes, socialist contract	no	yes	4
Việt Thắng Jeans Ltd. (2007, 2008)	yes, class action	no information	yes	4
Hoàn Cầu (1998, 2008)	yes	yes	yes (piece-rate, 2002; cicada, 2008)	5
Shilla Bags (2004)	yes	yes	yes	5
Top One (2004)	yes	yes	unclear	5
Freetrend (2005, 2008)	yes	yes	yes	5
Kollan (2005)	yes	no	yes	5
Quảng Việt (2004, 2008)	yes	yes	yes	5
Viva-Blast (2005)	yes	yes	yes	5
Haimin (from 2005)	yes	yes	yes	5
C&N Security Service (2005)	no	no	yes	5
Minh Nghệ shoe (2006)	yes, collective action	yes, dignity, justice	not explicit	6
Thời Ích electric/rubber (2005)	no	implicit	yes	6
Đông Á textile (2005)	yes, implicit: "collective benefits of all workers"	no	yes	6
Sơn Kim garment (2005)	yes: "we are living in a socialist country"	unclear	yes	6

Cases (year; status)	Marx/ Socialist	Polanyi	Use of Law	Chapter
Dịch Vụ-Bảo Vệ (security guard services) (2005)	yes, socialist contract	implicit	yes	6
Huê Phong (from 1997; foreign ownership with Vietnamese front)	yes: "I worked as one."	yes : "long-term social problems for workers"	yes	6
Thanh Loan Thi Ltd. (2006; foreign ownership with Vietnamese front)	yes: "us brothers"	yes: "our jobs are dangerous"	yes	6
Phú Sĩ Washing & Ironing (2005; foreign ownership with Vietnamese front)	yes: "collective of thirty workers"	yes: "forced to work until we drop"	yes	6

APPENDIX C

HUÊ PHONG FACTORY (1992–2008): A REPRESENTATIVE SAMPLE OF PROTESTS AND INTERVENTION BY THE MEDIA AND STATE AGENCIES

1992: Huê Phong factory established as being Vietnamese-owned because the first listed owner, Tô Gia Đương, received a certificate "of Vietnamese origin" issued by the MPI and the Ministry of External Affairs.

September 1997: The first worker-led strike against abuses by Taiwanese specialists on the Huê Phong assembly line; Taiwanese technical specialist (*chuyên gia kỹ thuật*) Liu Tien Kuang disciplined 120 workers by making them stand under the hot sun; this led to a spontaneous strike immediately afterwards by all workers. After that, this company was fined only VND 2.8 million (about US$182) by the Ho Chi Minh City (HCMC) labor investigator (*Chánh Thanh Tra Lao Động Thành Phố*) for an administrative offense.

September 2000: More than four thousand workers went on strike; some workers trashed the cafeteria and the flower beds. Many were laid off.

September 20, 2000: After the strike, Gò Vấp People's Committee created an Inter-departmental Investigation Team to investigate labor violations at the Huê Phong factory. After the investigation, Gò Vấp People's Committee decided to levy a fine on Huê Phong management of about VND 10 million (approximately US $650).

October 16, 2000: Twelve workers who were laid off for participating in the strike went on a hunger strike right in front of the factory; four hours later, seven workers fainted out of exhaustion. Most of them were women.

October 23, 2000: The VGCL (Vietnamese General Confederation of Labor) confirmed the need to sustain the Inter-departmental Investigation Team to monitor and discipline violations at Huê Phong in a timely manner.

November 2000: MOLISA (Ministry of Labor, Invalids, and Social Affairs) reinforced the Inter-departmental Investigation Team so it could enforce the law at this factory, but no fine was imposed. Phạm Ngọc Đoàn, Gò Vấp District Labor Union Director, commented at the time that such weak enforcement of the law only encourages the owners of Huê Phong to disrespect the law and to violate it.

December 2004: *Người Lao Động* article, *"Monitoring then left as is,"* criticized local state officials for their weak monitoring of Huê Phong management and for not enforcing the law, so that violations continued to be rampant.

June 3, 2005: More than two thousand workers went on strike. This time they not only messed up the cafeteria, but also destroyed some property on the factory floor and in the office. This was the seventh strike at Huê Phong since it started operating at the end of 1992.

2005: Articles from *Người Lao Động* critically assessed repeated violations and updated labor–management relations at this factory:
- June 6, 2005: "A Strange Tale at Huê Phong"
- July 2005: A series of articles on the ten-year anniversary of this factory's establishment, entitled: "Re-opened the file on underground investment at Huê Phong." The series included: "Creating wealth on the sweat of workers" (*Tạo phồn vinh trên mồ hôi của Người Lao Động*) (July 18, 2005); "Skidding on the road of violations" (*Trượt dài trên con đường sai phạm*) (July 20, 2005); and "The needle had emerged from the bag" (*Cây kim trong bọc đã thò ra …*) (July 21, 2005)

August 2005: HCMC People's Committee reinforced its Inter-departmental Investigation Team to investigate all aspects of Huê Phong.

October 2005: Investigating team announced its findings to Huê Phong management.

February 13–16, 2006: Thousands of workers went on strike.

February 2006: Management agreed to pay its workers VND 560,000 instead of VND 330,000 (domestic minimum wage). This was still lower than the FDI minimum wage (VND 870,000).

January 2007: *"Huê Phong factory owes VND 5.2 billion to social insurance funds"* article.

July 18, 2007: Huê Phong paid its debt of US$325,000 to the HCMC social insurance office.

March 2008: Huê Phong failed to raise wages and allowances according to the inflation-adjusted rates effective at the beginning of 2008. On March 13, 2008, four thousand workers went on strike over wage and bonus issues.[1] Then, Huê Phong promised to revise workers' overtime payment (based on the new inflation-adjusted rates) and to improve the quality of meals for workers.[2]

April 9–11, 2008: Many strikes erupted after workers received their salary on April 9 and found that nothing had changed: again, Huê Phong did not fulfill its promise made in March 2008. So, on April 11, workers went on strike again. Some radical workers went to different departments to mobilize fellow workers to join the strike and "threaten to beat them up" if they chose not to strike. But security forces had been fortified to prevent this from happening. Some workers broke a security guard's camera when he tried to take photos of the incident.[3]

---

[1] Yến Trinh and Quốc Thanh, "Đình công tại công ty Huê Phong (TP.HCM): Cần can thiệp mạnh!" [Strikes at Huê Phong (Ho Chi Minh City): Need to intervene forcefully!], April 26, 2008, http://tuoitre.vn/Chinh-tri-Xa-hoi/252763/Dinh-cong-tai-cong-ty-Hue-Phong-TPHCM-Can-can-thiep-manh.html, accessed March 2012.

[2] Hà Diu, "Công nhân Huê Phong lại đình công" [Huê Phong Workers Went on Strike Again], http://www.tin247.com/cong_nhan _hue_phong_lai_dinh_cong-1-5492.html and http://vietnamnet.vn/xahoi/2008/04/777989, accessed March 4, 2012.

[3] Ibid. and http://vietnamnet.vn/xahoi/2008/04/777989, accessed March 4, 2012.

April 12, 2008: More than three hundred workers in the cutting/pressing department started the strike and went around the factory to mobilize workers in other departments to join them. A pregnant worker was slightly injured during this recruitment process. Workers presented their case to the state inter-departmental team that came to resolve the conflict. The three factors that led to the strike were: (1) Unequal social security contributions: Huê Phong contributed to the HCMC social security fund based on paying workers only VND 330,000 per month, whereas workers had to contribute 6 percent of the then-official minimum wage (VND 540,000); (2) Management increased production quotas without providing adequate compensation. This issue is related to the labor-fluctuation problem corresponding to the Vietnamese Lunar New Year, when many migrant workers (from the North and South) do not return to work when scheduled, yet the daily quota for the whole assembly line remains the same, thus putting an unbearable burden on each of the remaining workers; and (3) the productivity allowance (designed to make workers work harder and faster) and other small allowances (such as perfect-attendance bonus) were inadequate and *not* included in workers' take-home salary. This resulted in a *smaller* worker salary base on which Huê Phong calculated its social security and health insurance contributions for workers.[4]

April 26, 2008: After the strike had lasted two weeks, one of the longest strikes in Vietnam since 1994, the three branches of officials in Gò Vấp district—the people's committee, the department of labor (DOLISA), and the district labor union—intervened to resolve this conflict. They understood the root cause of this long-term conflict. According to a HCMC DOLISA report, Huê Phong had been using an excuse to not respond to workers' requests: management claimed that, as a supplier, it had to seek the opinion of and approval from its corporate buyers (or "the brands"). Huê Phong's practice of dragging its feet and failing to fulfill its promises had frustrated workers time and time again. Moreover, in a report to the HCMC People's Committee, the HCMC DOLISA office argued that Huê Phong had skillfully transferred the responsibility to resolve labor–management conflicts to local Vietnamese state offices: "Company representative had intentionally allowed the strike to last this long to pressure local state offices to stabilize the local condition on their behalf. Now, their responsibility to workers has become that of the state management offices."[5]

April 27, 2008: Huê Phong announced its hard-line position and gave workers an ultimatum: from April 28 onward, if workers stopped work for five consecutive days without reason, management would cancel the labor contract with those workers.[6] On April 28, a security guard tried to convince about twenty workers to return to work. Instead, those workers immediately protested and incited hundreds of other workers to stop the machines and join the strike. No one destroyed anything during this period. Only a thousand workers (out of about 4,600 total) remained working until the end of that shift. But among the hundreds of workers who walked out of that factory, about two hundred resigned for fear of retribution from management. The article reported that those two hundred workers received all of their entitlements soon after their resignations. Overall, workers gained a short-term victory when Huê Phong

[4] M. Hương and Q. lâm, "Vụ đình công tại Công ty Huê Phong (quận Gò Vấp, TPHCM): Lan rộng toàn công ty" [The Case of Strike at Huê Phong Company (Gò Vấp District, Ho Chi Minh City): Spread throughout the Factory], *Lao Động*, April 13, 2008, http://www.baomoi.com/Home/LaoDong/www.sggp.org.vn/Vu-dinh-cong-tai-Cong-ty-Hue-Phong-quan-Go-Vap-TPHCM--Lan-rong-toan-cong-ty/1539152.epi, accessed March 4, 2012.

[5] Trinh and Thanh, "Đình công tại công ty Huê Phong (TP.HCM).

[6] Vĩnh Tùng, "Công ty Huê Phong ra "tối hậu thư," [Huê Phong Company Issued "an Ultimatum"], *Người Lao Động*, April 27, 2008, http://nld.com.vn/ 222826P0C1010/cong-ty-hue-phong-ra-toi-hau-thu.htm, accessed March 2012.

agreed to pay workers a supplement: each worker would receive between VND 100,000 to 250,000 per person per month, effective from August 2008 (averaging about twelve US cents).[7]

---

[7] Công Đòan page, "Công ty TNHH giày da Huê Phong—TPHCM: Gần 200 công nhân xin thôi việc," [Huê Phong Ltd. in Ho Chi Minh City: About 200 Workers Resigned], *Lao Động*, April 28, 2008, http://laodong.com.vn/Home/Cong-ty-TNHH-giay-da-Hue-Phong--TPHCM-Gan-200-cong-nhan-xin-thoi-viec/20084/86547.laodong, accessed March 2012.

APPENDIX D

DANH SÁCH CÔNG
TY NỢ BẢO HIỂM XÃ HỘI

Companies with Social Insurance debts in 2007–08 (in billions of VND)

Limited Shoe Anjin (S. Korea, $4.4)

Limited Dae Yun (Vietnam–S. Korea, $2.9)

Limited Kwang Nam (S. Korea, $2.8)

Global Cybersoft (joint-venture, Vietnam–US, $2.8)

Liên Hiệp Công Nghiệp Saeyoung (S. Korea, $2.3)

Top Royal Flash (Vietnam–Taiwan, $2.3)

AMW (Vietnam–Hong Kong, $2.2)

Limited Yesum Vina (Vietnam–S. Korea, $1.8)

Ilshinwomo (S. Korea, $1.4)

Garment Phúc Yên (Vietnam, > $1)

Saigon CAP (Vietnam–S. Korea, $.895)

Astro Saigon (Vietnam–S. Korea, $.845)

H.World Vina Shoes (S. Korea, $.831)

Lucky (Vietnam–S. Korea, $.729)

Textile Hanshin Vina (Vietnam– S. Korea, $.659)

Limited Garment Dục Quân (Taiwan, $.603)

Liên Hiệp Công Nghiệp Sea Young (Gò Vấp—HCMC, amount unknown)

From 2011 through November 2012, the situation did not improve. It is increasingly difficult to determine the origins of owners/investors from public records, that is, whether the debtor firms are foreign- or domestic-owned. The majority of the twenty-three companies for which I found records (HCMC Social Security Accounts Receivable Office, November 2011–November 2012) still owed almost VND 30 billion. Of these twenty-three cases, only three companies paid all their debts. Among the others, three East Asian owners fled the country, and, in the case of two Vietnamese-owned companies, the owners were classified as: "enterprise owner gone hiding" (*chủ doanh nghiệp bỏ trốn*) or "unit not showing up to a district court" (*đơn vị không đến*).

Sources: Phạm Hồ, November 26, 2007 (citing HCMC Social Security Office); Nam Dương, February 18, 2008; HCMC Social Security–Account Receivables Office (Bảo Hiểm Xã Hội Thành Phố Hồ Chí Minh–Phòng Thu), through November 2012.

SELECTED BIBLIOGRAPHY

Althusser, Louis. "Ideology and Ideological State Apparatuses," in *Lenin and Philosophy, and Other Essays*, trans. Ben Brewster. New York, NY, and London: Monthly Review Press, 1970.

American Chamber of Commerce in Vietnam. "Letter to National Labour Relations Committee (NLRC) and other interested agencies re proposed amendments to Labour Code w Attachment (Eng)." July 18, 2011. Accessed September 19, 2012. http://www.amchamvietnam.com/download/1525

———. "National Employers Conference 2011–Labour Code Revision (AmCham Statement) on Industrial Relations and Labour Code Revision." Hà Nội: National Employers Conference. October 24, 2011. Accessed June 2012. http://www.amchamvietnam.com/5063

Anagnost, Ann. *National Past-Times: Narrative, Representation, and Power in Modern China*. Durham, NC: Duke University Press, 1997.

Balme, Stéphanie and Mark Sidel, eds. *Vietnam's New Order: International Perspectives on the State and Reform in Vietnam*. CERI Series in International Relations and Political Economy. New York, NY: Palgrave Macmillan, 2006.

Ban Bí Thư Trung Ương [Secretary of the Central Committee]. *Chỉ Thị 22 Về Xây Dựng Quan Hệ Lao Động Hài Hoà, Ổn Định, Tiến Bộ Trong Doanh Nghiệp* [Directive No. 22-CT/TW of the Central Committee of the Party: On the Development of Harmonious, Stable, and Progressive Labor Relations in Enterprises]. Paragraph No. 7, 2. Hà Nội: Central Committee of the Communist Party of Vietnam. June 5, 2008. Accessed July 2009. http://amchamvietnam.com/3451

Báo Dân Trí. "Hộ Khẩu KT3, Công Dân Thiệt Đủ Đường" [KT3 Household Registration Policy, Migrant Workers Got Shortchanged in Every Way]. May 8, 2005. Accessed June 8, 2009. http://dantri.com.vn/c20/s20-54015/ho-khau-kt3-cong-dan-thiet-du-duong.htm

Báo VietNamNet. "Công Ty Kwang Nam Xin Miễn 2,4 Tỷ Đồng Nợ BHXH" [Kwang Nam Company Asked to be Exempted from Its 2.4 billion VND Social Insurance Debt], September 21, 2004. Accessed June 2010. http://vietnamnet.vn/xahoi/laodong/2004/09/261765/

Barton, Clifton. "Trust and Credit: Some Observations Regarding Business Strategies of Overseas Chinese Traders in South Vietnam." In *The Chinese in Southeast Asia, Volume 1: Ethnicity and Economic Activity*, ed. Linda Y. C. Lim and Peter Gosling, 46–64. Singapore: Maruzen Asia, 1983.

BBC–Vietnamese section. "Phản Ứng Sau Phiên Xử Ba Nhà Hoạt Động Trẻ" [Reactions after the Trial of the Three Young Activists]. October 27, 2010. Accessed November 2010. http://www.bbc.co.uk/vietnamese/mobile/vietnam/2010/10/101027_activist_trial_reax.shtml?page=all#page2

BBC-Vietnamese section. "Một Vạn Công Nhân Đình Công Ở Trà Vinh" [Ten Thousand Workers Went on Strike in Trà Vinh]. February 2, 2010. Accessed November 2, 2010. http://www.bbc.co.uk/vietnamese/vietnam/2010/02/100202_labour_strike.shtml

Bellin, Eva R. "Contingent Democrats: Industrialists, Labor, and Democratization in Late-Developing Countries." *World Politics* 52, no. 2 (January 2000): 175–205.

Beresford, Melanie. *National Unification and Economic Development in Vietnam*. New York, NY: St. Martin's Press, 1989.

———. "Review of Carlyle A. Thayer and David G. Marr, *Vietnam and the Rule of Law*." *The Journal of Asian Studies* 54, no. 3 (August 1995): 910–12.

——— and Đặng Phong. *Economic Transition in Vietnam: Trade and Aid in the Demise of a Centrally Planned Economy*. Cheltenham: Edward Elgar, 2000.

——— and Chris Nyland. "The Labour Movement of Vietnam." *Labour History* 75 (November 1998): 57–80.

Bộ Lao Động [The Labor Ministry]. *Vài Hoạt Động Quan Trọng: 1965–1969* [Several Important Activities: 1965–1969]. Saigon: Labor Ministry, n.d.

Bradsher, Keith. "Investors Seek Asian Options to Costly China." *New York Times*, June 18, 2008. Accessed July 2010. http://www.nytimes.com/2008/06/18/business/worldbusiness/18invest.html?pagewanted=all&_r=0

Braverman, Harry. *Labor and Monopoly Capital: The Degradation of Work in the Twentieth Century*. New York, NY: Monthly Review Press, 1974.

Brown, Irving. "Memorandum to George Meany; Subject: South Vietnam, June 1, 1964." In *Reports*. Jay Lovestone's Collection. Stanford, CA: Hoover Institution Library and Archives, February 6, 1968, and March 26, 1968.

Bùi Thị Thanh Hà. *Công Nhân Công Nghiệp Trong Các Doanh Nghiệp Liên Doanh ở Nước Ta Thời Kỳ Đổi Mới* [Industrial Workers in Joint-Ventures in Vietnam in the Renovation Era]. Hà Nội: Social Science Publishing House, 2003.

Bùi Văn Toản. *Đấu Tranh Cánh Mạng của Đồng Bào Hoa Saigon–Thành Phố Hồ Chí Minh* [Revolutionary Struggle of the Hoa in Saigon—Hồ Chí Minh City]. Hồ Chí Minh City: Nhà Xuất Bản Trẻ, 2005.

Burawoy, Michael. *Manufacturing Consent: Changes in the Labor Process under Monopoly Capitalism*. Chicago, IL, and London: The University of Chicago Press, 1979.

———. *Politics of Production: Factory Regimes under Capitalism and Socialism*. Thetford, Norfolk: Verso, 1985.

Bureau for Asia, Agency for International Development. "Industry: United States Economic Assistance to Viet Nam, 1954–1975." *Viet Nam Terminal Report*. Washington, DC: Agency for International Development, December 1975.

Bửu Hoàn. "A Study of the Consequences of the Geneva Peace for the Vietnamese Economy," *Far Eastern Economic Review* XXV, no. 24 (December 11, 1958): 753–57; XXV, no. 25 (December 18, 1958): 789–98; and XXV, no. 26 (December 25, 1958): 839–42.

Camara, Helder. *Spiral of Violence.* London: Sheed and Ward Stagbooks Ltd., 1971.

Ca Dao Truyền Miệng Của Công Nhân Kêu Gọi Đấu Tranh Chống Chủ Tây Đánh Thợ [Oral Popular Poem of Workers Mobilizing Protest against the French Boss Hitting a Co-Worker]. Nam Định: Nam Định Archives, 1928.

Cao Văn Lượng. *Công Nhân Miền Nam Việt Nam Trong Cuộc Kháng Chiến Chống Mỹ Cứu Nước (1954–75)* [Workers in the South of Vietnam in the Anti-American Resistance to Save the Country (1954–75)]. Hà Nội: Nhà Xuất Bản Khoa Học Xã Hội, 1977.

Chae, Suhong. "Spinning Work and Weaving Life: The Politics of Production in a Capitalistic Multinational Textile Factory in Vietnam." PhD dissertation, City University of New York, 2003.

Chan, Anita, ed. *Vietnam Update Series: Labour in Vietnam.* Singapore: Institute of Southeast Asian Studies, 2011.

Chân Không. *Learning True Love: How I Learned and Practiced Social Change in Vietnam.* Berkeley, CA: Parallax Press, 1993.

Cheng, Tiejun and Mark Selden. "The Origins and Social Consequences of China's Hukou System." *The China Quarterly* 139 (September 1994): 644–68.

Chesneaux, Jean. "Stages in the Development of the Vietnam National Movement 1862–1940." *Past and Present* 7 (April 1955): 63–75.

China Political History Database. "China's External Relations—A History." Accessed April 2012. http://www.chinaforeignrelations.net/taxonomy/term/4

———. Convention of Tientsin [Tianjin], 1886 (Ratified by France by the Law of 30 November 1888). Accessed April 2012. http://www.chinaforeignrelations.net/node/165

———. "Treaty of Peace, Friendship, and Commerce between France and China [1885]." Accessed April 2012. http://www.chinaforeignrelations.net/node/164

Chọn. "Nhật Ký Trong Tù Của Tập Thể Công Nhân" [Prison Diaries of a Collective of Workers]. 18, no. 7–8 (October 1971): 25–39.

———. "Kết Luận" [Conclusion]. 6 (February 1971): 71–82.

Clarke, Simon, Chang-Hee Lee, and Đỗ Quỳnh Chi. "From Rights to Interests: The Challenge of Industrial Relations in Vietnam." *Journal of Industrial Relations* 49, no. 4 (2007): 545–68.

Cleary, Mark. "Land Codes and the State in French Cochinchina c. 1900–1940," *Journal of Historical Geography* 29 (July 2003): 356–75.

Coe, Neil, Philip Kelly, and Kris Olds. "Globalization, Transnationalism, and the Asia-Pacific." In *Remaking the Global Economy: Economic–Geographical Perspectives*, ed. Jamie Peck and Henry Wai-chung Yeung, 45–60. London: Sage Publications, 2003.

Comaroff, Jean and John L. Comaroff. "Millennial Capitalism: First Thoughts on a Second Coming." *Public Culture* 12, no. 2 (2000): 291–343. Accessed August 6, 2012. http://publicculture.dukejournals.org/content/12/2/291.full.pdf+html

Công Nhân Xưởng Dệt. *Bản Dịch Đơn Của Công Nhân Xưởng Dệt* [Translation of the Petition of Workers in the Weaving Plant]. Nam Định: Nam Định Archives, August 30, 1926.

Công Ty Tránh Nhiệm Hữu Hạn, Giày Da Huê Phong. "Báo Cáo Nguyên Nhân Và Cách Xử Lý Đình Công" [Report on the Causes and Ways to Resolve Strikes]. In *Hội Thảo Tranh Chấp Lao Động* [Conference on Labor Strikes]. Hồ Chí Minh City: Gò Vấp People's Committee, June 14, 2003.

Coy, Kevin J. "Colonel Edward Geary Lansdale and the Saigon Military Mission: The CIA in Vietnam, 1954–1955." *4th Triennial Symposium* (Lubbock, TX: Texas Tech University Vietnam Center, 2002). Accessed July 20, 2009. http://www.vietnam.ttu.edu/vietnamcenter/events/2002_Symposium/2002Papers_files/coy.htm#_ftn32

Dân Trí. "HCM City: Low Salaries Prompt Kindergarten Teachers to Give up Jobs." *VietnamNet Bridge*, May 27, 2008. Accessed June 2008. http://english.vietnamnet.vn/education/2008/05/785163/

Deitch, Joanne Weisman. *The Lowell Mill Girls: Life in the Factory—Perspectives on History Series*. Lowell, MA: Discovery Enterprises Ltd., 1991.

Department of Labor, Invalids, and Social Affairs (DOLISA). "Tình Hình Tranh Chấp Lao Động Trên Địa Bàn Quận Gò Vấp Từ Năm 2000 Đến Tháng 6/2003" [The Strike Situation in the Gò Vấp Vicinity from 2000 to June 2003]. *Tham luận của Phòng Lao Động—Thương Binh Xã Hội Quận Gò Vấp* [Proceedings of Gò Vấp DOLISA]. Hồ Chí Minh City: Gò Vấp People's Committee.

Định Á. *Bắt Được Cờ Đỏ Tại Nhà Máy Sợi* [Found a Red Flag at the Fiber Factory]. Nam Định: Nam Định Archives, March 18, 1930.

Đinh Lực. *Lịch Sử Đảng Cộng Sản Việt Nam, Tập 1* [History of the Vietnamese Communist Party, Volume 1]. Hà Nội: Nhà Xuất Bản Chính Trị Quốc Gia, 1993.

Đỗ Quang Hưng. *Công Hội Đỏ Việt Nam* [The Vietnamese Red Trade Union]. Hà Nội: Labor Publisher, 2004.

Đỗ Viết Hải. "Điều Kiện Và Thủ Tục Làm KT3" [Conditions and Procedure to Obtain KT3], Đoàn Luật Sư Thành Phố Hà Nội [The Lawyers Syndicate in Hà Nội City]. *Thu Vien Phap Luat*, June 2, 2012. Accessed November 2012. http://danluat.thuvienphapluat.vn/dieu-kien-va-thu-tuc-lam-kt3-69863.aspx#190854.

Đoàn Loan. "Hơn 19.000 Người Nhập Cư Sẽ Được Cấp Thẻ Công Dân" [Over 19,000 Migrant Workers Will be Issued Citizenship Cards]. *VNExpress*, June 7, 2006. Accessed June 8, 2009. http://www.vnexpress.net/GL/Xa-hoi/2006/06/3B9EA8C3/

"Đồng Bào Người Hoa ở Sài Gòn Đấu Tranh Chống Mỹ–Ngụy" [The Hoa in Saigon Fought against the Americans and the South Vietnamese Army]. In *Chung Một Bóng Cờ Và Lịch Sử Sài Gòn—Chợ Lớn Kháng Chiến 1945–1975*. Hà Nội: Chính trị Quốc gia Press, 1995). Accessed July 2008. www.hochiminhcity.gov.vn/left/ gioi_thieu/lich_su_van_hoa/lich_su/tp_chung_nhan_cua_dong_chay_ls/khang_ chien_chong_my/nguoihoa.htm?left_menu=1

Dương Minh Đức. "Sẽ Cưỡng Chế, Phát Mại Tài Sản Các DN Nợ BHXH" [Will Impose the Liquidation of the Property of the Companies that Owed Workers' Social Insurance]. *Lao Động*, April 3, 2008. Accessed July 2008. http://www. laodong.com.vn/Utilities/PrintView.aspx?ID=82930

———. "'Nát Bấy' Dự Thảo!" [Completely Destroyed Proposal!]. *Lao Động*, March 27, 2010. Accessed June 2010. http://www.laodong.com.vn/Utilities/PrintView. aspx?ID=178942

"Establishing of AID-supported and AFL-CIO-sponsored Institute to Strengthen CVT Participation in Rural and Revolutionary Development." Jay Lovestone's Collection, Stanford, CA: Hoover Institution Library and Archives.

Evans, Mark and Bùi Đức Hải. "Embedding Neoliberalism through Statecraft: The Case of Market Reform in Vietnam." In *Internalizing Globalization: The Rise of Neoliberalism and the Decline of National Varieties of Capitalism*, ed. Susanne Soederberg, Georg Menz, and Philip Cerny. Hampshire: Palgrave Macmillan, 2006.

Fforde, Adam and Stefan De Vylder. *From Plan to Market: The Economic Transition in Vietnam*. Boulder, CO: Westview Press, 1996.

Flanders, Laura. "Workers vs. Investors: Chicago Window Factory in Danger of Liquidation." *The Nation*, July 4, 2012. Accessed January 2013. www.thenation. com/blog/168727/workers-vs-investors-famous-windows-factory-danger- liquidation

Foreign Investment Agency, Ministry of Planning and Investment. "20 Năm Đầu Tư Nước Ngoài Tại Việt Nam (1988–2007)" [Twenty Years of FDI in Vietnam (1988– 2007)]. MPI March 22, 2008. Accessed August 2010. http://fia.mpi.gov.vn/ News.aspx?ctl=newsdetail&p=2.44&aID=507

———. "Đầu Tư Trực Tiếp Nước Ngoài Vào Việt Nam Năm 2009" [Direct Foreign Investment in Vietnam in 2009]. Accessed July 2010. http://fia.mpi.gov.vn/ Default.aspx?ctl=Article2&TabID=4&mID=265&aID =877

G. H. "Nhọc Nhằn Lao Động Nhập Cư" [Arduous Work of Migrant Workers]. *Lao Động*, December 4, 2006. Accessed June 2009. http://www.laodong.com.vn/ Utilities/PrintView.aspx?ID=13668.

Gillespie, John. "Understanding Legality in Vietnam." In *Vietnam's New Order*, ed. Balme and Sidel. 137–61.

Greenfield, Gerard. "The Development of Capitalism in Vietnam." In *Socialist Register 1994: Between Globalism and Nationalism*, ed. Ralph Miliband and Leo Panitch. 202–34. London: The Merlin Press, Ltd., 1994.

Hà Dịu. "Nhọc Nhằn Đời Lao Động Nhập Cư" [Hardships of the Life of Migrant Workers]. *Báo VietNamNet*, May 1, 2008. Accessed June 2009. http://www.Vietnamnet.vn/service/ printversion.vnn?article_id=1057357

Hansen, Peter. "The Virgin Heads South: Northern Catholic Refugees in South Vietnam, 1954–1964." PhD dissertation, Melbourne College of Divinity, 2009.

Hansson, Eva. *Trade Unions and Đổi Mới: The Changing Role of Trade Unions in the Era of Economic Liberalization in Vietnam*. Politics of Development Group for Stockholm University (PODSU) series, no. 2. Stockholm: Department of Political Science, Stockholm University, 1995.

Harianto, Farid. "Business Linkages and Chinese Entrepreneurs in Southeast Asia." In *Culture and Economy: The Shaping of Capitalism in Eastern Asia*, ed. Timothy Brook and Hy Van Luong. 137–54. Ann Arbor, MI: University of Michigan Press, 1997.

Harvey, David. *The Condition of Postmodernity: An Enquiry into the Origins of Cultural Change*. Cambridge, MA, and Oxford: Blackwell, 1990.

Heng, Russell. "Media in Vietnam and the Structure of its Management." In *Mass Media in Vietnam*, ed. David Marr. 27–53. Canberra: Australian National University, 1998.

Hồ Chí Minh City Labor Federation. "Báo Cáo: Tình Hình Công Nhân, Viên Chức, Lao Động Và Hoạt Động Công đoàn Thành phố 6 Tháng Đầu Năm 2012 [Report on The Conditions of Workers, Public Employees, and City Union Activities in the First Six Months of 2012].

———. "Phương Hướng Hoạt Động 6 Tháng Cuối Năm 2012" [Report on the Directions for Activities in the Last Six Months of 2012].

———. "Báo Cáo Tình hình Tranh Chấp Lao Động Tập Thể" [Report on the Situation in Collective Labor Conflicts]. 1995 to 2011.

Hồ Ngọc Nhuận. "Tại Sao Chính Quyền Can Thiệp?" [Why the Government Intervened?]. *Chọn Special Issue* (1971): 40–55.

Hồ Sơn Đài. "Introduction." In *Lịch Sử Phong Trào Công Nhân Cao Su Dầu Tiếng* [History of the Labor Movement in Dầu Tiếng Rubber Plantation], ed. Lê Văn Khoa, 14–17. Hồ Chí Minh City: Nhà Xuất Bản Lao Động, 2000.

Hoàng Hà. "Đồng Loạt Điều Chỉnh Lương Tối Thiểu Từ Ngày 1-1-2011" [Uniformly Adjusting the Minimum Wage from January 1, 2011]. *Người Lao Động*. November 9, 2010. Accessed November 10, 2010. http://nld.com.vn/20101109015453591 P0C1010/dong-loat-dieu-chinh-luong-toi-thieu-tu-ngay-112011.htm

Hoàng Lan. "Người Nước Ngoài Được Cấp Sổ Hồng, Sổ Đỏ Trong 30 Ngày" [Foreign Citizens Can Obtain the Red Cards within Thirty Days]. *VNExpress.net* June 8, 2009. Accessed June 15, 2009. http://www.vnexpress.net/GL/Kinh-doanh/Bat-Dong-san/2009/06/3BA0FE33/?q=1

Hoàng Quốc Việt. *The Trade Union Movement in Vietnam*. Hà Nội: Foreign Languages Publishing House/Vietnam Federation of Trade Unions, 1988.

Hoành Anh and Văn Nguyễn. "Chỉ Có Gió Và Cỏ: Tan Giấc Mơ Công Nhân" [Only Wind and (Wild) Grass: Gone with the Dream of Being Workers]. *Báo Nông nghiệp Việt Nam*. February 29, 2012. Accessed March 2012. http://nongnghiep. vn/nongnghiepvn/72/149/150/91008/Tan-giac-mo-cong-nhan-.aspx

Hương, M., and Q. Lâm. "Vụ Đình Công Tại Công ty Huê Phong (quận Gò Vấp, TPHCM)—Lan Rộng Toàn Công Ty" [Strike at Huê Phong Company (Gò Vấp, HCMC)—Spread to the Whole Factory]. *Baomoi.com*. April 13, 2008. Accessed March 2012. http://www.baomoi.com/Home/LaoDong/www.sggp.org. vn/Vu-dinh-cong-tai-Cong-ty-Hue-Phong-quan-Go-Vap-TPHCM--Lan-rong-toan-cong-ty/15 39152.epi

Hồng Đào. "Đối Mặt Với Tăng Giá" [Facing Rising Costs]. *Người Lao Động*. April 13, 2009. Accessed May 2009. http://nld.com. vn/20090412095249576P0C1010/doi-mat-voi-tang-gia.htm

———. "Đã Tặng 22 Tủ Sách Công Nhân" [Already Donated 22 Book Shelves (with books) for Workers]. *Người Lao Động*, December 29, 2006. http://nld.com.vn/ 175709P0C1010/da-tang-22-tu-sach-cong-nhan.htm

Huỳnh Ngọc Trảng. "Người Hoa ở Thành Phố Hồ Chí Minh" [The Hoa in Hồ Chí Minh City]. *Người Hoa Tại Thành Phố Hồ Chí Minh*. Nhà Xuất Bản Sở Văn Hoá Thông Tin, 2007.

Huỳnh Thị Ngọc Tuyết. "Báo Cáo Kết Quả Cuộc Khảo Sát Về 'Phòng Chống Mua Bán Phụ Nữ—Trẻ Em' và 'Tăng Cường Trách Nhiệm Xã Hội" [Findings of the Survey on the Trafficking of Women and Children and Strengthening Social Responsibility]. Hồ Chí Minh City: Gò Vấp District People's Committee, ActionAid Vietnam [Southern Office], and Development Assistance Project, 2005.

———. Nguyễn Thị Minh Châu, and Vũ Ngọc Hà. "Dự Án Tăng Cường Tiếp Cận Thông Tin Và Tư Vấn Pháp Luật Cho Người Lao Động Nhập Cư Của Tỉnh Đồng Nai" [Increasing Access to Information and Legal Assistance to Migrant Workers in Đồng Nai Province]. *Project Midterm Report*, August 2012.

The Indochina Communist Party. *Hỡi Anh Chị Em Thợ Thuyền Binh Lính và Nông Dân"* [To Brothers, Sisters, Workers, Soldiers, and Peasants]. Nam Định Nam: Định Archives, October 20, 1930.

Indochina International Consulting Co., LTD. Industrial Park and Investment Information Consulting Portal. Vietnam Industrial Parks Investment Promotion. Accessed June 6, 2012. http://viipip.com/homeen/?module=listip.

"Industrial Development of Vietnam," *Vietnam Information Series 5*. Washington, DC: Embassy of Vietnam, September 1969.

Intelligence Report: The Situation in South Vietnam. Central Intelligence Agency (CIA) Directorate of Intelligence. August 15, 1966.

The International Textile Garments and Leather Workers Federation. "A Collection of Success Stories in Organizing Women Workers and Trade Union Rights in the Philippine Export Processing Zones (EPZs)." Manila: ILO. December 2003. Accessed July 19, 2012. www.itglwf.org/docs/EPZStudy.doc

Jacobs, Seth. *Cold War Mandarin: Ngo Dinh Diem and the Origins of America's War in Vietnam, 1950–1963*. New York, NY: Rowman & Littlefield Publishers, 2006.

Joyce, Patrick, ed. *Class.* Oxford and New York, NY: Oxford University Press, 1995.

K. An. "Quận Gò Vấp—TPHCM: 21.508 Công Nhân Mua Điện Đúng Giá" [Gò Vấp District—HCMC: 21,508 Workers Paid Electricity at the Right Price]. *Người Lao Động,* October 13, 2010. http://nld.com.vn/20101012111539418P0C1010/21508-cong-nhan-mua-dien-dung-gia.htm

Kabeer, Naila. "Globalization, Labor Standards, and Women's Rights: Dilemmas of Collective (In)action in an Interdependent World." *Feminist Economics* (March 10, 2004): 3–35.

Karadjis, Michael. "State Enterprise Workers: 'Masters' or 'Commodities'?" In *Vietnam Update Series: Labour in Vietnam,* ed. Chan. 46–90.

Katznelson, Ira. "Levels of Class Formation." In *Class,* ed. Joyce. 142–49.

Kauffman, Christopher. "Politics, Programs, and Protests: Catholic Relief Services in Vietnam, 1954–1975." *The Catholic Historical Review* 91, no. 2 (April 2005): 223–51.

Kerkvliet, Benedict J. Tria. "Workers' Protests in Contemporary Vietnam." In *Vietnam Update Series: Labour in Vietnam,* ed. Chan. 160–210.

Kerkvliet, Melinda Tria. "Life Stories of Retired Workers in Hà Nội." *Proceedings of the EUROVIET III Bi-Annual Conference.* Amsterdam, July 2–4, 1997.

Khánh Bình. "Trốn, Né Đóng Bảo Hiểm Xã Hội: Chưa Có Thuốc Đặc Trị" [Evading and Avoiding Paying Social Insurance (for Workers): Still Lacking Special Solution]. *Saigon Giải Phóng,* July 2004. Accessed July 2006. http://www.sggp.org.vn/xahoi/nam2004/thang7/6991/

Khánh Chi. "Nắm Bắt Tâm Tư, Nguyện Vọng CN Tổ Tự Quản." *Người Lao Động,* September 28, 2010. Accessed November 5, 2010. http://nld.com.vn/201009280 21218209P0C1010/nam-bat-tam-tu-nguyen-vong-cn-to-tu-quan.htm

Kim, Chong-se. "The Economic Settlement of the Vietnam War: An Analysis of the Economic Impact of a Possible Truce." *International Studies Seoul* (December 1970): 100–114.

Kim, Jee Young. "How Does Enterprise Ownership Matter? Labor Conditions in Fashion and Footwear Factories in Southern Vietnam." In *Vietnam Update Series: Labour in Vietnam,* ed. Chan. 278–308.

Koh, David. "Law, Ethics, and Political Legitimacy." In *Vietnam's New Order,* ed. Balme and Sidel. 217–36.

Kuey, Tsai Maw. "Người Hoa Ở Miền Nam Việt Nam" [The Hoa in the South of Vietnam]. PhD Dissertation, Sorbonne University, 1968. Saigon: Bô Quốc Gia Giáo Dục; Ủy Ban Nghiên Cứu Sử Học Và Khoa Học [Ministry of Education; Committee on Research on History and Science].

Lam, Tom. "The Exodus of Hoa Refugees from Vietnam and their Settlement in Guangxi: China's Refugee Settlement Strategies." *Journal of Refugee Studies* 13, no. 4 (2000): 374–90.

Langguth, Jack. "A Labor Dispute in Saigon Easing: Appears Resolved by Mill's Concessions to Workers." *New York Times*. October 7, 1964.

Lê Đăng Doanh. "Equitization of State-Owned Enterprises: Crucial Test for Vietnam's Reform Process and the Role of SCIC." *Conference on Emergence of Vietnam as a Middle Income Country: Opportunities, Constraints, and Regional Implications*. Singapore: Institute of Southeast Asian Studies, October 30–31, 2008.

Lê Tấn Lợi. *Vietnamese Exports*. Saigon: The Vietnam Council on Foreign Relations, 1971.

Lệ Thủy. "Cổ Phần Hóa Doanh Nghiệp: Đừng Để Người Lao Động Trắng Tay. Yếu tố bền vững trong chính sách lao động bị xem nhẹ" [Equitized State Factories: Please Do Not Leave the Workers Empty Handed. The Sustainable Factor in Labor Policies Is Being Undermined]. *Người Lao Động*. April 2, 2007. Accessed July 2009. http://nld.com.vn/184870P0C1010/yeu-to-ben-vung-trong-chinh-sach-lao-dong-bi-xem-nhe.htm

———— and Nam Dương, "Quyết Định 1846 Của Bộ LĐ-TB-XH Về Thí Điểm Ký Thỏa Ước Lao Động Tập Thể Ngành Dệt May VN: Quá Nhiều Sai Sót" [Decision 1846 of MOLISA on the Pilot Collective Bargaining Agreement in the Vietnamese Textile and Garment Industries: Too Many Mistakes]. February 24, 2009. Accessed July 2009. http://nld.com.vn/2009022401325466P0C1012/qua-nhieu-sai-sot.htm

Lê Văn Đồng, *Sơ Lược Về Hiện Tình Các Vấn Đề Lao Động ở Việt Nam* [Preliminaries on Current Situations of Labor Issues in Vietnam]. Saigon: Labor Ministry, 1956.

Lee, Ching Kwan. *Against the Law: Labor Protests in China's Rustbelt and Sunbelt*. Berkeley, CA: University of California Press, 2007.

Lê Văn Khoa, ed. *Lịch Sử Phong Trào Công Nhân Cao Su Dầu Tiếng* [History of the Labor Movement in Dầu Tiếng Rubber Plantation]. Hồ Chí Minh City: Nhà Xuất Bản Lao Động, 2000.

Los, Jonathan Hoving. "The Rise of the Labor Movement in South Vietnam." Master's thesis, University of Texas at Austin, 1975.

Marr, David. *Vietnamese Tradition on Trial: 1920–1945*. Berkeley, CA: University of California Press, 1981.

Minh Nam. "Chuyện Bây Giờ Mới Kể Về Những CN Người Hoa" [The Stories Now Told about the Hoa Workers]. *Người Lao Động*, March 1, 2007. Accessed January 14, 2012. http://suckhoedinhduong.nld.com.vn/181644p0c1010/chuyen-bay-gio-moi-ke-ve-nhung-cn-nguoi-hoa.htm

Ministry of Industry and Commerce. "Thu Hút Đầu Tư Nước Ngoài Vào Dệt May—Những Chuyển Động Tích Cực" [Attracting Foreign Investment in Textile and Garment Industries—Some Positive Developments]. *Thông Tin Thương Mại Việt Nam*. February 21, 2008. Accessed May 2008. http://www.tinthuongmai.vn/IWINews.aspx?Catalog ID=1987&ID=67319

Ministry of Planning and Investment. "Report to the Prime Minister on Strikes in Đồng Nai, Bình Dương, Thành phố Hồ Chí Minh." 2004.

————. "Accumulated Inflow of FDI by the End of 2010." In *Guidebook on Business and Investment In Vietnam*. Berlin: Embassy of Socialist Republic of Vietnam to the Federal Republic of Germany, 2011.

————. "Tình Hình Đầu Tư Trực Tiếp Nước Ngoài 6 Tháng Đầu Năm 2012" [FDI Status in the First Six Months of 2012]. July 2, 2012. Accessed July 2012. http://fia.mpi.gov.vn/News.aspx?ctl=newsdetail&aID=1153

Morlat, Patrice. *La repression colonial au Vietnam (1908–40)*. Paris: L'Harmattan, 1990.

Musolf, Lloyd D. "Public Enterprise and Development, Perspectives in South Vietnam." *Asian Survey* 3 (August 1963): 357–71.

Nam Định Textile Combine Party Executive Committee. *Lịch Sử Đảng Bộ Công Ty Dệt Nam Định 1930–1975* [The History of the Party at Nam Định Textile Combine 1930–1975]. Nam Định: Nam Định Publisher, 2000.

Nam Dương. "Lương Tối Thiểu Không Phải Là Lương Căn Bản" [The Minimum Wage is Not Basic Wage]. *Người Lao Động*. January 22, 2008. Accessed July 2008. http://nld.com.vn/213304P1010C1012/luong-toi-thieu-khong-phai-la-luong-can-ban.htm

———— and Phạm Hồ. "Mỏi Mòn Chờ Trợ Cấp Sau Cổ Phần Hóa" [Desperately Waiting for Allowances/Subsidies after Equitization]. *Người Lao Động*, September 15, 2008. Accessed November 2008. http://nld.com.vn/239342P1010C1012/moi-mon-cho-tro-cap-sau-co-phan-hoa.htm.

Nghị Đoàn. "Đồng Bào Hoa tại Thành Phố Hồ Chí Minh Dưới Sự Lãnh Đạo của Đảng Cộng Sản Việt Nam" [The Hoa in Hồ Chí Minh City under the Leadership of the Vietnamese Communist Party]. In *Người Hoa Tại Thành Phố Hồ Chí Minh*. 30–70. Hồ Chí Minh City: Sở Văn Hoá Thông Tin Publisher, 2007.

————. *Người Hoa ở* Việt Nam—*Thành Phố Hồ Chí Minh* [The Hoa in Vietnam—Hồ Chí Minh City]. Hồ Chí Minh City: Thành Phố Hồ Chí Minh Publisher, 1999.

————. *Truyền Thống Cách Mạng của Đồng Bào Hoa Ở Thành Phố Hồ Chí Minh Dưới Sự Lãnh Đạo Của Đảng Cộng Sản Việt Nam* [The Revolutionary Tradition of the Hoa in Hồ Chí Minh City under the Leadership of the Vietnamese Communist Party]. Hồ Chí Minh City: Hồ Chí Minh Publisher, 1987.

Nghiêm, Liên Hương. "Work Culture, Gender, and Class In Vietnam: Ethnographies of Three Garment Workshops in Hà Nội." PhD dissertation, University of Amsterdam, 2006.

Ngô Quang Định. "Về Thế Mạnh Kinh Tế Của Người Hoa ở Quận 5 và Khu Vực Chợ Lớn Trước Năm 1975" [About the Economic Strength of the Hoa in District 5 and Cholon Area before 1975]. *University of Social Science and Humanities* 22, article no. 15 (n.d.).

Ngô Văn Hòa and Dương Kinh Quốc. *Giai Cấp Công Nhân Việt Nam Những Năm Trước Khi Thành Lập Đảng* [The Working Class before the Establishment of the Vietnamese Communist Party]. Hà Nội: Khoa Hoc Xa Hoi Publisher and Uy Ban Khoa Hoc Xa Hoi Vietnam, 1978.

Ngô Vĩnh Long. *Before the Revolution: Vietnamese Peasants under the French*. New York, NY: Columbia University Press, 1991.

Ngọc Lan. "Cổ phần hóa DNNN vẫn lúng túng" [Equitization of State-Owned Factories Still Struggling]. *Saigon Times*, July 14, 2008. Accessed August 2008. http://www.thesaigontimes.vn/home/doanhnghiep/phapluat/7469/

Nguyễn Hữu Vinh. *Policy Paper*. Harvard Asian Program, Fulbright Vietnam; 98/2009/NĐ-CP, October 30, 2009.

Nguyễn Ngọc Linh, ed. *The Working Man in Vietnam*. Saigon: Vietnam Council on Foreign Relations, 1970.

Nguyễn Quang Quýnh. "Công Nhân, Nghiệp Đoàn Và Cộng Sản" [Workers, Trade Unions, and Communism]. *Nghiên Cứu Hành Chánh* [Journal of the Association for Administrative Studies]. January/February 1965: 44–82.

———. *Quyển 1: Những Vấn Đề Lao Động* [Book No. 1: Labor Issues]. Saigon: Lửa Thiêng, 1974.

Nguyễn Quốc Việt. "Explaining the Transition to the Rule of Law in Vietnam: The Role of Informal Institutions and the Delegation of Powers to Independent Courts." PhD dissertation, Kassel University, Germany, 2006. Accessed August 6, 2012. http://kobra.bibliothek.uni-kassel.de/bitstream/urn:nbn:de:hebis:34-2006070313842/1/VietDiss-final.pdf

Nguyễn Quyết. "Giảm Đình Công, Tăng an Sinh Xã Hội" [Reducing Strikes, Increasing Social Security]. *Người Lao Động*, February 22, 2012. Accessed March 2012. http://nld.com.vn/20120222095732102p0c1010/giam-dinh-cong-tang-an-sinh-xa-hoi.htm, accessed March 2012.

Nguyễn Thị Mộng Tuyền. "Phong Trào Đấu Tranh Của Công Nhân Cao Su Thủ Dầu Một Trong 30 Năm Chiến Tranh Giải Phóng (1945–1975)" [The Struggle Movement of the Thủ Dầu Một Rubber Plantation Workers in 30-Year Liberation War (1945–1975)]. PhD dissertation, Vietnam Academy for Social Sciences/Southern Institute of Sustainable Development, 2010. Accessed October 2, 2010. www.sugia.vn/index.php?mod=news&cpid=12&nid=669&view=detail

Nguyễn Thị Sương Kiều. "Hiện Tình Nghiệp Đoàn Công Nhân Tại Việt Nam" [The Current Situation of Trade Unions in Việt Nam]. Graduation thesis, Học Viện Quốc Gia Hành Chánh, 1969.

Nguyễn Thị Thanh Mai. "Labor Disputes in HCM City: Resolutions and Recommendations." Department of Labor, Invalids, and Social Affairs. Accessed June 2012. http://www.amchamvietnam.com/1239

Nguyên Thủy. "Lao Động Nhập Cư Tại TP.HCM Phải Có 'Sổ Lao Động'" [Migrant Workers In Hồ Chí Minh City Must Have "Work Cards"]. *Việt Báo*, June 24, 2005. Accessed June 8, 2009. http://vietbao.vn/Xa-hoi/Lao-dong-nhap-cu-tai-TP-HCM-phai-co-so-lao-dong/45159503/157/

Nguyễn Tuấn Triết and Trịnh Thị Kiều Oanh. "Truyền Thống Đấu Tranh Cách Mạng và Thành Tựu Xây Dựng Chủ Nghĩa Xã Hội của Đồng Bào Hoa ở Quận 6 Thành Phố Hồ Chí Minh" [Revolutionary Tradition and Achievement in Building Socialism of the Hoa in District 6 in Hồ Chí Minh City]. In *Người Hoa ở Quận 6— Thành Phố Hồ Chí Minh*, ed. Phan An. Hồ Chí Minh City: Mặt Trận Tổ Quốc Việt Nam Quận 6, 1990.

Nguyễn Văn Thư. "Các Nghiệp Đoàn Tại Gia Định: Phong Trào Nghiệp Đoàn tại Gia Định; Vài Con Số Chính Yếu và Cách Định Trí" [Trade Unions in Gia Định: The Trade Union Movement in Gia Định; Some Important Statistics and Positionality]. *Nghiên Cứu Hành Chánh, Học Viện Quốc Gia Hành Chánh* [Administration Research, National Institute of Administration] 9, no. 9/10 (September/October 1965): 3–134.

Nguyễn, Xuân Lương. "Vần đề Quốc Tịch Của Người Hoa Ở Việt Nam." Hồ Chí Minh City: *Luật Học* [Legal Studies], No. 23 (1978): 7–16.

Nguyễn-võ Thu-hương, *The Ironies of Freedom: Sex, Culture, and Neoliberal Governance in Vietnam.* Seattle, WA, and London: University of Washington Press, 2008.

Norlund, Irene. "Democracy and Trade Unions in Vietnam: Riding a Honda in Low Gear." *The Copenhagen Journal of Asian Studies* (November 1996): 73–99.

Ong, Aihwa. *Spirits of Resistance and Capitalist Discipline: Factory Women in Malaysia.* Albany, NY: State University of New York Press, 1987.

———. "The Gender and Labor Politics of Postmodernity." In *The Politics of Culture in the Shadow of Capital*, ed. Lisa Lowe and David Lloyd. Durham, NC, and London: Duke University Press, 1997.

———. *Neoliberalism as Exception: Mutations in Citizenship and Sovereignty.* Durham, NC, and London: Duke University Press, 2006.

Pangsapa, Piya. *Textures of Struggle: The Emergence of Resistance among Garment Workers in Thailand.* Ithaca, NY: Cornell University ILR Press, 2007.

Perry, Elizabeth. *Challenging the Mandate of Heaven: Social Protest and State Power in China.* London: M. E. Sharpe, 2002.

———. *Shanghai on Strike: The Politics of Chinese Labor.* Stanford, CA: Stanford University Press, 1997.

Phạm Hồ. "Các Doanh Nghiệp Nợ BHXH 2.156 Tỉ Đồng: Bất Lực Phải Giải Quyết Dứt Điểm Bằng Biện Pháp Mạnh" [Enterprises Owed 2.156 Billions of Social Security Debt: Powerless. Must Resolve with a Tough Solution]. *Người Lao Động,* November 26, 2007. Accessed July 2009. http://www.nld.com.vn/tools/print.asp?news_id=208443

——— and Nam Dương, "Cổ Phần Hóa: Đừng Để Người Lao Động Trắng Tay/Mặt Trái Cổ Phần Hóa" [Equitization: Please Do Not Leave the Workers Empty-Handed/The Flip Side of Equitization]. *Người Lao Động,* March 29, 2007. http://www.nld.com.vn/tools/print.asp?news_id=184345

Phạm Nguyễn. "'Chuyện Lạ'" Ở Huê Phong" ["A Strange Tale" at Huê Phong]. *Người Lao Động,* June 6, 2005. Accessed July 2009. http://nld.com.vn/119833P0C1010/chuyen-la-o-hue-phong.htm

Phan An. *Người Hoa ở Nam Bộ* [The Hoa in the South of Vietnam]. Hồ Chí Minh City: Nhà Xuất Bản Khoa Học Xã Hội—Viện Khoa Học Xã Hội Vùng Nam Bộ, 2005.

———. "Người Hoa Trong Hoạt Động Kinh Tế Của Miền Nam Việt Nam Sau Năm 1975." [The Hoa in the South of Vietnam's Economic Activities After 1975]. *Phát Triển Kinh Tế.* 14 (October 1991).

———. "Người Hoa Trong Hoạt Động Kinh Tế Đối Ngoại Của Thành Phố Hồ Chí Minh" [The Hoa in Hochiminh City Economic Activities and Trade]. *Phát Triển Kinh Tế*. 15 (December 1991).

——— and Phan Xuân Biên. "Người Hoa trong hoạt động kinh tê của Miền Nam Việt Nam Trước Năm 1975" [The Hoa in the South of Vietnam's Economic Activities before 1975]. *Phát Triển Kinh Tế* [Economic Development Journal] 12 (October 1991): 21–22.

Phan Anh and Hồng Nhung. "Kiệt sức vì làm thêm" [Exhausted Due to Overtime Work]. *Người Lao Động*, December 9, 2011. Accessed December 2011. http://nld.com.vn/20111209103658773p0c1010/kiet-suc-vi-lam-them.htm

Phan Khắc Từ, *Bản Tin Lao Động: Ủy Ban Bảo Vệ Quyền Lợi Lao Động* [Labor Newsletter: The Committee for the Protection of Workers' Rights and Interests]. Saigon, issues in 1974.

Phan Khắc Từ. "Trang Thơ Tranh Đấu" [Resistance Poetry Page]. *Bản Tin Lao Động: Ủy Ban Bảo Vệ Quyền Lợi Lao Động* [Labor Newsletter: The Committee for the Protection of Workers' Rights]. February 1975.

Polanyi, Karl. *The Great Transformation: The Political and Economic Origins of Our Time*. Boston, MA: Beacon Press, 1944.

Report on April 1, 1929, to Marchand about the Leaflets Found in the Factory. Nam Định: Nam Định Archives.

Resch, R. *Althusser and the Renewal of Marxist Social Theory*. Berkeley, CA: University of California Press, 1992.

Roediger, David. *The Wages of Whiteness: Race and the Making of the American Working Class*. London and New York, NY: Verso, 1991.

Scott, James C. *Domination and the Arts of Resistance: Hidden Transcripts*. New Haven, CT, and London: Yale University Press, 1990.

———. *Weapons of the Weak*. New Haven, CT: Yale University Press, 1990.

Sidel, Mark. *Law and Society in Vietnam: The Transition from Socialism in Comparative Perspective*. Cambridge: Cambridge University Press, 2008.

Silver, Beverly J. *Forces of Labor: Workers' Movements and Globalization Since 1870*. Cambridge and New York, NY: Cambridge University Press, 2003.

Slaughter, Jane. "UE Occupies Chicago Window Plant Again and Wins Reprieve." *Labor Notes*, February 24, 2012. Accessed January 2013. http://www.labornotes. org/2012/02/ue-occupies-chicago-window-plant-again-and-wins-reprieve

Sunoo, Jan Jung-Min, Chang Hee Lee, and Đỗ Quỳnh Chi. *Vietnam: A Foreign Manager's HR Survival Guide*. Hà Nội: International Labour Organization, 2009.

Taylor, Milton C. "South Viet-Nam: Lavish Aid, Limited Progress." *Pacific Affairs* 34, no. 3 (Autumn 1961): 242–56.

T. Đ. "Trà Vinh: Xét Xử Vụ Án Phá Rối An Ninh" [Trà Vinh: Ruling on the Case of Disrupting Security]. *Lao Động* October 27, 2010. Accessed July 2012. http://www.laodong.com.vn/Tin-Tuc/Xet-xu-vu-an-pha-roi-an-ninh/18156

Thảo Lan. "Tác Động Của Khủng Hoảng Tài Chính Đối Với Công Nhân Nữ Nhập Cư Và Nguy Cơ Mua Bán Người" [The Consequences of the Financial Crisis on Female Migrant Workers and the Dangers of Human Trafficking]. Hà Nội: Ministry of Labor, Invalids, and Social Affairs, September 8, 2009. Accessed November 2012. http://www.molisa.gov.vn/news/detail/tabid/75/news id/49916/seo/Tac-dong-cua-khung-hoang-tai-chinh-doi-voi-cong-nhan-nu-nhap-cu-va-nguy-co-mua-ban-nguoi/language/vi-VN/Default.aspx

Thompson, Edward Palmer. "Class and Class Struggle." In *Class*, ed. Joyce. 133–41.

———. "Eighteenth Century English Society: Class Struggle without Class?" *Social History* 3 (1978): 133–65.

———. "The Making of Class." In *Class*, ed. Joyce. 131–32.

———. "Time, Work-Discipline, and Industrial Capitalism." *Past and Present Society* 38 (December 1967): 56–97.

Thùy Linh. "Ngập Ngừng … Tăng Lương Tối Thiểu" [Halting … Raising the Minimum Wage]. *Người Lao Động*, September 20, 2010. Accessed September 26, 2010. http://nld.com.vn/20100919105149803P1010C1012/ngap-ngung-tang-luong-toi-thieu.htm

Tiến Khải, ed. *Công Nhân Saigon–Chợ Lớn Trong Sự Nghiệp Giải Phóng Dân Tộc* [Workers in Saigon-Cho Lon and Their Role in National Liberation]. Hà Nội: Lao Động Publisher, 1993.

Tønnesson, Stein. *Vietnam 1946: How the War Began.* Berkeley, CA: University of California Press, 2010.

Top Secret: Section III, *Additional Measures in South Viet Nam*, declassified materials. National Archives and Records Administration (NARA), June 5, 1994.

Tr. Hoàng. Ra mắt Văn phòng Luật sư Công đoàn [The Opening of the Labor Unions Law Office]. *Người Lao Động*, December 2, 2010. Accessed July 2011. http://nld.com.vn/20101201115959323P1010C1012/ra-mat-van-phong-luat-su-cong-doan.htm

"Trade Union World Briefing." *International Confederation of Free Trade Unions*, 2005. Accessed July 19, 2012. http://www.icftu.org/www/PDF/LMSDossier8-05YouthEN.pdf

Trần, Angie Ngọc. "Alternatives to the 'Race to the Bottom' in Vietnam: Minimum Wage Strikes and Their Aftermath." *Labor Studies Journal* 32, no. 4 (December 2007): 430–51.

———. "Corporate Social Responsibility in Socialist Vietnam: Implementation, Challenges, and Local Solutions." In *Labour in Vietnam*, ed. Chan. 119–59.

———. "Global Subcontracting and Women Workers in Comparative Perspective." In *Globalization and Third World Socialism: Cuba and Vietnam*, ed. Claes Brundenius and John Weeks. 217–36. Houndmills, Basingstoke, Hampshire: Palgrave, 2001.

———. "Linking Growth With Equity? The Vietnamese Textile and Garment Industries Since Đổi Mới." In *Reaching for the Dream: Challenges of Sustainable Development in Vietnam*, ed. Melanie Beresford and Angie Ngọc Trần. 135–82. Copenhagen: Nordic Institute for Asian Studies Press, 2004.

———. "Sewing for the Global Economy: Thread of Resistance in Vietnamese Textile and Garment Industries." In *Critical Globalization Studies*, ed. William Robinson and Richard Appelbaum. 379–92. New York, NY, and London: Routledge, 2005.

———. "The Third Sleeve: Emerging Labor Newspapers and the Response of Labor Unions and the State to Workers' Resistance in Vietnam." *Labor Studies Journal* 32, no. 3 (September 2007): 257–79.

———. "Through the Eye of the Needle: Vietnamese Textile and Garment Industries Rejoining the Global Economy." *Crossroads: An Interdisciplinary Journal of Southeast Asian Studies* 10, no. 2 (1997): 83–126.

———. "Vietnamese Textile and Garment Industry in the Global Supply Chain: State Strategies and Workers' Responses." *International Journal of Institutions and Economies* 4, no. 3 (October 2012): 123–50.

——— and David Smith. "Cautious Reformers and Fence Breakers: Vietnam's Economic Transition in Comparative Perspective." *Humboldt Journal of Social Relations* 24, no. 1/2 (1998): 51–100.

Trần Đức Thanh Phong. *The Textile Industry in Vietnam*. Saigon: The Vietnam Council on Foreign Relations, 1970.

Trần Hữu Quyền. *Báo Cáo Tinh Thần* [The Spiritual Report], from The Third Congress, April 22–24, 1960: Ten-Year Anniversary of the Tổng Liên Đoàn Lao Công Việt Nam. Saigon: CVT, 1960.

Trần Khánh. *The Ethnic Chinese and Economic Development in Vietnam*. Singapore: Institute of Southeast Asian Studies, 1993.

———. "Tìm Hiểu Các Tổ Chức Xã Hội Và Nghiệp Đoàn Truyền Thống Của Người Hoa ở Việt Nam Trong Lịch Sử" [Understanding Traditional Social Associations and Trade Unions of the Hoa in Vietnam in Historical Perspective]. *Tạp chí Dân Tộc Học* [Ethnology Journal] 116 (February 2002): 3–13.

———. *Vai trò Người Hoa trong nền Kinh tế các nước Đông Nam Á* [The Role of the Hoa in the Economies of Southeast Asian Countries]. Hà Nội: Viện Đông Nam Á, 1992.

Trần Quốc Bửu. "Confidential Memorandum to the President of the United States of America, May 20, 1964." Jay Lovestone's Collection. Stanford, CA: Hoover Institution Library and Archives.

———. *The Vietnamese Confederation of Labor (CVT) Speaks to the Free World*. Saigon: Vietnamese Confederation of Labor, Department of Research-Publication-Education, 1966.

———. "Thông Cáo của Hội Đồng Tổng Liên Đoàn Lao Công Việt Nam" [Announcement of the Committee of the General Confederation of Vietnamese Workers]. August 30, 1964.

Trần Tử Bình. *The Red Earth: A Vietnamese Memoir of Life on a Colonial Rubber Plantation*, trans. John Spragens, Jr. Athens, OH: Ohio University Center for International Studies, 1985.

Trần Văn Giàu. *Giai Cấp Công Nhân Việt Nam: Sự Hình Thành và Sự Phát Triển của Nó từ Giai Cấp 'Tự Mình' đến Giai Cấp 'Cho Mình'* [The Vietnamese Workers' Class: Its Formation and Development from 'Class-In-Itself' to 'Class-For-Itself']. Hà Nội: Su That Publisher, 1961.

———. *Giai Cấp Công Nhân Việt Nam, Từ Đảng Cộng Sản Thành Lập Đến Cách Mạng Thành Công: Tập III, 1939–1945* [The Vietnamese Workers' Class, from the Formation of the Communist Party to the Revolution Victory: Volume III, 1939–1945]. Hà Nội: Nhà Xuất Bản Sử Học, 1963.

Trần Văn Hai. "Report on Phan Văn Chí to the Head of Bộ Nội Vụ on July 16, 1968 [Internal Security Department in Republic of Vietnam]." In *Phủ Tổng Thống Đệ Nhị 4161 v/v Tranh Chấp Quyền Lãnh Đạo Tại Tổng Liên Đoàn Lao Công Việt Nam, 1965–8 Archive*, Lưu Trữ Quốc Gia [National Archive] No. 2, Hồ Chí Minh City.

Trần Xuân Cầu. "Sức Ép Của Lao Động Nhập Cư Trong Các Khu Công Nghiệp Và Chính Sách Đối Với Họ" [The Pressure of Migrant Workers in Industrial Zones and Migrant Labor Policy]. Hồ Chí Minh City: Đại học Kinh tế Quốc Dân (National Economics University), August 22, 2008. Accessed June 2009. http://www.vienkinhte.hochiminhcity.gov.vn/xemtin.asp?idcha=1679&cap=3&id=4301.

Trang Công Đòan. "Công ty TNHH giày da Huê Phong—TPHCM: Gần 200 công nhân xin thôi việc" [Huê Phong Shoe Factory: About Two Hundred Workers Resigned]. *Lao Động*. April 28, 2008. Accessed July 2008. http://laodong.com.vn/Home/Cong-ty-TNHH-giay-da-Hue-Phong--TPHCM-Gan-200-cong-nhan-xin-thoi-viec/20084/86547.laodong

Trịnh Quang Quỹ. *Phong Trào Lao Động Việt Nam* [The Labor Movement in Vietnam]. Saigon: n.p., 1970.

Trương Bá Cần. "Catholics and Socialism." *Chọn Special Issue* 21 (October 20, 1974).

———. *Fifty Years Reflection: June 28, 1958 to June 28, 2008*. Hồ Chí Minh City: n.p., 2008.

Trịnh Chi, ed. *Questions and Answers about the History of the Vietnamese Communist Party*. Hà Nội: Thanh Niên Publisher, 1978.

Turley, William S. *The Second Indochina War: A Concise Political and Military History*. Lanham, MD: Rowman & Littlefield Publishers, 2009.

T.V.N. "Dệt Việt Thắng Chuyển Thành Công Ty Cổ Phần" [Việt Thắng Textile Became a Joint-Stock Company]. *Tuổi Trẻ Online*, December 18, 2006. Accessed November 10, 2010. http://tuoitre.vn/Kinh-te/178372/Det-Viet-Thang-chuyen-thanh-Cong-ty-co-phan.html

Việt Dũng. "Phạt Gần 81 Triệu Đồng Một Công Ty Gây Ô Nhiễm" [The Fine of Almost 81 Millions Đồng on a Polluting Factory]. *VTC News* July 14, 2009. Accessed July 2010. http://www.tin247.com/phat_gan_81_trieu_dong_mot_cong_ty_gay_o_nhiem-16-21453192.html

Việt - Hưng - Đủ. "Đồng Lương Đói" [The Starving Wage]. *Tuổi Trẻ Online*, January 15, 2006. Accessed November 10, 2010. http://tuoitre.vn/Chinh-tri-Xa-hoi/118614/Dong-luong-doi.html

Vietnam Federation of Trade Unions. *1965, A Year of Great Victories for the Workers' Movement in South Vietnam*. Hà Nội: Vietnam Federation of Trade Unions, January 1966.

Vietnam General Confederation of Labor. "Report on Strikes, Internal Report." July 2010.

VietNamNet Bridge. "Fewer Rural Workers Can Return For Tet." May 27, 2010. Accessed February 21, 2012. http://english.vietnamnet.vn/en/society/17999/fewer-rural-workers-can-return-for-tet.html

Vĩnh Tùng. "Báo Động Tình Trạng Nợ Lương Công Nhân" [Alert on the Problem of Owing Workers' Salaries]. *Người Lao Động*, April 26, 2006. Accessed July 2006. http://nld.com.vn/149183p0c1010/bao-dong-tinh-trang-no-luong-cong-nhan.htm.

———. "Giải Quyết Tình Trạng 'Vô Chủ' Tại Công ty HaiMin VN" [Resolving the Problem of "Missing Owner" at HaiMin Vietnam Factory]. *Người Lao Động*, May 11, 2007. Accessed November 2007. http://www.nld.com.vn/tintuc/cong-doan/188853.asp.

———. "Gian Nan Khởi Kiện, Rốt Cuộc Trắng Tay" [Struggling with the Lawsuit, Ending up Empty Handed]. *Người Lao Động*, August 5, 2009. Accessed July 2010. http://nld.com.vn/2009080411409640P0C1010/gian-nan-khoi-kien-rot-cuoc-trang-tay.htm

Vũ Ngọc Lý. *The Ancient Capital*. Nam Định: Sở Văn Hóa Thông Tin, 1997.

Vũ Xuân Hiểu. "Tường Thuật Vụ Tranh Chấp Giữa Công Nhân và Chủ Nhân Hãng Pin Con Ó" [Report of the Conflict between Workers and the Owner of the Eagle Battery Factory]. *Chọn Special Issue*: *Một Bài Học Cho Công Nhân Và Nghiệp Đoàn: Vụ Pin Con Ó* [A Lesson for Workers and Trade Unions: The Case of the Eagle Battery Factory]. Saigon: Lê Văn Duyệt, 1971.

Walder, Andrew G. *Communist Neo-Traditionalism: Work and Authority in Chinese Industry*. Berkeley, CA: University of California Press, 1986.

Wehrle, Edmund F. *Between a River and a Mountain: The AFL–CIO and the Vietnam War*. Ann Arbor, MI: University of Michigan Press, 2005.

———. "No More Pressing Task than Organization in Southeast Asia: The AFL–CIO Approaches the Vietnam War, 1947–1964." *Labor History* 42, no. 3 (August 2001): 277–95.

"World Report Chapter: Vietnam, 2009." Human Rights Watch. Accessed June 2010. http://www.hrw.org/en/world-report/2009/vietnam

Yến Trinh and Quốc Thanh. "Đình Công Tại Công Ty Huê Phong (TP.HCM): Cần Can Thiệp Mạnh!" [Strike at Huê Phong Company (HCMC): Need to Intervene Forcefully!]. *Tuổi Trẻ* April 26, 2008. Accessed March 2012. http://tuoitre.vn/Chinh-tri-Xa-hoi/252763/Dinh-cong-tai-cong-ty-Hue-Phong-TPHCM-Can-can-thiep-manh.html

Yeung, Henry. "The Political Economy of Transnational Corporations." *Political Geography* 17 (May 2008): 389–416.

Yeung, Henry and Kris Olds, eds., *Globalization of Chinese Business Firms.* New York, NY: St. Martin's Press, 2000.

Zarrow, Peter. *China in War and Revolution, 1895–1949*. London: Routledge, 2005.

INDEX

1886 Tianjin Commercial Convention, 67
1999 Enterprise Law, 127
1999 Law to Encourage Domestic Investment (Luật Khuyến Khích Đầu Tư Trong Nước), 125, 127, 234, 255–56, 261, 264–65, 275
2000 Foreign-Direct Investment Law, 127
2002 Fund to Assist Redundant Workers, 274
2003 State-Owned Enterprises Law, 127
2005 Enterprises Law (Luật Doanh Nghiệp), 127, 261
2005 Investment Law (Luật Đầu Tư), 264
2006 Minimum-wage law, 240, 255, 272, 284. see also minimum-wage levels
2009 Law on Unemployment Insurance, 274

A

Accusation Letter (Đơn Tố Cáo), 215
ActionAid, 234, 235
Action Committee for the Protection of Trade Union Movement (Ủy Ban Hành Động Bảo Vệ Phong Trào Nghiệp Đoàn), 76
"action teams" (đoàn công tác), 149–50
AFL-CIO, 74, 75, 76
Agency for International Development (AID), 68, 87
allowances/bonuses. see attendance bonus, hard-working bonus, Tết bonus
Althusser, Louis, 124
American Chamber of Commerce (AmCham), 116
American Federation of Labor and Congress of Industrial Organizations (AFL-CIO), 73

American War
    and Catholic worker movement, 82, 83, 109, 295
    and economic/labor system of the South, 65, 66, 67, 69, 70, 71, 72, 74, 78
    and "steely land," 212
Anagnost, Ann, 180
Anjin Shoe Factory, 281–82
An Nam, 16
annual workers' congress, 165, 167, 168, 283
arbitrary discretion of the state, 5, 287
"aristocracy of labor," 35
Article No. 17, 169
Association of Southeast Asian Nations (ASEAN), 113
Association of the Hoa in Vietnam (Hội Hoa Kiều Việt Nam), 25
attendance bonus (tiền chuyên cần), 155.
August 1945 Revolution, 39, 41

B

Ban Chuyên Mục Công Đoàn-Đài Truyền Hình Việt Nam, 156
Bản Tin Lao Động (Labor newsletter), 10
benefits. see benefits by type; entitlements
Bến Nghé port, 171–72
Beresford, Melanie, 4, 95, 120
Biên Hòa city, 286
Bình An brick factory, 169–70, 174
Bình Chánh district, 202
Bình Dương province, 50, 129, 169, 184, 200, 287
Bình Tây alcohol distillery, 24
"blue-shirted workers" (công nhân áo xanh), 26
Blum, Leon, 40, 48
boycott, 23, 193, 206, 208
brand-name companies, 131
brotherhood/sisterhood language, 214, 215, 220

"brown-shirted workers" (*công nhân áo nâu*), 27, 30, 33, 35, 61, 62
Buddhist workers and activists, 72, 74, 97, 103, 104
Bùi Đức Hải, 227
Bùi Lượng, 75
Bùi Quang Vinh, 184
Bùi Văn Thiện, 77
Burawoy, Michael, 7, 60

C

capital ownership types, 128–31
"Catholic labor soldiers" (*Chiến sĩ lao động công giáo*), 76, 82
Catholic migrants, 65, 78
Catholic priests and labor activists, 72, 81–84, 101. *see also* progressive Catholic organizations by name
Catholic Youth and Worker Movement (Phong trào Thanh Niên Lao Động Công Giáo [PTTNCG]), 81, 85
Center for Legal Assistance (Trung Tâm Tư Vấn Pháp Luật), 169
Center for the Development of Industrial Relations, 115
Central Committee Directives (Chỉ Thị Ủy Ban Trung Ương Đảng), 147–48
central planning model, 112–13
certificate of "*nguồn gốc Việt Nam*," 126
Chapter 14 (Labor Code), 116, 117, 118
Châu Giới Tăng, 87
Châu Nhật Bình, 251
Chiang Kai-shek, 25
child care, 45, 190, 192, 264
child labor, 33–34
China, 4, 39, 68, 239
China treaties, 21, 22
Chinese citizens, 21–22
Chinese Nationalist Kuomintang (KMT) government, 22
Chợ Lớn Chamber of Commerce, 20
Chợ Lớn district, 19, 24–25, 67, 70
Chongqing Treaty, 22
Chong-se Kim, 70
Chọn journal, 84, 86, 106
Choong Nam-Việt Thắng, 174, 175–78, 179, 283
cicada practices, 147, 148, 150, 216–22, 264, 267, 273, 278
citizenship, 65, 125–26
class consciousness, 6, 27–28, 103–5, 108, 179, 216, 223, 245–46, 291, 292, 296–97

class language, 42, 45, 62, 223, 231, 232, 233, 257, 297
class moments, 12, 31, 86, 96–98, 207, 208, 219, 223, 291, 292, 295–97
C & N Security Service Company, 221–22
Cochin China, 16
collective bargaining agreements (CBAs), 139, 148–49
collective consciousness. *see* class consciousness
Comaroff, Jean, 3, 33
Comaroff, John, 3, 33
Commercial Import Program (CIP), 66, 69, 75
Committee for the Protections of Workers' Rights, 82
Committee to Protect Vietnamese Workers (CPVW), 202
Committee to Renew State Enterprises (Ban Đổi Mới Doanh Nghiệp), 132
commodification of labor, 157, 203
complaint letters, 154, 155, 220, 230–31, 232–33. *see* "pen protests"
"Completely Destroyed Proposal," 116
Côn Đảo Island prison, 92, 93
Construction Corporation No. 4, 172–73
contract factories, 131
contract workers (*công nhân công tra*), 16–19
contributing capital (*tài sản góp vốn*), 127
corporate buyers, 130
cost-of-living adjustment, 199
court delays, 282, 285
Cửa Ông factory, 27
Củ Chi district, 212
Củ Chi district labor union, 267
cultural identity, 2, 7–9, 12, 50–52, 55–57, 91, 102, 223, 291, 292–93, 296. *see also* ethnic identity; gender identity; historical legacy; knowledge factor; native-place (*yếu tố đồng hương*) identification; religious identity; skills factor
CVT. *see* General Confederation of Workers (CVT [Tổng Liên Đoàn Lao Công Việt Nam])

D

DACOTEX (Kỹ Nghệ Dệt Đông Á), 78–79
Đại Lăng Cô, 91
Đặng Ngọc Tùng, 164, 182
Đặng Thị Thân, 84, 85

data sources, 9–11
Dầu Tiếng rubber plantation, 18–19, 49–54, 60–62
day of the sewing saint (giỗ tổ thợ may), 195
ĐD journal, 10. *see Đối Diện, Đồng Dao, Đứng Dậy* journals
Decree No. 2/CP/2003, 274, 277, 280
Decree No. 3/CP, 177
Decree No. 41/CP, 180
Decree No. 51/CP, 135, 190
Decree No. 70/CP, 139
Decree No. 110/CP, 133, 226
Decree No. 168/CP, 139
Democratic Republic of Vietnam (DRV), 64–65, 111–13
Department of Labor, Invalids, and Social Affairs (DOLISA), 118
de Vylder, Stefan, 5
"Diagnosing the Illness," 107
Điện Biên Phủ, 42
direct action, 1–2, 141, 209, 243, 247, 263, 278
disbursed capital (vốn thực hiện/vốn giải ngân), 128
division of (factory) labor, 37–38
Đối Diện journal, 85
Đổi Mới, 3, 111, 128, 152
DOLISA (Department of Labor, Invalids, and Social Affairs), 248–49, 250, 253
domestic private sector, 146, 166, 225–26, 227, 228, 264, 272, 274
Đông Á Garment and Textile factory, 230–31
Đồng Dao, 85
Đồng Nai city, 129
Đồng Nai Labor Federation, 286
Đồng Nai province, 170, 184, 200, 286
dormitories, 90
Dư Huệ Liên, 93
Đứng Dậy, 85
Dương Minh Đức, 116, 281

E
Eagle Battery factory, 63–64, 65, 86, 99
early retirement (nghỉ hưu sớm), 161–62
early worker activism, 24–30
East Asian investment, 66, 128, 129, 184, 195–97
Eastern European communist bloc, 113, 128
economic liberalism, 26

economic zones, 136–37
education levels of workers, 135, 154, 185, 186
"eighteen betel leaves villages" (mười tám thôn vườn trầu), 218
"elder sister" workers (đàn chị), 208
electricity cost, 135, 136, 190, 191, 224, 271
Enterprises Law (Luật Doanh Nghiệp), 127
enterprises' rights/responsibilities, 127–28
entitlements, 144, 155, 161, 169, 170, 172–73, 177, 180, 209, 223, 226, 283–85, 292, 300. *see also by benefit type*
environmental laws, 178
EPZs [export processing zones], general, 121–22, 184–86. *see also by name*
equitization (cổ phần hóa) and equitized companies, 3, 114, 120, 127, 131–34, 133, 146, 154, 156–74, 164, 226, 228, 283, 297, 300
Equitization Laws (2002–13), 156, 163
ethical obligations of companies, 131
ethnic Chinese, 19. *see also* Hoa
ethnic identity, 19–25, 37, 107, 245, 258
"Et-sam," 36
Eun Ho Kang, 281
European joint venture, 215
evacuation from the North, 75, 78
Evans, Mark, 227
export processing zones (EPZs). *see* EPZs, general; *see also by name*
external consciousness, 60

F
factory workers. *see* "blue-shirted workers" (công nhân áo xanh)
false consciousness, 7, 62, 223, 259, 297–99
Far East Battery Company (Công ty Pin Viễn Đông), 99
FDI sector. *see* foreign-direct investment (FDI) sector
Federation of Handicraft Weavers (Nghiệp Đoàn Thợ Dệt Thủ Công), 78
Federation of Trade Unions for the Liberation of South Vietnam (Hội Lao Động Giải Phóng Miền Nam [FTU]), 77
female workers. *see* women workers
"fence-breaking" (phá rào) 112–13
Fforde, Adam, 5
five-year plan, 122–23
flexible resistance, 299–301
foreign capital investment, 128–31

foreign-direct investment (FDI) sector
general, 114, 121–22, 125, 129, 130,
136–40, 200
worker agency, 203–16
formation of labor unions, 72–73
Formosa Taffeta Vietnam, 213
Four Reals (Bốn Thật) Directive, 148
framework of the book, 8–9, 11
Franco–Chinese Bank, 22
free-market system, 2, 112, 113
Freetrend shoe factory, 185, 209–11, 284
Free Viet Labor Federation, 202
French Catholic Trade Union, 74
French–Chinese commercial alliance, 20–23
French colonial rule, 1, 2, 8, 10, 11, 15, 16,
18, 20–24, 38
French Indochina, 15–19, 20–21
French Indochina Bank, 22, 23
French investment in Vietnam, 16, 30–31
French legal system, 57–59
French Popular Front government, 40
Fund to Assist Redundant Workers (Quỹ
hỗ trợ lao động dôi dư), 133, 163–64

G
"garbage priest," 82
garment factory protests, 157–58
gender, differences in handling wages,
194–95
gender, division of labor, 36
gender identity, 8, 31–33, 35–36, 61, 84–86,
99, 100, 102–3, 157, 183, 193, 207, 235,
236, 283, 292–93
General Confederation of Labor (Tổng
Liên Đoàn Lao Động Việt Nam), 73, 75–
78
General Confederation of Workers (CVT
[Tổng Liên Đoàn Lao Công Việt Nam]),
72–76, 79, 88, 94–95, 98, 99, 109
General Statistics Office of Vietnam, 10
Geneva Accords (July 1954), 64, 65, 75
Gia Định, 98
Gillespie, John, 4
global supply chain, 128–31
Gò Vấp district, 98, 168, 234, 236, 240, 248,
266
Gò Vấp district labor union, 252, 253
Gò Vấp District People's Committee, 234,
249, 253, 277
graffiti protest, 209–11, 247, 284
Great Britain, 68
Greater China Zone, 68, 70, 196, 197, 239

H
Haekwang Vina, 267
Haimin Vietnam embroidery factory, 218–
21, 278–81
Hải Phòng city, 23, 56, 78, 129
Hải Phòng province, 23, 30, 39
Hà Nam village, 56, 57, 59
handicraft camps, 78
Handicraft Development Center, 69
Hãng Pin con Ó. *see* Eagle Battery factory
Hanoi, 26, 39, 44, 84, 137, 146, 157, 158, 183
"hard-working" bonus (tiền chuyên cần)
[*also* "attendance bonus"], 155
Harvey, David, 33, 179
Hà Tăng, 86, 90, 93–94, 96–97, 98
HCMC Department of Labor, 251
HCMC Environmental Agency, 178
HCMC Labor Federation (Liên Đoàn Lao
Động Thành Phố Hồ Chí Minh), 10,
135, 148, 150, 167, 176, 177, 178, 191,
218, 248, 249, 250, 271, 279, 280, 287
HCMC legal assistance center (Trung Tâm
Tư Vấn Pháp Luật), 287
HCMC People's Committee, 121, 148, 178,
251, 276, 277
HCMC People's Court (Toà Án Nhân Dân
Thành Phố Hồ Chí Minh), 279, 281, 282
HCMC Social Insurance Office, 151
health insurance benefits, 115, 138, 151,
213, 238
HEPZA, 121–22, 182, 216, 250, 270
HEPZA Labor Federation, 122
HEPZA Labor Union, 122
historical legacy, 32–33, 179, 292, 293
Hoa
cadres, 90–91, 93, 98
capitalists, 19, 22, 25, 65–67, 70, 79, 196
class system, 23–24
connection to Taiwan, 70
ethnic identification, 19–25, 37–38
monopolies, 20, 21, 22, 23, 67, 100
relationship with Kinh, 23–24, 61, 102
role in labor movement, 79–80, 81
and textile industry, 68–69
trade associations, 20
and Vimytex, 87, 88–96
Hoàn Cầu factory sit-in, 203–6
Hoàng Quốc Việt, 41
Hoàng Thị Khánh, 80, 176
Ho Chi Minh City (HCMC), 135, 155, 167,
172, 178, 179, 181, 184, 185, 191, 192,
202, 225–26, 227

Ho Chi Minh City EPZs Authority (HEPZA). *see* HEPZA
Hóc Môn district, 1, 218, 219, 267, 278
Hóc Môn District Labor Union, 221, 279, 280, 284
Hóc Môn People's Court, 280
Hồng Hải, 263, 264
Hồ Ngọc Nhuận, 106
"hot Christmas" strike, 176
household registration (*hộ khẩu*) policy, 135–36, 190, 263
Hsiao, H. H. Michael, 196–97
Huê Phong factory, 234–40, 242–43, 252–54, 275–78
Huê Phong Footwear Co. Ltd., 239. *see also* Huê Phong factory
HUFOCO (Everglory Footwear Co. Ltd.), 239. *see also* Huê Phong factory
Huỳnh Liên, 107
Huỳnh Mỹ Tiên, 95, 97
Huỳnh Thị Ngọc Tuyết, 81, 277
Huỳnh Trí Dũng, 136
"hybrid transitional" economic model, 111–12

I
"illegal strikes," 117
implemented capital (*vốn thực hiện/vốn giải ngân*), 128
import subsidization program, 66
independent labor organizations, 72, 73, 78, 98, 109, 152, 246, 288
Indochina Communist Party (ICP), 30, 38
Industrial Development Center (IDC), 69
Industrial Development Division, 69
inflation, 182, 197, 198
Interior Security Ministry, 77
internal consciousness, 60
International Labor Organization (ILO), 116
International Workers' Day 1944, 41
Investment Law (Luật Đầu Tư), 127
IZs (Industrial Zones), 184–85

J
Japan, 66, 67, 68
Japanese-owned factories, 145, 181, 200
joint-stock/joint venture companies, 114, 127–28, 132, 146, 153, 155, 156, 165, 166, 167, 168, 174

K
Kexim, 278, 280
Khmer ethnic group, 50
Kiên Giang province, 234, 240
Kinh (Người Việt)
    and class, 61
    and division of labor, 37–38
    relationship with Hoa, 23–24, 61, 79, 102
    role in colonial Vietnam, 19–25
    and unions, 100
    women workers, 108–9, 292, 293
knowledge factor, 37, 168, 293
Koh, David, 271, 272
Kollan factory, 211–12
Korean-owned factories, 175–76, 181, 200, 206–7, 217–20, 273, 281, 285
KT3 residency permit, 135–36, 190, 192
Kwang Nam, 281

L
Labor Code, 41, 48, 49, 88, 115–16, 117, 118, 274
labor confederations, 72, 73, 75, 78, 109
labor contracts
    and FDIs, 212, 214, 221–22
    general, 17, 133, 136, 144, 148, 173, 215
    and SOEs, 161, 167, 172–74
    and underground foreign investment factories, 232–33, 244, 256, 257, 258
    see also collective bargaining agreements
Labor Investigation Office, 101
labor-management relations, 115, 249–51, 261–62
labor-management-state relations, 287–89
Labor Newsletter (Bản Tin Lao Động), 82, 107
labor press, 123–24, 147–48, 163–66, 189–90, 198, 215, 224, 233, 247–48, 271–82, 301. *see also specific titles of newspapers/newsletters*
labor system development, 64–65
Labor Union Program–Vietnam TV, 156
Labor Unions Page (Công Đoàn), 273
laid-off workers. *see* "redundant" workers (lao động dôi dư)
land-use rights, 126, 162
Lao Động (Labor), 124, 156, 163, 221, 271, 273, 281
lavatory messages. *see* graffiti protest
lay-offs and lay-off stipulations. *see* "redundancy" policy

Leather Garment 30-4 joint-stock company, 163–64

Lee, Ching Dwan, 4, 8, 180

legal assistance centers (*trung tâm tư vấn pháp luật*), 286, 287

legal capital (*vốn điều lệ*), 128

legal workshops, 286

Lê Kim Ngọc Tuyết, 100

Lệ Thủy, 275, 278

Lê Văn Vũ, 279

Lê Văn Y, 99, 100

Liberation Newsletter (*Bản tin Giải Phóng*), 81

Liberation Newspaper (*Báo Giải Phóng*), 81

library-for-workers (*tủ sách công nhân*), 189–90

limited liability companies, 132, 171

Linh Trung I and II (EPZs), 121, 185, 200, 268

living conditions, 190, 235

local resident status, 135

Long An province, 184

L'Union Commerciale Indochinoise (L'UCI), 26

Lưu Quế , 86, 90–93

M

Machine Assembly and Construction 45-4 company, 170–71

Magnicon factory, 217

male-worker bonding, 194–95

management codes of conduct, 131

manufacturing hierarchies, 130–31

"market economy with social orientation" (*Kinh tế thị trường, Định hướng xã hội chủ nghĩa*), 3, 4, 113–14

Marxist-Leninist ideology, 3, 39, 64, 123

Marxist-type resistance, 8, 12, 39, 62, 223, 283, 285, 291–92, 299–300

May Day parade (1966), 97

methodology of book, 9–11

methods of protest, 9–11

Michelin Company, 50

military-owned factories, 156, 157, 172

Minh Nghệ leather shoe factory, 228–29

minimum-wage levels. *see also* 2006 minimum-wage law

in the domestic sector, 136–38, 140–41

in the FDI sector, 136–40, 200

in state-owned companies, 262–64

minimum-wage strikes

nationwide statistics, 141–47

specific, 198–200, 209, 211, 215, 224–28, 262–64, 283, 298

Ministry of External Affairs (Bộ Ngoại Vụ), 126, 250

Ministry of Finance, 133

Ministry of Foreign Relations, 126

Ministry of Justice, 127

Ministry of Labor, Invalids, and Social Affairs. *see* MOLISA

Ministry of Planning and Investment (MPI), 126–27, 250, 280–81

MOLISA, 115, 116, 132, 133, 151, 226

"Mr. Jen," 87

multiple-language organizing, 93–94

Mỹ Lộc, 32

My Phong shoe factory, 200, 263, 288

N

Nam Á Shoe joint-stock company, 163

Nam Định, 15, 16, 159, 160

Nam Định Museum, 10, 15

Nam Định province, 235

Nam Định Textile Combine, 15, 18, 26–27, 30–34, 37–42, 63

Nam Trực, 32

Nanjing Agreement, 22

National Congress of Trade Unions, 41

National Employers' Conference 2011, 117

Nationalist Party government of China, 25

nationality law (November 1963), 65

National Liberation Front (NLF), 75, 88, 212

native-place (*yếu tố đồng hương*) identification, 8, 32, 55, 158–61, 194–95, 235, 236, 240–41, 246, 258, 268–71

neoliberal era and the global market system, 128, 153, 222, 262, 301

neoliberal era and the law, 3, 4, 113, 292, 301

newspapers. *see by name*; labor press; state media

Người Lao Động (Laborer)

equitization, 163

and foreign-investment factories, 191, 207, 220–21, 224, 228–29, 230–31, 251

Labor Law Consultancy section, 213–14

Labor Unions Page (Trang Công Đoàn), 273

library-for-workers campaign, 189

as public forum, 124

Quảng Việt protest, 213
and state worker agency, 178
and state–worker relations, 271, 272,
273, 275, 278, 279, 284, 285
Unions Page, 275
Người Việt. see Kinh
người Việt gốc Hoa (Vietnamese of Chinese
origin). see Hoa
Nguyễn An, 29–30
Nguyễn Đức Cảnh, 39, 40
Nguyễn Mạnh Cường, 115
Nguyễn Minh Hà, 207–8
Nguyễn Nghị, 81, 85
Nguyễn Ngọc Linh, 71, 74, 75
Nguyễn Quốc Việt, 4, 6, 272
Nguyễn Tấn Dũng, 201
Nguyễn Thị Thanh Mai, 117
Nguyễn Thị Vá, 43
Nguyễn Tiến Cảnh, 27, 29, 38
Nguyễn Tiến Mạo, 84
Nguyễn Văn Thư, 73, 74, 77, 91
Nguyễn-võ Thu-hương, 262
Nhiệm Hồng Bảo, 87
Nhơn Trạch district, 286
Norlund, Irene, 120
"no violence" strategy, 243–44

O
occupational rituals, 195
"one stop service" principle, 121
Ong, Aihwa, 3, 31
Ordinance No. 48, 65
Ordinance No. 53, 128
origins of capital (*quốc tịch của doanh
nghiệp*), 127
overtime stipulations, 101, 116, 198, 213,
231, 232, 235, 242
Oxfam Belgium Solidarity, 286
Oxfam–Vietnam, 286

P
peasants-turned-workers. see "brown-
shirted workers" (*công nhân áo nâu*)
"pen protests," 156–58, 283
Perry, Elizabeth, 35
petitions, 214, 221–22
Phạm Hồ, 277
Phạm Ngọc Đoàn, 252, 253–54
Phan Khắc Từ, 82, 107

Phan Văn Chí, 77, 99, 102
Phú Riềng rubber plantation, 18–19, 49–50,
54–62
Phú Sĩ Washing and Ironing Services, 257–
58
piece-rate pay system, 17–18
Pin Con Ó (Eagle Battery) factory. *see*
Eagle Battery factory
Polanyi-type resistance, 8, 12, 25–26, 27,
62, 223, 283, 291–92, 299–300
police brutality, 102–4
Popular Front government, 48
post-equitization period (giai đoạn *hậu cổ
phần hóa*), 153–54, 165
Pou Yuen Vietnam, 130–31, 198, 202
President Ngô Đình Diệm, 65
President Nguyễn Khánh, 88
Prime Minister decrees: Decree No. 2, 274,
277, 280; Decree No. 3, 177; Decree No.
41, 180; Decree No. 51, 135, 190; Decree
No. 70, 139; Decree No. 98, 136–37;
Decree No. 110, 133, 226; Decree No.
168, 139
Prime Minister Decision 276/2006, 136
prison diaries (*Nhật Ký Trong Tù Của Tập
Thể Công Nhân*), 64, 86, 100, 102, 108,
296
privatization. *see* equitization (*cổ phần hóa*)
and equitized companies
privatization laws. *see* Equitization Laws
(2002–13)
proactive Catholic movement (Công Giáo
Tiến Hành), 84
Proposal No. 3 (Labor Code), 116, 117–18
Proposed Labor Code Revision,
Stipulation No. 92, Section 1, 182
protest letters, 228–29, 254–58, 284
protests. *see by type and by factory/company*
Provisional Executive Council of the
Committee for the Protection of
Workers' Rights, 82

Q
Quách Nhạn, 100
Quảng Nam region, 50–51
Quảng Ninh mines, 27
Quảng Trị region, 50–51
Quảng Việt factory strikes, 212–15

R

"race to the bottom," 128

Rạch Chiếc River, 178

Radio Vietnam, 156

"rearrangement of SOEs" (*Sắp xếp lại công ty nhà nước*), 132

Reception and Resettlement Committee, 78

"red thread," 291

Red Trade Union Federation (RTUF), 24, 30, 38, 39, 41, 59, 119. *see also* Vietnamese Federation of Trade Unions (VFTU)

"redundancy" policy, 167–68, 173, 226

"redundant" workers (*lao động dôi dư*), 132, 133, 155, 161, 163, 170

registered capital (*vốn đăng ký*), 128

religious identity, 8, 84–85, 107, 195

Republic of Vietnam (RVN [the South]) policies, 64–66

residency law (*Luật Cư Trú*), 135

resistance. *see by type and by factory/company*

Resolution of Labor Disputes, 116

Revolutionary Youth League, 39

rice, 20, 66, 67

rights-based language, 214, 215

rights (*quyền*) *versus* interests (*lợi ích*), 117–18

rubber, 16–17, 66

rule by law *versus* rule of law, 4–6

rule of law, 3–6, 12–13, 282, 284–86, 287, 297

rural workers and minimum wage, 137–38

S

sabotage, 60, 119

Sagoda Leather Shoe company, 168–69

Saigon, 16–17, 19, 24–25, 78, 97

Saigon-Chợ Lớn labor movement, 71, 79, 80, 86, 93, 97, 99

Saigon Department of Labor, 71–72, 101, 105

Saigon Labor Court, 102, 105

samizdat, 10, 299

schools for migrant workers' children, 192–93

Scott, James C., 7

"selling young rice" (*"bán lúa non"*), 164

service sector, 123

severance pay, 161–62, 163, 168, 169, 170, 171, 226, 231

"shadow-foreign enterprises." *see* underground investment factories (*đầu tư chui*),

Shanghai study of labor resistance, 35

Shilla Bags company, 206–8

"short sale" of shares (*"bán lúa non"*), 164

Sidel, Mark, 5–6, 180

sisterhood/brotherhood language, 214, 215, 220

skilled factory workers. *see* "blue-shirted workers" (*công nhân áo xanh*)

skills differentiation of workers, 36, 61, 125, 205, 293

skills factor, 35–37

social contract, 157, 158, 173, 282, 283, 300

social insurance benefits, 150–51, 172, 213, 215, 245, 247, 251, 264, 274–75, 280

socialist contract/ideals, 157, 158, 168, 175, 179, 180, 232, 233, 285, 300

Socialist Republic of Vietnam, 111, 125, 171

social justice consciousness, 108

social-opinion cells (*tổ dư luận xã hội*), 265, 267, 268–71

Sóc Sơn district, 267

SOEs. *see* state-owned enterprises

soldiers to protect trade union units (*chiến sĩ*), 76

Sơn Kim garment factory, 231–32

Southeast Asian investors, 196

South Korea, 175, 176

South Vietnam. *see* Republic of Vietnam (RVN [the South])

Soviet commercial relations, 113, 125–26

state media, 9, 123, 152, 156, 169, 213, 271, 282, 288

state-owned enterprises (SOEs), 113–14, 120, 123, 127, 131–34, 142, 146, 153–80, 226, 282, 283, 300

state pro-investment policies, 199

"state segregation," 272

state surveillance, 265–67

state worker agency

    and equitization policy, 154, 156–61

    and equitized joint-stock companies, 166–74

    in HCMC state-owned enterprises, 154–56

    layoffs, 153

    pre-equitization period, 156–61

    and rule of law, 282–83

    and Việt Thắng, 174–79

strike hotspots, 129

strike mediation and Labor Code, 118

strike protests, 141–47, 167–68, 181, 197–203

structure of labor force in market economy, 113–14

Students and Scholars against Corporate Misbehavior (SACOM), 203

subcontracting hierarchies, 130–31

Suhong Chae, 175

T

Taiwan, 25, 66, 67, 68, 70, 88

Taiwanese investment, 103, 121, 129, 184, 196–97, 200, 240

Tân Phú People's Court, 280

Tân Thuận EPZ, 121, 185, 268, 269

Tầu Cuốc joint-stock company, 167–68

temporary residency permit (KT3), 135–36

Tết bonus (or thirteenth-month bonus), 101, 155, 175

textiles, 66, 69

Thái Bình province, 234, 235, 240

Thanh Hóa province, 235

Thanh Hoá region, 50–51

Thanh Lao Công (TLC), 83–85, 99, 101, 105–7

Thanh Loan Thi Ltd. (TLT), 256

Thiệu-Kỳ government, 65

thirteenth-month bonus. *see* Tết bonus

Thirty-Nine-Letter Sample, 11

Thời Ích rubber company, 229–30

Thompson, E. P., 6, 27, 31

Thợ Xưởng Dệt, 47

Thủ Đức district, 89, 175

Tianjin Commercial Convention, 21

Tiền Giang, 268, 269, 270, 271

"tiger cage," 92

TLC. *see* Thanh Lao Công (TLC)

Tô Gia Đương, 237

Tonkin, 16

Tôn Nhơn Khanh, 87

Top One lunch boycott, 208

Tô Sang, 99, 100

Tô Thanh Tuyền, 99, 102

Trade Union of Workers in the Far East Battery Company (Nghiệp Đoàn Công Nhân Công ty Pin Viễn Đông), 99

Trade Union of Workers of the Vietnamese Battery Company (Nghiệp Đoàn Công Nhân Hãng Pin Việt Nam), 99

tradition, 32–33

Trần Đăng Thanh, 187

Trần Hữu Quyền, 75, 78, 79

Trảng Bom district, 286

Trần Lượng, 100

Trần Nam Dương, 165, 166

Trần Quốc Bửu, 74, 75, 76, 78, 88, 95, 97

transparent wage table, 245

Trần Thị Kim Đường, 32, 38

Trần Thị Lệ, 279, 280

Trần Tử Bình, 55, 56, 57, 58, 59

Trần Văn Giàu, 6, 23, 28, 29, 31, 35, 38

Trần Văn Hai, 77

Trần Văn Lý, 143

Trần Xuân Cầu, 185

Trà Vinh city, 200

Trà Vinh province, 263

Treaty of Peace, Friendship, and Commerce, 21

Tria Kerkvliet, Melinda, 158

Trịnh Quang Quỹ, 73, 74, 77

Trực Ninh, 32

Trương Bá Cần, 82, 84, 106

Trương Bá Huê, 99, 100

Trương Lâm Danh, 116, 218, 280

U

underground investment factories (*đầu tư chui*), 225, 234–58

unemployment insurance, 151

Unions Page, 275

urban-rural wage disparity, 262–63

US Agency for International Development (USAID), 68, 87

US Central Intelligence Agency (CIA), 74, 75, 98

use of law, 98, 221–22, 223–24, 228–29, 230, 233, 246–48, 274–75, 291

US investment, 66–70, 69, 129

US Operations Mission (USOM), 69, 75, 76, 87

US President Johnson [LBJ], 76

US trade embargo, 112, 113, 125, 255

US–Vietnamese relations, 113, 128

US–Vietnam War. *see* American War

utility costs, 135, 136, 191

V

VC. *see* Việt Cộng

VCP. *see* Vietnamese Communist Party

VCP-Mandated Directive (Chỉ Thị) 22, 147–48

Vidopin. *see* Eagle Battery factory

Vietnamese Communist Party (VCP), 24, 38, 39, 40, 41, 86, 96, 119, 120, 147, 156–57, 269
Vietnamese Communist Party (VCP) congresses, 4, 13, 112–13, 122, 125, 249
Vietnamese Confederation of Catholic Workers (Confederation Vietnamienne du Travail Catholique [CVTC]), 74
Vietnamese Confederation of Workers (Confederation Vietnamienne du Travail [CVT]), 74
Vietnamese Federation of Trade Unions (VFTU), 41, 119
Vietnamese General Confederation of Labor (VGCL), 10, 119, 120–22, 123, 151, 152, 165, 201, 251, 265
Vietnamese National Assembly, 4
Vietnam Security Guard Services (Công Ty Dịch Vụ Bảo Vệ Việt Nam), 232–33
Vietnamese Textile and Apparel Association (VITAS), 116
Vietnamese Victory Textile. *see* Việt Thắng Factory
Vietnam War. *see* American War
Việt Cộng (VC), 81
Việt Thắng Factory, 87, 174–75, 179. *see also* Vimytex
Việt Thắng Jeans Limited Company, 178–79, 283
Việt Thắng Textile combine, 158–59
Việt Thắng Textile Limited, 174
Việt Thắng-Vicoluch, 174, 283
Vimytex, 69, 70. *see also* Việt Thắng Factory
Vimytex textile factory, 86, 87–99
Vimytex Trade Union (Phân Bộ Nghiệp Đoàn Vimytex), 94
Vimytex Workers Trade Federation (Nghiệp Đoàn Công Nhân Vimytex), 94
Vina Duke factory, 267
Vinatex, 134
Vinatexco, 70
Vĩnh Phúc province, 263
Vĩnh Tùng, 278
violations of law by companies/owners, 201–2, 228–29, 230, 232, 242, 251, 276–77, 284, 285
Viva-Blast Prezioso labor dispute, 215–16
Voice of the People radio station, 169
Vương Khải Hồng, 100

W
wages/salary. *see* minimum-wage levels
wage zones, 263
Wang, Hong-Zen, 196–97
Wehrle, Edmund F., 74
welfare entitlements, 226
West Germany, 68
women workers
    aspirations of, 187–88
    class consciousness, 102, 103, 104, 105, 108
    food boycott, 206–8
    and gender bonding, 292
    graffiti protest, 209–12
    native-place bonding, 235–36, 240–42
    protests in French colonial period, 27, 31, 33, 34, 36, 37, 42, 48, 58, 59, 61, 63–64
    rights, 27
    and skills, 293
    stipulations in the Labor Code, 115, 116
worker cells, 265–68
worker housing (*làng*), 179, 185
worker self-management cells (*tổ công nhân tự quản*), 265, 266
Workers Newspaper (Báo Công Nhân), 81
worker surveillance. *see* worker cells
worker voice, 123–24
working conditions, 154, 171–72, 179, 187, 189, 226, 236, 242
workplace accidents, 171–72
World Bank, 133
World Trade Organization (WTO), 3, 272
World War I, 16, 49, 50

X
X32 Shoe and Garment Factory, 172

Y
Young Catholic Worker movement (Thanh Lao Công [TLC]), 81, 82, 83, 84
Young Christian Workers (YCW) movement, 83–84

SOUTHEAST ASIA PROGRAM PUBLICATIONS
Cornell University

Studies on Southeast Asia

Number 62   *Ties that Bind: Cultural Identity, Class, and Law in Vietnam's Labor Resistance,* Trần Ngọc Angie. 2013. ISBN 978-0-87727-762-0 (pb.)

Number 61   *A Mountain of Difference: The Lumad in Early Colonial Mindanao,* Oona Paredes. 2013. ISBN 978-0-87727-761-3 (pb.)

Number 60   *The* Kim Vân Kieu *of Nguyen Du (1765–1820),* trans. Vladislav Zhukov. 2013. ISBN 978-0-87727-760-6 (pb.)

Number 59   *The Politics of Timor-Leste: Democratic Consolidation after Intervention,* ed. Michael Leach and Damien Kingsbury. 2013. ISBN 978-0-87727-759-0 (pb.)

Number 58   *The Spirit of Things: Materiality and Religious Diversity in Southeast Asia,* ed. Julius Bautista. 2012. ISBN 970-0-87727-758-3 (pb.)

Number 57   *Demographic Change in Southeast Asia: Recent Histories and Future Directions,* ed. Lindy Williams and Michael Philip Guest. 2012. ISBN 978-0-87727-757-6 (pb.)

Number 56   *Modern and Contemporary Southeast Asian Art: An Anthology,* ed. Nora A. Taylor and Boreth Ly. 2012. ISBN 978-0-87727-756-9 (pb.)

Number 55   *Glimpses of Freedom: Independent Cinema in Southeast Asia,* ed. May Adadol Ingawanij and Benjamin McKay. 2012. ISBN 978-0-87727-755-2 (pb.)

Number 54   *Student Activism in Malaysia: Crucible, Mirror, Sideshow,* Meredith L. Weiss. 2011. ISBN 978-0-87727-754-5 (pb.)

Number 53   *Political Authority and Provincial Identity in Thailand: The Making of Banharn-buri,* Yoshinori Nishizaki. 2011. ISBN 978-0-87727-753-8 (pb.)

Number 52   *Vietnam and the West: New Approaches,* ed. Wynn Wilcox. 2010. ISBN 978-0-87727-752-1 (pb.)

Number 51   *Cultures at War: The Cold War and Cultural Expression in Southeast Asia,* ed. Tony Day and Maya H. T. Liem. 2010. ISBN 978-0-87727-751-4 (pb.)

Number 50   *State of Authority: The State in Society in Indonesia,* ed. Gerry van Klinken and Joshua Barker. 2009. ISBN 978-0-87727-750-7 (pb.)

Number 49   *Phan Châu Trinh and His Political Writings,* Phan Châu Trinh, ed. and trans. Vinh Sinh. 2009. ISBN 978-0-87727-749-1 (pb.)

Number 48   *Dependent Communities: Aid and Politics in Cambodia and East Timor,* Caroline Hughes. 2009. ISBN 978-0-87727-748-4 (pb.)

Number 47   *A Man Like Him: Portrait of the Burmese Journalist, Journal Kyaw U Chit Maung,* Journal Kyaw Ma Ma Lay, trans. Ma Thanegi, 2008. ISBN 978-0-87727-747-7 (pb.)

Number 46   *At the Edge of the Forest: Essays on Cambodia, History, and Narrative in Honor of David Chandler,* ed. Anne Ruth Hansen and Judy Ledgerwood. 2008. ISBN 978-0-87727-746-0 (pb).

Number 45   *Conflict, Violence, and Displacement in Indonesia,* ed. Eva-Lotta E. Hedman. 2008. ISBN 978-0-87727-745-3 (pb).

Number 44   *Friends and Exiles: A Memoir of the Nutmeg Isles and the Indonesian Nationalist Movement*, Des Alwi, ed. Barbara S. Harvey. 2008. ISBN 978-0-877277-44-6 (pb).

Number 43   *Early Southeast Asia: Selected Essays*, O. W. Wolters, ed. Craig J. Reynolds. 2008. 255 pp. ISBN 978-0-877277-43-9 (pb).

Number 42   *Thailand: The Politics of Despotic Paternalism* (revised edition), Thak Chaloemtiarana. 2007. 284 pp. ISBN 0-8772-7742-7 (pb).

Number 41   *Views of Seventeenth-Century Vietnam: Christoforo Borri on Cochinchina and Samuel Baron on Tonkin*, ed. Olga Dror and K. W. Taylor. 2006. 290 pp. ISBN 0-8772-7741-9 (pb).

Number 40   *Laskar Jihad: Islam, Militancy, and the Quest for Identity in Post-New Order Indonesia*, Noorhaidi Hasan. 2006. 266 pp. ISBN 0-877277-40-0 (pb).

Number 39   *The Indonesian Supreme Court: A Study of Institutional Collapse*, Sebastiaan Pompe. 2005. 494 pp. ISBN 0-877277-38-9 (pb).

Number 38   *Spirited Politics: Religion and Public Life in Contemporary Southeast Asia*, ed. Andrew C. Willford and Kenneth M. George. 2005. 210 pp. ISBN 0-87727-737-0.

Number 37   *Sumatran Sultanate and Colonial State: Jambi and the Rise of Dutch Imperialism, 1830-1907*, Elsbeth Locher-Scholten, trans. Beverley Jackson. 2004. 332 pp. ISBN 0-87727-736-2.

Number 36   *Southeast Asia over Three Generations: Essays Presented to Benedict R. O'G. Anderson*, ed. James T. Siegel and Audrey R. Kahin. 2003. 398 pp. ISBN 0-87727-735-4.

Number 35   *Nationalism and Revolution in Indonesia*, George McTurnan Kahin, intro. Benedict R. O'G. Anderson (reprinted from 1952 edition, Cornell University Press, with permission). 2003. 530 pp. ISBN 0-87727-734-6.

Number 34   *Golddiggers, Farmers, and Traders in the "Chinese Districts" of West Kalimantan, Indonesia*, Mary Somers Heidhues. 2003. 316 pp. ISBN 0-87727-733-8.

Number 33   *Opusculum de Sectis apud Sinenses et Tunkinenses (A Small Treatise on the Sects among the Chinese and Tonkinese): A Study of Religion in China and North Vietnam in the Eighteenth Century*, Father Adriano de St. Thecla, trans. Olga Dror, with Mariya Berezovska. 2002. 363 pp. ISBN 0-87727-732-X.

Number 32   *Fear and Sanctuary: Burmese Refugees in Thailand*, Hazel J. Lang. 2002. 204 pp. ISBN 0-87727-731-1.

Number 31   *Modern Dreams: An Inquiry into Power, Cultural Production, and the Cityscape in Contemporary Urban Penang, Malaysia*, Beng-Lan Goh. 2002. 225 pp. ISBN 0-87727-730-3.

Number 30   *Violence and the State in Suharto's Indonesia*, ed. Benedict R. O'G. Anderson. 2001. Second printing, 2002. 247 pp. ISBN 0-87727-729-X.

Number 29   *Studies in Southeast Asian Art: Essays in Honor of Stanley J. O'Connor*, ed. Nora A. Taylor. 2000. 243 pp. Illustrations. ISBN 0-87727-728-1.

Number 28   *The Hadrami Awakening: Community and Identity in the Netherlands East Indies, 1900-1942*, Natalie Mobini-Kesheh. 1999. 174 pp. ISBN 0-87727-727-3.

Number 27   *Tales from Djakarta: Caricatures of Circumstances and their Human Beings*, Pramoedya Ananta Toer. 1999. 145 pp. ISBN 0-87727-726-5.

Number 26   *History, Culture, and Region in Southeast Asian Perspectives*, rev. ed., O. W. Wolters. 1999. Second printing, 2004. 275 pp. ISBN 0-87727-725-7.

Number 25   *Figures of Criminality in Indonesia, the Philippines, and Colonial Vietnam*, ed. Vicente L. Rafael. 1999. 259 pp. ISBN 0-87727-724-9.

Number 24   *Paths to Conflagration: Fifty Years of Diplomacy and Warfare in Laos, Thailand, and Vietnam, 1778-1828*, Mayoury Ngaosyvathn and Pheuiphanh Ngaosyvathn. 1998. 268 pp. ISBN 0-87727-723-0.

Number 23   *Nguyễn Cochinchina: Southern Vietnam in the Seventeenth and Eighteenth Centuries*, Li Tana. 1998. Second printing, 2002. 194 pp. ISBN 0-87727-722-2.

Number 22   *Young Heroes: The Indonesian Family in Politics*, Saya S. Shiraishi. 1997. 183 pp. ISBN 0-87727-721-4.

Number 21   *Interpreting Development: Capitalism, Democracy, and the Middle Class in Thailand*, John Girling. 1996. 95 pp. ISBN 0-87727-720-6.

Number 20   *Making Indonesia*, ed. Daniel S. Lev, Ruth McVey. 1996. 201 pp. ISBN 0-87727-719-2.

Number 19   *Essays into Vietnamese Pasts*, ed. K. W. Taylor, John K. Whitmore. 1995. 288 pp. ISBN 0-87727-718-4.

Number 18   *In the Land of Lady White Blood: Southern Thailand and the Meaning of History*, Lorraine M. Gesick. 1995. 106 pp. ISBN 0-87727-717-6.

Number 17   *The Vernacular Press and the Emergence of Modern Indonesian Consciousness*, Ahmat Adam. 1995. 220 pp. ISBN 0-87727-716-8.

Number 16   *The Nan Chronicle*, trans., ed. David K. Wyatt. 1994. 158 pp. ISBN 0-87727-715-X.

Number 15   *Selective Judicial Competence: The Cirebon-Priangan Legal Administration, 1680–1792*, Mason C. Hoadley. 1994. 185 pp. ISBN 0-87727-714-1.

Number 14   *Sjahrir: Politics and Exile in Indonesia*, Rudolf Mrázek. 1994. 536 pp. ISBN 0-87727-713-3.

Number 13   *Fair Land Sarawak: Some Recollections of an Expatriate Officer*, Alastair Morrison. 1993. 196 pp. ISBN 0-87727-712-5.

Number 12   *Fields from the Sea: Chinese Junk Trade with Siam during the Late Eighteenth and Early Nineteenth Centuries*, Jennifer Cushman. 1993. 206 pp. ISBN 0-87727-711-7.

Number 11   *Money, Markets, and Trade in Early Southeast Asia: The Development of Indigenous Monetary Systems to AD 1400*, Robert S. Wicks. 1992. 2nd printing 1996. 354 pp., 78 tables, illus., maps. ISBN 0-87727-710-9.

Number 10   *Tai Ahoms and the Stars: Three Ritual Texts to Ward Off Danger*, trans., ed. B. J. Terwiel, Ranoo Wichasin. 1992. 170 pp. ISBN 0-87727-709-5.

Number 9   *Southeast Asian Capitalists*, ed. Ruth McVey. 1992. 2nd printing 1993. 220 pp. ISBN 0-87727-708-7.

Number 8   *The Politics of Colonial Exploitation: Java, the Dutch, and the Cultivation System*, Cornelis Fasseur, ed. R. E. Elson, trans. R. E. Elson, Ary Kraal. 1992. 2nd printing 1994. 266 pp. ISBN 0-87727-707-9.

Number 7   *A Malay Frontier: Unity and Duality in a Sumatran Kingdom,* Jane Drakard. 1990. 2nd printing 2003. 215 pp. ISBN 0-87727-706-0.

Number 6   *Trends in Khmer Art,* Jean Boisselier, ed. Natasha Eilenberg, trans. Natasha Eilenberg, Melvin Elliott. 1989. 124 pp., 24 plates. ISBN 0-87727-705-2.

Number 5   *Southeast Asian Ephemeris: Solar and Planetary Positions, A.D. 638–2000,* J. C. Eade. 1989. 175 pp. ISBN 0-87727-704-4.

Number 3   *Thai Radical Discourse: The Real Face of Thai Feudalism Today,* Craig J. Reynolds. 1987. 2nd printing 1994. 186 pp. ISBN 0-87727-702-8.

Number 1   *The Symbolism of the Stupa,* Adrian Snodgrass. 1985. Revised with index, 1988. 3rd printing 1998. 469 pp. ISBN 0-87727-700-1.

SEAP Series

Number 23   *Possessed by the Spirits: Mediumship in Contemporary Vietnamese Communities.* 2006. 186 pp. ISBN 0-877271-41-0 (pb).

Number 22   *The Industry of Marrying Europeans,* Vũ Trọng Phụng, trans. Thúy Tranviet. 2006. 66 pp. ISBN 0-877271-40-2 (pb).

Number 21   *Securing a Place: Small-Scale Artisans in Modern Indonesia,* Elizabeth Morrell. 2005. 220 pp. ISBN 0-877271-39-9.

Number 20   *Southern Vietnam under the Reign of Minh Mạng (1820-1841): Central Policies and Local Response,* Choi Byung Wook. 2004. 226pp. ISBN 0-0-877271-40-2.

Number 19   *Gender, Household, State: Đổi Mới in Việt Nam,* ed. Jayne Werner and Danièle Bélanger. 2002. 151 pp. ISBN 0-87727-137-2.

Number 18   *Culture and Power in Traditional Siamese Government,* Neil A. Englehart. 2001. 130 pp. ISBN 0-87727-135-6.

Number 17   *Gangsters, Democracy, and the State,* ed. Carl A. Trocki. 1998. Second printing, 2002. 94 pp. ISBN 0-87727-134-8.

Number 16   *Cutting across the Lands: An Annotated Bibliography on Natural Resource Management and Community Development in Indonesia, the Philippines, and Malaysia,* ed. Eveline Ferretti. 1997. 329 pp. ISBN 0-87727-133-X.

Number 15   *The Revolution Falters: The Left in Philippine Politics after 1986,* ed. Patricio N. Abinales. 1996. Second printing, 2002. 182 pp. ISBN 0-87727-132-1.

Number 14   *Being Kammu: My Village, My Life,* Damrong Tayanin. 1994. 138 pp., 22 tables, illus., maps. ISBN 0-87727-130-5.

Number 13   *The American War in Vietnam,* ed. Jayne Werner, David Hunt. 1993. 132 pp. ISBN 0-87727-131-3.

Number 12   *The Voice of Young Burma,* Aye Kyaw. 1993. 92 pp. ISBN 0-87727-129-1.

Number 11   *The Political Legacy of Aung San,* ed. Josef Silverstein. Revised edition 1993. 169 pp. ISBN 0-87727-128-3.

Number 10   *Studies on Vietnamese Language and Literature: A Preliminary Bibliography,* Nguyen Dinh Tham. 1992. 227 pp. ISBN 0-87727-127-5.

Number 8   *From PKI to the Comintern, 1924–1941: The Apprenticeship of the Malayan Communist Party,* Cheah Boon Kheng. 1992. 147 pp. ISBN 0-87727-125-9.

Number 7   *Intellectual Property and US Relations with Indonesia, Malaysia, Singapore, and Thailand*, Elisabeth Uphoff. 1991. 67 pp. ISBN 0-87727-124-0.

Number 6   *The Rise and Fall of the Communist Party of Burma (CPB)*, Bertil Lintner. 1990. 124 pp. 26 illus., 14 maps. ISBN 0-87727-123-2.

Number 5   *Japanese Relations with Vietnam: 1951–1987*, Masaya Shiraishi. 1990. 174 pp. ISBN 0-87727-122-4.

Number 3   *Postwar Vietnam: Dilemmas in Socialist Development*, ed. Christine White, David Marr. 1988. 2nd printing 1993. 260 pp. ISBN 0-87727-120-8.

Number 2   *The Dobama Movement in Burma (1930–1938)*, Khin Yi. 1988. 160 pp. ISBN 0-87727-118-6.

Cornell Modern Indonesia Project Publications

All CMIP titles available at http://cmip.library.cornell.edu

Number 75   *A Tour of Duty: Changing Patterns of Military Politics in Indonesia in the 1990s.* Douglas Kammen and Siddharth Chandra. 1999. 99 pp. ISBN 0-87763-049-6.

Number 74   *The Roots of Acehnese Rebellion 1989–1992*, Tim Kell. 1995. 103 pp. ISBN 0-87763-040-2.

Number 72   *Popular Indonesian Literature of the Qur'an*, Howard M. Federspiel. 1994. 170 pp. ISBN 0-87763-038-0.

Number 71   *A Javanese Memoir of Sumatra, 1945–1946: Love and Hatred in the Liberation War*, Takao Fusayama. 1993. 150 pp. ISBN 0-87763-037-2.

Number 69   *The Road to Madiun: The Indonesian Communist Uprising of 1948*, Elizabeth Ann Swift. 1989. 120 pp. ISBN 0-87763-035-6.

Number 68   *Intellectuals and Nationalism in Indonesia: A Study of the Following Recruited by Sutan Sjahrir in Occupation Jakarta*, J. D. Legge. 1988. 159 pp. ISBN 0-87763-034-8.

Number 67   *Indonesia Free: A Biography of Mohammad Hatta*, Mavis Rose. 1987. 252 pp. ISBN 0-87763-033-X.

Number 66   *Prisoners at Kota Cane*, Leon Salim, trans. Audrey Kahin. 1986. 112 pp. ISBN 0-87763-032-1.

Number 64   *Suharto and His Generals: Indonesia's Military Politics, 1975–1983*, David Jenkins. 1984. 4th printing 1997. 300 pp. ISBN 0-87763-030-5.

Number 62   *Interpreting Indonesian Politics: Thirteen Contributions to the Debate, 1964–1981*, ed. Benedict Anderson, Audrey Kahin, intro. Daniel S. Lev. 1982. 3rd printing 1991. 172 pp. ISBN 0-87763-028-3.

Number 60   *The Minangkabau Response to Dutch Colonial Rule in the Nineteenth Century*, Elizabeth E. Graves. 1981. 157 pp. ISBN 0-87763-000-3.

Number 57   *Permesta: Half a Rebellion*, Barbara S. Harvey. 1977. 174 pp. ISBN 0-87763-003-8.

Number 52   *A Preliminary Analysis of the October 1 1965, Coup in Indonesia (Prepared in January 1966)*, Benedict R. Anderson, Ruth T. McVey, assist. Frederick P. Bunnell. 1971. 3rd printing 1990. 174 pp. ISBN 0-87763-008-9.

Number 48   *Nationalism, Islam and Marxism,* Soekarno, intro. Ruth T. McVey. 1970.

Number 37   *Mythology and the Tolerance of the Javanese,* Benedict R. O'G. Anderson. 2nd edition, 1996. Reprinted 2004. 104 pp., 65 illus. ISBN 0-87763-041-0.

Copublished Titles

The Ambiguous Allure of the West: Traces of the Colonial in Thailand, ed. Rachel V. Harrison and Peter A. Jackson. Copublished with Hong Kong University Press. 2010. ISBN 978-0-87727-608-1 (pb.)

The Many Ways of Being Muslim: Fiction by Muslim Filipinos, ed. Coeli Barry. Copublished with Anvil Publishing, Inc., the Philippines. 2008. ISBN 978-0-87727-605-0 (pb.)

Language Texts

INDONESIAN

Beginning Indonesian through Self-Instruction, John U. Wolff, Dédé Oetomo, Daniel Fietkiewicz. 3rd revised edition 1992. Vol. 1. 115 pp. ISBN 0-87727-529-7. Vol. 2. 434 pp. ISBN 0-87727-530-0. Vol. 3. 473 pp. ISBN 0-87727-531-9.

Indonesian Readings, John U. Wolff. 1978. 4th printing 1992. 480 pp. ISBN 0-87727-517-3

Indonesian Conversations, John U. Wolff. 1978. 3rd printing 1991. 297 pp. ISBN 0-87727-516-5

Formal Indonesian, John U. Wolff. 2nd revised edition 1986. 446 pp. ISBN 0-87727-515-7

TAGALOG

Pilipino through Self-Instruction, John U. Wolff, Maria Theresa C. Centeno, Der-Hwa V. Rau. 1991. Vol. 1. 342 pp. ISBN 0-87727—525-4. Vol. 2., revised 2005, 378 pp. ISBN 0-87727-526-2. Vol 3., revised 2005, 431 pp. ISBN 0-87727-527-0. Vol. 4. 306 pp. ISBN 0-87727-528-9.

THAI

A. U. A. Language Center Thai Course, J. Marvin Brown. Originally published by the American University Alumni Association Language Center, 1974. Reissued by Cornell Southeast Asia Program, 1991, 1992. Book 1. 267 pp. ISBN 0-87727-506-8. Book 2. 288 pp. ISBN 0-87727-507-6. Book 3. 247 pp. ISBN 0-87727-508-4.

A. U. A. Language Center Thai Course, Reading and Writing Text (mostly reading), 1979. Reissued 1997. 164 pp. ISBN 0-87727-511-4.

A. U. A. Language Center Thai Course, Reading and Writing Workbook (mostly writing), 1979. Reissued 1997. 99 pp. ISBN 0-87727-512-2.

KHMER

Cambodian System of Writing and Beginning Reader, Franklin E. Huffman. Originally published by Yale University Press, 1970. Reissued by Cornell Southeast Asia Program, 4th printing 2002. 365 pp. ISBN 0-300-01314-0.

Modern Spoken Cambodian, Franklin E. Huffman, assist. Charan Promchan, Chhom-Rak Thong Lambert. Originally published by Yale University Press, 1970. Reissued by Cornell Southeast Asia Program, 3rd printing 1991. 451 pp. ISBN 0-300-01316-7.

Intermediate Cambodian Reader, ed. Franklin E. Huffman, assist. Im Proum. Originally published by Yale University Press, 1972. Reissued by Cornell Southeast Asia Program, 1988. 499 pp. ISBN 0-300-01552-6.

Cambodian Literary Reader and Glossary, Franklin E. Huffman, Im Proum. Originally published by Yale University Press, 1977. Reissued by Cornell Southeast Asia Program, 1988. 494 pp. ISBN 0-300-02069-4.

HMONG

White Hmong-English Dictionary, Ernest E. Heimbach. 1969. 8th printing, 2002. 523 pp. ISBN 0-87727-075-9.

VIETNAMESE

Intermediate Spoken Vietnamese, Franklin E. Huffman, Tran Trong Hai. 1980. 3rd printing 1994. ISBN 0-87727-500-9.

Proto-Austronesian Phonology with Glossary, John U. Wolff, 2 volumes, 2011. ISBN vol. I, 978-0-87727-532-9. ISBN vol. II, 978-0-87727-533-6.

To order, please contact:
Mail:
Cornell University Press Services
750 Cascadilla Street
PO Box 6525
Ithaca, NY 14851 USA

E-mail: orderbook@cupserv.org

Phone/Fax, Monday–Friday, 8 am – 5 pm (Eastern US):
Phone: 607 277 2211 or 800 666 2211 (US, Canada)
Fax: 607 277 6292 or 800 688 2877 (US, Canada)

Order through our online bookstore at:
www.einaudi.cornell.edu/southeastasia/publications/